Practical Guide to PKI with Windows Server

Second Edition

Matthew Burr

mjcb.ca

Practical Guide to PKI with Windows Server - Second Edition

by Matthew Burr

Copyright © 2025 Matthew Burr (*https://mjcb.ca/*)

ISBN: 978-1-7774422-3-1
ISBN: 978-1-7774422-4-8
ISBN: 978-1-7774422-6-2

Trademarks

The following products and/or companies are referenced in this book. Their associated trademarks are as follows:

- 1.1.1.1 is trademarked to Cloudflare, Inc.
- Active Directory Certificate Services, Active Directory Domain Services, Azure Stack HCI, Edge, File Explorer, Hyper-V, Internet Explorer, Internet Information Services, Microsoft Azure, Microsoft Certificate Server, Microsoft Hyper-V Server, Microsoft Virtual PC, System Center Virtual Machine Manager, Windows (NT, NT 4.0, 2000, XP, Vista, 7, 8, 8.1, 10 and 11), Windows Admin Center, Windows Server (NT, NT 4.0, 2000, 2003, 2003 R2, 2008, 2008 R2, 2012, 2012 R2, 2016, 2019 and 2022), Windows Subsystem for Linux, Windows Update, and Windows Virtual PC are trademarked to the Microsoft Corporation.
- AlmaLinux is trademarked to the AlmaLinux OS Foundation.
- Android and chromeOS are trademarked to Google LLC.
- Apache HTTP Server is trademarked to the Apache Software Foundation.
- Firefox is trademarked to the Mozilla Foundation.
- iOS, iPad, iPadOS, iPhone, macOS, and Safari are trademarked to Apple Inc.
- Linux is trademarked to Linus Torvalds in the U.S. and other countries.
- Nginx is trademarked to F5 Networks, Inc.
- OpenSSL is trademarked to the OpenSSL Software Foundation.
- Parallels Desktop is trademarked to Parallels International GmbH.
- VirtualBox is trademarked to Oracle.
- Virtual PC is trademarked to Connectix Corporation.
- VMware Workstation is trademarked to Broadcom Inc.

Warning and Disclaimer

It is strongly recommended to test the steps and procedures provided in this book prior to using it in a production environment. Details on how to test the steps and procedures in this book are provided.

The author reserves the right to change, modify, transfer, or otherwise revise this publication without notice.

Revision History

2021-09-13 - First Edition Release
2025-09-16 - Second Edition Release

Additional Information

See *https://mjcb.ca/publications/practical-guide-to-pki-with-windows-server-second-edition/* for additional details, updates, and any online resources for this book.

See *https://docs.mjcb.ca/publications/practical-guide-to-pki-with-windows-server/second-edition/command-listing/* for a complete list of commands that are used in this book.

WQE02271125137

I would like to dedicate this book to my wife, who has supported me for all the time that I spent working on this book, and on all the other projects that I enjoy working on.

Contents at a Glance

Table of Contents

About the Author

Matthew Burr is an IT Professional who has worked in the IT industry for over 16 years in the Greater Toronto Area. During that time, he has worked in the energy, financial, government, healthcare, retail, scientific, social media, and software development industries. He attended Cambrian College in Sudbury, Ontario from 2006 to 2009, where he studied Computer Networking and Systems Administration.

Matthew is a Network Architect and Network Security expert who has provided his services to multiple companies during his career. Aside from working in those roles, he has also worked as a Systems Administrator for networks running both Windows and Linux. For the last few years, he has also worked on multiple cloud implementations using various platforms.

Aside from working in the IT industry at various companies, Matthew also holds several industry certifications from various vendors, and regularly attends training courses and conferences to stay current.

Matthew founded Ten Fifteen Solutions (*https://tenfifteen.ca/*) in early 2016 to better serve clients and to work on consulting services in the Toronto area.

Matthew also runs a website (*https://mjcb.ca/*) where he discusses various IT related topics and hosts other projects that he is working on.

Preface

The purpose of this book is to demonstrate how to create a functioning Public Key Infrastructure using Active Directory Certificate Services (AD CS), which is a role within Windows Server. This is a topic that has become more important in the last few years as security has become more critical to the daily operations of every company. The outcome of this book is to create a Certificate Authority using Active Directory Certificate Services with Windows Server. This book offers a comprehensive step-by-step guide that demonstrates how to successfully create a Certificate Authority using those technologies.

This book explains each step, the necessity of that step, and the importance of that step within the creation of a Certificate Authority. The result of this book will create a Certificate Authority that can issue certificates internally within an organization in a secure manner, using best practices. This book also explains at critical steps how to modify those steps to accommodate infrastructure in other environments.

This book is meant for Developers, Network Administrators and Systems Administrators who have a basic understanding of Windows Server, as well as Public Key Infrastructures and need to deploy a Certificate Authority rapidly within their environment for various purposes. By using the steps provided in this book, there will be a Certificate Authority framework created that can be customized for whatever requirements are needed in any environment.

This book is also meant to be used by Developers, Network Administrators and Systems Administrators who can interpret this guide and modify it for their existing environment.

Simply following this guide will not implement a functioning PKI for an organization, steps will need to be modified accordingly to make it function properly. This means creating different servers, modifying steps for different Active Directory domains, modifying LDAP settings, modifying file paths, creating different certificates, and other critical steps as needed. Instructions are present that explain how to modify the provided steps for a particular environment.

The contents of this book are presented in a thorough, but easy to follow format. Screenshots are provided for important steps for verification purposes and to demonstrate how the environment should be configured. Screenshots and other examples are included to ensure that there are as few issues as possible in the creation of a Certificate Authority.

This book was written to offer a complete guide on this subject in an efficient and straightforward manner. In this case, creating a PKI is an extremely complex subject which involves multiple complex steps that must be completed correctly. This book is meant to be as straightforward as possible in the creation of a Certificate Authority using Windows Server.

Acknowledgements

I received a lot of feedback for the first edition of this book, and I am grateful to the people that took the time to send me emails or leave reviews about it. I read every single piece of feedback, and most of it was positive in nature. I am happy to say that I have taken almost all of that feedback and applied it to this new edition. I can't thank anyone in particular, but I am happy to say that all feedback that I received has been applied to this new edition in one way or another, whether it be positive or negative in nature.

For negative feedback, it wasn't the greatest thing to hear, but I am happy to have received it. I know that there were issues with the first edition, and I hope that I have fixed those issues.

I would like to thank all of the people who purchased the first edition of this book, which showed me that there was a demand for the second edition. For people that have been waiting for this new edition, sorry it took so long.

Introduction

Goals of This Book

The main goal of this book is to successfully deploy a functioning and secure Two-Tier Certificate Authority and Public Key Infrastructure (PKI) using Active Directory Certificate Services (AD CS) with Windows Server. This book provides a complete guide on implementing a complete PKI with detailed steps, instructions, and background information.

Creating a properly functioning and secure Certificate Authority is a complicated process that requires multiple complex steps. There are also validation steps that need to occur to ensure that there are no errors in the Certificate Authority implementation at certain key steps. Effort has been made to document every single step that is needed, as missing even the smallest step or detail can cause issues that are difficult to correct later.

This book will focus on the fictional **TFS Labs** domain. This environment is basic in design, and it will easily demonstrate how to build a Two-Tier Certificate Authority using Active Directory Certificate Services (AD CS) with Windows Server. Steps are provided on how to create this test environment, as well as what needs to be updated for an implementation on another domain to be successful. This book is written in such a way that all steps provided are incorporated into a complete Certificate Authority, and steps that are optional are specified.

There are multiple ways to create a test environment for creating a Certificate Authority, and this book will focus on using the Hyper-V virtualization platform to accomplish this goal. By using Hyper-V over other virtualization platforms, there is no need to utilize any other third-party software for completing the steps in this book, but that does not mean that other providers can be used. Hyper-V is a hypervisor platform that was developed by Microsoft for virtualizing other operating systems in a Windows environment.

Since all the required tools are provided by Microsoft and are already available in Windows Server, there is technically no requirement for any third-party software as absolutely everything is provided. If a Windows Server 2022 and a Windows 11 installation source is available, there is no need for an internet connection at all to complete the steps in this book. The only thing needed to complete the steps in this book is a workstation or server that can run the software with the necessary hardware requirements.

By using this book as a guide, the provided instructions can be modified for an existing Active Directory domain. It is advised to go through the steps in this book at least once to see what needs to be done for creating a Certificate Authority before attempting to implement it in an existing organization. This will ensure that a functioning Certificate Authority is created and normal operation is observed, which will help in troubleshooting any issues that may arise.

What This Book Won't Cover

While this book will cover the creation of a PKI using Active Directory Certificate Services on Windows Server 2022, there are many topics that will not be covered. Creating a working Two-Tier Certificate Authority with Active Directory Certificate Services is the primary goal of this book, but there are many applications of this that will not be covered. Among the features that will not be covered in this book includes the following:

- 802.1X authentication
- Document and code signing
- Encrypting file systems
- Email signing and encryption
- Smart Card authentication
- SSL decryption

Attempting to cover additional features such as the ones that were just listed would be complicated and is usually specific to the organization that wants to implement those features. These features require considerable planning depending on what vendors are involved and are beyond the scope of this book. By implementing a proper PKI using this book, the framework will be established to add features like this in the future.

What is also missing from this book is the option to perform a completely scripted version of the PKI installation and configuration. This is not because it is not possible, but it is difficult to automate many of the configuration steps that are performed in this book. Since there is a requirement to have an offline server with no network connections, this prevents automatically transferring files between servers.

There are also a few issues with building a Two-Tier PKI using an Offline Root CA with an unattended setup using PowerShell for automation, as there is no way to easily transmit files and issue commands remotely on a server that is supposed to be offline. A workaround to this would be to temporarily enable network connections to the Offline Root CA during the setup process, but that would defeat the purpose of the security of the Offline Root CA. Also, some features such as the Online Responder role do not support CLI options without requiring overly complex steps. Because of these reasons, a fully automated PKI deployment is not covered in this book.

Conventions Used in This Book

There are several text and design conventions that are used to make it easier to understand the contents of this book. These conventions are also used to understand what needs to be done to follow the steps in this book. Some of the conventions are also used for additional information that the reader should be aware of, including potential issues that could arise under certain circumstances, or additional information on technologies or features that can be implemented in the future.

Text Conventions

There are multiple references to running PowerShell or the Command Prompt in an elevated state. In the context of this book, this means running these applications as an administrator. By not running these commands as an administrator, it may result in unexpected behaviour as a result which can be difficult to troubleshoot. Depending on what is being configured and on what server, it will either be a local administrator or a Domain Administrator account that is needed.

There are also multiple text conventions that are used in this book, and all are used for instructional purposes. The main text conventions that will be found in this book include:

Convention	Meaning and Purpose
Menu Commands and Console Trees	Menu commands or console trees that need to be followed are referenced using the **>** symbol and **bolded** to emphasize the steps. For example, open the **File > New** menu, and click the **Text Document** option to create the text document needed for the configuration file.
Bold Text	Text that is in bold is used to highlight important items in a set of instructions or to highlight specific commands. For example, open the **Server Manager** console to find information on a particular server.
Italics Text	Text that is in italics is used to reference a URL that may be used as part of a configuration, and in some cases is an external link to an outside resource. It may be required to test a URL to ensure that items have been configured correctly.
Plus Sign (+)	Keyboard shortcuts are indicated using a plus sign (+) which separates multiple keys. For example, reading CTRL + ALT + DELETE means that the CTRL, ALT and DELETE keys needs to be pressed simultaneously to perform an action.

Table: Text conventions that are used in this book and how to interpret them.

Steps are provided in numerical order and should always be followed in the correct order to ensure that the task being performed is setup in the correct manner. Skipping steps or performing them in the incorrect order can cause issues with setting up the Certificate Authority, so it is strongly recommended to perform the steps in the correct order in this book to ensure everything works as intended.

Steps that are optional for the Certificate Authority implementation are stated, and not performing those steps will not cause any issues with the functionality of the Certificate Authority. Those steps add additional functionality to the Certificate Authority, and those functions may not be necessary for all environments or organizations. In most cases, those steps can be completed at a later time if they are required.

Information Boxes

There are several types of informational boxes that appear throughout this book. These boxes are used to provide additional information or highlight important steps, and each colour represents different types of information that is needed during the implementation in this book:

Customization Box

Anything that appears in a Customization Box is a step that needs to be modified for a different environment. These steps need to be adapted to work in different Active Directory domains.

Information Box

Anything that appears in an Information Box is provided for reference purposes or for additional details for a particular topic. The instructions or explanations provided in these boxes will not affect the deployment of a Certificate Authority in this book but can also provide additional details on how to configure specific functions.

Notice Box

Anything that appears in a Notice Box is provided to highlight a potential issue in the Certificate Authority implementation that could cause issues if not addressed correctly.

Warning Box

Anything that appears in a Warning Box is provided to highlight a potential issue in the Certificate Authority implementation that could cause issues if not addressed correctly.

Configuration Boxes

There are two types of configuration boxes that appear throughout this book. These are used for configuring services that are related to AD CS, and are usually modified for different environments:

```
C:\configuration.inf

Anything that appears in a Configuration File Box is required for configuring the roles
and features within Windows Server that is used in this book. The path to the file that
is being configured will be in the Configuration File Box header, including the file
extension for the file.
```

There is also an additional box that is used for commands that need to be inputted through the CLI and used for inputting configuration items in configuration boxes. The contents in these boxes should be inputted exactly as shown:

```
Input the contents in this box exactly as it appears to make the appropriate changes.
```

Terminal Commands

There are multiple ways to enter commands using the CLI, and that is with PowerShell, the Command Prompt and with the Linux Terminal:

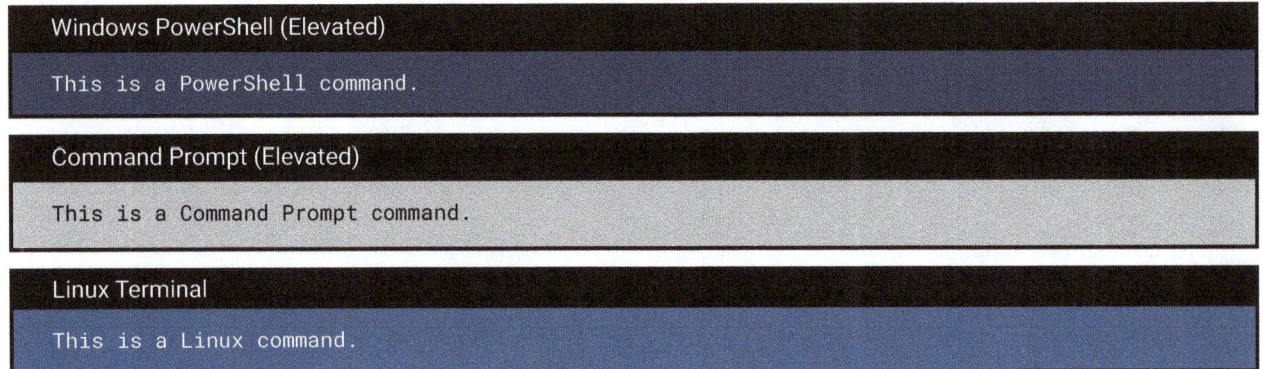

> **Windows PowerShell (Elevated)**
>
> ```
> This is a PowerShell command.
> ```

> **Command Prompt (Elevated)**
>
> ```
> This is a Command Prompt command.
> ```

> **Linux Terminal**
>
> ```
> This is a Linux command.
> ```

There are references to running a PowerShell or Command Prompt in an elevated state, which means it needs to be run as an administrator. This is required to apply commands on a system level, which is not always done by default.

Prerequisites

Before starting with the steps in this book, there are a few things that will need to be ready. This book only requires three virtual machines running Windows Server 2022 and one virtual machine running Windows 11 Pro. It also requires at least one workstation or server that can host four virtual machines needed for the TFS Labs test environment. No additional third-party software is required, as all necessary features are already available within the Windows operating system. There is an optional step in a later chapter which demonstrates certificate deployment on a Linux server, but it is completely optional.

This book uses virtualization software for creating the TFS Labs test environment. The choice of a virtualization platform is not important, but this book uses the Hyper-V platform. Hyper-V runs natively on 64-bit versions of Windows Server 2008 and above, as well as on any Education, Enterprise and Pro versions of Windows 10 and Windows 11.

Software Requirements

All servers in this book are created using Windows Server 2022, which is available on the Microsoft Evaluation Center website on a trial basis. There should be no issues in using Windows Server 2016 or Windows Server 2019 for creating the same Certificate Authority, the only potential issue being the Active Directory Functional Level. Earlier versions of Windows Server are not covered in this book as they are no longer supported by Microsoft.

For the workstation component, Windows 11 Pro is also available on a trial basis on the Microsoft website. There should be no issues with using supported versions of Windows 10 Pro in place of Windows 11 Pro. Earlier versions of Windows, including Windows 8.1 and Windows 7 are no longer supported by Microsoft and there are no guarantees that those versions of Windows will operate correctly using the steps in this book.

AD CS Installation and Configuration Options

As part of creating a functioning PKI using the steps that are in this book, Active Directory Domain Services (AD DS) and Active Directory Certificate Services (AD CS) will be configured on three servers running Windows Server 2022. Command line installation and configuration in the Windows operating system has come a long way since earlier versions, and it is entirely possible to configure most of the features in Windows without using the GUI. This book will present the option for installing and configuring the needed server roles using the CLI whenever possible. Some users are more comfortable with the GUI configuration as it is easier and faster in most cases, so those options are presented as well. A quick start guide is included in this book that demonstrates how to quickly build a PKI with only the essential components and minimum required steps using only the CLI.

Virtualization Requirements

This book uses Hyper-V as the virtualization platform for creating the TFS Labs test environment. Hyper-V is available as a role in Windows Server 2022 and as an optional feature in Windows 11 Education, Enterprise and Pro. No additional third-party software is required to use and install it.

For Hyper-V to function correctly, it requires the following features to be available on the workstation or server (these requirements do not factor in any virtual machines that are being used):

- 64-bit Processor with Second Level Address Translation (SLAT) and No-Execute bit (NX bit)
- CPU support for hardware-assisted virtualization (VT-x on Intel Processors, AMD-V on AMD Processors)
- Minimum of 2 GB memory

Any modern computer or server will most likely support the necessary virtualization features without any issues if it was manufactured after 2018. The only exception is computers that are 32-bit only, as those features are not possible. Hyper-V is only compatible with 64-bit processors.

For Hyper-V to operate correctly on a particular workstation or server, there may be various settings within the BIOS that would need to be enabled. These settings vary based on the manufacturer, but there is usually a virtualization option within the BIOS where those settings are configured. If unsure about the settings, refer to the manufacturer's documentation to determine how to enable those features.

A workstation or server is required that has at least 16 GB of memory to properly host the four virtual machines that are needed to support the steps provided in this book. The option to allocate less memory to the virtual machines is available if the host system does not have that amount of memory, but it may affect performance. With Hyper-V, the option to utilize dynamic memory is available, and this would only allocate needed memory for the virtual machines as it is needed. This should be acceptable for testing purposes but should be avoided for production deployments.

> **Supported Virtualization Platforms**
>
> The steps that are outlined in this book should work perfectly fine using the Hyper-V, VirtualBox or VMware platforms for virtualization. If the virtualization platform supports Windows 11 Pro, Windows Server 2022, virtual floppy disks, and basic networking that allows for multiple virtual machines to be connected to each other, the steps in this book should work correctly.

Organization of This Book

This book is organized into fifteen chapters to properly break down the deployment, and proper configuration of a Certificate Authority using Active Directory Certificate Services. There is also a full glossary of all important terms, a full list of all commands that are used in this book, and a complete index. The chapters that are included in this book are as follows:

Chapter 1 - Public Key Infrastructure Overview

This chapter provides an overview of what a Public Key Infrastructure and Certificate Authority is, how hierarchies work, and how certificates work.

Chapter 2 - AD CS Overview

This chapter provides an overview of the Active Directory Certificate Services role, and how it can be used to create a Certificate Authority using Windows Server.

Chapter 3 - Test Environment Overview

This chapter explains the TFS Labs test environment that is being used in this book for creating the Certificate Authority with Windows Server 2022.

Chapter 4 - Hyper-V Setup and Configuration

This chapter provides an overview of the Hyper-V virtualization platform, how it works, and how it can be used with Windows for creating virtual machines.

Chapter 5 - Domain and Workstation Setup

This chapter explains how to install an Active Directory Domain Controller and workstation. This will setup the necessary Active Directory infrastructure for supporting Active Directory Certificate Services.

Chapter 6 - Offline Root CA Setup

This chapter explains how to setup and secure an Offline Root Certificate Authority using Windows Server and Active Directory Certificate Services.

Chapter 7 - Subordinate CA Setup

This chapter explains how to setup and secure a Subordinate Certificate Authority that is capable of issuing, managing, and revoking certificates using Active Directory Certificate Services.

Chapter 8 - Deploy CA Certificates

This chapter explains how the Root and Subordinate certificates are deployed to an Active Directory domain using Group Policy.

Chapter 9 - Online Responder Role

This chapter explains how to enable the Online Responder role Service in Active Directory Certificate Services, which allows for OCSP to be used in the TFS Labs domain.

Chapter 10 - Private Key Archive and Recovery

This chapter explains how to backup private keys for certificates that are issued internally, and how it can be automated and backed up with Active Directory.

Chapter 11 - Certificate Templates

This chapter explains how to customize Certificate Templates in Active Directory Certificate Services to ensure that those certificates fit the needs of an organization.

Chapter 12 - Certificate Enrollment

This chapter explains how to deploy Certificate Templates automatically and manually within an Active Directory domain. It also demonstrates how to deploy certificates to other platforms such as Linux, iOS, and Android.

Chapter 13 - AD CS Maintenance Tasks

This chapter provides an overview of what tasks need to be completed to maintain a Certificate Authority that is using Active Directory Certificate Services.

Chapter 14 - AD CS on an Existing Domain

This chapter demonstrates how to safely test the deployment of Active Directory Certificate Services on an existing Active Directory domain without affecting a production network.

Chapter 15 - AD CS Quick Start

This chapter demonstrates how to quickly deploy a basic Two-Tier Certificate Authority using mostly command line tools, without all features included in this book.

Changes in This Edition

This book primarily covers the process for creating a Certificate Authority using Active Directory Certificate Services on Windows Server 2022. The previous version of this book used Windows Server 2019 for this purpose. Aside from updating the Windows Server version, additional content has also been added to supplement the process for creating the Certificate Authority.

There are too many changes from the first edition to individually list, but these are the major changes that have been made to for the second edition:

- Updated the Windows Server version from Windows Server 2019 to Windows Server 2022.
- Updated the Windows Client version from Windows 10 21H1 to Windows 11 24H2.
- Changed the main focus on using CLI commands instead of using the GUI for installation and configuration of the Certificate Authority. Either method can be used for most steps in this book, and both methods are present when both options are available.
- Added new CLI commands to several configuration steps that were missing.
- Added new screenshots and diagrams, and updated multiple existing screenshots to reflect updated software versions.
- Added a new information box that focuses on how to customize a step in the book for an existing environment.
- Added information on how to utilize virtualization checkpoints in several sections of the book, which can be used for testing purposes during the deployment of the Certificate Authority.
- Reorganized several sections into different chapters to improve the flow of the book.
- Added three new chapters which focus on Active Directory Certificate Services, Hyper-V, and testing AD CS on an existing domain.

A lot of content was added and updated in this edition of the book, but some content was removed for various reasons:

- Removed the steps on configuring iOS and macOS with certificates from AD CS.
- Removed the steps on configuring Android with certificates from AD CS.

Overall, the second edition of this book expands on the first edition in many ways. Multiple issues were corrected, new content was added, and the book is more complete as a result of the changes.

Chapter 1 - Public Key Infrastructure Overview

A Public Key Infrastructure (PKI) exists to facilitate the secure transfer of information between networks and is used primarily to keep sensitive data protected. Information that is protected includes anything, including email, websites, storage devices and authentication. This allows the internet, and networks in general to be considerably more secure as sensitive data would not be transmitted in plain text, and all traffic would be encrypted in a standard way.

A certificate provides the primary foundation of a PKI and is the most commonly facing method of interacting with a PKI. Certificates can represent users, workstations, servers, and other devices. These certificates are issued by a Certificate Authority, which can manage those certificates. Certificates that are issued by a Certificate Authority are associated with a public key and private key pair.

The main certificates in a Certificate Authority are typically the Root and Subordinate certificates. In some cases, it may be necessary to revoke a certificate before it expires, and this is usually performed using a Certificate Revocation List (CRL).

A certificate will typically contain the following information:

- Information on the Certificate Authority that issued the certificate.
- Information on how to determine the revocation status of the certificate as well as the validity of that certificate.
- Information about the user, workstation or device that holds the private key that corresponds to the certificate.
- Information on what encryption protocols is being used with the certificate.
- The public key of the certificate, which is used to encrypt data and send it to the device that holds the private key.

The currently accepted standard for defining a certificate in a Public Key Infrastructure is with the X.509 standard, which is defined in RFC 5280.

This chapter will review the fundamentals of what a Public Key Infrastructure is, how a certificate is structured, how a Certificate Authority hierarchy works, and how a Certificate Authority normally operates with all necessary components. It will also review how it applies to Windows Server and Active Directory Certificate Services.

> **Public Key Infrastructure Overview**
>
> If there is no need to review how a Public Key Infrastructure operates and how Certificate Authorities are organized, then this chapter can be skipped.

Public Key Infrastructure Overview - What Is a PKI?

A Public Key Infrastructure (PKI) is a collection of server roles, software, policies, and procedures that are used to create, distribute, and manage Certificates. The most common application of PKI that most people are familiar with is securing websites using SSL, but there are many more applications of a PKI such as:

- Allowing for email encryption and digital signatures.
- Increasing security for Remote Desktop services on internal servers.
- Issuing internal certificates for VPN services.
- Issuing internal certificates for wireless users and access points.
- Replacing insecure self-signed certificates on internal network devices.
- Signing code for internal applications.
- Utilizing internal certificates for applications and services.
- Utilizing internal certificates for disk and file system encryption.
- Utilizing internal certificates for SSL decryption on firewalls and proxy devices.

There are several ways to utilize a Public Key Infrastructure. There is the option of purchasing certificates from an online Certificate Authority or hosting a Certificate Authority internally within an organization. Both solutions have their advantages and disadvantages, and which solution is chosen is dependent on the needs of an organization and whether customization is required that is not available through an online Certificate Authority.

The entire basis for PKI is dependent on Public-Private Key Encryption, which depends on using pairs of public and private keys for the encryption and decryption of data. The public keys are distributed to whoever needs to send encrypted data, and the private keys are known only to the destination that needs to decrypt the secure data. The ability to create, distribute and manage those keys in an effective, automatic, and secure manner is the entire reason that Certificate Authorities exist.

Due to the open nature of Public Key Infrastructure, Certificate Authorities can be created using multiple platforms and solutions. The ability to "tier" a Certificate Authority into specific roles depending on the desired function is an important aspect of creating a modern PKI.

> ### Certificate Authorities and Public Key Infrastructure Terminologies
>
> The Certificate Authority (CA) and Public Key Infrastructure (PKI) terms are interchangeable since they are the same thing, with different software implementations depending on what is used to create those systems. A PKI is the entire solution for providing secure certificates, and a CA is the individual components needed to provide those services.
>
> Whether a Certificate Authority is a single system or multiple systems working together is entirely dependent on the solution that is used to create it.

From a cost and overhead perspective of running a Certificate Authority within an organization, it is really what works best for that environment. It used to be common for organizations to simply purchase a wildcard certificate for their environment from a commercial Certificate Authority and just use that for internal services, but that is no longer a solution that works for several reasons:

- Commercial Certificate Authorities will not typically issue certificates for internal domains, especially if it is a subdomain within an internal domain. Non-routable domains are not able to be verified and that is a primary requirement for commercial Certificate Authorities.
- Commercial Certificate Authorities cannot normally issue custom certificates that are able to be used for non-standard and custom purposes, especially in a development environment.
- Commercial Certificate Authorities can be extremely expensive when many certificates need to be issued. If a specific service requires dozens or hundreds of certificates to be issued, the cost of purchasing and deploying those certificates can become extremely expensive.

There is certainly an administrative overhead and associated cost of setting up and maintaining a PKI in an organization, but the benefits of having a proper PKI are worth the time and effort in creating one.

Self-Signed Certificates

One of the key benefits to implementing a proper Certificate Authority within an organization is the ability to eliminate self-signed certificates. A self-signed certificate is technically free and can be easily setup, but there are many disadvantages to using those types of certificates:

- Web browsers do not trust self-signed certificates unless it has been explicitly added to the list of Trusted Certificates on a workstation. On a single workstation this is not normally an issue but correcting this on an entire network can be extremely difficult.
- Modern web browsers show errors that a certificate is self-signed and should not be trusted. Web browsers alert users to this to keep them safe on a website that may not be taking their security seriously.
- Some vendors that issue self-signed certificates with network appliances do not always use the strongest encryption options. There may also be duplicate certificates in use, which present security risks on devices where security needs to be a priority.

Adding a Certificate Authority certainly adds overhead and maintenance to an organization to maintain it, but the benefits to getting rid of self-signed certificates are worth it from a security perspective and optics from users.

SSL Decryption

SSL decryption is a method of decrypting traffic that is secured with SSL, and this is done for the purpose of examining all traffic that goes in and out of a network. When traffic that is secured with SSL traverses a network, the contents of that traffic is hidden to everyone except for the device that initiated the traffic, and the destination of the traffic. Details such as the DNS name of the destination is usually always known, since that is required to facilitate the connection, but that is usually all that is known.

SSL decryption is performed for many reasons, the most common reasons being:

- Enforce web filtering on SSL sites.
- Examining the contents of encrypted traffic to search for malicious activity.
- Monitor for unwanted uploads and downloads.
- Search downloads and uploads for malware.

SSL decryption is typically performed on firewalls, proxies and in some cases, dedicated SSL decryption devices. SSL decryption works by placing certificates on a device and using it to sign SSL traffic on that device. There is always another copy of the certificate on a device that performs the SSL decryption using same certificate.

Typically, it is best practice to exclude certain sites from SSL decryption, including government, finance, and healthcare websites. This is to ensure that potentially sensitive information is not decrypted and potentially stored.

Public Key Infrastructure Overview - Certificate Authority Hierarchies

When deploying a Certificate Authority and a Public Key Infrastructure, it is typically setup in a hierarchical deployment, with a Root Certificate Authority at the top, and going all the way down to the issued certificates.

The Root Certificate Authority signs the certificate for itself, and that certificate is used to sign any Subordinate certificates that are in the Certificate Authority. In between there can be multiple Subordinate Certificate Authorities that perform separate functions in the Certificate Authority. These types of Certificate Authority hierarchies are known as a One-Tier, Two-Tier and Three-Tier Certificate Authority. All three of these tiers are supported in Windows Server using Active Directory Certificate Services (AD CS).

This book focuses entirely on a Two-Tier Certificate Authority as it is the most common Certificate Authority deployment for organizations, as it is the easiest to setup and support, and is also recommended by Microsoft with Active Directory Certificate Services. Overviews of the other available Certificate Authority hierarchies are also provided for reference purposes, should those types of hierarchies be encountered. The complexity of every Certificate Authority hierarchy increases every time an additional tier is introduced, or whenever additional servers are added to increase the functionality of the Certificate Authority.

Public Key Infrastructure Overview - Certificate Authority Hierarchies - One-Tier CA

A One-Tier Certificate Authority consists of a single Certificate Authority that is usually hosted on a single server and represents the most basic way to issue certificates:

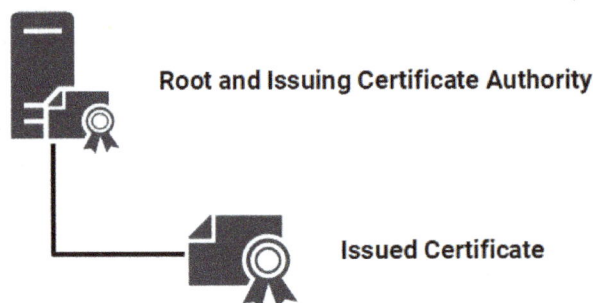

Root and Issuing Certificate Authority

Issued Certificate

Figure 1.2.1.1: A One-Tier Certificate Authority consists of just one Certificate Authority server that is used to issue and manage certificates to users and workstations in an organization.

This single Certificate Authority is the Root CA as well as the Issuing CA, which means it is responsible for all roles of the Certificate Authority. A One-Tier Certificate Authority is never recommended for a production environment for multiple reasons:

- Compromising a single CA server will immediately compromise the entire PKI. This would mean if the Certificate Authority were ever compromised in any way, all certificates ever issued would need to be re-issued to ensure that the certificates can be trusted again.
- For large environments, having just a single CA could potentially become a bottleneck if the CA server is unavailable, or if many certificates need to be issued at a single time.
- If certificate policy requirements for certificates need to be changed in the future, having a single CA can make that change extremely difficult, and it can be difficult to scale out from a single CA server.
- In a production environment, a One-Tier Certificate Authority is a single point of failure for the entire PKI. This type of CA is not scalable, and if the needs of an organization change in the future it can cause serious issues.

There are some instances where a One-Tier Certificate Authority is used, mostly for one-off applications that require just a single certificate to be issued for things like application signing or for test environments. These types of scenarios do not require a robust Certificate Authority to work correctly and are typically only used when there is a specific need for such a setup.

> ❌ **One-Tier Certificate Authorities and Domain Controllers**
> Never install a Root Certificate Authority on an Active Directory Domain Controller in an environment under any circumstances. Even though the server role can easily be added to an existing Domain Controller, it is not advisable to have the Active Directory Certificate Services role installed on the same server that is also a Domain Controller. This can cause multiple unexpected issues, the most common occurring if a recovery needs to occur on the Domain Controller. This can cause any issued certificates within the environment to be broken and invalid. Since the requirements for running a Certificate Authority are quite low, it is advised to run a Certificate Authority on a separate server, especially when virtualization is being used in an environment.

Public Key Infrastructure Overview - Certificate Authority Hierarchies - Two-Tier CA

A Two-Tier Certificate Authority consists of an Offline Root Certificate Authority and at least one online Subordinate Issuing Certificate Authority. It is the most common and most practical way to issue certificates using Active Directory Certificate Services, and is the primary focus of this book.

A typical Two-Tier Certificate Authority will look something like this:

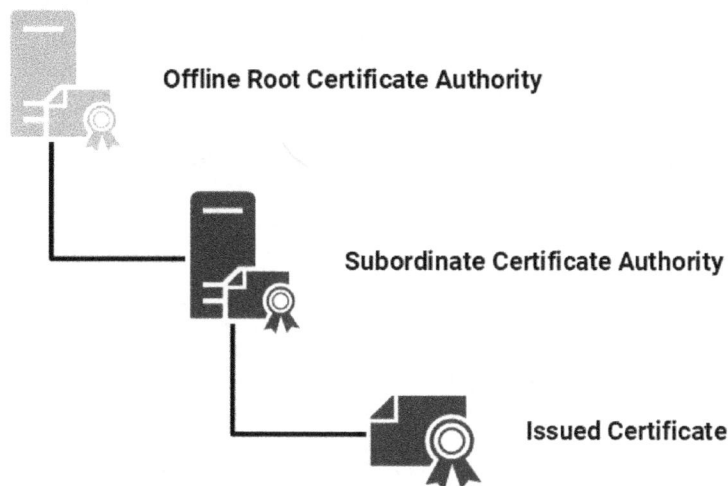

Figure 1.2.2.1: A Two-Tier Certificate Authority consists of at least one Root CA and at least one Subordinate CA, which is used to issue and manage certificates for an organization.

Most organizations utilize a Two-Tier Certificate Authority as it has the best balance between security and in ease in managing Subordinate Certificate Authorities. Compared to a One-Tier Certificate Authority, a Two-Tier Certificate Authority has several advantages:

- The Root Certificate Authority server is usually setup and configured as a server that is not a member of the Active Directory domain and is usually kept in an offline state unless it is needed for standard maintenance tasks (such as renewing a CRL). These servers will also have no network connections configured, so there is no way for traffic to reach them.
- The Root Certificate Authority server can be locked down and hardened separately from the rest of the servers on the domain, so it can have the strictest security policies applied to it without becoming an administration issue. Since it is always in an offline state, and not part of the domain, any Group Policy Object changes will not affect it as there is no way to apply those changes.
- An offline Root Certificate Authority can protect the private keys for the Root certificate, so that it is much more difficult to compromise.
- With a separate tier for Subordinate Certificate Authorities, it is much easier to separate those roles onto different servers for different purposes (such as location, operating systems, applications, etc.) than if it was located on just one server. This gives much greater flexibility to the architecture and operation of the Certificate Authority, as it allows for more specific features to be configured without affecting the entire PKI.
- If a Subordinate Certificate Authority is compromised, it can be easily revoked, and a new Subordinate certificate can be issued from the Offline Root CA. While there is still time and effort required to perform these tasks, it will prevent the entire Certificate Authority from needing to be recreated.

A Two-Tier Certificate Authority is the most common Certificate Authority deployment that will most likely be used in a production environment. It is a balanced mix between a One-Tier and a Three-Tier Certificate Authority, and it can be scaled up should requirements change and additional functionality is required.

By introducing a Subordinate Certificate Authority and using an Offline Root CA, the security of the PKI is increased and allows for more customization of the Certificate Authority. Microsoft recommends that a Two-Tier Certificate Authority be used wherever possible with the Active Directory Certificate Services role.

> **Offline Root Certificate Authority Tasks**
>
> When dealing with an Offline Root CA there are tasks that are normally handled automatically when the server is always online. When a Certificate Authority is offline, the CRL is not automatically updated and distributed to the necessary servers. If the CRL expires it can cause multiple issues with the online Subordinate CA and the entire PKI under certain circumstances.
>
> It is advised to set calendar reminders on a yearly recurring basis to bring the Root CA online temporarily to update these records and publish them to the Subordinate CA. This will ensure that there are no issues with the PKI in an organization. The time that the CRL is set to expire on the Root CA will also determine what interval is needs to perform maintenance tasks to keep the environment updated.
>
> Performing these tasks are not difficult and are relatively easy to do. How to perform this task is demonstrated in a later chapter.

Public Key Infrastructure Overview - Certificate Authority Hierarchies - Three-Tier CA

A Three-Tier Certificate Authority consists of an offline Root Certificate Authority, an Intermediate Certificate Authority (usually offline, but not always) and at least one Subordinate Issuing Certificate Authority. This represents one of the most complex ways to issue certificates using Active Directory Certificate Services to build a Certificate Authority.

A Three-Tier Certificate Authority can have multiple configurations, but the simplest version of this type of hierarchy would look like this:

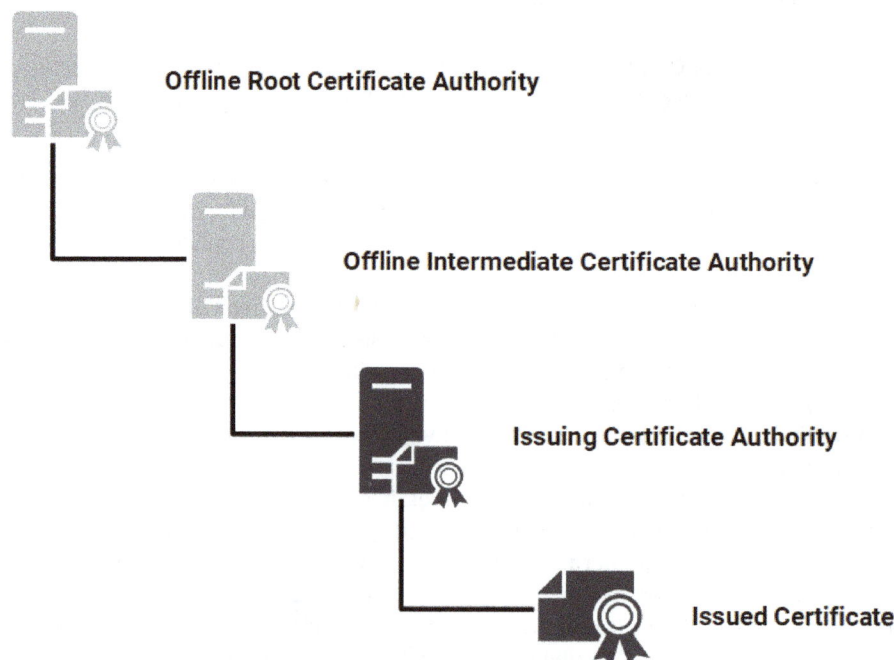

Offline Root Certificate Authority

Offline Intermediate Certificate Authority

Issuing Certificate Authority

Issued Certificate

Figure 1.2.3.1: A Three-Tier Certificate Authority consists of at least one Root CA, one Subordinate CA, and at least one independent Issuing CA. Depending on the size of the Certificate Authority, there may be other servers involved as well that may perform other Certificate Authority tasks.

This is the most difficult type of Certificate Authority to setup and maintain, but it does provide the most amount of flexibility and security. It does have many of the same advantages as a Two-Tier Certificate Authority, but does introduce some other advantages:

- The ability to revoke Certificate Authorities for only a specific part of the PKI. If there is an issue with a particular Subordinate CA in the PKI hierarchy, only that server and certificate would need to be revoked without affecting the entire PKI.
- Additional security by putting more of the Certificate Authority into an offline or inaccessible state for potential attacks.
- If one of the Issuing Certificate Authorities is compromised, the Offline Root Certificate Authority does not need to be brought online to replace it, as the other Subordinate Certificate Authorities would be able to issue a new certificate for that purpose.

A Three-Tier Certificate Authority is most often found in external Certificate Authorities that are used for securing websites using SSL. While it is more complex than a Two-Tier Certificate Authority, it does have the most flexibility for organizations that require it. A Three-Tier Certificate Authority is found internally in large organizations and is usually maintained by a dedicated team due to the complexity of it. The importance of keeping the Certificate Authority operating is a mission critical component of the network infrastructure as a result.

> **Three-Tier Hierarchy for a PKI**
>
> Due to the complexity of creating and maintaining a Three-Tier Certificate Authority, it is strongly recommended to take the necessary time to thoroughly plan what the PKI will look like and how it will operate. Due to the multiple Subordinate CA servers that are required to properly make this type of Certificate Authority operate correctly, and especially if those servers will be offline, it is important to factor in the availability of those servers when tasks such as updating the CDP and AIA records need to occur.

Public Key Infrastructure Overview - Certificate Authority Terminologies

There are a lot of terms that are used when dealing with Certificate Authorities and Public Key Infrastructures in general, and it is easy to get confused since a lot of those terms can be interchangeable with Active Directory Certificate Services. When dealing with Microsoft there are even more terms that are introduced that are also interchangeable as well. So far in this book, the following Certificate Authority terms have been brought up:

- Root CA
- Intermediate CA
- Enterprise CA
- Issuing CA
- Subordinate CA (SubCA)

The Root CA is self-explanatory as it is always the top of the Certificate Authority or the PKI Hierarchy depending on which definition is used. For a One-Tier hierarchy, the Root CA is the entire Certificate Authority, and it handles everything related to issuing and managing certificates.

An Intermediate CA and a Subordinate CA is the same thing, especially when using that term in a Microsoft Certificate Authority. An Intermediate CA exists between the Root CA and Issuing CA servers, and this is a more common term to use in a Three-Tier hierarchy. A Subordinate CA exists in a Two-Tier hierarchy when there is just a Root CA, and the Subordinate CA handles the issuing of certificates. From a Microsoft perspective, the Enterprise CA, Intermediate CA, and Subordinate CA terms are used interchangeably as they are the same thing, and provide similar functionality in a Certificate Authority.

Public Key Infrastructure Overview - X.509 Certificates

A certificate is used to link a user, computer, server, or a services identity to a public key to allow for secure transfer of data between those clients using that public key. There are accepted standards for these certificates to allow for interoperability between various clients, and the currently accepted standard for certificate is with the X.509 standard, specifically version 3 of the standard.

Certificates that are issued by a Certificate Authority are structured to meet certain standards to ensure that they are usable on any device that requires a certificate, and those standards were established by the Internet Engineering Task Force (IETF).

On a high-level, the structure of an X.509 certificate is as follows:

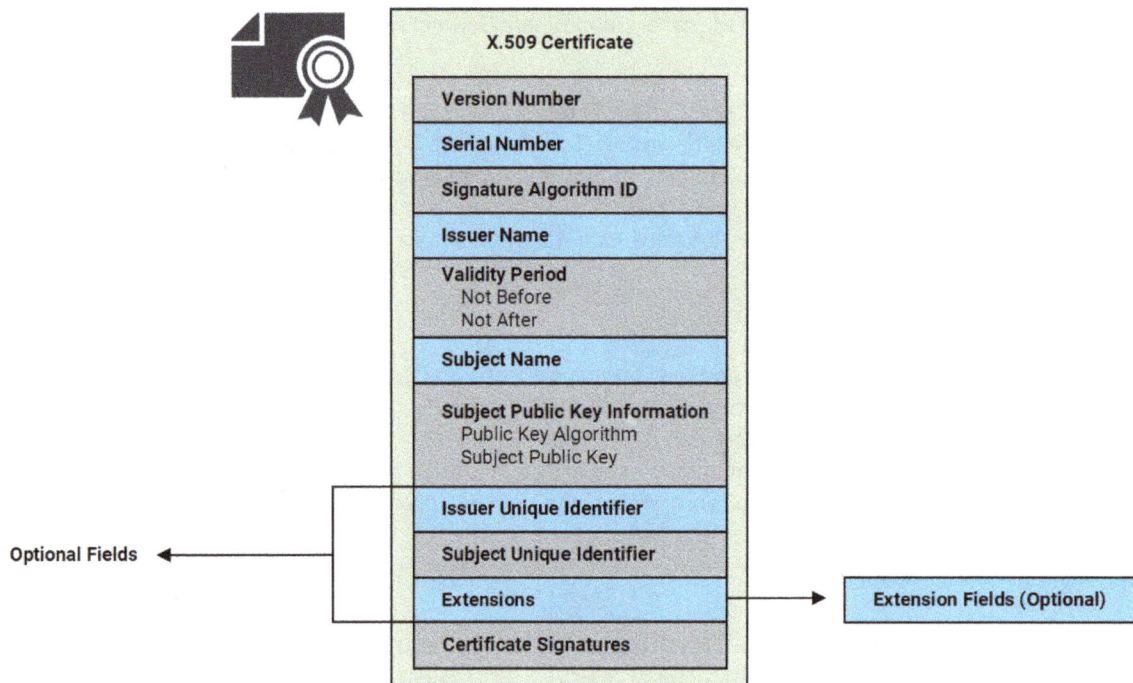

Figure 1.4.1: An X.509 certificate consists of multiple fields that can be used for defining a certificate and can be customized for various purposes. Some fields are used in every certificate and some fields are completely optional.

The X.509 version 3 certificate supports the following fields by default, some of which have been supported since X.509 version 1:

- **Version Number** - This is the version number for the certificate, which is usually V3.
- **Serial Number** - This is a unique identifier for each certificate that is issued by a Certificate Authority.
- **Signature Algorithm ID** - This is the algorithm that was used to sign the certificate.
- **Issuer Name** - This is the distinguished name of the Certificate Authority that issued the certificate.
- **Validity Period** - This is time frame for the validity of the certificate.
    - **Not Before** - The date that the certificate is valid from.
    - **Not After** - The date that the certificate is valid to.
- **Subject Name** - This is the name of the computer, user, server, or service that the certificate is issued to.
- **Subject Public Key Information** - This is the public key information that was used to create the certificate.
    - **Public Key Algorithm** - This is the algorithm that was used to sign the certificate.
    - **Subject Public Key** - This is the public key of the certificate.
- **Issuer Unique Identifier** - This is an optional value that is used to make the certificate unique if used by different entities.
- **Subject Unique Identifier** - This is an optional value that is used to make it possible for the same Subject Name to be reused.
- **Extensions** - These are optional values that can be added to an X.509 version 3 certificate for various purposes.
    - **Extension Fields** - These are additions to the certificates that are used for various purposes, which is expressed as an OID. Unrecognized extensions are ignored.

In addition to the normal X.509 fields, there are also Extension Fields that are available for certificates. All extensions are optional, but the most common ones found on a certificate are:

- **Authority Information Access (AIA)** - The AIA extension provides one or more URLs for certificate revocation purposes, including the OCSP URL if it is present.
- **CRL Distribution Points (CDP)** - The CDP extension provides the URLs or other locations where a client can retrieve the CRLs for checking if certificates have been revoked.
- **Subject Alternative Name** - This allows for the inclusion of different information in the certificate such as a user's email address or LDAP information. This allows for alternate names for various purposes, most of which are used for authentication purposes. The most common usage of this field is for different FQDN entries for a server. This Extension Field can also be referred to as a Unified Communications Certificate (UCC).
- **Certificate Policies** - This is used to describe what an organization does to validate the identity of the Certificate Requestor before a certificate is issued.

To view the fields that are configured for an issued certificate, open any certificate and select the Details tab:

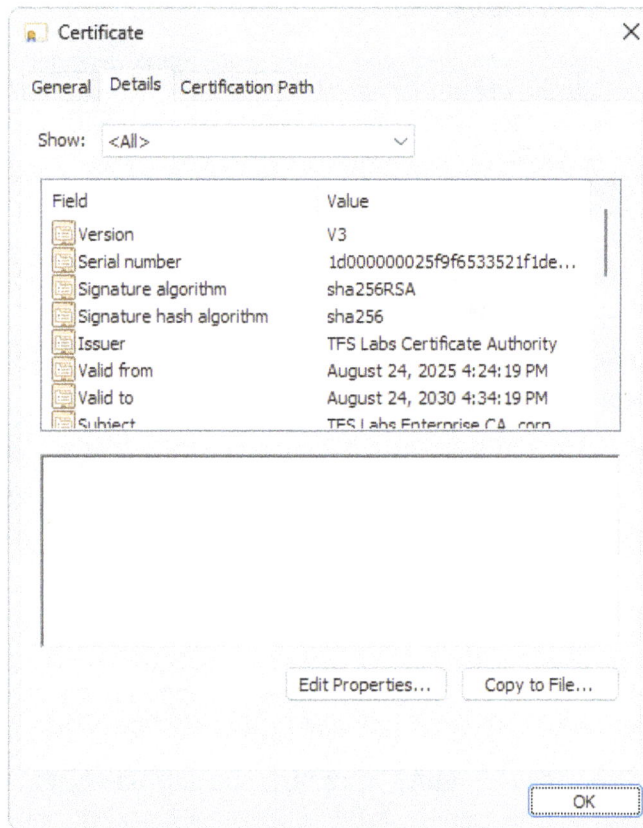

Figure 1.4.2: The certificate fields of an X.509 certificate being viewed on a Windows device. Most of these fields are usually configured automatically by the Certificate Authority at the time of certificate creation, while some are configured by the requestor.

There is certainly a lot more to go over on the format of a certificate and how it is structured, but that is not relevant for the purposes of this book. It is important to know that these fields are there, and that they are configurable if needed based on the needs of an organization.

Public Key Infrastructure Overview - Certificate Attributes

There are several attributes that are defined with an X.509 certificate that can be used within a Certificate Authority, and these attributes can be viewed on every issued certificate. The subject attribute has several fields as well that can be defined, all of which are usually configured at the time when a certificate is requested and issued. The most used subject attributes include:

- **C** - Country
- **ST** - State
- **L** - Locality
- **O** - Organization Name
- **OU** - Organization Unit Name
- **CN** - Common Name
- **E** - Email Address
- **SAN** - Subject Alternative Name (also known as a UCC certificate)

Depending on the certificate that is being issued, it is up to the user that is requesting the certificate, or the administrator that is creating a Certificate Template to ensure that the necessary attributes are specified at the time of creation. Once a certificate is issued, there is no way to amend or correct a certificate with the updated settings.

SAN Certificates with Modern Web Browsers

There are two ways to define DNS names in an SSL certificate, one is using the CN attribute and the other using the SAN attribute. The use of the Common Name attribute has been phased out, as defined in RFC 2818. Certificates that are used for web servers or for email services most commonly require multiple DNS records per certificate to allow for all required services to function.

There are a few reasons why the CN attribute has been phased out, mostly because it is easier to spoof a domain name using the CN attribute. One of the major web browsers currently in use is Google Chrome, which has enforced the use of the SAN attribute for DNS names. Since version 65 of Google Chrome, the use of the CN attribute has been deprecated, and the use of the SAN attribute is enforced by default. When trying to view a website that only has the CN attribute set, the following error code may be shown:

NET::ERR_CERT_COMMON_NAME_INVALID

This issue is difficult to avoid since most modern web browsers are based on Google Chrome. The most recent versions of Microsoft Edge, Mozilla Firefox, and Apple Safari also no longer honour the CN attribute for the same reason.

SAN Certificates with Active Directory Certificate Services

Earlier versions of Active Directory Certificate Services had issues with issuing SAN certificates, especially when using the Web Enrollment website service. A workaround to this was to issue a command on an Enterprise CA or Issuing CA to allow for SAN certificates to be issued:

certutil.exe -setreg policy\EditFlags +EDITF_ATTRIBUTESUBJECTALTNAME2

Issuing this command can introduce several risks to a Certificate Authority which could harm users and introduce other security issues to an environment. This command will allow anyone to add additional information to a certificate request and potentially impersonate other users or servers in the environment. Microsoft also recommends not enabling this feature in a Certificate Authority. It is best practice to maintain the Certificate Templates within the Certificate Authority to ensure that required features are not only enabled for usage, but also done in a safe manner.

Public Key Infrastructure Overview - Certificate Revocation Lists

All certificates that are issued always include an expiration date, and that date usually varies depending on the type of certificate, or by the Certificate Authority that issues the certificate. There are some cases where a certificate must be revoked earlier than expected and that is where a Certificate Revocation List (CRL) comes in. A CRL is used to centrally manage the list of certificates that have been revoked on that Certificate Authority and the reason it was revoked. There are a few reasons why a certificate would need to be revoked earlier than planned:

- **Affiliation Changed** - This is used when an employee is terminated or suspended.
- **Certificate Authority Compromise** - This is used when a CA certificate is compromised.
- **Certificate Hold** - This is used when a certificate needs to be put temporarily on hold.
- **Cessation of Operation** - This is used when an issued certificate is replaced.
- **Key Compromise** - This is used when a certificate is known to be stolen or no longer trusted.
- **Remove from CRL** - This is used when a CA is removed.
- **Superseded** - This is used if the legal name of an employee has changed.
- **Unspecified** - This is used when a certificate is revoked for any other reason.

In Active Directory Certificate Services, there are seven options that are available for revoking a certificate:

- CA Compromise
- Cease of Operation
- Certificate Hold
- Change of Affiliation
- Key Compromise
- Superseded
- Unspecified

Active Directory Certificate Services supports two types of Certificate Revocation Lists, which are known as a Base CRL and a Delta CRL:

- A Base CRL contains the serial numbers of all certificates that have been revoked on a Certificate Authority that are within their expiration time, as well as the reason they were revoked. The Base CRL is only published on a pre-determined schedule, or whenever a CA certificate is renewed or published.
- A Delta CRL contains only the serial numbers of all certificates that have been revoked on a Certificate Authority since the last time that the Base CRL was published. A Delta CRL is used to provide faster updates to the Base CRL, which is typically only published on a pre-determined schedule. All Delta CRL changes are added to the Base CRL whenever it is updated. The Delta CRL is much smaller than the Base CRL, so it is much easier to update and send to clients as needed.

There are a few issues with Certificate Revocation Lists, and it mostly applies to how often they are generated and how quickly they are generated. Whenever a client checks the Certificate Revocation List, this requires the client to check the complete list and this can create a lot of overhead. If a certificate is revoked after the Base CRL and Delta CRL is generated, a client can unknowingly accept a certificate that has already been revoked without being aware of it.

More recently, there are more sophisticated methods and protocols for informing clients about certificates that have been revoked. To allow for more rapid checking of revoked certificates, the Online Certificate Status Protocol (OCSP) can be used to check certificates much more rapidly than with a CRL. Instead of downloading and processing an entire CRL, the client can individually determine the status of a certificate. By using OCSP, the client can determine the status of a certificate, the responses being as "good", "revoked", or "unknown". By using OCSP instead of a CRL, the method is much more reliable, it is updated constantly and used less overhead. OCSP is fully supported with Active Directory Certificate Services with the Online Responder Role.

Public Key Infrastructure Overview - Certificate Types

There are several commonly used filename extensions and formats that are used for X.509 certificates. Many of these formats are used for different purposes, such as exporting or importing public and private keys, so choosing the correct format is important. The format of the certificate will also vary depending on its purpose and what application will be utilizing that certificate.

When dealing with the Windows Certificate Store and Active Directory Certificate Services, there are several formats of certificates that are normally used. There are several reasons why one format should be used over another, and it depends on how the certificate files are intended to be used. There are several common file extensions and formats used with X.509 Certificates, but the most common formats in the Windows operating system are the following:

- **Base-64 Encoded Binary X.509 (*.CER)**
    - This format stores the certificate in Base-64 format, which allows the certificate to be viewed in ASCII text.
    - The file extension of the certificate can vary, and be CER, CRT or DER.
- **Cryptographic Message Syntax Standard - PKCS #7 Certificates (*.P7B)**
    - The P7B format stores the certificate in the Cryptographic Message Syntax Standard format, which is a binary format.
    - When exporting a certificate in this format, there is an option to also include all the certificates in the certificate chain as well.
    - This is the format most commonly used for exporting certificates within Active Directory Certificate Services, as it has the most flexibility.
- **DER Encoded Binary X.509 (*.CER)**
    - This format stores the certificate in the Distinguished Encoding Rules (DER) format, which stores the certificate in binary format.
    - The file extension of the certificate can vary, and be CER, CRT or DER depending on what method is used for interacting with the certificate.
- **Microsoft Serialized Certificate Store (*.SST)**
    - The SST format is used for storing multiple certificates in a single file for easier distribution and is a proprietary Microsoft format that is only used in Windows.
    - This format is convenient for Certificate Authorities, as it can allow multiple certificates to be distributed much more rapidly to devices that support the format.
- **Personal Information Exchange - PKCS #12 (*.PFX)**
    - The PFX certificate format stores the certificate in the Personal Information Exchange format, which is a binary format.
    - This format allows for the export of private keys and allows the certificate to be encrypted with TripleDES-SHA1 or AES256-SHA256 for added protection.

The certificate file extension of *.CER is usually interchangeable with *.CRT, which is used in other operating systems and applications. Certificates in the DER format might sometimes have the file extension of *.DER and Base-64 formats might also have the file extension of *.PEM.

Changing the file extension is usually the easiest way to convert between certificate formats, but it is not always that easy. Depending on the requirements it may require exporting the certificate in a different format or converting it to the correct format entirely. Making these conversions is not difficult, and there are tools available to do these conversions.

> ⚠️ **Private Key Security**
>
> Ensure that whenever a certificate is exported that includes the private key, a strong password is always used when the option is given. Even if a certificate is exported for use within a production environment, always use a strong password to secure and protect the private key if the file is misplaced or deleted.
>
> Using a strong password for private key exports will prevent unnecessary revocation of certificates when it is known that those certificates have been lost or compromised in any way.

Public Key Infrastructure Overview - Private Enterprise Numbers

When dealing with an internal Certificate Authority there is usually no need to deal with utilizing a properly registered Private Enterprise Number (PEN), but it is something that is supported with Active Directory Certificate Services should it be required. The Private Enterprise Number is defined with an OID, which is a unique identifier that is defined at the time when the Certificate Authority is created. A Private Enterprise Number is only ever required if a Certificate Authority is used outside of an organization, or if custom applications or certificates require it. Configuring a Private Enterprise Number is beyond the scope of this book, but it only requires minor modifications to the OID Number that is used in two configuration files at the time of implementation. In Active Directory Certificate Services, this is in the CAPolicy.inf file, which is located in the root of the Windows folder.

There are a few available options for assigning a Private Enterprise Number. One of the easiest methods is to register an organization with the Internet Assigned Numbers Authority (IANA), and they can provide a valid number for usage. Applying for a Private Enterprise Number is easy and can be done free of charge. It does take several days for the application to be reviewed and approved, so factor that in if a Private Enterprise Number is used for a production deployment.

To apply for a Private Enterprise Number, it can be done online at the IANA website:

https://www.iana.org/assignments/enterprise-numbers/assignment/apply/

Private Enterprise Numbers that are issued and managed through the IANA are public information, and can be freely viewed online at any time at this website address:

https://www.iana.org/assignments/enterprise-numbers/

If a Private Enterprise Number is not required for an organization for whatever reason, use the OID of **1.2.3.4.1455.67.89.5** instead. This OID number is used within Microsoft's documentation for Active Directory Certificate Services and there should be no issues using it within an environment. The only downside to using this OID is that there may be issues with having another organization trust certificates if they use the same OID. For testing purposes this OID is perfectly okay to use, but for production environments, consider using a properly assigned and unique OID.

> ⚠️ **Private Enterprise Number Requirement**
>
> If there is even a possibility that a Private Enterprise Number is required for an organization in the future, consider registering for one prior to the deployment of the Certificate Authority. Adding a Private Enterprise Number later to an existing Certificate Authority is possible, but is complicated and could cause issues if not done correctly.
>
> Adding a Private Enterprise Number to an existing Certificate Authority is beyond the scope of this book. It requires a reconfiguration of the Certificate Authority, and the certificates will all need to be recreated.

Public Key Infrastructure Overview - Offline Root CA

There are multiple reasons to use an Offline Root CA in an environment, and it all comes down to securing a critical part of the infrastructure. It is almost expected that any Certificate Authority that is created today will have the Root CA in an always offline state. Unauthorized access to a Certificate Authority can put an organization at considerable risk and can cause a lot of headaches to fix. If the PKI is depended on for critical functions in an environment, the trust of that infrastructure is not something that can be compromised on.

The Root CA is critical to a PKI, and the risk of having the Root CA compromised and having the private keys leaked is something to be aware of and be concerned about. This would effectively invalidate every single certificate in an organization, and would require every certificate to be re-issued as existing certificates could no longer be trusted. For smaller organizations this may not be a problem, but for large-scale certificate deployments this can be a time-consuming problem to fix should it ever happen.

The best way to protect the Root CA is to have it always be unavailable and inaccessible. Access to the Root CA is not needed for day-to-day operations, so having it online at all times is completely unnecessary. Further to that point, it is not enough to just have it turned off until needed, it should not be accessible by anyone even when it is temporarily powered on.

It may be extreme, but having a network connection to the Root CA is dangerous, so it is not uncommon to use mediums such as virtual floppy disks to transfer data between the Root CA and other servers. It is cumbersome, but this happens so infrequently that it should not be an issue. Some virtualization platforms allow for copy and paste functions in virtual machines, but that should be disabled for the Root CA to minimize the attack surface on it as those are features that could potentially be exploited.

No Network Access vs Network Isolation

There is a difference between having an Offline Root CA that has no access to a network, and an Offline Root CA that is in contained in an isolated network segment. The most common and cost-effective way to utilize an Offline Root CA is to use a virtual machine that has no network adapters attached to it, and have it powered off until it is needed. Another way to setup an Offline Root CA is to use a dedicated laptop or workstation that only runs the Offline Root CA, but both solutions cost money for equipment that is only used at most, once or twice a year. Devices should always utilize full disk encryption to ensure that the Root CA is protected when it is powered off.

Another way to utilize an Offline Root CA is to use an isolated network segment (either with an inaccessible VLAN or management network), but this is not always recommended. It is not always possible to block access to these networks, and an attacker can always find their way into these networks if given enough time to do so.

Public Key Infrastructure Overview - Windows Certificate Management

Knowing how the operating system manages certificates that are currently issued to it is important in building and supporting a proper PKI and Certificate Authority. In every client and server version of the Windows operating system, certificates are stored and managed using the Certificate Store, which is used specifically for this purpose. From this context, a Store is where certificates are located, and this varies based on that usage. This centralized location provides a complete overview of all certificates that are installed and available within the operating system.

The Certificate Store can be managed by administrators by using Active Directory and Group Policy, which is useful for rapid deployment and management of certificates:

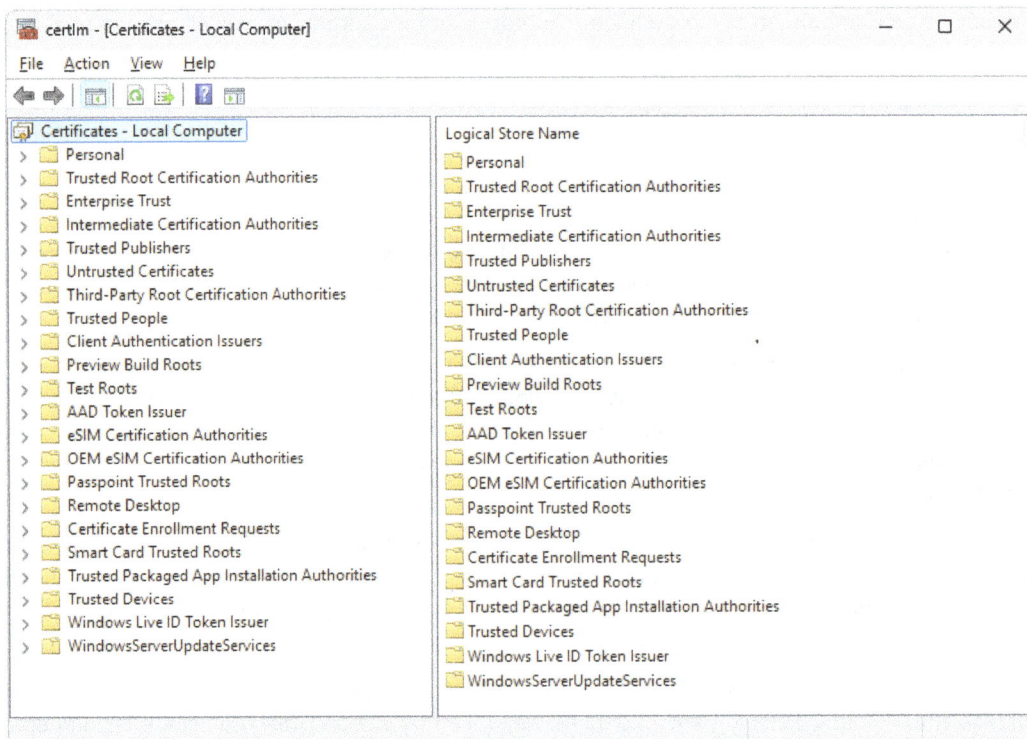

Figure 1.10.1: The Windows Certificate Manager can be used to view all certificates that are installed on a Windows device. Certificates are contained in Stores, which group certificates based on their usage.

There are three main Certificate Stores that are used within the Windows operating system which all have separate purposes:

- **Local Computer Store** - Stores certificates that are local to the device and available to all users on the workstation.
- **Service Account Store** - Stores certificates that are used for Windows services that are local on the workstation.
- **User Account Store** - Stores certificates that are used for individual users that utilize the workstation. These certificates can potentially "follow" users if they use other workstations in the Active Directory domain.

The Local Computer Store and the User Account Store are the most common Certificate Stores that are used on a Windows device. The Service Account Certificate Store is used for services or service accounts on the workstation, and is something that is not likely to have to be managed unless there is a specific application that requires it. There are several different folders within these Stores that are used to place certificates in:

Windows Certificate Store Name	Purpose
Personal	The Personal Store contains certificates that have a private key controlled by the user or workstation.
Trusted Root Certification Authorities	The Trusted Root Certification Authorities Store contains certificates that belong to implicitly trusted Certificate Authorities.
Enterprise Trust	Contains certificates that are issued from other organizations.
Intermediate Certification Authorities	Contains certificates issued to Subordinate Certificate Authorities in the certificate hierarchy.
Active Directory User Object	Contains the user object certificate or certificates published in Active Directory.
Trusted Publishers	Contains certificates installed from trusted Certificate Authorities.
Untrusted Certificates	Contains certificates that have been explicitly identified as untrusted.
Third Party Root Certification Authorities	Contains trusted Root Certificates from Certificate Authorities outside of the internal PKI hierarchy.

Table 1.10.1: There are multiple Certificate Store folders that can be found on a Windows device.

There are locations within the Windows Registry and within the Certificate Store where certificates are located and can be utilized. Most of the time these details are not relevant, but for Developers, Network Administrators or Systems Administrators these details become relevant for implementation and troubleshooting purposes.

Windows Certificate Management with MMC

The Certificate Store utilizes the Microsoft Management Console (MMC) for managing certificates within the Windows operating system. There are two MMC Management Saved Console (MSC) files available on Windows (both client and server versions) which makes it easy to rapidly view certificates:

- **certlm.msc** - Shows certificates located in the Local Computer Store.
- **certmgr.msc** - Shows certificates located in the User Account Store.

For the Service Account Certificate Store, this can be viewed by adding the Certificates Snap-in, and selecting the Service account option when selecting an available Snap-in.

Public Key Infrastructure Overview - Chapter Summary

Now that the basic fundamentals of a PKI have been reviewed, the next step in this book is to explore and understand how Active Directory Certificate Services is used with Windows Server to create a Certificate Authority.

Chapter 2 - AD CS Overview

Active Directory Certificate Services (AD CS) is a server role that has been available in Windows Server releases since Windows Server 2008. Active Directory Certificate Services allows for the creation of a Public Key Infrastructure and Certificate Authority in a Windows environment, with or without the use of Active Directory. Active Directory Certificate Services is a fully featured PKI solution that can be used to issue certificates for multiple purposes, which can include the following:

- Digital Signatures
- Encrypting File System
- IPSec
- MDM Certificates
- S/MIME
- Secure LDAP (LDAPS) with Active Directory
- Smart Cards
- SSL Client Certificates
- VPN Access
- Wireless Network Access

With the Active Directory Certificate Services role, certificates can be issued and managed for various purposes as defined and required by an organization. Active Directory Certificate Services supports various Certificate Authority hierarchy configurations and other options depending on the needs of an organization. Also supported are several deployment scenarios, and AD CS can be "tiered", which breaks up a Certificate Authority into multiple servers by adding different layers to the Certificate Authority. This can be done to factor in future scalability, security, and for custom deployments in an organization. There are third-party utilities and vendors that provide the same functionality as Active Directory Certificate Services. In some cases, additional functionality is present with other vendor solutions, but there are several advantages to using Active Directory Certificate Services within a Windows Server environment:

- Active Directory Certificate Services is available as a role within Windows Server, which means that it can be added or removed at any time. Since the role is already provided with Windows Server, there is no additional software required for implementation as it is already present.
- Active Directory Certificate Services is designed to be scalable and backwards compatible with earlier versions of Windows Server to allow for easier and faster migration paths to new versions of the Active Directory Certificate Services role.
- Active Directory Certificate Services offers complex integrations with Active Directory, which is a benefit in an organization that primarily utilizes the Windows operating system. It can get information about users and workstations automatically when issuing and managing certificates, which saves a considerable amount of time.
- Active Directory Certificate Services is an on-premises solution, which means that it allows for customizations that are not always possible through a third-party provider.
- With Active Directory and Group Policy, deploying certificates within an Active Directory domain is easy and can be automated with minimal effort.
- With Active Directory domains with unsupported top-level domain names, it is extremely difficult to issue certificates to those domains through a third-party vendor since there is no way to validate that the domain is valid. Active Directory Certificate Services supports custom domains that may be present within an Active Directory domain.

This chapter will focus on the Active Directory Certificate Services role and how it can be used as a Certificate Authority in a Windows domain.

Active Directory Certificate Services Overview

Most of the information in this chapter is for reference purposes only, and skipping this chapter will not affect the deployment of the Certificate Authority.

AD CS Overview - Active Directory Certificate Services History

Active Directory Certificate Services is a mature and well supported PKI solution that Microsoft has supported in one way or another since 1997. The predecessor to Active Directory Certificate Services was a product known as Microsoft Certificate Server. This product was originally released for Windows NT 4.0 Server as an optional feature with the Windows NT 4.0 Option Pack. It offered basic and limited Certificate Authority features to Windows, and was not easy to install or manage. It was fairly limited compared to modern PKI solutions, but the product continued to evolve in later versions of Windows Server.

There were subsequent versions of the Microsoft Certificate Server application released for Windows 2000 Server, Windows Server 2003 and finally for Windows Server 2003 R2. Some of the basic features of that product can still be found in modern versions of Active Directory Certificate Services. For example, the Certification Authority console has remained mostly unchanged in later versions of Windows Server, and most of the changes are related to updated cryptography options and Active Directory integration:

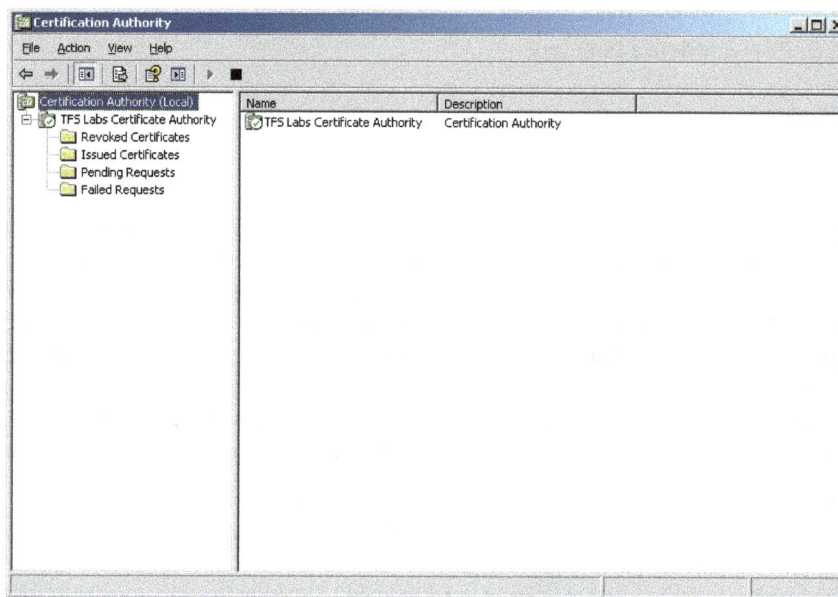

Figure 2.1.1: The Certification Authority console as it appears on Windows Server 2003 R2 Standard. This is the last version of Microsoft Certificate Server before it was retired and replaced with Active Directory Certificate Services, which was first released with Windows Server 2008.

When Windows Server 2008 was released, the Microsoft Certificate Server application was retired in favour of the Active Directory Certificate Services role. The role has continued to be updated since that initial release, and has remained a critical role in Windows Server. There is considerably more Active Directory integrations present in these versions, which allows for greater flexibility on certificate deployment.

> **Active Directory Certificate Services Backwards Compatibility**
>
> There is a degree of backwards compatibility that exists with Active Directory Certificate Services, and the general rule is that AD CS can coexist with versions of Windows Server that is no more than 2 versions behind. For example, AD CS should work correctly with Windows Server 2022 and Windows Server 2016, but Windows Server 2022 and Windows Server 2012 R2 could potentially have compatibility issues.
>
> This is an important factor to consider for the lifecycle of a Certificate Authority. For Root CA servers, ensure that the version of Windows Server does not differ too much from any of the Subordinate CA servers that are located within the domain.

AD CS Overview - Active Directory Certificate Services Roles

Active Directory Certificate Services is currently split into six separate roles, which provides additional options and flexibility for various deployment scenarios:

Certification Authority - This role is used to issue and manage certificates, with the ability to create Root and Subordinate Certificate Authorities. Multiple Certificate Authorities can be linked together and "tiered" to form a complete PKI. Currently the AD CS role allows for the creation of Certificate Authorities with or without the use of Active Directory:

- **Standalone CA** - These are servers that may or may not be members of an Active Directory domain and can operate without it entirely. A Standalone CA can be used in an online or offline state and is most often used as a Root Certificate Authority in most organizations.
- **Enterprise CA** - These are servers that are a member of an Active Directory domain and are typically used as a Subordinate or Issuing Certificate Authority. These types of servers are typically always online and available, and handle the normal tasks of a Certificate Authority such as issuing certificates to users and devices.

Certificate Enrollment Policy Web Service - The Certificate Enrollment Policy Web Service role allows users and computers to request and obtain certificates when they are not members of an Active Directory domain or are located outside of the Active Directory network. It is used together with the Certificate Enrollment Web Service to issue certificates.

Certificate Enrollment Web Service - The Certificate Enrollment Web Service role allows users and computers to enroll and renew certificates when they are not members of an Active Directory domain or are located outside of the Active Directory network. It is used together with the Certificate Enrollment Policy Web Service.

Certification Authority Web Enrollment - The Certification Authority Web Enrollment role adds a simple web interface using Internet Information Services over the HTTPS protocol that allows users to request and manage certificates, as well as retrieve the Certificate Revocation List (CRL) files for the Certificate Authority.

Network Device Enrollment Service - The Network Device Enrollment Service (NDES) role gives the AD CS role the ability to issue and manage certificates for network devices such as switches, routers, and firewalls. These types of devices typically do not have Active Directory accounts associated with them, so they are not able to automatically request certificates.

Online Responder - The Online Responder role adds OCSP functionality to Active Directory Certificate Services, which allows for rapid revocation of certificates in large environments without relying entirely on a CRL to be updated and deployed to the Certificate Authority.

Even though there are multiple roles available with Active Directory Certificate Services, it does not necessarily mean that all roles are needed in a particular organization. Certain roles have a particular set of requirements, which means that some environments would never need to use certain roles at all if they are not needed.

Active Directory Certificate Services Roles and Multiple Servers

Typically, all the Active Directory Certificate Services roles are not used in every organization. If multiple Active Directory Certificate Services roles are used, they are typically not installed on the same server. This is to reduce the complexity of the servers that are used in the PKI, as well as to enable greater flexibility in complex environments. For a large-scale Active Directory Certificate Services deployment that utilizes all roles, there would be individual servers used for each role at a minimum.

It is also not uncommon to split up servers if the usage becomes too high for a single server. For example, the Online Responder role can be installed on the same server as the Subordinate CA and initially encounter no issues. In the future, should the amount of traffic increase and start to become a problem, the role could be migrated to a separate server without impacting the Certificate Authority.

AD CS Overview - Active Directory Certificate Services Cryptography Options

Active Directory Certificate Services supports multiple cryptography options for creating certificates, and offers a great deal of flexibility on how those certificates are configured. When creating a Certificate Authority using Active Directory Certificate Services, there are several cryptography options that need to be configured for the certificate at the time of creation:

- **Cryptographic Provider** - The cryptographic provider defines what features are available in a Certificate Authority and what types of certificates can be issued. This will vary based on the usage of a Certificate Authority, and how a particular organization will utilize certificates.
- **Key Length** - The key length will determine the length of the keys that are generated by the Certificate Authority for any issued certificates. Typically, larger key lengths offer better security, but can affect performance on some devices.
- **Hash Algorithm** - The hash algorithm determines how certificates are signed and encrypted, which is a critical aspect of the security of certificates that are issued by a Certificate Authority. Weaker hash algorithms are easier to break, and hash algorithms such as SHA1 and MD5 are considered obsolete as they are no longer secure enough for certificates in most cases.

Active Directory Certificate Services offers a great deal of flexibility when configuring the cryptographic options for a Certificate Authority, and supports multiple options:

Cryptographic Provider	Key Lengths	Hash Algorithms
DSA#Microsoft Software Key Storage Provider	512, 1024, 2048	SHA1
ECDSA_P256#Microsoft Smart Card Key Storage Provider	256	SHA1, SHA256, SHA384, SHA512
ECDSA_P384#Microsoft Smart Card Key Storage Provider	384	SHA1, SHA256, SHA384, SHA512
ECDSA_P521#Microsoft Smart Card Key Storage Provider	521	SHA1, SHA256, SHA384, SHA512
ECDSA_P256#Microsoft Software Key Storage Provider	256	SHA1, SHA256, SHA384, SHA512
ECDSA_P384#Microsoft Software Key Storage Provider	384	SHA1, SHA256, SHA384, SHA512
ECDSA_P521#Microsoft Software Key Storage Provider	521	SHA1, SHA256, SHA384, SHA512
Microsoft Base Cryptographic Provider v1.0	512, 1024, 2048, 4096	SHA1, MD2, MD4, MD5
Microsoft Base DSS Cryptographic Provider	512, 1024	SHA1
Microsoft Base Smart Card Crypto Provider	1024, 2048, 4096	SHA1, MD2, MD4, MD5
Microsoft Enhanced Cryptographic Provider v1.0	512, 1024, 2048, 4096	SHA1, MD2, MD4, MD5
Microsoft Strong Cryptographic Provider	512, 1024, 2048, 4096	SHA1, MD2, MD4, MD5
RSA#Microsoft Smart Card Key Storage Provider	1024, 2048, 4096	SHA1, SHA256, SHA384, SHA512, MD2, MD4, MD5
RSA#Microsoft Software Key Storage Provider	512, 1024, 2048, 4096	SHA1, SHA256, SHA384, SHA512, MD2, MD4, MD5

Table 2.3.1: Cryptographic provider options, key lengths, and hash algorithms that are available in Active Directory Certificate Services running on Windows Server 2022. The **RSA#Microsoft Software Key Storage Provider** is the default cryptographic provider for Active Directory Certificate Services.

During the configuration of the Certificate Authority, the cryptographic options can be setup as necessary based on the requirements that the certificate will use:

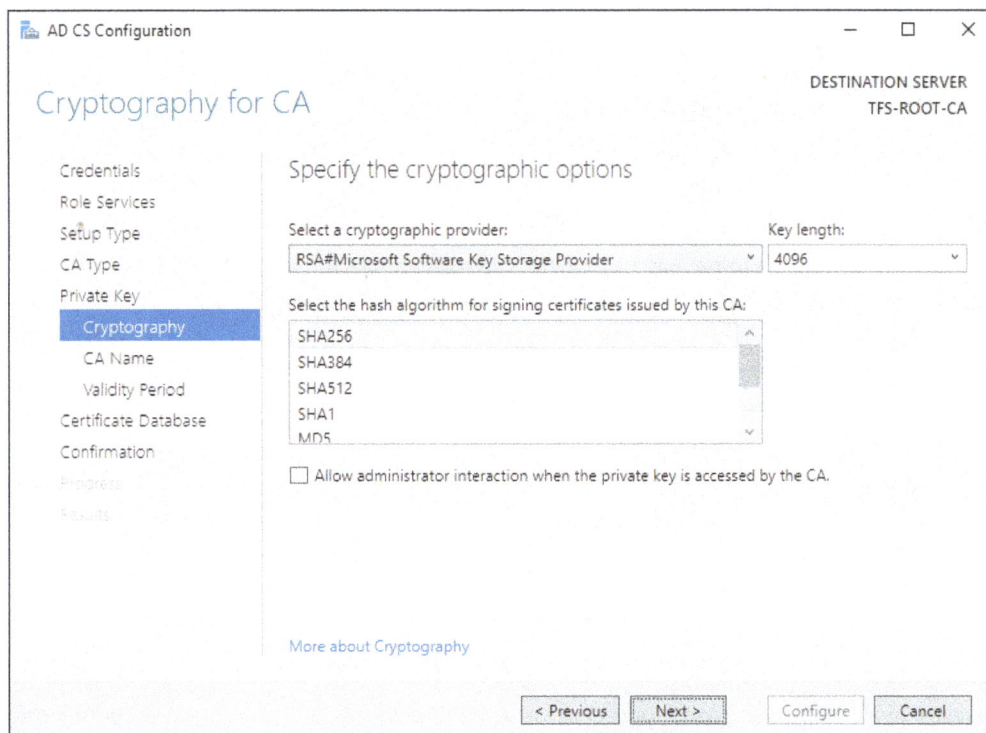

Figure 2.3.1: During the configuration of a Certificate Authority using Active Directory Certificate Services, there are options for setting the cryptographic provider, the key length and the hash algorithm for the certificate. This example shows a configuration used for a Root certificate, which is configured later in this book.

These settings cannot be changed later, and if a different cryptographic provider is required for the Certificate Authority, the certificate will need to be recreated with the correct settings.

> **Active Directory Certificate Services Cryptographic Options**
>
> The cryptographic options used in this book for the Root and Subordinate certificates use the **RSA#Microsoft Software Key Storage Provider** as the cryptographic provider, with a key length of **4096**, and the **SHA256** hash algorithm. These options provide the highest level of compatibility with modern operating systems and web browsers. If different settings are required, ensure that they are correctly configured for both the Root and Subordinate certificates.

AD CS Overview - Active Directory Certificate Services Key Components

There are multiple components to consider when dealing with Active Directory Certificate Services, especially when it comes to regular operation of a Certificate Authority:

Certificate Authority CAPolicy.inf File - The CAPolicy.inf file is used to configure Active Directory Certificate Services, specifically during the initial creation of a Certificate Authority. It can be used to specify default settings, define certificate templates, set the OID, and other settings. It is only used when the Certificate Authority is created and whenever the CA certificate is renewed. The complete path for this file is **C:\Windows\CAPolicy.inf**, and can usually be found on any Certificate Authority using AD CS.

Certificate Authority Database - The database holds all information that is related to the Certificate Authority. This includes all certificates, including ones that have been issued, revoked and all pending requests. If the Certificate Authority is configured to use Private Key Archive, those private keys will also be stored in the database. The database and associated files can be found in the **C:\Windows\System32\CertLog** folder.

Certificate Authority Private Key - The private key is critical to the Certificate Authority operation, and if the private key is ever compromised the PKI can no longer be trusted. The private key is stored in an encrypted state, and can be found in the **C:\ProgramData\Application Data\Microsoft\Crypto** folders.

Windows Server Registry Settings - There are multiple configuration options that are stored in the Windows Registry that are specifically related to the configuration and operation of Active Directory Certificate Services. These settings can be found in the **HKLM\SYSTEM\CurrentControlSet\Services\CertSvc\Configuration** location.

These are some of the components to be aware of when Active Directory Certificate Services is being used as a Certificate Authority. More information on how these components are utilized and configured are included in later chapters in this book, as they are configured as part of demonstrating how to create a Certificate Authority.

> **Active Directory Certificate Services Backup and Restore**
>
> Aside from using the native Windows Server Backup tool and other third-party tools for creating backups, there is also a tool included with Active Directory Certificate Services dedicated specifically for backing up the Certificate Authority. Instructions on how to use this tool for backup and restoring AD CS are included in a later chapter in this book.

AD CS Overview - Active Directory Certificate Services Management Tools

There are several methods that can be used for managing Active Directory Certificate Services, both locally and remotely depending on how an environment is configured. There are tools that are available for managing AD CS using the GUI which are well supported, and there are also tools available using the CLI using PowerShell. These tools for managing AD CS are well supported, and offer a great deal of flexibility for managing a Certificate Authority.

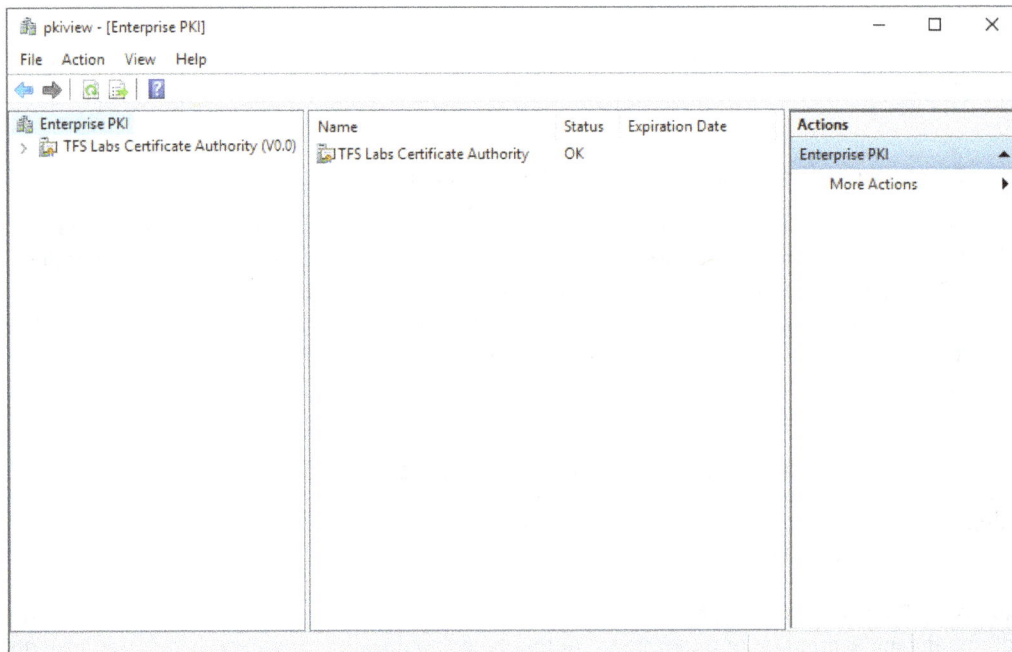

Figure 2.5.1: The Enterprise PKI tool that is included with the Active Directory Certificate Services management tools allows an administrator to verify the health of the Certificate Authority, specifically on an Enterprise CA.

Many of the graphical tools that are used for managing Active Directory Certificate Services utilize MMC with several snap-ins. These tools offer the ability to manage the Certificate Authority without the use of the command line if necessary. The **certutil.exe** tool is a command line tool that performs many administrative tasks for Active Directory Certificate Services, as well as many certificate tasks on Windows devices.

Since the introduction of PowerShell in Windows Server 2008, Active Directory Certificate Services has several Cmdlets available for administrators to use for managing the Certificate Authority. These Cmdlets are used during the deployment of the Certificate Authority in later chapters in this book, and a detailed listing of the available Cmdlets are provided as well.

AD CS Overview - Chapter Summary

The next step in this book is to explore and understand the TFS Labs test environment that is used in this book for creating the TFS Labs Certificate Authority. This will provide a complete overview of the test environment so that the requirements are understood, what needs to be done, and how everything will work in a complete Certificate Authority using Active Directory Certificate Services.

Chapter 3 - Test Environment Overview

Creating a Certificate Authority requires a considerable amount of planning to ensure that it is setup correctly. This involves several important steps, which requires answering the following questions before servers are even provisioned for a PKI:

- What type of Certificate Authority is being created?
- What servers are required to be created?
- What are the names of the servers that are required?
- What names are going to be used for the Root and Subordinate certificates?
- What is the validity period of the issued certificates?
- Are there any legacy requirements that need to be considered for the environment?

Determining the answers to these questions will determine how the Certificate Authority will function once it has been created. Planning this out properly is the most crucial part of the entire PKI implementation, and if any mistakes are made in the planning process or something is overlooked, correcting the problem later can be extremely difficult.

This chapter will focus on the test environment that this book will be using for creating a Certificate Authority with Active Directory Certificate Services.

> **Active Directory Certificate Services GUI and CLI Installations**
>
> Even though this book focuses on the fictional TFS Labs domain, the instructions and guidelines provided in this chapter can be easily adapted to fit with other organizations. Take note of the servers and Certificate Authority details provided in this chapter and start thinking about how it can be applied to other domains that will be used with Active Directory Certificate Services.

Test Environment Overview - TFS Labs Domain

This book uses a simplified and basic Active Directory environment for demonstration purposes. This Active Directory domain demonstrates the bare minimum that is required for Active Directory Certificate Services to operate correctly with Windows Server 2022. The Active Directory domain that is going to be used in this book is the TFS Labs domain (corp.tfslabs.com), which is being used by a small IT company that is based in Toronto, Ontario, Canada.

In total, there are three Windows servers and one Windows workstation that will be used to build and test the TFS Labs environment:

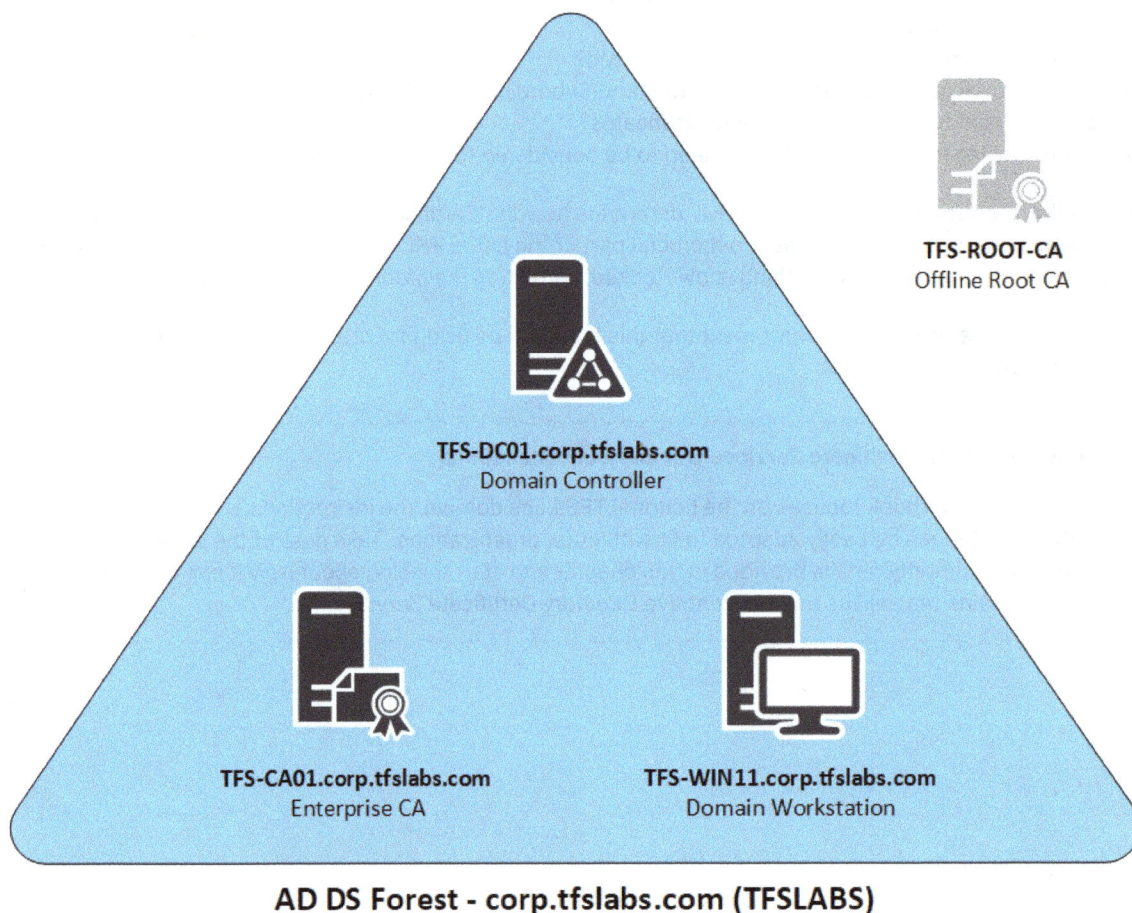

TFS-ROOT-CA
Offline Root CA

TFS-DC01.corp.tfslabs.com
Domain Controller

TFS-CA01.corp.tfslabs.com
Enterprise CA

TFS-WIN11.corp.tfslabs.com
Domain Workstation

AD DS Forest - corp.tfslabs.com (TFSLABS)

Figure 3.1.1: The TFS Labs Active Directory domain consists of three servers and one workstation. This domain represents the bare minimum environment that is required to demonstrate and test Active Directory Certificate Services.

The virtual machines that are being used in this book for the test environment are using the following specifications:

VM	Operating System	CPU	Memory	Disk	IP Address	Hyper-V Generation
TFS-DC01	Windows Server 2022	2	4096 MB	40 GB	10.100.1.100	2
TFS-WIN11	Windows 11 Pro 24H2	2	4096 MB	64 GB	10.100.1.110	2
TFS-ROOT-CA	Windows Server 2022	2	4096 MB	40 GB	N/A	1
TFS-CA01	Windows Server 2022	2	4096 MB	40 GB	10.100.1.101	1

Table 3.1.1: TFS Labs domain virtual machine specifications and network settings.

There is a mixture of Hyper-V Generation 1 and Generation 2 virtual machines used for the TFS Labs environment. This is due to requiring a virtual floppy drive on certain virtual machines, and only Generation 1 virtual machines offer that functionality. A virtual floppy disk is used to transfer files between the servers that are hosting the Offline Root CA and the Subordinate CA. If Hyper-V Generation 1 virtual machines are being used, there is no need to add a virtual floppy drive at the time of provisioning of the virtual machine, it is always present by default.

For networking purposes all virtual machines in this test environment are using the 10.100.1.0/24 network. Since there is only a handful of virtual machines involved, all IP addresses are set to static and there is no DHCP server present to automatically distribute IP addresses. This network will vary depending on different environments, so keep that in mind when provisioning a test environment. Information on how networking in Hyper-V is configured and operates is provided in a later chapter.

Virtual Networking Configuration

For the TFS Labs environment, use whatever IP address scheme works best as there are not many requirements for connecting the virtual machines. Since there are only three virtual machines, of which only two of them require network connectivity, the test environment can be configured with private networking so that those virtual machines have no access to the network.

External Network Connections

Before determining how the virtual machines will connect to the virtual network, determine if testing the Certificate Authority with external devices such as an iOS or an Android device is required. There are several ways to configure the networking to allow for shared access from the virtual network to the physical network, and there is a lot of flexibility in virtual networks to allow for this connection. Since this is just being used for a test environment, setting up the virtual network is much simpler than in a production environment.

Software Versions

All versions of Windows Server 2022 are using Standard Edition (Desktop Experience) in this book. There is no difference in the implementation if Windows Server 2022 Datacenter Edition (Desktop Experience) is used instead. For the version of Windows 11 Pro, the 24H2 release was used in this book. There should be no issues with using earlier versions of Windows 11 Pro, but consider using versions that are currently under active support from Microsoft. For the specific versions of the software that was used for the creation of this book, they are as follows:

- Windows Server 2022 - Version 21H2 (Build 20348.4052)
- Windows 11 Pro - Version 24H2 (Build 26100.4946)
- Microsoft Edge - Version 139.0.3405.102

Earlier or later versions of Windows Server 2022 and Windows 11 should work correctly.

Windows Server Core

The version of Windows Server that is used in this book is Windows Server 2022 Standard Edition (Desktop Experience). Windows Server Core is a method of using Windows Server that removes a considerable part of the user interface to reduce the attack surface on Windows Server, and most configuration on this type of server is performed remotely with RSAT (Remote Server Administration Tools) or with command line tools. It is entirely possible to deploy Active Directory Certificate Services using Windows Server Core and remotely manage the installation and configuration. It is possible with remote administration features that are available in Windows Server to manage this type of environment, but this is beyond the scope of this book.

Here is a breakdown of the servers and workstations that are being used in the TFS Labs environment:

- **TFS-DC01** is the Domain Controller for the TFS Labs Active Directory domain. It is also used to allow for automatic distribution of certificates using Group Policy to the TFS Labs domain. The Active Directory Forest and Domain Functional Levels are set to Windows Server 2016 Functional Levels, which is the latest version available for Active Directory.
- **TFS-WIN11** is a workstation that is a member of the TFS Labs domain, and it is used to ensure that the certificates that are issued by the Certificate Authority is operating correctly. This workstation is also used to ensure that Group Policy deployment of certificates is working correctly.
- **TFS-ROOT-CA** is the Root Certificate Authority for the TFS Labs domain, which is a Standalone CA that is using the Active Directory Certificate Services role. It is used to create the Root certificate and is also used to sign the certificate for the Subordinate Certificate Authority. It is left in an offline state unless there is an issue with the Subordinate Certificate Authority or the CRL needs to be updated. It is not a member of the TFS Labs domain and is technically just a workgroup server. There is also no additional software or services installed on the server, except for BitLocker, should that be used. Once the implementation of the Certificate Authority is complete it can be shut down (but not deleted). This server has no network access to provide additional security.
- **TFS-CA01** is the Subordinate Certificate Authority in the TFS Labs domain. It is an Enterprise CA that is using the Active Directory Certificate Services role. It is used to issue all certificates within the domain, except for the Root certificate that is issued by the Root Certificate Authority that is located on the TFS-ROOT-CA server. It is also used to handle the OCSP role and primary CRL roles for certificate revocation. It is a TFS Labs domain member.

Now that the virtual machines that are needed for the TFS Labs domain have been defined, there are several design considerations that will need to be made.

> **Active Directory Certificate Services GUI and CLI Installations**
>
> The installation and configuration for Active Directory Certificate Services can be done almost entirely through the CLI, but there are some steps that require the GUI to complete the configuration. Most of the installation and configuration is performed using the CLI, but the GUI instructions are also provided as an alternative. Whichever method is used to configure the Certificate Authority is not important, but the CLI installation and configuration are typically much faster to perform.

Test Environment Overview - Certificate Authority Design Considerations

The focus of this book is to demonstrate the deployment of Active Directory Certificate Services on the TFS Labs domain as a Two-Tier Certificate Authority. On a high-level, the following design considerations will be made for this deployment:

- SHA-1 will not be used since it has been deprecated by online Certificate Authorities and by most vendors since it is incredibly insecure. The Certificate Authority that will be created in this example for TFS Labs will use SHA-2 (SHA256) by default. It will also use a key length of 4096 bits wherever possible.
- The Certificate Authority deployment will utilize an Offline Root CA.
- The deployment will utilize a Subordinate CA for issuing certificates to the TFS Labs domain. The Subordinate CA will always be online and will be used to issue all certificates to the TFS Labs domain.
- The Root certificate will be valid for 10 years and the Subordinate certificate will be valid for 5 years. All issued certificates from the Subordinate CA will be valid for only 1 year.
- All files that need to be transferred to and from the Root CA server is done with a virtual floppy disk through the virtualization platform used for creating it. This virtual floppy disk will be deleted at the end of the implementation phase to protect the files that were needed to be transferred as part of the implementation. When needed in the future, a new virtual floppy disk should be created and then immediately deleted once it is no longer required.
- For connectivity purposes, CNAME records will be used whenever possible to allow for the Subordinate CA server to be split up in the future if needed. The Active Directory Certificate Services role is designed to be easily broken up and reconfigured should the need arise.

- Server roles will be minimized and only the required roles will be used, as it is bad practice to run multiple server roles on the same servers that are running Active Directory Certificate Services. Certificate Authority servers should never run other server roles, as this increases complexity on the server and can introduce issues that are difficult to troubleshoot.
- Certificate Templates will use the highest available compatibility settings whenever possible and will not work properly on older versions of Windows.
- Auditing is enabled for all available Certificate Authority functions for troubleshooting and compliance purposes. All auditing logs are stored in the Windows Event Logs, which can be viewed at any time.

These design considerations do not factor in any type of legacy applications or services that may be present in some network environments. It is important to determine if these settings are appropriate a particular network, and that is why it is important to fully plan and thoroughly test the Certificate Authority before putting it into production. Determining which requirements are needed for the Certificate Authority when it is deployed in an environment is always different, and the requirements will always vary based on the organization and what applications will utilize the Certificate Authority with the issued certificates.

Test Environment Overview - Certificate Hierarchy Overview

For the certificates that will be issued for the TFS Labs domain, there will be one Root certificate and one Subordinate certificate in a Two-Tier Certificate Authority. Here is an overview of what that certificate hierarchy will look like once it is completed:

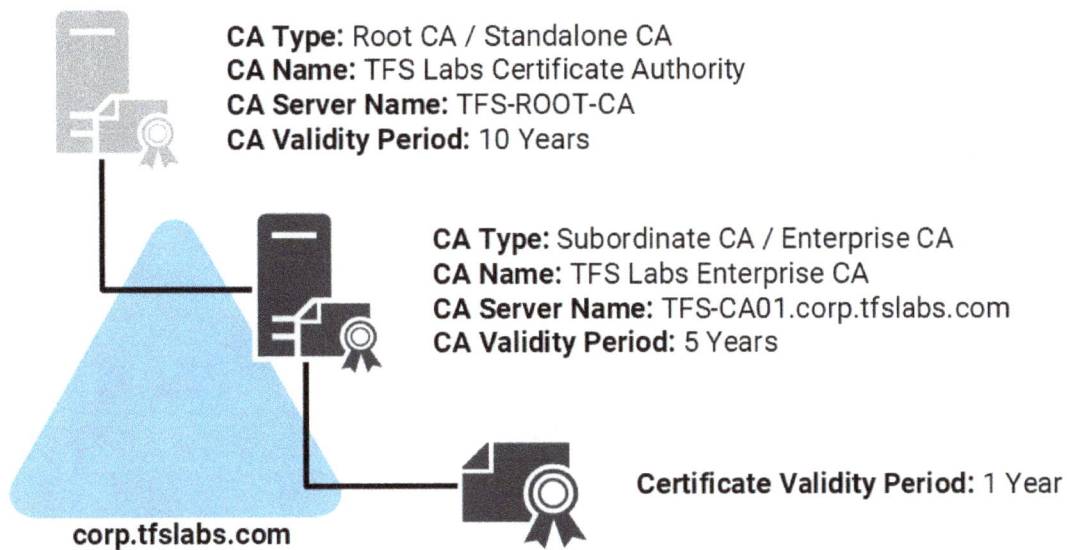

CA Type: Root CA / Standalone CA
CA Name: TFS Labs Certificate Authority
CA Server Name: TFS-ROOT-CA
CA Validity Period: 10 Years

CA Type: Subordinate CA / Enterprise CA
CA Name: TFS Labs Enterprise CA
CA Server Name: TFS-CA01.corp.tfslabs.com
CA Validity Period: 5 Years

Certificate Validity Period: 1 Year

corp.tfslabs.com

Figure 3.3.1: The TFS Labs Certificate Authority is a Two-Tier Certificate Authority consisting of a Root and Subordinate Certificate Authority.

The certificate structure and associated servers for the TFS Labs domain are as follows:

Certificate Name	Certificate Type	Validity	Virtual Machine
TFS Labs Certificate Authority	Root Certificate	10 years	TFS-ROOT-CA
TFS Labs Enterprise CA	Subordinate Certificate	5 years	TFS-CA01
N/A	Issued Certificate	1 year	N/A

Table 3.3.1: TFS Labs Certificate Authority structure and validity periods.

The validity period for the certificates in the TFS Labs domain will be set to the following:

- The Root CA certificate is set to expire after 10 years. This certificate is the Root of the entire PKI for the TFS Labs domain. The validity period of 10 years is perfectly acceptable for a Root CA, and that server will need to be brought online once every 52 weeks to update the CRL for the Root CA. It is possible to have a longer validity period for the Root CA, but that is not recommended.
- The Subordinate CA certificate is set to expire after 5 years. This certificate is used to sign all certificates that are issued in the TFS Labs domain. Unlike the Root CA, it will always be online and available, as users and devices will request certificates from the server. From an Active Directory Certificate Services role perspective, it is an Enterprise CA.
- All certificates that are issued from the Subordinate CA is limited to 1 year only for the validity period. Many vendors, the most recent being Apple, have specifically restricted SSL lifetimes to 1 year only for security purposes. This forces vendors to keep their SSL certificates up to date and to make sure that modern security practices and technologies are being used to protect their users. Most modern web browsers enforce strict SSL security to keep users safe, so this is the primary reason this is being done. Even though the TFS Labs Certificate Authority is internal only and not publicly accessible, it should still follow best practices whenever possible to avoid potential issues.

Once a fully functioning Certificate Authority is deployed on the TFS Labs domain, the complete Certificate Authority hierarchy for the TFS Labs domain can be seen on the Subordinate certificate. Open the Subordinate certificate to view the configuration for it:

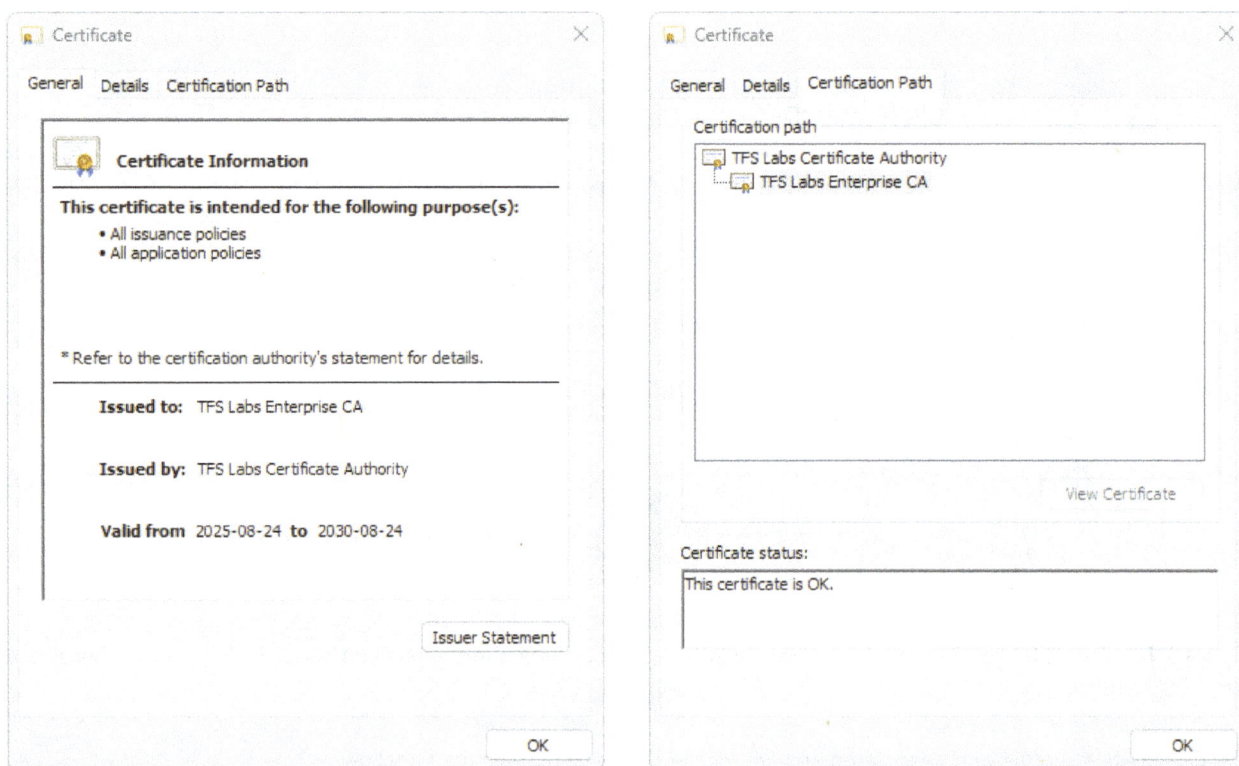

Figure 3.3.2: The TFS Labs Certificate Authority and TFS Labs Enterprise CA certificate can be viewed in the completed certificates for the TFS Labs domain. These two certificates make up the Two-Tier Certificate Authority, and make up the foundation of the PKI.

By looking at the Subordinate certificate details, the TFS Labs Enterprise CA is a Subordinate certificate of the TFS Labs Certificate Authority Root certificate. The TFS Labs Certificate Authority was used to sign the certificate for the TFS Labs Enterprise CA. The validity period for the Root certificate is set to 10 years, and the validity period for the Subordinate certificate is set to 5 years as specified above.

Certificate Validity Periods

It is up to an organization to determine how long certificates should be valid for when they are issued. It used to be common to have Root certificates that would have validity periods of over 20 years, and with that type of setup it was not a lot of work to maintain those Certificate Authorities. If an organization does not require interoperability with certain vendors, then there can be certificate validity periods for as long as needed, but that could change at any time.

For example, vendors could force a change to disallow certificates with long validity periods within their web browsers. This could mean that certificates with long expiration times could become invalidated at any time, and it usually only requires one vendor to make the change to get the other vendors to do the same.

Test Environment Overview - AD CS Internal URLs

All the internal URLs that will be in use for the Active Directory Certificate Services role will point to the TFS-CA01 server and utilize CNAME records. The following URLs will be in use once the Active Directory Certificate Services implementation has been completed:

Active Directory Certificate Services Role	Internal URL
IIS 10.0 HTTP Server Instance	*http://tfs-ca01.corp.tfslabs.com/*
Certificate Practice Statement	*http://pki.corp.tfslabs.com/cps.html*
Root CA Certificate Revocation List	*http://pki.corp.tfslabs.com/CertData/*
Enterprise CA Certificate Revocation List	*http://pki.corp.tfslabs.com/CertEnroll/*
Certificate Internal Download Location	*http://pki.corp.tfslabs.com/Certificates/*
Online Certificate Status Protocol	*http://ocsp.corp.tfslabs.com/ocsp/*
Active Directory Web Enrollment Service	*https://pki.corp.tfslabs.com/CertSrv/*

Table 3.4.1: Active Directory Certificate Services internal URLs for the TFS Labs Certificate Authority.

These URLs will be needed to properly implement a Certificate Authority using Active Directory Certificate Services. Even though some of them do not appear to be important, or in some cases even appear to have anything associated with them, they are needed to ensure that clients and services that are using the PKI can do so successfully. IIS will be used for hosting the files for the Certificate Authority in the TFS Labs domain.

Despite there being CNAME records in place to create these URLs for the PKI, they will still work with the regular FQDN of the TFS-CA01 server.

SSL Enabled Services with Active Directory Certificate Services

SSL is not enabled for many of the websites that a Certificate Authority uses, and this is mostly to support the deployment and validation of certificates. The reason that SSL cannot be used is because it cannot be assumed that the devices connecting to an SSL website has the correct Root and Subordinate certificates installed on it when it is internal. When new devices are added to the domain they will typically be missing these certificates as they have not been installed yet, and are otherwise not available.

The one exception to this is the Active Directory Web Enrollment Service website, since it is used to securely submit a Certificate Request to the Enterprise CA.

Public Facing PKI Websites

It is extremely bad practice to ever allow the internal websites for the Active Directory Certificate Services role to be publicly facing on the internet. Allowing these websites to be available on the public internet exposes an organization to many potential security risks, such as potentially leaking information about Active Directory information and any certificates that have been issued.

If there is ever a requirement to make the Active Directory Certificate Services role publicly facing on the internet, there is an issue with the requirements for that type of deployment. The internal websites for the Active Directory Certificate Services role should never be publicly facing, and if the request is ever made to allow this, push back on that requirement and deny it.

Active Directory Certificate Services is not meant to be used for issuing certificates on the public internet, so there is no requirement for the role to be available in that manner. Users that are external to the network should utilize a VPN to request and update certificates if they are located outside of the network.

Test Environment Overview - AD CS Important Files

At the end of the Active Directory Certificate Services deployment, there will be several important file locations on several servers that are needed to host important files needed to support the Certificate Authority.

Test Environment Overview - AD CS Important Files - TFS-CA01

The TFS-CA01 server is the Subordinate CA as well as an Enterprise CA for the TFS Labs domain. It is the only part of the Certificate Authority that is always online, so it contains the needed files for both the Root and Subordinate Certificate Authority, as well as all web services needed to support both of those functions.

The important folders that are used for Active Directory Certificate Services located on the TFS-CA01 server include:

Location	Purpose
C:\CertData	Contains the Root CA CRL files.
C:\Certificates	Contains the Root and Subordinate certificates needed for internal web deployment.
C:\CertRecovery	Contains any certificate that has been restored if the private key is lost.
C:\inetpub\wwwroot\cps.html	The CPS HTML document that is referenced in the CAPolicy.inf file for the Root and Subordinate certificates.
C:\Windows\System32\CertLog	Contains the database and log files for the Enterprise CA.
C:\Windows\System32\CertSrv\CertEnroll	Contains the Subordinate CA CRL files.
C:\Windows\System32\CertSrv\en-US	Contains the Web Enrollment website files.
C:\Windows\SystemData\ocsp	Contains the files needed for the OCSP role web service.

Table 3.5.1.1: Important files related to Active Directory Certificate Services located on the TFS-CA01 server.

Aside from the files and folders that are located on the TFS-CA01 server, there is also an important location in the Windows Registry that is used to store critical settings needed for Active Directory Certificate Services:

HKLM\SYSTEM\CurrentControlSet\Services\CertSvc\Configuration

This Registry location is used with Active Directory Certificate Services regardless of the type of Certificate Authority that is setup and configured.

Test Environment Overview - AD CS Important Files - TFS-DC01

The TFS-DC01 server is the Domain Controller for the TFS Labs domain and is used primarily to deploy certificates to the domain using Group Policy. The important folders that are used for Active Directory Certificate Services located on the TFS-DC01 server include:

Location	Purpose
C:\Certificates	Contains the Root and Subordinate certificates for Group Policy deployment.

Table 3.5.2.1: Important files related to Active Directory Certificate Services located on the TFS-DC01 server.

Since Active Directory Certificate Services is not installed on the TFS-DC01 server, there is nothing specifically stored in the Windows Registry related to that role. There is information stored in Active Directory relating to the Certificate Authority since there is an Enterprise CA in the domain, and this can be viewed using the Active Directory Sites and Services (dssite.msc) console.

Test Environment Overview - AD CS Important Files - TFS-ROOT-CA

The TFS-ROOT-CA server is the Root Certificate Authority for the TFS Labs domain. It is an Offline CA, so it does not have any network connections. Any files that are needed for normal operation of the Root Certificate Authority will be hosted on the TFS-CA01 server, which is an Enterprise CA. The important folders that are used for Active Directory Certificate Services located on the TFS-ROOT-CA server include:

Location	Purpose
C:\RootCA	Contains many of the implementation files that are needed for the Certificate Authority deployment.
C:\Windows\System32\CertLog	Contains the database and log files for the Root CA.
C:\Windows\System32\CertSrv\CertEnroll	Contains the Root CA CRL files which are updated once per year.

Table 3.5.3.1: Important files related to Active Directory Certificate Services located on the TFS-ROOT-CA server.

Like the TFS-CA01 server, there is also an important location in the Windows Registry that is used to store critical settings needed for Active Directory Certificate Services:

HKLM\SYSTEM\CurrentControlSet\Services\CertSvc\Configuration

This Registry location is used with Active Directory Certificate Services regardless of the type of Certificate Authority that is setup and configured.

Test Environment Overview - AD CS Security Considerations

There are a few security considerations that should be factored in before deploying Active Directory Certificate Services in an environment, and most of those considerations are just best practices. This is to ensure that the integrity of the PKI is always maintained, and that there are no issues in supporting it. The most common security considerations for Active Directory Certificate Services include:

- Never install any Active Directory Certificate Services roles on a Domain Controller.
- Always install Active Directory Certificate Services roles on dedicated servers whenever possible. Keeping AD CS servers more isolated than other servers is beneficial for security purposes.
- Avoid mixing and matching Windows Server versions with Active Directory Certificate Services. Try and keep all associated AD CS roles on the same operating system versions and editions whenever possible.
- Ensure that regular backups are kept for Active Directory Certificate Services servers. Test the backups to ensure that the PKI infrastructure can be successfully restored if needed.

- Ensure that Active Directory Certificate Services servers are kept up to date.
- Avoid using obsolete or legacy encryption technologies.
- Create specific Active Directory groups for AD CS administration purposes. Reduce the number of users that have access to those servers to minimize risk to the PKI infrastructure.
- Avoid auto-enrollment for Certificate Templates that do not require it.
- Keep Offline Root Certificate Authorities in a secure location that cannot be easily accessed.

If the network and server environment are secure and everything is configured correctly, then there is not much to worry about for the security of the Active Directory Certificate Services deployment. With that said, it is important to understand that a compromised Certificate Authority is a major issue for an organization, so keeping it secure is critical for IT staff members and the organization in general. Certificates can be used for critical infrastructure such as VPN and server authentication, so if there are security issues with a Certificate Authority, there can be instances when those critical services are not available to the end user.

Test Environment Overview - Certificate Authority Naming Conventions

It is important to create a proper naming convention for the Certificate Authority and everything that is associated with the Certificate Authority. Determining the name of the Certificate Authority is an important first step before servers are provisioned, and it is extremely difficult to change the name of a Certificate Authority after one has been created.

Some things that should be taken into consideration before starting a Certificate Authority are the following:

- Use descriptive names whenever possible, even if those names can be redundant in some instances.
- For customizable items, such as a Certificate Template, try and prefix the name of the Certificate Template so that users are aware that the Certificate Template is for them and that it is something that they should use instead of the default options that may still be available within the environment.
- Ensure that the Certificate Authority incorporates the name of the organization, and is not something generic that can potentially cause confusion for end users.
- Do not use the default names for the Certificate Authority, as they are not user-friendly and do not look professional in a production environment. Using default names can also expose the names of the servers that host the Certificate Authority, which is not always something that an organization would want for security or compliance purposes.
- Avoid using server names for important internal links, use CNAME records to make them more user-friendly whenever possible.
- Only advertise the links to internal Certificate Authority services using CNAME records whenever possible.

Worrying about how to name a Certificate Authority may not seem important and somewhat trivial, but it is important. Ensuring that a proper naming convention is in place will save a lot of trouble later, especially if things are not setup correctly. Fixing the name of a Certificate Authority after it has been created it not easy to do, so it is best to just determine the naming convention before provisioning the servers that are needed for it.

Test Environment Overview - Virtual Machine Checkpoints

There are several steps in this book where virtualization Checkpoints are used during the implementation of the Certificate Authority. Creating a Certificate Authority using Active Directory Certificate Services is a complex process, and there are multiple steps where an error in the implementation can cause issues. Using Checkpoints (or whatever equivalent feature) can make the implementation easier, and will prevent the process from being restarted. These Checkpoints are entirely optional, and they do not need to be used if they are not required for testing.

Test Environment Overview - Chapter Summary

Now that the TFS Labs test environment has been thoroughly explained, the next step in this book is to review how Hyper-V works, and how to use it to create the virtual machines needed for later chapters in this book.

Chapter 4 - Hyper-V Setup and Configuration

Hyper-V is a hypervisor and virtualization platform that was created by Microsoft for the Windows operating system. Like other virtualization solutions, it is capable of creating and running multiple virtual machines in an isolated environment for multiple purposes. Hyper-V is an optional feature that has been available since Windows Server 2008 was released, and it requires no additional licensing costs to be used on a default installation of Windows. A reduced feature version of Hyper-V (referred to as Windows Client Hyper-V) is also available on the Pro, Enterprise and Education versions of Windows starting with Windows 8. Hyper-V is the successor to the Microsoft Virtual PC and Windows Virtual PC virtualization applications, which were deprecated by Microsoft in 2011.

By using Hyper-V for virtualization, there are several benefits that are offered:

- Create a private cloud environment for running multiple production or development virtual machines.
- Run software in a sandbox to prevent it from causing issues with other computers.
- Run software that requires older versions of the Windows operating system or other operating systems.
- Test and develop applications and more rapidly without affecting the main operating system.
- Use hardware more effectively by running multiple virtual machines with less resources.

Like other virtualization platforms, Hyper-V allows for the creation of virtual hard disks, virtual switches, and all other virtual devices that are required to emulate computer hardware. Unlike other virtualization solutions, Hyper-V is not suitable for emulating older operating systems without using complicated workarounds. Hyper-V is meant for modern, production virtual machines and not for legacy operating systems.

Hyper-V requires 64-bit versions of Windows to operate, but is fully capable of emulating supported 32-bit operating systems. There is limited support for Hyper-V on the ARM architecture, but Windows Server 2022 is currently not available for that architecture.

This chapter will focus on the following aspects of Hyper-V:

- Provide an overview on Hyper-V and what its capabilities are, and how to use Hyper-V features for virtualizing test environments in a safe and secure manner.
- Provide information on the different versions of Hyper-V that are available, and what the differences are between those versions.
- How to Install and configure Hyper-V using Windows 11 Pro from start to finish, which is what is used for virtualizing the TFS Labs test environment in this book.
- Demonstrate how to create and manage virtual machines on Hyper-V.

The underlying architecture and design of Hyper-V is quite complex, and is beyond the scope of this book.

> **Hyper-V and Other Virtualization Platforms**
>
> If a different virtualization platform other than Hyper-V is being used for creating the TFS Labs environment, there will be a mention of what the equivalent feature will need to be used to accomplish certain steps in the book.

> **Virtualization Platform Options**
>
> If Hyper-V is already being used and there is no need for any assistance with setting it up or using it, skip this chapter as it is not needed. If another virtualization platform is being used instead, skip this chapter if it is not applicable.

Hyper-V Setup and Configuration - Hyper-V History

Hyper-V is the successor to the Microsoft Virtual PC and Windows Virtual PC virtualization applications, which were deprecated by Microsoft in 2011. These products were derived from the Virtual PC application that was created by Connectix, which was acquired by Microsoft in 2003. Unlike Virtual PC and its derivatives that were created after it was acquired by Microsoft, Hyper-V was written from the ground up and released several months after Windows Server 2008 reached general availability. Hyper-V has been released with every version of Windows Server since that initial release, and multiple variations of the software exists. During the development of Hyper-V, it was referred to with the codename of "Viridian" and was renamed to Hyper-V prior to being released.

Hyper-V is an optional feature in Windows Server that can be easily added to an existing server. A version of Hyper-V is also available on the Pro, Enterprise and Education versions of Windows starting with Windows 8. This version of Hyper-V only includes a subset of the features that are available in Hyper-V and is primarily designed for developers and for testing purposes. Aside from the versions of Hyper-V that are included in the server and workstation versions of Windows, there was also a standalone version of Hyper-V that was released, which has been superseded by Azure Stack HCI. More information on the different versions of Hyper-V that are available for deployment is discussed later in this chapter.

From an architectural perspective, Hyper-V is a Type-1 hypervisor, while other virtualization solutions such as Parallels Desktop, VirtualBox and VMware Workstation are Type-2 hypervisors. There are advantages and disadvantages to both types of hypervisors. The main difference is that a Type-1 hypervisor typically runs directly on the hardware, where a Type-2 hypervisor runs on top of an operating system:

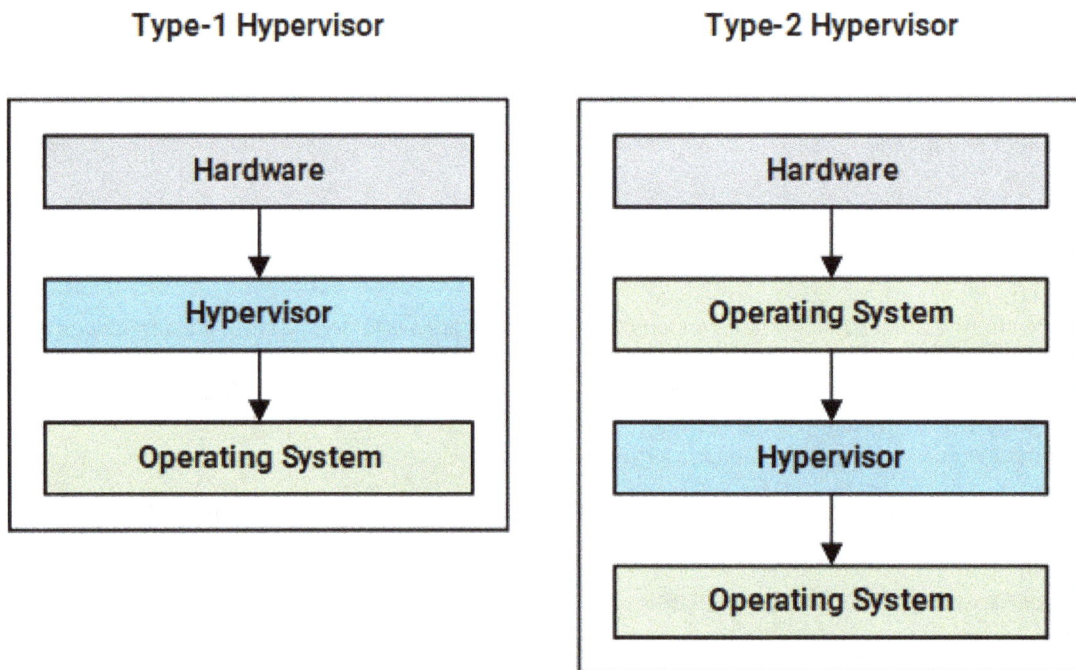

Figure 4.1.1: Type-1 and Type-2 hypervisors are both designed to run multiple virtual machines on physical hardware. The major difference is that a Type-1 hypervisor runs directly on the hardware and a Type-2 hypervisor runs on top of an operating system.

Even though Hyper-V is a Type-1 hypervisor, Microsoft has architected it differently than a traditional Type-1 hypervisor and it operates differently as a result. When Hyper-V is installed on an existing Windows installation, it is installed beneath the already running Windows installation. Once Hyper-V has been installed, all virtual machines will then use Hyper-V as the hypervisor. The main difference is that the host operating system is given priority access to the hardware on the system which gives it a performance advantage over the other virtual machines.

Hyper-V Setup and Configuration - Hyper-V Requirements

As stated earlier in this chapter, Hyper-V is an optional feature in Windows Server that can be easily added to an existing server. A version of Hyper-V is also available on the Pro, Enterprise and Education versions of Windows starting with Windows 8. Hyper-V is not available on any Home edition of Windows and there is no option to install the feature. Hyper-V requires a 64-bit processor to function, but Hyper-V does have limited support for the ARM architecture. Since Windows Server is not compiled for the ARM architecture at this time, it cannot be used on Hyper-V as a virtual machine, but this behaviour may change in the future.

From a hardware support perspective, here are the basic requirements for installing and running Hyper-V on any system:

- 64-bit Processor with Second Level Address Translation (SLAT) and No-Execute bit (NX bit)
- CPU support for hardware-assisted virtualization (VT-x on Intel Processors, AMD-V on AMD Processors)
- Minimum of 2 GB memory

The 2 GB memory requirement is just a guideline for using Hyper-V, and it does not always accurately reflect the performance of the device that is running Hyper-V. Even though there are minimum requirements for running Hyper-V, there is also additional memory requirements for any virtual machines that are running on the same device. These memory requirements can vary, and it is up the administrator or end user to properly allocate the appropriate amount of memory to ensure that everything that needs to be run on Hyper-V is able to be run on it.

Hyper-V Memory Allocation Options

For memory requirements, 2 GB is the minimum that is required to install and run Hyper-V, but that is not enough memory to run all the virtual machines needed to setup the TFS Labs test environment. A minimum of 16 GB of memory is recommended to properly test all virtual machines needed for the steps in this book. If a device with that amount of memory is not available, there are workarounds within Hyper-V to allow for those virtual machines to operate correctly. The most obvious workaround is to just allocate less memory for the virtual machines needed for the test environment, but there are also additional options in Hyper-V to allocate a dynamic amount of memory instead of a fixed amount.

There is the option to assign a fixed amount of memory for a virtual machine, and there is a way to assign a dynamic amount of memory for a virtual machine. There are advantages and disadvantages to both methods, but the main advantage of using dynamic memory in a virtual machine is that is potentially allows for much less memory usage.

Dynamic memory is especially useful for testing purposes, and is useful on a regular computer where it is not ideal to unnecessarily allocate a large amount of memory for no reason. It is not recommended for a production virtual machine under most circumstances, as it can potentially lead to over-provisioning of the resources that are available to Hyper-V and other virtualization platforms.

Prior to installing the Hyper-V in Windows, it is easy to determine if there would be any problems with installing the role. The System Information application is a utility that can allow for quickly determining if a device can run Hyper-V:

1. Click on the **Start menu**, type in **msinfo32.exe** and press the **Enter** key to open the program.
2. The **System Information** program will open.
3. In the **System Summary** window, scroll to the bottom of the page.
4. Check that the following **Items** are present:
    - **Virtualization-based security**
    - **Virtualization-based security Required Security Properties**
    - **Virtualization-based security Available Security Properties**
    - **Virtualization-based security Service Configured**
    - **Virtualization-based security Services Running**

The output of the System Information application should look similar to this if Hyper-V is able to be used:

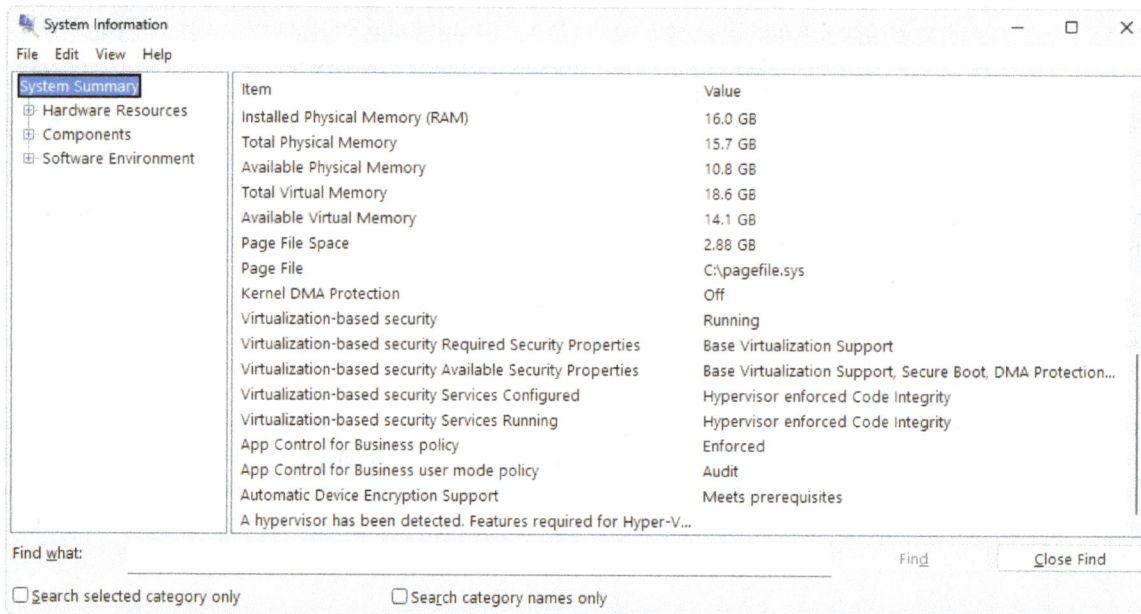

Item	Value
Installed Physical Memory (RAM)	16.0 GB
Total Physical Memory	15.7 GB
Available Physical Memory	10.8 GB
Total Virtual Memory	18.6 GB
Available Virtual Memory	14.1 GB
Page File Space	2.88 GB
Page File	C:\pagefile.sys
Kernel DMA Protection	Off
Virtualization-based security	Running
Virtualization-based security Required Security Properties	Base Virtualization Support
Virtualization-based security Available Security Properties	Base Virtualization Support, Secure Boot, DMA Protection...
Virtualization-based security Services Configured	Hypervisor enforced Code Integrity
Virtualization-based security Services Running	Hypervisor enforced Code Integrity
App Control for Business policy	Enforced
App Control for Business user mode policy	Audit
Automatic Device Encryption Support	Meets prerequisites
A hypervisor has been detected. Features required for Hyper-V...	

Figure 4.2.1: The System Information application can be used to view extensive information for a Windows host. In this screenshot from a Windows 11 24H2 computer, it is showing the virtualization status and availability.

If all Hyper-V settings are present and available in the System Summary window, then Hyper-V should be able to be installed and run without any issues. If Hyper-V or another virtualization solution is already installed on the same device and is running, a message stating **A hypervisor has been detected. Features required for Hyper-V will not be displayed.** This message can also appear before Hyper-V has been installed, so it is not unusual to see this on a new installation of Windows.

If a Server Core installation of Windows Server is being used, use the **systeminfo.exe** utility instead. It is the command line version of the System Information utility and outputs the exact same information.

Multiple Virtualization Platforms

Windows does not always easily support multiple virtualization platforms that are installed at the same time. For example, Hyper-V and VMware Workstation cannot always be installed at the same time and work correctly. If there is an issue getting Hyper-V to operate, ensure that there is no other virtualization platform installed and in use.

In recent versions of Windows 10 (version 1809 and later) and Windows 11 (RTM), there is a Windows feature called **Virtual Machine Platform** that makes it much easier for virtualization platforms to co-exist on the same Windows installation. Prior to this feature being introduced, it was possible to change the system boot parameters to not load Hyper-V if needed.

Enabling Virtualization Options for Hyper-V

For Hyper-V to operate correctly there may be various settings within the BIOS that would need to be enabled. These settings vary based on the manufacturer, but there is usually a virtualization section in the computer or server BIOS where those settings are configured. If there is an issue with confirming this, refer to the manufacturer's documentation for the particular system to determine how to enable the necessary virtualization features.

Hyper-V Setup and Configuration - Hyper-V Versions

There are several different versions of Hyper-V that are available depending on what operating system it is to be installed on, and the capabilities can vary depending on what operating system it is installed on. There are also variations on what management capabilities are available, and what is required to manage Hyper-V locally and remotely.

Since Hyper-V has existed as a feature in Windows since it was initially released for Windows Server 2008, there are several different variations of Hyper-V that exist:

- Windows Server Hyper-V
- Windows Client Hyper-V
- Microsoft Hyper-V Server
- Azure Stack HCI

The capabilities of these versions of Hyper-V vary slightly, and each version has different advantages and disadvantages. Some of these versions are no longer supported by Microsoft and have been superseded by other products.

Hyper-V Setup and Configuration - Hyper-V Versions - Windows Server Hyper-V

Hyper-V is available as an optional feature in Windows Server starting with Windows Server 2008, and there are no additional licensing requirements for installing it. Even though there are no additional licensing fees for having Hyper-V installed, that does not include any licensing requirements for virtual machines that are installed on Hyper-V. Licensing for virtual machines that require it is something that is left up to the user if necessary. The requirements for installing Hyper-V on an existing Windows Server is the same as the requirements that were stated earlier in this chapter.

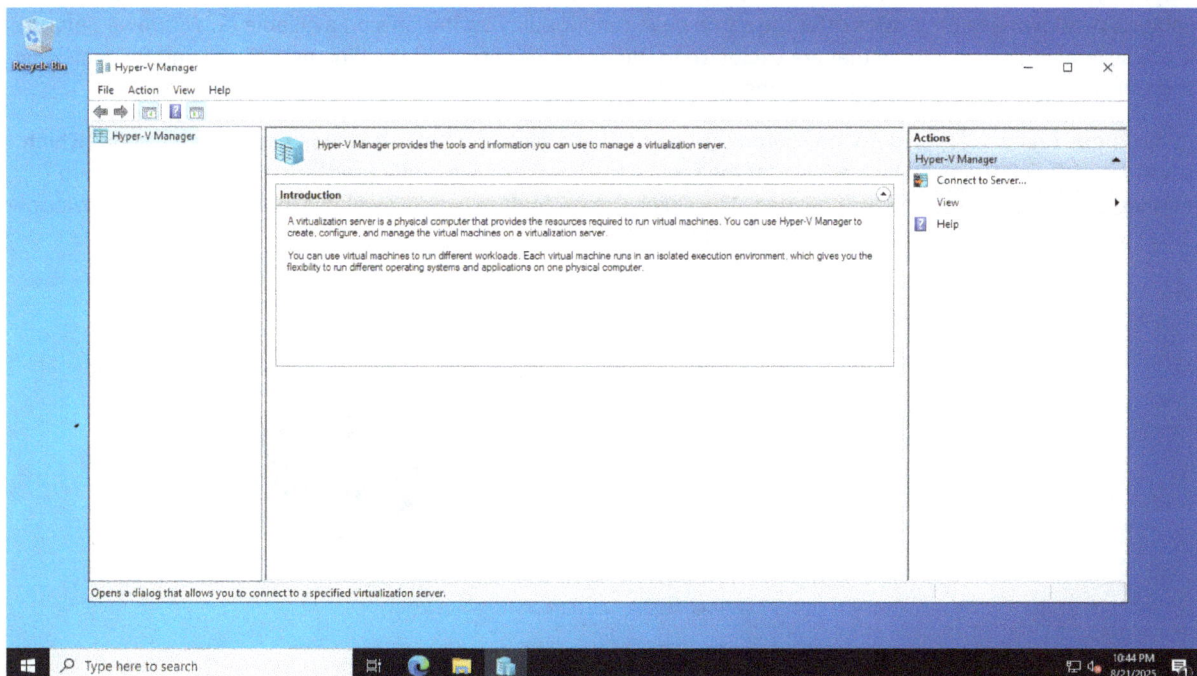

Figure 4.3.1.1: Windows Server Hyper-V running on a Windows Server 2022 Standard installation. Hyper-V Manager is the default management console for managing Hyper-V using the GUI.

There are several features that are only available on the Windows Server version of Hyper-V and are not found in the Windows Client Hyper-V version. These features include:

- **Discrete Device Assignment** - This feature allows a virtual machine to access a physical PCI device that is located on the Hyper-V server.
- **Failover Clustering** - This feature combines multiple Hyper-V servers into a cluster which is used to aggregate all available resources.
- **Hyper-V Replica** - This feature is used to replicate Hyper-V virtual machines from one Hyper-V host to another.
- **Live Virtual Machine Migration** - This feature allows for a live migration of a Hyper-V virtual machine from one host to another without shutting down the virtual machine.
- **Shared VHDX Files** - This feature allows for shared VHDX files between multiple Hyper-V virtual machines.
- **SR-IOV Networking** - This feature allows for increased throughput and reduced latency on a network adapter that is used for Hyper-V virtual machines.
- **Virtual Fibre Channel** - This feature allows a virtual machine to use a physical adapter to connect to a Fibre Channel storage device.

Windows Server Hyper-V can be installed on a Windows Server with the full Desktop Experience, or on Server Core. Once it has been installed it can be managed with several different methods:

- Locally or remotely with Hyper-V Manager and Windows Admin Center.
- Locally or remotely with PowerShell Cmdlets.
- Remotely with System Center Virtual Machine Manager (VMM).

In a production environment, an installation of Windows Server Hyper-V is the most common deployment scenario that will most likely be encountered. It is easy to setup and maintain, while being extremely reliable and stable.

Hyper-V Setup and Configuration - Hyper-V Versions - Windows Client Hyper-V

Windows Client Hyper-V is available on the Pro, Enterprise and Education versions of Windows starting with Windows 8. Just like Hyper-V for Windows Server, it is available as an optional feature that can be installed at any time. The version of Hyper-V that is available in the client versions of Windows is not exactly the same as the version that is available in Windows Server. It does offer the same base functionality as the version available on Windows Server, but there are several missing features that are exclusive to Windows Server. All of the high availability and failover options are missing, and advanced networking options are also missing.

The only unique features for Hyper-V on client versions of Windows is the **Default Switch** networking option (which uses NAT), and **Quick Create**, which allows for the rapid deployment of pre-configured virtual machines that are maintained by Microsoft and locally if needed. The Quick Create feature is only available in later versions of Windows 10 (1709 and higher), and in all versions of Windows 11:

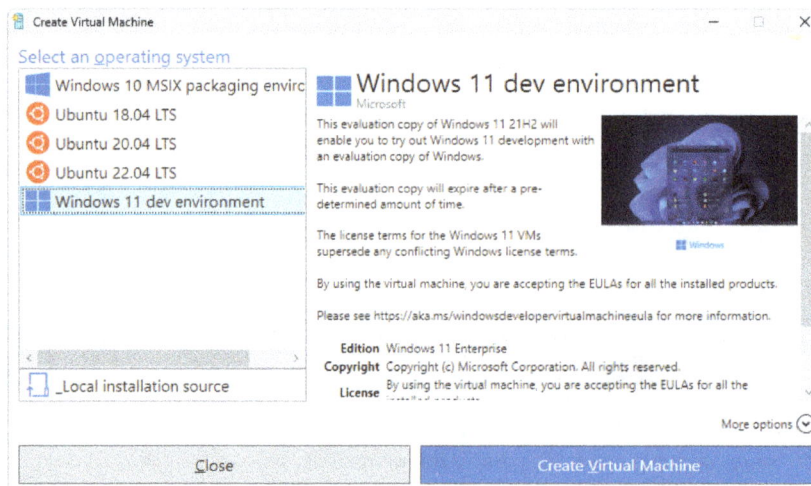

Figure 4.3.2.1: The Hyper-V Quick Create tool (VMCreate.exe) that is available on Windows Client Hyper-V allows a user to rapidly deploy pre-configured Hyper-V virtual machines. This is the tool as seen on Windows 11 24H2.

The limitations that are present in the client version of Hyper-V should not cause issues for most people as those missing features are mostly used in large-scale deployments of Hyper-V. These features are especially helpful in datacentre deployments of Hyper-V and would not affect users on a regular computer.

Overall, Client Hyper-V is really only meant for testing and development purposes and is not meant for any production workloads.

Hyper-V Setup and Configuration - Hyper-V Versions - Microsoft Hyper-V Server

Microsoft Hyper-V Server was a standalone version of Hyper-V that was released by Microsoft in 2008. It was initially released after the first version of Hyper-V was made generally available in Windows Server 2008, and it was available as a free download. Microsoft Hyper-V Server had almost all of the capabilities of Windows Server Hyper-V, with only a few exceptions. The major difference with Microsoft Hyper-V Server was that it was based on Server Core and had no GUI, and there was no option to install one.

Microsoft Hyper-V Server is only capable of being managed on the local device through the command line, or remotely with Microsoft management tools:

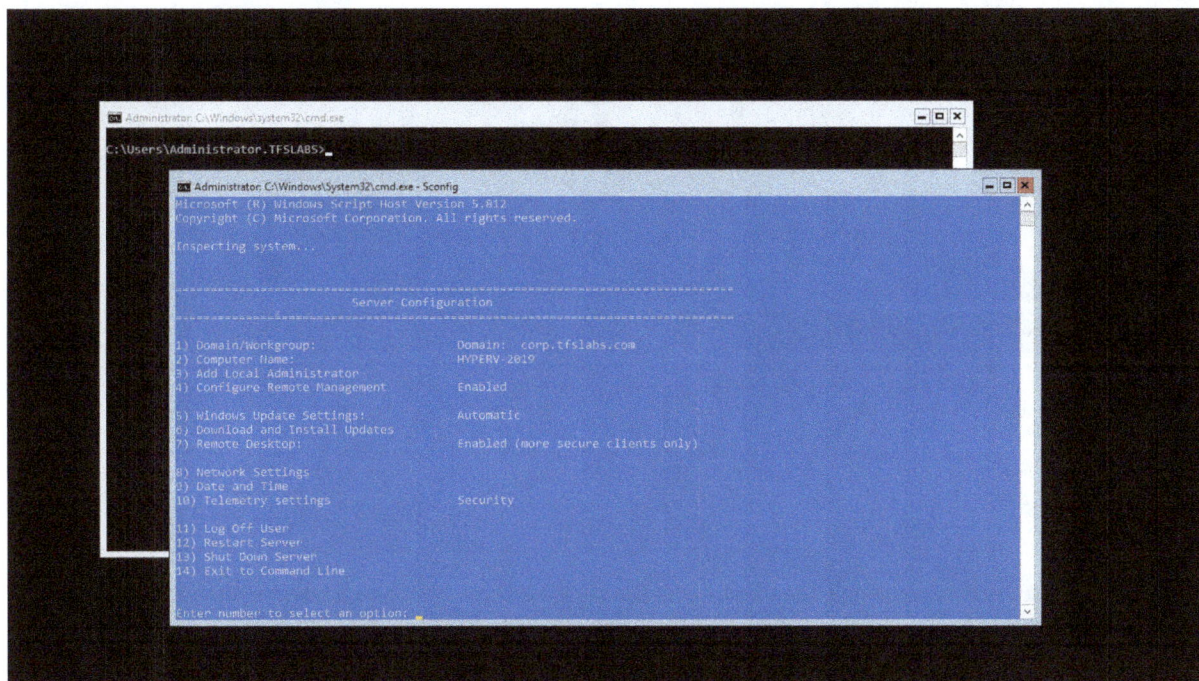

Figure 4.3.3.1: Microsoft Hyper-V Server 2019 is a Server Core deployment, and offers no graphical interface tools for configuring or managing the operating system.

There were six major versions of Microsoft Hyper-V Server that were released by Microsoft, all of which corresponded to the equivalent Windows Server releases:

- Microsoft Hyper-V Server 2008
- Microsoft Hyper-V Server 2008 R2
- Microsoft Hyper-V Server 2012
- Microsoft Hyper-V Server 2012 R2
- Microsoft Hyper-V Server 2016
- Microsoft Hyper-V Server 2019

Microsoft ended mainstream support of Microsoft Hyper-V Server 2019 on January 9, 2024, and extended support for that product will end on January 9, 2029. Microsoft Hyper-V Server 2019 is the last version of this product line, and it has been superseded by Azure Stack HCI.

Hyper-V Setup and Configuration - Hyper-V Versions - Azure Stack HCI

Azure Stack HCI is a hyper-converged infrastructure (HCI) product that can be used for virtualizing multiple instances of Windows or Linux hosts. The first version of Azure Stack HCI was released by Microsoft in 2020, and it was originally based on Windows Server 2019. It is a hybrid product that is designed to run on-premises, but it also connects to Microsoft Azure to expand on its functionality. It uses Hyper-V as its underlying virtualization technology, but unlike previous versions of Hyper-V it uses validated hardware and has stricter requirements. A major difference between typical installations of Hyper-V is that Azure Stack HCI runs in a cluster (2 servers minimum) to ensure high-availability and redundancy. This makes the setup and deployment of Azure Stack HCI more complex and expensive to implement than a standard Hyper-V installation.

When Azure Stack HCI is installed on a server, it is installed using Server Core and there is no GUI to manage the server locally. From a management perspective, Azure Stack HCI can be managed using either PowerShell or Windows Admin Center:

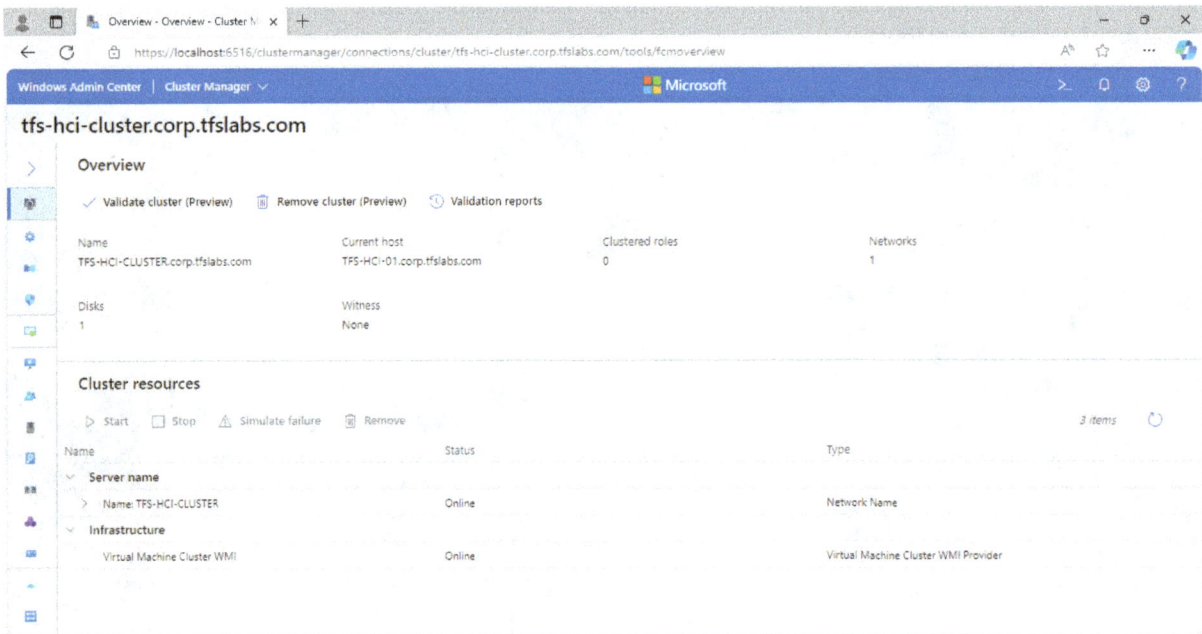

Figure 4.3.4.1: The Overview landing page of an Azure Stack HCI cluster that is being managed with Windows Admin Center on Windows Server 2022. In this screenshot there is a single node in an Azure Stack HCI 22H2 cluster.

As discussed earlier, Azure Stack HCI is a much more complex product that regular Windows Server Hyper-V and Microsoft Hyper-V Server. The system requirements are stricter, and there is a list of certified hardware that can be used with the product. For example, Azure Stack HCI does not support a cluster if the servers are not the same manufacturer and model. The other major issue with Azure Stack HCI is the requirement to have an active Microsoft Azure subscription, so if an organization does not use that service, it may not be an appropriate solution.

> **Azure Stack HCI Limitations**
>
> Azure Stack HCI is not a one-to-one replacement for standalone Microsoft Hyper-V Server installations. Due to the added complexities of creating a cluster and the costs of acquiring the appropriate hardware, it is not a suitable solution for many organizations.
>
> The most common migration path for organizations that are using Microsoft Hyper-V Server would be to use Windows Server and the Hyper-V role. This configuration allows for the most amount of hardware options and ease in licensing, while having the most available options for hardware support.

Hyper-V Setup and Configuration - Hyper-V Installation

There are several methods for installing Hyper-V if a computer or server meets the necessary requirements for running it. Hyper-V can be installed using PowerShell with a Cmdlet, the Control Panel, or through the Deployment Imaging Servicing and Management (DISM) tool. All three methods will install the Hyper-V role, and only one method is required to install the role. The steps outlined below will install Hyper-V on Windows 11 Pro (Windows Client Hyper-V).

Installing the Hyper-V Role

If the steps in this book are being tested using a personal computer, then there should be no issues with installing Hyper-V if the computer meets the requirements for it. Typically, in a corporate environment the IT department will not allow for the installation of additional roles and features within Windows for security purposes.

Hyper-V Hardware Compatibility

As mentioned earlier in this book, there are certain hardware requirements that must be met for Hyper-V to be enabled properly. These requirements include hardware options that are present within the processor, and some options that are available in the BIOS. Ensure that those options are correct and enabled before proceeding with enabling the Hyper-V role. There is virtually zero risk in installing the Hyper-V role if a computer or server supports it.

Hyper-V is available in all versions of Windows that supports it and there is no need to download any additional software to install the Hyper-V role, as the necessary files are already available within the operating system. The installation of Hyper-V will require at least one restart to successfully complete the installation.

Hyper-V Setup and Configuration - Hyper-V Installation - Enable Hyper-V Using PowerShell

Hyper-V and all associated features can also be installed using PowerShell on a Windows 11 Pro workstation by using the **Enable-WindowsOptionalFeature** Cmdlet. This Cmdlet is used to install additional features after Windows has been installed.

To install the Hyper-V role and all associated features using PowerShell, open an **elevated PowerShell prompt** and run the following command:

```
Windows PowerShell (Elevated)

Enable-WindowsOptionalFeature -Online -FeatureName Microsoft-Hyper-V -All
```

After the PowerShell Cmdlet has been executed, it will prompt to restart the computer for the installation of the Hyper-V role to be successfully completed. Once the computer has been restarted, all Hyper-V tools and features will be accessible and ready to be used.

PowerShell Cmdlet Execution

If there is an issue with the PowerShell command being executed properly, then the command is not being executed as an administrator. The command will also not work if it is being executed in the Command Prompt. This is because it is not possible to run a Cmdlet from the Command Prompt, so the command will always fail if it is executed incorrectly.

PowerShell can be manually started from the Command Prompt by executing the **powershell.exe** command, which will switch the session to PowerShell.

Hyper-V Setup and Configuration - Hyper-V Installation - Enable Hyper-V Using the Control Panel

To install the Hyper-V role using the Control Panel on a Windows 11 Pro workstation, perform the following steps:

1. Click on the **Start menu**, type in **appwiz.cpl** and press the **Enter** key to open the **Programs and Features** window.
2. In the **Programs and Features** window, click on the **Turn Windows features on or off** link in the left side of the window.
3. In the **Windows Features** window, select all options under **Hyper-V**, and click the **OK** button to continue:

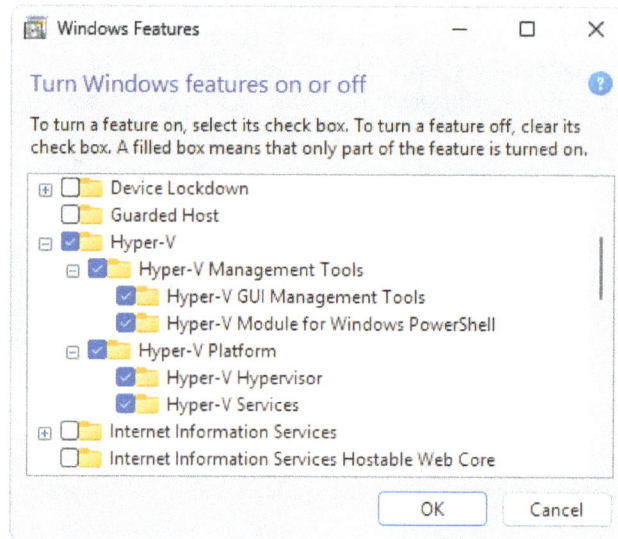

After the installation is completed, restart the computer for the installation of Hyper-V to be completed. Once the computer has been restarted, all Hyper-V tools and features will be accessible.

Hyper-V Setup and Configuration - Hyper-V Installation - Enable Hyper-V Using DISM

Another method to install Hyper-V and all associated features is to use the Deployment Image Servicing and Management (DISM) command line tool to add the Hyper-V feature to the Windows device that is going to be using it. DISM is normally used to prepare and customize Windows images, but it can be used to enable features in Windows once it is installed.

To install the Hyper-V role and all associated features using DISM, open an **elevated PowerShell prompt** and run the following command:

```
Windows PowerShell (Elevated)

DISM.exe /Online /Enable-Feature /All /FeatureName:Microsoft-Hyper-V
```

After the DISM command has been executed, there will be a prompt to restart the computer for the installation of Hyper-V to be completed. Once the computer has been restarted, all Hyper-V tools and features will be accessible.

> ⚠️ **DISM Command Execution Issues**
>
> If there are any issues with the DISM command being executed properly, the most likely issue was that the command was not executed as an administrator. Unlike installing the Hyper-V role using a PowerShell Cmdlet, the DISM command can be executed from an elevated Command Prompt as well. The Command Prompt will also need to be run as an administrator for the command to execute correctly.

Hyper-V Setup and Configuration - Hyper-V Management

There are multiple methods for administering Hyper-V servers and virtual machines, all of which are able to be managed locally or remotely. Most of the tools for managing Hyper-V are provided directly by Microsoft, and those tools are included with the Hyper-V role as an optional feature. There are also third-party tools available as well that are capable of managing Hyper-V servers and virtual machines, but that is beyond the scope of this book. The four primary tools that are available from Microsoft for managing Hyper-V include:

- Hyper-V Manager
- PowerShell Cmdlets
- System Center Virtual Machine Manager
- Windows Admin Center

There are different reasons for using each method of managing Hyper-V, and it is mostly due to the size of the organization and the complexity of the Hyper-V environment that is setup. The basic Hyper-V management tools that are provided are more than capable of managing large Hyper-V deployments, but they do not scale well when there are potentially dozens of Hyper-V servers and hundreds of virtual machines in an organization.

For the purposes of the steps provided in this book, all Hyper-V management is performed using Hyper-V Manager and PowerShell.

> **Hyper-V Remote Management Considerations**
>
> There are certain requirements for allowing remote management of Hyper-V from another host, and those requirements vary depending on which version of Windows Server is being used, and how the Active Directory domain is configured. There are certain firewall ports that need to be opened, and there are several policies that must be in place that allows the remote connections to occur. These requirements can also differ if Hyper-V is being used in a non-domain environment.
>
> Configuring a Windows host to allow for Hyper-V remote management is beyond the scope of this book, but it is something to be aware of should it be something that is required for administrative purposes.

Hyper-V Setup and Configuration - Hyper-V Management - Hyper-V Manager

Hyper-V Manager is the most common administrative tool that is used for managing the Hyper-V role. Hyper-V Manager provides a GUI interface that allows for management of Hyper-V environments, and it is available in the **Hyper-V GUI Management Tools** feature. It is a very stable and reliable tool, and it can be used on Windows Server and supported Windows Client versions. Hyper-V Manager is capable of creating and managing virtual machines that are running locally or remotely and provides a single interface for that purpose.

By using Hyper-V Manager to manage Hyper-V, is can be used to configure settings such as disk locations, network settings and replication settings. Hyper-V Manager also allows an administrator the ability to easily manage Hyper-V Checkpoints, which can be used to revert to earlier versions of a virtual machine.

Hyper-V Setup and Configuration - Hyper-V Management - PowerShell Cmdlets

PowerShell is another management tool that is available for Hyper-V that allows for the management of Hyper-V from the command line, and it is available in the **Hyper-V Module for Windows PowerShell** feature. There is a single PowerShell Cmdlet available that contains all of the necessary functionality for managing a Hyper-V deployment on a local or remote server. At the time of this writing, the Hyper-V Cmdlet contains over 200 commands that can be used to manage Hyper-V. The ability to automate Hyper-V functionality and script virtual machine deployment is one of the most powerful features that PowerShell allows for. There are also third-party PowerShell Cmdlets that are available for Hyper-V, but those are beyond the scope of this book.

There is a learning curve for using PowerShell for managing Hyper-V and it may not be an appropriate tool for someone who is not familiar with PowerShell or scripting in general.

Hyper-V Setup and Configuration - Hyper-V Management - System Center VMM

System Center Virtual Machine Manager (VMM) is a management platform created by Microsoft that is designed for large scale server deployments using Windows Server. It contains Hyper-V management tools that offer enhanced features that are not available in the standard tools that are provided by Microsoft. Deploying VMM requires considerable resources to operate correctly and is meant for organizations that have dozens of Hyper-V server and hundreds of virtual machines.

Due to the complexities and costs of deploying System Center Virtual Machine Manager, it is only common in large organizations that require it and is almost never used with small Hyper-V deployments. Installing and configuring System Center Virtual Machine Manager is beyond the scope of this book, and it will not be used for any configuration of Active Directory Certificate Services.

Hyper-V Setup and Configuration - Hyper-V Management - Windows Admin Center

Windows Admin Center is a modern management tool that was released by Microsoft in early 2018 that is browser-based and is capable of managing most components in Windows Server operating systems. It is fully capable of managing Hyper-V hosts and virtual machines, both in small and large deployments. Aside from managing regular Hyper-V hosts, Windows Admin Center is also used to manage Azure Stack HCI deployments. Windows Admin Center is available for download for free from the Microsoft website. Installing and configuring Windows Admin Center is beyond the scope of this book, and it will not be used for any configuration of Active Directory Certificate Services.

Hyper-V Setup and Configuration - Hyper-V VMConnect Application

When a virtual machine is created using Hyper-V it is not immediately useful if there is no method of connecting to that virtual machine to perform any installations or configurations on it. The exception to this is if a virtual machine is installed in an automated manner where the operating system is automatically deployed, the credentials are configured, networking is configured, and remote access is enabled. Azure deploys Linux and Windows hosts in this manner, but this can also be done on regular Hyper-V servers as well with automation scripts and tools. Included with the Hyper-V management tools is an application that enables a connection to the virtual machine, and that is the Virtual Machine Connection (vmconnect.exe) application, which is also known as VMConnect.

The Virtual Machine Connection application can connect to Hyper-V virtual machines either locally or remotely over the network and connects to the "console" of the virtual machine. This means that the Virtual Machine Connection works as if someone is physically working with the virtual machine. By default, the keyboard and mouse input are all sent to a virtual machine when interacting with a virtual machine using this application. The Virtual Machine Connection application is similar to the Remote Desktop Connection (mstsc.exe) application that is used to connect over RDP to Windows devices. Start the Virtual Machine Connection application manually through the Start Menu, or by running the **vmconnect.exe** command. Once the application is opened, connect to Hyper-V virtual machines that are local to that server, or on virtual machines that are located on other Hyper-V servers on the network:

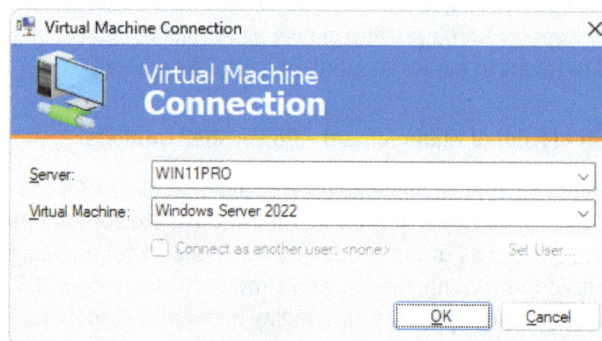

Figure 4.6.1: The Hyper-V Virtual Machine Connection (VMConnect) application supports connections to Hyper-V virtual machines on the local device or over the network. There is an option to select virtual machines on different servers if the environment is configured for that. This is how the application appears on Windows 11 24H2.

The Virtual Machine Connection application can also be opened by double-clicking on a virtual machine that is listed in the Hyper-V Manager application. This can also be accomplished by right-clicking on a virtual machine and selecting the **Connect...** option. When connecting to the Virtual Machine Connection application, this window will be presented for the virtual machine that needs to be administered:

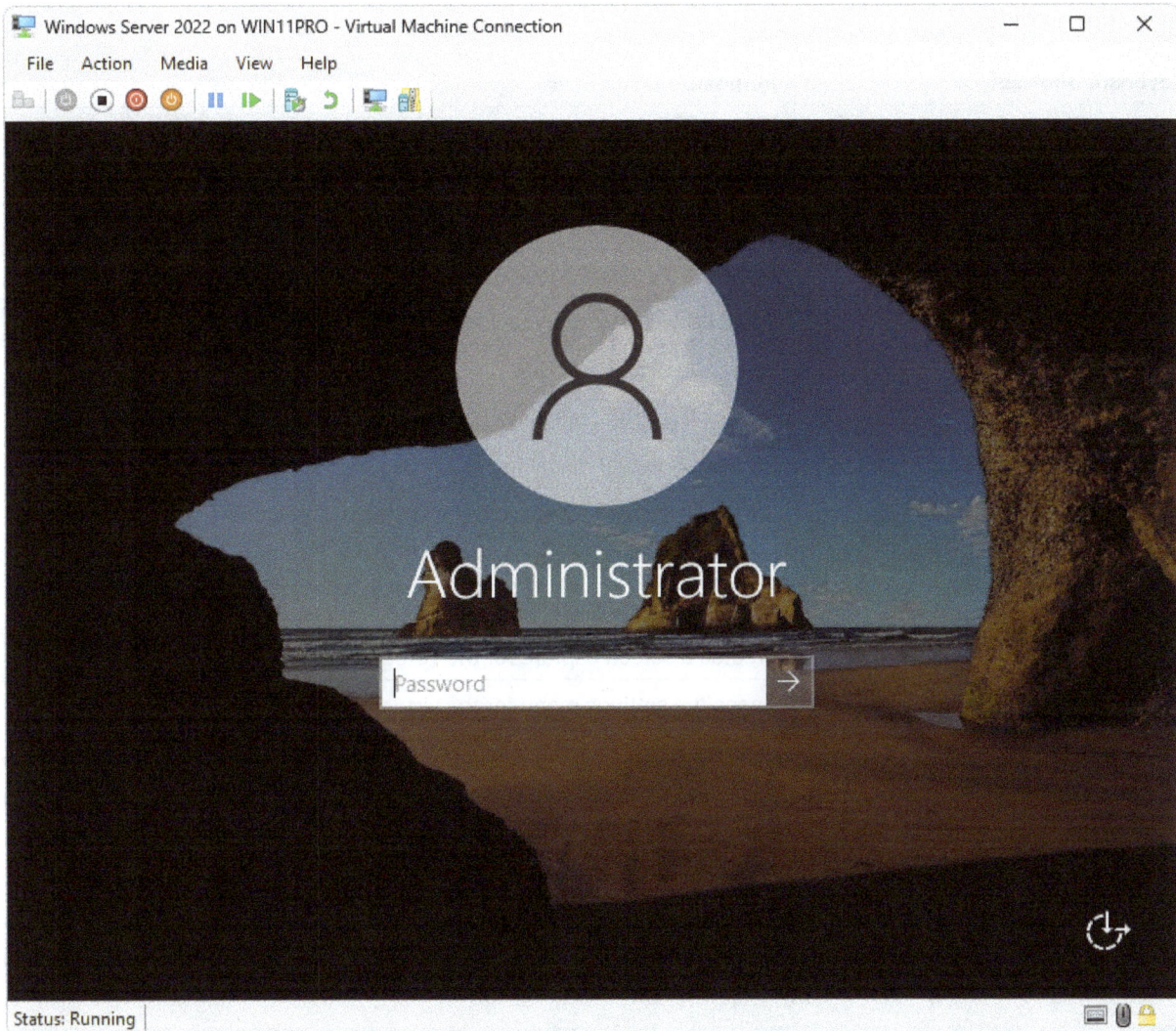

Figure 4.6.2: The Hyper-V Virtual Machine Connection (VMConnect) application allows direct interaction with the virtual machine as if it were a physical machine. Compared to the Remote Desktop Protocol, this is the equivalent of connecting to the console of the virtual machine. This is how the application appears on Windows 11 24H2.

Aside from connecting to a virtual machine and allowing interaction with it, the Virtual Machine Connection application also offers the following features for managing other aspects of a virtual machine with Hyper-V:

- Send custom keyboard commands to a virtual machine such as CTRL + ALT + DEL.
- Perform actions to a virtual machine such as start, turn off, shut down, save, pause, and reset.
- Create and revert Hyper-V Checkpoints on a virtual machine.
- Switch from a Basic Session to an Enhanced Session.
- Add external media to a virtual machine, such as a disc image (ISO) or a virtual floppy disk image (VFD).
- Access and manage the shared clipboard for a virtual machine.
- View a virtual machine in full screen mode.
- Copy and paste files to and from the virtual machine (if supported).

There are several keyboard shortcuts that are specifically available for the Virtual Machine Connection application. These keyboard shortcuts do not perform any actions for the underlying host operating system, and to ensure that the Virtual Machine Connection application has focus, use the mouse and click within the virtual machine window before using the following commands (some of these commands do not work for every host operating system).

Keyboard shortcuts that can be used for the Virtual Machine Connection application to control virtual machines on a Hyper-V host include:

Keyboard Shortcut	Purpose
CTRL + ALT + BREAK	Switches a virtual machine from full screen mode back to windowed mode.
CTRL + ALT + LEFT Arrow Key	Releases the mouse from the virtual machine and returns it to the host.
CTRL + ALT + END	Enters CTRL + ALT + DELETE for the virtual machine.
CTRL + S	Turns off the virtual machine.
CTRL + D	Shuts down the virtual machine.
CTRL + A	Saves the virtual machine.
CTRL + P	Pauses the virtual machine.
CTRL + R	Resets the virtual machine.
CTRL + N	Creates a Hyper-V Checkpoint for the virtual machine.
CTRL + E	Reverts to a Hyper-V Checkpoint.
CTRL + H	Exports a virtual machine.
CTRL + C	Creates a screen capture for the virtual machine.
CTRL + O	Opens the settings menu for the virtual machine.

Table 4.6.1: Hyper-V Virtual Machine Connection (VMConnect) keyboard shortcuts that are available on Windows 11 Pro. Depending on what operating system is being virtualized, not all keyboard shortcuts will apply to a particular virtual machine.

Overall, the Virtual Machine Connection application offers an easy and convenient method of accessing virtual machines that are hosted on Hyper-V servers. The Virtual Machine Connection application is critical for installing and configuring an operating system when it is provisioned, and is extremely useful in the event that there is an issue with a virtual machine that cannot be normally accessed over the network.

> **Virtual Machine Connection and Remote Desktop Protocol**
>
> The Remote Desktop Connection (RDP) application can be more responsive than the Virtual Machine Connection application and allows actions such as copy and paste to be performed much easier on virtual machines. When accessing Hyper-V virtual machines, it is usually easier and faster to use the Remote Desktop Connection application whenever possible. Hyper-V has a feature called Enhanced Session Mode which provides an experience similar to RDP when connecting to virtual machines using the Virtual Machine Connection application.
>
> Typically, in a production environment most connections to a virtual machine happen over RDP and not directly on the Hyper-V host. The only exception for not using RDP to connect to virtual machines are ones that are not on the network, such as the Offline Root CA. In that case, use the Virtual Machine Connection application to interact with that virtual machine as it is not available on the network and does not accept any connections from other hosts by design. Virtual machines configured in this manner are not common in a production environment, and are only found in certain cases such as an Offline Root CA.

Hyper-V Setup and Configuration - Hyper-V VMConnect Application - Enhanced Session Mode

There are two operational modes that are available with the Virtual Machine Connection application, Basic Session Mode and Enhanced Session Mode. Basic Session Mode provides a simple connection to a virtual machine, limited to mouse and keyboard input as well as basic graphics options. Enhanced Session Mode offers a better experience when connecting to a virtual machine, similar to an RDP connection. Enhanced Session Mode adds the following functionality to the Virtual Machine Connection application:

- Improved remote audio recording and playback.
- Shared clipboard access.
- Access to local drives, and Plug and Play devices, printers, Smart Cards, and USB devices.
- Allows for resizable screens in the Virtual Machine Connection application (if the virtual machine supports it).
- Allows for file sharing with copy and pasting.

Enhanced Session Mode is usually enabled by default when the host running Hyper-V supports it, but it can be easily enabled if it has been disabled for any reason. To enable Enhanced Session Mode from the command line, open an **elevated PowerShell prompt** on the Hyper-V host and run the following command:

```
Windows PowerShell (Elevated)

Set-VMHost -EnableEnhancedSessionMode $true
```

Enhanced Session Mode can also be enabled from Hyper-V Manager. To enable Enhanced Session Mode, perform the following steps in Hyper-V Manager on the Hyper-V host:

1. Open the **Hyper-V Manager** (virtmgmt.msc) console.
2. In the **Actions** pane, click the option for **Hyper-V Settings...** under the name of the Hyper-V server.
3. In the **Hyper-V Settings** window, select the option for **Enhanced Session Mode Policy** in the **User** pane.
4. In the **Enhanced Session Mode** pane, enable the option for **Use enhanced session mode**. Click the **OK** button to close the window:

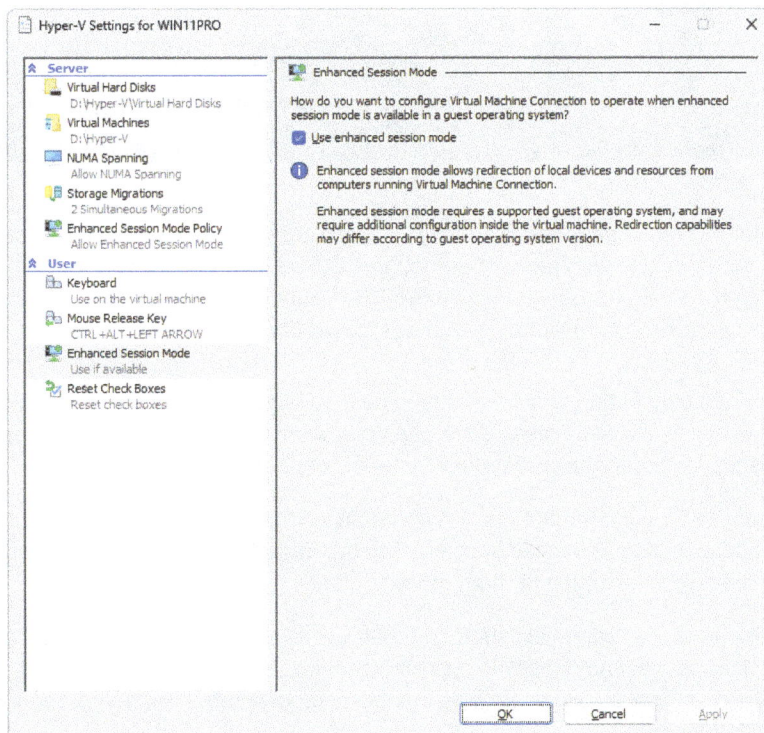

Enhanced Session Mode is usually enabled by default on Windows hosts that are running on a Hyper-V server, and no further action is required unless it specifically needs to be enabled or disabled for an individual virtual machine. To enable Enhanced Session Mode on a virtual machine running Linux, run the following command in an **elevated PowerShell prompt** for the specific virtual machine (use the complete name of the virtual machine to enable Enhanced Session Mode on that particular VM):

```
Windows PowerShell (Elevated)

Set-VM -VMName "Virtual Machine Name" -EnhancedSessionTransportType HvSocket
```

When Enhanced Session Mode is enabled on a Hyper-V host and virtual machine, the Virtual Machine Connection application will automatically use that feature. The most common way to determine if Enhanced Session Mode is working correctly is to connect to a virtual machine and see if the option to modify display options and local resources appears:

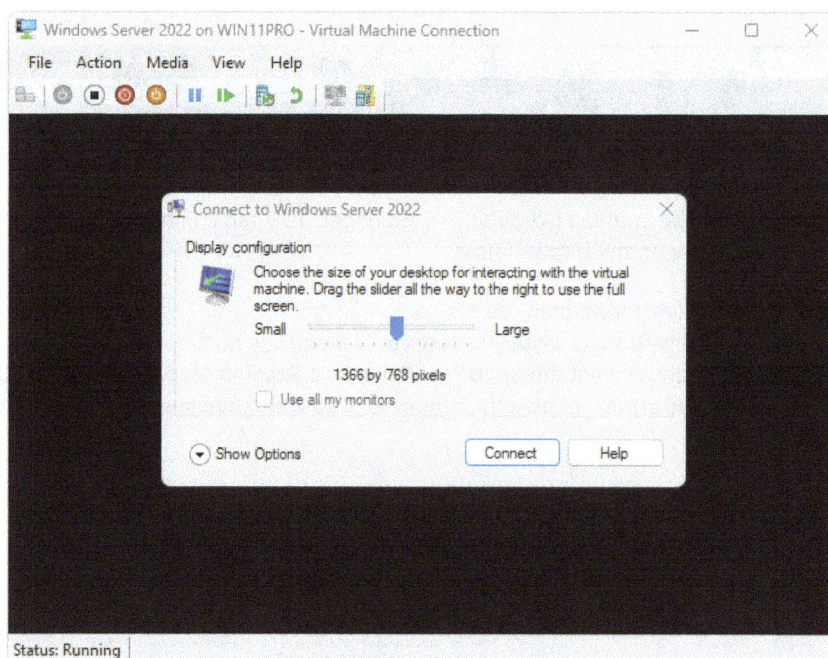

Figure 4.6.1.1: The Connect window provides the ability to configure display options and local resources that can be made available to the virtual machine with the Virtual Machine Connection application. This is similar to the way that RDP connections occur on the Windows operating system. The Connect window shows the options on a Windows 11 Pro workstation, and it will appear on virtual machines that support Enhanced Session Mode.

There may be situations when connecting to a virtual machine may require Enhanced Session Mode to be enabled or disabled. An example of where it should be disabled is when connecting to an Offline Root CA server, which will ensure that the number of connection types to the virtual machine is kept at a minimum.

To enable or disable Enhanced Session Mode for a virtual machine, it can be done in two ways. One method is by going to the **View** menu and selecting **Enhanced session**. The other method is to click the **Basic session** or **Enhanced session** button in the toolbar, which is on the far right of the toolbar.

Overall, the Enhanced Session Mode feature allows for a better overall experience when using the Virtual Machine Connection application when connecting directly to a virtual machine. While it provides a lot of conveniences, it is not common to use this application once a virtual machine has been successfully configured, but it is useful for times when a direct connection is required.

Hyper-V Setup and Configuration - Hyper-V Integration Services

Hyper-V Integration Services is a collection of services that are available within Windows and Linux hosts that improves the performance of virtual machines that are hosted on a Hyper-V server. These services are available by default with Windows hosts starting from Windows 10 and Windows Server 2016, but can be made available in earlier versions should it be required. There is also support available for Linux hosts using a kernel module that is available with recent distributions.

Hyper-V Integration Services enhances functionality in virtual machines, adding important features such as:

- Backup (using volume shadow copy)
- Data exchange
- Guest services
- Heartbeat
- Operating system shut down
- Time synchronization

As part of the Hyper-V Integration Services, there are several services that are installed on a Windows virtual machine, and several daemons that are installed on a Linux virtual machine to support it:

Service Name	Windows Service	Linux Daemon	Essential Service
Hyper-V Data Exchange Service	vmickvpexchange	hv_kvp_daemon	Yes
Hyper-V Guest Service Interface	vmicguestinterface	hv_fcopy_daemon	No
Hyper-V Guest Shutdown Service	vmicshutdown	hv_utils	Yes
Hyper-V Heartbeat Service	vmicheartbeat	hv_utils	Yes
Hyper-V PowerShell Direct Service	vmicvmsession	N/A	No
Hyper-V Time Synchronization Service	vmictimesync	hv_utils	Yes
Hyper-V Volume Shadow Copy Requestor	vmicvss	hv_vss_daemon	No

Table 4.7.1: Hyper-V Integration Services and related Windows services and Linux daemons that can be installed on supported virtual machines.

In cases where Hyper-V Integration Services are not available due to the age of the operating system, they can be manually installed from within Hyper-V. This only applies to older operating systems that does not already include the necessary Hyper-V features by default.

There may be cases where it is necessary to enable or disable certain Hyper-V Integration Services for a virtual machine, but it is not common to disable these features in most environments. Should it be required, this can be accomplished by accessing the settings for a virtual machine, or with the command line by using PowerShell with the **Enable-VMIntegrationService** and **Disable-VMIntegrationService** Cmdlets.

> **Virtualization Shared Features**
>
> Hyper-V Integration Services is similar to other virtual machine integration features that are offered in other virtualization platforms. VMware and VirtualBox offer similar features as well, and just like these other platforms it may be necessary to manually install these services as they are not likely to be present by default.
>
> Installing and configuring integration options are essential to ensuring that there are no issues with a virtual machine on a particular platform. If a service such as time synchronization is unavailable, it can cause unintended side effects on the normal operation of a virtual machine.

Hyper-V Setup and Configuration - Hyper-V Folder Locations

There are several folder locations where Hyper-V stores files that are related to Hyper-V virtual machines and virtual hard disks. These folder locations vary depending on what operating system the Hyper-V role is installed on, and whether it is the Windows Server Hyper-V version or Windows Client Hyper-V version. These folder locations are assigned by default when the Hyper-V role is installed, but the locations can be modified as needed. The folder locations can be modified for all virtual machines running on the Hyper-V host or can be modified for specific virtual machines if required.

On Windows 11 Pro (which is running Windows Client Hyper-V), the default Hyper-V folder locations are:

Folder	Path
Virtual Hard Disk Files	C:\ProgramData\Microsoft\Windows\Virtual Hard Disks\
Virtual Machine Configuration Files	C:\ProgramData\Microsoft\Windows\Hyper-V\

Table 4.8.1: Default folder locations for Hyper-V on Windows 11 Pro (Windows Client Hyper-V).

On Windows Server 2022 (which is running Windows Server Hyper-V), the default Hyper-V folder locations are slightly different:

Folder	Path
Virtual Hard Disk Files	C:\Users\Public\Documents\Hyper-V\Virtual Hard Disks\
Virtual Machine Configuration Files	C:\ProgramData\Microsoft\Windows\Hyper-V\

Table 4.8.2: Default folder locations for Hyper-V on Windows Server 2022 (Windows Server Hyper-V).

For Hyper-V virtual machine configuration files, a directory is automatically created called **Virtual Machines** in the root of the virtual machine configuration files folder. This folder is automatically created regardless of what version of Hyper-V is used, and it does not need to be specified if the folder is relocated elsewhere.

Hyper-V Checkpoints Folder

The default location for the Checkpoints folder is found in the same folder where the virtual machine configuration files are found. The first time that a Hyper-V Checkpoint is created, a folder called **Snapshots** is automatically created, and the configuration for the virtual machines is stored inside.

More information about Hyper-V Checkpoints and how they work can be found later in this chapter.

Hyper-V Virtual Machine Folder Locations

Hyper-V virtual machines and all associated files must be stored in a subfolder. This folder is created automatically whenever a virtual machine is provisioned on a Hyper-V server. Virtual machine configuration files cannot be stored in the root of a drive or a network folder. For example, a virtual machine configuration folder cannot be stored in the root of the **C:** drive, or on the root of a network folder such as **\\HYPERV-01**.

Hyper-V must also have the necessary permissions to modify and control all files related to a virtual machine configuration file. This cannot be accomplished on the root of a drive or a network folder. This limitation does not exist for virtual hard drives or virtual floppy disks that might be used by a virtual machine.

When Hyper-V is installed on Windows 11 Pro the folder locations for Hyper-V are configured by default, but can be modified later if required. Regardless of the operating system version being used, Hyper-V folders can be moved later, and this can be done using the command line with PowerShell or with Hyper-V Manager. In this example, the Hyper-V folders will be moved from their default location to the **D:\Hyper-V** folder, which is located on a separate hard drive. Within this folder the virtual machine configuration files and virtual hard disk files will be located, and the default path will be modified to use the new folder locations.

> **Hyper-V Default Path Relocation**
>
> For testing purposes there is no requirement to relocate any of the default Hyper-V folders. If there is no requirement to relocate any of the Hyper-V folders in an environment, the following steps can be ignored. The Hyper-V folder can be relocated to any other location as long as it meets the necessary requirements and is accessible with the correct permissions.

> **Hyper-V Virtual Hard Disk Relocation**
>
> When the default path for Hyper-V virtual machines configuration files is changed, the existing virtual machine configuration files will be automatically relocated to the new location. Changing the path of Hyper-V virtual hard disks does not relocate existing virtual hard disks and this must be done manually.

Hyper-V Setup and Configuration - Hyper-V Folder Locations - Base Folder Creation

Prior to relocating the virtual machine configuration and virtual hard disks folders, the base folders for Hyper-V will need to be created first. This can be done by creating the folders using the command line with PowerShell, or with Windows File Explorer (if preferred). To create the folders using PowerShell, perform the following steps:

1. Open an **elevated PowerShell prompt**.
2. Run the following command to create the base folder for Hyper-V:

```
Windows PowerShell (Elevated)

mkdir D:\Hyper-V
```

3. Run the following command to create the folder for virtual hard disks:

```
Windows PowerShell (Elevated)

mkdir "D:\Hyper-V\Virtual Hard Disks"
```

4. Optionally, run the following command to create a folder for virtual floppy disks:

```
Windows PowerShell (Elevated)

mkdir "D:\Hyper-V\Virtual Floppy Disks"
```

5. Once the folders for Hyper-V have been created, close the **PowerShell prompt**.

Once the Hyper-V folders have been created, proceed to modifying the default path for Hyper-V.

> **Hyper-V Virtual Machine Configuration Folder Creation**
>
> The virtual machine configuration folder will be created automatically in the root of the Hyper-V folder when the default path is changed, or a virtual machine is created in that folder. There is no need to manually create the folder.

Hyper-V Setup and Configuration - Hyper-V Folder Locations - CLI Configuration

To relocate the default Hyper-V folders to a new location using the command line, perform the following steps:

1. Open an **elevated PowerShell prompt**.
2. Run the following command to move the base folders for Hyper-V:

```
Windows PowerShell (Elevated)

Set-VMHost `
-ComputerName "WIN11PRO" `
-VirtualHardDiskPath "D:\Hyper-V\Virtual Hard Disks" `
-VirtualMachinePath "D:\Hyper-V"
```

3. Once the folders for Hyper-V have been moved, close the **PowerShell prompt**.

Once the virtual machine configuration and virtual hard disk folders for Hyper-V have been relocated to a different folder, any existing virtual machines will be automatically relocated. Any virtual hard disks will need to be manually relocated, and the configuration for the affected virtual machine will need to be updated to reflect the new location.

> **Hyper-V Default Path Relocation**
>
> In the example above, the Cmdlet is making a reference to **WIN11PRO**, which is the name of the computer that Hyper-V is installed on for demonstration purposes. Substitute the appropriate name for the Hyper-V host when running this command, otherwise it will not execute correctly.

Hyper-V Setup and Configuration - Hyper-V Folder Locations - GUI Configuration

To relocate the virtual machine configuration files and virtual hard disks to another location using Hyper-V Manager, perform the following steps:

1. Open the **Hyper-V Manager** (virtmgmt.msc) console.
2. In the **Actions** pane, click the option for **Hyper-V Settings...** under the name of the Hyper-V server.
3. In the **Hyper-V Settings** window, select the option for **Virtual Hard Disks** in the **Server** pane.
4. In the **Virtual Hard Disks** pane, click the **Browse...** button.
5. In the **Select Folder** window, select the **D:\Hyper-V** folder and click the **Select Folder** button.
6. In the **Hyper-V Settings** window, select the option for **Virtual Machines** in the **Server** pane.
7. In the **Virtual Machines** pane, click the **Browse...** button.
8. In the **Select Folder** window, select the **D:\Hyper-V\Virtual Hard Disks** folder and click the **Select Folder** button.
9. Click the **OK** button to close the window.

Once the virtual machine configuration and virtual hard disk folders for Hyper-V have been relocated to a different folder, any existing virtual machines will be automatically relocated. Any virtual hard disks will need to be manually relocated, and the configuration for the affected virtual machine will need to be updated to reflect the new location.

> **Hyper-V Move Virtual Machine Wizard**
>
> Within Hyper-V Manager is a feature for easily relocating virtual machines and virtual hard disks. This feature is accessed through Hyper-V Manager, and it allows for the ability to relocate a virtual machine and all related files (including virtual hard disks) to another location as required. This simplifies the process of relocating existing virtual machines after they have been created, and removes much of the administrative work involved in performing that task.
>
> Unfortunately, Windows Client Hyper-V does not completely support this functionality, so if the feature is accessed through Hyper-V Manager some features will not be available.

Hyper-V Setup and Configuration - Hyper-V File Types

There are several file types that are used to store information related to virtual machines for Hyper-V. The file types can vary depending on which version of Hyper-V is being used, and on which operating system it is installed on. On a Windows 11 Pro computer, the following file types are commonly used for Hyper-V:

File Type	Extension	Purpose
AVHD	*.avhd	Differencing Virtual Hard Disk (Legacy), used with Checkpoints.
AVHDX	*.avhdx	Differencing Virtual Hard Disk, used with Checkpoints.
VFD	*.vfd	Virtual Floppy Disk
VHD	*.vhd	Virtual Hard Disk (Legacy)
VHDX	*.vhdx	Virtual Hard Disk
VMCX	*.vmcx	Virtual Machine Configuration File, stores virtual machine data.
VMGS	*.vmgs	Virtual Machine Guest State, stores the state of a virtual machine.
VMRS	*.vmrs	Virtual Machine Runtime State File, stores the running memory of a virtual machine.

Table 4.9.1: Common file types for Hyper-V files and their primary purpose.

Aside from common file types that are related specifically to Hyper-V, the most common file type that likely to be used with Hyper-V is an ISO file. This is a disc image format that is commonly used for installing operating systems, and it is universally supported in every modern operating system. When a virtual machine is deployed using Hyper-V, it will create several files located over several locations. In this example, a virtual machine named **Windows Server 2022** was created on a Windows 11 Pro computer:

Virtual Machine File	Purpose
D:\Hyper-V\Virtual Hard Disks\Windows Server 2022.vhdx	Virtual hard disk.
D:\Hyper-V\Virtual Machines\D70CA193-47FC-4B7F-8C38-1995C6365F83\	Virtual machine directory.
D:\Hyper-V\Virtual Machines\D70CA193-47FC-4B7F-8C38-1995C6365F83.vmcx	Virtual machine configuration.
D:\Hyper-V\Virtual Machines\D70CA193-47FC-4B7F-8C38-1995C6365F83.vmgs	Virtual machine state file.
D:\Hyper-V\Virtual Machines\D70CA193-47FC-4B7F-8C38-1995C6365F83.vmrs	Virtual machine memory file.

Table 4.9.2: Virtual machine configuration and virtual hard disk files for a virtual machine created in Windows 11 Pro. This is not using the default Hyper-V folder locations for storing virtual machine configuration files or virtual hard disks.

When a virtual machine is created it will always use a UUID for that virtual machine. This UUID is tied to the virtual machine, and aside from the virtual hard disk that can use a more human-readable format for naming, this UUID is used for all other configuration files. This can cause an issue with identifying which virtual machine corresponds to a particular virtual machine, which can cause issues with troubleshooting. Determining which UUID belongs to which virtual machine can be done using PowerShell and the **Get-VM** Cmdlet:

```
Windows PowerShell (Elevated)

PS C:\Windows\system32> Get-VM | Format-Table VMName, VMId


VMName                  VMId
------                  ----
Windows Server 2022     d70ca193-47fc-4b7f-8c38-1995c6365f83
```

Hyper-V Setup and Configuration - Hyper-V Virtual Machine Generation

Hyper-V currently supports multiple configurations of virtual machines, and those configurations are created with the Hyper-V generation feature. There are two generations of virtual machines that are currently available in Hyper-V, Generation 1, and Generation 2. There are several technical reasons to choose one virtual machine generation over another, and that depends on what requirements are needed for a virtual machine. Generation 1 virtual machines are legacy and have been available since the first version of Hyper-V. Generation 2 virtual machines have been available in Hyper-V since Windows Server 2012 R2 and are designed for more modern operating systems. It is important to understand the differences between the two generations, as it can affect how a virtual machine operates and which features are available to it.

Hyper-V Generation 1 and Generation 2 Support

At the time of this writing, Generation 1 virtual machines are still supported and are needed for specific use cases. Generation 1 virtual machines are used in this book for some of the Windows Server 2022 servers due to a requirement for virtual floppy disks, which is a feature not available in Generation 2 virtual machines. This requirement could potentially change in the future, so it is something to be aware of.

Hyper-V Default Virtual Machine Generation

The default virtual machine generation in Windows 11 and Windows Server 2022 is Generation 1.

There are several differences between Generation 1 and Generation 2 virtual machines, and it is mostly due to legacy hardware support for operating systems. There are a few scenarios where a Generation 1 virtual machine is needed over a Generation 2 virtual machine, and it almost always because of supporting legacy operating systems or devices. A Generation 1 virtual machine is commonly used in the following situations:

- Installing an older operating system that does not fully support UEFI.
- Installing an older operating system that is only available on the 32-bit architecture.
- Migrating to a legacy Hyper-V host machine that does not support Generation 2 virtual machines.
- Support for COM ports, virtual floppy drives, and virtual network adapters.

Requirements will also vary depending on the operating system that needs to be installed, and what features are required to utilize a virtual machine. A Generation 2 virtual machine differs from a Generation 1 virtual machine in the following ways:

- Allows for adding or removing a virtual network adapter while the virtual machine is powered on.
- Allows for UEFI, TPM and secure boot support.
- Allows for the shielded virtual machine feature.

Modern operating systems such as Windows 11 only support Generation 2 virtual machines, and there is no supported method for installing Windows 11 as a Generation 1 virtual machine. This requirement is entirely dependent on the operating systems ability to support legacy hardware.

Converting Virtual Machines Between Hyper-V Generations

Microsoft does not officially support a way to convert a Generation 1 virtual machine to a Generation 2 virtual machine in Hyper-V, and vice versa. Ensure that when creating a virtual machine in Hyper-V that it is created with the correct Generation as required, as there is no way to easily fix that issue that is done in a supported manner.

There are third-party solutions that may be able to convert between Generation 1 virtual machines and Generation 2 virtual machines in Hyper-V. Those solutions are beyond the scope of this book and not supported by Microsoft and may or may not work correctly.

Hyper-V Setup and Configuration - Hyper-V Virtual Switches

The networking architecture in Hyper-V is fairly simple in nature, and involves two main components for connectivity for virtual machines. A virtual switch is used to connect to a network, and a virtual network adapter connects a virtual switch to a virtual machine. This is similar to how networking operates in other virtualization solutions, and it offers a great deal of flexibility for providing networking access to a virtual machine. It is also capable of restricting networking access for a virtual machine using various methods. Networking requirements will always vary depending on the purpose of a particular virtual machine, but the networking options within Hyper-V should be sufficient for most organizations. Hyper-V offers three types of virtual switches for connecting virtual machines to a network:

- **External Virtual Switch** - This is a virtual switch that binds to a physical network adapter on the Hyper-V host computer so that virtual machines can access the network just like a physical device.
- **Internal Virtual Switch** - This is a virtual switch that does not connect to a physical network in any way. Any virtual machine that is connected to this virtual switch will be able to communicate with other virtual machines that are connected on the same virtual switch, as well as the host operating system.
- **Private Virtual Switch** - This is a virtual switch that is similar to an internal virtual switch, except the host operating system is not able to communicate with the virtual machines on that virtual switch.

The most common type of Hyper-V virtual switch is the External virtual switch. This is the easiest type of virtual switch to setup, and it offers the most flexibility for connecting virtual machines to networks. The other types of virtual switches are designed and intended for larger scale datacentre environments with specific security requirements, or for specific testing requirements.

Virtual switches in Hyper-V support VLAN tags to allow for more complex networking requirements. Hyper-V also supports the ability to share the management interface of Hyper-V with the network adapter that is being used to reduce the number of required network adapters that are needed. This is especially useful for Windows Client Hyper-V, since it is most likely being used on a computer that likely has only one network adapter. For users with laptops that utilize wireless networking, it is also compatible with Hyper-V networks and allows for devices with different hardware configurations the ability to use Hyper-V with various configurations.

> **Hyper-V Default Virtual Switch**
>
> In Windows Client Hyper-V versions of the Hyper-V role, an Internal virtual switch will automatically be created at the time of installation of the Hyper-V role. This virtual switch is bridged to the Hyper-V host ethernet adapters and uses NAT to provide virtual machines access to the local network. It also automatically provides IP addresses to the virtual machines as required using DHCP. This type of virtual switch is unique to Windows Client Hyper-V and cannot be used on other platforms.

There are several ways to determine what Hyper-V virtual switches are currently configured on a Hyper-V host. The two most common methods for verification are by using the Hyper-V Manager console, and it can also be verified with a Cmdlet using PowerShell. To get a list of the currently configured virtual switches on a Hyper-V host, open an **elevated PowerShell prompt** and run the **Get-VMSwitch** Cmdlet:

```
Windows PowerShell (Elevated)

PS C:\Windows\system32> Get-VMSwitch


Name            SwitchType    NetAdapterInterfaceDescription
----            ----------    ------------------------------
Default Switch  Internal
```

The Cmdlet will return the list of all configured virtual switches, which type of virtual switch it is, and which network adapter the virtual switch is configured to use.

To view the configured virtual switches that are on a Hyper-V host using Hyper-V Manager, perform the following steps:

1. Open the **Hyper-V Manager** (virtmgmt.msc) console.
2. In the **Actions** pane, click the option for **Virtual Switch Manager...** under the name of the Hyper-V server.
3. In the **Virtual Switch Manager** window, the currently configured virtual switches are listed in the **Virtual Switches** pane, below the option for **New virtual network switch**:

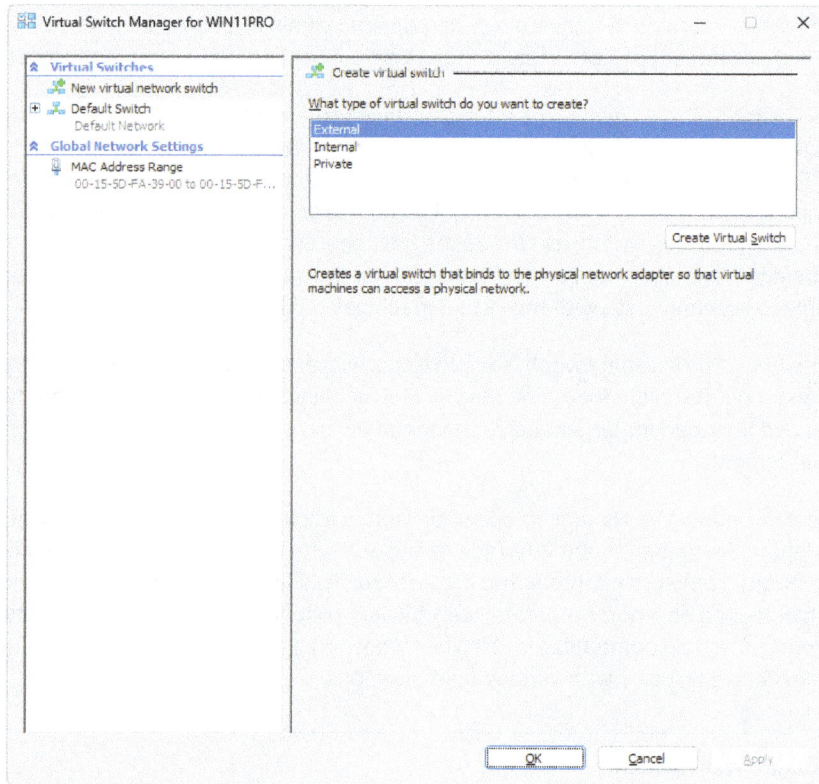

4. Click the **OK** button to close the window.

Managing virtual switches that are configured with Hyper-V is not difficult to do, and there is a great deal of flexibility on adding, editing, and deleting virtual switches as needed.

Hyper-V Virtual Switch Options

The purpose of this book is to create a test environment for demonstrating the setup of a Two-Tier Certificate Authority. If testing this environment does not require any external devices (such as iOS or Android devices), an Internal virtual switch is sufficient for testing. The Default Virtual Switch provided with Windows Client Hyper-V works well for this purpose. If external devices are needed for testing the deployment of the Certificate Authority, an External virtual switch is more appropriate since it will allow for the test environment virtual machines to connect to a network where those devices are located.

Hyper-V Internal and Private Networks

These types of virtual switches are more restricted in the types of network connections that are permitted compared to an External virtual switch, but it is still not recommended to use these types of networks with an Offline Root Certificate Authority. This server should never accept network connections from other devices since there is no guarantee that those devices are not compromised, even in a presumed secure environment.

In the following example, an External virtual switch named **Hyper-V External Switch** will be configured and attached to a network adapter called **Ethernet (Intel Ethernet I219-LM)**. This virtual switch will allow management access as well. This can be accomplished using the command line with PowerShell, or with Hyper-V Manager. Only one method is required, and either method will accomplish the same task.

> **Hyper-V Virtual Switch Management Access**
>
> When creating an External virtual switch there is an option for allowing the management operating system to share the network adapter that the virtual switch is configured with. Typically, on a dedicated Hyper-V server there are usually multiple network adapters for the server and the virtual machines to use, and it is good practice to separate which network adapters are used for management purposes. This ensures that there is always access to the Hyper-V server in the event of an issue, and allows for the management network to be located on an isolated network if required.
>
> On Windows Client Hyper-V versions, the Hyper-V role is typically used with computers that do not have multiple network adapters, and it is not always possible to have a dedicated network adapter strictly for management purposes. In this case it is necessary to share the network adapter with both the Hyper-V host operating system. The default virtual switch that is installed is configured in a manner that allows for this automatically, and requires no configuration.

> **Hyper-V External Virtual Switch Network Interruptions**
>
> Configuring an External virtual switch on a network adapter will cause temporary network interruptions while the network adapter is reconfigured. Ensure that there is access to the Hyper-V host in the event that network connectivity is lost due to IP address changes.

Hyper-V Setup and Configuration - Hyper-V Virtual Switches - CLI Configuration

Before adding a virtual switch using PowerShell, the correct name of any available network adapters will need to be determined. This can be accomplished by using the **Get-NetAdapter** Cmdlet from an **elevated PowerShell prompt**:

```
Windows PowerShell (Elevated)

PS C:\Windows\system32> Get-NetAdapter

Name           InterfaceDescription        ifIndex Status   MacAddress           LinkSpeed
----           --------------------        ------- ------   ----------           ---------
Ethernet       Intel Ethernet I219-LM           14 Up       00-11-22-33-44-55    1 Gbps
```

The correct name of the ethernet adapter is the one under the **Name** column, and this is what will be used to configure the virtual switch. Once the name of the ethernet adapter has been determined, the External virtual switch can now be created using the **New-VMSwitch** Cmdlet from an **elevated PowerShell prompt**:

```
Windows PowerShell (Elevated)

New-VMSwitch `
-Name "Hyper-V External Switch" `
-NetAdapterName "Ethernet" `
-AllowManagementOS:$true
```

Once the new virtual switch has been created, it can now be added to any virtual machine that is located on the Hyper-V host.

Hyper-V Setup and Configuration - Hyper-V Virtual Switches - GUI Configuration

To create an External virtual switch using Hyper-V Manager, perform the following steps:

1. Open the **Hyper-V Manager** (virtmgmt.msc) console.
2. In the **Actions** pane, click the option for **Virtual Switch Manager...** under the name of the Hyper-V server.
3. In the **Virtual Switch Manager** window, in the **Virtual Switches** pane, click the option for **New virtual network switch** (if it is not already selected).
4. In the **Crate virtual switch** pane, select the option as **External**, and click the **Create Virtual Switch** button.
5. In the **Virtual Switch Properties** pane, make the following changes to the new virtual switch:
   - **Name**: Hyper-V External Switch
   - **Connection Type**: External network
   - **Network Adapter**: Ethernet (Intel Ethernet I219-LM)
   - **Allow management operating system to share this network adapter**: Yes
6. Click the **OK** button to create the virtual switch.
7. A warning stating that **Pending changes may disrupt network connectivity** will appear, click the **Yes** button to continue. The window will automatically close.

Once the new virtual switch has been created, it can now be added to any virtual machine that is located on the Hyper-V host.

Hyper-V Setup and Configuration - Hyper-V Virtual Network Adapters

Similar to how other virtualization solutions offer networking to virtual machines, Hyper-V is capable of adding virtual network adapters to a virtual machine to allow for communication to internal and external networks. Hyper-V offers two types of virtual network adapters that can be added to a virtual machine, the **Legacy Network Adapter** and the **Network Adapter**. The types of virtual network adapters that are available are to virtual machines is entirely dependent on the generation version of the virtual machine, so there is some consideration on which one to use depending on what virtual network adapter is required.

The Hyper-V **Legacy Network Adapter** is available on Generation 1 virtual machines only. There are a few things to consider if this type of virtual network adapter is required:

- The virtual network adapter is being used for legacy operating systems that do not fully support Hyper-V, and do not support the most recent Hyper-V Integration Services.
- The virtual network adapter is needed to emulate a basic, well supported network adapter that has the most support available for virtual machines.
- The virtual network adapter is required for PXE booting for legacy virtual machines.

The Hyper-V **Network Adapter** is available on Generation 1 and Generation 2 virtual machines, so it offers the most amount of compatibility should it be required. It offers several differences from the **Legacy Network Adapter**:

- The virtual network adapter does not rely on emulation for the network adapter hardware, so it has better performance than the legacy network adapter.
- The virtual network adapter is supported by default on all modern Windows operating systems, and Linux operating systems that have the necessary kernel modules available.
- The virtual network adapter offers better performance and higher speeds.
- The virtual network adapter supports VLAN tagging for network access.

The virtual network adapters can be added or removed where needed, but depending on the generation of the particular virtual machine it may require the virtual machine to be powered off to make the change.

> **Hyper-V Virtual Network Adapter Management**
>
> Virtual network adapters can be modified using the command line with the **Add-VMNetworkAdapter** and **Rename-VMNetworkAdapter** Cmdlets, or with Hyper-V Manager as required.

Hyper-V Setup and Configuration - Hyper-V Checkpoints

Hyper-V has the Checkpoints feature, which is the ability to save the state of a virtual machine and revert changes to a virtual machine if there is an issue. This feature exists with other virtualization solutions, and in Hyper-V they are called Checkpoints (previously known as Snapshots in older versions of Hyper-V). A Checkpoint is a copy of a virtual machine at a particular time, which captures everything about the virtual machine at that point.

Hyper-V Checkpoints are primarily used to revert or undo changes to a virtual machine if an issue occurs during an update or during a major configuration change. Multiple Checkpoints can be made for a virtual machine, which can be useful for testing purposes. Even though Hyper-V Checkpoints can be a useful feature for specific scenarios, they are not an adequate backup solution and should never be used in that manner. For example, changes that are made to Active Directory cannot be reverted by using Checkpoints if there are multiple Domain Controller in an Active Directory Forest.

There are few things to know about Hyper-V Checkpoints prior to using them on virtual machines:

- Hyper-V Checkpoints can be explicitly enabled or disabled for a virtual machine, as well as set to be created automatically if needed or required.
- Hyper-V Checkpoints are helpful for testing purposes and can be used to undo changes to a virtual machine in only a few minutes.
- Hyper-V Checkpoints can be given meaningful names at the time that they are created to ensure that the Checkpoint is easily identifiable.
- Hyper-V stores virtual machine Checkpoints in two locations when they are created. The differencing virtual hard disks for a virtual machine are stored as an AVHD or AVHDX file whenever they are created (the file type depends on the type of virtual hard disk), and it is located in the same folder as the accompanying virtual hard disk. The virtual machine state and other information is stored in the Snapshots folder, which is located in the root of the Hyper-V Virtual Machine Configuration Files folder.

There are two types of Checkpoints that are supported in recent versions of Hyper-V, Production Checkpoints and Standard Checkpoints. Both types of Checkpoints offer different features:

- Production Checkpoints are used to capture the state of everything on a virtual machine at the time when it was created, and it leverages the native backup features located within the virtual machine. This type of Checkpoint is the most widely supported, and offers the best compatibility compared to Standard Checkpoints. This is the default type of Checkpoint that is created, and can be changed should it be required.
- Standard Checkpoints are a legacy version of Checkpoints that only captures the basic state of a virtual machine, and is more appropriate for reverting a virtual machine to an earlier version if there is an immediate issue.

Hyper-V Checkpoints are a useful feature for quickly reverting to a previous point in time if there is an issue with a virtual machine, but they do not replace the necessity for a proper backup solution for critical virtual machines in an organization.

> **Hyper-V Checkpoints and Managing Disk Space**
>
> An important thing to consider before using Hyper-V Checkpoints is that once one is created, they can begin to slowly take up a considerable amount of disk space if they are not properly managed. When a virtual hard disk is provisioned, the size of the virtual hard disk can be specified and Hyper-V will not allocate more to the disk space if it is used up. Hyper-V will treat the virtual hard disk as if it is a physical hard disk, which cannot be resized after it is manufactured. With Checkpoints, the differencing files can grow to whatever size is needed, which can fill up an entire hard drive or storage location if left unchecked.
>
> Ensure that if Hyper-V Checkpoints are being used, either delete the Checkpoint or merge in into the main virtual hard disk to prevent the size from growing out of control. A Checkpoint that is not managed correctly can cause a Hyper-V server to crash if disk space is exhausted, and recovering from this issue is difficult and time consuming.

Hyper-V Setup and Configuration - Hyper-V Virtual Machine Creation

Creating a virtual machine with Hyper-V is not difficult to do, and the only important requirement to consider is managing the resources on the device that is running Hyper-V (or any virtualization platform for that matter). The most important factor to consider when provisioning virtual machines is to not over-provision them on the virtualization host. This can cause resource issues for the host machine running the Hyper-V role, and affect other existing virtual machines if there are insufficient resources to run the virtual machines.

In this example a Windows Server 2022 virtual machine will be created using Hyper-V on a Windows 11 Pro computer. The following specifications will be used for the test virtual machine:

Virtual Machine Name	Windows Server 2022
Virtual Machine Generation	1
Virtual Processors	2
Virtual Memory	4 GB (4096 MB)
Virtual Hard Disk	40 GB
Virtual Network Adapters	1

Table 4.14.1: Virtual machine specifications for the Windows Server 2022 virtual machine being created on Hyper-V.

In this example, the Hyper-V settings for the Windows 11 Pro computer is configured as follows:

Hyper-V Virtual Machine Path	D:\Hyper-V\
Hyper-V Virtual Hard Disk Path	D:\Hyper-V\Virtual Hard Disks\
Hyper-V Network Type	External
Hyper-V Network Name	Hyper-V External Switch
ISO Image Path	D:\ISO Images\Windows Server 2022.iso

Table 4.14.2: Hyper-V folder path locations and virtual switch settings for the Windows 11 Pro computer.

This section demonstrates how to create a virtual machine on the Hyper-V platform using two different methods. There is an option to use the CLI with PowerShell, and there is another option to use the GUI with Hyper-V Manager. Use whichever method to create the virtual machine, but only one method is required.

> **Hyper-V Test Environment**
>
> This section assumes that the location of the Hyper-V virtual machines is known, the name of the Hyper-V network switch is known, and the location of an installation ISO is known. Information on how to determine this information can be found earlier in this chapter. Adjust the configuration of the virtual machine as needed before proceeding.

> **Hyper-V Test Virtual Machine**
>
> This Windows Server 2022 virtual machine is only for testing and demonstration purposes. It is not used in the Active Directory Certificate Services implementation in any way whatsoever. If there is no need to test how to create virtual machines with Hyper-V, then skip this section. **If this virtual machine is created for the demonstration in this chapter, it can be safely deleted at the end of the chapter as it is not used in any later steps in this book.**

Hyper-V Setup and Configuration - Hyper-V Virtual Machine Creation - CLI Configuration

To create a Hyper-V virtual machine for Windows Server 2022 using the command line, open an **elevated PowerShell prompt** and run the following commands:

1. Create the **Windows Server 2022** virtual machine and virtual hard disk using the **New-VM** Cmdlet:

```
Windows PowerShell (Elevated)

New-VM `
-Name "Windows Server 2022" `
-Generation 1 `
-MemoryStartupBytes 4GB `
-BootDevice VHD `
-NewVHDPath "D:\Hyper-V\Virtual Hard Disks\Windows Server 2022.vhdx" `
-NewVHDSizeBytes 40GB `
-Switch "Hyper-V External Switch"
```

2. Set the number of virtual processors for the **Windows Server 2022** virtual machine to **2** using the **Set-VMProcessor** Cmdlet:

```
Windows PowerShell (Elevated)

Set-VMProcessor "Windows Server 2022" -Count 2
```

3. Mount the ISO image that will be used to install the operating system on the **Windows Server 2022** virtual machine using the **Set-VMDvdDrive** Cmdlet:

```
Windows PowerShell (Elevated)

Set-VMDvdDrive `
-VMName "Windows Server 2022" `
-Path "D:\ISO Images\Windows Server 2022.iso"
```

4. Power on the **Windows Server 2022** virtual machine using the **Start-VM** Cmdlet:

```
Windows PowerShell (Elevated)

Start-VM -Name "Windows Server 2022"
```

5. Connect to the **Windows Server 2022** virtual machine using the **Virtual Machine Connection** tool:

```
Windows PowerShell (Elevated)

vmconnect.exe localhost "Windows Server 2022"
```

6. At this point the **Windows Server 2022** operating system can now be installed as it normally would be.

There is no need to proceed with the installation as this was just a test to demonstrate how to create a virtual machine and connect to it using PowerShell. If there is a need to test how virtual floppy disks operate, install the operating system with the default options. If no issues were encountered with creating the virtual machine, it can be deleted as it is no longer required. This task can be completed later in this chapter.

> ⚠️ **Hyper-V Generation Virtual Machine Startup Options**
>
> There is a difference in the way that Generation 1 virtual machines and Generation 2 virtual machines handle the boot order when installing an operating system. Generation 1 virtual machines do not require any changes by default, but Generation 2 virtual machines require a modification to ensure that external media is used when starting the virtual machine. The **Set-VMFirmware** Cmdlet can be used for this.

Hyper-V Setup and Configuration - Hyper-V Virtual Machine Creation - GUI Configuration

To create a Hyper-V virtual machine for Windows Server 2022 using Hyper-V Manager, perform the following steps:

1. Open the **Hyper-V Manager** (virtmgmt.msc) console:

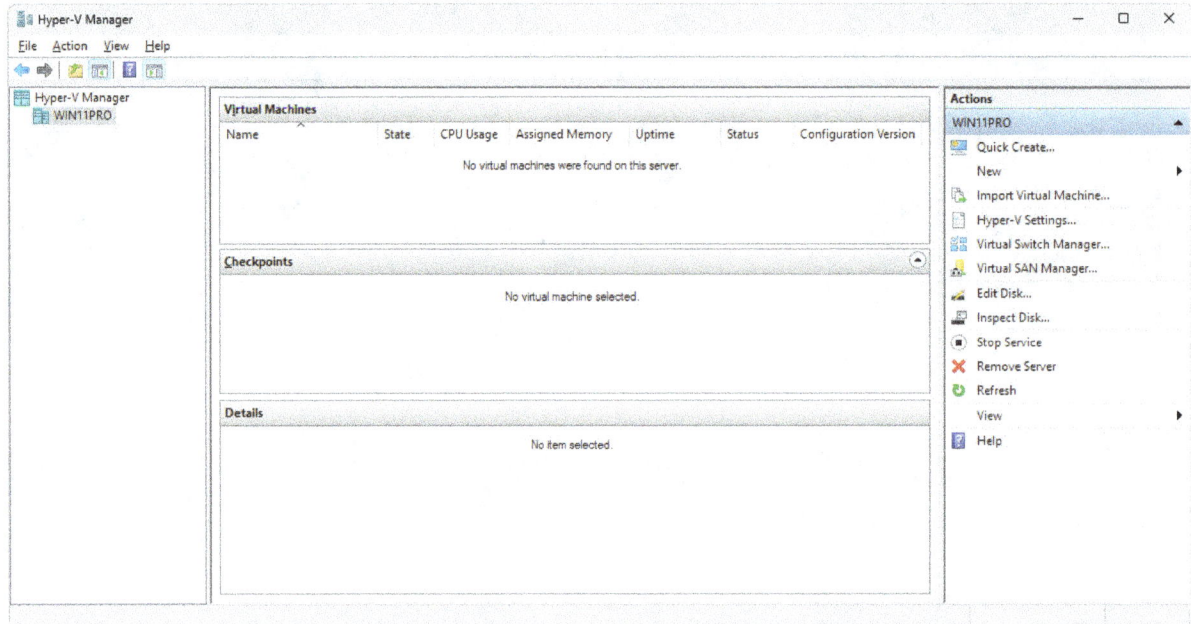

2. In the **Actions** pane, click **New**, and when the menu appears select the **Virtual Machine...** option.
3. The **New Virtual Machine Wizard** window will appear.
4. On the **Before You Begin** screen, click the **Next** button to continue:

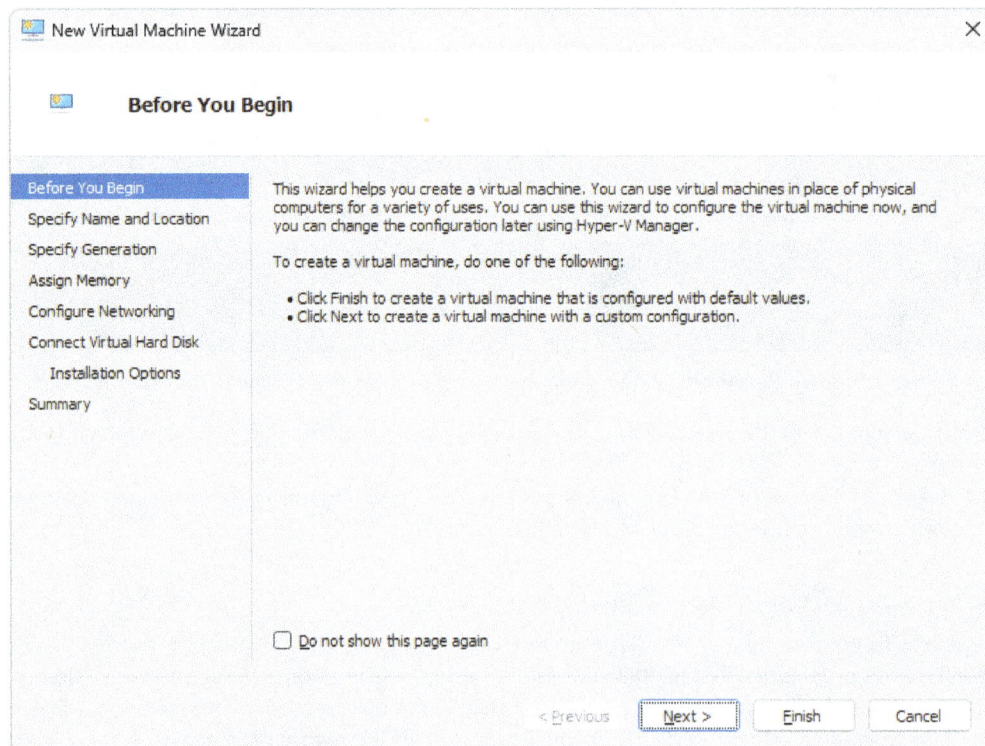

5. On the **Specify Name and Location** screen, enter **Windows Server 2022** as the name for the virtual machine in the **Name** field. Click the **Next** button to continue:

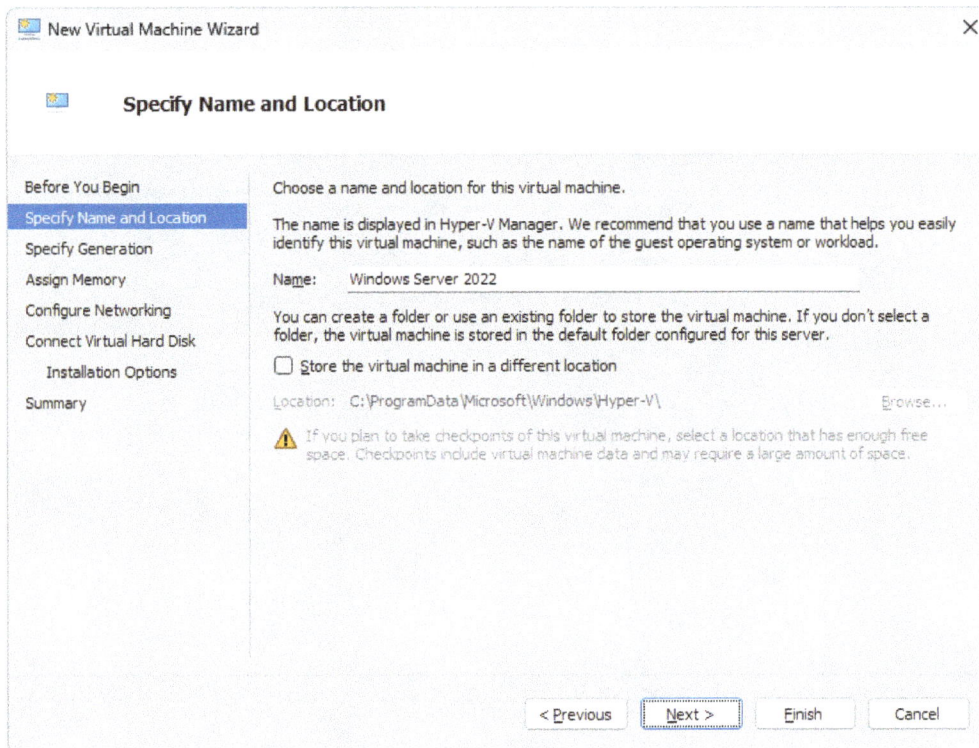

6. On the **Specify Generation** screen, ensure that the **Generation 1** setting is selected for the virtual machine. Click the **Next** button to continue:

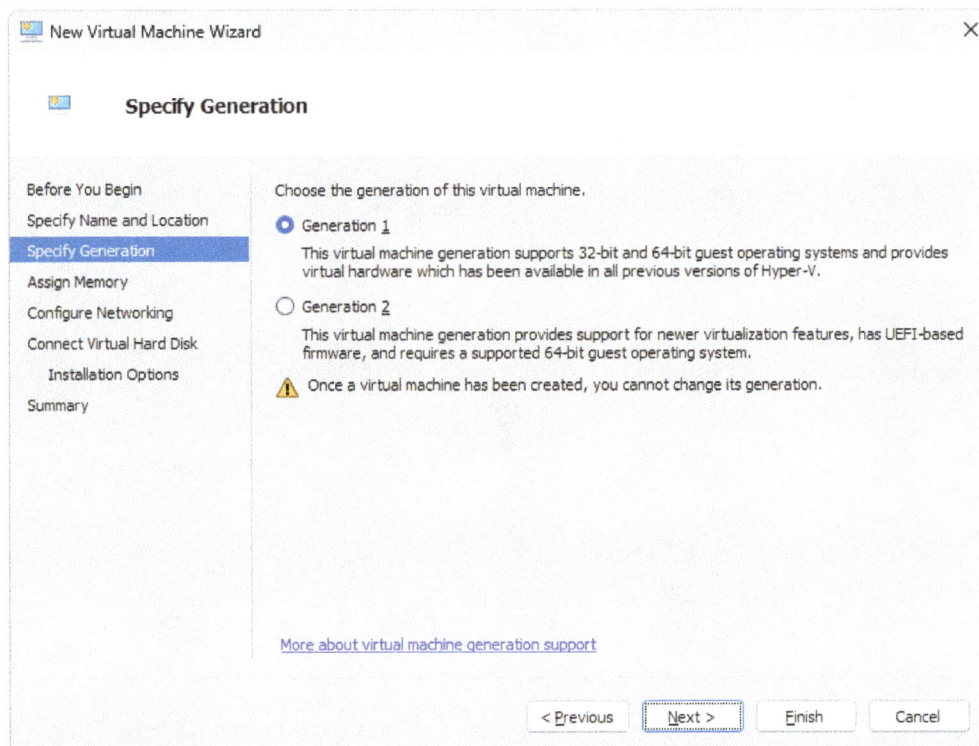

7. On the **Assign Memory** screen, set the amount of **Startup memory** for the virtual machine to **4096 MB**. If required, unselect the **Use Dynamic Memory for this virtual machine** option and click the **Next** button to continue:

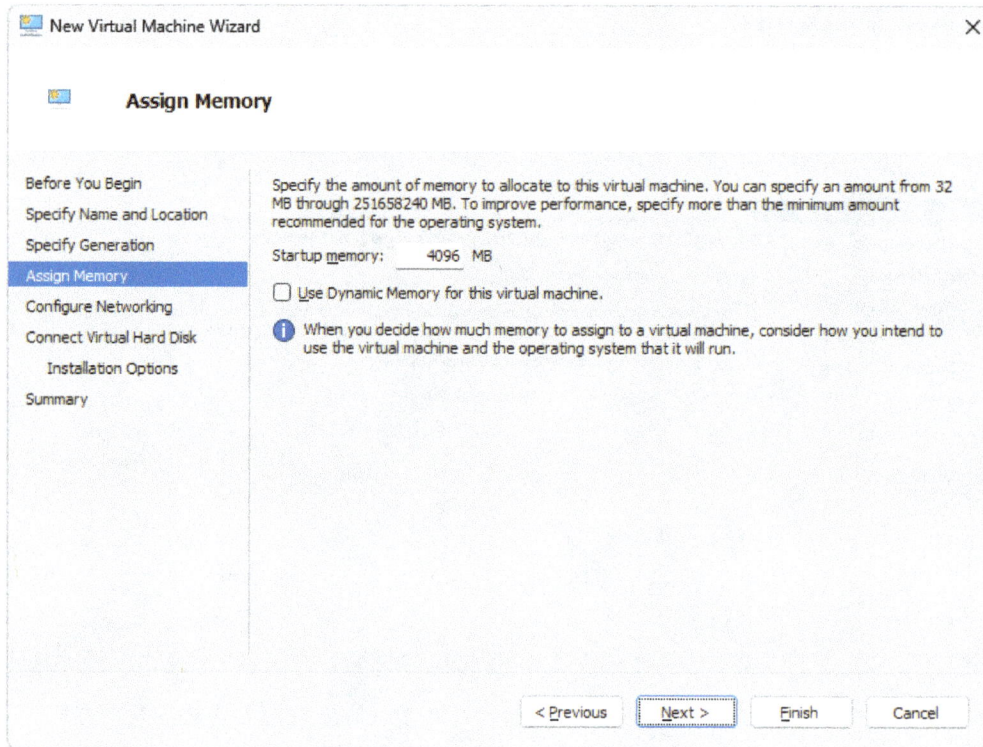

New Virtual Machine Wizard ☒ ✕

Assign Memory

Before You Begin
Specify Name and Location
Specify Generation
Assign Memory
Configure Networking
Connect Virtual Hard Disk
   Installation Options
Summary

Specify the amount of memory to allocate to this virtual machine. You can specify an amount from 32 MB through 251658240 MB. To improve performance, specify more than the minimum amount recommended for the operating system.

Startup memory: 4096 MB

☐ Use Dynamic Memory for this virtual machine.

ⓘ When you decide how much memory to assign to a virtual machine, consider how you intend to use the virtual machine and the operating system that it will run.

< Previous   Next >   Finish   Cancel

8. On the **Configure Networking** screen, select the **Hyper-V External Switch** network to use in the **Connection** list and click **Next** to continue:

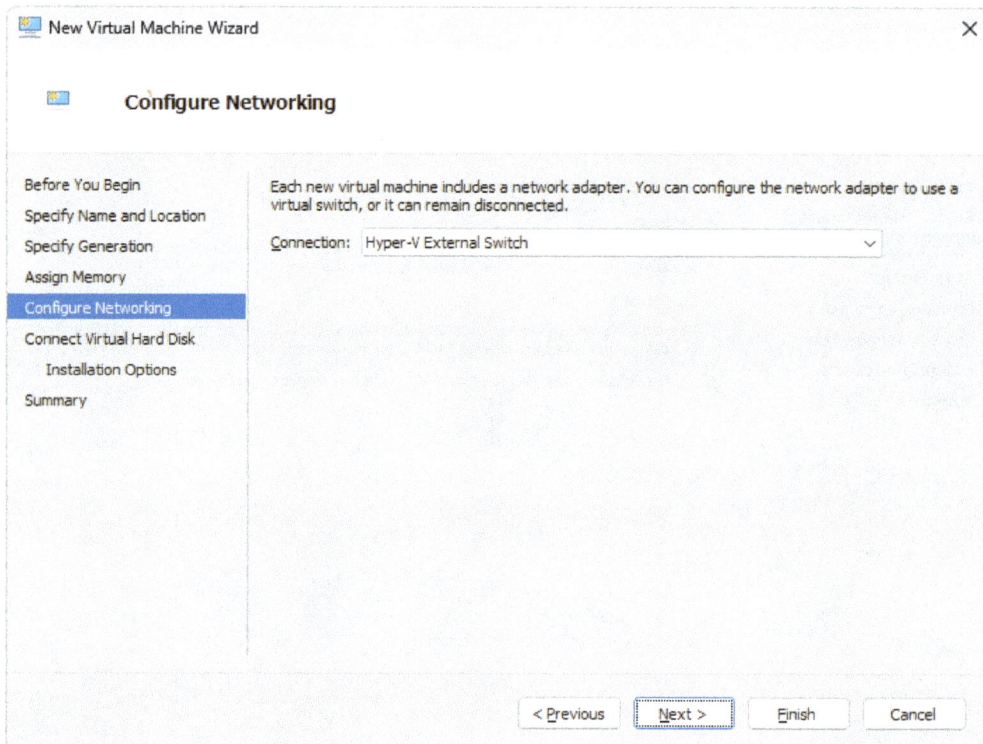

New Virtual Machine Wizard ☒ ✕

Configure Networking

Before You Begin
Specify Name and Location
Specify Generation
Assign Memory
Configure Networking
Connect Virtual Hard Disk
   Installation Options
Summary

Each new virtual machine includes a network adapter. You can configure the network adapter to use a virtual switch, or it can remain disconnected.

Connection: Hyper-V External Switch ⌄

< Previous   Next >   Finish   Cancel

9. On the **Configure Virtual Hard Disk** screen, change size of the virtual hard disk to **40 GB**. Click the **Next** button to continue:

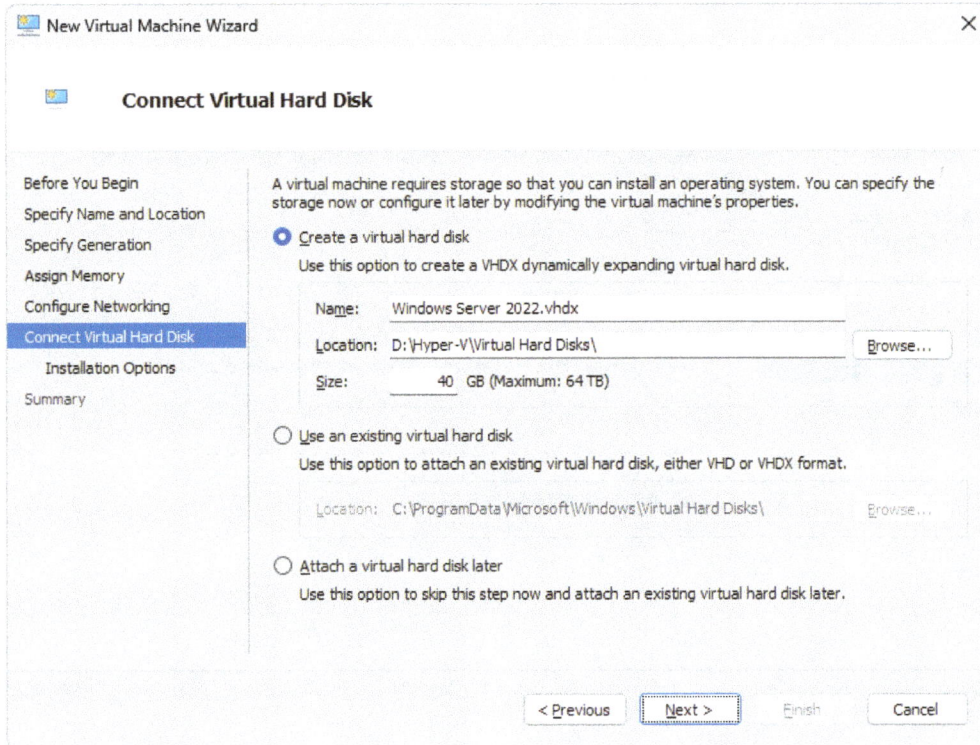

10. On the **Installation Options** screen, specify where the Windows Server 2022 ISO image is located. Click the **Next** button to continue:

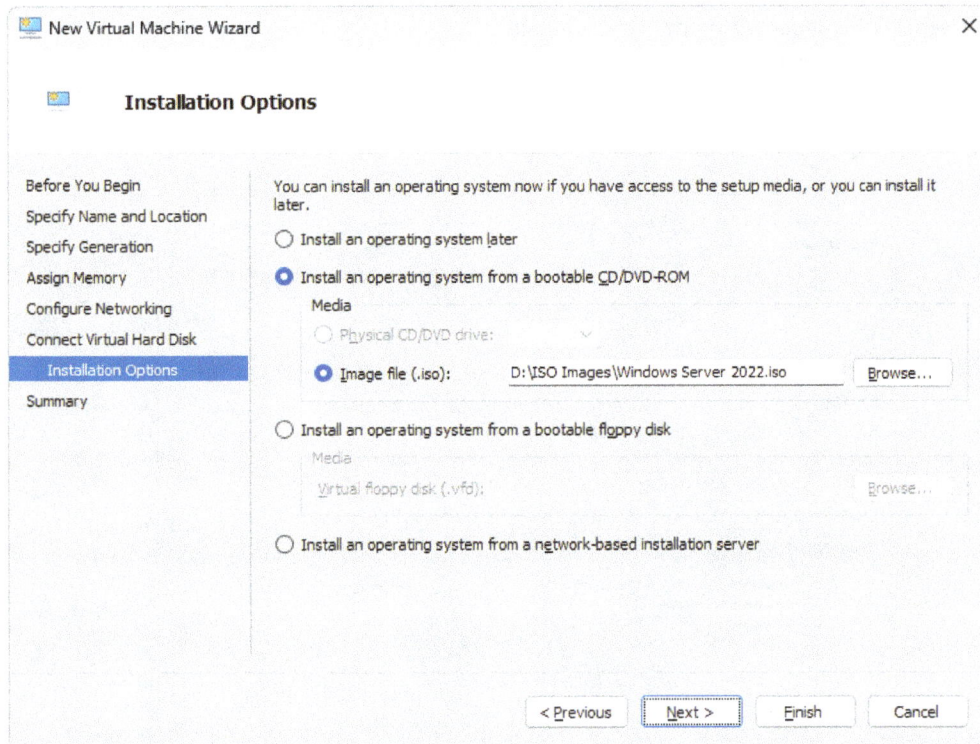

11. On the **Completing the New Virtual Machine Wizard** screen, click the **Finish** button to continue:

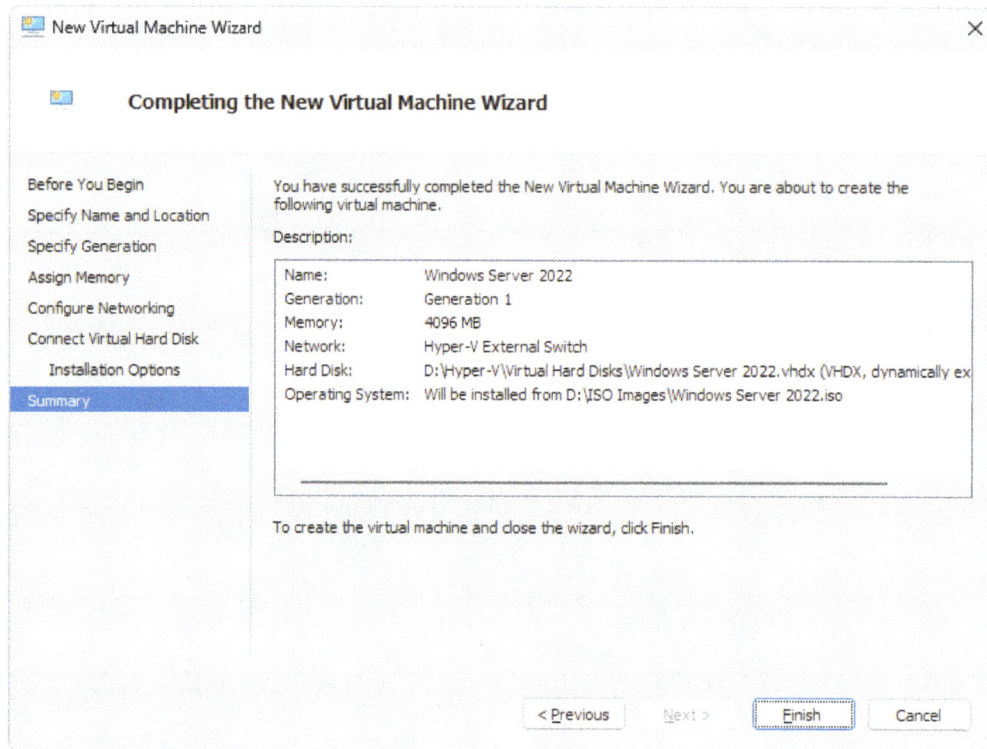

At this point the virtual machine has been created and additional settings can now be configured. The next step needed for configuring the virtual machine is to modify the settings to use more than one virtual processor. This configuration change can be completed using Hyper-V Manager:

1. Open the **Hyper-V Manager** (virtmgmt.msc) console.
2. Select the **Windows Server 2022** virtual machine in the **Virtual Machines** pane.
3. In the **Actions** pane, under the **Windows Server 2022** virtual machine, click the **Settings...** option:

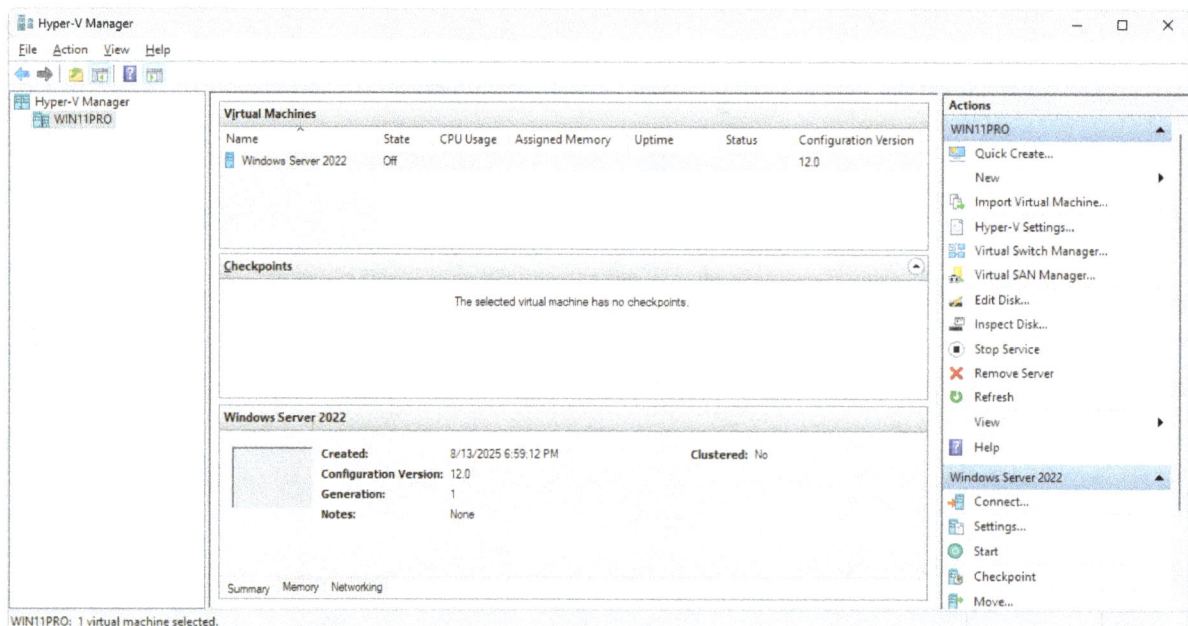

4. In the settings window for the **Windows Server 2022** virtual machine, select the **Processor** option in the **Hardware** pane.
5. In the **Processor** settings for the virtual machine, set the **Number of virtual processors** to **2**. Click the **OK** button to apply the change and close the window:

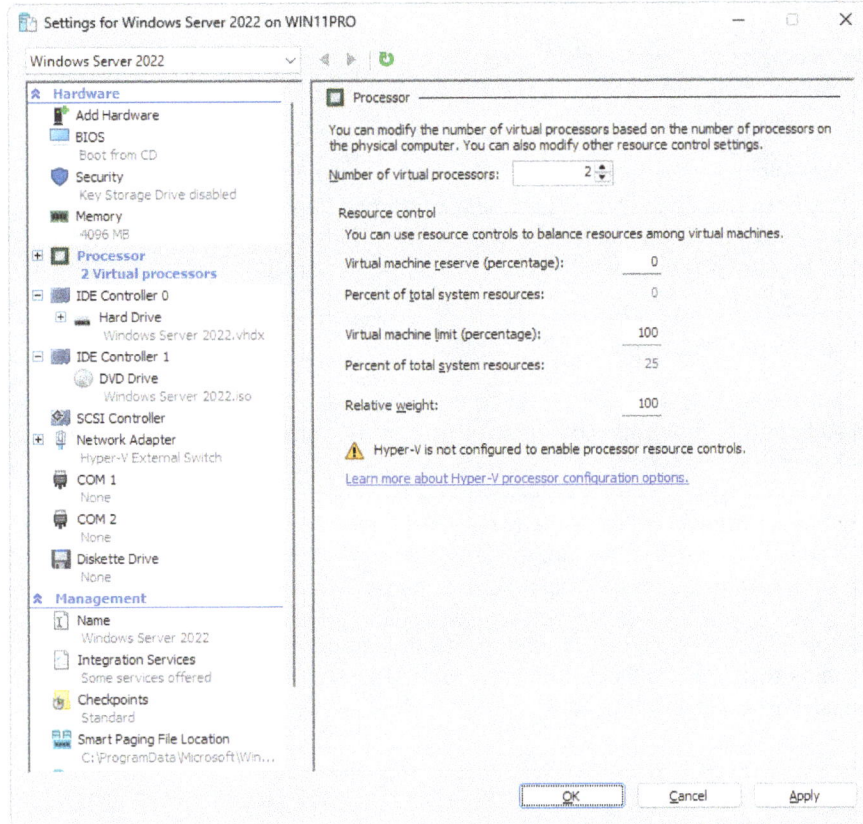

Once the virtual machine has all of the correct settings configured correctly it can be powered on. Once powered on it can be connected to using the Virtual Machine Connection tool, and the installation of an operating system can be performed. Both of these actions can be performed using Hyper-V Manager:

1. Open the **Hyper-V Manager** (virtmgmt.msc) console.
2. Select the **Windows Server 2022** virtual machine in the **Virtual Machines** pane.
3. Right-click on the **Windows Server 2022** virtual machine and select the **Start** option.
4. Right-click on the **Windows Server 2022** virtual machine and select the **Connect...** option. This will open the **Virtual Machine Connection** window and connect to the virtual machine.
5. At this point the operating system can now be installed as it normally would be.

There is no need to proceed with the installation as this was just a test to demonstrate how to create a virtual machine and connect to it using PowerShell. If there is a need to test how virtual floppy disks operate, install the operating system with the default options. If no issues were encountered with creating the virtual machine, it can be deleted as it is no longer required. This task can be completed later in this chapter.

> **Virtual Machine Generation Differences**
>
> Examining the settings for a virtual machine using Hyper-V Manager clearly shows the hardware differences between Generation 1 and Generation 2 virtual machines. Legacy devices such as serial ports and floppy drives are not available, and the use of IDE hard drive controllers for the virtual hard disks instead of SCSI hard drive controllers.

Hyper-V Setup and Configuration - Hyper-V Virtual Floppy Disks

Floppy disks are an obsolete media format which is largely unused today on modern computers. They have many limitations compared to modern storage solutions:

- Lack of physical hardware to read and write floppy disks.
- Long-term reliability issues.
- Low availability of new floppy disks.
- Low storage capacity.
- Slow read and write speeds.

There are scenarios where floppy disks can be useful on a modern operating system. They are most commonly used for adding drivers at the time of an operating system installation, and they can also be used for transferring small files between legacy devices. In this book, a virtual floppy disk is useful for transferring files related to the installation and operation of the Certificate Authority between servers.

> **Hyper-V Virtual Floppy Disk Support**
>
> Virtual floppy disks are fully supported with Hyper-V when Generation 1 virtual machine are used. It is not possible to add a virtual floppy disk to a Generation 2 virtual machine. Ensure that when creating a virtual machine using Hyper-V to select the correct Hyper-V Generation type as it cannot be changed later.
>
> The majority of virtual machines do not require virtual floppy disk support, and it is common to use Generation 2 virtual machines in the vast majority of cases with Hyper-V. If there is a possibility that a virtual floppy disk is required for a virtual machine, then a Generation 1 virtual machine is required.
>
> Windows Server 2022 and Windows 11 do not natively support reading virtual floppy disk files directly, and they cannot be mounted without third-party tools. This limitation does not exist with virtual hard disk files, as this support is natively available.

Virtual floppy disks are saved with the **VFD** extension. When virtual disk types are created in Hyper-V they are not formatted by default, and that will need to occur before the virtual floppy disk can be used with a virtual machine. Due to the age of the floppy disk media type, the only file system that is supported with the Windows operating system is the File Allocation Table (FAT) file system. Since the storage size is limited for a floppy disk, this is not an issue.

> **Hyper-V USB Passthrough**
>
> Other virtualization solutions offer varying levels of support for USB devices that can be accessed through a virtual machine. USB passthrough support in Hyper-V is cumbersome, and requires many steps to be used.
>
> Accessing USB devices through Remote Desktop or the Virtual Machine Connection application is possible, but is not recommended for servers that are hosting sensitive information. Allowing this level of access between a host and a server can potentially put the data on that server at risk. For a server that is involved in a Certificate Authority, this can potentially comprise the PKI and is not advised.

> **Virtual Floppy Disk Deletion**
>
> It is advised that after the implementation of the Certificate Authority that the virtual floppy disk be deleted as it is no longer needed. This will prevent any sensitive data that is stored on the virtual floppy disk from being left on a server or workstation where it could be found. When files need to be transferred between the Root CA and the Subordinate CA (such as the CRL when it needs to be renewed), Create a new virtual floppy disk for the task and then delete it again when finished with it. This is a yearly task in most cases, and is not a regular occurrence.

Virtual floppy disks can be created and managed using the CLI with PowerShell, and with the GUI using Hyper-V Manager. Use whichever method to create and manage the virtual floppy disk, but only one method is required. The **Windows Server 2022** virtual machine that was created earlier can be used to test the virtual floppy disk.

> **Virtual Floppy Disk Storage Location**
>
> In this example a virtual floppy disk named **Test-Floppy.vfd** will be created in the **D:\Hyper-V\Virtual Floppy Disks** directory on the workstation that is running Hyper-V. This directory is not created by default when the Hyper-V role is configured. A virtual floppy disk does not have the same limitations with other Hyper-V files, and can be located anywhere that Hyper-V is able to read/write to. Virtual floppy disks are not linked to specific virtual machines like virtual hard disks are, and can be located anywhere. They are treated like portable media just like their physical counterparts, and Hyper-V treats them in the same manner.

Hyper-V Setup and Configuration - Hyper-V Virtual Floppy Disks - CLI Configuration

To create a virtual floppy disk using PowerShell, use the **New-VFD** Cmdlet from an **elevated PowerShell prompt**:

```
Windows PowerShell (Elevated)

New-VFD "D:\Hyper-V\Virtual Floppy Disks\Test-Floppy.vfd"
```

To add an existing virtual floppy disk to a virtual machine named **Windows Server 2022** using PowerShell, use the **Set-VMFloppyDiskDrive** Cmdlet from an **elevated PowerShell prompt**:

```
Windows PowerShell (Elevated)

Set-VMFloppyDiskDrive `
-VMName "Windows Server 2022" `
-Path "D:\Hyper-V\Virtual Floppy Disks\Test-Floppy.vfd"
```

Removing a virtual floppy disk from a virtual machine can also be done using the **Set-VMFloppyDiskDrive** Cmdlet from an **elevated PowerShell prompt**:

```
Windows PowerShell (Elevated)

Set-VMFloppyDiskDrive -VMName "Windows Server 2022" -Path $null
```

Virtual floppy disks can be formatted when they are connected to a supported virtual machine, steps for which can be found in the next section.

Hyper-V Setup and Configuration - Hyper-V Virtual Floppy Disks - GUI Configuration

To create a virtual floppy disk using Hyper-V Manager, perform the following steps:

1. Open the **Hyper-V Manager** console (virtmgmt.msc).
2. In the **Actions** pane, click the **New** button and select **Floppy Disk...** from the menu.
3. On the **Create Virtual Floppy Disk** window, browse to the **D:\Hyper-V\Virtual Floppy Disks** directory to save the virtual floppy disk.
4. Input **Test-Floppy.vfd** as the name for the virtual floppy disk in the **File name** field, and click the **Create** button.

To add a virtual floppy disk to a virtual machine using the VMConnect application, perform the following steps:

1. Open the **Virtual Machine Connection** (vmconnect.exe) window for the virtual machine that the virtual floppy disk is being added to.
2. Click on the **Media** menu, select the **Diskette Drive** menu and click the **Insert Disk...** option.
3. On the **Open** window, browse to the **D:\Hyper-V\Virtual Floppy Disks** directory, select the **Test-Floppy.vfd** file, and click the **Open** button.
4. The virtual floppy disk is now added to the virtual machine and accessed.

To remove the virtual floppy disk, it only requires a few steps as well (ensure that there are no open files on the virtual floppy disk when it is ejected):

1. Open the **Virtual Machine Connection** (vmconnect.exe) window for the virtual machine that the virtual floppy disk needs to be removed from.
2. Click on the **Media** menu, select the **Diskette Drive** menu and click the **Eject Test-Floppy.vfd** option.
3. The virtual floppy disk has now been removed from the virtual machine.

A virtual floppy disk can also be inserted and removed using the Hyper-V Manager console as well. Virtual floppy disks can be formatted when they are connected to a supported virtual machine, steps for which can be found in the next section.

Hyper-V Setup and Configuration - Hyper-V Virtual Floppy Disks - Disk Formatting

There are multiple ways to format storage devices in Windows, and this task can be performed using the command line or with graphical tools. There are no third-party tools required to format storage devices in Windows, but they are available for special cases where the native tools are insufficient. **The virtual floppy disk needs to be added to a virtual machine before it can be formatted, and a virtual floppy disk only needs to be formatted once.**

Formatting a virtual floppy disk can be done using the command line with the **format.exe** command from an **elevated Command Prompt**. The command requires no options since it defaults to using FAT as the filesystem. The command is interactive and will prompt the user several times to complete the formatting of the floppy disk. The default options are sufficient for a floppy disk, and a virtual floppy disk in Hyper-V will always be found at the **A:** location:

```
Command Prompt (Elevated)

format.exe A:
```

To format a virtual floppy disk using the graphical tools in Windows, perform the following steps:

1. Open **Windows File Explorer** (explorer.exe) and go to **This PC**. Right-click on **Floppy Disk Drive (A:)** and select the **Format...** option.
2. On the **Format Floppy Disk Drive (A:)** window, accept all of the default options and click the **Start** button.
3. When the window appears warning about deleting the contents of the disk, click the **OK** button.
4. When the disk formatting has completed, click the **OK** button.
5. Click the **Close** button to complete the formatting of the virtual floppy disk.

Once the virtual floppy disk has been formatted it can be used as external storage for virtual machines that support it. Since this virtual floppy disk was created for testing purposes and is not used in any steps in later chapters, it can be safely deleted.

Hyper-V Setup and Configuration - Hyper-V Virtual Machine Deletion

Managing the lifecycle of a virtual machine is important, and part of that lifecycle is removing virtual machines that are no longer required as they can cause an unnecessary drain on resources. Deleting old virtual machines, especially ones that are used for testing purposes should be a task that is performed regularly and when they are no longer required. Deleting virtual machines is not a difficult task, and the only extra step that needs to be performed is deleting any virtual hard disks that are associated with a virtual machine.

Deleting virtual machines is not difficult, and can be performed using the CLI with PowerShell, or with the GUI using Hyper-V Manager. In this example, the **Windows Server 2022** virtual machine that created in the previous section will be deleted. Both methods to delete the virtual machine work the same way, and both methods will delete a virtual machine. Only one method is required, there is no need to use both.

> **Virtual Machine Backups and Retention Policies**
>
> The purpose of this book is to demonstrate how to create a Certificate Authority with AD CS using Hyper-V. This is purely a test environment, and none of the virtual machines that are created are meant to be used in a production environment. Deleting virtual machines on a personal computer that are used for testing is not an issue, but deleting virtual machines on a corporate network can sometimes me more complicated. There could be retention policies for virtual machines that need to be followed, and those would be dictated by IT policies for an organization.

Hyper-V Setup and Configuration - Hyper-V Virtual Machine Deletion - CLI Configuration

There are four major steps that need to be completed to delete a Hyper-V virtual machine and all associated files using PowerShell:

1. Shut down the virtual machine.
2. Determine which virtual hard disks are associated with the virtual machine.
3. Delete the virtual machine configuration files.
4. Delete any virtual hard disks that belonged to the virtual machine.

To delete a virtual machine named **Windows Server 2022** running on a Hyper-V server, run the following commands using an **elevated PowerShell prompt**:

1. Shut down the **Windows Server 2022** virtual machine if it is currently running:

```
Windows PowerShell (Elevated)

Stop-VM -Name "Windows Server 2022" -Force
```

2. List the virtual hard disks that are currently associated with the **Windows Server 2022** virtual machine:

```
Windows PowerShell (Elevated)

Get-VMHardDiskDrive -VMName "Windows Server 2022" | Format-Table Path
```

3. Delete the virtual machine configuration files for the **Windows Server 2022** virtual machine:

```
Windows PowerShell (Elevated)

Remove-VM -Name "Windows Server 2022" -Force
```

4. Delete the virtual hard disks for the **Windows Server 2022** virtual machine (repeat this step for every file if there is more than one virtual hard disk):

```
Windows PowerShell (Elevated)

Remove-Item "D:\Hyper-V\Virtual Hard Disks\Windows Server 2022.vhdx"
```

5. Once the virtual machine files have been deleted, close the **PowerShell prompt**.

Hyper-V does not easily allow for the deletion of all files related to a Hyper-V virtual machine, and it is a manual process regardless of how it is done. This is to ensure that if a virtual machine is deleted by mistake it can be recovered. The virtual machine configuration files can be easily recreated if necessary, but the virtual hard disk files are permanently gone if they are deleted by accident if no backups exist.

Hyper-V Setup and Configuration - Hyper-V Virtual Machine Deletion - GUI Configuration

There are four major steps that need to be completed to delete a Hyper-V virtual machine and all associated files using Hyper-V Manager and Windows File Explorer:

1. Shut down the virtual machine.
2. Determine which virtual hard disks are associated with the virtual machine. Virtual hard drives that are associated with the virtual machine will need to be deleted manually after the virtual machine configuration has been deleted.
3. Delete the virtual machine configuration files.
4. Delete any virtual hard disks that belonged to the virtual machine.

To delete a virtual machine named **Windows Server 2022** running on a Hyper-V server, perform the following steps:

1. Open the **Hyper-V Manager** (virtmgmt.msc) console.
2. Select the **Windows Server 2022** virtual machine in the **Virtual Machines** pane.
3. Right-click on the **Windows Server 2022** virtual machine and select the **Shut Down...** option.
4. When the virtual machine has been shut down, right-click on the **Windows Server 2022** virtual machine and select the **Settings...** option.
5. In the settings window for the **Windows Server 2022** virtual machine, select the **Hard Drive** option under the **IDE Controller** in the **Hardware** pane (for Generation 2 virtual machines, this will appear as **SCSI Controller**). Close the settings window for the **Windows Server 2022** virtual machine.
6. Right-click on the **Windows Server 2022** virtual machine and select the **Delete...** option. In the **Delete Selected Virtual Machines** prompt, click the **Delete** button to continue.
7. Open **Windows File Explorer** (explorer.exe), browse to the folder where the virtual hard disks for the **Windows Server 2022** virtual machine were located and delete them.

Hyper-V does not easily allow for the deletion of all files related to a Hyper-V virtual machine, and it is a manual process regardless of how it is done. This is to ensure that if a virtual machine is deleted by mistake it can be recovered. The virtual machine configuration files can be easily recreated if necessary, but the virtual hard disk files are permanently gone if they are deleted by accident if no backups exist.

Hyper-V Setup and Configuration - Chapter Summary

This chapter reviewed many aspects of Hyper-V and how it can be used for virtualizing the test environment for the Certificate Authority. Other aspects related to Hyper-V were also covered in this chapter:

- Reviewed the available versions of Hyper-V and what platforms are supported for those versions.
- Reviewed the process for installing the Hyper-V role.
- Reviewed the process for configuring the Hyper-V role.
- Reviewed the process for creating a virtual machine.
- Reviewed the process for creating and managing virtual floppy disks.
- Reviewed the process for deleting a virtual machine.

In the next chapter the process for creating an Active Directory Domain Controller and a Windows 11 workstation will be reviewed. This is a prerequisite for completing the installation of Active Directory Certificates Services (AD CS) and creating the TFS Labs Certificate Authority.

Chapter 5 - Domain and Workstation Setup

The TFS Labs domain that is used in this book is configured using a single Domain Controller in the **corp.tfslabs.com** domain. This Active Directory domain is used for critical functions in the TFS Labs test environment and is necessary for a proper Active Directory Certificates Services (AD CS) deployment to be completed. The TFS-DC01 server will be used as the Domain Controller for this domain, and this chapter will focus on how to set it up for that purpose.

While acting as the Domain Controller for the TFS Labs domain, the TFS-DC01 server will also be responsible for hosting the DNS services and DNS Zone for the TFS Labs domain. It will also be used for managing Group Policy, which will be used for deploying certificates to workstations and servers that are joined to the domain. To create an Active Directory domain, the Active Directory Domain Services (AD DS) role that is available in Windows Server needs to be installed and configured.

Once the AD DS role has been successfully installed and configured on the TFS-DC01 server, the following features will become available for managing Active Directory:

- Active Directory Sites and Services
- Active Directory Users and Computers
- DNS Management
- Group Policy Management
- Windows PowerShell Cmdlets (for command line administration)

These features are all required to properly support Active Directory, as well as configuring a Certificate Authority using AD CS. These features are available as separate applications that are automatically installed on the server and can be managed through the Microsoft Management Console (MMC), or through the command line.

Aside from creating an Active Directory domain and a Domain Controller for the TFS Labs domain, there are several other tasks that are completed in this chapter:

- Create an Organizational Unit (OU) structure for managing Active Directory objects.
- Create test user accounts in Active Directory for testing certificate deployment.
- Create a Windows 11 workstation that will be used for testing certificate deployment.
- **Optional:** Create a Checkpoint for the virtual machines which can be used for testing purposes.

Once the steps in this chapter have been completed, the infrastructure that is needed to support Active Directory Certificate Services will be in place.

> **TFS Labs Domain Controller**
>
> Regardless of what type of Certificate Authority is created using the steps in this book, the Domain Controller configuration is common and necessary for AD CS unless specified otherwise. The steps in this chapter do not change or differ regardless of the type of Certificate Authority that is being created.

> **Active Directory Certificate Services and Active Directory Domain Services Changes**
>
> Since changes are made to Active Directory when an Enterprise CA is added to the configuration, it is not recommended to reuse a Domain Controller when testing the steps in this book more than once. This could cause deployment issues that are difficult to troubleshoot, and requires the old AD CS configurations to be fully removed.

Domain and Workstation Setup - Prerequisites

At the end of this chapter there will be a functional Active Directory domain that will be used to setup and configure Active Directory Certificate Services for the TFS Labs domain. There are no special configurations required for Active Directory, and aside from creating an Organizational Unit (OU) structure and several test user accounts. Nothing else needs to be done to the Domain Controller to properly support Active Directory Certificate Services. There are no customizations required for Active Directory to support Active Directory Certificate Services, it is natively supported without any additional configuration or any third-party software.

Prior to beginning the steps in this chapter, there are several passwords that are needed to complete the configuration for Active Directory. These passwords are required to complete the setup, and should be recorded at each step that requires a password.

The passwords that need to be created and recorded from this chapter include:

- The local administrator account password for the TFS-DC01 server. This password will eventually become the Domain Administrator password for the TFS Labs domain once the TFS-DC01 server is promoted to a Domain Controller, and will be used on other servers to complete the AD CS implementation.
- The Directory Services Restore Mode (DSRM) password for the TFS-DC01 server. This password is required should there ever be an issue logging into the TFS-DC01 server, but that is unlikely to occur in this test environment.
- The local administrator account password for TFS-WIN11 workstation. This password will only be used for the implementation in this chapter and will not be used again. Once the workstation is joined to the domain, the password is no longer required.
- The passwords for the Active Directory test user accounts.

Since this is a test environment, and security is not an issue, it is safe to use the same password for all accounts. In a production environment, this is extremely bad practice to reuse passwords and should be avoided.

Testing an Existing Active Directory Domain

It is recommended to go through the steps in this book at least once using the TFS Labs domain for testing purposes. This will demonstrate what a proper Active Directory Certificate Services configuration and deployment will look like from start to finish.

Once the deployment of AD CS has been successfully tested, it is recommended to test this deployment on a Domain Controller that is part of an existing domain, but in a controlled and non-damaging manner. With virtualization it is a trivial process to safely test a deployment of Active Directory Certificate Services without damaging a production environment.

There are several methods to safely test an existing Active Directory domain with AD CS, and they all take advantage of virtualization:

- Clone an existing Domain Controller to a new virtual machine.
- Provision a new Domain Controller from an existing Active Directory domain in a virtual machine, and allow all Active Directory data to synchronize with it.

When the virtual Domain Controller has been created, it can be isolated in a virtual network that has no access to the other servers or workstations on the network. By isolating the virtual machine in this manner, it is possible to safely test the deployment of Active Directory Certificate Services without causing any potential problems.

Once a Domain Controller has been created as a virtual machine, and is properly isolated in a virtual network, then any testing of the deployment of Active Directory Certificate Services can be safely performed. This process is explained in further detail in a later chapter in this book, and should be completed to ensure there are no issues.

Domain and Workstation Setup - Domain Controller Setup

In this chapter, a virtual machine named TFS-DC01 will be created using Hyper-V, and will use Windows Server 2022 Standard (Desktop Experience) as the operating system. This virtual machine will become the Domain Controller for the TFS Labs domain. There are several steps that need to be completed to create the virtual machine that will be used for the Domain Controller for the **corp.tfslabs.com** domain:

- Provision a virtual machine for the TFS-DC01 server using Hyper-V and ensure it is connected to a virtual switch that is able to connect to other virtual machines.
- Install Windows Server 2022 Standard (Desktop Experience) on the virtual machine.
- Configure the local administrator password and hostname of the TFS-DC01 server.
- Configure the network settings of the TFS-DC01 server.
- **Optional:** Update the TFS-DC01 server using Windows Update.

The TFS-DC01 virtual machine will have the following specifications:

Virtual Machine Generation	2
Virtual Processors	2
Virtual Memory	4 GB (4096 MB)
Virtual Hard Disk	40 GB
Virtual Network Adapters	1

Table 5.2.1: Virtual machine specifications for the TFS-DC01 server.

The TFS-DC01 virtual machine will be configured with the following network settings:

IP Address	10.100.1.100
Netmask	255.255.255.0
Gateway	10.100.1.1
DNS Server 1	1.1.1.1

Table 5.2.2: Network configuration and DNS settings for the TFS-DC01 server.

The network settings for the TFS-DC01 server are important, as all other servers and workstations in the TFS Labs domain will all need to be configured in a similar manner so that Active Directory can function correctly. This is essential for joining the other virtual machines to the TFS Labs domain, with the exception of the Offline Root CA server (TFS-ROOT-CA) which will never be connected to the network.

> **Domain Controller Virtual Machine and Networking Configuration**
>
> The virtual machine as configured in this section uses specific settings for the path locations for the virtual hard disk and the location of an installation ISO image for Windows Server 2022. The virtual machine specifications are also configured in such a manner to allow the virtual machine to have sufficient performance to complete the tasks within this book. The network settings that are used for the virtual machine is also specific to the test environment for creating the Certificate Authority.
>
> The network that is used for the TFS-DC01 server will also be used for the other virtual machines later in the book. The external DNS server being used is a publicly accessible service managed by Cloudflare.
>
> Modify these settings as required for a particular test environment. Ensure that if these settings are modified, that the settings are also modified in later steps in this book.

Domain and Workstation Setup - Domain Controller Setup - Virtual Machine Setup

To create a Hyper-V virtual machine for the TFS-DC01 server using the command line, open an **elevated PowerShell prompt** and run the following commands on the Hyper-V host:

1. Create the **TFS-DC01** virtual machine and virtual hard disk using the **New-VM** Cmdlet:

```
Windows PowerShell (Elevated)

New-VM `
-Name "TFS-DC01" `
-Generation 2 `
-MemoryStartupBytes 4GB `
-BootDevice VHD `
-NewVHDPath "D:\Hyper-V\Virtual Hard Disks\TFS-DC01.vhdx" `
-NewVHDSizeBytes 40GB `
-Switch "Hyper-V External Switch"
```

2. Set the number of virtual processors for the **TFS-DC01** virtual machine to **2** using the **Set-VMProcessor** Cmdlet:

```
Windows PowerShell (Elevated)

Set-VMProcessor "TFS-DC01" -Count 2
```

3. Add a virtual DVD drive to the **TFS-DC01** virtual machine, and mount the installation ISO image that will be used to install the operating system with the **Add-VMDvdDrive** Cmdlet:

```
Windows PowerShell (Elevated)

Add-VMDvdDrive `
-VMName "TFS-DC01" `
-Path "D:\ISO Images\Windows Server 2022.iso"
```

4. Set the virtual DVD drive as the first startup device for the **TFS-DC01** virtual machine using the **Set-Firmware** Cmdlet:

```
Windows PowerShell (Elevated)

Set-VMFirmware `
-VMName "TFS-DC01" `
-FirstBootDevice $(Get-VMDvdDrive -VMName "TFS-DC01")
```

5. Power on the **TFS-DC01** virtual machine using the **Start-VM** Cmdlet:

```
Windows PowerShell (Elevated)

Start-VM -Name "TFS-DC01"
```

6. Connect to the **TFS-DC01** virtual machine using the **Virtual Machine Connection** tool:

```
Windows PowerShell (Elevated)

vmconnect.exe localhost "TFS-DC01"
```

Alternatively, the TFS-DC01 virtual server can be created and configured without PowerShell by using Hyper-V Manager instead. Only one method is required to create the virtual machine. Regardless of which method is used to create the virtual machine, Windows Server 2022 can be installed normally with all default options. In this book, **Windows Server 2022 Standard (Desktop Experience)** is the version that all servers will use. When the operating system has been successfully installed, there are a few steps left to complete.

When the installation of Windows Server 2022 has successfully completed, the first step is to configure the local administrator password for the TFS-DC01 server. This step occurs automatically before the server can be logged into, and is the first screen that is displayed after the successful installation of Windows Server 2022:

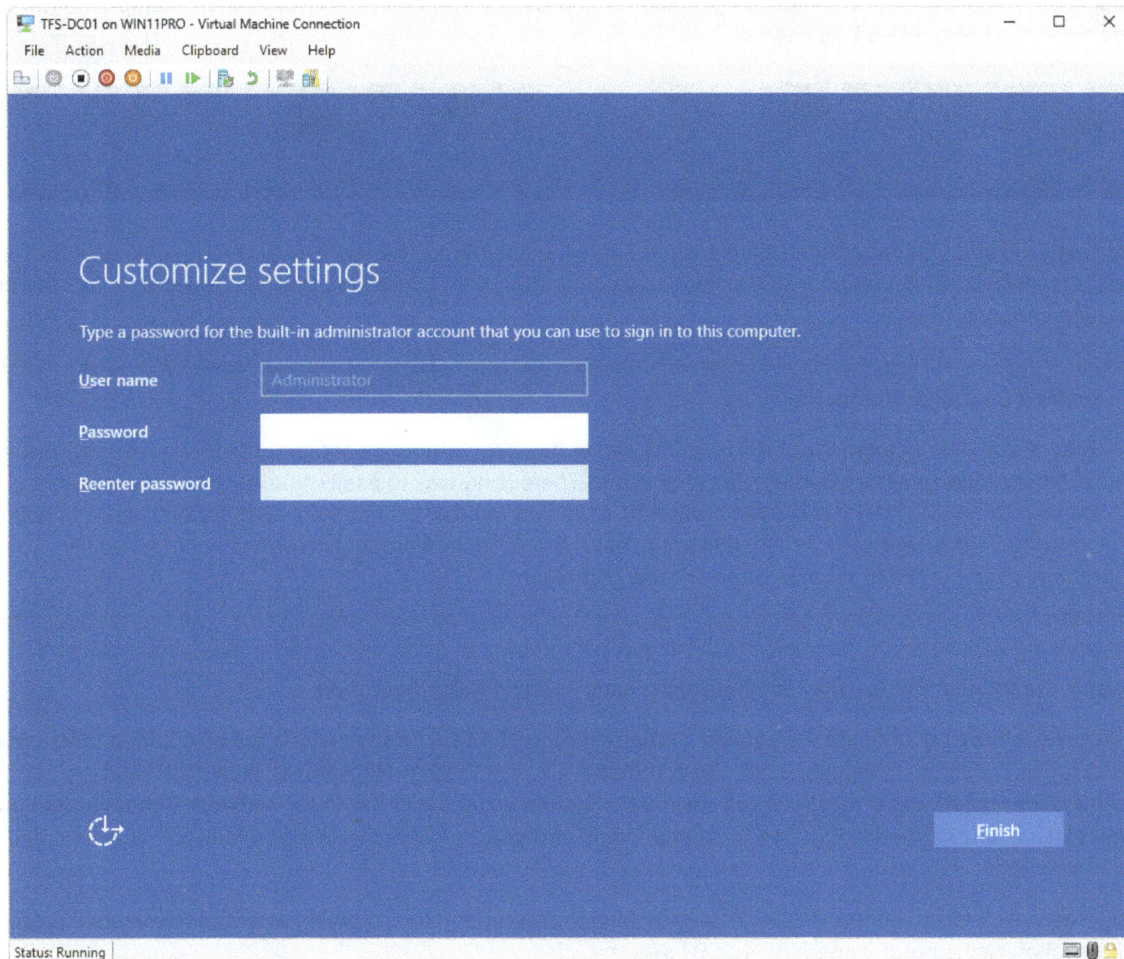

Figure 5.2.1.1: Setting the local administrator account password is the first step that needs to be completed on a new installation of Windows Server 2022. Immediately after setting the local administrator password, the login screen for the server will appear and the server can be further configured.

With automated deployments of Windows Server 2022 and Windows 11, the option to configure the local administrator password is usually not shown to the user and can be configured automatically in advance.

> **TFS Labs Domain Administrator Account Password**
>
> The local administrator account that is used during the initial setup of the TFS-DC01 server will become the Domain Administrator account for the TFS Labs domain once the server has been promoted to a Domain Controller.
>
> Once the Active Directory installation has been completed, the local administrator account that is on the TFS-DC01 server will become the **TFSLABS\Administrator** account, which is the Domain Administrator account for the TFS Labs domain.
>
> The Domain Administrator account will be used for the remainder of the Certificate Authority implementation, except on the Offline Root CA server which uses a local administrator account.

When the local administrator account password has been set, login to the server using the new password. Renaming a Windows server can be performed using the command line with the **Rename-Computer** Cmdlet. Alternatively, the hostname can be configured using the Server Manager console in the Local Server configuration section.

To configure the hostname of the server using the command line, open an **elevated PowerShell prompt** and run the following command on the TFS-DC01 server:

```
Windows PowerShell (Elevated)

Rename-Computer "TFS-DC01" -Restart
```

The command will automatically restart the server to apply the hostname change. The only remaining task that is required for the TFS-DC01 server prior to installing and configuring Active Directory Domain Services is the network configuration changes.

> **Domain Controller Hostname**
>
> Ensure that the hostname for the TFS-DC01 server has been properly configured before going any further with the Active Directory Domain Services setup. There is no way to easily change the hostname on a Domain Controller after it has been promoted, so it best to have the hostname set correctly prior to being promoted. For a test environment it is not a major issue, but in a production environment it usually requires moving FSMO roles to other domain controllers.

Domain and Workstation Setup - Domain Controller Setup - Network Configuration

There are several ways to configure the network settings for the TFS-DC01 server which will be configured to use a static IP address. It can be configured using the command line with the **Get-NetAdapter**, **New-NetIPAddress**, and **Set-DnsClientServerAddress** Cmdlets. It can also be configured using the GUI with the **Network Connections** Control Panel applet. Only one method is required to change the IP address and DNS server addresses on the server, there is no need to use both.

To configure the IP address on the TFS-DC01 server using the command line, open an **elevated PowerShell prompt** and run the following command on the TFS-DC01 server:

```
Windows PowerShell (Elevated)

New-NetIPAddress `
-AddressFamily IPv4 `
-IPAddress 10.100.1.100 `
-PrefixLength 24 `
-DefaultGateway 10.100.1.1 `
-InterfaceIndex (Get-NetAdapter).InterfaceIndex
```

To configure the DNS server addresses on the TFS-DC01 server using the command line, open an **elevated PowerShell prompt** and run the following command:

```
Windows PowerShell (Elevated)

Set-DnsClientServerAddress `
-ServerAddresses ("1.1.1.1") `
-InterfaceIndex (Get-NetAdapter).InterfaceIndex
```

Alternatively, the IP address and DNS server addresses for the server can be configured without using the command line by using the **Network Connections** Control Panel applet. To configure the IP address and the DNS server addresses for the TFS-DC01 server, perform the following steps:

1. Open the **Network Connections** Control Panel applet (ncpa.cpl).
2. In the **Network Connections** window, right-click on the **Ethernet** network adapter and select the **Properties** option.
3. In the **Ethernet Properties** window, scroll to the **Internet Protocol Version 4 (TCP/IPv4)** connection and select it. Click the **Properties** button.
4. In the **Internet Protocol Version 4 (TCP/IPv4) Properties** window, make the following changes to configure the IP address:
   - Select the option for **Use the following IP address**
   - Set the **IP address** to **10.100.1.100**
   - Set the **Subnet mask** to **255.255.255.0**
   - Set the **Default Gateway** to **10.100.1.1**
5. In the **Internet Protocol Version 4 (TCP/IPv4) Properties** window, make the following changes to configure the DNS server addresses:
   - Select the option for **Use the following DNS server addresses**.
   - Set the **Preferred DNS server** to the **1.1.1.1** address.
   - Leave the **Alternate DNS server** blank.
6. Click the **OK** button to apply the IP and DNS address changes.
7. Click the **OK** button to close the **Ethernet Properties** window.

Changes to the IP and DNS server addresses are applied immediately, and there is no need to restart the server.

> ⚠️ **Active Directory External DNS Servers**
>
> Once the TFS-DC01 server has been successfully promoted to a Domain Controller, the DNS settings for that server should be automatically updated to utilize any servers that may have been added prior the installation. The TFS-DC01 server will become the primary DNS server for the domain, and any servers or workstations will need to use the Domain Controller IP address for DNS resolution.
>
> The TFS-DC01 server IP address will be added as the first DNS server in the network settings, and the original DNS entries should be automatically updated once it is promoted to a Domain Controller.
>
> If there are any DNS resolution issues after the Domain Controller promotion, validate that the DNS settings are correct on the TFS-DC01 server to ensure that there are forwarding DNS servers configured to access external resources.

Once the local administrator password, hostname, and network has been setup correctly on the server, proceed to installing any Windows Updates on the TFS-DC01 server.

Domain and Workstation Setup - Domain Controller Setup - Windows Update

While it is not necessary to run Windows Update on any of the servers in this book as they are for testing purposes, now would be the best time to run those updates if it is required. Windows Update can be accessed through the Settings app, or through the command line by opening an **elevated PowerShell prompt** and running the following command:

```
Windows PowerShell (Elevated)

Start-Process ms-settings:windowsupdate
```

Installing all available updates will take time to complete and will require several restarts of the server. Once completed, proceed to setting up the TFS-DC01 server as a Domain Controller by installing the Active Directory Domain Services role.

Domain and Workstation Setup - AD DS Role Installation

The Active Directory Domain Services (AD DS) role needs to be installed on the TFS-DC01 server prior to configuring it as a Domain Controller for the TFS Labs domain. This role is not installed on Windows Server by default, so the AD DS role will need to be manually installed prior to configuring and promoting a server to a Domain Controller.

The Active Directory Domain Services role can be installed either through the command line with PowerShell or by using the Server Manager console. The installation using PowerShell is much faster than using Server Manager, and is the preferred method for installing roles in Windows Server. Only one method for installing the Active Directory Domain Services role is required, and both methods have the exact same outcome.

A restart of the TFS-DC01 server is not required to add the AD DS role, but a restart will be required after the configuration of the AD DS role later in this chapter.

Domain and Workstation Setup - AD DS Role Installation - CLI Installation

The installation for Active Directory Domain Services will utilize the **Install-WindowsFeature** Cmdlet, which is used to add features to Windows Server from the command line. Aside from just adding the Active Directory Domain Services role, the necessary administration features will also need to be added at the same time.

Perform the following steps on the TFS-DC01 server using PowerShell to add the Active Directory Domain Services role:

1. Open an **elevated PowerShell prompt**.
2. Run the following command to install the **Active Directory Domain Services** role and the necessary **Remote Server Administration Tools** required for managing Active Directory:

```
Windows PowerShell (Elevated)

Install-WindowsFeature AD-Domain-Services, RSAT-ADDS
```

3. The command will automatically install the **Active Directory Domain Services** role and output a **Success** status of **True**:

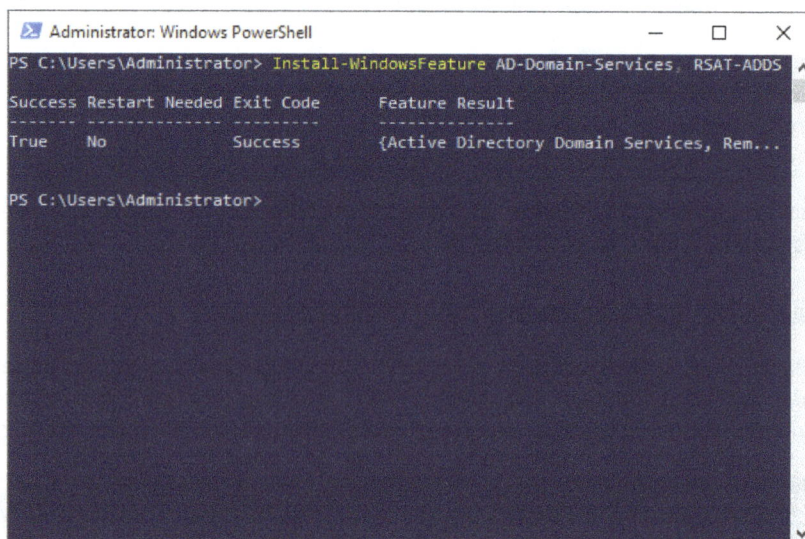

4. Once the installation for **Active Directory Domain Services** has completed, close the **PowerShell prompt**.

Once the Active Directory Domain Services role has been successfully installed on the TFS-DC01 server, proceed to the validation step for the Active Directory Domain Services installation.

Domain and Workstation Setup - AD DS Role Installation - GUI Installation

To perform the Active Directory Domain Services installation using the Server Manager console, perform the following steps on the TFS-DC01 server:

1. Open the **Server Manager** console (servermanager.exe), click on the **Manage** menu, and then click on **Add Roles and Features** to start the installation wizard:

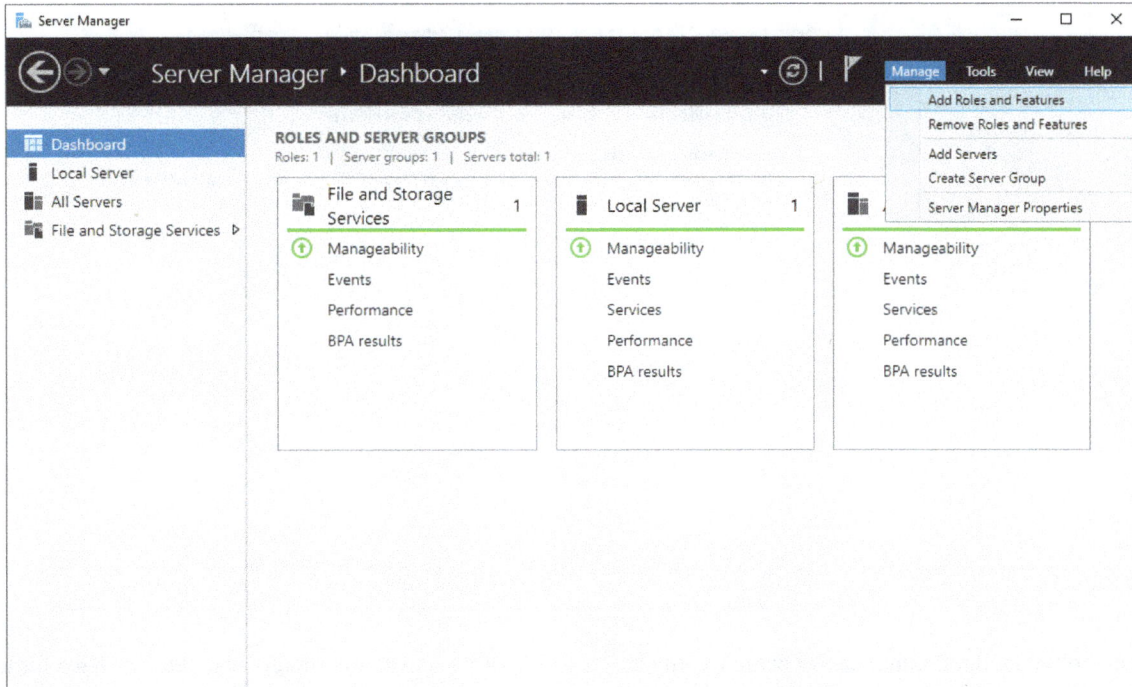

2. On the **Before you begin** screen, click the **Next** button to continue:

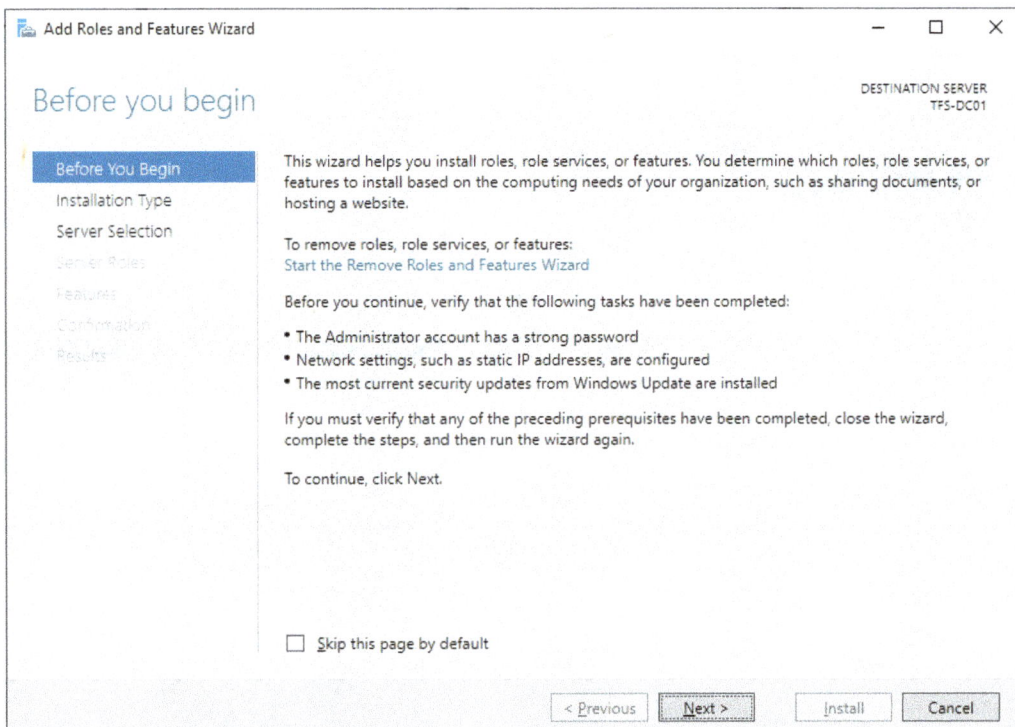

3. On the **Select installation type** screen, select the option for **Role-based or feature-based installation** and click the **Next** button to continue:

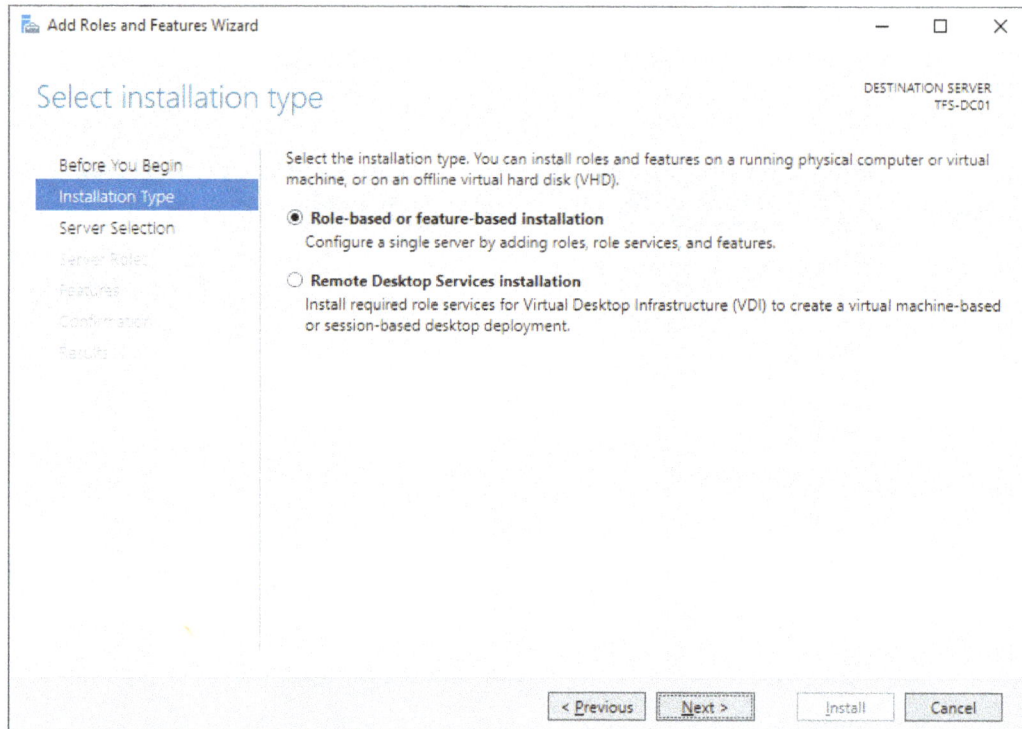

4. On the **Select destination server** screen, verify that the **TFS-DC01** server is selected, and click the **Next** button to continue:

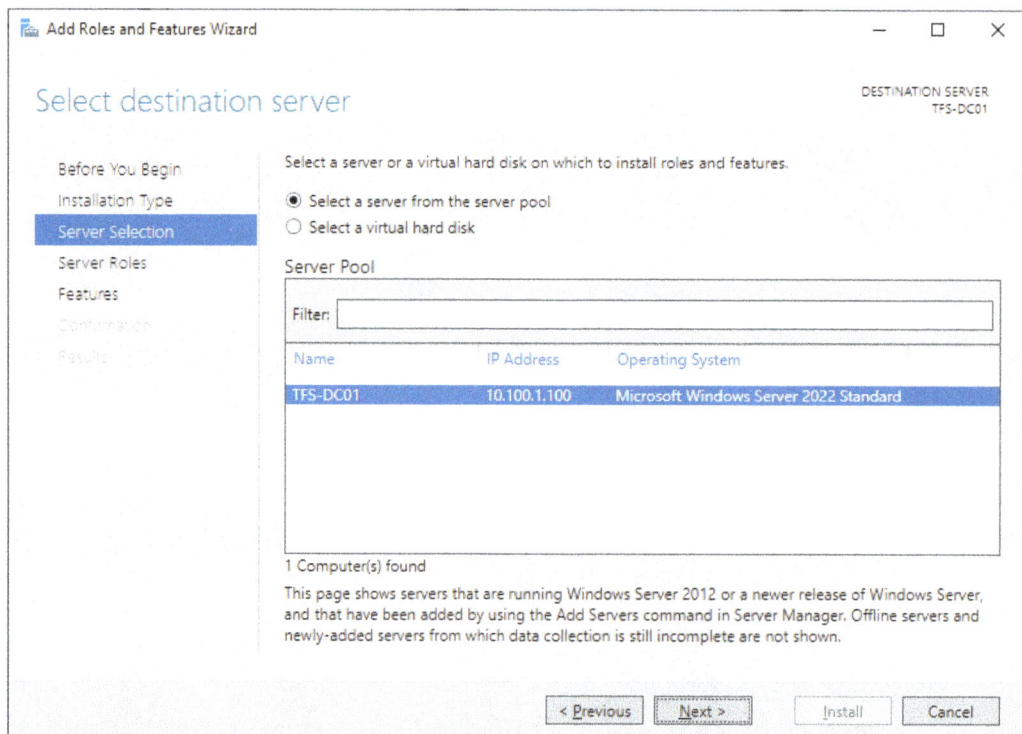

5. On the **Select server roles** screen, select the **Active Directory Domain Services** option:

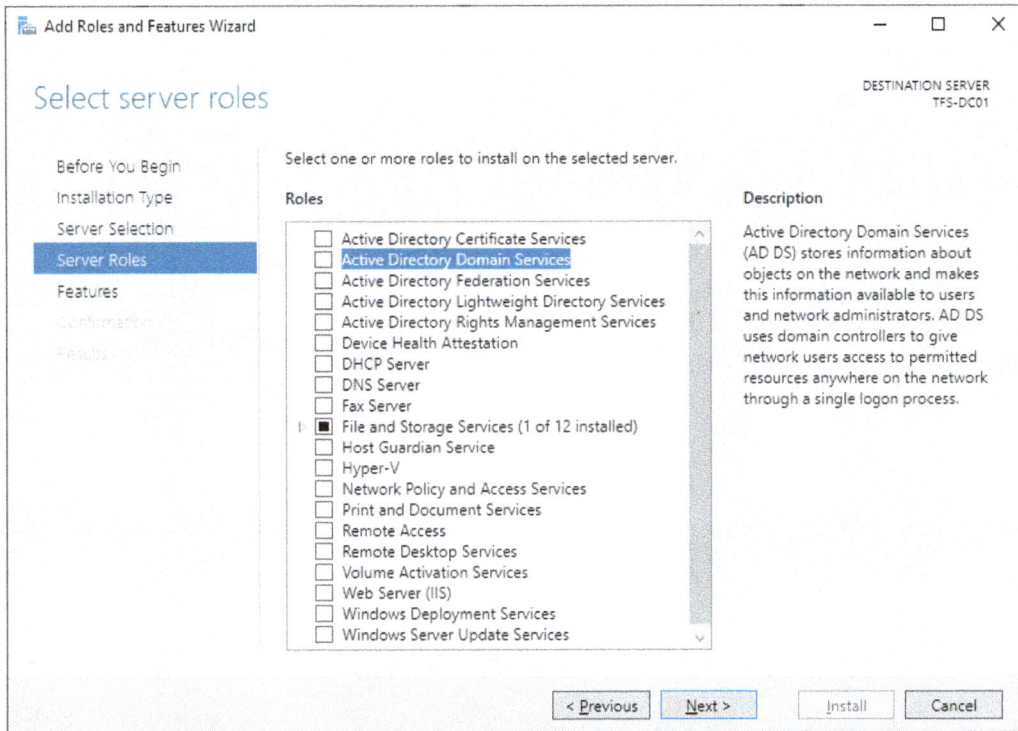

6. The installation wizard will ask to install any additional features that are required for the **Active Directory Domain Services** role. Select the option to **Include management tools (if applicable)** to install the necessary management tools for the role. Click the **Add Features** button to continue.
7. On the **Select server roles** screen, click the **Next** button to continue:

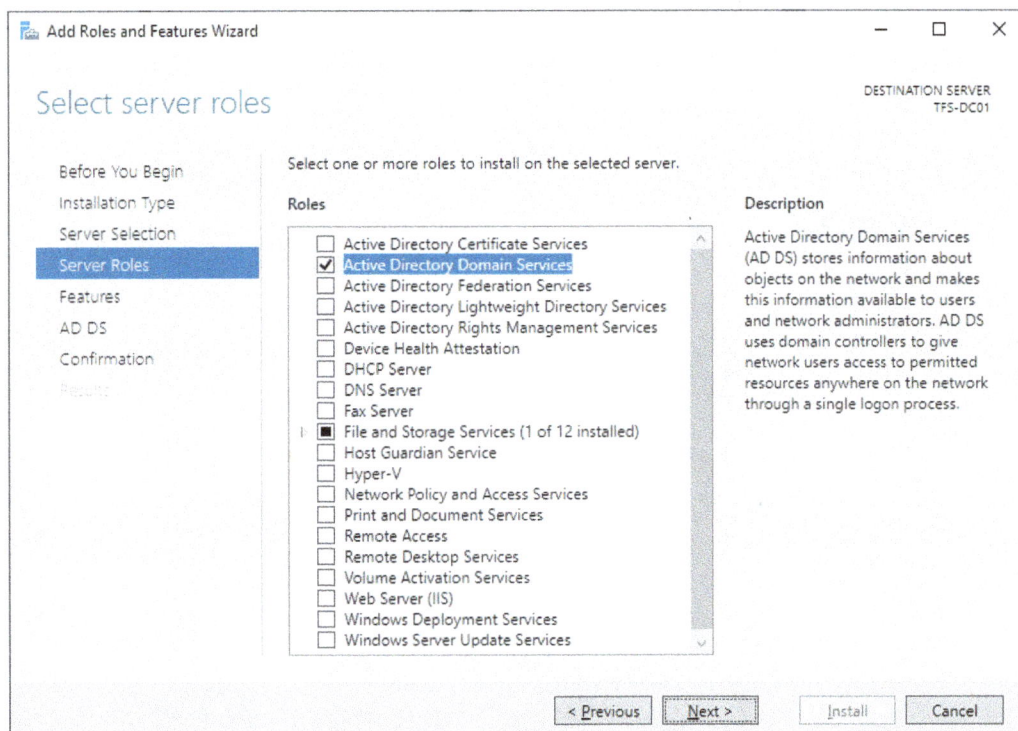

8. On the **Select features** screen, click the **Next** button to continue:

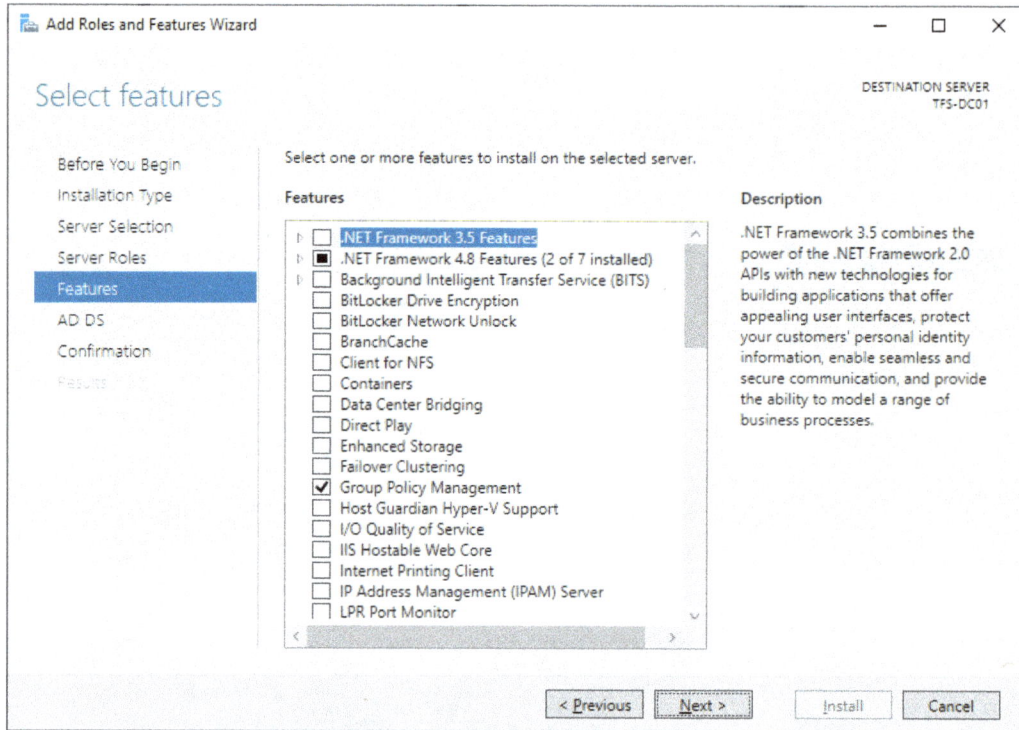

9. On the **Active Directory Domain Services** screen, click the **Next** button to continue:

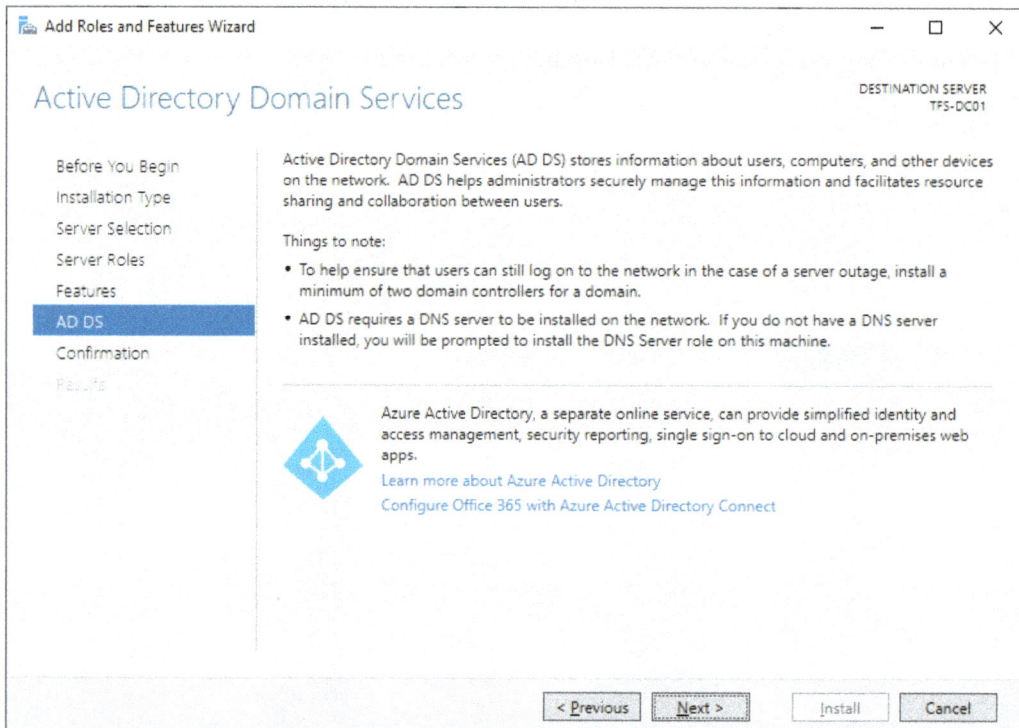

10. On the **Confirm installation selections** screen, click the **Install** button to continue:

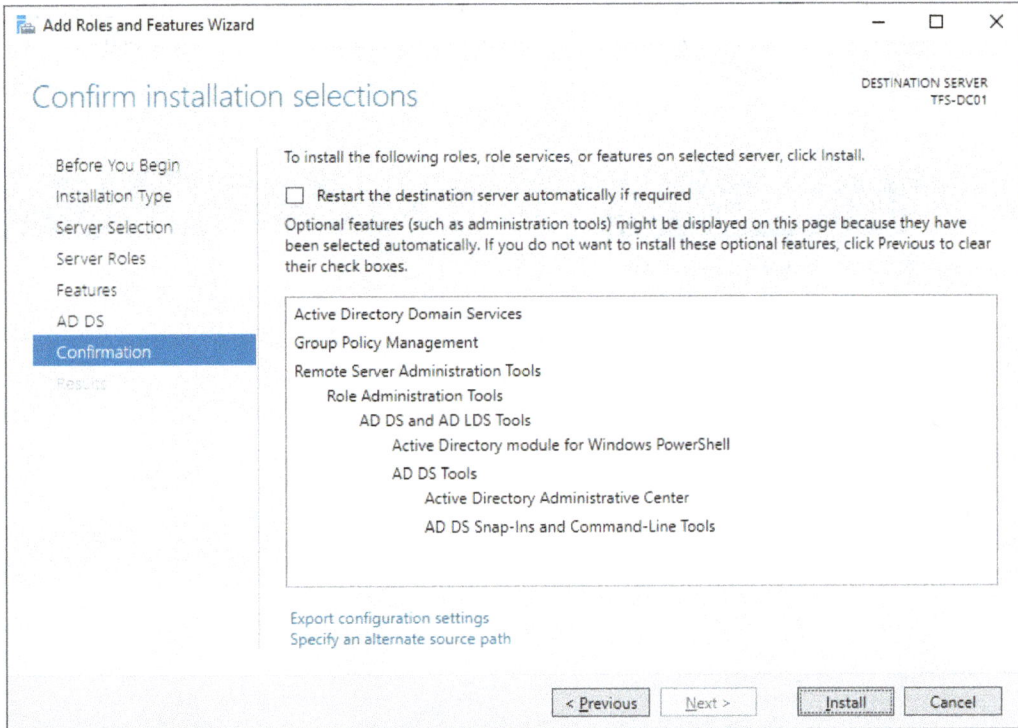

11. Once the installation is completed, click the **Close** button:

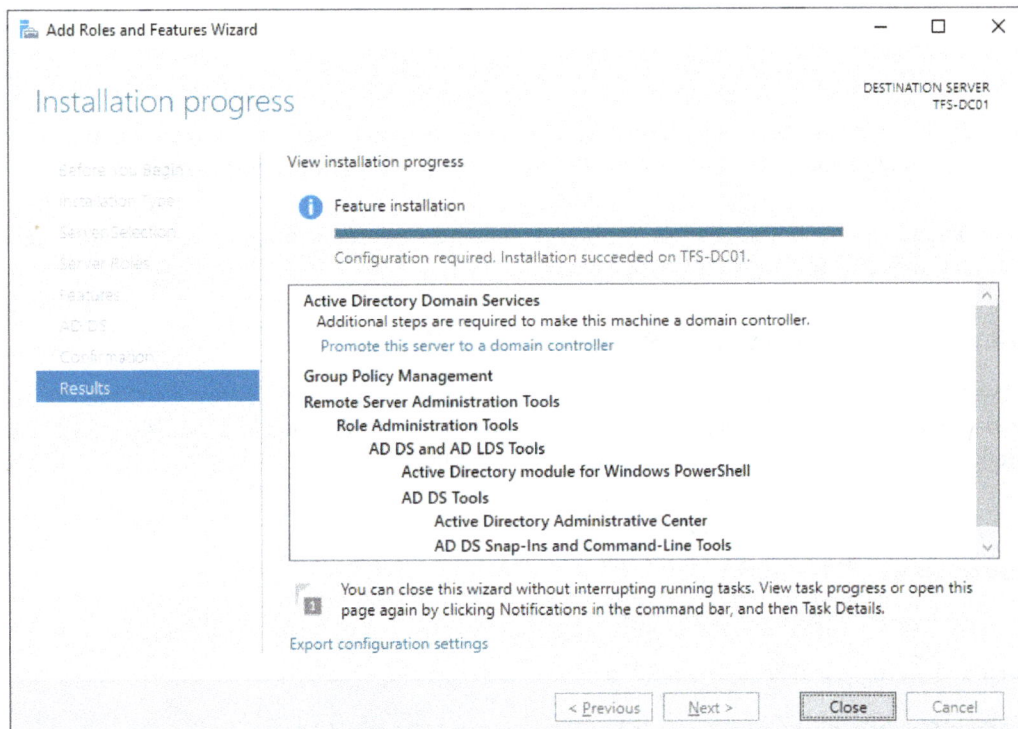

Once the Active Directory Domain Services role has been successfully installed on the TFS-DC01 server, proceed to the validation step for the Active Directory Domain Services installation.

Domain and Workstation Setup - AD DS Role Installation - Validation

Once the Active Directory Domain Services role has been installed on the TFS-DC01 server, the option to promote the server to a Domain Controller will become available. The option to promote the server to a Domain Controller can be seen in the Server Manager notifications:

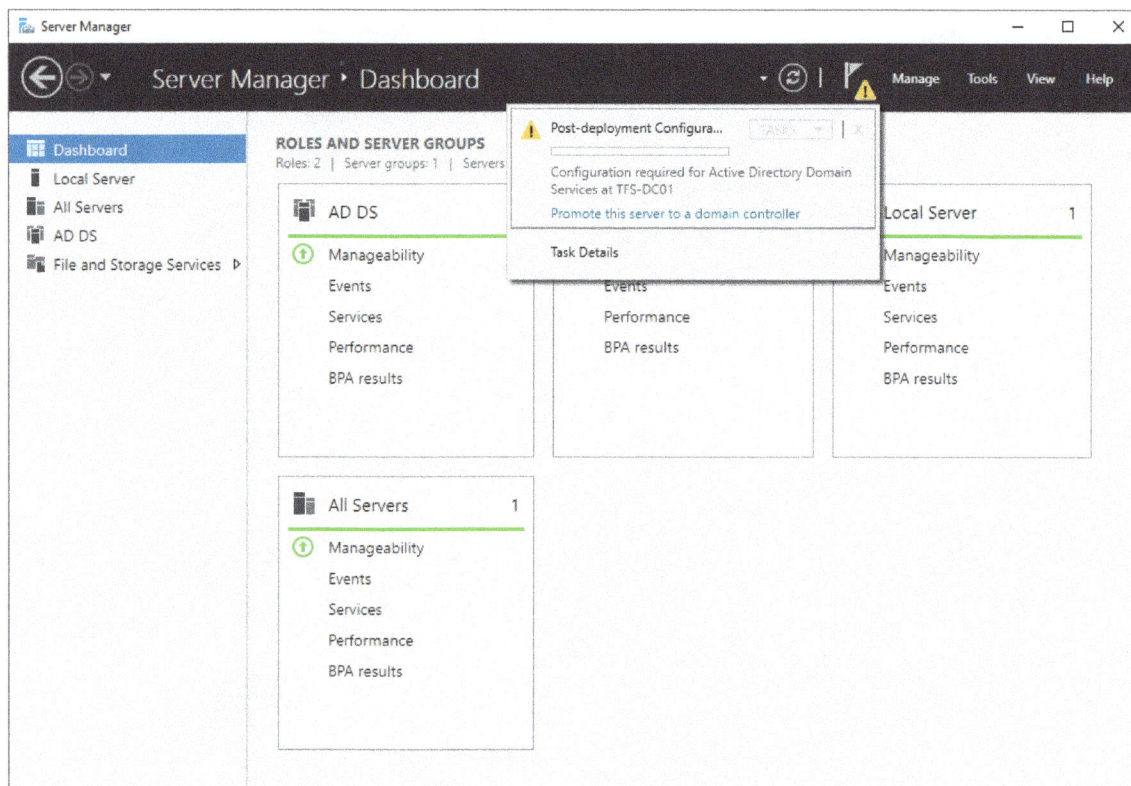

Figure 5.3.3.1: When the Active Directory Domain Services role has been installed, the Server Manager console will prompt the user to configure the server as a Domain Controller in a new or an existing domain.

Once the Active Directory Domain Services role has been installed successfully, proceed to configuring the TFS-DC01 server as a Domain Controller for the TFS Labs domain.

Domain and Workstation Setup - AD DS Role Configuration

When the Active Directory Domain Services role has been installed on the TFS-DC01 server it will need to be properly configured to become a Domain Controller for the TFS Labs domain. In the process of configuring the TFS Labs domain, the following Active Directory domain settings will be configured:

Forest Name	corp.tfslabs.com
NetBIOS Domain Name	TFSLABS
Forest Functional Level	Windows Server 2016
Domain Functional Level	Windows Server 2016

Table 5.4.1: Active Directory domain configuration options for the TFS Labs domain.

The Active Directory Domain Services role can be configured through the command line with PowerShell, or by using the Server Manager console. Only one method is needed for configuring the Active Directory Domain Services role.

Active Directory Domain Configuration

The Active Directory domain that is used in this book is just for demonstration purposes, and is not meant to be used in a production environment. This domain is setup using the latest version of Windows Server, and the latest Forest and Domain Functional Levels. There are also no legacy issues with the domain as it is a new deployment, and there are no third-party extensions or applications being used.

Modify the Active Directory configuration to match an environment to ensure that the installation of Active Directory Certificate Services is compatible with a particular domain. This includes changing the domain name, as well as the Forest and Domain Functional Levels if required.

Active Directory Forest and Domain Functional Levels

The Forest and Domain Functional Levels for the TFS Labs domain is set to Windows Server 2016. When using the **Install-ADDSForest** Cmdlet there are two parameters that are used to set the Forest and Domain Modes, **DomainMode** and **ForestMode**.

Depending on which Forest and Domain Functional Levels is required for an Active Directory domain, there are a few different options that can be used at the time of configuration:

- **Win2003** - Windows Server 2003
- **Win2008** - Windows Server 2008
- **Win2008R2** - Windows Server 2008 R2
- **Win2012** - Windows Server 2012
- **Win2012R2** - Windows Server 2012 R2
- **WinThreshold** - Windows Server 2016

The Forest and Domain Functional Levels prior to Windows Server 2008 R2 are obsolete and would likely never be used in a new deployment of Active Directory. The only exception would be if there was a specific feature in earlier versions that is no longer available or for backwards compatibility.

There is no specific Forest or Domain Functional Level for Windows Server 2022, and the **WinThreshold** option represents the latest version that has been available since Windows Server 2016. With Active Directory, the Forest and Domain Functional Levels can always be upgraded, or "raised" at any point after installation. There is no option to downgrade a domain to an earlier version, and an upgrade cannot be easily reversed.

Upgrading the Forest and Domain Functional Levels is not a trivial task, and requires extensive testing and research before it is applied to a production domain.

The default option for the **Install-ADDSForest** Cmdlet in Windows Server 2022 is to set the Forest and Domain to the **Windows Server 2016** Functional Level.

Directory Services Restore Mode (DSRM) Password

It is essential that the Directory Services Restore Mode password (DSRM) is set and documented if there is a major issue with Active Directory. In the event that a restore needs to be performed for Active Directory, this password must be used to regain access to a Domain Controller within the domain. Once the DSRM password has been set, it should be documented in a secure location if it is needed.

For an existing Active Directory domain, there are methods to reset the DSRM password without causing any production issues or downtime if the password is unknown or has been lost. This task is beyond the scope of this book, but is thoroughly documented on Microsoft's website should it be required to recover the password.

Domain and Workstation Setup - AD DS Role Configuration - CLI Configuration

The Active Directory Domain Services configuration can be performed in much fewer steps using PowerShell. The following commands will setup the TFS Labs domain in the exact same way as using the Server Manager console to configure the domain. The configuration will utilize the **Install-ADDSForest** Cmdlet, which can configure the Active Directory Domain Services role from the command line. Perform the following steps on the TFS-DC01 server using PowerShell to configure the Active Directory Domain Services role:

1. Open an **elevated PowerShell prompt**.
2. Run the following command to import the **ADDSDeployment** PowerShell module which is needed to configure **Active Directory Domain Services**:

Windows PowerShell (Elevated)

```
Import-Module ADDSDeployment
```

---

3. Run the following command to configure **Active Directory Domain Services** using the following configuration settings for **Active Directory**:

Windows PowerShell (Elevated)

```
Install-ADDSForest `
-CreateDnsDelegation:$false `
-DatabasePath "C:\Windows\NTDS" `
-DomainMode "WinThreshold" `
-DomainName "corp.tfslabs.com" `
-DomainNetbiosName "TFSLABS" `
-ForestMode "WinThreshold" `
-InstallDns:$true `
-LogPath "C:\Windows\NTDS" `
-NoRebootOnCompletion:$false `
-SysvolPath "C:\Windows\SYSVOL" `
-Force:$true
```

---

4. The command will prompt to set the **SafeModeAdministratorPassword**, which is the **Directory Services Restore Mode (DSRM)** password as specified in the GUI installation. Enter a complex password for this, and the command will prompt for confirmation of the password before proceeding (ensure that this password is recorded in case it is needed in the future):

5. The **Active Directory Domain Services** configuration will take several minutes to complete:

6. The **TFS-DC01** server will automatically restart when the configuration has completed.

Once the Active Directory Domain Services configuration is complete, there will be a functioning Domain Controller for the TFS Labs domain.

Domain and Workstation Setup - AD DS Role Configuration - GUI Configuration

To perform the Active Directory Domain Services configuration using the Server Manager console, perform the following steps on the TFS-DC01 server:

1. To begin the configuration of **Active Directory Domain Services**, open the **Server Manager** console (servermanager.exe). Click the **Notifications** icon in the upper-right hand corner and click the **Promote this server to a domain controller** link in the **Post-deployment Configuration box**:

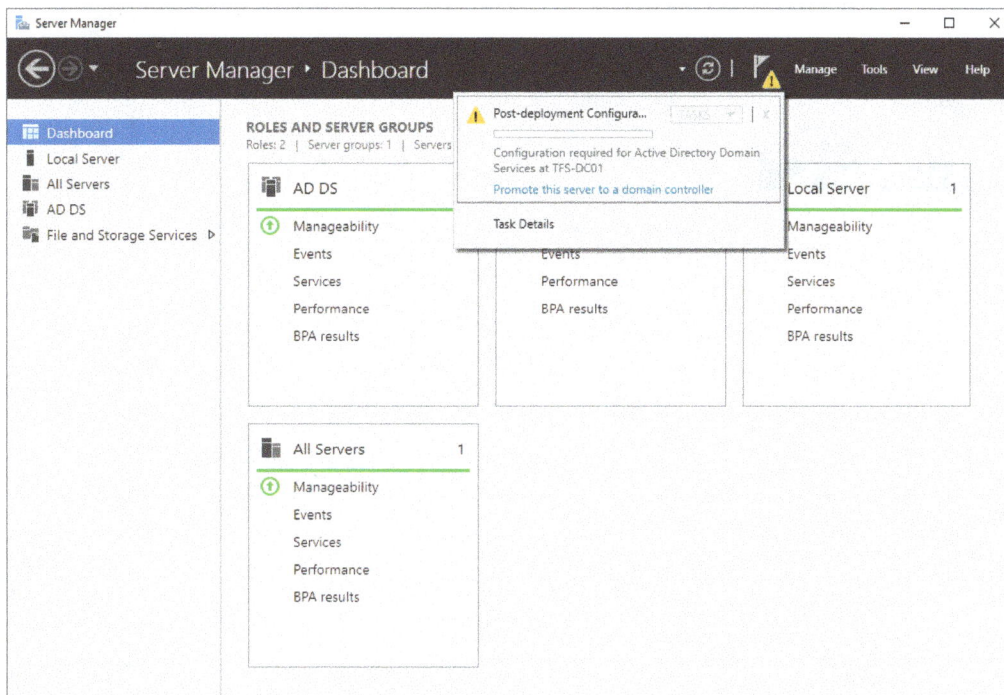

2. On the **Deployment Configuration** screen, select the option for **Add a new forest**. For the **Root domain name**, enter **corp.tfslabs.com** and click **Next** to continue:

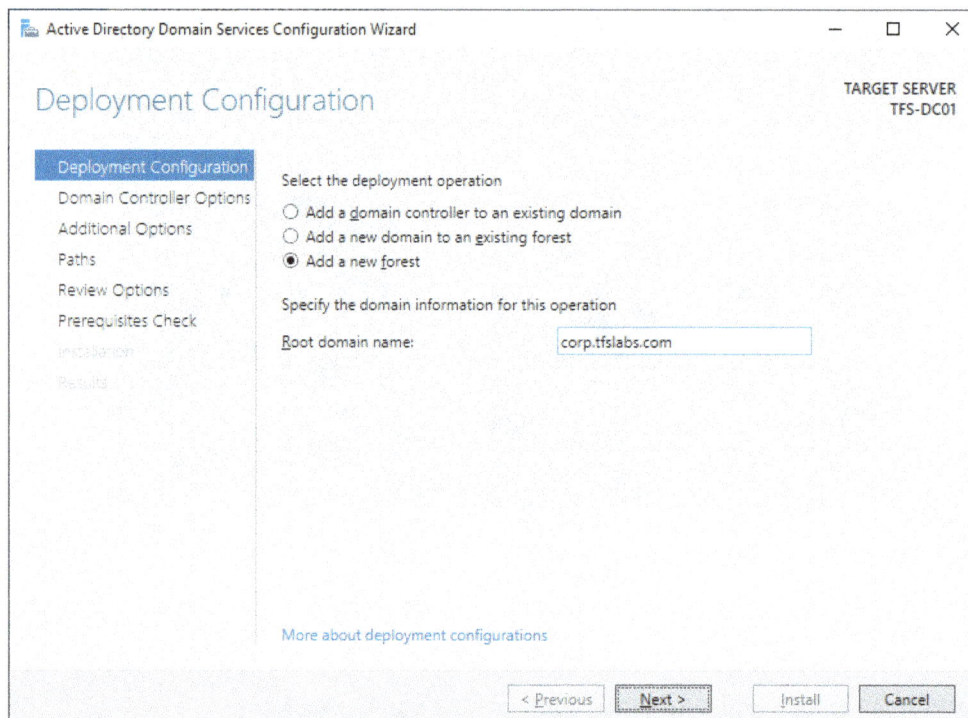

3. On the **Domain Controller Options** screen, ensure that the **Forest functional level** and **Domain functional level** are both set to **Windows Server 2016**. Ensure that the options for **Domain Name System (DNS) server** and **Global Catalog (GC)** are both selected. For the **Directory Services Restore Mode (DSRM)** password, enter a complex password in both fields (record this password for future usage). Once completed, click **Next** to continue:

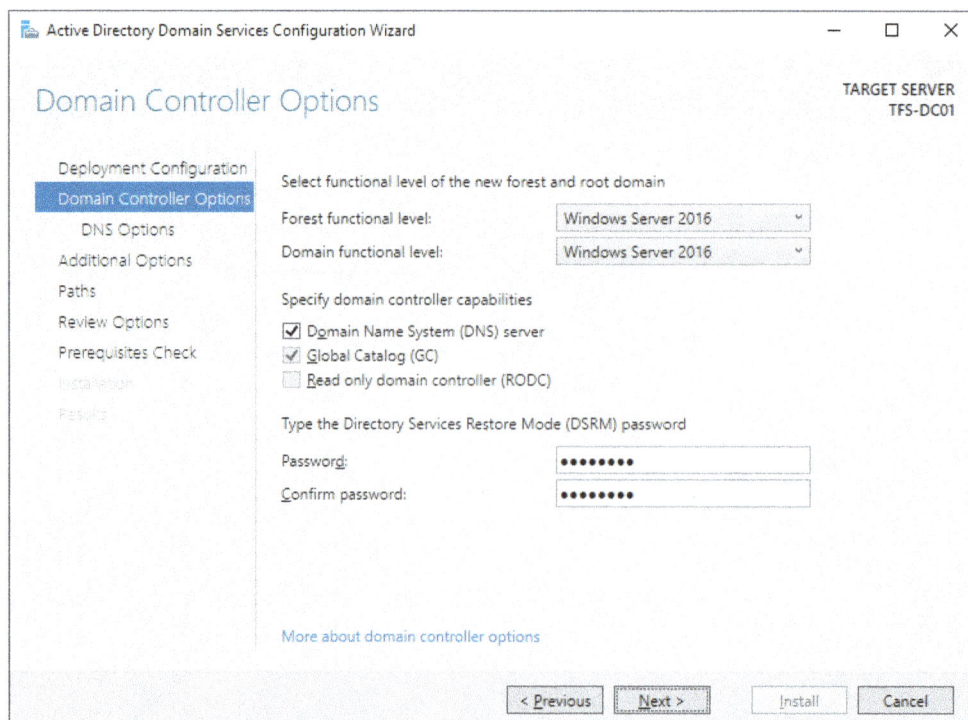

4. On the **DNS Options** screen, ignore the warning message about **DNS Delegation** (this is due to there being no existing DNS Infrastructure at this point) and click **Next** to continue:

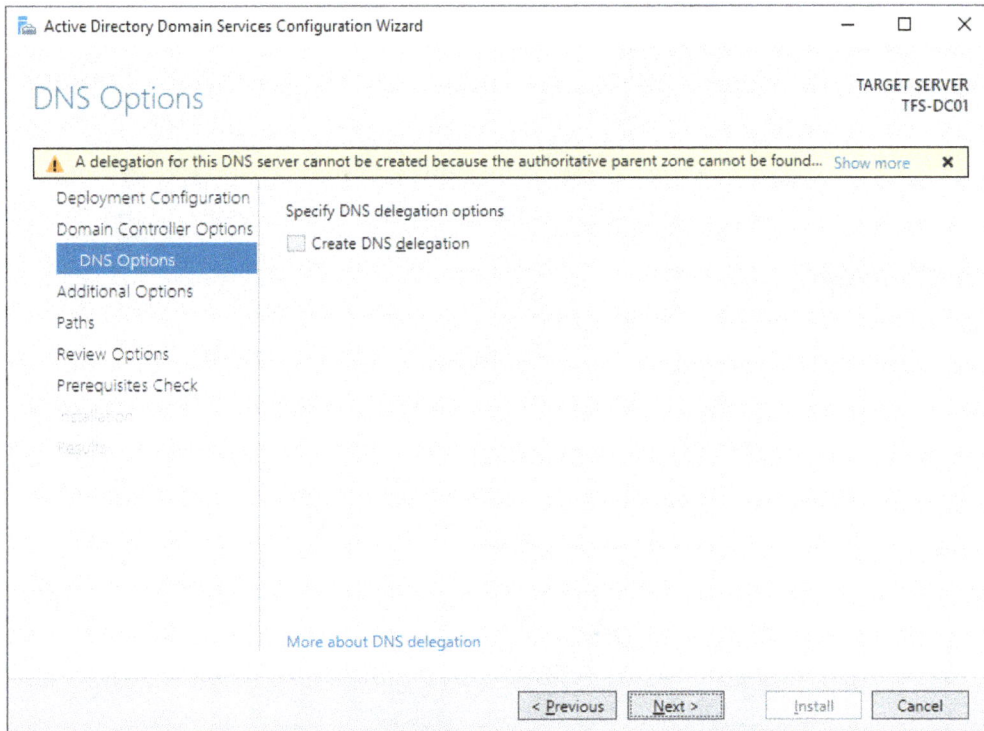

5. On the **Additional Options** screen, for the **NetBIOS domain name** enter **TFSLABS** and click **Next** to continue:

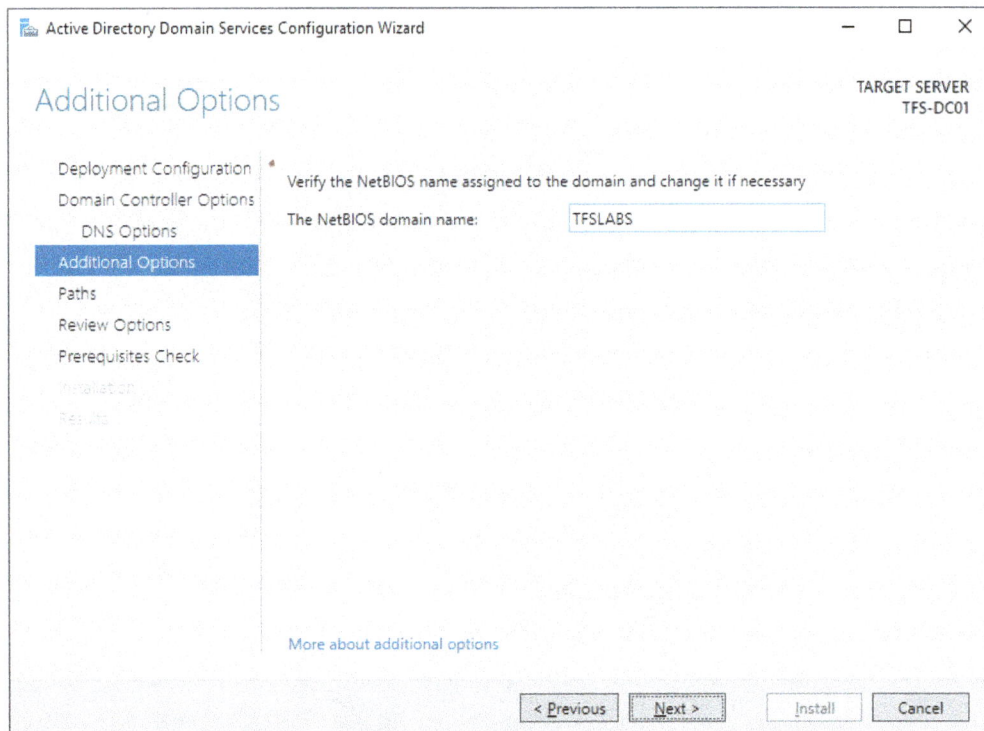

6. On the **Paths** screen, do not modify the default folder paths for Active Directory Domain Services, and click **Next** to continue:

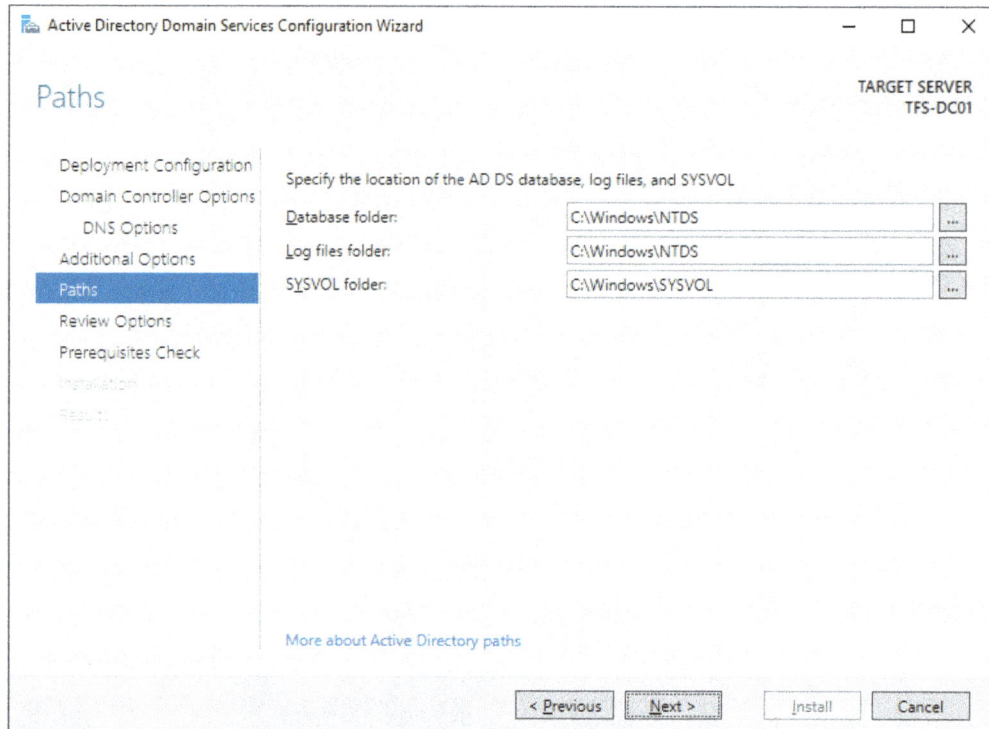

7. On the **Review Options** screen, click **Next** to continue:

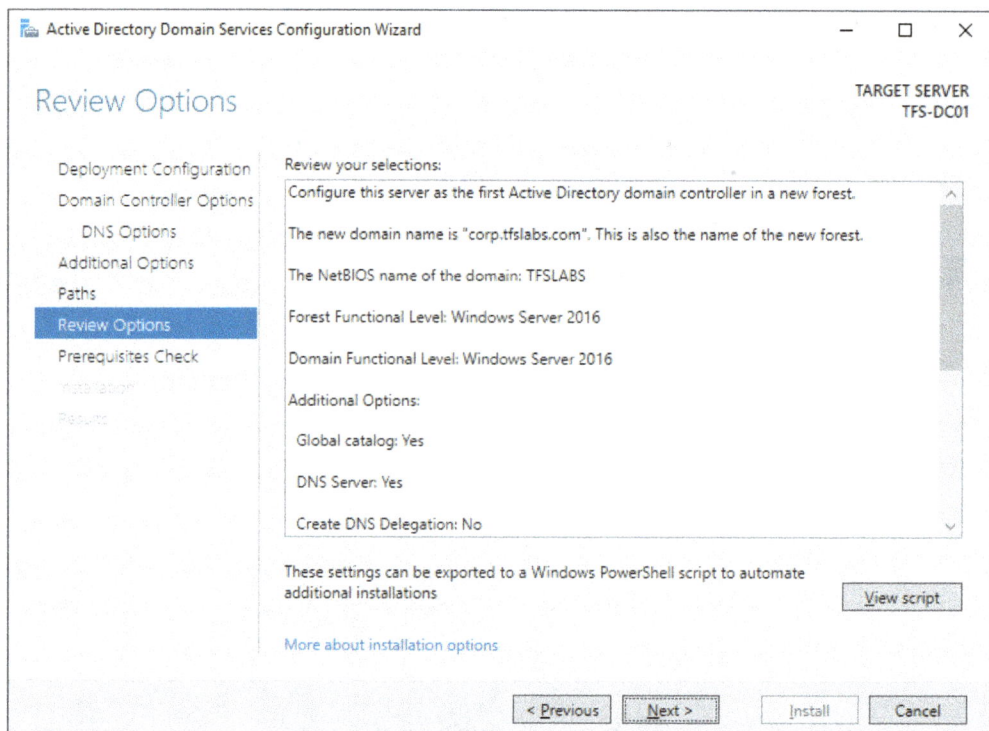

8. On the **Prerequisites Check** screen, ignore any warnings for the Active Directory Domain Services configuration, and click **Install** to continue:

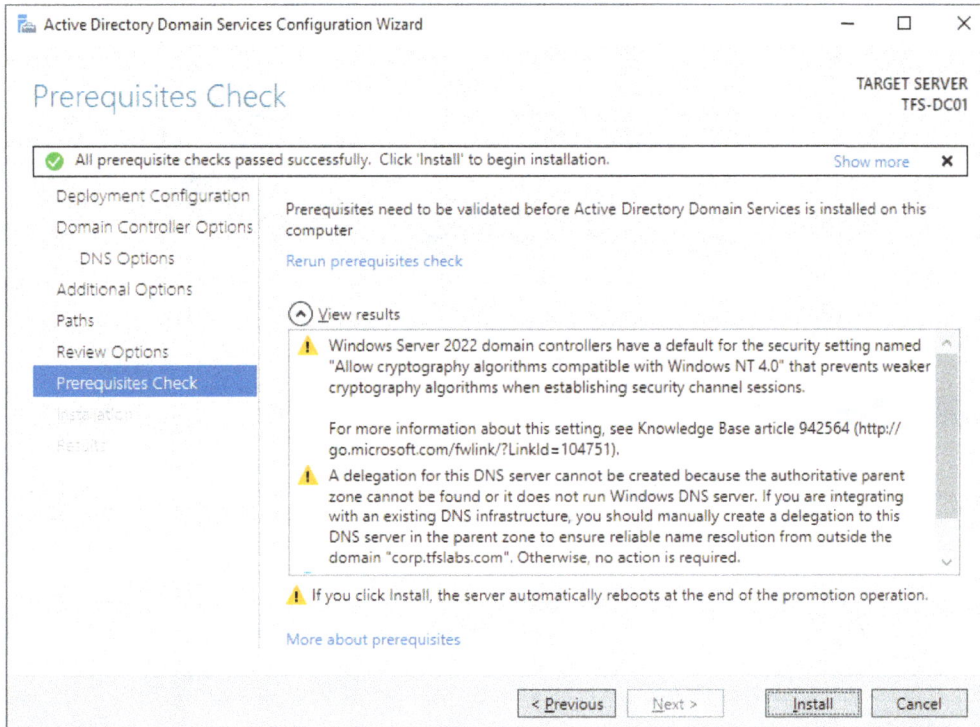

9. On the **Installation** screen, **Active Directory Domain Services** will be configured, and no actions are required until it has completed the configuration:

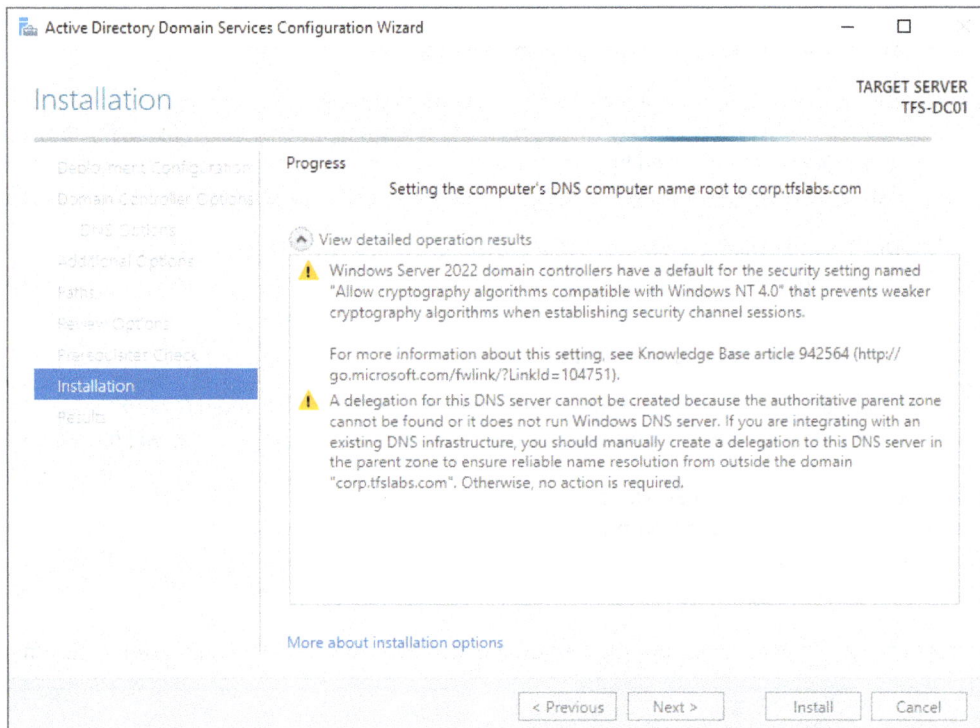

10. On the **Results** screen, click the **Close** button to exit the wizard:

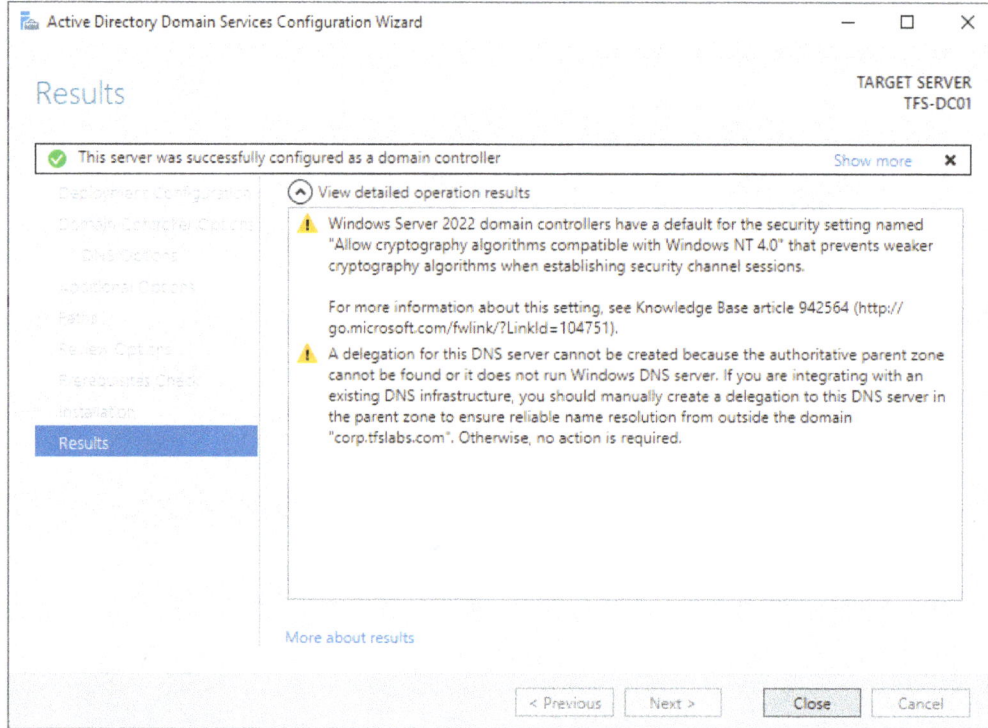

11. The **TFS-DC01** server will automatically restart when the AD DS configuration has completed.

Once the Active Directory Domain Services configuration is complete, there will be a functioning Domain Controller for the TFS Labs domain.

Domain and Workstation Setup - AD DS Role Configuration - Validation

Once the Active Directory Domain Services role has been successfully installed and configured on the TFS-DC01 server, the Windows login screen will now specify the domain when logging in. Use the **TFSLABS\Administrator** account to login to the TFS-DC01 server, which is the Domain Administrator account. The local administrator account that was previously configured on the TFS-DC01 server no longer exists, and there is no way to login with that account.

At this point, the TFS-DC01 server will have the necessary roles and features installed to properly act as a Domain Controller for the TFS Labs domain.

> **Active Directory Domain Services Roles and Features**
>
> When logging into the TFS-DC01 server after it has been promoted to a Domain Controller, ensure that the following tools are now available for Active Directory administration tasks as they will be required later:
>
> - Active Directory Sites and Services
> - Active Directory Users and Computers
> - DNS Management
> - Group Policy Management
>
> These tools can all be accessed from the Server Manager console, the Start menu or the command line.

Once the Active Directory Domain Services role has been successfully configured, proceed to configuring the OU structure for the TFS Labs domain.

Domain and Workstation Setup - Create an OU Structure

It is good practice to create a proper Organizational Unit (OU) structure prior to adding any users, computers, or servers to an Active Directory domain. An Organizational Unit is a type of folder in Active Directory that has many features that are useful for managing and maintaining Active Directory:

- Allows for easier management and organization of Active Directory users, computers, and servers.
- Allows for easier application of Group Policy Objects to the domain.
- Forces administrators to keep Active Directory objects organized.

The OU structure for the TFS Labs domain is not complex, and consists of the following OU structure:

TFS Labs	TFS Labs Root OU
TFS Labs\TFS Servers	Stores all TFS Labs Servers
TFS Labs\TFS Users	Stores all TFS Labs Users
TFS Labs\TFS Workstations	Stores all TFS Labs Workstations

Table 5.5.1: OU structure for the TFS Labs domain for the servers, users, and workstations.

There are two ways to add an OU structure to the TFS Labs domain, one is with the command line using PowerShell and the other is with using the Active Directory Users and Computers console. Only one method is required to create the OU structure.

> **Domain Controller Default Organizational Unit**
>
> Any Domain Controller in an Active Directory Domain will always be found in the Domain Controllers OU by default. Do not move any Domain Controllers from this OU unless the Domain Controller has been demoted and is no longer being used for Active Directory. Since the Domain Controllers are in a separate OU from the structure that will be created, it will need to be factored when applying Group Policy Objects to those servers.

Domain and Workstation Setup - Create an OU Structure - CLI Configuration

To create the OU structure using PowerShell, perform the following steps on the TFS-DC01 server:

1. Open an **elevated PowerShell prompt**.
2. Run the following commands to create the OU structure using the **New-ADOrganizationalUnit** Cmdlet:

```
Windows PowerShell (Elevated)

New-ADOrganizationalUnit `
-Name "TFS Labs" -Path "DC=corp,DC=tfslabs,DC=com"

New-ADOrganizationalUnit `
-Name "TFS Servers" -Path "OU=TFS Labs,DC=corp,DC=tfslabs,DC=com"

New-ADOrganizationalUnit `
-Name "TFS Users" -Path "OU=TFS Labs,DC=corp,DC=tfslabs,DC=com"

New-ADOrganizationalUnit `
-Name "TFS Workstations" -Path "OU=TFS Labs,DC=corp,DC=tfslabs,DC=com"
```

3. Close the **PowerShell prompt**.

Once the OU structure has been created, proceed to validating the OU structure for the TFS Labs domain.

Domain and Workstation Setup - Create an OU Structure - GUI Configuration

To create the OU structure using the Active Directory Users and Computers console, perform the following steps on the TFS-DC01 server:

1. Open the **Active Directory Users and Computers** console (dsa.msc):

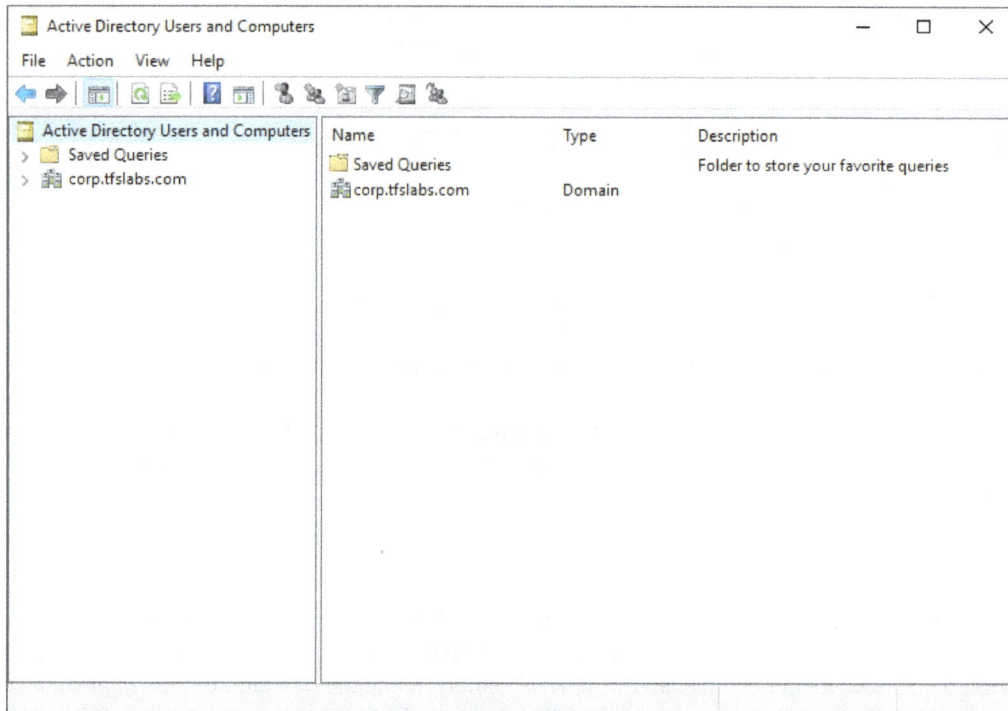

2. Click on the **corp.tfslabs.com** domain in the left side of the window:

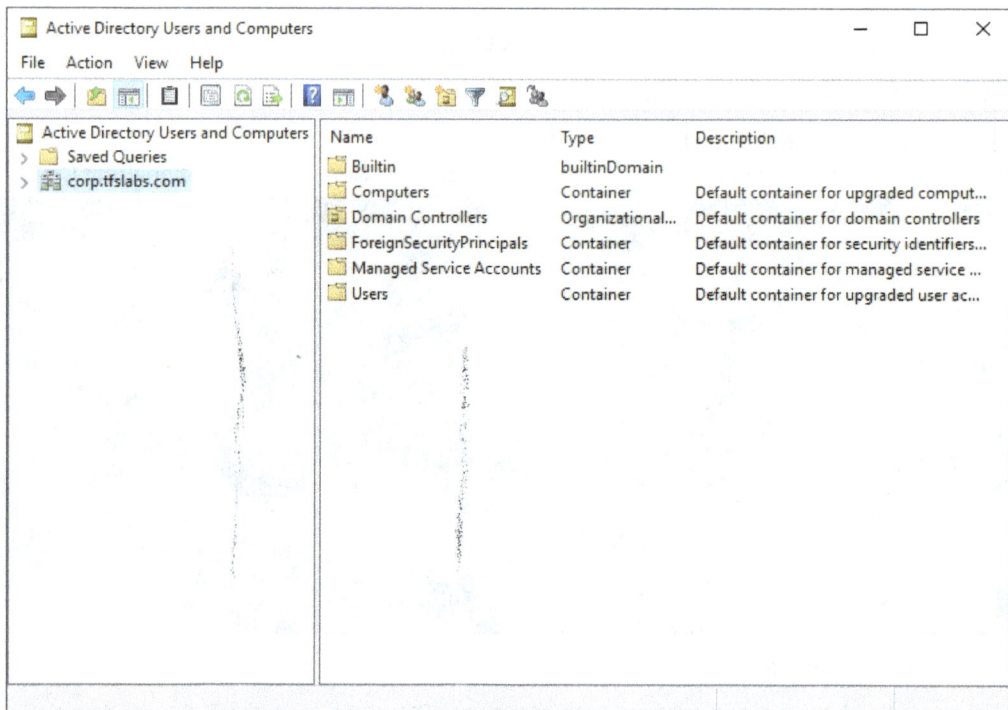

3. Right-click on the **corp.tfslabs.com** domain, select the **New** option, and select **Organizational Unit**:

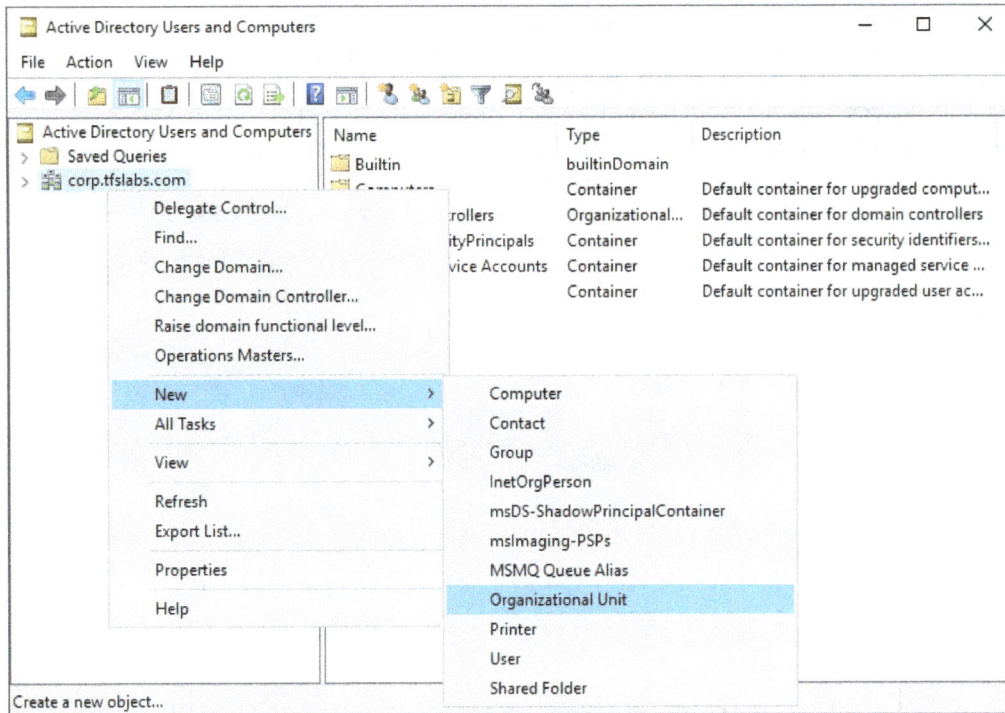

4. In the **New Object - Organizational Unit** window, for the **Name**, enter **TFS Labs**. Ensure that the option to **Protect container from accidental deletion is selected** and click the **OK** button.
5. The **TFS Labs** OU should now appear in the **corp.tfslabs.com** domain:

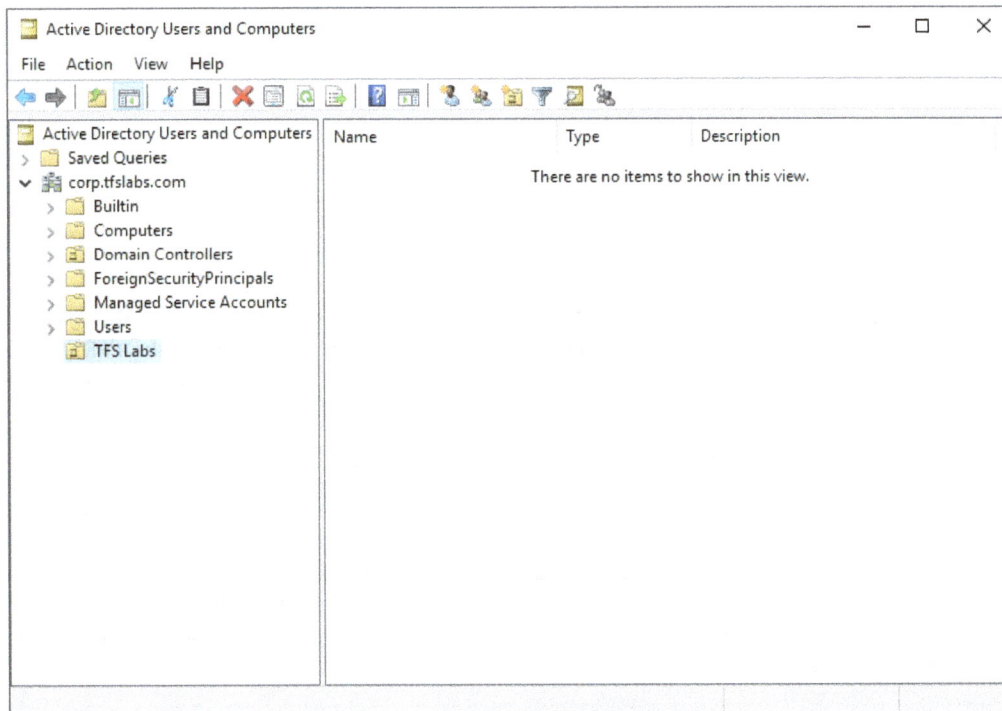

6. Right-click on the **TFS Labs** OU, go to **New**, and select **Organizational Unit**.

7. In the **New Object - Organizational Unit** window, for the **Name**, enter **TFS Servers**. Ensure that the option to **Protect container from accidental deletion is selected** and click **OK**.
8. Right-click on the **TFS Labs** OU, go to **New**, and select **Organizational Unit**.
9. In the **New Object - Organizational Unit** window, for the **Name**, enter **TFS Users**. Ensure that the option to **Protect container from accidental deletion is selected** and click **OK**.
10. Right-click on the **TFS Labs** OU, go to **New**, and select **Organizational Unit**.
11. In the **New Object - Organizational Unit** window, for the **Name**, enter **TFS Workstations**. Ensure that the option to **Protect container from accidental deletion is selected** and click **OK**.
12. In the **corp.tfslabs.com** domain, there should now be three OUs within the **TFS Labs** OU:

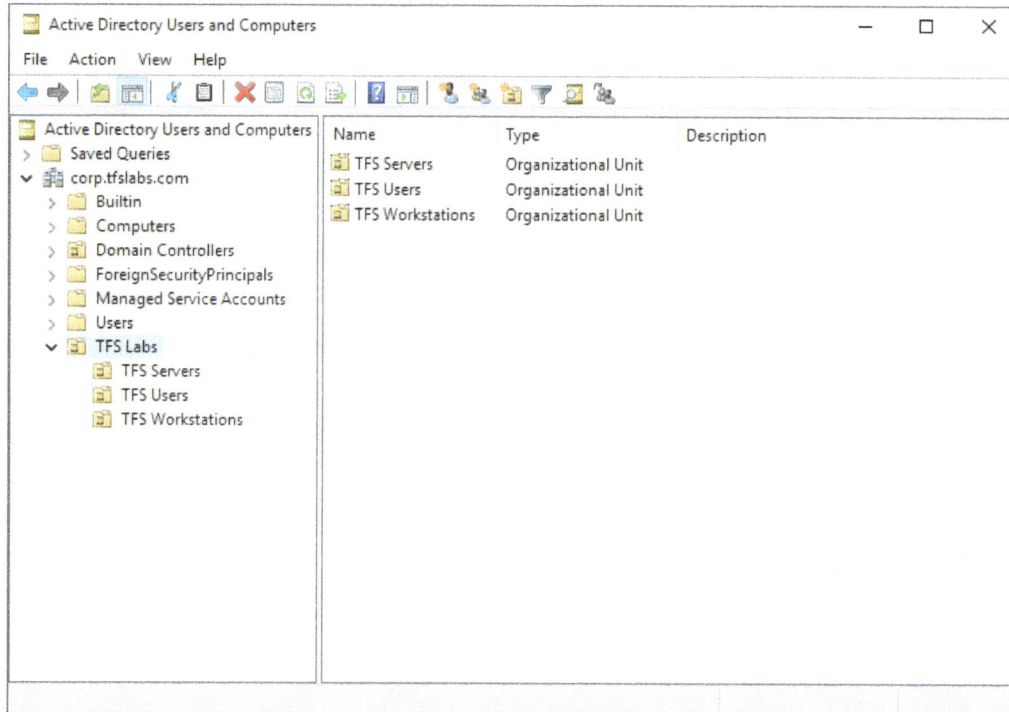

13. Close the **Active Directory Users and Computers** console.

Once the OU structure has been created, proceed to validating the OU structure for the TFS Labs domain.

Domain and Workstation Setup - Create an OU Structure - Validation

Regardless of the method used to create the OU structure, it can be validated by using the **Get-ADOrganizationalUnit** Cmdlet, or by opening the **Active Directory Users and Computers** console and searching for the **TFS Labs** OU in the root of the domain. This OU structure will be used to store all Active Directory objects that are created in this book.

> **Organizational Unit Structure Requirements**
>
> An OU structure for an Active Directory domain is not standardized, and is practically an optional feature in Active Directory. It is possible to have an Active Directory domain and never use an OU structure, and the only downside is the lack of management capabilities. This book creates an OU structure for several reasons, and it is mostly to allow for easier deployment of certificates using Group Policy. If there are no plans on using a custom OU structure for an Active Directory domain, then this OU structure is not required and can be disregarded in deployment steps in this book.

Now that there is a basic OU structure in place in the TFS Labs domain, several test user accounts can now be created that will be used in later chapters for testing purposes.

Domain and Workstation Setup - Create Domain User Accounts

On the TFS Labs domain there is currently only one Active Directory account that is available, and that is the Domain Administrator account that was created by default. For production Active Directory domains this is typically not the case as there are regular domain user accounts that are used for day-to-day administration tasks, and for regular users. Several regular user accounts should be created to test the Active Directory Certificate Services functionality. This will ensure that user certificates that are issued are working correctly, and to test that private key recovery is working with Active Directory Certificate Services. For the purposes of this book, the following three Active Directory accounts will be created for testing purposes:

User Account Name	Active Directory Account	Email Address
Mary Smith	TFSLABS\msmith	msmith@corp.tfslabs.com
Michael Brown	TFSLABS\mbrown	mbrown@corp.tfslabs.com
Robert Johnson	TFSLABS\rjohnson	rjohnson@corp.tfslabs.com

Table 5.6.1: TFS Labs user test accounts. This table includes the name of the user account, the name of the associated Active Directory account, and the email address for the user.

There are several ways to add Active Directory user accounts to the TFS Labs domain. One method is using the command line using PowerShell, and the other method is with the Active Directory Users and Computers console.

> ⚠️ **Active Directory User Email**
>
> Ensure that the email addresses for the test user accounts are entered correctly, otherwise there may be issues with the automatic deployment of user certificates to those accounts in later chapters of this book. The email addresses are not routable as there are no email services in place.

Domain and Workstation Setup - Create Domain User Accounts - CLI Configuration

To create the Active Directory user accounts on the TFS-DC01 server using PowerShell, perform the following steps:

1. Open an **elevated PowerShell prompt**.
2. Using the **New-ADUser** Cmdliet, run the following command to create a user account (there will be a prompt to create a password for the user account):

```
Windows PowerShell (Elevated)

New-ADUser `
-DisplayName "Mary Smith" `
-Name "Mary Smith" `
-GivenName "Mary" `
-Surname "Smith" `
-SamAccountName "msmith" `
-EmailAddress "msmith@corp.tfslabs.com" `
-Path "OU=TFS Users,OU=TFS Labs,DC=corp,DC=tfslabs,DC=com" `
-AccountPassword (Read-Host -AsSecureString "User Password") `
-ChangePasswordAtLogon $false `
-Enabled $true
```

3. Modify the previous command and run it for each user account that needs to be created. The **DisplayName**, **Name**, **GivenName**, **Surname**, **SamAccountName**, and **EmailAddress** options will need to be modified.
4. Close the **PowerShell prompt**.

Once the test user accounts have been created on the TFS-DC01 server, proceed to validating the accounts.

Domain and Workstation Setup - Create Domain User Accounts - GUI Configuration

To create user accounts using the Active Directory Users and Computers console, perform the following steps on the TFS-DC01 server:

1. Open the **Active Directory Users and Computers** console (dsa.msc):

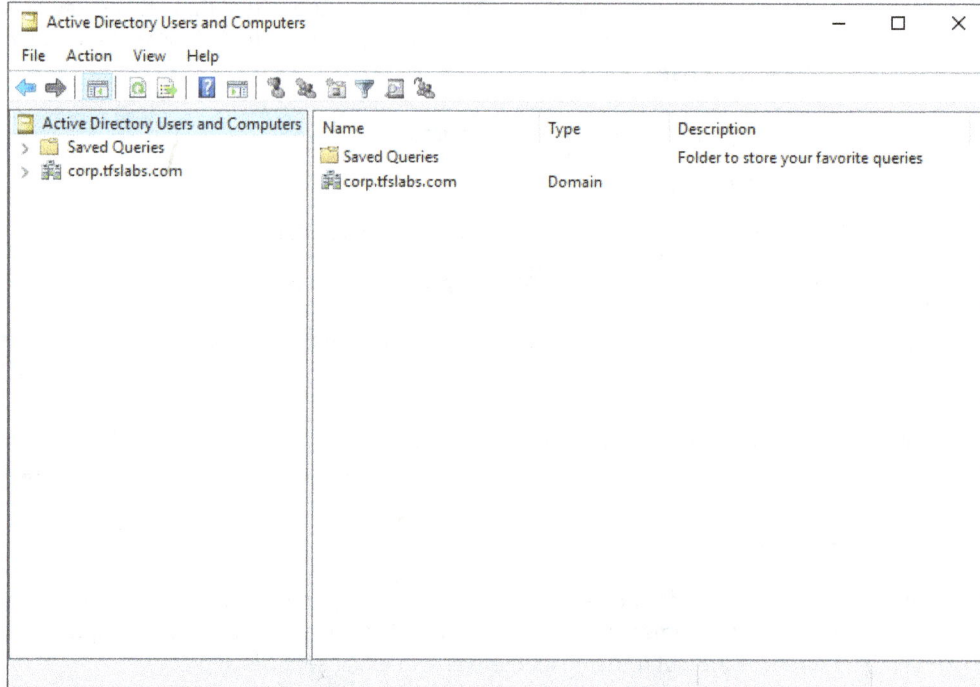

2. Click on the **corp.tfslabs.com** domain, and then click the arrow to the left of the domain to expand the domain structure.
3. Expand the **TFS Labs** OU and select the **TFS Users** OU:

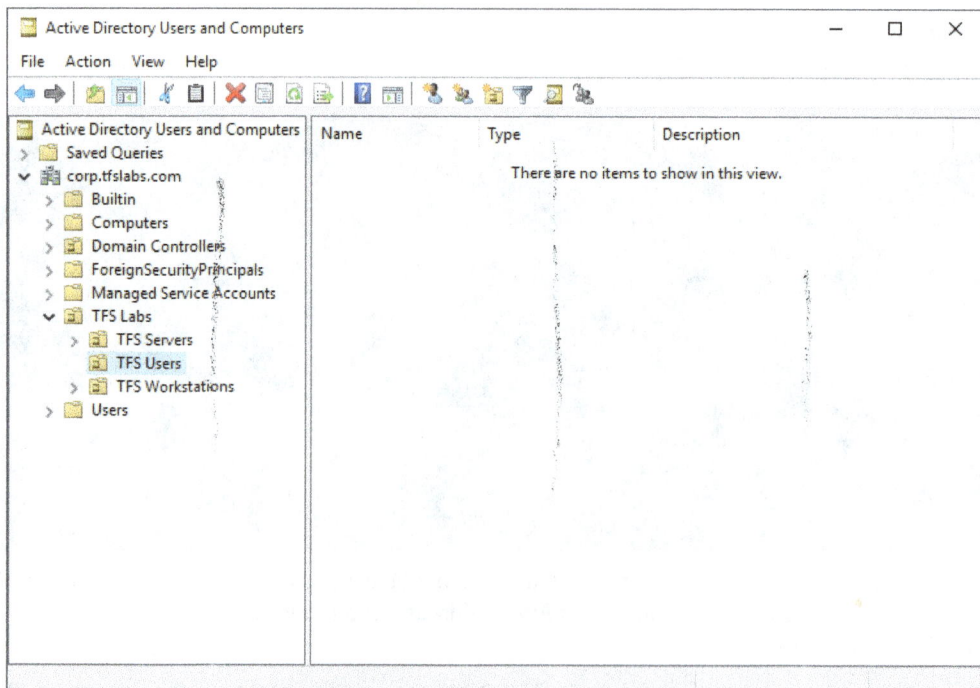

4. Right-click on the **TFS Users** OU, select **New**, and then select **User**.
5. On the **New Object - User** window, enter the details for the user account (First name, Last name, Full name, and User logon name) and click **Next** to continue:

6. On the next window enter a password for the user account. Uncheck the option for **User must change password at next logon** option, as this is not necessary for testing purposes (this will most likely not be the case for a production environment). Click the **Next** button to continue.
7. On the next window, ensure that the account details are correct and click the **Finish** button to continue.
8. Repeat steps 4 to 7 to add the additional user accounts for the **TFS Labs domain** until all user accounts have been added:

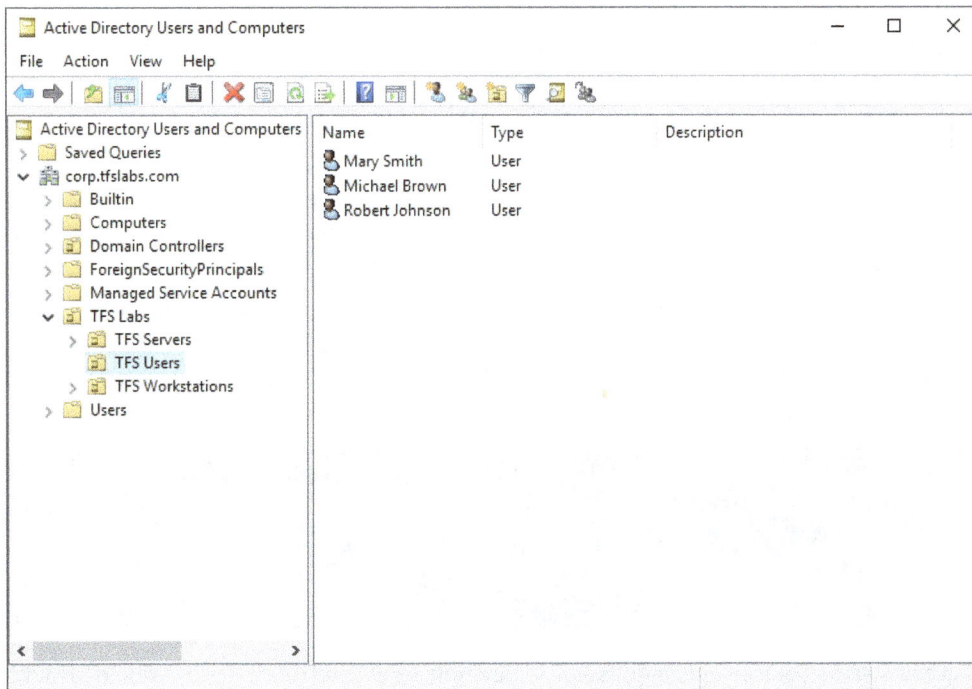

9. To ensure that there are no issues with generating user certificates later in this book, the email addresses of the users will need to be configured on each account. Right-click on one of the user accounts and select the **Properties** option.

10. On the **User Properties** window, on the **General** tab, enter the **E-mail** address for the user account. Click the **Apply** button and then click the **OK** button. Repeat this step for all user accounts until the email address is added to all accounts:

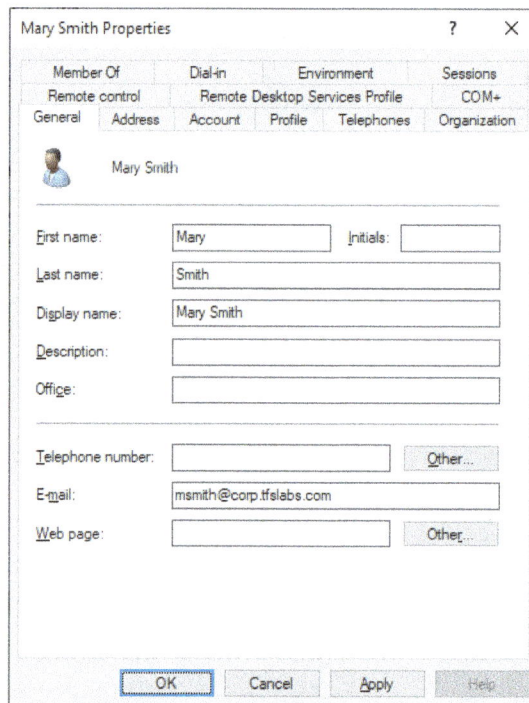

11. Close the **Active Directory Users and Computers** console.

Once the test user accounts have been created on the TFS-DC01 server, proceed to validating the accounts.

Domain and Workstation Setup - Create Domain User Accounts - Validation

Once the test user accounts have been created, it is now possible to demonstrate that the certificates issued by the Certificate Authority are working correctly. The test user accounts should not be used on the TFS-DC01 server, as they are regular accounts and should never be used on a Domain Controller. These accounts should be tested on a Windows 11 workstation that is joined to the domain, which is setup later in this chapter.

Before moving on from creating the test user accounts for the TFS Labs domain, the Domain Administrator account should have the email address field set as well. This field is not set by default, and can cause issues in the future for certificate deployment. The change can be made using the **Set-ADUser** Cmdlet from an **elevated PowerShell prompt** with the following command:

```
Windows PowerShell (Elevated)

Set-ADUser `
-Identity Administrator `
-EmailAddress "administrator@corp.tfslabs.com"
```

Alternatively, this can also be done by opening the Active Directory Users and Computers console (dsa.msc) and adding the **administrator@corp.tfslabs.com** email address to the Domain Administrator account. The Domain Administrator account can be found in the Users OU in the TFS Labs domain (this account is not moved at all in this book, so it should be found there by default).

These user accounts will be able to be used for testing purposes in later chapters with certificate deployment. Once the user account validation has been completed, proceed to setting up the Windows 11 workstation.

Domain and Workstation Setup - Workstation Setup

The next step in this chapter is to create a Windows 11 virtual machine named TFS-WIN11 using Hyper-V that is used to test Active Directory Certificate Services. The test user accounts that were created previously in this chapter will be tested on this virtual machine, and certificate deployments will be tested as well. There are several steps that need to be completed to create the virtual machine that will be used for the Windows 11 Pro workstation that will be used to test Active Directory Certificate Services on the **corp.tfslabs.com** domain:

- Provision a virtual machine for the TFS-WIN11 workstation using Hyper-V and ensure it is connected to a virtual switch that can communicate with the TFS-DC01 server.
- Install Windows 11 24H2 Pro on the virtual machine.
- Configure the local administrator password and hostname of the TFS-WIN11 workstation.
- Configure the network settings of the TFS-WIN11 workstation.
- Move the TFS-WIN11 computer object the correct OU in Active Directory.
- **Optional:** Update the TFS-WIN11 workstation using Windows Update. It is important to ensure that the major version of Windows 11 is not changed in this step.

The TFS-WIN11 virtual machine will have the following specifications:

Virtual Machine Generation	2
Virtual Processors	2
Virtual Memory	4 GB (4096 MB)
Virtual Hard Disk	64 GB
Virtual Network Adapters	1
Secure Boot	Enabled
Trusted Platform Module	Enabled

Table 5.7.1: Virtual machine specifications for the TFS-WIN11 workstation.

The TFS-WIN11 virtual machine will be configured with the following network settings:

IP Address	10.100.1.110
Netmask	255.255.255.0
Gateway	10.100.1.1
DNS Server 1	10.100.1.100

Table 5.7.2: Network configuration settings for the TFS-WIN11 workstation.

Unlike the TFS-DC01 server, the network settings are not as important for workstations in the TFS Labs domain. As long as the TFS-WIN11 workstation is on the same network as the TFS-DC01 server, and has the TFS-DC01 server configured as a DNS server, there should be no issues with the remaining steps in this book.

> **Windows Client Version Support for Active Directory Certificate Services**
>
> The steps in this book will work correctly with supported versions of Windows 10 and Windows 11 workstations. Modern versions of Windows are updated at an accelerated rate, and those versions should work correctly despite being out of support. As long as the Windows workstation is able to join an Active Directory domain, it should not be an issue for testing purposes. Security is also not a major concern since this is a test environment, but this will not be the case for a production environment.

Workstation Virtual Machine and Networking Configuration

The virtual machine as configured in this section uses specific path locations for the virtual hard disk and the location of an installation ISO image for Windows 11. The virtual machine specifications are also configured in such a manner to allow the virtual machine to have the minimum requirements to install it, and to complete the tasks within this book.

The network settings that are used for the virtual machine is also specific to the test environment for creating the Certificate Authority. The network that is used for the TFS-WIN11 workstation must be the same network as the TFS-DC01 server, which is the Domain Controller for the TFS Labs domain.

Modify these settings as needed for a particular test environment. Ensure that if these settings are modified, that it is also modified in later steps in this book.

Windows 11 System Requirements

Unlike previous versions of Windows, Windows 11 has strict hardware requirements which also apply in cases where Windows 11 is installed as a virtual machine. If the hardware requirements are not met, the installation of Windows 11 cannot occur. The minimum hardware requirements that are needed for Windows 11 are as follows:

- **Processor:** 1 Ghz or faster (with 2 or more cores)
- **Architecture:** 64-bit only (there is no 32-bit support in Windows 11)
- **Memory:** 4 GB
- **Storage:** 64 GB
- **Secure Boot:** UEFI and Secure Boot capable
- **Trusted Platform Module:** TPM version 2.0

For virtualization purposes, these requirements can be fulfilled using Hyper-V, but are not all required options are enabled by default. Windows 11 requires a Generation 2 virtual machine, as that is the only configuration that offers all necessary virtual hardware options.

Other virtualization solutions such as Parallels Desktop, VirtualBox and VMware Workstation are capable of virtualizing Windows 11, but that is beyond the scope of this book.

Windows 11 Microsoft Account Requirements

There is a requirement during the initial setup of Windows 11 for using a Microsoft Account to create a local user account. This requirement can sometimes be difficult to bypass, especially when a local user account is required in a domain environment. It can also be challenging to overcome this requirement if there are network connection issues, especially with DNS. Since the TFS-WIN11 workstation will be joined to the TFS Labs domain, there is no reason for using a Microsoft Account once it has been joined to the domain.

The easiest method to bypass the Microsoft Account login requirement is to select the option to join a domain during the setup process, and then creating a local user account to login with. After the local user account has been created, the workstation can be joined to the TFS Labs domain once the network settings are properly configured.

There are other workarounds that can be used for creating a local user account during the initial setup of Windows 11 and removing the requirement for a Microsoft Account entirely, but that is beyond the scope of this book. Some of these methods require automation tools, the use of third-party tools, or modifying the Windows installation files, and is not recommended.

Now that the requirements for creating the Windows 11 test workstation have been reviewed, proceed to creating the virtual machine and configuring the TFS-WIN11 workstation for the TFS Labs domain. There are several steps required, and it is important to ensure that the virtual machine is configured correctly before proceeding to the next section of the book.

Domain and Workstation Setup - Workstation Setup - Virtual Machine Setup

To create a Hyper-V virtual machine for the TFS-WIN11 workstation using the command line, open an **elevated PowerShell prompt** and run the following commands on the Hyper-V host:

1. Create the **TFS-WIN11** virtual machine and virtual hard disk using the **New-VM** Cmdlet:

```
Windows PowerShell (Elevated)

New-VM `
-Name "TFS-WIN11" `
-Generation 2 `
-MemoryStartupBytes 4GB `
-BootDevice VHD `
-NewVHDPath "D:\Hyper-V\Virtual Hard Disks\TFS-WIN11.vhdx" `
-NewVHDSizeBytes 64GB `
-Switch "Hyper-V External Switch"
```

2. Set the number of virtual processors for the **TFS-WIN11** virtual machine to **2** by using the **Set-VMProcessor** Cmdlet:

```
Windows PowerShell (Elevated)

Set-VMProcessor "TFS-WIN11" -Count 2
```

3. Configure the key protector for the **TFS-WIN11** virtual machine by using the **Set-VMKeyProtector** Cmdlet:

```
Windows PowerShell (Elevated)

Set-VMKeyProtector -VMName "TFS-WIN11" -NewLocalKeyProtector
```

4. Enable the virtual TPM option for the **TFS-WIN11** virtual machine by using the **Enable-VMTPM** Cmdlet:

```
Windows PowerShell (Elevated)

Enable-VMTPM -VMName "TFS-WIN11"
```

5. Add a virtual DVD drive to the **TFS-WIN11** virtual machine, and mount the installation ISO image that will be used to install the operating system with the **Add-VMDvdDrive** Cmdlet:

```
Windows PowerShell (Elevated)

Add-VMDvdDrive `
-VMName "TFS-WIN11" `
-Path "D:\ISO Images\Windows 11 24H2.iso"
```

6. Set the virtual DVD drive as the first startup device for the **TFS-WIN11** virtual machine by using the **Set-Firmware** and **Get-VMDvdDrive** Cmdlets:

```
Windows PowerShell (Elevated)

Set-VMFirmware `
-VMName "TFS-WIN11" `
-FirstBootDevice $(Get-VMDvdDrive -VMName "TFS-WIN11")
```

7. Power on the **TFS-WIN11** virtual machine using the **Start-VM** Cmdlet:

```
Windows PowerShell (Elevated)

Start-VM -Name "TFS-WIN11"
```

8. Connect to the **TFS-WIN11** virtual machine using the **Virtual Machine Connection** tool:

```
Windows PowerShell (Elevated)

vmconnect.exe localhost "TFS-WIN11"
```

Alternatively, the TFS-WIN11 virtual workstation can be created and configured without using PowerShell by using Hyper-V Manager instead. Creating the virtual machine using Hyper-V Manager requires several additional steps to ensure that Windows 11 will install and operate correctly:

1. Using the **Hyper-V Manager** (virtmgmt.msc) console, create a new virtual machine for the **TFS-WIN11** workstation. Ensure that the following settings are configured using the **New Virtual Machine Wizard**:
    - **Virtual Machine Name**: TFS-WIN11
    - **Virtual Machine Generation:** 2
    - **Virtual Memory:** 4 GB (4096 MB)
    - **Virtual Network:** Hyper-V External Network
    - **Virtual Hard Disk:** 64 GB
    - **Installation ISO Image:** D:\ISO Images\Windows 11 24H2.iso
2. Once the virtual machine has been created, there are two changes that need to be configured to ensure that it is compatible with Windows 11. The number of **virtual processors** needs to be updated, and the **Trusted Platform Module** needs to be enabled.
3. In the **Hyper-V Manager** console, select the **TFS-WIN11** virtual machine in the **Virtual Machines** pane.
4. Right-click on the **TFS-WIN11** virtual machine and select the **Settings...** option.
5. In the **Settings for TFS-WIN11** window, make the following changes to the configuration for the **TFS-WIN11** virtual machine:
    - In the **Processor** options pane, set the number of processors to **2**.
    - In the **Security** options pane, check the option for **Enable Trusted Platform Module**.
6. Close the settings window.
7. Right-click on the **TFS-WIN11** virtual machine and select the **Start** option to turn the virtual machine on.
8. Right-click on the **TFS-WIN11** virtual machine and select the **Connect...** option to connect to the virtual machine.

Windows 11 can be installed normally with all default options regardless of which method is used to create and configure the virtual machine. In this book, **Windows 11 Pro** (version 24H2) is the version that the test workstation will use for verifying that Active Directory Certificate Services is functioning correctly.

Whether a Microsoft Account or local user account is configured during the initial setup of Windows 11, a user account with local administration privileges will be available at the end of the installation. This local administrator account can be used to complete the configuration of the TFS-WIN11 workstation.

Domain and Workstation Setup - Workstation Setup - Local Administrator Configuration

The local administrator account in Windows 11 is disabled by default and will need a password to be configured on the account before it can be enabled. Unless Windows is deployed with automated tools, the password for the local administrator is not known to the user. The local administrator account can be configured using the command line with PowerShell, or with the Computer Management console. Only one method is required to configure the local administrator account, so there is no need to perform the steps twice.

The password for the local administrator account can be set using the **Set-LocalUser** Cmdlet with PowerShell. When setting the password for the account, it can be entered securely by using the **Read-Host** Cmdlet, but it can be entered in plain text as well. Choose a complex password for the local administrator account and ensure that it is documented if it is required later.

Run the following commands from an **elevated PowerShell prompt** on the TFS-WIN11 workstation to set the password for the local administrator account:

```
Windows PowerShell (Elevated)

$password = Read-Host -AsSecureString "Administrator Password"
$username = Get-LocalUser -Name "Administrator"
$username | Set-LocalUser -Password $password
```

Once the local administrator account has a password configured, the account can be enabled by using the **Enable-LocalUser** Cmdlet:

```
Windows PowerShell (Elevated)

Enable-LocalUser -Name "Administrator"
```

To enable the local administrator account and set the password using the Computer Management console, perform the following steps on the TFS-WIN11 workstation:

1. Open the **Computer Management** console (compmgmt.msc).
2. In the **Computer Management** console, in the left-hand pane under **System Tools**, expand **Local Users and Groups**, and select **Users**.
3. In the center pane, right-click on the **Administrator** account and select the **Set Password...** option.
4. In the **Set Password for Administrator** window, there is a warning about changing the password for a user account, but since this account has never had a password configured the warning can be ignored. Click the **Proceed** button to continue.
5. In the **Set Password for Administrator** window, enter the password for the local administrator account twice, and click the **OK** button. When the **Local Users and Groups** window appears, click the **OK** button to close it.
6. In the center pane, right-click on the **Administrator** account and select the **Properties** option.
7. In the **Administrator Properties** window, uncheck the option for **Account is disabled** and click the **OK** button.
8. Close the **Computer Management** console.

Regardless of the type of account that is created during the initial setup of Windows 11, the local administrator account should always be enabled and a password should be configured. This will ensure that there is always a way to login to the TFS-WIN11 workstation, and this can be useful for troubleshooting purposes. Proceed to configuring the hostname for the TFS-WIN11 workstation.

> **⚠ Domain Administrator Account Login**
>
> The Domain Administrator account that is created with Active Directory is capable of logging into every workstation and server on the domain. While this may be convenient for testing purposes, it is considered bad practice to use this account in this manner. If the Domain Administrator account is used on a compromised workstation, the entire domain is at risk since an account with that privilege level can be used on every domain device.

Domain and Workstation Setup - Workstation Setup - Hostname Configuration

In recent versions of Windows 11 the hostname is usually created during the initial setup process, but in most cases the hostname of a Windows workstation or server is usually randomly generated at the time of installation. With automated tools, the hostname can be set automatically at the time of installation, but for the purposes of this book those tools are not used. The hostname of the TFS-WIN11 workstation can be configured using the command line with PowerShell, or with the System Properties Control Panel applet. Only one method is required to configure the hostname, so there is no need to perform the steps twice. A restart of the workstation is required to complete the process, and that restart should be performed before joining the workstation to the TFS Labs domain.

Renaming a Windows workstation can be performed using the command line with the **Rename-Computer** Cmdlet. To configure the hostname on the workstation using the command line, open an **elevated PowerShell prompt** and run the following command on the TFS-WIN11 workstation (the command will automatically restart the workstation without requiring any manual intervention):

```
Windows PowerShell (Elevated)

Rename-Computer "TFS-WIN11" -Restart
```

To rename the workstation using the System Properties Control Panel applet, perform the following steps on the TFS-WIN11 workstation:

1. Open the **System Properties** Control Panel applet (sysdm.cpl).
2. In the **System Properties** window, click the **Change...** button at the bottom of the **Computer Name** tab.
3. In the **Computer Name/Domain Changes** window, set the **Computer name** field to **TFS-WIN11** and click the **OK** button.
4. In the **Computer Name/Domain Changes** box, there will be a notification that the computer will need to be restarted to apply the hostname change. Click the **OK** button to continue.
5. In the **System Properties** window, click the **Close** button.
6. When prompted, click the **Restart Now** button to immediately restart the **TFS-WIN11** workstation.

Regardless of which method is used to rename the TFS-WIN11 workstation, once the workstation has restarted the hostname should be correctly configured. Proceed to configuring the network settings for the TFS-WIN11 workstation.

Domain and Workstation Setup - Workstation Setup - Network Configuration

There are several ways to configure the network settings for the TFS-WIN11 workstation, which will be configured to use a static IP address. It can be configured using the command line with the **Get-NetAdapter**, **New-NetIPAddress**, and **Set-DnsClientServerAddress** Cmdlets. It can also be configured using the GUI with the **Network Connections** Control Panel applet. Only one method is required to change the IP address and DNS server addresses on the workstation, there is no need to use both.

To configure the IP address on the TFS-WIN11 workstation using the command line, open an **elevated PowerShell prompt** and run the following command on the TFS-WIN11 workstation:

```
Windows PowerShell (Elevated)

New-NetIPAddress `
-AddressFamily IPv4 `
-IPAddress 10.100.1.110 `
-PrefixLength 24 `
-DefaultGateway 10.100.1.1 `
-InterfaceIndex (Get-NetAdapter).InterfaceIndex
```

To configure the DNS server addresses on the TFS-WIN11 workstation using the command line, open an **elevated PowerShell prompt** and run the following command:

```
Windows PowerShell (Elevated)

Set-DnsClientServerAddress `
-ServerAddresses ("10.100.1.100") `
-InterfaceIndex (Get-NetAdapter).InterfaceIndex
```

Alternatively, the IP address and DNS server addresses for the server can be configured without using the command line by using the **Network Connections** Control Panel applet. To configure the IP address and the DNS server addresses for the TFS-WIN11 workstation, perform the following steps:

1. Open the **Network Connections** Control Panel applet (ncpa.cpl).
2. In the **Network Connections** window, right-click on the **Ethernet** network adapter and select the **Properties** option.
3. In the **Ethernet Properties** window, scroll to the **Internet Protocol Version 4 (TCP/IPv4)** connection and select it. Click the **Properties** button.
4. In the **Internet Protocol Version 4 (TCP/IPv4) Properties** window, make the following changes to configure the IP address:
   - Select the option for **Use the following IP address**
   - Set the **IP address** to **10.100.1.110**
   - Set the **Subnet mask** to **255.255.255.0**
   - Set the **Default Gateway** to **10.100.1.1**
5. In the **Internet Protocol Version 4 (TCP/IPv4) Properties** window, make the following changes to configure the DNS server addresses:
   - Select the option for **Use the following DNS server addresses**.
   - Set the **Preferred DNS server** to the **10.100.1.100** address.
   - Leave the **Alternate DNS server** blank.
6. Click the **OK** button to apply the IP and DNS address changes.
7. Click the **OK** button to close the **Ethernet Properties** window.

Regardless of which method is used to apply the network configuration to the TFS-WIN11 workstation, any changes to the IP and DNS server addresses are applied immediately and there is no need to restart the workstation. Proceed to joining the TFS-WIN11 workstation to the TFS Labs domain.

Network Configuration Validation

Before proceeding any further it is important to validate the network configuration settings and ensure that the TFS-WIN11 workstation is able to communicate correctly with the TFS-DC01 Domain Controller. This can be done by pinging the domain name for the TFS Labs domain (**corp.tfslabs.com**), and the IP address should resolve to a Domain Controller in the Active Directory domain:

```
Windows PowerShell

ping corp.tfslabs.com
```

Since there is only one Domain Controller configured in the TFS Labs domain, the IP address for the domain should only resolve to the IP address of the TFS-DC01 server (10.100.1.100). If there are no issues with the network configuration or the DNS configuration, the TFS-WIN11 workstation can be joined to the TFS Labs domain.

Domain and Workstation Setup - Workstation Setup - Domain Join

Joining a Windows workstation to an Active Directory domain is a fairly simple task to perform as long as the following requirements are met:

- The workstation is using a supported version of Windows (Pro, Enterprise and Education) that is capable of joining an Active Directory domain.
- The workstation is connected to a network where there is an available Domain Controller.
- The workstation has the correct DNS settings that can resolve the domain name of the Active Directory domain which is accessible.
- There is an account on the Active Directory domain with sufficient privileges available to add the workstation to the domain when prompted.

There are several options available for joining a Windows workstation to an Active Directory domain. It can be joined to the domain using the command line with the **Add-Computer** Cmdlet. It can also be joined to the domain with the System Properties Control Panel applet. Only one method is required to join the TFS-WIN11 workstation to the TFS Labs domain, there is no need to use both methods.

To join the test workstation to the TFS Labs domain, open an **elevated PowerShell prompt** and run the following command on the TFS-WIN11 workstation:

```
Windows PowerShell (Elevated)

Add-Computer -DomainName corp.tfslabs.com -Restart
```

When the **Add-Computer** Cmdlet is used, a window will appear asking for valid credentials to join the workstation to the domain. The Domain Administrator account (**TFSLABS\Administrator**) can be used to join the workstation to the domain. If there are no issues with the credentials, the TFS-WIN11 workstation will automatically restart to complete the process of adding it to the domain.

To join the test workstation to the TFS Labs domain using the System Properties Control Panel applet, perform the following steps on the TFS-WIN11 workstation:

1. Open the **System Properties** Control Panel applet (sysdm.cpl).
2. In the **System Properties** window, click the **Change...** button at the bottom of the **Computer Name** tab.
3. In the **Computer Name/Domain Changes** window, select the option for **Domain** in the **Member of** box. For the **Domain**, enter **corp.tfslabs.com** and click the **OK** button.
4. A window will appear asking for valid credentials to join the workstation to the domain. The Domain Administrator account (**TFSLABS\Administrator**) can be used to join the workstation to the domain. Enter the username and password and click the **OK** button.
5. In the **Computer Name/Domain Changes** box, there will be a notification that the computer will need to be restarted to join the domain. Click the **OK** button to continue.
6. In the **Computer Name/Domain Changes** box, there will be a notification that the computer has been joined to the domain. Click the **OK** button to continue.
7. In the **System Properties** window, click the **Close** button.
8. When prompted, click the **Restart Now** button to immediately restart the **TFS-WIN11** workstation and complete the Active Directory join.

After the restart has been completed, and if there were no issues with the network or with the credentials, the TFS-WIN11 workstation will now be joined to the TFS Labs domain.

Active Directory Modifications to Windows Clients

When a Windows client or server is added to Active Directory, several changes occur that allow it to be used on a domain:

- Group Policy will be available on the Windows device, and Group Policy Objects will be applied to any devices where those objects are applied (only valid Group Policy Objects will be applied to a Windows device). Group Policy has the ability to automatically deploy valid software packages and configurations to Windows devices that support them.
- Active Directory user accounts and associated permissions will be available on the Windows device, as well as any security settings that are associated with those accounts.
- Security settings from Active Directory will be applied to the Windows device. This includes file and share permissions on domain-joined servers and file shares.

Many of these features are utilized by Active Directory Certificate Services, specifically with certificate deployment to users and workstations.

Once the TFS-WIN11 workstation has been joined to the TFS Labs domain, the Windows login screen will be updated to allow for different options for logging in with user accounts:

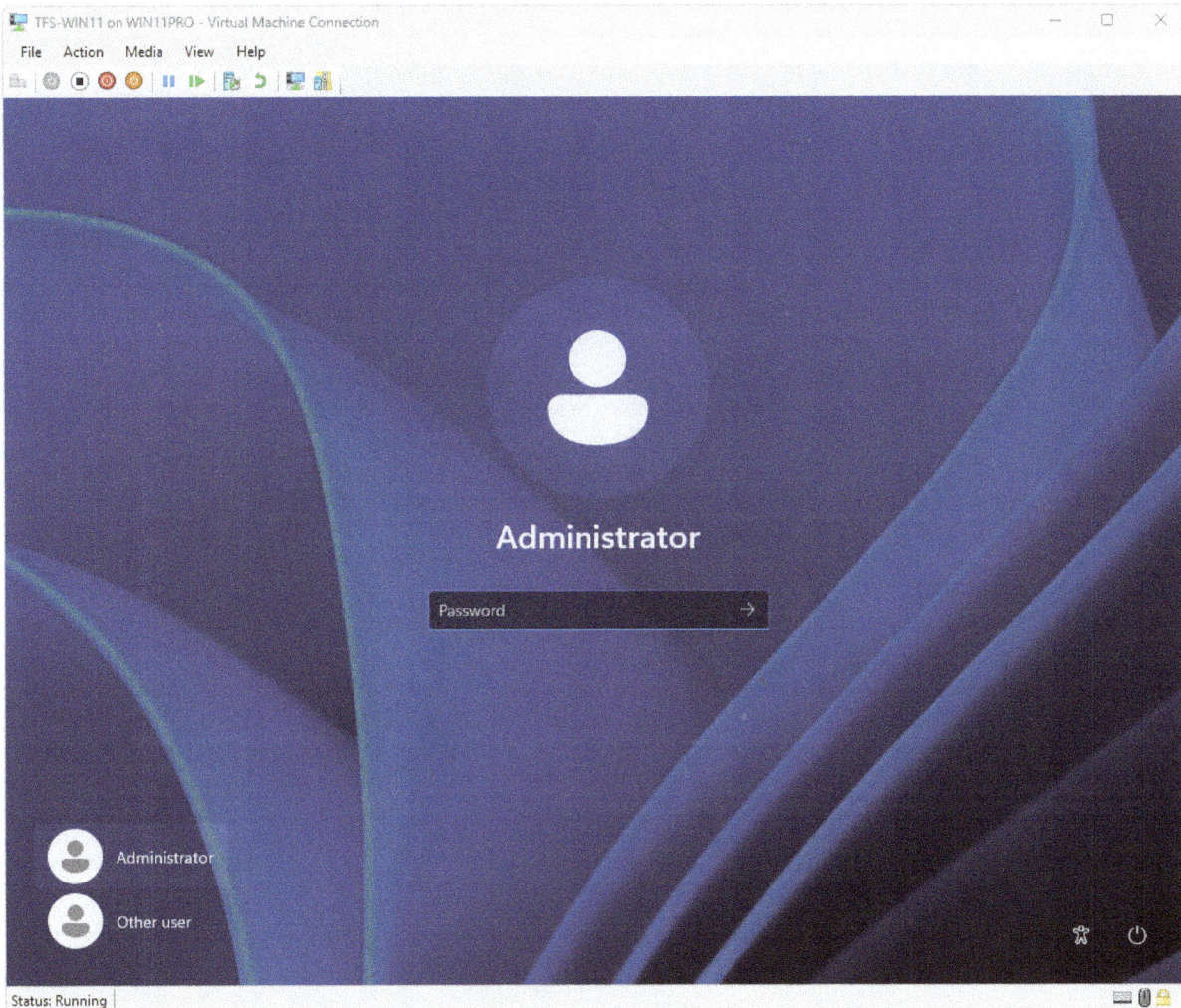

Figure 5.7.4.1: The TFS-WIN11 workstation once it has been joined to the TFS Labs domain. The Windows login screen now gives the option to login as other users on the TFS Labs domain.

From the Windows login screen the option to login as an Active Directory user is available under the **Other user** option in the lower-left corner of the login screen:

- To login as an Active Directory user, select the **Other user** option and login using the Active Directory username of the desired account. This can be done using the username itself (**msmith**), the username with the domain (**TFSLABS\msmith**), or the email address (**msmith@corp.tfslabs.com**) of the user account (only if the option is configured on the domain and the user account).
- To login as a local user, add the hostname of the workstation before the username (**TFS-WIN11\Administrator**) in the **User name** field.
- The Domain Administrator should not be used on a regular workstation, but the domain name is required to be specified for that account to be used. Without the domain name specified, the workstation will default to the local administrator account on the workstation.

To test that there are no issues with the user accounts for Active Directory that were created earlier in the chapter, login to the TFS-WIN11 workstation with one of those accounts. Once that has been completed, proceed to relocating the TFS-WIN11 computer object in the TFS Labs domain.

Remote Connections and Domain User Accounts

There may be an issue with connecting to the TFS-WIN11 workstation with the Virtual Machine Connection application when using a domain user account. This is due to the way that Hyper-V handles connections with the Virtual Machine Connection application, which is similar to Remote Desktop. This issue also applies to Remote Desktop connections as well, so the configuration changes are also required if that is how connections will be used for the workstation.

Additional permissions are required to allow for domain users to login correctly when using Virtual Machine Connection or Remote Desktop. By default, all users in Active Directory are added to the **Domain Users** group, and that is how users in this book are configured. Typically, in a production domain environment, changes like this would be managed with Group Policy since there is usually more than one workstation available. Since this is a test environment, it only needs to be applied to a single workstation and the change only needs to be performed once.

To facilitate testing for the steps in this book, the **Domain Users** group will need to be added to the TFS-WIN11 workstation to allow for domain users to login. On the TFS-WIN11 workstation, make the following changes to the **Remote Desktop Users** group:

1. Login to the **TFS-WIN11** workstation using the local administrator account.
2. Open the **Computer Management** console (compmgmt.msc).
3. In the **Computer Management** console, in the left-hand pane, expand **Local Users and Groups** and select **Groups**.
4. Select the **Remote Desktop Users** group, right-click and select **Properties**.
5. On the **General** tab, under the **Members** window, click the **Add...** button.
6. On the **Select Users, Computers, Service Accounts, or Groups** window, enter **Domain Users** and click the **OK** button.
7. If prompted, enter the **Domain Administrator** credentials to authenticate to the **TFS Labs** domain.
8. The **TFSLABS\Domain Users** group should now be listed in the window.
9. Click the **OK** button to close the window.
10. Restart the **TFS-WIN11** workstation to complete the configuration.

At this point the TFS-WIN11 workstation should be ready for domain users to login with the Virtual Machine Connection application. They should also be able to login using the Remote Desktop application as well if that feature is enabled on the workstation (Remote Desktop is disabled by default).

Domain and Workstation Setup - Workstation Setup - Relocate Computer Object

To ensure that there are no issues in later steps in the book, the TFS-WIN11 workstation should be moved from the default **Computer** OU in Active Directory to one of the dedicated OUs that were created earlier in this chapter for the TFS Labs domain. This will facilitate easier application of Group Policy Objects which are needed for Active Directory Certificate Services and other configuration options to be deployed. This change can be made on any Domain Controller in an Active Directory domain.

Organizational Units and Group Policy Objects

There is no requirement to use Organizational Units to manage objects in Active Directory. The use of them allows for better organization in Active Directory, specifically in separating objects based on their function and location. They also allow for easier application of Group Policy, since applying Group Policy Objects to the root of the domain can cause serious issues if there are problems with those policies.

If there are no plans to utilize Organizational Units for an existing domain, or there are none currently in place, then factor that in while deploying any related Group Policy Objects in later steps in this book.

There are several ways to move the computer object in Active Directory. One method is with the command line using PowerShell, and the other method is using the Active Directory Users and Computers console. Only one method is required to move the computer object.

The TFS-WIN11 computer object can be moved using the **Get-ADComputer** and **Move-ADObject** Cmdlets by running the following command from an **elevated PowerShell prompt** on the TFS-DC01 server:

```
Windows PowerShell (Elevated)

Get-ADComputer "TFS-WIN11" | `
Move-ADObject -TargetPath "OU=TFS Workstations,OU=TFS Labs,DC=corp,DC=tfslabs,DC=com"
```

Alternatively, the TFS-WIN11 computer object can be moved using the Active Directory Users and Computers console by performing the following steps on the TFS-DC01 server:

1. Open the **Active Directory Users and Computers** console (dsa.msc).
2. Expand the **corp.tfslabs.com** domain and go to the **Computers** OU.
3. Right-click on the **TFS-WIN11** computer and click on **Move...**.
4. In the **Move** window, expand the **TFS Labs** OU and select **TFS Workstations** and click **OK**. If there is a warning message about moving the computer object, click the **Yes** button to confirm.
5. Close the **Active Directory Users and Computers** console.

Once the TFS-WIN11 workstation has been moved to the correct OU in Active Directory, it is ready to be used for testing of the Certificate Authority deployment in the later chapters in this book. Proceed to installing any Windows Updates to the TFS-WIN11 workstation if required.

Organizational Units and Group Policy Changes

When a computer or user object is relocated in Active Directory, the Group Policy Objects that are associated with the new OU may potentially be different from the source location. If an object is relocated in Active Directory, it may take time for the new Group Policy changes to take effect. The changes can also be different depending on if a computer object or user object was moved, as those policies can be different.

Group Policy Objects are applied at regular intervals, and are usually applied every 90 minutes by default. However, some policies are only applied when a user logs in, or when the computer is started. To ensure that there are no issues with policies being applied, it is good practice to restart the computer after it has been moved. This will ensure that the correct Group Policy Objects are being applied to the computer and user without needing to wait for the change to be automatically applied.

Domain and Workstation Setup - Workstation Setup - Windows Update

While it is not necessary to run Windows Update on any of the workstations in this book, now would be a good time to run those updates if it is required. Windows Update can be accessed through the Settings app, or through the command line by opening an **elevated PowerShell prompt** and running the following command:

```
Windows PowerShell (Elevated)

Start-Process ms-settings:windowsupdate
```

Installing all available updates will take time to complete and will likely require several restarts of the workstation. Once completed, there is nothing further to configure on the TFS-WIN11 workstation, and it is ready to be used for the remaining steps in this book.

Windows 11 Major Release Updates

Ensure that when running Windows Update on the TFS-WIN11 workstation that the option to upgrade to a newer version of Windows 11 is not selected and installed. While the steps in this book will most likely work correctly with more recent versions of Windows 11, it has not been tested and it is not guaranteed to work with Active Directory Domain Services.

Domain and Workstation Setup - Checkpoints

Test Environment Checkpoints

This section is entirely optional. If there is no need to use Checkpoints for testing purposes, skip this section and any other sections in other chapters about this topic.

At this point in the process of creating the test environment for the TFS Labs domain it is suggested to create a Checkpoint (or equivalent) for the TFS-DC01 server and the TFS-WIN11 workstation. This is useful for testing purposes and has several benefits:

- The Active Directory domain and the test workstation are correctly configured at this stage in the book, and are ready to have the Active Directory Certificate Services role configured for the TFS Labs Certificate Authority.
- The steps for configuring Active Directory Certificate Services in later sections of this book will make changes to Active Directory, and this is the last point before those changes occur.
- Removing the configuration for Active Directory Certificate Services is complex, and if not performed correctly can have unintended side effects. Avoiding this issue during testing will save a lot of time.
- The TFS-DC01 server and TFS-WIN11 workstation are always setup in the same manner, so there is no need to repeat the steps in this chapter again if the process needs to be restarted.

The configuration of Active Directory Certificate Services is complex, and there is a chance that mistakes can occur during the implementation. This book demonstrates a test environment using the TFS Labs domain which is a new implementation, so it is easier to restart the process of creating the Certificate Authority instead of troubleshooting existing configuration issues. Creating an Active Directory domain and a workstation is the simplest part of the entire process and is not the main focus of this book, so there is nothing to gain by going through the steps in this chapter repeatedly. In this section, a Checkpoint named **Pre-ADCS-Implementation** will be created after the previous steps in this chapter have been successfully completed.

Checkpoints and Virtualization Solutions

This book uses Hyper-V for virtualization of the TFS Labs environment which is used to test the deployment of Active Directory Certificate Services. The Checkpoint feature in Hyper-V allows for a complete snapshot of a virtual machine at a specific point in time. If a different virtualization solution is being used, it most likely supports an equivalent feature. Details on how to use Checkpoints with other virtualization solutions are beyond the scope of this book.

Virtual Machine Checkpoints and Hard Disk Space

An important thing to consider before using Hyper-V Checkpoints is that once they are used, they can begin to slowly take up a considerable amount of disk space if they are not properly managed. When a virtual hard disk is provisioned, the size of the virtual hard disk can be specified and Hyper-V will not allocate more to the disk space if it is used up. Hyper-V will treat the virtual hard disk as if it is a physical hard disk, which cannot be resized after it is manufactured. With Checkpoints, the differencing files can grow to whatever size is needed, which can fill up an entire hard drive or storage location.

Domain and Workstation Setup - Checkpoints - Create a Checkpoint

There are two virtual machines related to the TFS Labs domain at this point in the book, and both of those virtual machines will require a Checkpoint to be created. These Checkpoints should be created at the same time to ensure that there are no issues in restoring them later (if necessary). A Checkpoint can be created with PowerShell by using the **Checkpoint-VM** Cmdlet, and it can also be created using Hyper-V Manager or the Virtual Machine Connection application. Checkpoints are created and managed on the Hyper-V host, and not on the virtual machine.

To create a Checkpoint named **Pre-ADCS-Implementation** for the TFS-DC01 server, run the following command from an **elevated PowerShell prompt** on the Hyper-V host where the virtual machine is running:

```
Windows PowerShell (Elevated)

Checkpoint-VM -Name TFS-DC01 -SnapshotName "Pre-ADCS-Implementation"
```

To create a Checkpoint named **Pre-ADCS-Implementation** for the TFS-WIN11 workstation, run the following command from an **elevated PowerShell prompt** on the Hyper-V host where the virtual machine is running:

```
Windows PowerShell (Elevated)

Checkpoint-VM -Name TFS-WIN11 -SnapshotName "Pre-ADCS-Implementation"
```

Once the virtual machine Checkpoints have been created, they can be used to restore the state of the virtual machines later on if there is an issue during the AD CS deployment.

Domain and Workstation Setup - Checkpoints - Restore a Checkpoint

Similar to the creation of the Checkpoints for the two virtual machines related to the TFS Labs domain, the virtual machines should be restored at the same time to ensure that there are no issues. When a virtual machine is restored from a Checkpoint, the default action is to have the virtual machine in a shut down state.

A Checkpoint can be restored with PowerShell by using the **Restore-VMSnapshot** Cmdlet, and it can also be restored using Hyper-V Manager or the Virtual Machine Connection application. Checkpoints are restored and managed on the Hyper-V host, and not on the virtual machine.

To restore a Checkpoint named **Pre-ADCS-Implementation** for the TFS-DC01 server, run the following command from an **elevated PowerShell prompt** on the Hyper-V host where the virtual machine is running:

```
Windows PowerShell (Elevated)

Restore-VMSnapshot -Name "Pre-ADCS-Implementation" -VMName TFS-DC01 -Confirm:$false
```

To restore a Checkpoint named **Pre-ADCS-Implementation** for the TFS-WIN11 workstation, run the following command from an **elevated PowerShell prompt** on the Hyper-V host where the virtual machine is running:

```
Windows PowerShell (Elevated)

Restore-VMSnapshot -Name "Pre-ADCS-Implementation" -VMName TFS-WIN11 -Confirm:$false
```

Once the virtual machines have been restored from their Checkpoints, they will need to be started before they can be used. Factor this is whenever a virtual machine Checkpoint is restored, as it can cause production issues.

Domain and Workstation Setup - Checkpoints - Checkpoint Management

When a Checkpoint is no longer required for a virtual machine, it should be deleted so that it can no longer consume resources on the virtualization host. The process of deleting a Checkpoint will merge the changes into the virtual hard disk of a virtual machine, and this should only be performed if there are no issues.

To delete a Checkpoint named **Pre-ADCS-Implementation** for the TFS-DC01 server, run the following command from an **elevated PowerShell prompt** on the Hyper-V host where the virtual machine is running:

```
Windows PowerShell (Elevated)

Get-VM -Name TFS-DC01 | Get-VMSnapShot -Name "Pre-ADCS-Implementation" | Remove-VMSnapshot
```

To delete a Checkpoint named **Pre-ADCS-Implementation** for the TFS-WIN11 workstation, run the following command from an **elevated PowerShell prompt** on the Hyper-V host where the virtual machine is running:

```
Windows PowerShell (Elevated)

Get-VM -Name TFS-WIN11 | Get-VMSnapShot -Name "Pre-ADCS-Implementation" | Remove-VMSnapshot
```

Maintaining any Checkpoints for virtual machines should always be a priority, and it is bad practice to leave them in place indefinitely.

Domain and Workstation Setup - Chapter Summary

This chapter reviewed the creation of the Active Directory domain that is used for the test environment for the Certificate Authority. Other aspects related to the TFS Labs domain were also covered in this chapter:

- Created the TFS-DC01 virtual machine, which is the Domain Controller for the TFS Labs domain.
- Promoted the TFS-DC01 server to a Domain Controller, and created the TFS Labs domain.
- Created an OU structure for the TFS Labs domain, as well as several test accounts.
- Created the TFS-WIN11 virtual machine, which is a Windows 11 Pro workstation.
- Joined the TFS-WIN11 workstation to the TFS Labs domain for testing purposes.
- Optionally, created Checkpoints for the virtual machines, which can be used to revert back to the end of this chapter if there is an issue with later steps in this book.

In the next chapter the process for creating the Offline Root Certificate Authority will be reviewed. This is a prerequisite for completing the installation of Active Directory Certificates Services (AD CS), since this will be the basis for the TFS Labs Certificate Authority.

Chapter 6 - Offline Root CA Setup

The Root Certificate Authority server is setup as a standalone Windows server and is never meant to be a member of an Active Directory domain. There are no network connections to the Root CA server and there never should be in this type of Two-Tier Certificate Authority setup. There are no domain policies being applied to the server, which means that it will require some local security modifications that are normally handled through Group Policy from Active Directory. Since there are no connections to Active Directory, these Group Policy changes will need to be applied locally and are specific only to this server. These modifications only need to be performed once on the server, as those settings will never be changed and will remain persistent.

Aside from having no network connections to and from the Root Certificate Authority server, there are also additional security considerations that are in place as well. BitLocker full disk encryption can be used to secure the server when it is in an offline state to protect the Root Certificate private keys. Using BitLocker is optional, but the instructions are still provided to enforce greater security for the Root CA server when it is in an offline state.

Moving files to and from the Root Certificate Authority server will be accomplished with the use of a virtual floppy disk. This allows the Offline Root CA to have minimal interaction with other devices within the environment and removes the requirement to have a network connection on that server. There are ways to move these files without using a virtual floppy disk, but those methods are not discussed in this book.

The Root Certificate Authority server should be considered an air gapped server with minimal interactions with other servers, workstations and devices on the network. Keeping the server offline at all times can prevent the PKI from being compromised.

This chapter will focus on how to install and configure an Offline Root CA server using Active Directory Certificate Services. There are several other tasks that are completed in this chapter:

- Configure local security policies to secure the Offline Root CA server.
- Configure auditing on the Offline Root CA server.
- Export the Root CRL, which will be needed for the deployment of the Enterprise CA.
- **Optional:** Configure BitLocker on the Root CA server to ensure that the data cannot be accessed when the virtual machine is offline.
- **Optional:** Create a Checkpoint for the Offline Root CA server to allow for faster testing should there be an issue with the Active Directory Certificate Services deployment.

Once the steps in this chapter have been completed, the necessary infrastructure that is needed to create the Enterprise CA in the next chapter will be in place.

> **DNS and LDAP Configuration**
>
> There are several steps in this chapter that reference specific DNS records and LDAP entries that are dependent on the Active Directory configuration of a particular domain. Ensure that when modifying the steps in this chapter for a different environment that these variables are accounted for. The configuration that is applied in this chapter for another environment will not work as they are specific to the TFS Labs domain.

> **Offline Root CA Configuration**
>
> Creating a Certificate Authority using Active Directory Certificate Services is a complex process, and it is easy to make mistakes when configuring everything. It is important to follow each step correctly, and make sure that steps are not skipped. It is not always possible to go back and fix certain mistakes, and this book will not go into every single potential issue that can occur.

Offline Root CA Setup - Prerequisites

At the end of this chapter there will be a functional Offline Root Certificate Authority for the TFS Labs domain. Similar to the Active Directory configuration, there are no special configurations that need to occur and there is no third-party software required to create the Root Certificate Authority. Since the Root Certificate Authority is offline, there is no interaction with any of the other virtual machines created so far. This will occur in later chapters in this book, but it will only require small files to be transferred with the use of a virtual floppy disk. There are no network connections at all on the Offline Root CA, and that is to keep the PKI as secure as possible.

An important aspect of this chapter, and the book as a whole is to keep the Offline Root CA as isolated as possible. To facilitate this, there are several considerations being taken to accommodate this:

- No network adapters will be available on the Root CA. It is not enough that a network adapter is disabled or not connected to a network, it is safer for the Root CA server to not have one available at all.
- A virtual floppy drive will be used on the virtual machine.
- The local accounts on the Root CA server will be reconfigured to not be the default account names.
- Local security policies will be configured to enhance security on the server. Group Policy from Active Directory is not available since the Root CA server is not connected to the network, so this will be configured locally.
- Optionally, BitLocker will be enabled on the Root CA server to ensure that the data cannot be accessed when the virtual machine is offline.

Unlike the other virtual machines in this book, this server will have a local administrator account and will not use Active Directory. This password will need to be documented as it is used whenever the Root CRL needs to be renewed, or the Root certificate needs to be renewed. Both of these tasks happen infrequently, and it is important to ensure that access to the Root CA server is not lost when it is needed.

> **ℹ️ Hyper-V and Other Virtualization Solutions**
>
> There are many references in this chapter that are specific to Hyper-V and how it is used to host the virtual machine for the Root CA server. There are equivalent features in other virtualization solutions, and those features should be used whenever possible for the purposes of keeping the Root CA isolated from the rest of the network.

Offline Root CA Setup - Installation and Configuration

The Windows server that is hosting the Root Certificate Authority requires minimal resources to operate correctly, as it only performs basic tasks and is not used for regular day-to-day activities. It will only to ever be used for issuing any Subordinate certificates to other TFS Labs Certificate Authority servers and is also used to revoke or add new Subordinate certificates if necessary. The Root CA will be used to refresh the Base CRL at least once a year to keep the PKI working correctly, since the CRL is required for all components of a PKI. The Root Certificate Authority server for the TFS Labs domain will be called TFS-ROOT-CA. There are several steps that need to be completed to create the virtual machine that will be used for the Root CA server for the **corp.tfslabs.com** domain:

- Provision a virtual machine for the TFS-ROOT-CA server using Hyper-V and ensure it has no network adapters associated with the virtual machine.
- Install Windows Server 2022 Standard (Desktop Experience) on the virtual machine.
- Configure the local administrator password, hostname, and the workgroup of the TFS-ROOT-CA server.
- Disable the shared virtualization features on the virtual machine to enhance security.
- Disable the Windows Update service on the TFS-ROOT-CA server.
- Configure the storage locations for certificate files and the virtual floppy disk.
- **Optional:** Configure the TFS-ROOT-CA server to use BitLocker.

Since there are no active network connections to and from the TFS-ROOT-CA virtual machine due to the lack of a network adapter, a virtual floppy disk will need to be created for transferring files to and from the TFS-ROOT-CA server.

The virtual floppy disk will be used several times during the Certificate Authority implementation. In this book, the virtual floppy disk that is used is called **RootCAFiles.vfd** and it is stored it in a location that is available for all virtual machines that require it. This virtual floppy disk will be required until the end of the Certificate Authority implementation, and can be recreated as needed in the future for maintenance tasks such as CRL renewal. Instructions on how to create his virtual floppy disk is provided in an earlier chapter.

> **Virtual Floppy Disks and File Transfers**
>
> This book uses virtual floppy disks to transfer files between the Root CA server and the other servers involved in the Certificate Authority implementation. There are other methods that can be used for moving files between servers without network connections, but the security of those methods is not guaranteed. The process for moving files with tools available with certain virtualization platforms are not covered in this book.

The TFS-ROOT-CA virtual machine will have the following specifications:

Virtual Machine Generation	1
Virtual Processors	2
Virtual Memory	4 GB (4096 MB)
Virtual Hard Disk	40 GB
Virtual Network Adapters	0

Table 6.2.1: Virtual machine specifications for the TFS-ROOT-CA server.

Unlike other servers and workstations being used for the TFS Labs test environment, there are no network settings to configure on the virtual machine since there is no network connectivity on the TFS-ROOT-CA server.

> **Offline Root CA Server and Network Adapters**
>
> It is not enough to disable an unused network adapter on the virtual machine that is used for the Offline Root CA server, there should be no network adapters available at all. By removing the network adapter from the virtual machine, there is no chance of it being accidentally connected to the network.
>
> The steps for creating the virtual machine for the Offline Root CA server removes the network adapter before the installation of Windows Server 2022 occurs.

Offline Root CA Setup - Installation and Configuration - Virtual Machine Setup

To create a Hyper-V virtual machine for the TFS-ROOT-CA server using the command line, open an **elevated PowerShell prompt** and run the following commands on the Hyper-V host:

1. Create the **TFS-ROOT-CA** virtual machine and virtual hard disk using the **New-VM** Cmdlet:

```
Windows PowerShell (Elevated)

New-VM `
-Name "TFS-ROOT-CA" `
-Generation 1 `
-MemoryStartupBytes 4GB `
-BootDevice VHD `
-NewVHDPath "D:\Hyper-V\Virtual Hard Disks\TFS-ROOT-CA.vhdx" `
-NewVHDSizeBytes 40GB
```

2. Set the number of virtual processors for the **TFS-ROOT-CA** virtual machine to **2** using the **Set-VMProcessor** Cmdlet:

```
Windows PowerShell (Elevated)

Set-VMProcessor "TFS-ROOT-CA" -Count 2
```

3. Mount the ISO image that will be used to install the operating system on the **TFS-ROOT-CA** virtual machine using the **Set-VMDvdDrive** Cmdlet:

```
Windows PowerShell (Elevated)

Set-VMDvdDrive `
-VMName "TFS-ROOT-CA" `
-Path "D:\ISO Images\Windows Server 2022.iso"
```

4. Remove the network adapter on the **TFS-ROOT-CA** virtual machine using the **Remove-VMNetworkAdapter** Cmdlet:

```
Windows PowerShell (Elevated)

Remove-VMNetworkAdapter -VMName "TFS-ROOT-CA" -VMNetworkAdapterName "Network Adapter"
```

5. Power on the **TFS-ROOT-CA** virtual machine using the **Start-VM** Cmdlet:

```
Windows PowerShell (Elevated)

Start-VM -Name "TFS-ROOT-CA"
```

6. Connect to the **TFS-ROOT-CA** virtual machine using the **Virtual Machine Connection** application:

```
Windows PowerShell (Elevated)

vmconnect.exe localhost "TFS-ROOT-CA"
```

Alternatively, the TFS-ROOT-CA virtual server can be created and configured without using PowerShell by using Hyper-V Manager instead (ensure that after the virtual machine is created that the configuration is modified as needed). Only one method is required to create the virtual machine for the TFS-ROOT-CA virtual machine.

Regardless of which method is used to create the virtual machine, Windows Server 2022 can be installed normally with all default options. In this book, **Windows Server 2022 Standard (Desktop Experience)** is the version that all servers will use. When the installation of Windows Server 2022 has successfully completed, the first step is to configure the local administrator password for the TFS-ROOT-CA server. This step occurs automatically before the server can be logged into, and is the first screen that is displayed after the successful installation of Windows Server 2022.

> ⚠️ **Root Certificate Authority Local Administrator Account Password**
>
> The local administrator account that is used during the initial setup of the TFS-ROOT-CA server will be required for all administrative tasks on the server. This server will not be connected to the TFS Labs domain, so any of the user accounts on the domain cannot be used on the TFS-ROOT-CA server. In a step later in this section the local administrator account will be renamed for security purposes. Ensure that the password for the local administrator account is properly documented and is a complex password.

When the local administrator account password has been set, login to the server using the new password. Renaming a Windows server can be performed using the command line with the **Rename-Computer** Cmdlet and this should be the first task performed on the server before continuing. Alternatively, the hostname can be configured using the Server Manager console in the Local Server configuration section.

To configure the hostname of the server using the command line, open an **elevated PowerShell prompt** and run the following command on the TFS-ROOT-CA server:

```
Windows PowerShell (Elevated)

Rename-Computer "TFS-ROOT-CA" -Restart
```

The command will automatically restart the server to apply the hostname change. Once the server has been restarted, the workgroup of the server will need to be changed from the default name. This can be done using the command line with the **Add-Computer** Cmdlet. Alternatively, the workgroup can be configured using the Server Manager console in the Local Server configuration section.

To configure the workgroup of the server using the command line, open an **elevated PowerShell prompt** and run the following command on the TFS-ROOT-CA server:

```
Windows PowerShell (Elevated)

Add-Computer -WorkgroupName "TFS-CA" -Restart
```

The command will automatically restart the server to apply the workgroup name change. Once the restart has been completed, there are still a few remaining tasks that need to be completed prior to installing and configuring Active Directory Certificate Services on the Root CA server. Proceed to disabling Hyper-V virtualization features on the TFS-ROOT-CA server in the next section.

Offline Root CA Setup - Installation and Configuration - Disable Virtualization Features

When provisioning the TFS-ROOT-CA server, features that allow for easily copying files to and from the virtual machine from the Hyper-V host using the Virtual Machine Connection application should be disabled. These features offer a convenient option for moving files to and from virtual machines, but it can compromise the security of a virtual machine in certain situations. This includes the shared clipboard feature that is available for copying and pasting text between virtual machines. Even though disabling these features can make dealing with the TFS-ROOT-CA somewhat cumbersome during the implementation and configuration phase, the added security features are worth it to protect the Root Certificate Authority from threats. The Offline Root CA is dealt with so infrequently after it has been setup and configured that it should not be an issue.

Normally when interacting with a virtual machine running Windows, the Remote Desktop application would be used to connect to it. However, since there are no network connections enabled on the TFS-ROOT-CA server, the option for connecting with RDP is not available. The Virtual Machine Connection application can be used to connect directly to virtual machines locally on a Hyper-V host, or remotely if necessary. This application will need to be restricted to ensure the security of the Root Certificate Authority server. The **Guest Services** and **Enhanced Session Mode** features should be disabled when interacting with the TFS-ROOT-CA server.

The first step to disabling these virtualization features should be to ensure that **Guest Services** is disabled on the TFS-ROOT-CA virtual machine. This feature should already be disabled as it is not commonly used on modern versions of Hyper-V, but the option is still available. This setting is specifically applied to particular virtual machines and can be configured using the **Disable-VMIntegrationService** Cmdlet, or with Hyper-V Manager. Only one method is required to change the configuration option, there is no need to configure the option more than once.

To ensure that the **Guest services** integration feature is disabled, open an **elevated PowerShell prompt** and run the following command on the Hyper-V host:

```
Windows PowerShell (Elevated)

Disable-VMIntegrationService -VMName "TFS-ROOT-CA" -Name "Guest Service Interface"
```

The Virtual Machine Connection application supports two operational modes, **Basic Session Mode** and **Enhanced Session Mode**. Basic Session Mode provides a simple connection to a virtual machine, limited to mouse and keyboard input as well as basic graphics options. Enhanced Session Mode offers a better experience when connecting to a virtual machine, similar to an RDP connection. Enhanced Session Mode adds the following functionality to the Virtual Machine Connection application:

- Allows for file sharing with copy and pasting within virtual machines.
- Access to local drives, and Plug and Play devices, printers, Smart Cards, and USB devices.
- Allows for resizable screens in the Virtual Machine Connection application (if the virtual machine supports it).
- Improved remote audio recording and playback capabilities.
- Shared clipboard access between the host machine and the virtual machine.

When connecting to the TFS-ROOT-CA virtual machine, Enhanced Session Mode should not be used with the Virtual Machine Connection application. The Enhanced Session Mode feature is enabled or disabled on the Hyper-V host server, and cannot be explicitly enabled or disabled for a particular virtual machine. When connecting to a virtual machine with the Virtual Machine Connection application, the option to use Enhanced Session Mode is shown to the user if it is supported:

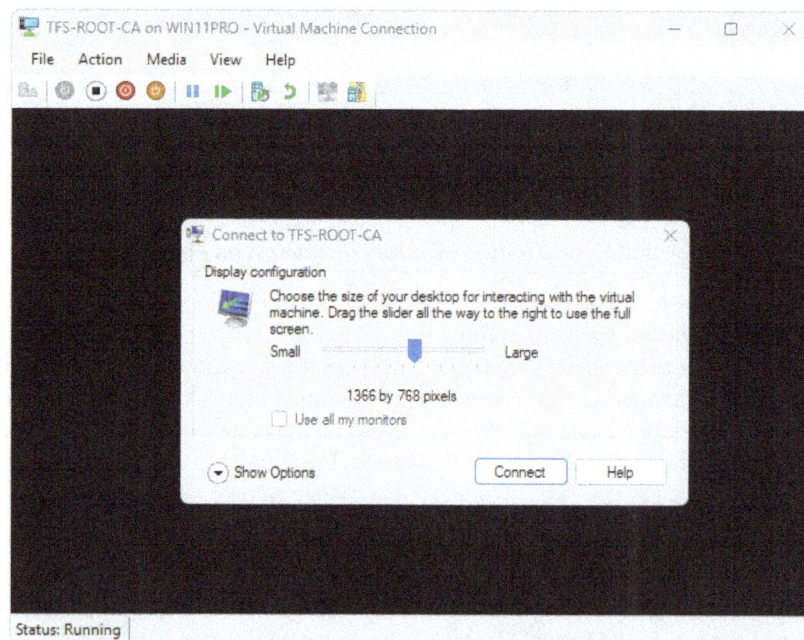

Figure 6.2.2.1: If a virtual machine supports Enhanced Session Mode, the Connect window will appear when connecting to the VMConnect application. Clicking the **X** in the upper-right corner of the window will disable Enhanced Session Mode and force Basic Session Mode to be used instead.

By closing the window without clicking the **Connect** button, Enhanced Session Mode will be disabled in the Virtual Machine Connection application for that particular session. This will need to be performed every time a new connection is made to the TFS-ROOT-CA virtual machine. Enhanced Session Mode can also be disabled in the Virtual Machine Connection application by going to the **View** menu, and disabling the **Enhanced session** option.

> **Hyper-V and Shared Clipboard Access**
>
> The shared clipboard feature with Hyper-V is a convenient feature for performing some of the steps in this book, as there is a lot of text to input to configure the Root CA server. To paste text into the TFS-ROOT-CA server with the Virtual Machine Connection application, go to the **Clipboard** menu and select the **Type clipboard text** option.

Other Virtualization Platform Shared Features

If Hyper-V is used for the virtualization platform, the settings for disabling certain virtualization features are easy to access and configure. If other solutions such as VMware Workstation is used, this setting can be disabled in the **Guest Isolation** settings. For every other virtualization platform, there should be a way to disable those features as well, but those steps are beyond the scope of this book.

Enhanced Session Mode and Production Hyper-V Servers

The **Enhanced Session Mode** feature is useful with Hyper-V, but it is only applicable when accessing virtual machines locally on a Hyper-V server. In a test environment it may be common to use the Virtual Machine Connection application to interact with virtual machines for convenience purposes, but in a production environment this is most likely not the case. Remote Desktop is most commonly used for accessing virtual machines in a Windows environment.

It is advisable to disable **Enhanced Session Mode** on production Hyper-V servers as it is not needed, and reduces that attack surface on virtual machines. This is a system-wide setting, and will be applied to all virtual machines on that particular Hyper-V host.

Once the Hyper-V virtualization features have been disabled, proceed to disabling Windows Update on the TFS-ROOT-CA server.

Offline Root CA Setup - Installation and Configuration - Disable Windows Update

Since the TFS-ROOT-CA server is always in an offline state due to the lack of network adapters on the virtual machine, there is no way for the server to ever connect to the Windows Update service and install any updates for the operating system. This should not be an issue since the Offline Root CA server is never intended to be used for anything other than various Certificate Authority maintenance tasks, and is not meant to be used for extended periods of time. It is possible to manually install critical updates to the server by utilizing offline installers for the updates and copying them to the virtual machine, but that should not be necessary unless it is for a specific reason.

Making changes to the Offline Root CA server should be avoided whenever possible, and installing updates can sometimes cause unintended consequences that can be difficult to correct. An update can easily break functionality in certain Windows services and reversing these changes is not trivial, especially with AD CS and AD DS. Disabling Windows Update is only a minor configuration change to the Offline Root CA server and it will not cause any issues. Since the TFS-ROOT-CA server is never connected to a network, disabling the Windows Update service mostly prevents unnecessary notifications which cannot be actioned anyways. There are multiple methods that can be used for disabling the Windows Update service on a Windows host, but two methods can be quickly used on the TFS-ROOT-CA server to accomplish this:

- Disable the Windows Update service in the Services console.
- Use the **SConfig** utility to disable Windows Update, which is used to manage Windows Server functions from the command line.

Only one of these methods is needed to disable Windows Update, there is no need to use both methods. To disable the Windows Update service using the Services console, perform the following steps on the TFS-ROOT-CA server:

1. Open the **Services** console (services.msc) on the **TFS-ROOT-CA** server.
2. Search for the **Windows Update** service. Right-click on the service and select the **Stop** option.
3. Right-click on the **Windows Update** service and select the **Properties** option.
4. On the **Windows Update Properties (Local Computer)** window, click on the **General** tab.
5. Go to the **Startup type** drop-down list and select the **Disabled** option.
6. Click the **OK** button to close the window.
7. Close the **Services** console.

To disable the Windows Update service using the SConfig utility, perform the following steps on the TFS-ROOT-CA server:

1. Open an **elevated PowerShell prompt**.
2. Run the following command to start the **SConfig** utility:

```
Windows PowerShell (Elevated)

SConfig.cmd
```

3. If a warning message about **No active network adapters found** is displayed, click the **OK** button to continue. The **Server Configuration** screen should then be displayed:

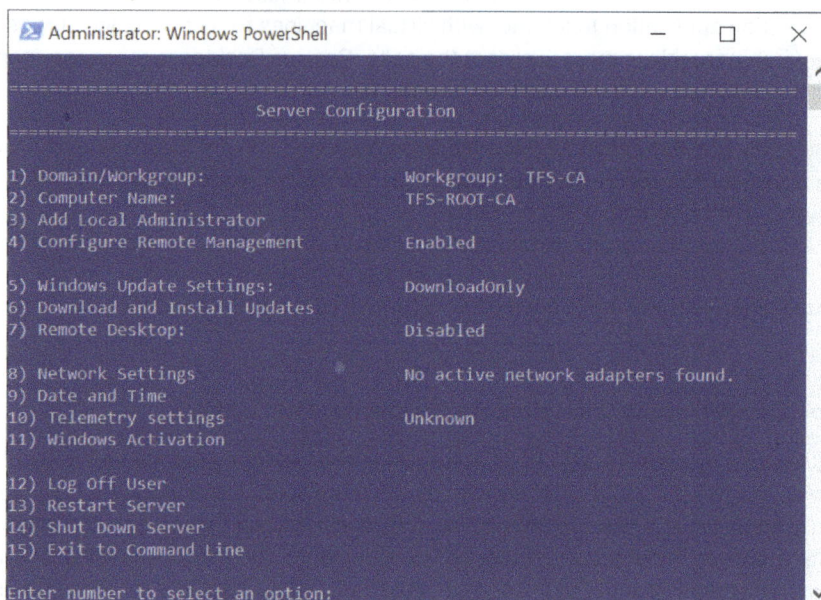

4. On the **Server Configuration** screen, select option **5** and press **Enter** to configure the **Windows Update Settings**.
5. When prompted to configure the **Windows Update Settings**, select option **M** and press **Enter** to set the option to manual:

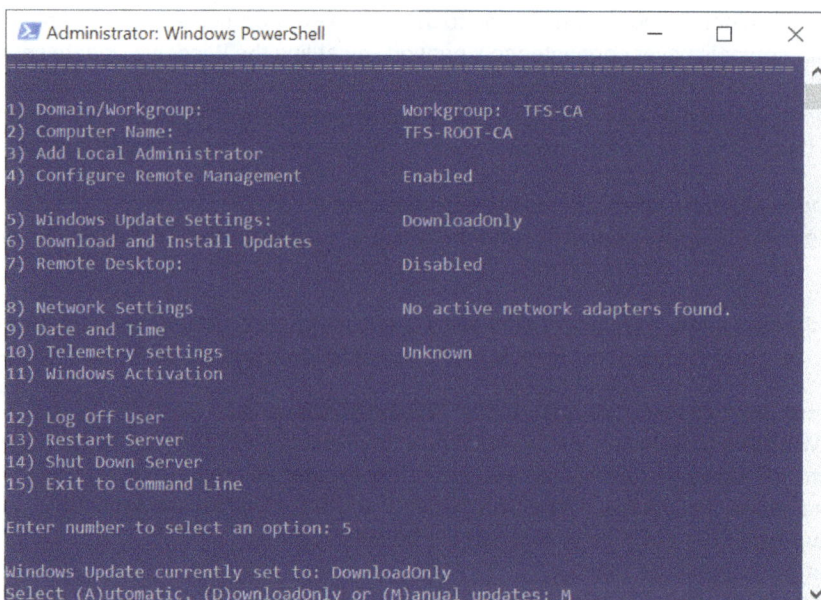

6. When the **Update Settings** message appears, click the **OK** button.
7. The **Windows Update Settings** should now be set to **Manual**:

8. Select option **15** and press **Enter** to close the **Sconfig** utility.
9. Close the **PowerShell prompt**.

Regardless of which method is used to disable the Windows Update service, performing this action can reduce potential issues in the future for the TFS-ROOT-CA server. Proceed to creating the virtual floppy disk for the TFS-ROOT-CA server in the next section.

Offline Root CA Setup - Installation and Configuration - Configure Storage and Virtual Floppy Disk

There are several steps that need to be performed to facilitate the transfer of files to and from the Root Certificate Authority server and the server that will eventually be used to host the Subordinate Certificate Authority server. Centralizing these files into a single location will ensure that they are properly tracked and accounted for, and will reduce the need to find those files in the future should they be required. The virtual floppy disk that is used to move files between those servers will also be created and formatted, as it will be required it later steps in this book. In this section the following items will be configured:

- Configure a folder on the TFS-ROOT-CA server where any Certificate Authority files will be stored during the implementation process. This folder can also be used for future PKI tasks, including CRL updates that will need to be performed.
- Create a virtual floppy disk on the Hyper-V host server which will be used for file transfers.
- Insert the virtual floppy disk on the TFS-ROOT-CA server and format the virtual floppy disk.

On the TFS-ROOT-CA server, create a folder on the root of the **C:\ drive** called **RootCA** (C:\RootCA). This folder will store the Root certificate, Subordinate certificate, CRL files and any other certificate files that are needed during the entire Certificate Authority implementation process. This folder will persist after the Certificate Authority has been created as it will be used in future maintenance tasks.

> ℹ **Virtual Floppy Disk Location**
> The location for the virtual floppy disk can vary and will always be located on the virtualization host system that is hosting the TFS Labs environment. Ensure that wherever the virtual floppy disk is located that it is accessible from the TFS-ROOT-CA (Root CA) and TFS-CA01 (Subordinate CA) servers. The virtual floppy disk will be deleted at the end of the Certificate Authority implementation.

There are several ways to create a virtual floppy disk on a Hyper-V host, but the fastest method is to use PowerShell. To create a virtual floppy disk using PowerShell, use the **New-VFD** Cmdlet from an **elevated PowerShell prompt** on the Hyper-V host:

```
Windows PowerShell (Elevated)

New-VFD "D:\Hyper-V\Virtual Floppy Disks\RootCAFiles.vfd"
```

To add the virtual floppy disk to the TFS-ROOT-CA virtual machine with PowerShell, use the **Set-VMFloppyDiskDrive** Cmdlet from an **elevated PowerShell prompt** on the Hyper-V host:

```
Windows PowerShell (Elevated)

Set-VMFloppyDiskDrive `
-VMName "TFS-ROOT-CA" `
-Path "D:\Hyper-V\Virtual Floppy Disks\RootCAFiles.vfd"
```

Once the virtual floppy disk has been added it will need to be formatted before it can used. There is no way to format a virtual floppy disk directly on a Hyper-V host without using third-party software, but it can be formatted on a virtual machine that supports virtual floppy disks. To format the virtual floppy disk, use the **format.exe** command from an **elevated Command Prompt** on the TFS-ROOT-CA server:

```
Command Prompt (Elevated)

format.exe A:
```

Removing a virtual floppy disk from a virtual machine can be done using the **Set-VMFloppyDiskDrive** Cmdlet from an **elevated PowerShell prompt** on the Hyper-V host:

```
Windows PowerShell (Elevated)

Set-VMFloppyDiskDrive -VMName "TFS-ROOT-CA" -Path $null
```

Once the virtual floppy disk has been created and formatted, it can then be used for further steps in this book. To recreate the virtual floppy disk in the future, the same steps can be used. Proceed to installing BitLocker on the TFS-ROOT-CA server in the next section.

Offline Root CA Setup - Installation and Configuration - Install BitLocker

One of the steps that should be taken on the Root Certificate Authority server before starting the configuration of Active Directory Certificate Services is to install, enable, and test the BitLocker feature. BitLocker is a full disk encryption solution that is available in Windows Server and some Windows client versions. BitLocker can fully encrypt the contents of a virtual hard disk while it is offline to keep it protected. This is critical for a Root Certificate Authority since without disk encryption the virtual hard disk could be opened and the private key could be compromised.

> ⚠️ **Test Environment and BitLocker Encryption Requirement**
>
> Encrypting the virtual hard disk for the Offline Root Certificate Authority server is entirely optional and this section can be skipped if it is not required in a particular environment. Encrypting the virtual hard disk for the TFS-ROOT-CA server does not affect the functionality of the server.

Even though this section is entirely optional, there are a few reasons why BitLocker should be used to encrypt and secure the TFS-ROOT-CA server:

- The information that is stored on the TFS-ROOT-CA server will be secure when the server is in an offline state. This is important since the virtual machine may be stored elsewhere and this will prevent users from accessing the virtual hard drive.
- BitLocker is a native feature in Windows Server, so there is no cost associated with using BitLocker since it is already part of the operating system. Since BitLocker is a native feature in Windows Server, there is no concern about using third-party encryption software that may require additional licensing or fees to use it.
- BitLocker is easily supported with virtualization software.
- BitLocker does not require any additional dependencies to operate and can be used without any outside software or services. It is available by default and does not require any downloads to enable the feature.

Using BitLocker to encrypt the TFS-ROOT-CA server is a reliable and effective way to protect the data on that server to ensure that the Root Certificate Authority is secure.

Third-Party Full Disk Encryption Applications

Typically, in a production environment there should be a managed full disk encryption solution in place to manage the encryption and unlocking of encrypted disks, as well as managing recovering keys if there is an issue. In the case of the Root CA server, it is recommended to avoid those types of third-party solutions for an Offline Root CA to reduce the need for extra third-party software on the server. These encryption solutions typically require network connectivity, and that is not available on the TFS-ROOT-CA server. Encryption solutions can also change over time, and can cause compatibility issues in the future.

BitLocker Encryption Verification

It may seem as though enabling BitLocker should be one of the last tasks performed in the Certificate Authority implementation process, but the reason that it is advisable to enable and test BitLocker at this stage is to ensure that there are no issues with it.

If BitLocker is enabled after creating the Root CA and there is an issue, it is possible that access the Root CA is permanently lost and the entire process will need to be restarted.

If BitLocker is used to secure the TFS-ROOT-CA server, these steps must be performed to add the BitLocker feature to the TFS-ROOT-CA server. The BitLocker feature can be installed using the command line with PowerShell, or with the Server Manager console. Only one method is required for installing the BitLocker Drive Encryption feature on the TFS-ROOT-CA server.

Offline Root CA Setup - Installation and Configuration - Install BitLocker - CLI Installation

The BitLocker Drive Encryption feature installation can be performed using PowerShell, which requires much fewer steps to accomplish. Perform the following steps on the TFS-ROOT-CA server:

1. Open an **elevated PowerShell prompt**.
2. Run the following command to install the **BitLocker Drive Encryption** feature, which will also install the necessary **BitLocker Administration Tools** using the **Install-WindowsFeature** Cmdlet:

```
Windows PowerShell (Elevated)

Install-WindowsFeature BitLocker `
-IncludeAllSubFeature `
-IncludeManagementTools `
-Restart
```

3. The command will install the **BitLocker Drive Encryption** feature and output a **Success** status of **True**:

4. Once the installation has completed, the **TFS-ROOT-CA** server will automatically restart.

The TFS-ROOT-CA server should automatically restart once the BitLocker feature has been installed (restart the server manually if it does not restart automatically). Once the server has restarted, it will require some additional configuration to allow BitLocker to be enabled.

Offline Root CA Setup - Installation and Configuration - Install BitLocker - GUI Installation

To perform the BitLocker Drive Encryption installation using the Server Manager console, perform the following steps on the TFS-ROOT-CA server:

1. Open the **Server Manager** console (servermanager.exe), click on the **Manage** menu, and click on **Add Roles and Features** to start the installation wizard:

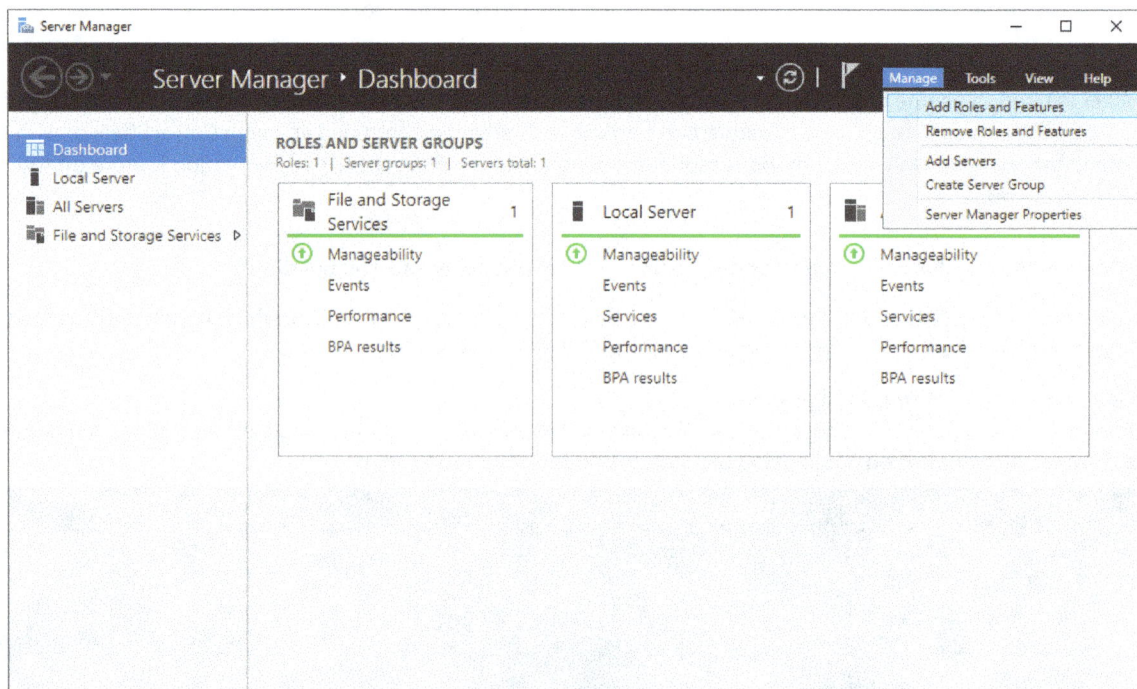

2. On the **Before you begin** screen, click the **Next** button to continue:

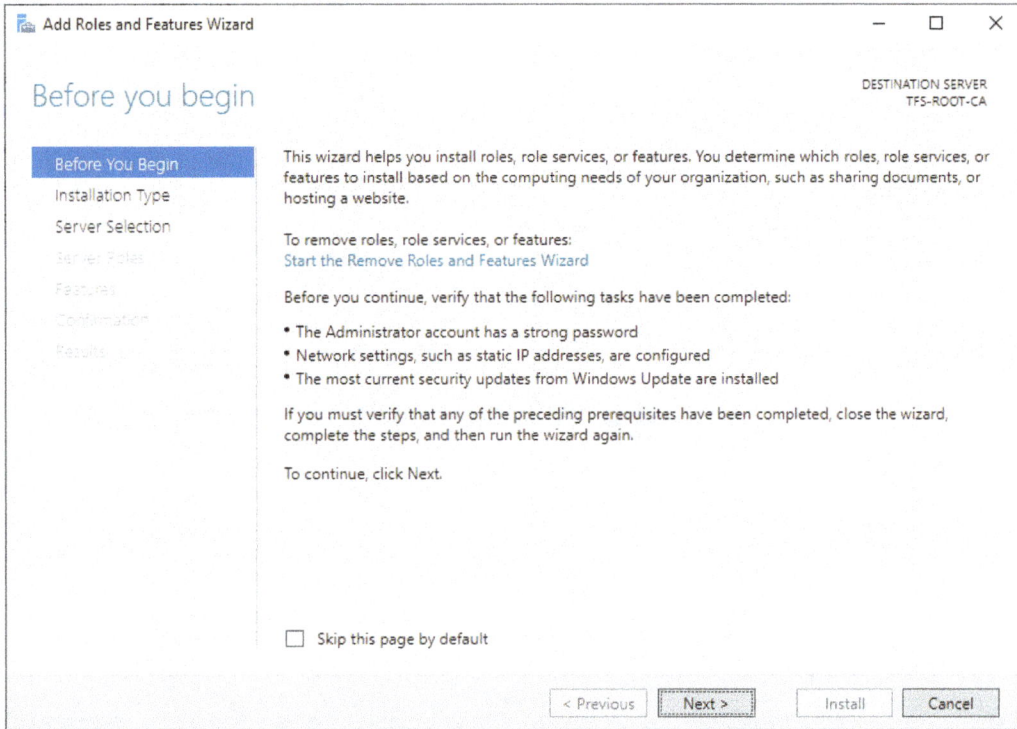

3. On the **Select installation type** screen, select the option for **Role-based or feature-based installation** and click the **Next** button to continue:

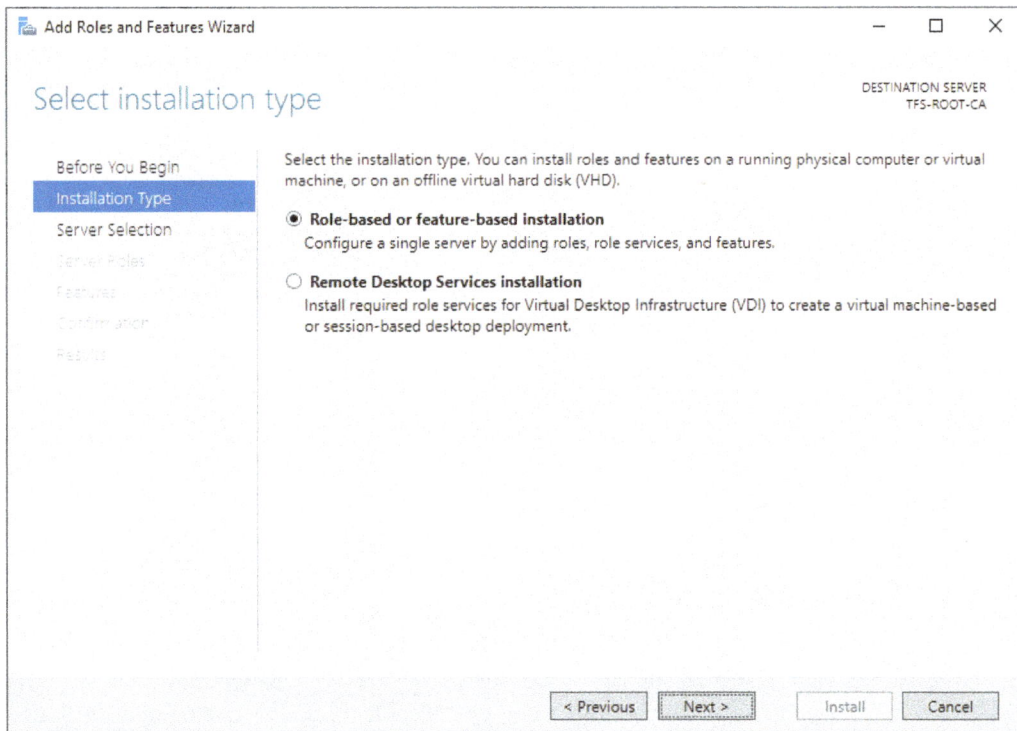

4. On the **Select destination server** screen, verify that the **TFS-ROOT-CA** server is selected and click the **Next** button to continue:

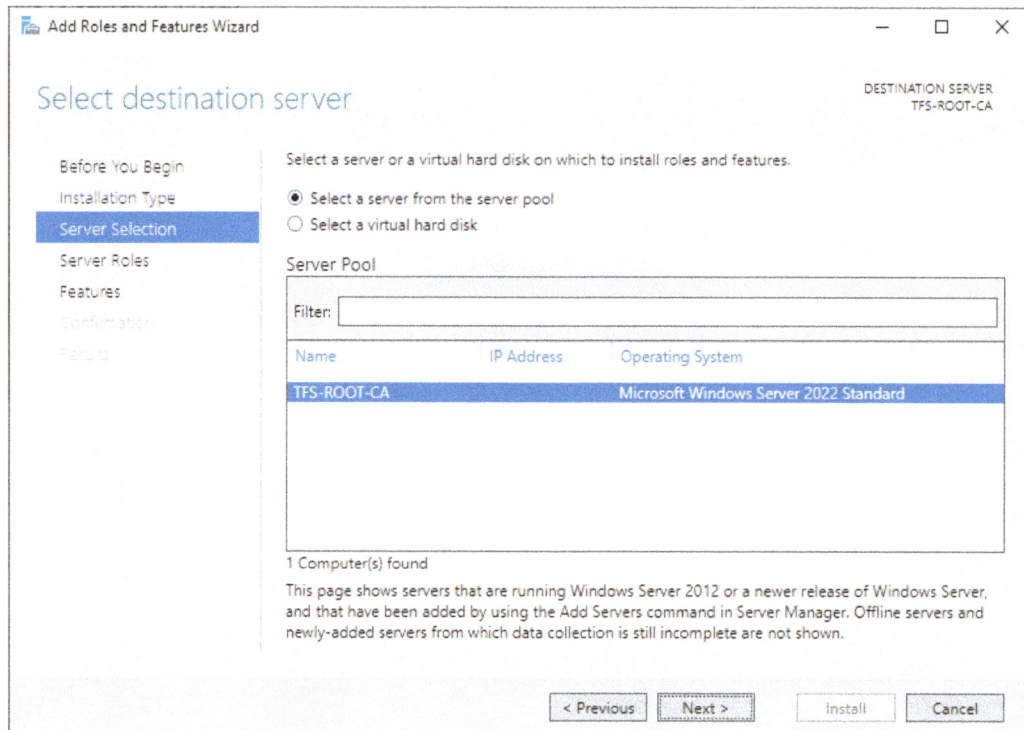

5. On the **Select server roles** screen, click the **Next** button to continue:

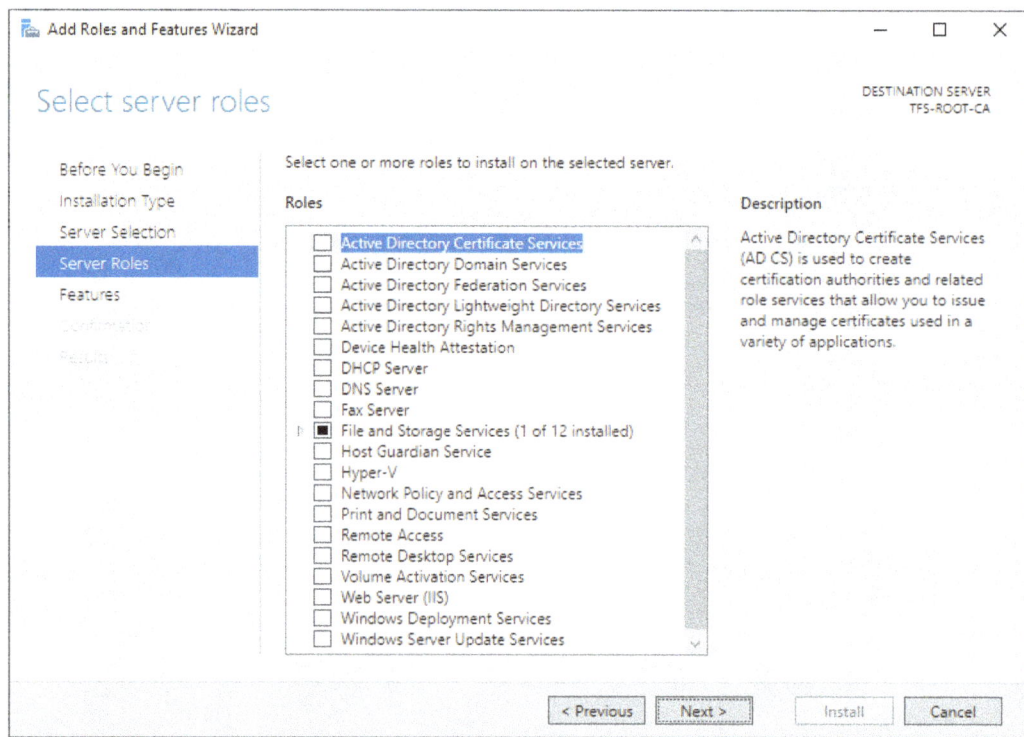

6. On the **Select features** screen, select the **BitLocker Drive Encryption** feature:

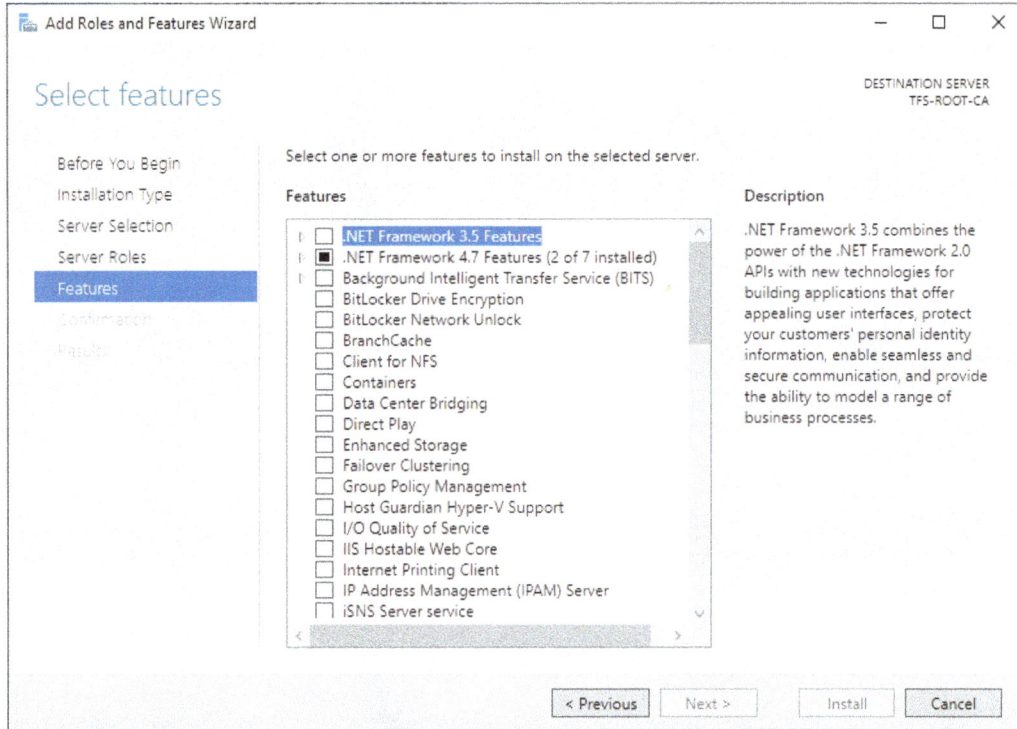

7. The installation wizard will ask to install any additional features required for the **BitLocker Drive Encryption** feature. Select the option to **Include management tools (if applicable)** to install the management tools for the role. Click the **Add Features** button to continue.

8. On the **Select features** screen, click the **Next** button to continue:

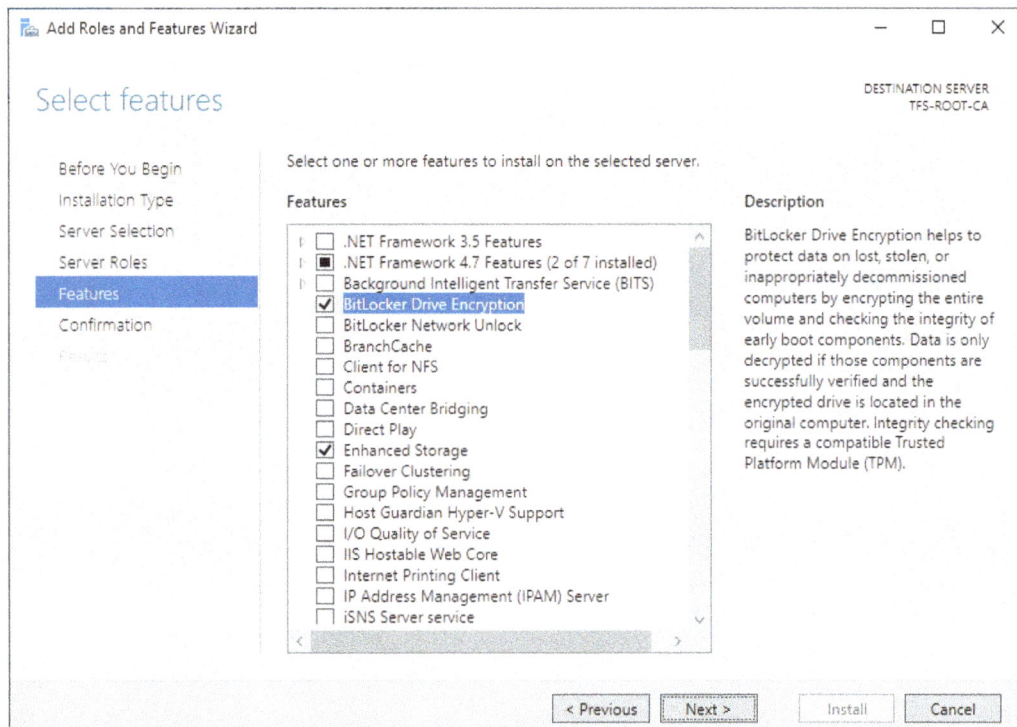

9. On the **Confirm installation selections** screen, select the option to **Restart the destination server automatically if required**:

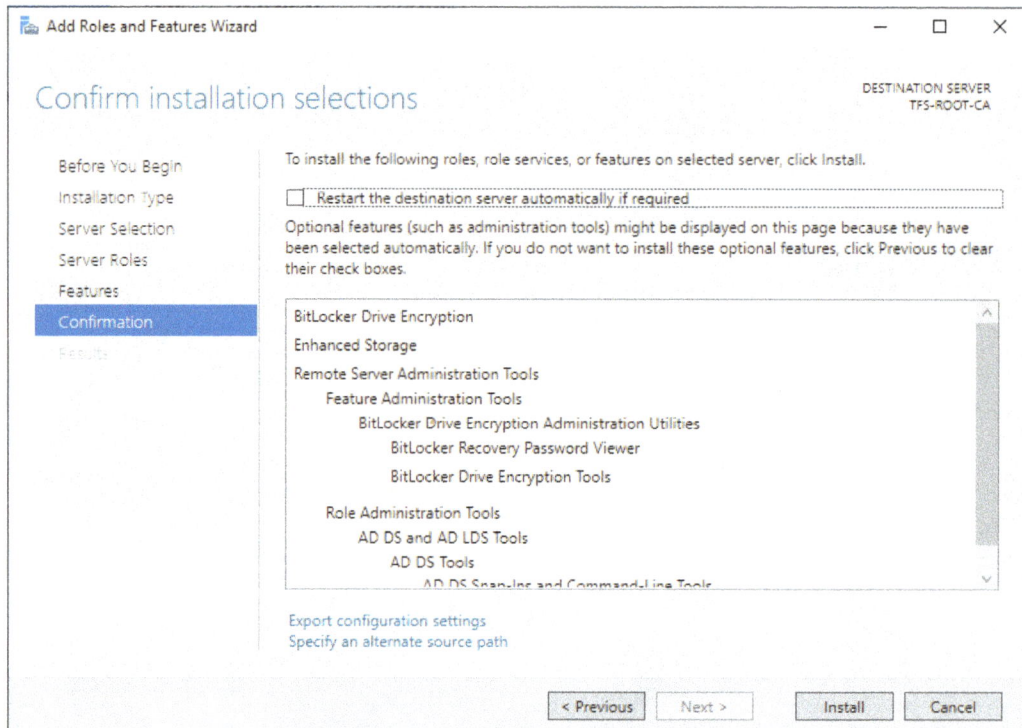

10. When prompted with a warning about restarting the server, click the **Yes** button.
11. On the **Confirm installation selections** screen, click the **Install** button to continue:

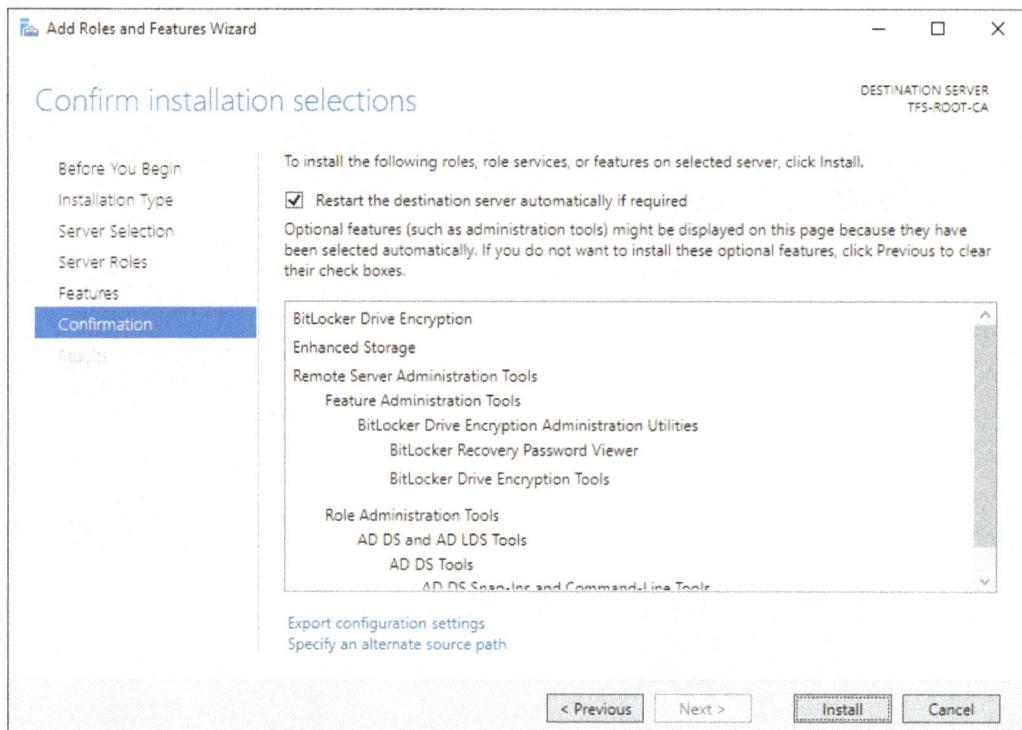

12. Once the installation is completed, click the **Close** button:

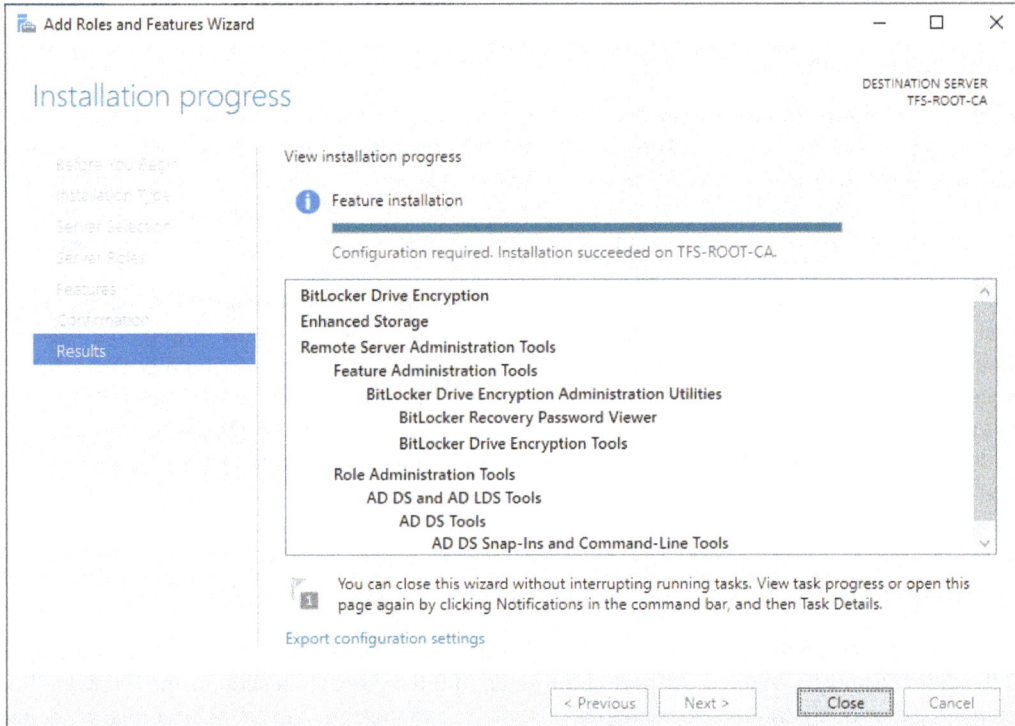

The TFS-ROOT-CA server should automatically restart once the BitLocker feature has been installed (restart the server manually if it does not restart automatically). Once restarted, additional configuration to the TFS-ROOT-CA server is required to allow BitLocker to be enabled.

Offline Root CA Setup - Installation and Configuration - Configure BitLocker Group Policy

Once the BitLocker feature has been successfully installed there are several Group Policy settings that need to be configured to allow for enabling a BitLocker startup password on the TFS-ROOT-CA server. These changes are required to allow for the activation of BitLocker without a proper TPM device present. Virtualization platforms do not always emulate a valid TPM device, so changes to the Group Policy settings are required to allow for BitLocker to be successfully enabled in those situations.

To configure the appropriate Group Policy settings for BitLocker, perform the following steps on the TFS-ROOT-CA server:

1. Open the **Local Group Policy Editor** console (gpedit.msc) on the **TFS-ROOT-CA** server.
2. Open the **Computer Configuration > Administrative Templates > Windows Components > BitLocker Drive Encryption > Operating System Drives** policy settings.
3. Double-click on the **Require additional authentication at startup** policy setting.
4. Make the following changes to the Policy Setting and apply the settings:
   (a) **Require additional authentication at startup** - Enabled
   (b) **Allow BitLocker without a compatible TPM (requires a password or a startup key on a USB flash drive)** - Enabled
   (c) **Configure TPM startup:** Allow TPM
   (d) **Configure TPM startup PIN:** Allow startup PIN with TPM
   (e) **Configure TPM startup key:** Allow startup key with TPM
   (f) **Configure TPM startup key and PIN:** Allow startup key and PIN with TPM
5. Close the **Local Group Policy Editor** window.
6. Restart the **TFS-ROOT-CA** server to ensure that the **Local Group Policy** settings have been successfully applied.

Ensure that the TFS-ROOT-CA server has been restarted before attempting to enable BitLocker on the server, otherwise the setup process will not complete successfully in the next step of the process.

Trusted Platform Module

The Trusted Platform Module is a physical chip that is present on most computers that have been manufactured in the last 10 years. The purpose of the TPM chip is to provide a hardware encryption device that is made available to the operating system. The most common application of the TPM is to allow for full disk encryption with solutions such as BitLocker using the Windows operating system. The TPM can also be used with other encryption software on different operating systems such as Linux.

The issue with requiring TPM by default with BitLocker is that it does not always work correctly with virtual machines since the TPM is difficult to emulate. This also means that by relying on a TPM from one device means that portability of the virtual machine would be affected. It is recommended to just disable the checking of a TPM when enabling BitLocker. Hyper-V Generation 1 virtual machines also do not emulate a TPM, which is the type of virtual machine required for the TFS-ROOT-CA server. Modern versions of virtualization platforms provide alternatives to make the TPM emulation easier to accomplish, so this is something to consider as time goes on.

Offline Root CA Setup - Installation and Configuration - Enable BitLocker

Once the BitLocker feature has been added to the TFS-ROOT-CA server, and the Local Group Policy settings have been configured, BitLocker can now be enabled. As part of the setup of BitLocker in this section, the BitLocker Recovery Key will be backed up to a previously created virtual floppy disk which can then be backed up later to another server. BitLocker can be enabled using the command line using PowerShell, and it can also be enabled through the BitLocker Drive Encryption management console. Only one method is required for enabling BitLocker, there is no need to use both methods on the TFS-ROOT-CA server.

BitLocker Key Terminology

There are several components to a BitLocker encrypted drive that may be referenced in this section:

- **BitLocker Encryption Key** - This is the encryption key that is created by Windows to encrypt the data stored on a drive. It will vary depending on the type of system, and the particular encryption options that are available at the time of encryption.
- **BitLocker Key ID** - This is a 32-digit unique alphanumeric identifier that is associated with a BitLocker Recovery Key. It is used to associate a BitLocker Recovery Key with a specific drive. Without this identifier, it would be difficult to know the correct key if there are multiple BitLocker drives that needs to be recovered.
- **BitLocker Recovery Key** - This is a 48-digit numerical key that can be used to unlock a BitLocker drive if there is an issue with accessing the drive. This can happen for multiple reasons, and this key can always be used to unlock a drive if there is an issue.

When a drive is encrypted using BitLocker, it is critical that the BitLocker Recovery Key is backed up.

BitLocker Recovery Key Backup

It is important to not misplace the BitLocker Recovery Key for the TFS-ROOT-CA server as there is absolutely no way to unlock the BitLocker drive without the BitLocker Recovery Key. If the BitLocker Recovery Key is lost, then the TFS-ROOT-CA server will never be able to be accessed again. BitLocker does not allow the recovery key to be backed up to the same device that has been encrypted, and that is why removable media is typically used to backup the BitLocker Recovery Key. The BitLocker Recovery Key will be backed up and tested in this chapter.

Offline Root CA Setup - Installation and Configuration - Enable BitLocker - CLI Configuration

To enable BitLocker using PowerShell, perform the following steps on the TFS-ROOT-CA server:

1. Insert the **RootCAFiles.vfd** virtual floppy disk on the **TFS-ROOT-CA** server.
2. Open an **elevated PowerShell prompt**.
3. Create the **BitLocker Recovery Key** using the **Add-BitLockerKeyProtector** Cmdlet which can be used to unlock the drive if there is an issue with the password:

```
Windows PowerShell (Elevated)

Add-BitLockerKeyProtector -MountPoint "C:" -RecoveryPasswordProtector | Out-Null
```

4. Create a backup of the **BitLocker Recovery Key** on the virtual floppy disk using the **Get-BitLockerVolume** Cmdlet:

```
Windows PowerShell (Elevated)

(Get-BitLockerVolume -MountPoint C).KeyProtector | Out-File A:\TFS-ROOT-CA-Key.txt
```

5. Open the recovery file that was saved on **A:\ Drive** and document the **48-digit BitLocker Recovery Key**.
6. Eject the **RootCAFiles.vfd** virtual floppy disk which now contains the BitLocker Recovery Key before continuing. This is critical in case there is an issue with the BitLocker password. The BitLocker Recovery Key can be backed up using the **TFS-CA01** server in the next chapter.
7. Set the password that will be used to unlock the virtual hard disk at startup using the **Enable-BitLocker** Cmdlet. Ensure that this password is properly documented, otherwise it will require the BitLocker Recovery Key to get back into the **TFS-ROOT-CA** virtual machine. Ensure that a complex password is used, and that it is at least 14 characters in length:

```
Windows PowerShell (Elevated)

$password = Read-Host -AsSecureString "BitLocker Password"
Enable-BitLocker -MountPoint "C:" -Password $password -PasswordProtector
```

8. Restart the **TFS-ROOT-CA** virtual machine using the **Restart-Computer** Cmdlet:

```
Windows PowerShell (Elevated)

Restart-Computer -Force
```

9. When the server is starting there will be a prompt for a password to unlock the hard drive. Enter the BitLocker password that was set for the drive to ensure that it is working correctly.
10. Login to the **TFS-ROOT-CA** server when the server has restarted successfully. A notification that the hard drive is encrypting should appear after the login is completed.

When BitLocker has been installed and verified to be working correctly, the virtual hard drive for the Root Certificate Authority server has been successfully secured when it is in an offline state. The next step is to test that the recovery options for BitLocker are working correctly.

Offline Root CA Setup - Installation and Configuration - Enable BitLocker - GUI Configuration

To enable BitLocker using the BitLocker Drive Encryption management console, perform the following steps on the TFS-ROOT-CA server:

1. Insert the **RootCAFiles.vfd** virtual floppy disk on the **TFS-ROOT-CA** server.
2. Open **Windows File Explorer** (explorer.exe) and go to **This PC**. Right-click on the **C:\ drive** and select the **Turn on BitLocker** option.
3. On the **BitLocker Drive Encryption setup** screen click the **Next** button to continue.
4. On the **Preparing your drive for BitLocker** screen click the **Next** button to continue.

5. On the **BitLocker Drive Encryption setup** screen, click the **Next** button to continue.
6. On the **Choose how to unlock your drive at startup** screen, select the option to **Enter a password**.
7. On the **Create a password to unlock this drive** screen, enter the password that will be used to unlock the drive at boot up. Ensure that this password is properly documented, otherwise it will require the BitLocker Recovery Key to get back into the **TFS-ROOT-CA** virtual machine. Ensure that a complex password is used, and that it is at least 14 characters in length. Click the **Next** button to continue.
8. On the **How do you want to back up your recovery key?** screen, select the option to **Save to a file**. Save the file to the **A:\ Drive** (which is the **RootCAFiles.vfd** virtual floppy disk). Click the **Next** button to continue.
9. Open the recovery file that was saved on **A:\ Drive** and document the 48-digit BitLocker Recovery Key.
10. Eject the **RootCAFiles.vfd** virtual floppy disk which now contains the BitLocker Recovery Key before continuing. This is critical in case there is an issue with the BitLocker password. The BitLocker Recovery Key can be backed up using the **TFS-CA01** server in the next chapter.
11. On the **Choose how much of your drive to encrypt** screen, select the option to **Encrypt entire drive (slower but best for PCs and drives already in use)** and click the **Next** button.
12. On the **Choose which encryption mode to use** screen, select the option for **New encryption mode (best for fixed drives on this devices)** and click the **Next** button to continue.
13. On the **Are you ready to encrypt this drive?** screen, ensure that the **Run BitLocker system check** box is selected and then click the **Continue** button, which will close the window.
14. Restart the **TFS-ROOT-CA** server when a notification appears stating the encryption has started. If this notification is missed, restart the server manually:

15. When the server is starting there will be a prompt for a password to unlock the hard drive. Enter the BitLocker password that was set for the drive to ensure that it is working correctly:

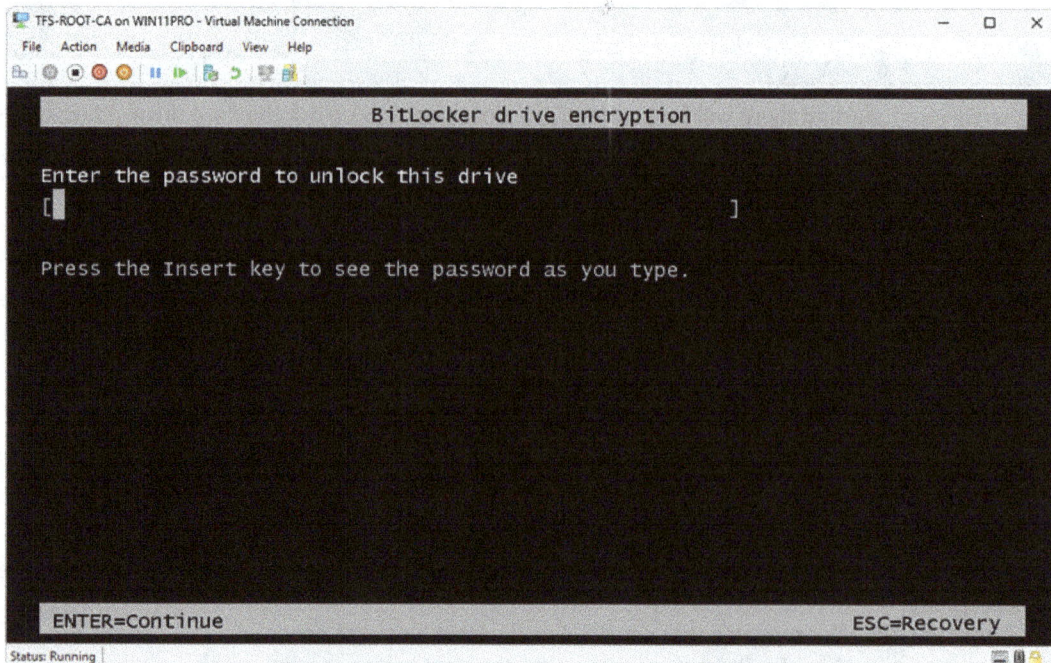

16. Login to the **TFS-ROOT-CA** server when the server has restarted successfully. A notification that the hard drive is encrypting should appear after the login is completed. The status of BitLocker can be checked at any time by going to **Windows File Explorer** (explorer.exe), then to **This PC**, right-clicking on the **C:\ drive** and selecting the **Manage BitLocker** option:

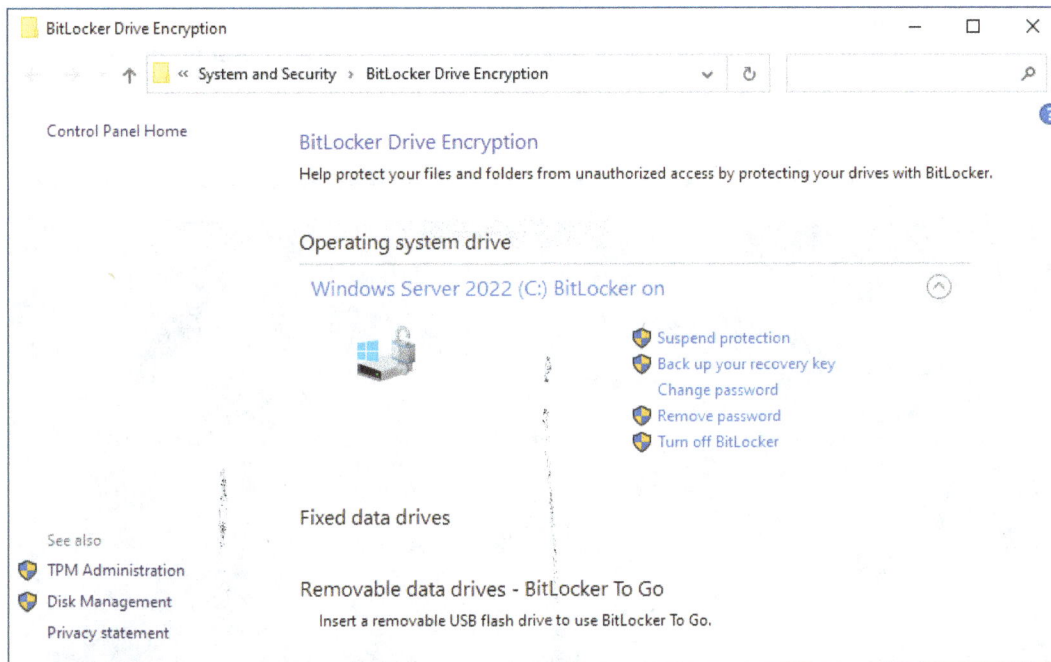

When BitLocker has been installed and verified to be working correctly, the virtual hard drive for the Root Certificate Authority server has been successfully secured when it is in an offline state. The next step is to test that the recovery options for BitLocker are working correctly.

> **BitLocker Encryption Time**
>
> The time to fully encrypt a virtual hard drive using BitLocker will vary based on the size of the drive, and the type of drive being encrypted. Even though the drive will take time to fully encrypt, the server is able to be used the entire time. Be aware that performance may be impacted during the encryption process.

Offline Root CA Setup - Installation and Configuration - Test BitLocker

There are a few tests that can be performed to ensure that the BitLocker encryption has been successfully configured on the TFS-ROOT-CA server before going any further. One test that can be performed is ensuring that the BitLocker Recovery Key can be successfully used at startup, and another test is to mount the virtual hard disk for the TFS-ROOT-CA server on another device to ensure that it can be accessed.

A backup of the BitLocker Recovery Key was completed during the BitLocker encryption section earlier in this chapter, and this process can be repeated should it be lost.

> **BitLocker Encryption and Corrupted VHD Files**
>
> If a virtual hard disk that is encrypted with BitLocker is damaged or corrupted in any way, there will be no way of retrieving the contents of that virtual hard disk. This is due to the way that BitLocker operates, and regular disk repair utilities will not work correctly on an encrypted disk. Ensure that proper backups of encrypted virtual hard disks are created to ensure that the data on that disk is never lost.

Offline Root CA Setup - Installation and Configuration - Test BitLocker - Test Recovery Key

Testing the BitLocker Recovery Key for a virtual hard disk is a simple process, and only requires a few steps to confirm that it is working correctly. The BitLocker Recovery Key that was generated and backed up in the previous section will be required. Perform the following steps to test the BitLocker Recovery Key:

1. Power on or restart the **TFS-ROOT-CA** server.
2. At the **BitLocker drive encryption** screen, press the **ESC** key to access the **BitLocker Recovery** options:

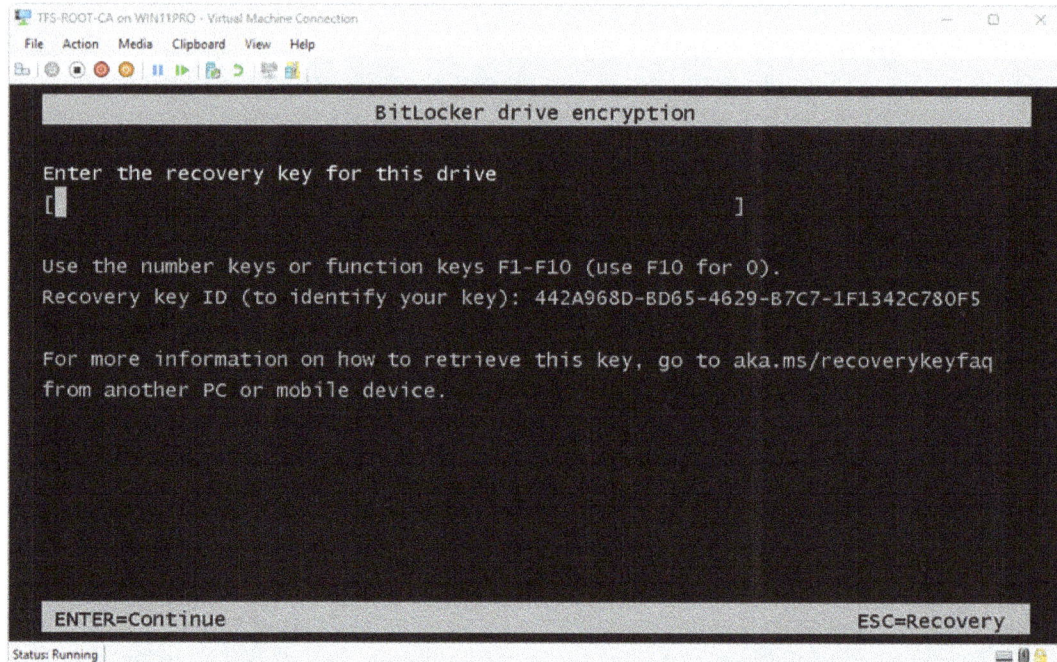

3. Input the **48-digit BitLocker Recovery Key** and press **Enter** to continue. This **BitLocker Recovery Key** should be the one that is associated with the **BitLocker Key ID**.
4. If the **BitLocker Recovery Key** works correctly, then the boot process will continue, and the Windows Login Screen should appear as expected.

If the BitLocker Recovery Key was able to start the virtual machine and get to the Windows Login Screen, then the BitLocker Recovery Key is working correctly. This key needs to be documented so that it is available in the future if there are any issues starting the TFS-ROOT-CA server.

> **BitLocker Recovery Key and Virtual Hard Disks**
>
> The BitLocker Recovery key can also be used to mount the virtual hard disk for the TFS-ROOT-CA server on another device should there be an issue that prevents Windows Server from booting correctly. This can easily be done on recent versions of Windows Server and Windows Client versions, and can also be added to an existing Hyper-V virtual machine. The process of mounting a virtual hard disk in this manner is beyond the scope of this book.

Offline Root CA Setup - Installation and Configuration - Test BitLocker - Backup Key

If the BitLocker Recovery Key for a hard disk has been misplaced a new backup of the key should be created as soon as possible. There are several methods that can be used to perform a backup of the BitLocker Recovery Key, and these methods will only work if the device can be started up and logged into. In the examples in this section, a virtual floppy disk is used to backup the BitLocker Recovery Key so the key can be backed up to another device. This can be the same virtual floppy disk that was previously created in this chapter, or a new one can be used for backing up the key.

> **⚠ BitLocker Recovery Key Backup**
>
> The BitLocker Recovery Key was already backed up in a previous section in this chapter. Unless the BitLocker Recovery Key has been lost there is no need to perform the steps in this section.

The BitLocker Recovery Key can be backed up using PowerShell with the **Get-BitLockerVolume** Cmdlet on the TFS-ROOT-CA server:

1. Insert a formatted virtual floppy disk on the **TFS-ROOT-CA** server.
2. Open an **elevated PowerShell prompt**.
3. Create a backup of the **BitLocker Recovery Key** on the virtual floppy disk:

```
Windows PowerShell (Elevated)

(Get-BitLockerVolume -MountPoint C).KeyProtector | Out-File A:\TFS-ROOT-CA-Key.txt
```

4. Close the **PowerShell prompt**.
5. Eject the virtual floppy disk which now contains the **BitLocker Recovery Key**, which can be backed up using a compatible Hyper-V virtual machine.

The BitLocker Recovery Key can also be backed up using the BitLocker Drive Encryption Control Panel applet on the TFS-ROOT-CA server:

1. Insert a formatted virtual floppy disk on the **TFS-ROOT-CA** server.
2. Open the **BitLocker Drive Encryption** Control Panel applet (control.exe /name Microsoft.BitLockerDriveEncryption):

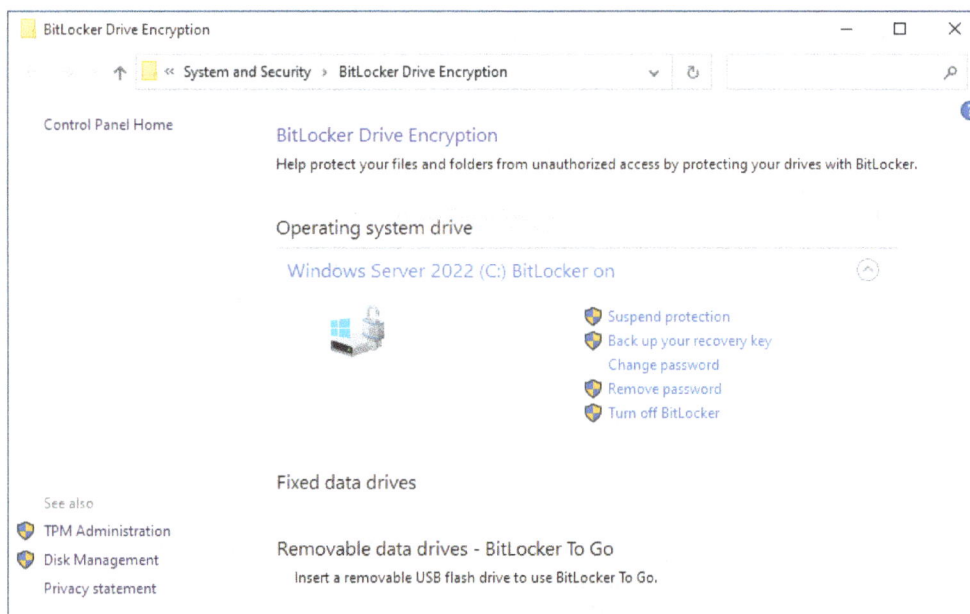

3. Under the **Operating system drive**, select the **Back up your recovery key** option.
4. When the **BitLocker Drive Encryption (C:)** window appears, select the option to **Save to a file**.
5. Browse to the **A:** and click the **Save** button. Use the default file name for the **BitLocker Recovery Key**.
6. Click the **Finish** button to complete the backup of the **BitLocker Recovery Key**.
7. Eject the virtual floppy disk which now contains the **BitLocker Recovery Key**, which can be backed up using a compatible Hyper-V virtual machine.

Whichever method is used to backup the BitLocker Recovery Key, it is important to make sure that a copy is securely stored should it ever be needed to recover the TFS-ROOT-CA server. Proceed to modifying the Local Group Policy and Local Security Policies for the TFS-ROOT-CA server in the next section.

Offline Root CA Setup - Local Policy Modifications

Once the TFS-ROOT-CA server has been setup and the operating system has been configured, the Local Group Policy settings and Local Security Policies can now be modified to increase the security of the local administrator account. Normally these types of changes are made using Group Policy with Active Directory, but since the TFS-ROOT-CA server is not on a domain the changes need to be made locally. The following policy settings will be applied to the TFS-ROOT-CA server:

- Disallow Microsoft accounts from logging into the server.
- Disable the guest account entirely if it is enabled.
- Rename the local administrator account to **CA-Admin**. Use this account after this section.
- Rename the local guest account to Administrator.
- Never display the last user that logged in on the server.
- Never display any user that logged in on the server.
- Disable LAN Manager hashes on passwords to increase password security.
- Use only the strongest LAN Manager authentication requests.
- Remember 24 previous passwords and force a password change every 90 days.
- Enforce password complexity with a minimum of 14 characters, and a minimum age of 14 days.
- Lock out the server after 5 failed login attempts for 30 minutes.

Some of these settings are not completely necessary since the TFS-ROOT-CA server is never supposed to have any active network connections to it, as there are no network adapters present on the virtual machine. Despite that configuration being applied, defining these options can prevent issues in the future should the server accidentally be connected to a network.

> **ⓘ** **Local Group Policy and Local Security Policy Changes**
>
> The Local Group Policy and Local Security Policy settings that are configured in this section are intended to provide an additional level of security to the Offline Root Certificate Authority server. The renaming of the local administrator account, and the changes to the password settings will provide additional protection for the TFS-ROOT-CA server when it is powered on for any Certificate Authority related tasks. While these changes may seem excessive, any additional security settings should be applied.
>
> If the Group Policy and Security Policy settings are not required, then this section can be skipped. If the local administrator account is not renamed, then in future steps in this chapter the **CA-Admin** account will not be used for local tasks on the TFS-ROOT-CA server.

Perform the following steps to configure the Local Group Policy settings on the TFS-ROOT-CA server:

1. Open the **Local Group Policy Editor** console (gpedit.msc), confirm the following settings, and make any changes if necessary:
   - (a) Modify the **Local Computer Policy > Computer Configuration > Windows Settings > Security Settings > Local Policies > Security Options** settings:
     - i. **Accounts: Administrator account status** - Enabled
     - ii. **Accounts: Block Microsoft accounts** - Users can't add or log on with Microsoft Accounts
     - iii. **Accounts: Guest account status** - Disabled
     - iv. **Accounts: Rename administrator account** - CA-Admin
     - v. **Accounts: Rename guest account** - Administrator
     - vi. **Interactive Logon: Don't display last signed-in** - Enabled
     - vii. **Interactive Logon: Don't display username at sign-in** - Enabled
     - viii. **Network security: Do not store LAN Manager hash value on next password change** - Enabled
     - ix. **Network security: LAN Manager authentication level** - Send NTLMv2 response only. Refuse LM & NTLM (click **Yes** when prompted to confirm the change)
2. Close the **Local Group Policy Editor** console.

Perform the following steps to configure the Local Security Policy settings on the TFS-ROOT-CA server:

1. Open the **Local Security Policy** console (secpol.msc), confirm the following settings, and make any changes if necessary:
   (a) Modify the **Security Settings > Account Policies > Password Policy** settings:
      i. **Enforce password history** - 24 passwords remembered
      ii. **Maximum password age** - 90 days
      iii. **Minimum password age** - 1 days
      iv. **Minimum password length** - 14 characters
      v. **Password must meet complexity requirements** - Enabled
      vi. **Store passwords using reversible encryption** - Disabled
   (b) Modify the **Security Settings > Account Policies > Account Lockout Policy** settings:
      i. **Account lockout threshold** - 5 invalid login attempts (click **OK** when prompted to confirm the change)
      ii. **Account lockout duration** - 30 minutes
      iii. **Reset account lockout counter after** - 30 minutes
2. Close the **Local Security Policy** console.
3. Restart the **TFS-ROOT-CA** server to apply the updated settings before continuing.

When the TFS-ROOT-CA server restarts, use the **CA-Admin** account to login. This is the local administrator account that was initially setup, but the name has changed and will be used for all remaining steps in this book for the TFS-ROOT-CA server.

The Local Group Policy and Local Security Policy settings are required since the TFS-ROOT-CA server is not a part of an Active Directory domain and therefore would never receive any policies from a Domain Controller. By default, the policies on Windows Server are weak when it comes to security settings for password complexity, account lockouts, and password age. By modifying the policies directly on the TFS-ROOT-CA server, there are adequate protections in place on the server and that they will always be in place as they cannot be modified.

> **Local Administrator Account Login Changes**
>
> After the steps in this section have been successfully completed, and after the TFS-ROOT-CA server has been restarted, the local administrator account on the TFS-ROOT-CA server will be renamed to **CA-Admin**. This new account name will be used for all tasks on the TFS-ROOT-CA server going forward. This includes all tasks that are used for configuring any features, and for the login credentials. Attempting to use the **Administrator** account for any tasks will fail, as the renamed account will not be enabled or have valid credentials for logging into the server.
>
> Since the local administrator account has already been used for the initial configuration, the path for the account will remain the same. This is not an issue since Windows will correctly map the username to the old folder. As part of the changes made to the TFS-ROOT-CA server, the username is no longer remembered on the Windows Login screen. This means that the full credentials will need to be inputted every time that the server is powered on or restarted.

> **Local Administrator Account Password Expiration**
>
> Since the Offline Root CA will only be used at least once a year and with the password settings that are being applied to this virtual machine, the password to the local administrator account will need to be reset every single time the TFS-ROOT-CA virtual machine is powered on.
>
> Ensure that the password for the local administrator account on the TFS-ROOT-CA server is always maintained, and updated as required.

With the Local Group Policy and Security Policy settings configured on the TFS-ROOT-CA server, the CAPolicy.inf file can now be created. This file is essential for configuring crucial settings for the Root Certificate, and those settings must be available at the time of creation.

Offline Root CA Setup - CAPolicy.inf Installation

The CAPolicy.inf file is used to add configuration details to the Certificate Authority at the time when the Root certificate is created. On the TFS-ROOT-CA server, create a file in the C:\Windows folder called CAPolicy.inf (ensure that the file is saved with the correct file extension otherwise these settings will be ignored).

Copy the following contents into the CAPolicy.inf file and save the file before continuing:

```
C:\Windows\CAPolicy.inf

[Version]
Signature = "$Windows NT$"

[PolicyStatementExtension]
Policies = AllIssuancePolicy, InternalPolicy
Critical = FALSE

[AllIssuancePolicy]
; Enables all Certificate Templates.
OID = 2.5.29.32.0

[InternalPolicy]
OID = 1.2.3.4.1455.67.89.5
Notice = "The TFS Labs Certification Authority is an internal only resource."
URL = http://pki.corp.tfslabs.com/cps.html

[Certsrv_Server]
; Renewal information for the Root CA.
RenewalKeyLength = 4096
RenewalValidityPeriod = Years
RenewalValidityPeriodUnits = 10

; Disable support for issuing certificates using RSASSA-PSS.
AlternateSignatureAlgorithm = 0

; The CRL publication period is the lifetime of the Root CA.
CRLPeriod = Years
CRLPeriodUnits = 10

; The option for Delta CRL is disabled since this is a Root CA.
CRLDeltaPeriod = Days
CRLDeltaPeriodUnits = 0
```

Once the CAPolicy.inf file has been created and saved, proceed to installing the AD CS role on the TFS-ROOT-CA server.

> **CAPolicy.inf Customization Options**
>
> The settings that are contained within the CAPolicy.inf file are used to create the Root or Subordinate certificates for a Certificate Authority. There are some configuration items that should be customized before the certificates are created, as modifying those items later is not always possible, which is why it is important to ensure that the settings are correct. In the case of the CAPolicy.inf file being used for the Root CA in this example, items that should be modified include the **Notice** and **URL** for the Certification Practice Statement (CPS). The DNS entry for the URL can be configured in the next chapter.

Certificate Authority OID Number

The OID number that is defined in the **InternalPolicy** section of the CAPolicy.inf file can be modified if necessary for an organization. The OID number in this example is used in Microsoft technical documentation, but it should work for any organization if it is only ever going to be used internally. If a customized OID number is required for a Certificate Authority, a Private Enterprise Number can be registered through the IANA.

If a custom OID number is required for the Certificate Authority, modify the OID line in the **InternalPolicy** section to **OID = 1.3.6.1.4.1.X** (replace the X with the PEN number that was previously registered).

Ensure that if a custom OID is configured for the Root certificate that the same OID number is used when creating the CAPolicy.inf file for the Subordinate certificate. If these numbers do not match, there could be issues with certificates that are issued.

Delta CRL with Root Certificate Authorities

A Delta CRL is not normally required for a Root Certificate Authority, especially one that is offline since it is not normally handling certificate revocations in a PKI. The Root CA is only ever used to issue a Base CRL when there are Subordinate Certificate Authorities present in the PKI. The Base CRL is updated on a yearly basis as per the configuration of the CAPolicy.inf file that is used in this example, and that file is copied to an online Certificate Authority (typically the Subordinate CA) whenever it is updated.

The only certificates that are typically revoked by a Root CA are Subordinate certificates, and that would necessitate the deployment of a new Base CRL instead of a Delta CRL when the certificate is revoked and a new one is issued.

Signature Algorithm Support Issues

The **AlternateSignatureAlgorithm = 0** flag in the CAPolicy.inf file explicitly uses SHA256 for the algorithm instead of the legacy RSASSA-PSS algorithm. This can cause issues with some devices (especially iOS) and by ensuring that it is disabled there should be no issues with certificates issued by the Certificate Authority.

CAPolicy.inf File Name and Locations

Ensure that the CAPolicy.inf file has been properly saved in the C:\Windows folder (%WINDIR%). Also make sure that the file extension is set to INF and not TXT. A common mistake is to accidentally save the file as CAPolicy.inf.txt which is not valid.

If the CAPolicy.inf file is not saved in the correct directory and without the correct file extension, all settings in the file will be ignored at the time when the Certificate Authority is created. An error message will not be displayed if the file is not named correctly, and the only way to verify that the settings are correct is to check the Root certificate after it has been created. If there is an error with the settings in the CAPolicy.inf file, the Root certificate will not be created.

Offline Root CA Setup - AD CS Role Installation

Once the TFS-ROOT-CA server has been configured properly and the CAPolicy.inf file has been created, the Active Directory Certificate Services role needs to be installed. The Active Directory Certificate Services role can be installed using PowerShell or with the Server Manager console. Either method for installing the Active Directory Certificate Services role can be used, and there is no need to use both methods for the installation.

Offline Root CA Setup - AD CS Role Installation - CLI Installation

The Active Directory Certificate Services installation can be performed using PowerShell, which requires much fewer steps to accomplish. Perform the following steps on the TFS-ROOT-CA server to install the Active Directory Certificate Services role and associated management features:

1. Open an **elevated PowerShell prompt**.
2. Run the following command to install the **Active Directory Certificate Services** role and the necessary **Management Tools** for the role:

```
Windows PowerShell (Elevated)

Add-WindowsFeature -Name ADCS-Cert-Authority -IncludeManagementTools
```

3. The command will automatically install the **Active Directory Certificate Services** role and output a **Success** status of **True** if there were no issues.
4. Once the installation for **Active Directory Certificate Services** has successfully completed, close the **PowerShell prompt**.

Once the Active Directory Certificate Services role has been installed, the role can now be configured and the Root certificate for the TFS Labs domain can be created.

Offline Root CA Setup - AD CS Role Installation - GUI Installation

To perform the Active Directory Certificate Services role installation using the Server Manager console, perform the following steps on the TFS-ROOT-CA server to install the AD CS role and associated management features:

1. Open the **Server Manager** console (servermanager.exe), click on the **Manage** menu, and click on **Add Roles and Features** to start the installation wizard:

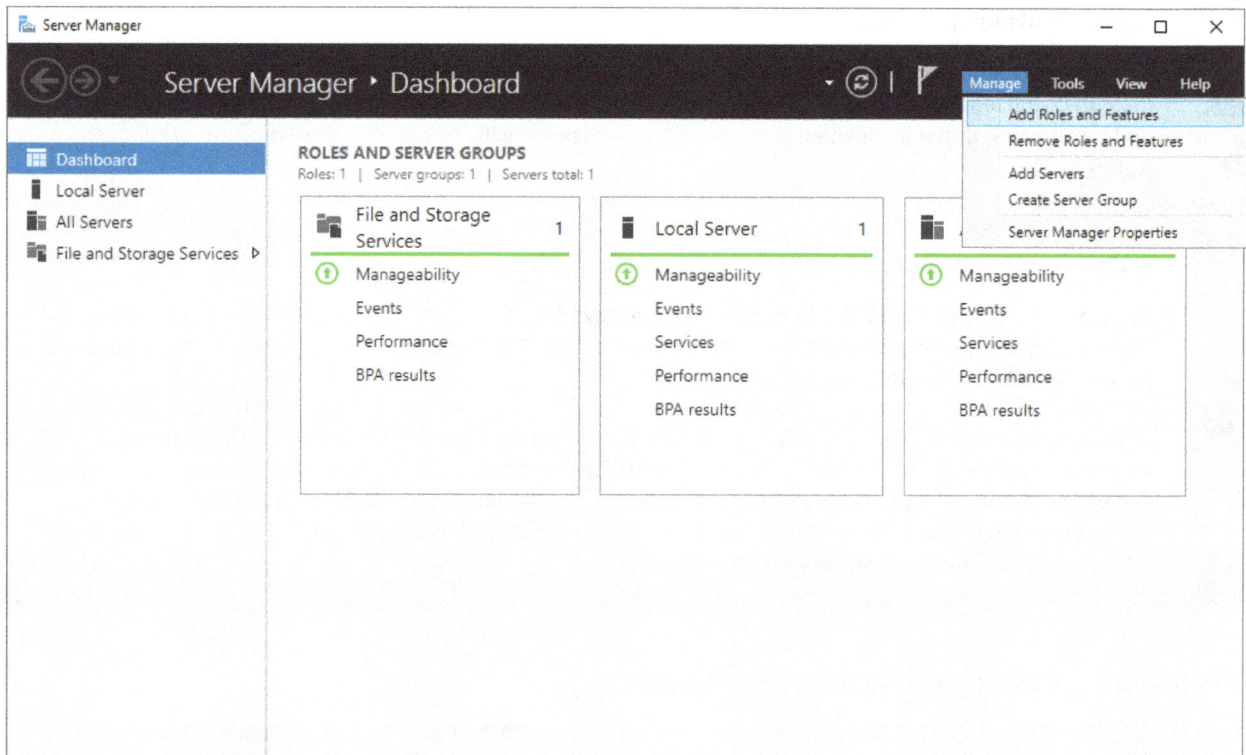

2. On the **Before you begin** screen, click the **Next** button to continue:

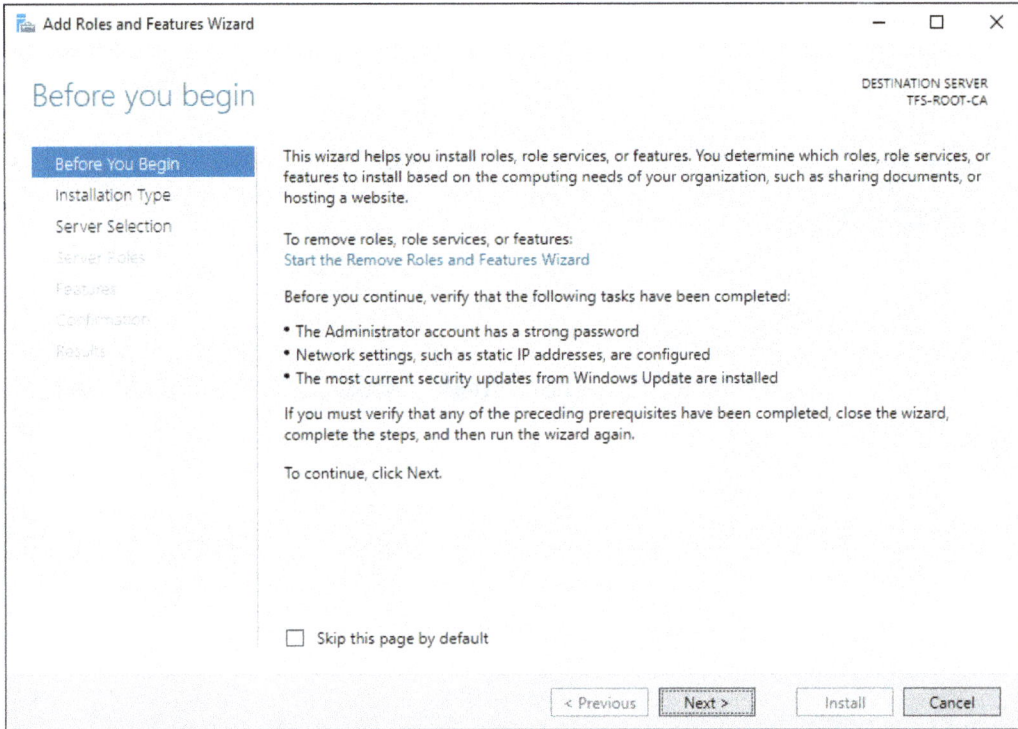

3. On the **Select installation type** screen, select the option for **Role-based or feature-based installation** and click **Next** to continue:

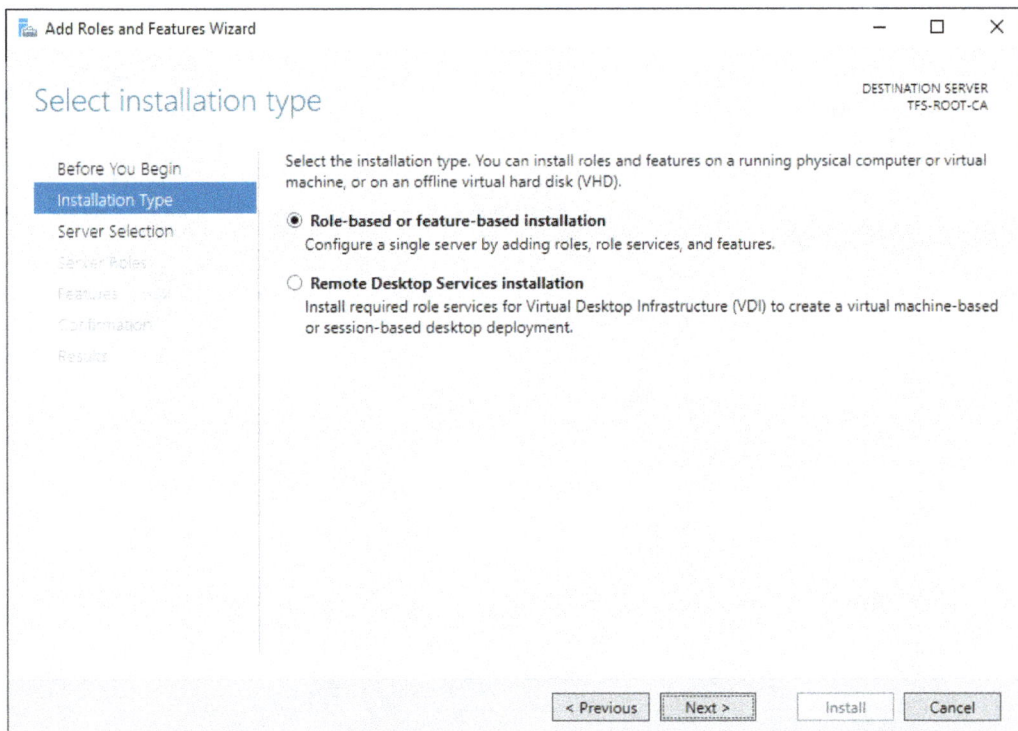

4. On the **Select destination server** screen, verify that the **TFS-ROOT-CA** server is selected and click **Next**:

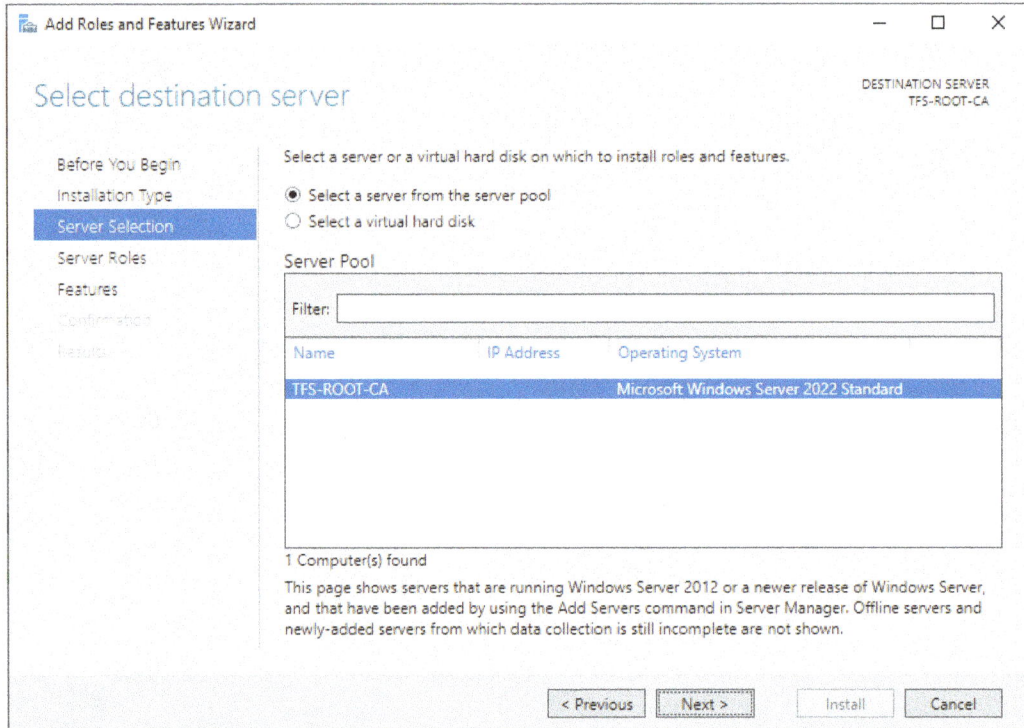

5. On the **Select server roles** screen, select the **Active Directory Certificate Services** option:

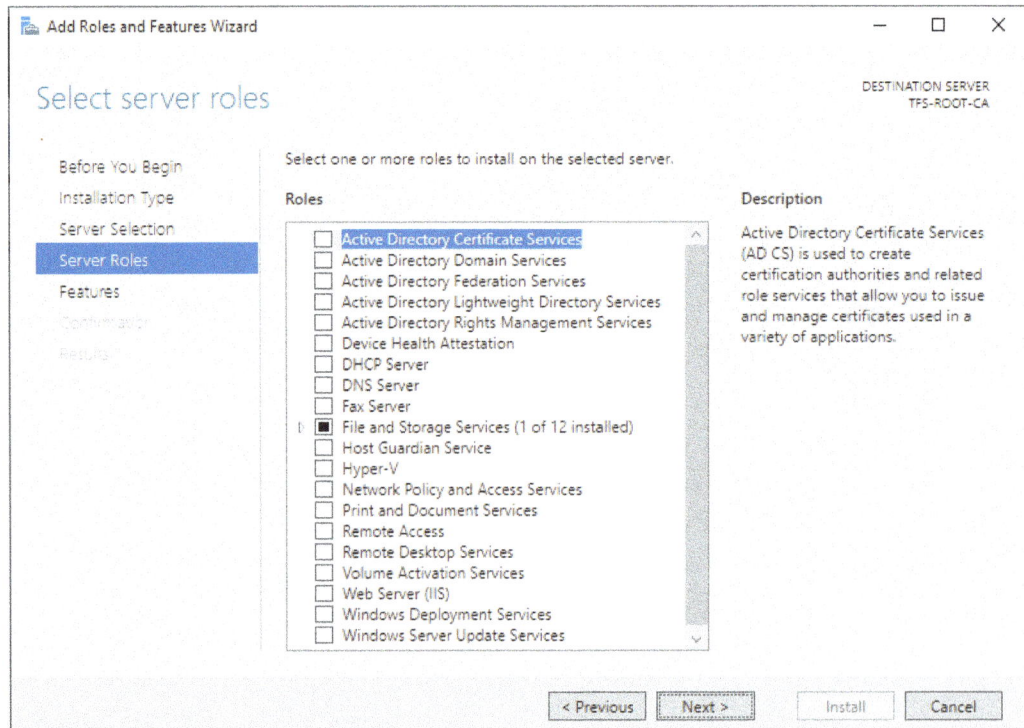

6. The installation wizard will ask to install any additional features required for the **Active Directory Certificate Services** role. Select the option to **Include management tools (if applicable)** to install the management tools for the role. Click the **Add Features** button to continue.

7. On the **Select server roles** screen, click the **Next** button to continue:

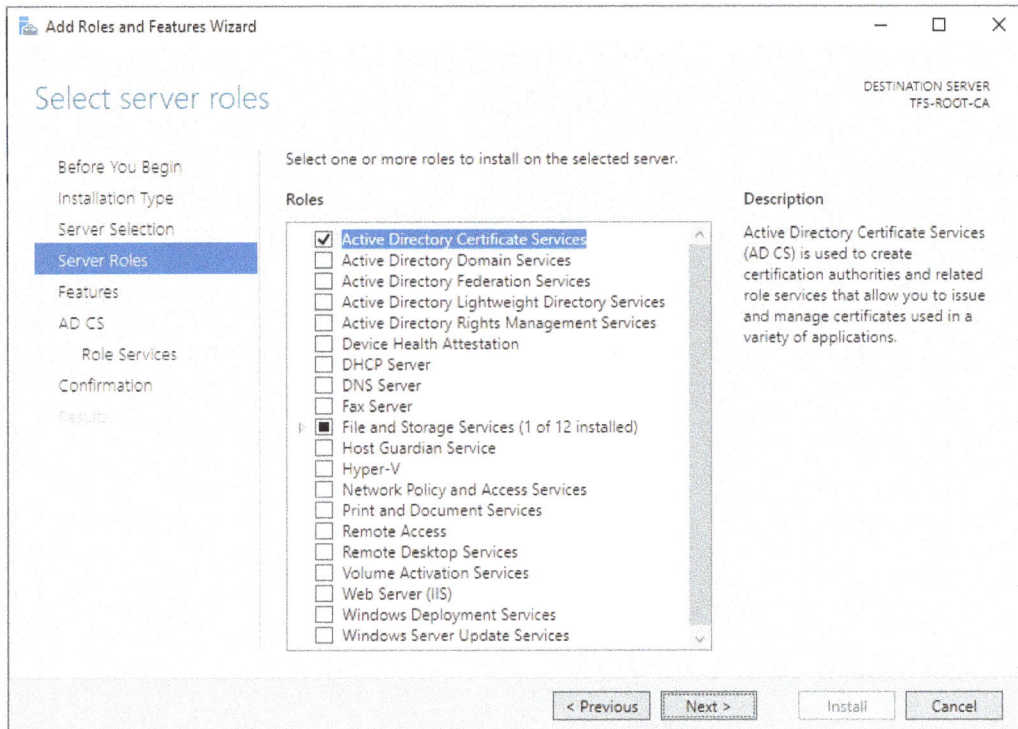

8. On the **Select features** screen, click the **Next** button to continue:

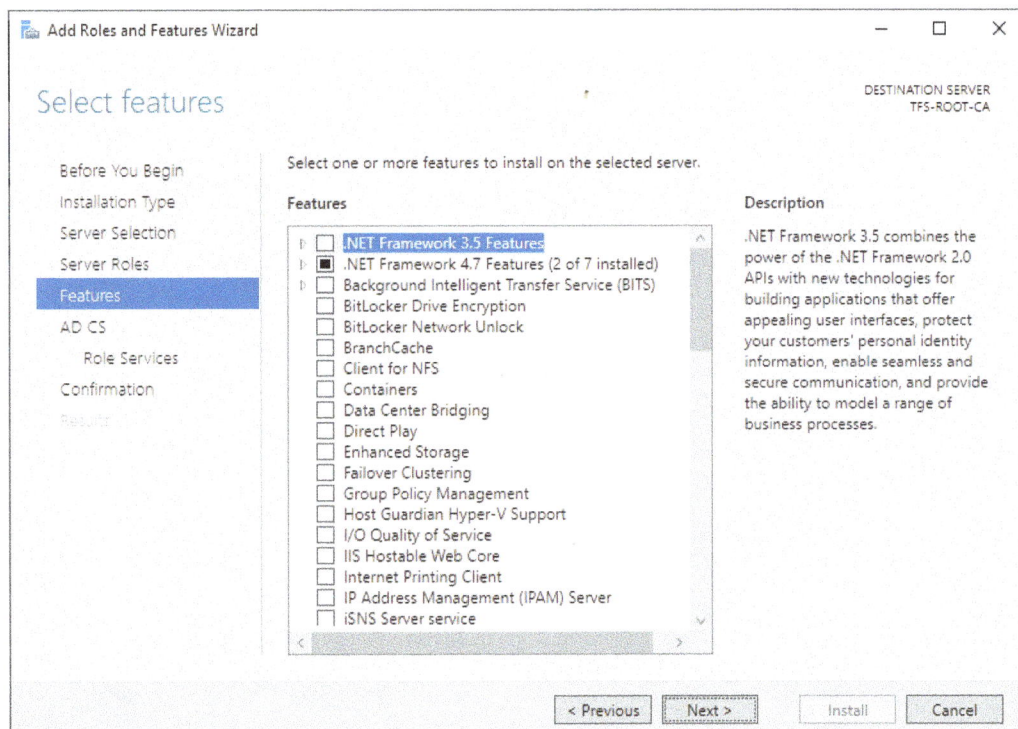

9. On the **Active Directory Certificate Services** screen, click the **Next** button to continue:

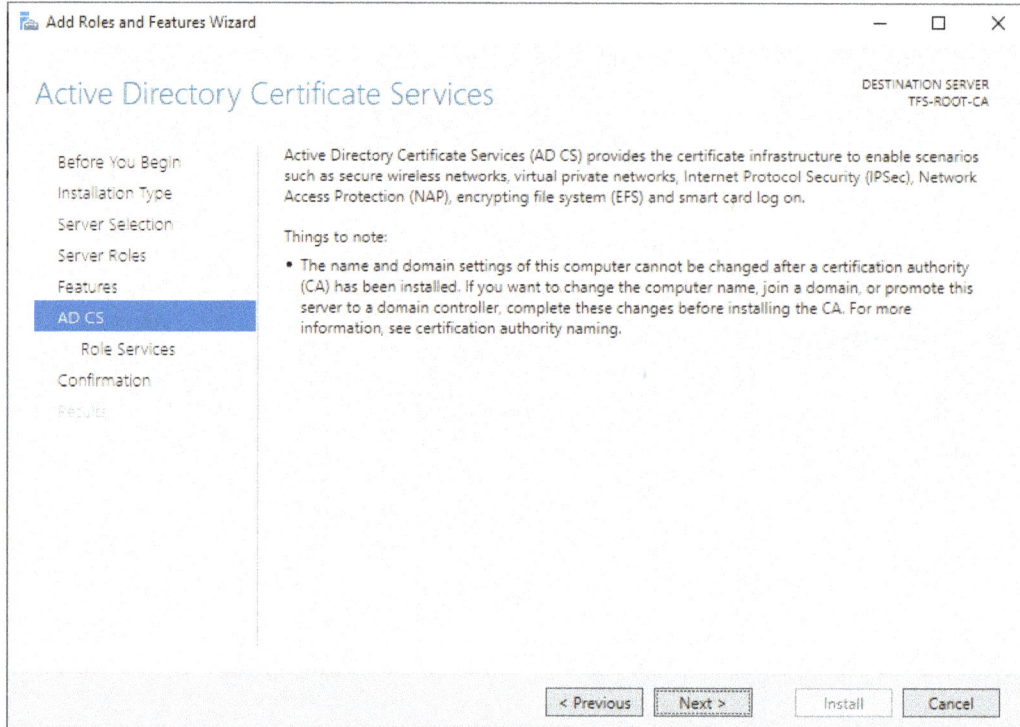

10. On the **Select role services** screen, select the option for **Certification Authority** and click the **Next** button to continue:

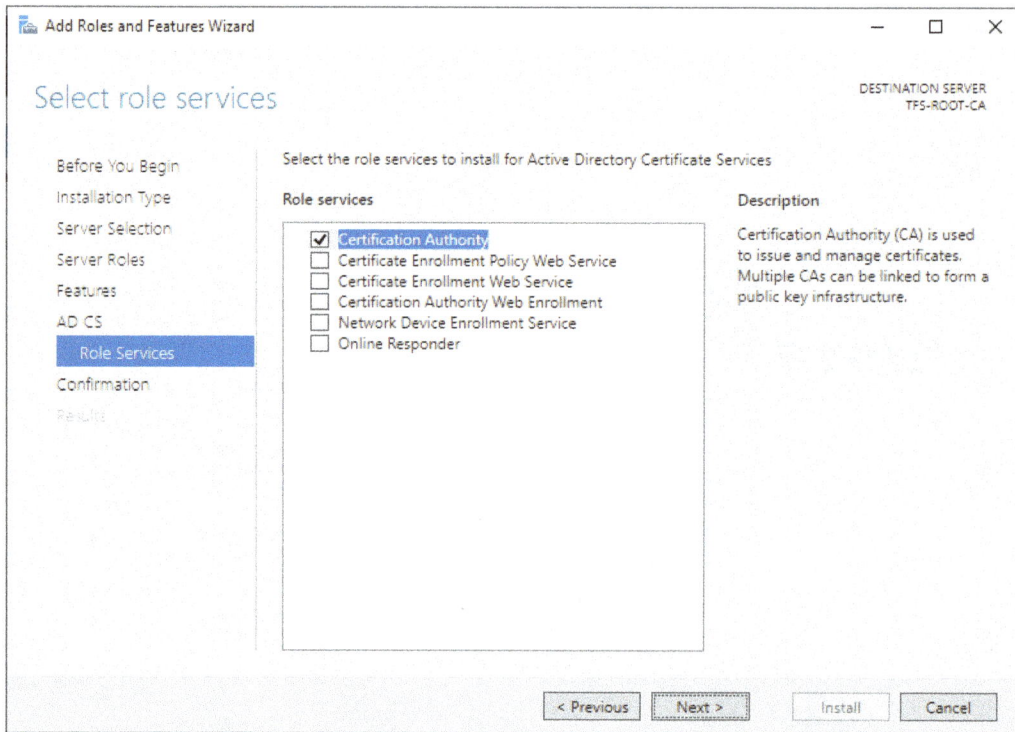

11. On the **Confirm installation selections** screen, click the **Install** button to continue:

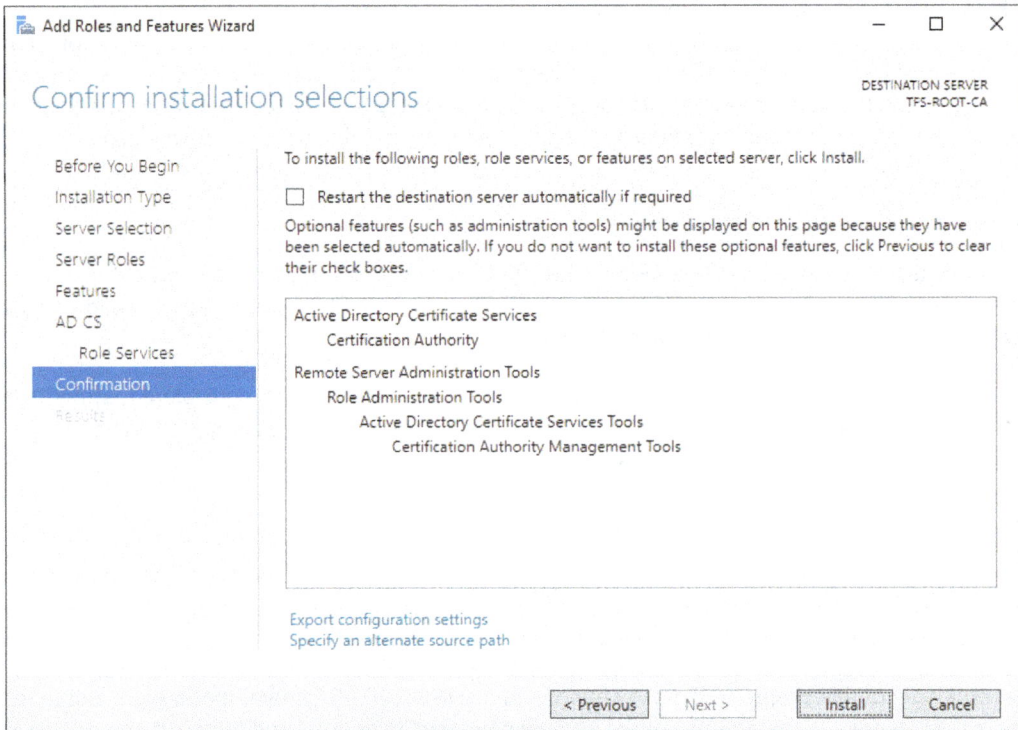

12. Once the installation is completed, click the **Close** button:

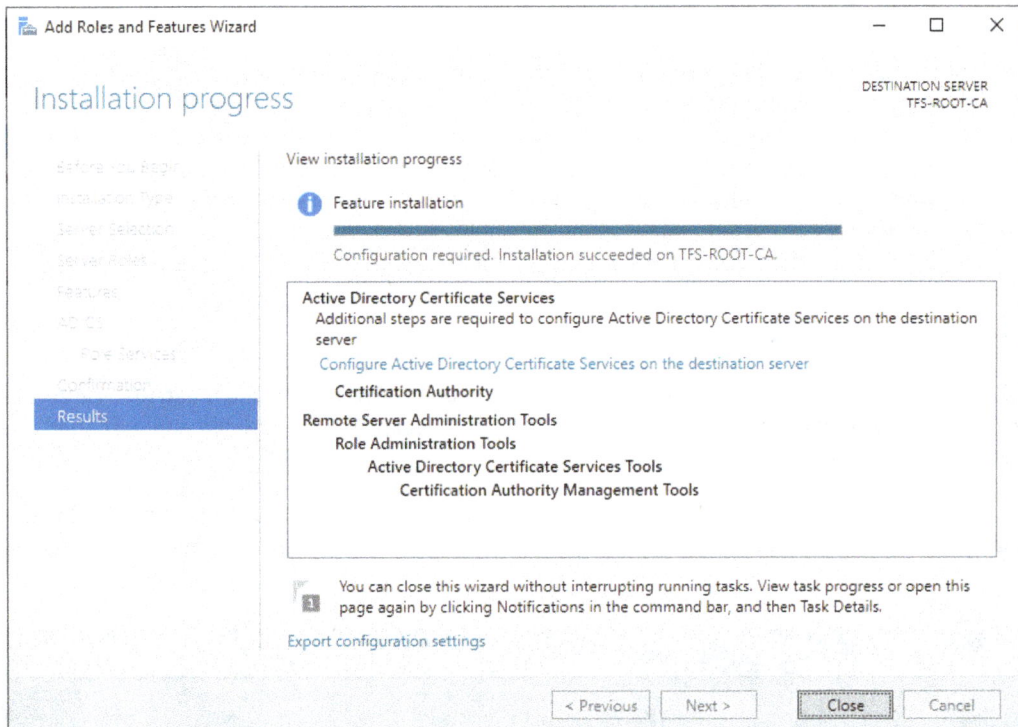

Once the Active Directory Certificate Services role has been installed, the role can be configured and the Root certificate for the TFS Labs domain can be created.

Offline Root CA Setup - Checkpoint

At this point in the process of creating the Root Certificate Authority for the TFS Labs domain, it is suggested, but not required to create a Checkpoint (or equivalent) for the TFS-ROOT-CA server. In this section, a Checkpoint named **Pre-ADCS-Implementation** will be created after the previous steps in this chapter have been successfully completed. If the process of creating the Root Certificate Authority needs to be restarted due to a mistake in the configuration, this Checkpoint can be used so that the earlier steps in this chapter do not need to be performed again.

Checkpoints and Virtualization Solutions

This book uses Hyper-V for virtualization of the TFS Labs environment which is used to test the deployment of Active Directory Certificate Services. The Checkpoint feature in Hyper-V allows for a complete snapshot of a virtual machine at a specific point in time.

If a different virtualization solution is being used, it most likely supports an equivalent feature. Details on how to use Checkpoints with other virtualization solutions are beyond the scope of this book.

Offline Root Certificate Authority Checkpoint

The steps that have been performed so far in this chapter have been on setting up the virtual machine for the TFS-ROOT-CA server, as well as configuring several local policies for the server. The Active Directory Certificate Services role has been installed, but not yet configured.

The remainder of this chapter will make changes to the TFS-ROOT-CA server that are difficult to reverse. This is the last point in this chapter where a Checkpoint can be created and restored, should there be an issue with the server.

Virtual Machine Checkpoints and Hard Disk Space

An important thing to consider before using Hyper-V Checkpoints is that once they are used, they can begin to slowly take up a considerable amount of disk space if they are not properly managed. When a virtual hard disk is provisioned, the size of the virtual hard disk can be specified and Hyper-V will not allocate more to the disk space if it is used up. Hyper-V will treat the virtual hard disk as if it is a physical hard disk, which cannot be resized after it is manufactured. With Checkpoints, the differencing files can grow to whatever size is needed, which can fill up an entire hard drive or storage location.

Offline Root CA Setup - Checkpoint - Create a Checkpoint

A Checkpoint can be created with PowerShell by using the **Checkpoint-VM** Cmdlet, and it can also be created using Hyper-V Manager or the Virtual Machine Connection application. Checkpoints are created and managed on the Hyper-V host, and not on the virtual machine itself.

To create a Checkpoint named **Pre-ADCS-Implementation** for the TFS-ROOT-CA server, run the following command from an **elevated PowerShell prompt** on the Hyper-V host where the virtual machines for the TFS Labs environment are running:

```
Windows PowerShell (Elevated)

Checkpoint-VM -Name TFS-ROOT-CA -SnapshotName "Pre-ADCS-Implementation"
```

Once the virtual machine Checkpoint has been created, it can be used to restore the state of the virtual machine later on if there is an issue during the AD CS deployment.

Offline Root CA Setup - Checkpoint - Restore a Checkpoint

A Checkpoint can be restored with PowerShell by using the **Restore-VMSnapshot** Cmdlet, and it can also be restored using Hyper-V Manager or the Virtual Machine Connection application. Checkpoints are restored and managed on the Hyper-V host, and not on the virtual machine.

To restore a Checkpoint named **Pre-ADCS-Implementation** for the TFS-ROOT-CA server, run the following command from an **elevated PowerShell prompt** on the Hyper-V host where the virtual machines for the TFS Labs environment are running:

```
Windows PowerShell (Elevated)

Restore-VMSnapshot -Name "Pre-ADCS-Implementation" -VMName TFS-ROOT-CA -Confirm:$false
```

When a virtual machine is restored from a Checkpoint, the default action is to have the virtual machine in a shut down state. The virtual machine will need to be powered on immediately after a restore to begin using it again.

Once the TFS-ROOT-CA virtual machine has been restored from the original Checkpoint, the server will need to be started before it can be used.

Offline Root CA Setup - AD CS Role Configuration

Once the Active Directory Certificate Services role has been installed it will need to be configured to work as the Root Certificate Authority. In the process of configuring the Active Directory Certificate Services role for the TFS Labs domain, the following Root certificate will be created:

Certificate Authority Setup Type	Standalone CA
Certificate Authority Type	Root CA
Cryptographic Provider	RSA#Microsoft Software Key Storage Provider
Key Length	4096 Bits
Signature Hash Algorithm	SHA256
CA Common Name	TFS Labs Certificate Authority
Validity Period	10 years

Table 6.7.1: Active Directory Certificate Services configuration for the Root Certificate Authority.

The Active Directory Certificate Services role can be configured through the command line with PowerShell, or by using the Server Manager console. Only one method is needed to configure the Active Directory Certificate Services role, there is no need to perform the configuration twice.

> ⚠️ **Root Certificate Validity Period**
>
> It is not advised to have the Root certificate and the Subordinate certificate set to have the same validity period. The expiration dates should always be different, and this needs to be factored in when designing a Certificate Authority. For example, if both certificates have a 5 year expiration date, it is possible that the Root certificate will expire before the Subordinate certificate since it was signed first.

Once the Active Directory Certificate Services role has been configured, all associated services will be started automatically since it is the Root Certificate Authority.

Offline Root CA Setup - AD CS Role Configuration - CLI Configuration

The Active Directory Certificate Services configuration can be completed using PowerShell by performing the following steps on the TFS-ROOT-CA server:

1. Open an **elevated PowerShell prompt**.
2. Using the **Install-AdcsCertificationAuthority** Cmdlet, run the following command to configure the **Active Directory Certificate Services** role and create the **Root certificate**:

```
Windows PowerShell (Elevated)

Install-AdcsCertificationAuthority `
-CAType StandaloneRootCA `
-CACommonName "TFS Labs Certificate Authority" `
-KeyLength 4096 `
-HashAlgorithm SHA256 `
-CryptoProviderName "RSA#Microsoft Software Key Storage Provider" `
-ValidityPeriod Years `
-ValidityPeriodUnits 10 `
-DatabaseDirectory $(Join-Path $env:SystemRoot "System32\CertLog") `
-Force
```

3. The command will automatically configure the **Active Directory Certificate Services** role, and if there are no issues it will output an **ErrorID** status of **0**.
4. Once the configuration for **Active Directory Certificate Services** has completed, close the **PowerShell prompt**.

At this point the Root Certificate for the TFS Labs domain has been created. The Certificate Authority and Root certificate will be validated in the next section.

Certificate Authority Deployment Modifications

There are few modifications that need to be made to the command to configure Active Directory Certificate Services. Most of the settings are already configured using the CAPolicy.inf file that was previously configured in this chapter.

The only configuration item that needs to be modified is the **CACommonName** parameter. This parameter sets the name of the Root Certificate Authority that will appear on all certificates in the PKI.

Certificate Authority Deployment on an Offline CA

There is an issue with running the **Install-AdcsCertificationAuthority** Cmdlet on a server that does not have any active network connections. When a server that is running Active Directory Certificate Services performs the configuration of the role, there are multiple calls to UNC paths that are not accessible. Even though it is for the local server, the configuration will fail since there are no functioning network adapters on the server. This issue does not occur when using the Server Manager console to configure the Active Directory Certificate Services role.

The **DatabaseDirectory $(Join-Path $env:SystemRoot "System32\CertLog")** option in the **Install-AdcsCertificationAuthority** command skips the checks for any network connection, and allows the configuration to complete with only local connections on the server.

Offline Root Setup - AD CS Role Configuration - GUI Configuration

To perform the Active Directory Certificate Services role configuration using the Server Manager console, perform the following steps on the TFS-ROOT-CA server:

1. To begin the configuration of **Active Directory Certificate Services** on **TFS-ROOT-CA**, open the **Server Manager** console (servermanager.exe). Click the **Notifications** icon in the upper-right hand corner and click the **Configure Active Directory Certificate Services on the destination server** link in the **Post-deployment Configuration** box:

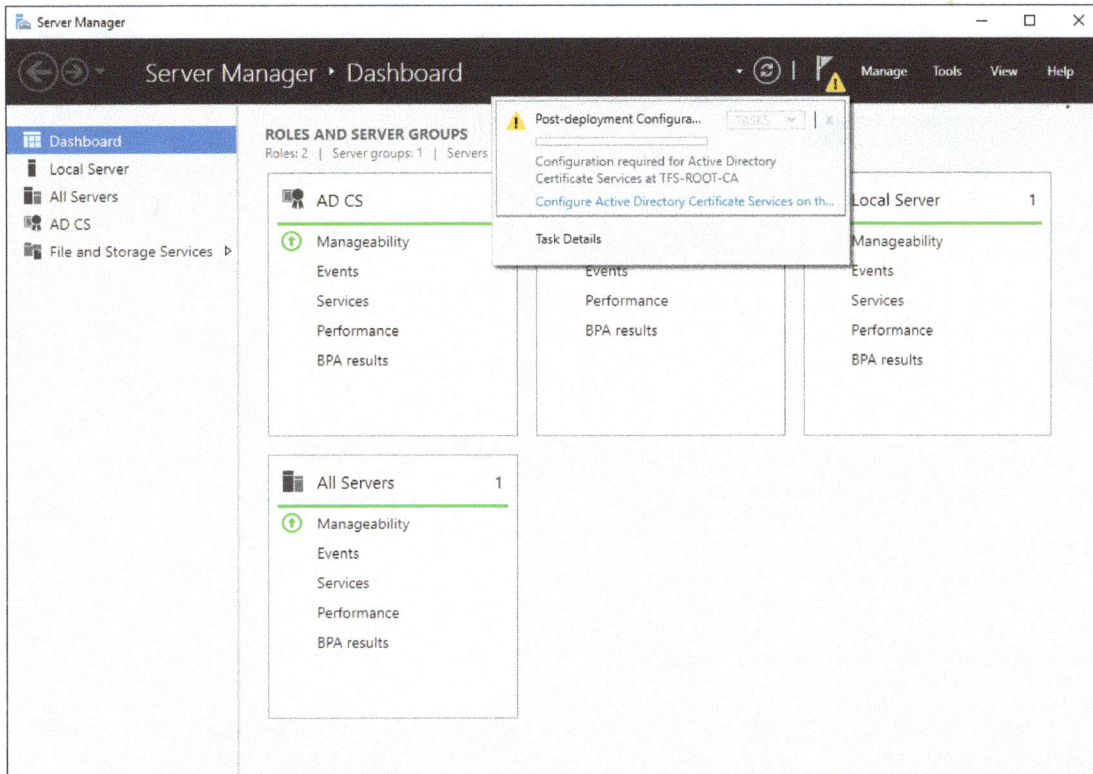

2. On the **Credentials** screen, verify that the credentials are set to **TFS-ROOT-CA\CA-Admin** and click **Next** to continue:

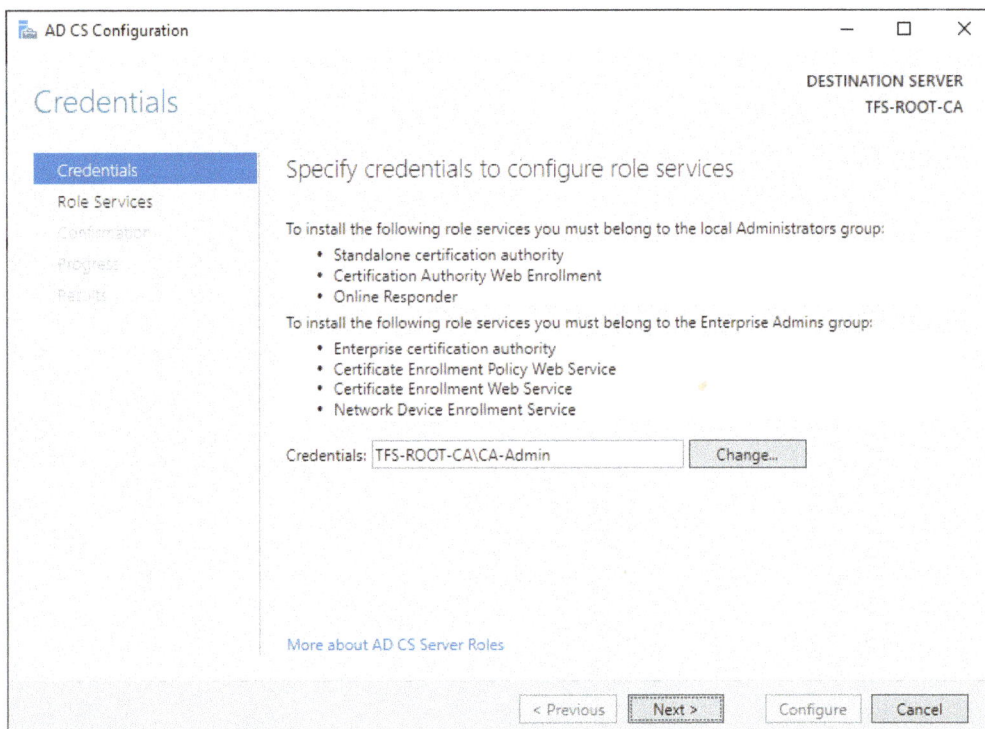

3. On the **Role Services** screen, select the option for **Certification Authority** and click the **Next** button to continue:

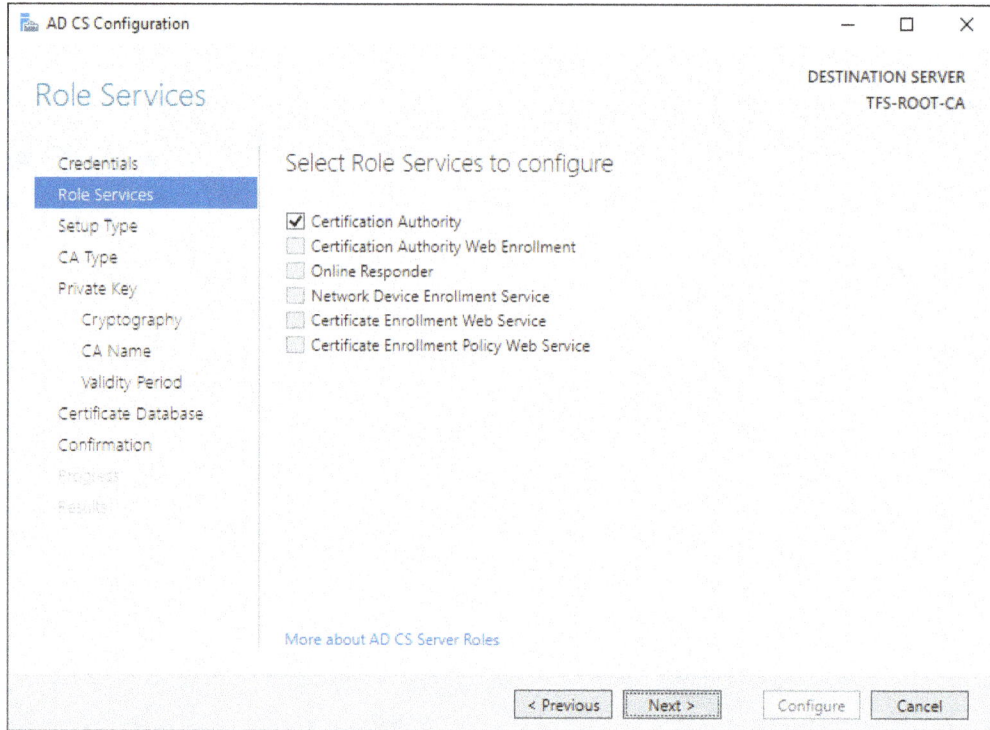

4. On the **Setup Type** screen, the option for **Standalone CA** should be selected. The option for Enterprise CA is not available since this server is not a domain member server. Click the **Next** button to continue:

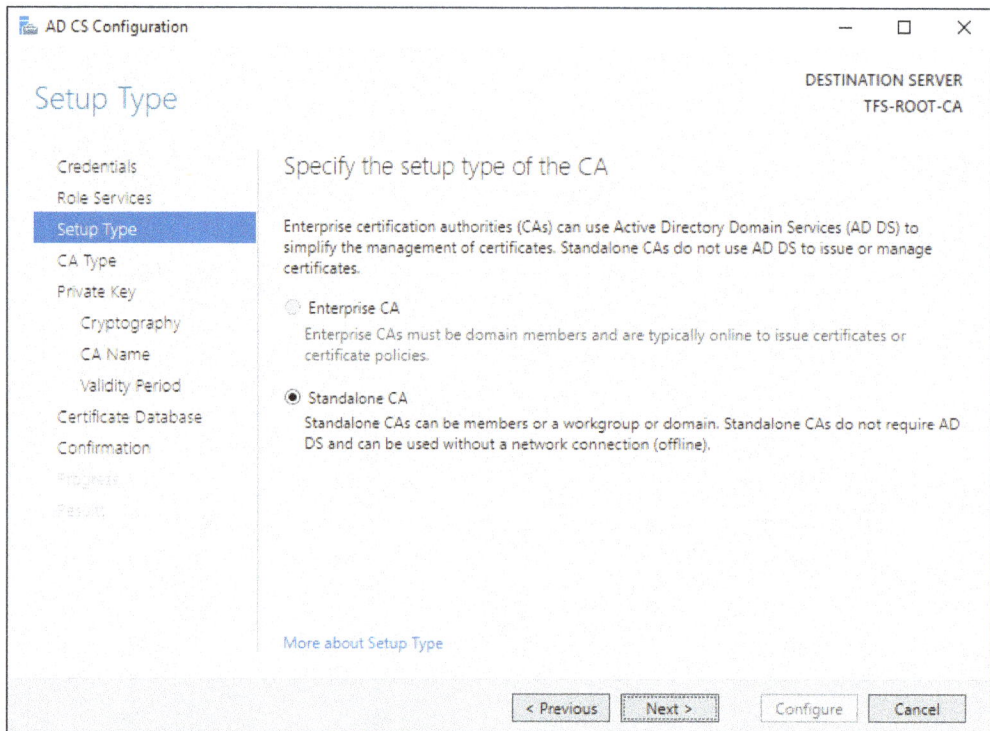

5. On the **CA Type** screen, ensure that the **Root CA** option is selected (the Subordinate CA option will be used later for the Enterprise CA). Click the **Next** button to continue:

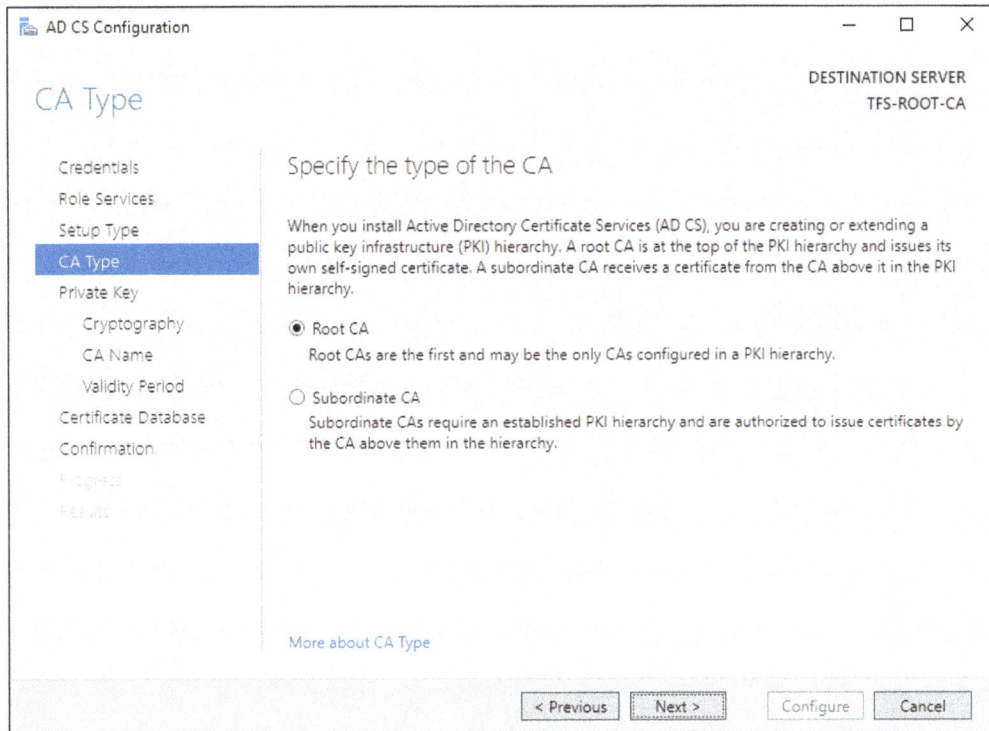

6. On the **Private Key** screen, verify that the **Create a new private key** option is selected. Click the **Next** button to continue:

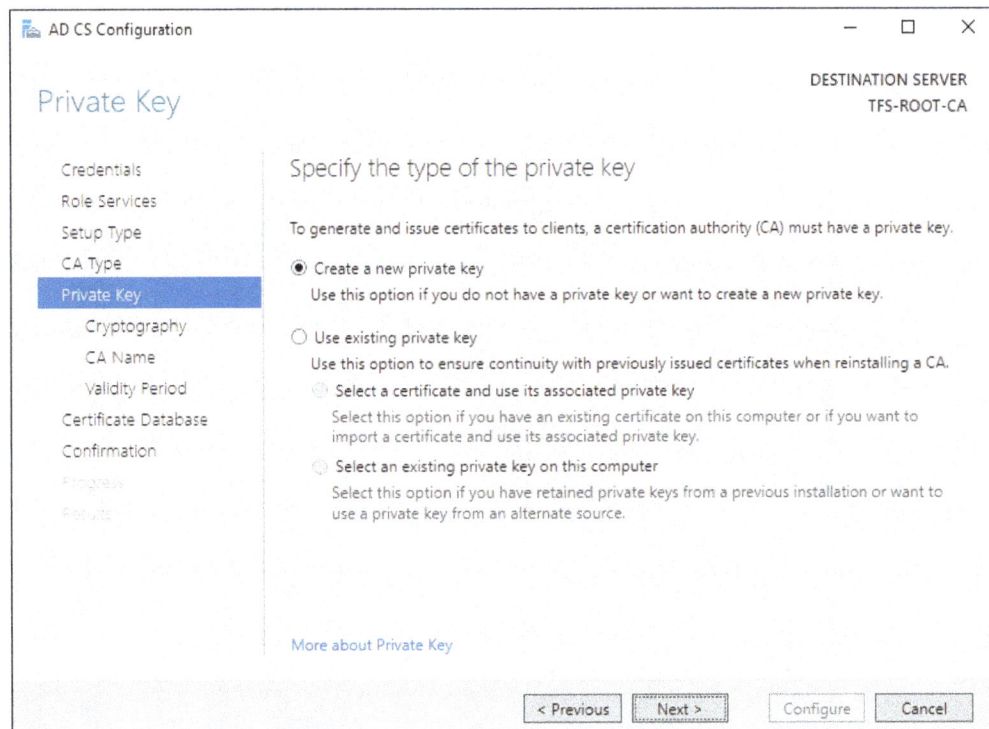

7. On the **Cryptography for CA** screen, set the **Cryptographic Provider** to **RSA#Microsoft Software Key Storage Provider**, the **Key Length** to **4096**, and the **Hash Algorithm** to **SHA256**. Click the **Next** button to continue:

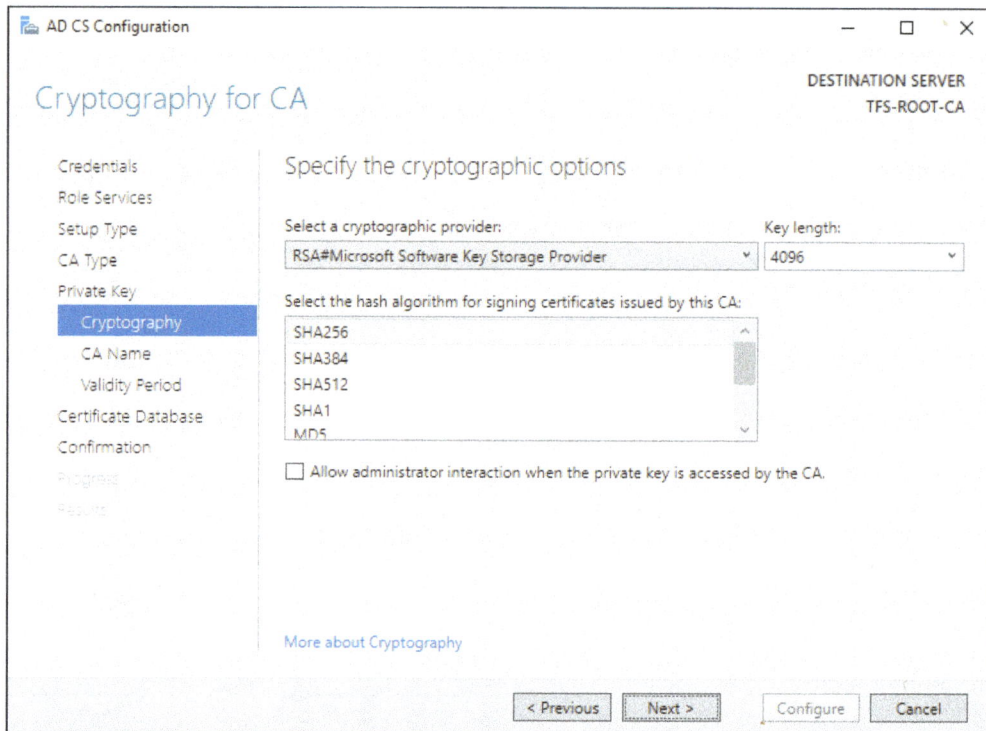

8. On the **CA Name** screen, set the **Common Name (CN)** for the CA to **TFS Labs Certificate Authority** and click the **Next** button to continue:

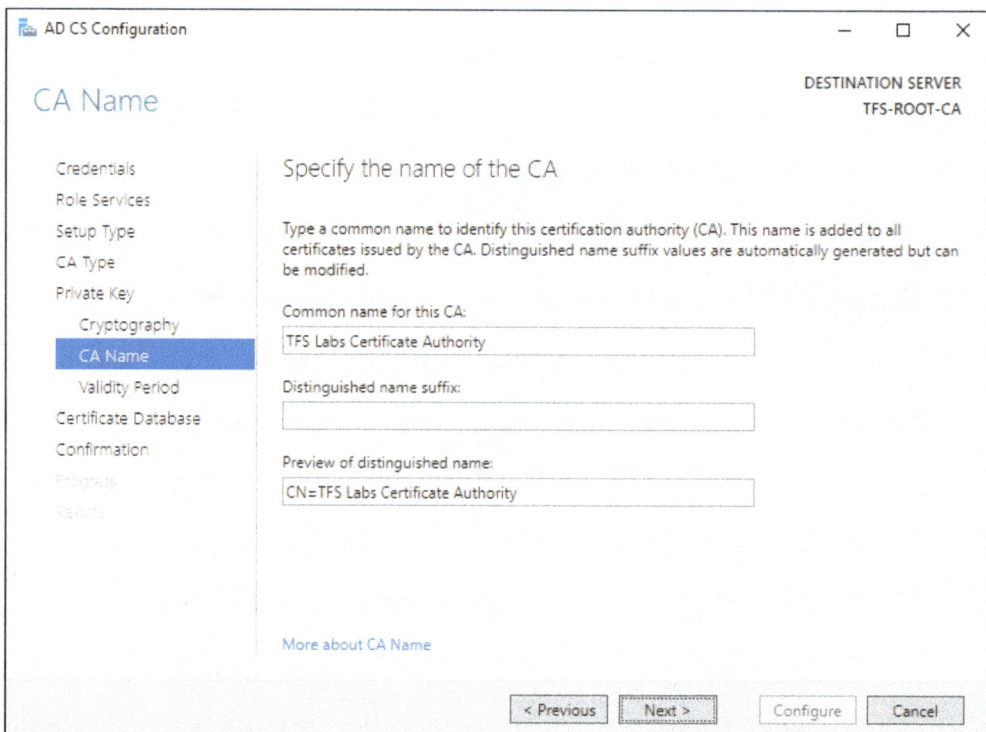

9. On the **Validity Period** screen, set the validity period to **10 Years** and click the **Next** button to continue:

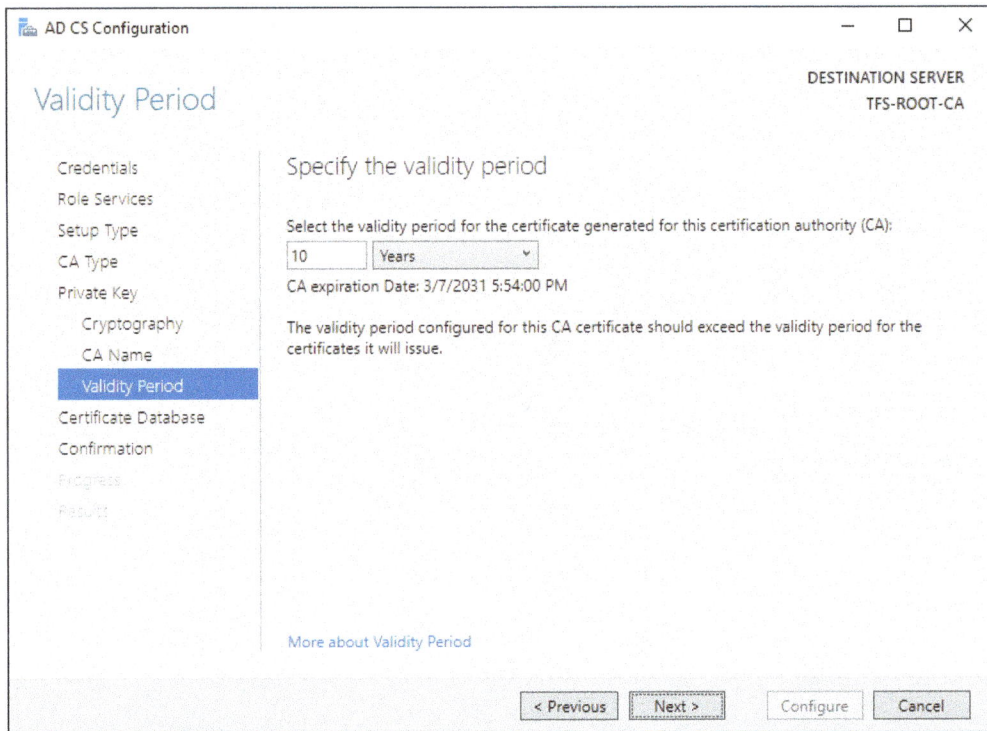

10. On the **CA Database** screen, make no changes to the database location and click the **Next** button to continue:

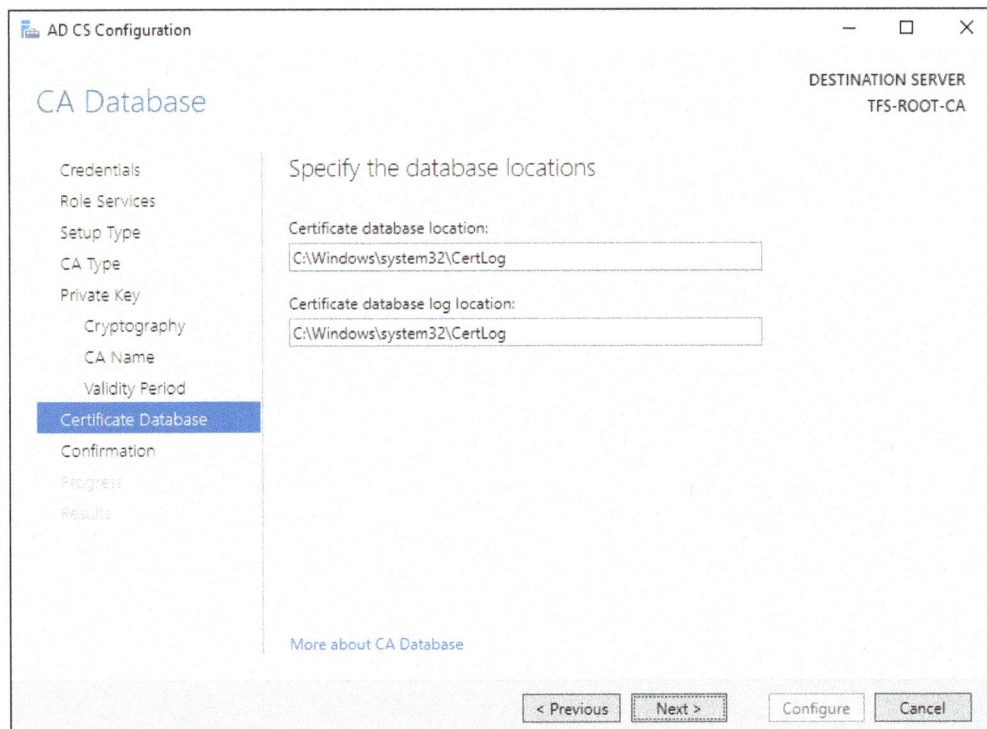

11. On the **Confirmation** screen, verify that the options are correct and click the **Configure** button to commit the changes and create the Root certificate:

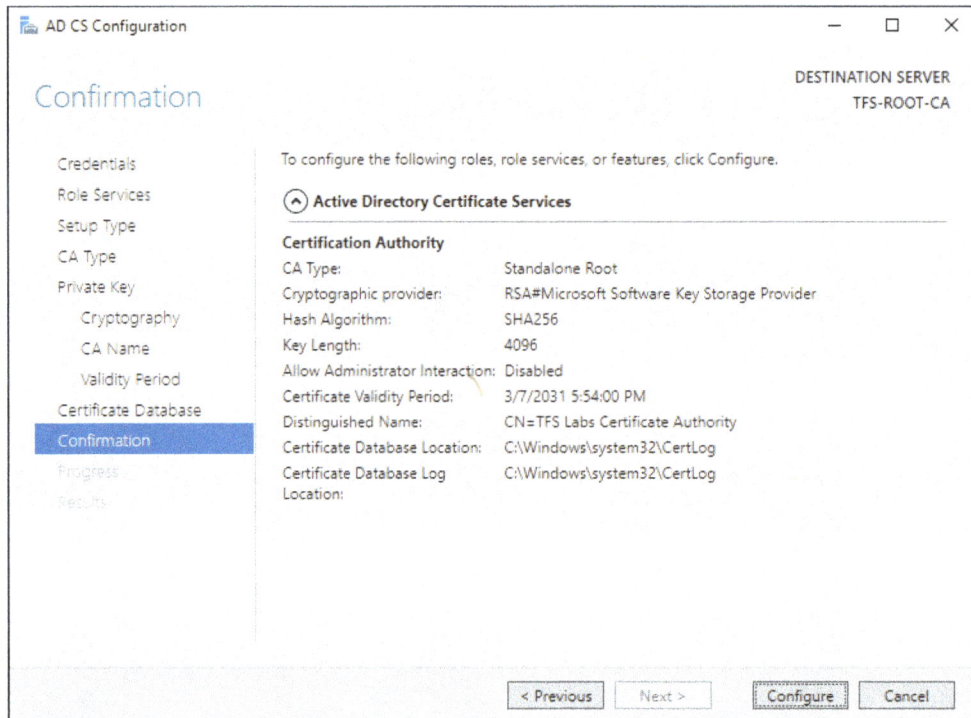

12. On the **Results** screen, click the **Close** button:

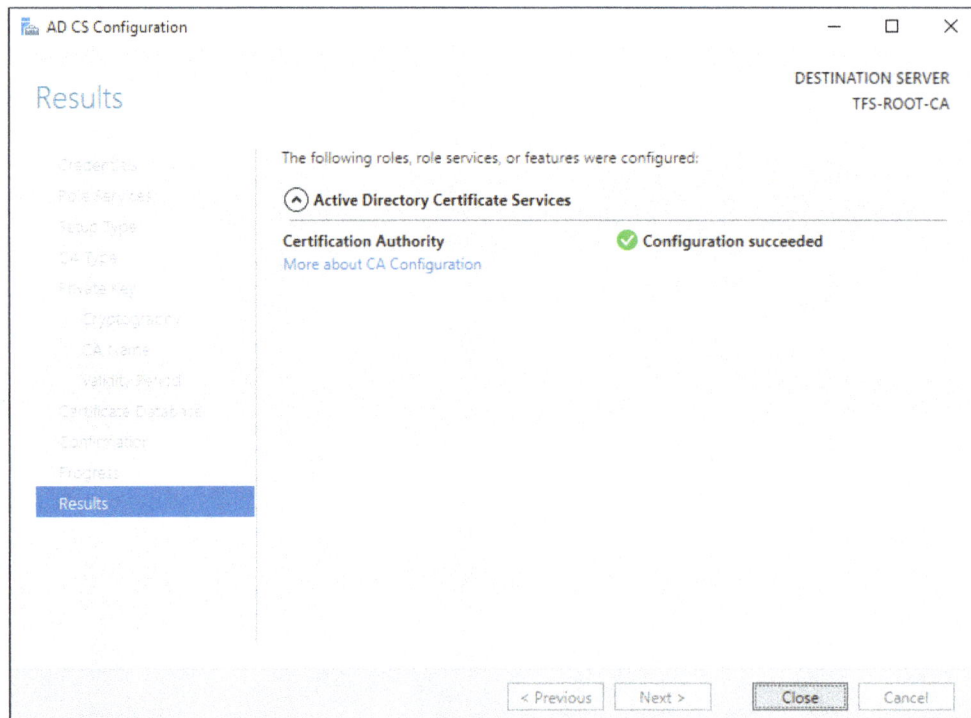

At this point the Root certificate for the TFS Labs domain has been created. The Certificate Authority and Root certificate will be validated in the next section.

Offline Root CA Setup - AD CS Role Validation

At this point there is now a functioning Certificate Authority and Root certificate for the TFS Labs domain. There are a few configuration items that still need to be completed prior to creating a Subordinate certificate, and those items include:

- Configuring the Distinguished Name for the TFS Labs domain.
- Configuring the validity period for the Subordinate CA.
- Configuring the CRL renewal for the Root CA.
- Configuring auditing on the Root CA.
- Configuring the CDP and AIA locations for the Root CA.
- Exporting the Root certificate and Root CRL files.

To verify that the Active Directory Certificate Services role has been successfully configured and the Root certificate was created, open the Certification Authority console (certsrv.msc) on the TFS-ROOT-CA server to check the status of the Certificate Authority:

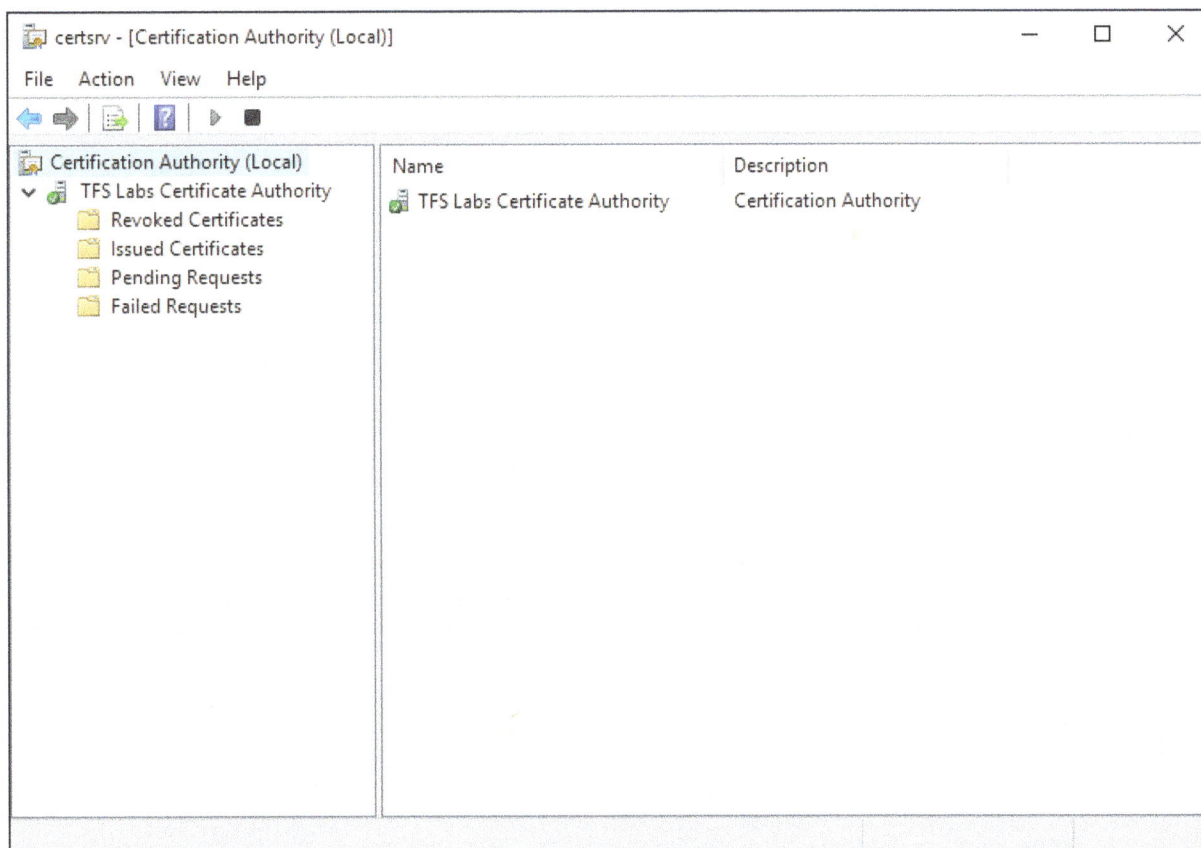

Figure 6.8.1: The Certification Authority console is used to manage the CA and allows administrators to issue and revoke certificates. This console also allows further customization of the CA.

Standalone Certificate Authority

At this point in the configuration of Active Directory Certificate Services, the Root certificate is a Standalone Root Certificate Authority for the TFS Labs domain. There are no dependencies on any other server, and the Root certificate can be used to issue certificates. This is the first part of a Two-Tier Certificate Authority, and the Root certificate will be used to sign the certificate for the Subordinate CA.

The Root certificate can also be verified that it was created with the correct values that were setup during the Active Directory Certificate Services configuration, and this can be checked by opening the Root certificate and checking the **Valid from** field on the certificate:

Figure 6.8.2: The TFS Labs Certificate Authority issued the Root certificate to itself, as it is the root of the PKI for the domain. The validity period for the Root certificate is important, since that will affect any Subordinate certificates that are issued.

When the Subordinate Certificate Authority is created on the TFS-CA01 server in the next chapter, it can also be validated that the Offline CA is functioning correctly when the certificate is created. The CDP and AIA settings still requires some customization to work with the TFS Labs domain, and those settings will be configured on the Root Certificate Authority in the next section.

Offline Root CA Setup - CRL Configuration

The Certificate Revocation List configuration for the Root CA that is configured in this section is meant to give greater control over when the CRL expires and needs to be renewed. The time is being extended to 52 weeks for renewal since the CRL does not need to be updated that often on the Root CA. The changes in this section also ensures that the Subordinate CA lifetime is extended to 5 years (the default is 1 year).

Also configured is the DSConfigDN settings for the Root Certificate Authority. This is needed to inform the Root Certificate Authority on the structure of the TFS Labs domain, since the Root CA has zero visibility to the domain since it is offline and not joined to the domain. All the commands in this section are just making changes to the Windows Registry using the certutil.exe command. This is a convenient way of making changes, as the command will ensure that invalid entries are not added, which could cause issues with the Certificate Authority.

The settings for the Certificate Authority can be viewed by opening the Windows Registry (regedit.exe), and going to the following location:

HKLM\SYSTEM\CurrentControlSet\Services\CertSvc\Configuration

To configure the CRL settings for the Root CA, perform the following steps on the TFS-ROOT-CA server:

1. Open an **elevated PowerShell prompt**.
2. To define the **Active Directory Configuration Partition Distinguished Name**, run the following command (replace **DC=corp,DC=tfslabs,DC=com** with the distinguished name of the Active Directory domain):

```
Windows PowerShell (Elevated)

certutil.exe -setreg `
CA\DSConfigDN "CN=Configuration,DC=corp,DC=tfslabs,DC=com"
```

3. To define the **Validity Period Units** for all issued certificates by the Root CA, run the following commands:

```
Windows PowerShell (Elevated)

certutil.exe -setreg CA\ValidityPeriodUnits 5
certutil.exe -setreg CA\ValidityPeriod "Years"
```

4. To define the **CRL Period Units** and **CRL Period**, run the following commands:

```
Windows PowerShell (Elevated)

certutil.exe -setreg CA\CRLPeriodUnits 52
certutil.exe -setreg CA\CRLPeriod "Weeks"
```

5. To define the **CRL Overlap Period Units** and **CRL Overlap Period**, run the following commands:

```
Windows PowerShell (Elevated)

certutil.exe -setreg CA\CRLOverlapPeriodUnits 12
certutil.exe -setreg CA\CRLOverlapPeriod "Hours"
```

6. Restart the **Active Directory Certificate Services** service to apply the changes:

```
Windows PowerShell (Elevated)

net stop CertSvc
net start CertSvc
```

7. Close the **PowerShell prompt**.

Once the CRL settings have been configured on the Root Certificate Authority, auditing can be enabled and configured on the Root CA.

Determining the Active Directory Configuration Partition Distinguished Name

There are several ways to determine the Active Directory Configuration Partition Distinguished Name in an Active Directory domain. One of the easiest ways to determine the correct format of this name can be accomplished by using the Active Directory Users and Computers console on a Domain Controller, which can be performed using the following steps:

1. On the **TFS-DC01** server, open the **Active Directory Users and Computers** console (dsa.msc).
2. Go to the **View** menu and select **Advanced Features**.
3. Right-click on **corp.tfslabs.com** and select **Properties**.
4. Go to the **Attribute Editor** tab.
5. Scroll down and find the **distinguishedName** attribute field, and click the **View** button:

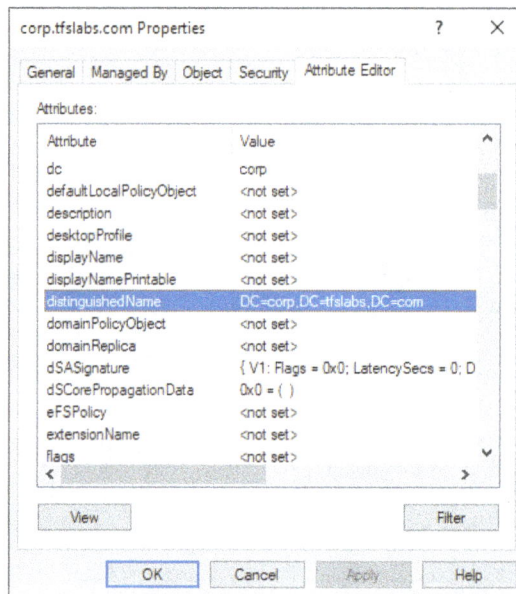

6. The **String Attribute Editor** window will appear for the **distinguishedName** attribute. Copy the value in the **Value** field, as this is the information needed for configuring the CRL.

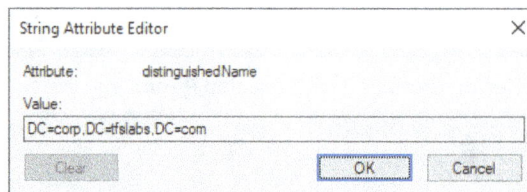

7. Close the **Active Directory Users and Computers** console.

Aside from using the Active Directory Users and Computers console to retrieve the Distinguished Name, the ADSI Edit tool (adsiedit.msc) can also be used to obtain the same result. The **Get-ADUser** Cmdlet can also be used to obtain the Distinguished Name from the CLI:

```
Windows PowerShell (Elevated)

(Get-ADUser -Identity Administrator).DistinguishedName
```

Offline Root CA Setup - Enable Advanced Auditing

Auditing is not necessary on servers that are running Active Directory Certificate Services, but it is highly recommended for best practices. Auditing is often required for compliance purposes, and it is important to know when certificates have been issued or revoked. When Active Directory Certificate Services has auditing enabled, it will create log entries in the Windows Event Log on the local server under the following circumstances:

- When a certificate is issued.
- When a certificate is revoked.
- When the CRL is updated.
- When the Certificate Authority configuration is modified.
- When the certificate archive keys are created and retrieved.
- When the Certificate Authority is backed up using the available methods within Active Directory Certificate Services.
- When administrative tasks are performed on the server, such as starting and stopping the AD CS service.

Even if the more advanced auditing options are not enabled for the Certificate Authority, there will always be Active Directory Certificate Services events written to the Windows Event Log. The settings configured in this section will enable the advanced auditing features for the service, which can be useful for troubleshooting purposes.

To configure auditing on the Root Certificate Authority, perform the following steps on the TFS-ROOT-CA server:

1. Open an **elevated PowerShell prompt** on the **TFS-ROOT-CA** server.
2. Enable the options to audit **Success** and **Failure** attempts on the **Audit object access** setting. This change is made in the **Local Security Policy** with the following command:

```
Windows PowerShell (Elevated)

auditpol.exe /set /category:"Object Access" /failure:enable /success:enable
```

3. Enable auditing for all events on the Certificate Authority by running the following command:

```
Windows PowerShell (Elevated)

certutil.exe -setreg CA\AuditFilter 127
```

4. Restart the **Active Directory Certificate Services** service to apply the changes:

```
Windows PowerShell (Elevated)

net stop CertSvc
net start CertSvc
```

5. Close the **PowerShell prompt**.

If the AD CS service is not restarted after auditing has been enabled, there will be no events written to the Windows Event Log. Auditing options can be verified by opening the Certification Authority console (certsrv.msc) and checking the properties of the TFS Labs Certificate Authority. Once auditing has been enabled on the Root Certificate Authority, the CDP and AIA settings on the Root Certificate Authority can be configured.

> **Third-Party Logging Solutions**
>
> There may be requirements in some organizations for sending logging events from Windows servers to third-party logging solutions. This is usually for monitoring purposes, and to use a tool such as a SIEM for aggregating logs into one location. Since the Root Certificate Authority is offline, these tools cannot be used and that needs to be factored in when designing the PKI. The Root Certificate Authority is only used for certain tasks, and there is not much logging events that can be monitored. The Subordinate Certificate Authority will be online, and those tools can be utilized as that server is handling requests.

Active Directory Certificate Services Auditing

With auditing enabled and configured for Active Directory Certificate Services, events that are enabled for auditing will be logged to the Windows Event Log. These events can be viewed using the Event Viewer Console (eventvwr.msc) on the local server:

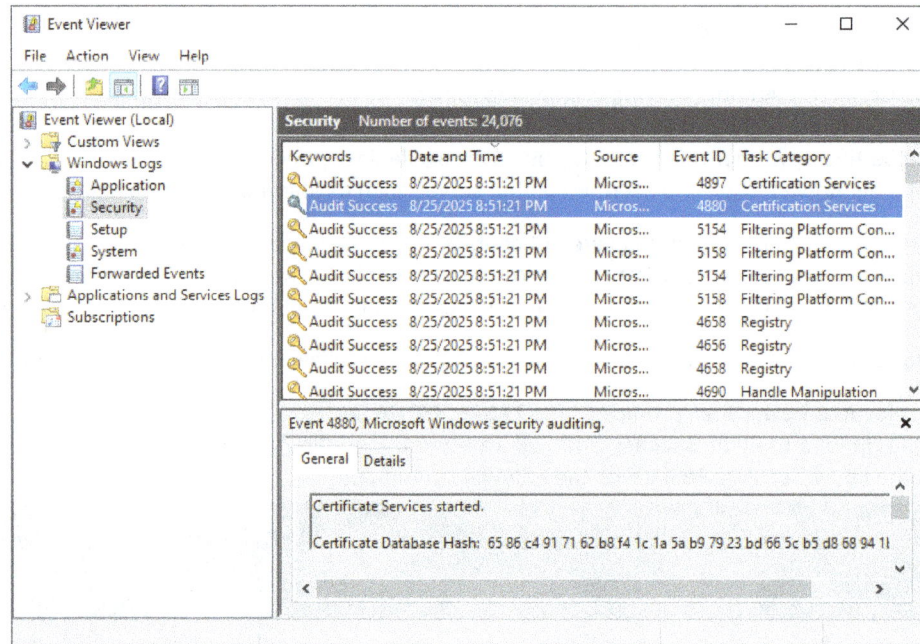

Opening one of the events will show more details on the Active Directory Certificate Services details will give further details on that event:

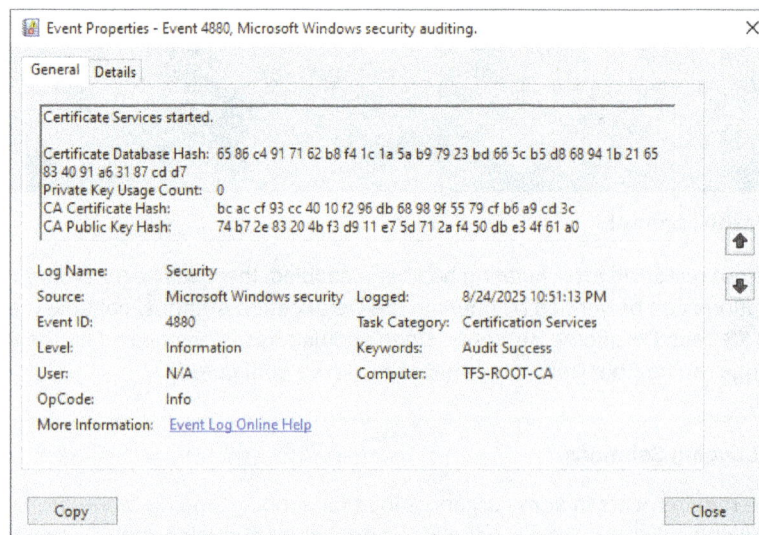

There are 30 Active Directory Certificate Services related events that can be logged in the Windows Event Viewer with an Event ID between 4868 and 4898. Events are also logged with a Task Category of Certification Services to allow for an alternative sorting and filtering method.

Offline Root CA Setup - CDP and AIA Configuration

Before the remainder of the TFS Labs Certificate Authority can be configured, the Certificate Revocation List needs to be configured on the Root Certificate Authority server. The CRL files that are provided by the Root CA are distributed with the Subordinate CA, and this is because the Root CA is not available on the network since it is always offline. There needs to be a way for devices to access the CRL files for the Root certificate, otherwise the PKI will be incomplete.

To correct this issue, the CRL Distribution Point (CDP) and Authority Information Access (AIA) settings are configured on the Root CA by specifying certain DNS records and pointing them to the TFS-CA01 server. The Base CRL will be configured and exported as part of this section, and the Delta CRL will be published on the Subordinate CA in the next chapter. The settings for OCSP are optionally configured in a later chapter in this book, as there are no configuration options required for the Root Certificate Authority.

There are multiple options where the CDP and AIA locations can be configured for the Root Certificate Authority, and there are four locations that are configured by default when the Root certificate is created with Active Directory Certificate Services:

- Local File System
- LDAP
- HTTP
- SMB

To complete the configuration of the CDP and AIA for the Root Certificate Authority, several of the locations will be deleted as they are not required, and a new location will be added that will point to the Subordinate Certificate Authority. This location will be on the TFS-CA01 server using the *http://pki.corp.tfslabs.com/CertData/* address, which will be configured in the next chapter.

The CDP and AIA configuration on the Root Certificate Authority can be performed through the command line using PowerShell, or by using the Certification Authority console.

DNS for CDP and AIA Locations

Ensure that in this section the URL for the CDP and AIA path is correct. This URL relies on a CNAME entry that will eventually point to the TFS-CA01 server (Subordinate CA). The reason that a CNAME entry is used instead of the hostname of the TFS-CA01 server is to provide flexibility in the future should the PKI structure need to be modified.

Any *http://pki.corp.tfslabs.com/CertData/* entries in this section should be modified to fit an existing Active Directory environment. Replace any references to this URL in the CLI and GUI sections with the correct one in this section, and in the next chapter when needed.

Default CRL and AIA Locations

For the purposes of the Root Certificate Authority, most of the default options for CDP and AIA are not valid or even required in most environments. The only location that cannot be removed or modified is the location on the local file system, as it is required for normal operation:

- The local file system location is always required so the Certificate Authority server can access the CDP and AIA data. If this location is missing, the Root CA will not be able to issue the Base CRL.
- The LDAP location entry is not required as this is a Root CA which has no access to Active Directory.
- The HTTP location which is using the DNS name of the Root CA server is not valid as it is an offline server with no network access.
- The SMB location is not required as this is a Root CA and there is no access to the network.

In any case, it is always important to validate the CDP and AIA locations, as it can cause issues with the PKI if there are invalid entries present.

Offline Root CA Setup - CDP and AIA Configuration - CLI Configuration

The CDP and AIA location settings can be configured using the command line with PowerShell by performing the following steps on the TFS-ROOT-CA server:

1. Open an **elevated PowerShell prompt**.
2. Run the following command to configure the **CDP** settings for the Root certificate (execute this command as a single line with no breaks):

```
Windows PowerShell (Elevated)

certutil.exe -setreg CA\CRLPublicationURLs "65:C:\Windows\system32\CertSrv\
CertEnroll\%3%8%9.crl\n6:http://pki.corp.tfslabs.com/CertData/%3%8%9.crl"
```

3. Run the following command to configure the **AIA** settings for the Root certificate (execute this command as a single line with no breaks):

```
Windows PowerShell (Elevated)

certutil.exe -setreg CA\CACertPublicationURLs "1:C:\Windows\system32\CertSrv\
CertEnroll\%1_%3%4.crt\n2:http://pki.corp.tfslabs.com/CertData/%1_%3%4.crt"
```

4. Restart the **Active Directory Certificate Services** service to apply the changes:

```
Windows PowerShell (Elevated)

net stop CertSvc
net start CertSvc
```

5. Close the **PowerShell prompt**.

Now that the CDP and AIA location settings have been successfully configured on the TFS-ROOT-CA server, the settings should be validated to ensure that there are no issues. Once the settings have been confirmed, the CRL for the Root CA can be published.

DNS Entries for CDP and AIA

Ensure that in this section the URL for the CDP and AIA path is correct. This URL relies on a CNAME entry that will eventually point to the TFS-CA01 server (Subordinate CA). The reason that a CNAME entry is used instead of the hostname of the TFS-CA01 server is to provide flexibility in the future should the PKI structure need to be modified.

The *http://pki.corp.tfslabs.com/CertData/* configuration is all performed in the next chapter. The DNS records will be created and the folder will be configured using IIS on the TFS-CA01 server.

Command Line Entry for CDP and AIA Locations

In this section there are two commands (step 2 and step 3) that are used to modify the CDP and AIA locations for the Root CA. These commands need to be executed as a single line, with no line breaks. They are shown with line breaks so that the entire command is visible, but they cannot be executed as they are displayed. Copy the entire command first, remove the line breaks while preserving the existing characters, and then execute the commands in each step.

If there is an error with the configuration in this section, it can cause unexpected issues with the Certificate Authority. Ensure that before proceeding to the next section in this chapter that all issues with the CDP and AIA entries and correct.

Offline Root CA Setup - CDP and AIA Configuration - GUI Configuration

To configure the CDP and AIA locations on the Root Certificate Authority using the Certification Authority console, perform the following steps on the TFS-ROOT-CA server:

1. Open the **Certification Authority** console (certsrv.msc) on the **TFS-ROOT-CA** server:

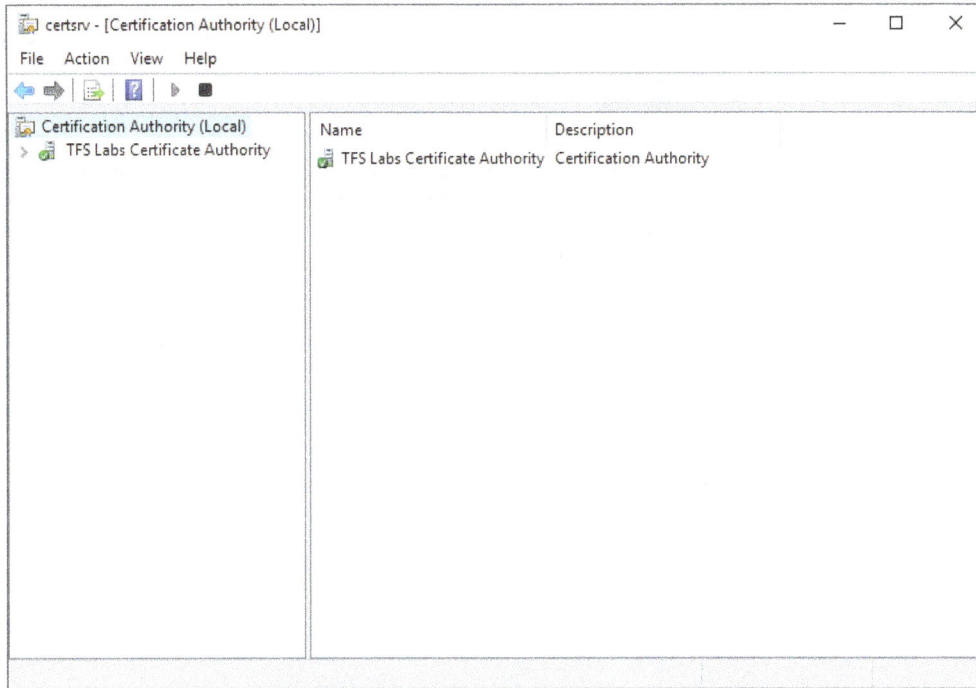

2. Right-click on the **TFS Labs Certificate Authority** server and select **Properties**.
3. Select the **Extensions** tab, verify that the **CRL Distribution Point (CDP)** extension is selected under the **Select extension** field, and click the **Add** button:

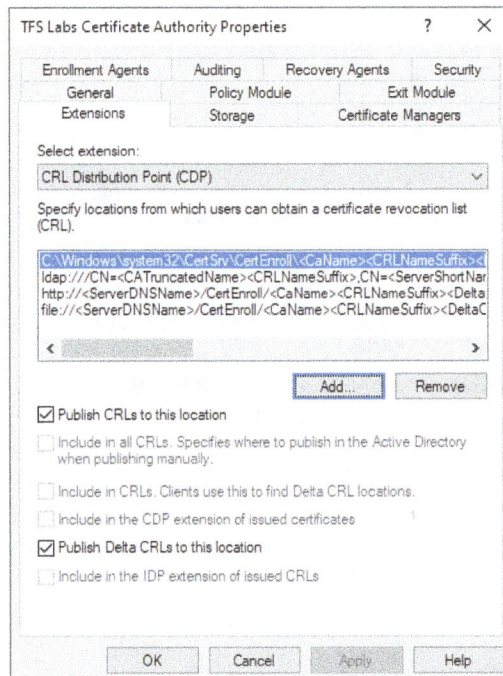

4. In the **Add Location** window, under the **Location** field, enter the following address and click the **OK** button:

```
http://pki.corp.tfslabs.com/CertData/<CaName><CRLNameSuffix><DeltaCRLAllowed>.crl
```

5. On the **Extensions** tab, verify that the **Include in CRLs. Clients use this to find Delta CRL locations.** and **Include in the CDP extension of issued certificates** options are selected for the location that was just entered.
6. Select **ldap:///CN=<CATruncatedName><CRLNameSuffix>,CN=<ServerShortName>,CN=CDP,CN=Public Key Services,CN=Services,<ConfigurationContainer><CDPObjectClass>** from the list and click the **Remove** button. Click the **Yes** button to confirm the location removal.
7. Select **http://<ServerDNSName>/CertEnroll/<CaName><CRLNameSuffix><DeltaCRLAllowed>.crl** from the list and click the **Remove** button. Click the **Yes** button to confirm the location removal.
8. Select **file://<ServerDNSName>/CertEnroll/<CaName><CRLNameSuffix><DeltaCRLAllowed>.crl** from the list and click the **Remove** button. Click the **Yes** button to confirm the location removal.
9. On the **Extensions** tab, verify that under the **Selection extension** field, the **Authority Information Access (AIA)** extension is selected, and click the **Add** button:

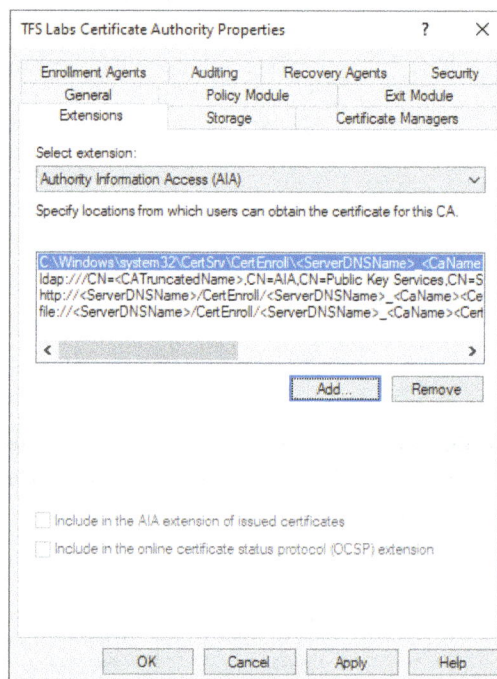

10. In the **Add Location** window, under the **Location** field, enter the following address and click the **OK** button:

```
http://pki.corp.tfslabs.com/CertData/<ServerDNSName>_<CaName><CertificateName>.crt
```

11. On the **Extensions** tab, verify that the **Include in the AIA extension of issued certificates** option is selected for the location that was just entered.
12. Select **ldap:///CN=<CATruncatedName>,CN=AIA,CN=Public Key Services,CN=Services,<ConfigurationContainer><CDPObjectClass>** from the list and click the **Remove** button. Click the **Yes** button to confirm the location removal.
13. Select **http://<ServerDNSName>/CertEnroll/<ServerDNSName>_<CaName><CertificateName>.crt** from the list and click the **Remove** button. Click the **Yes** button to confirm the location removal.
14. Select **file://<ServerDNSName>/CertEnroll/<ServerDNSName>_<CaName><CertificateName>.crt** from the list and click the **Remove** button. Click the **Yes** button to confirm the location removal.
15. Once the CDP and AIA extensions have been configured, click the **OK** button to commit the changes.
16. On the **Certification Authority** window, when prompted to restart **Active Directory Certificate Services**, click the **Yes** button.
17. Close the **Certification Authority** console.

Now that the CDP and AIA location settings have been successfully configured on the TFS-ROOT-CA server, the settings should be validated to ensure that there are no issues. Once the settings have been confirmed, the CRL can be published.

Offline Root CA Setup - CDP and AIA Configuration - Validation

There is a simple way to validate that the CDP and AIA location settings have been applied correctly to the Root CA by using the **certutil.exe** command. The command will output the settings as they have been configured for the Certificate Authority, but will show different variables from the configuration.

From an **elevated PowerShell prompt** on the TFS-ROOT-CA server, run the following command to verify the CDP locations:

Windows PowerShell (Elevated)
certutil.exe -getreg CA\CRLPublicationURLs

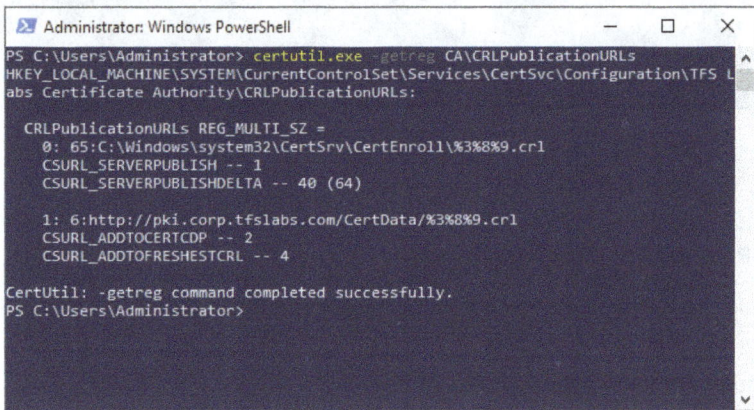

```
Administrator: Windows PowerShell                                    —   □   ×

PS C:\Users\Administrator> certutil.exe -getreg CA\CRLPublicationURLs
HKEY_LOCAL_MACHINE\SYSTEM\CurrentControlSet\Services\CertSvc\Configuration\TFS L
abs Certificate Authority\CRLPublicationURLs:

  CRLPublicationURLs REG_MULTI_SZ =
    0: 65:C:\Windows\system32\CertSrv\CertEnroll\%3%8%9.crl
    CSURL_SERVERPUBLISH -- 1
    CSURL_SERVERPUBLISHDELTA -- 40 (64)

    1: 6:http://pki.corp.tfslabs.com/CertData/%3%8%9.crl
    CSURL_ADDTOCERTCDP -- 2
    CSURL_ADDTOFRESHESTCRL -- 4

CertUtil: -getreg command completed successfully.
PS C:\Users\Administrator>
```

From the same **elevated PowerShell prompt**, run the following command to verify the AIA locations:

Windows PowerShell (Elevated)
certutil.exe -getreg CA\CACertPublicationURLs

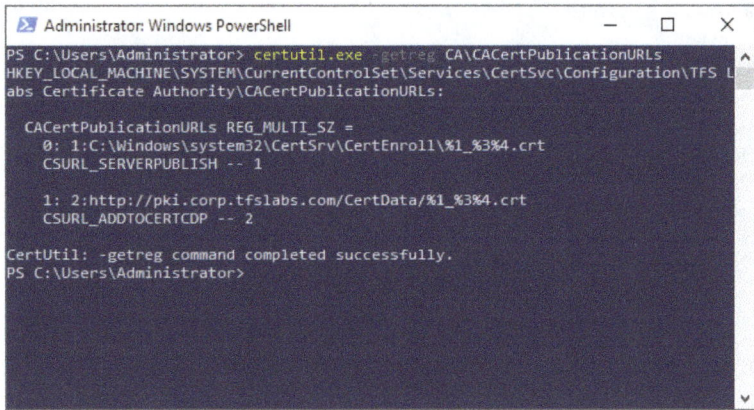

```
Administrator: Windows PowerShell                                    —   □   ×

PS C:\Users\Administrator> certutil.exe -getreg CA\CACertPublicationURLs
HKEY_LOCAL_MACHINE\SYSTEM\CurrentControlSet\Services\CertSvc\Configuration\TFS L
abs Certificate Authority\CACertPublicationURLs:

  CACertPublicationURLs REG_MULTI_SZ =
    0: 1:C:\Windows\system32\CertSrv\CertEnroll\%1_%3%4.crt
    CSURL_SERVERPUBLISH -- 1

    1: 2:http://pki.corp.tfslabs.com/CertData/%1_%3%4.crt
    CSURL_ADDTOCERTCDP -- 2

CertUtil: -getreg command completed successfully.
PS C:\Users\Administrator>
```

If there are no issues with the CDP and AIA locations for the Root certificate, then the CRL for the Root Certificate Authority can be published. Publishing the Root CRL can be performed in the next section.

Offline Root CA Setup - Publish CRL

Once the CDP and AIA configuration has been successfully completed for the Root Certificate Authority, the CRL can be published. The Root CA will publish the Base CRL for the TFS Labs domain, and the associated files will be copied to the Subordinate CA in the next chapter.

> **CRL Renewal Tasks for Root Certificate Authorities**
>
> Publishing the CRL is an on-going maintenance task that is required for the normal operation of a Certificate Authority using Active Directory Certificate Services and must be performed at regular intervals. More details on how to perform this task are provided in a later chapter of the book.

Offline Root CA Setup - Publish CRL - CLI Method

The CRL can be published using the **certutil.exe** command. From an **elevated PowerShell prompt** on the TFS-ROOT-CA server, run the following command to publish the CRL:

```
Windows PowerShell (Elevated)

certutil.exe -crl
```

Once the CRL has been published, the CRL and the Root certificate can now be exported so that the Subordinate CA server can host it for the TFS Labs domain.

Offline Root CA Setup - Publish CRL - GUI Method

The CRL can also be published using the Certificate Authority console by performing the following steps on the TFS-ROOT-CA server:

1. Open the **Certification Authority** console (certsrv.msc).
2. In the **Certification Authority** console, expand the **TFS Labs Certificate Authority**, right-click on **Revoked Certificates** under **TFS Labs Certificate Authority** and select **All Tasks > Publish**:

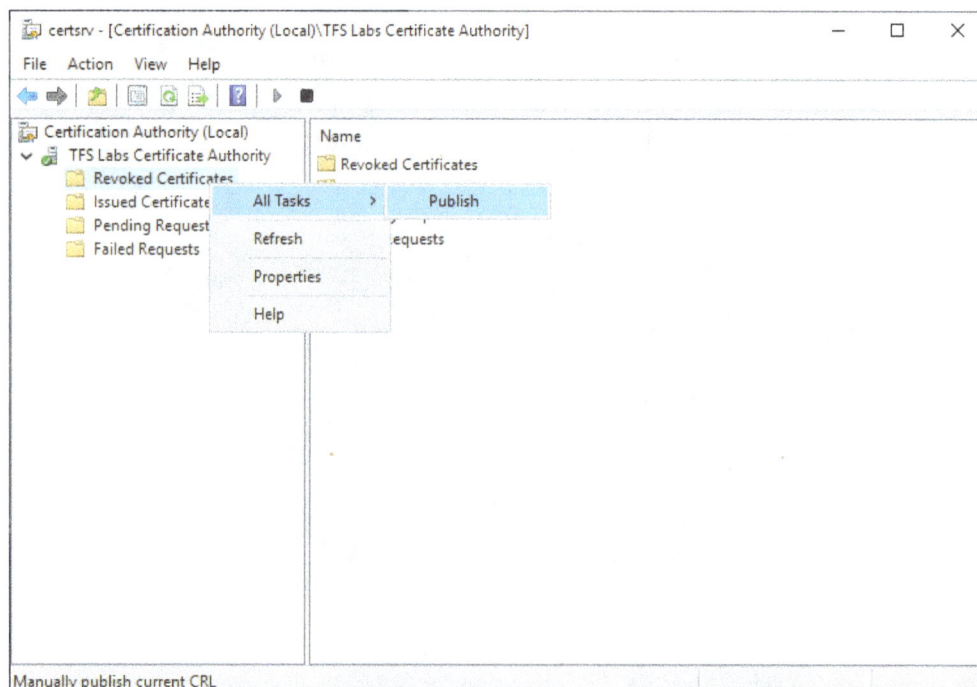

3. On the **Publish CRL** window, verify that **New CRL** is selected and click the **OK** button:

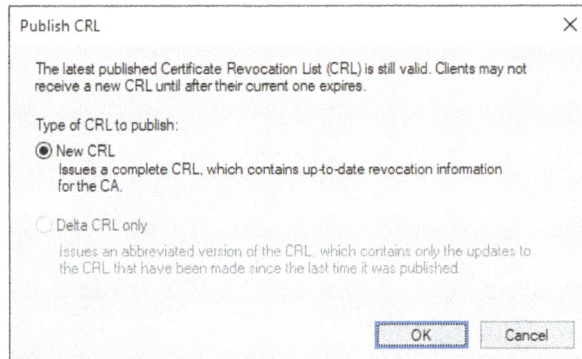

```
Publish CRL                                                      ×

   The latest published Certificate Revocation List (CRL) is still valid. Clients may not
   receive a new CRL until after their current one expires.

   Type of CRL to publish:
   ⦿ New CRL
      Issues a complete CRL, which contains up-to-date revocation information
      for the CA.

   ○ Delta CRL only
      Issues an abbreviated version of the CRL, which contains only the updates to
      the CRL that have been made since the last time it was published.


                                            [    OK    ]    [  Cancel  ]
```

4. Close the **Certification Authority** console.

Once the CRL has been published, the CRL and the Root certificate can now be exported so that the Subordinate CA server can host it for the TFS Labs domain.

Offline Root CA Setup - Root Certificate CRL Export

Exporting the CRL for the Root Certificate Authority is needed to make it available on the TFS-CA01 server, and for the rest of the TFS Labs domain. The links to these files are referenced in the Root certificate CDP and AIA configuration, so they will need to be copied to the Subordinate CA server to make them accessible. To copy the Root CRL files, perform the following steps on the TFS-ROOT-CA server:

1. Copy the contents of the **C:\Windows\System32\CertSrv\CertEnroll** folder to the **C:\RootCA** folder.
2. The following files should be present in the **C:\RootCA** folder:
   - C:\RootCA\TFS Labs Certificate Authority.crl
   - C:\RootCA\TFS-ROOT-CA_TFS Labs Certificate Authority.crt
3. Add the **RootCAFiles.vfd** virtual floppy disk to the **TFS-ROOT-CA** virtual machine.
4. Copy the contents of the **C:\RootCA** folder to the **A:\ drive**.
5. Eject the **RootCAFiles.vfd** virtual floppy disk.

Once the Root CRL files have been successfully copied to the virtual floppy disk, all initial tasks for the TFS-ROOT-CA server are now complete.

Offline Root CA Setup - Server Restart

It is advisable to restart the Root CA server before continuing with any additional configuration of the TFS Labs Certificate Authority. This will ensure that all changes to the Root CA have been successfully committed and applied. The server will need to remain powered on to complete steps in the next chapter.

Offline Root CA Setup - Chapter Summary

Now that the Root Certificate Authority and Root certificate have been successfully created, the Subordinate Certificate Authority and the Subordinate certificate for the TFS Labs domain can now be created. The next chapter will outline the process for creating the Subordinate Certificate Authority server, and how to create the Certificate Request for the Subordinate certificate. Multiple tasks for configuring the Root CA and Subordinate CA will also be performed in the next chapter, as the Subordinate Certificate Authority contains most of the configuration for the PKI.

If BitLocker was configured for encrypting the TFS-ROOT-CA server, the BitLocker Recovery Key should also be located on the **RootCAFiles.vfd** virtual floppy disk (or whatever virtual floppy disk was used). In the next chapter when the TFS-CA01 server is provisioned, the virtual floppy disk can be mounted on that server and the BitLocker Recovery Key can be copied to it and backed up accordingly.

Chapter 7 - Subordinate CA Setup

The Subordinate Certificate Authority server is setup as a Windows server on the TFS Labs Active Directory domain. Unlike the Root CA server, it is meant to always be online, and is primarily used to issue and manage certificates for the TFS Labs domain. The Subordinate CA server can also be referred to as an Enterprise CA, and can also be referred to as an Issuing CA. These terms will be used interchangeably throughout the remainder of this book, but they are essentially the same thing. The SubCA term can also be used to refer to the Subordinate CA server in most cases.

Since the Subordinate CA will be setup on an Active Directory domain, it is necessary to make changes to the Windows Defender Firewall on the server to ensure that other devices on the domain can communicate with AD CS services. It is extremely bad practice to disable the Windows Defender Firewall on a production Windows server, so this chapter will demonstrate what changes should be made to the Windows Defender Firewall to allow for proper communication without compromising security.

The Root CA that was setup in the previous chapter used BitLocker full disk encryption, but that step is skipped for this chapter. Since it is assumed that the Subordinate CA will be a member of an Active Directory environment, it is likely that full disk encryption would be setup differently if it were being used in that environment. The instructions for configuring BitLocker are still valid should they also be used for this server. This chapter will focus on how to install and configure a Subordinate CA server using Active Directory Certificate Services. There are several main tasks that are completed in this chapter:

- Configure DNS records for PKI services for the TFS Labs domain.
- Create folders in IIS for Root CA CRL distribution.
- Modify the certificate age for all certificates issued by the Subordinate CA.
- Configure auditing on the Subordinate CA server.
- Configure the Certification Practice Statement for the TFS Labs domain.
- Configure the Windows Defender Firewall for allow AD CS communication.

Once the steps in this chapter have been completed, the infrastructure that is needed create the remainder of the PKI will be available. Further chapters in this book will focus on deployment and further customization of the Certificate Authority for the TFS Labs domain.

DNS and LDAP Configuration

There are several steps in this chapter that reference specific DNS records and LDAP entries that are dependent on the Active Directory configuration of a particular domain. Ensure that when modifying the steps in this chapter for a different environment that these variables are accounted for. Applying the steps in this chapter for another environment will not work as they are specific to the TFS Labs domain.

BitLocker Recovery Key Backup

An optional step in the previous chapter placed the BitLocker Recovery Key for the TFS-ROOT-CA server on a virtual floppy disk. If this step was completed, the BitLocker Recovery Key should be securely backed up before the end of this chapter.

Existing Active Directory Domains and AD CS

There are little to no changes required on an existing Active Directory domain to support the installation of Active Directory Certificate Services. Standard configurations such as DNS settings do not change because of using AD CS, but changes will be made to the Active Directory configuration as a result of deploying AD CS.

Subordinate CA Setup - Prerequisites

At the end of this chapter there will be a functional Subordinate Certificate Authority and Enterprise CA for the TFS Labs domain. This will complete the PKI for the TFS Labs domain, and certificates will be able to be issued on the domain. Similar to the Active Directory configuration, there are no special configurations that need to occur, and there is no third-party software required to create the Subordinate Certificate Authority. Unlike the Root Certificate Authority, the Subordinate Certificate Authority is online at all times. The server requires access to a Domain Controller on the TFS Labs domain, as well as limited access to the Root CA server. The virtual floppy disk that was created in the previous chapter will also be used as part of the process for creating the Subordinate certificate.

> **Hyper-V and Other Virtualization Solutions**
>
> There are many references in this chapter that are specific to Hyper-V and how it is used to host the virtual machine for the Subordinate CA server. Unlike the Root CA server, the limitation to keep the server offline is not in place, so shared virtualization features such as copy and paste are not a limiting issue with this server and can be used.

Subordinate CA Setup - Installation and Configuration

Similar to the Windows Server that is hosting the Root Certificate Authority, the Subordinate Certificate Authority requires minimal resources to operate correctly. Even though the server is online and performs more tasks than the Root CA server, these tasks will operate correctly with minimal hardware specifications. In a production environment these requirements will vary depending on the size of the organization, and how often the Certificate Authority is used. The specifications for the virtual machine can be modified at any time should the performance become an issue.

The Subordinate Certificate Authority server for the TFS Labs domain will be called TFS-CA01. There are several steps that need to be completed to create the virtual machine that will be used for the Subordinate CA server for the **corp.tfslabs.com** domain:

- Provision a virtual machine for the TFS-CA01 server using Hyper-V.
- Install Windows Server 2022 Standard (Desktop Experience) on the virtual machine.
- Configure the local administrator password and hostname for the TFS-CA01 server.
- Configure the network settings for the TFS-CA01 server.
- Join the TFS-CA01 server to the TFS Labs domain.
- Move the TFS-CA01 server to the correct Organizational Unit (OU) in Active Directory.

The TFS-CA01 server will be a member of the TFS Labs domain, so the Group Policy modifications that were required for the Root CA server are not necessary for this server as these settings should be applied through Active Directory.

> **Virtual Floppy Disks and File Transfers**
>
> This book uses virtual floppy disks to transfer files between the Root CA server and the other servers involved in the Certificate Authority implementation. There are other methods that can be used for moving files between servers without network connections, but the security of those methods is not guaranteed. The process for moving files with tools available with certain virtualization platforms are not covered in this book.

> **BitLocker Disk Encryption**
>
> Unlike the Root CA server which is an offline server that is meant for a specific purpose, the Subordinate CA server is a member of an Active Directory domain which can use those resources. There may be requirements for full disk encryption software for the TFS-CA01 server, and it may be different than BitLocker. Encrypting the virtual hard disk for the TFS-CA01 server is beyond the scope of this book.

The TFS-CA01 virtual machine will have the following specifications:

Virtual Machine Generation	1
Virtual Processors	2
Virtual Memory	4 GB (4096 MB)
Virtual Hard Disk	40 GB
Virtual Network Adapters	1

Table 7.2.1: Virtual machine specifications for the TFS-CA01 server.

The TFS-CA01 virtual machine will have the following network configuration:

IP Address	10.100.1.101
Netmask	255.255.255.0
Gateway	10.100.1.1
DNS Server 1	10.100.1.100

Table 7.2.2: Network configuration settings for the TFS-CA01 server.

Since the TFS-CA01 server will be part of the TFS Labs domain, the network configuration settings need to be configured so that there is connectivity with the TFS-DC01 Domain Controller. If there is an issue with the DNS settings, then it will not be possible to join the TFS-CA01 server to the TFS Labs domain.

The TFS-CA01 server can now be created and configured for the TFS Labs domain. If there are issues with joining the TFS-CA01 server to the TFS Labs domain, check the network settings and validate connectivity to the TFS-DC01 server.

> **Generation 1 Virtual Machine**
>
> The TFS-CA01 virtual machine needs to be configured as a Generation 1 virtual machine so that it has access to a virtual floppy drive. This virtual floppy drive is required to transfer files to and from the Root CA server, as the Root CA cannot transfer files over the network due to the lack of an available network connection.

Subordinate CA Setup - Installation and Configuration - Virtual Machine Setup

To create a Hyper-V virtual machine for the TFS-CA01 server using the command line, open an **elevated PowerShell prompt** and run the following commands on the Hyper-V host:

1. Create the **TFS-CA01** virtual machine and virtual hard disk using the **New-VM** Cmdlet:

```
Windows PowerShell (Elevated)

New-VM `
-Name "TFS-CA01" `
-Generation 1 `
-MemoryStartupBytes 4GB `
-BootDevice VHD `
-NewVHDPath "D:\Hyper-V\Virtual Hard Disks\TFS-CA01.vhdx" `
-NewVHDSizeBytes 40GB `
-Switch "Hyper-V External Switch"
```

2. Set the number of virtual processors for the **TFS-CA01** virtual machine to **2** using the **Set-VMProcessor** Cmdlet:

Windows PowerShell (Elevated)

```
Set-VMProcessor "TFS-CA01" -Count 2
```

3. Mount the ISO image that will be used to install the operating system on the **TFS-CA01** virtual machine using the **Set-VMDvdDrive** Cmdlet:

Windows PowerShell (Elevated)

```
Set-VMDvdDrive `
-VMName "TFS-CA01" `
-Path "D:\ISO Images\Windows Server 2022.iso"
```

4. Power on the **TFS-CA01** virtual machine using the **Start-VM** Cmdlet:

Windows PowerShell (Elevated)

```
Start-VM -Name "TFS-CA01"
```

5. Connect to the **TFS-CA01** virtual machine using the **Virtual Machine Connection** application:

Windows PowerShell (Elevated)

```
vmconnect.exe localhost "TFS-CA01"
```

Alternatively, the TFS-CA01 virtual server can be created and configured without using PowerShell by using Hyper-V Manager instead (ensure that after the virtual machine is created that the configuration is modified as needed). Only one method is required to create the virtual machine for the TFS-CA01 virtual machine.

Regardless of which method is used to create the virtual machine, Windows Server 2022 can be installed normally with all default options. In this book, **Windows Server 2022 Standard (Desktop Experience)** is the version that all servers will use. When the installation of Windows Server 2022 has successfully completed, the first step is to configure the local administrator password for the TFS-CA01 server. This step occurs automatically before the server can be logged into, and is the first screen that is displayed after the successful installation of Windows Server 2022.

> ⚠️ **Subordinate Certificate Authority Local Administrator Account Password**
>
> The local administrator account that is used during the initial setup of the TFS-CA01 server will only be required for the initial configuration tasks on the server. All administrative tasks on the Subordinate CA will be performed using a Domain Administrator account, as the Certificate Authority configuration makes changes to Active Directory. Ensure that the password for the local administrator account is a complex password and is properly documented should it be needed in the future.

When the local administrator account password has been set, login to the server using the new password. Renaming a Windows server can be performed using the command line with the **Rename-Computer** Cmdlet and this should be the first task performed on the server before continuing. Alternatively, the hostname can be configured using the Server Manager console in the Local Server configuration section.

To configure the hostname of the server using the command line, open an **elevated PowerShell prompt** and run the following command on the TFS-CA01 server:

Windows PowerShell (Elevated)

```
Rename-Computer "TFS-CA01" -Restart
```

The command will automatically restart the server to apply the hostname change. Once the server has been restarted, the network settings for the server can now be configured prior to joining it to the TFS Labs domain.

Subordinate CA Setup - Installation and Configuration - Network Configuration

There are several ways to configure the network settings for the TFS-CA01 server which will be configured to use a static IP address. The settings can be configured using the command line with the **Get-NetAdapter**, **New-NetIPAddress**, and **Set-DnsClientServerAddress** Cmdlets. The settings can also be configured using the GUI with the **Network Connections** Control Panel applet. Only one method is required to change the IP address and DNS server addresses on the server, there is no need to use both. To configure the IP address on the TFS-CA01 server using the command line, open an **elevated PowerShell prompt** and run the following command on the TFS-CA01 server:

```
Windows PowerShell (Elevated)

New-NetIPAddress `
-AddressFamily IPv4 `
-IPAddress 10.100.1.101 `
-PrefixLength 24 `
-DefaultGateway 10.100.1.1 `
-InterfaceIndex (Get-NetAdapter).InterfaceIndex
```

To configure the DNS server addresses on the TFS-CA01 server to point to the TFS-DC01 server using the command line, open an **elevated PowerShell prompt** and run the following command:

```
Windows PowerShell (Elevated)

Set-DnsClientServerAddress `
-ServerAddresses ("10.100.1.100") `
-InterfaceIndex (Get-NetAdapter).InterfaceIndex
```

Alternatively, the IP address and DNS server addresses for the server can be configured without using the command line by using the **Network Connections** Control Panel applet. To configure the IP address and the DNS server addresses for the TFS-CA01 server, perform the following steps:

1. Open the **Network Connections** Control Panel applet (ncpa.cpl).
2. In the **Network Connections** window, right-click on the **Ethernet** network adapter and select the **Properties** option.
3. In the **Ethernet Properties** window, scroll to the **Internet Protocol Version 4 (TCP/IPv4)** connection and select it. Click the **Properties** button.
4. In the **Internet Protocol Version 4 (TCP/IPv4) Properties** window, make the following changes:
   - Select the option for **Use the following IP address**
   - Set the **IP address** to **10.100.1.101**
   - Set the **Subnet mask** to **255.255.255.0**
   - Set the **Default Gateway** to **10.100.1.1**
5. In the **Internet Protocol Version 4 (TCP/IPv4) Properties** window, make the following changes to configure the DNS server addresses:
   - Select the option for **Use the following DNS server addresses**.
   - Set the **Preferred DNS server** to the **10.100.1.100** address.
   - Leave the **Alternate DNS server** blank.
6. Click the **OK** button to apply the IP and DNS address changes.
7. Click the **OK** button to close the **Ethernet Properties** window.

Regardless of which method is used to apply the network configuration to the TFS-CA01 server, any changes to the IP and DNS server addresses are applied immediately and there is no need to restart the server. Once the network settings have been configured, proceed to joining the TFS-CA01 server to the domain.

Network Configuration Validation

Before proceeding any further it is important to validate the network configuration settings and ensure that the TFS-CA01 server is able to communicate correctly with the TFS-DC01 Domain Controller. This can be done by pinging the domain name for the TFS Labs domain (**corp.tfslabs.com**), and the IP address should resolve to any available Domain Controllers in the Active Directory domain:

```
Windows PowerShell

ping corp.tfslabs.com
```

Since there is only one Domain Controller configured in the TFS Labs domain, the IP address for the domain should only resolve to the IP address of the TFS-DC01 server (10.100.1.100). If there are no issues with the network configuration or the DNS configuration, the TFS-CA01 server can be joined to the TFS Labs domain.

Subordinate CA Setup - Installation and Configuration - Domain Join

There are several options available for joining a Windows server to an Active Directory domain. It can be joined to the domain using the command line with the **Add-Computer** Cmdlet. It can also be joined to the domain with the System Properties Control Panel applet. Only one method is required to join the TFS-CA01 server to the TFS Labs domain, there is no need to use both methods.

To join the Subordinate CA server to the TFS Labs domain, open an **elevated PowerShell prompt** and run the following command on the TFS-CA01 server:

```
Windows PowerShell (Elevated)

Add-Computer -DomainName corp.tfslabs.com -Restart
```

When the **Add-Computer** Cmdlet is used, a window will appear asking for valid credentials to join the server to the domain. The Domain Administrator account (**TFSLABS\Administrator**) can be used to join the server to the domain. If there are no issues with the credentials, the TFS-CA01 server will automatically restart to complete the process of adding it to the domain.

To join the Subordinate CA server to the TFS Labs domain using the System Properties Control Panel applet, perform the following steps on the TFS-CA01 server:

1. Open the **System Properties** Control Panel applet (sysdm.cpl).
2. In the **System Properties** window, click the **Change...** button at the bottom of the **Computer Name** tab.
3. In the **Computer Name/Domain Changes** window, select the option for **Domain** in the **Member of** box. For the **Domain**, enter **corp.tfslabs.com** and click the **OK** button.
4. A window will appear asking for valid credentials to join the workstation to the domain. The Domain Administrator account (**TFSLABS\Administrator**) can be used to join the workstation to the domain. Enter the username and password and click the **OK** button.
5. In the **Computer Name/Domain Changes** box, a notification that the computer will need to be restarted to join the domain will appear. Click the **OK** button to continue.
6. In the **Computer Name/Domain Changes** box, a notification that the computer has been joined to the domain will appear. Click the **OK** button to continue.
7. In the **System Properties** window, click the **Close** button.
8. When prompted, click the **Restart Now** button to immediately restart the **TFS-CA01** server and complete the Active Directory join.

After the restart of the server has been completed, and if there were no issues with the network or with the credentials, the TFS-CA01 will now be joined to the TFS Labs domain. The Domain Administrator account can now be used on the TFS-CA01 server, which will be used for the remainder of the Active Directory Certificate Services configuration in this chapter, and in future chapters in this book.

When the TFS-CA01 server restarts, login using the Domain Administrator account. This will ensure that there are no issues with configuring Active Directory Certificate Services for the TFS Labs domain. Once that has been completed, proceed to relocating the server object in Active Directory.

Subordinate CA Setup - Installation and Configuration - Relocate Server Object

The TFS-CA01 server should be moved from the default Computer OU in Active Directory to one of the dedicated OUs that was created earlier for the TFS Labs domain. This will facilitate easier application of Group Policy objects, which are needed for Active Directory Certificate Services. This change can be made on any Domain Controller in an Active Directory domain.

There are several ways to move the computer object in Active Directory. One method is with the command line using PowerShell, and the other method is using the Active Directory Users and Computers console. Only one method is required to move the computer object.

The TFS-CA01 server object can be moved using the **Get-ADComputer** and **Move-ADObject** Cmdlets by running the following command from an **elevated PowerShell prompt** on the TFS-DC01 server:

```
Windows PowerShell (Elevated)

Get-ADComputer "TFS-CA01" | `
Move-ADObject -TargetPath "OU=TFS Servers,OU=TFS Labs,DC=corp,DC=tfslabs,DC=com"
```

Alternatively, the TFS-CA01 server object can be moved using the Active Directory Users and Computers console by performing the following steps on the TFS-DC01 server:

1. Open the **Active Directory Users and Computers** console (dsa.msc) on the **TFS-DC01** server.
2. Expand the **corp.tfslabs.com** domain and go to the **Computers** OU.
3. Right-click on the **TFS-CA01** computer and click on **Move…**.
4. In the **Move** window, expand the **TFS Labs** OU and select **TFS Servers** and click **OK**. If a warning message about moving the computer object appears, click the **Yes** button to continue.
5. Close the **Active Directory Users and Computers** console.

Once the TFS-CA01 server has been moved to the correct OU in Active Directory, it is ready to be used for configuring the Subordinate CA with Active Directory Certificate Services. Proceed to creating the necessary DNS records needed to support AD CS on the TFS Labs domain in the next section.

Organizational Units and Group Policy Changes

When a computer or user object is relocated in Active Directory, the Group Policy Objects that are associated with the new OU may potentially be different from the source location. If an object is relocated in Active Directory it may take time for the new Group Policy changes to take effect. The changes can also be different depending on if a computer object or user object was moved, as those policies can be different from one another.

Group Policy Objects are applied at regular intervals, and are usually applied every 90 minutes by default. However, some policies are only applied when a user logs in, or when the computer is started. To ensure that there are no issues with policies being applied, it is good practice to restart the server after it has been moved. This will ensure that the correct Group Policy Objects are being applied to the server without needing to wait for the change to be automatically applied.

Subordinate CA Setup - Create DNS Records

By creating separate CNAME records for the Active Directory Certificate Services role, it will make it possible to split up the Subordinate CA server in the future if needed. In the process of creating the TFS Labs Certificate Authority, there are two DNS records that need to be created in the DNS Zone to support the functions of the PKI. These DNS records will be used by clients to retrieve certificates, and perform important lookups for Certificate Revocation.

There are two CNAME records that need to be created to support the PKI on the TFS Labs domain:

- OCSP.corp.tfslabs.com
- PKI.corp.tfslabs.com

There are two methods for creating CNAME records in DNS using Windows Server, one is through the command line using PowerShell, and the other is with the DNS Manager console. Only one method is required to create the CNAME records, there is no need to use both methods.

> **Optional PKI Features and DNS Records**
>
> At a minimum, the **PKI** DNS record is required to allow access to the Root CRL files as those files are needed to complete the PKI for the TFS Labs domain. The **OCSP** DNS record is an optional record for domains that use the OCSP (Online Responder) functionality with Active Directory Certificate Services. If that functionality is not being used for a particular deployment, then that record does not need to be created now, but can be added later if it is needed.
>
> Ensure that the DNS records created in this section match the records that were configured in the previous chapter, as those records are referenced in the CDP and AIA configurations for the Root CA. If the records are different, then there will be issues in validating the PKI.

Subordinate CA Setup - Create DNS Records - CLI Configuration

The DNS records needed for the PKI on the TFS Labs domain can be added through the command line using PowerShell on the TFS-DC01 server:

1. Open an **elevated PowerShell prompt**.
2. Enter the following command to create a **CNAME** record for **OCSP.corp.tfslabs.com**:

```
Windows PowerShell (Elevated)

Add-DnsServerResourceRecordCName `
-Name "OCSP" `
-HostNameAlias "TFS-CA01.corp.tfslabs.com" `
-ZoneName "corp.tfslabs.com"
```

3. Enter the following command to create a **CNAME** record for **PKI.corp.tfslabs.com**:

```
Windows PowerShell (Elevated)

Add-DnsServerResourceRecordCName `
-Name "PKI" `
-HostNameAlias "TFS-CA01.corp.tfslabs.com" `
-ZoneName "corp.tfslabs.com"
```

4. Close the **PowerShell prompt**.

Once the DNS records have been created, the CAPolicy.inf file that is needed to create the Subordinate certificate can be configured in the next section.

Subordinate CA Setup - Create DNS Records - GUI Configuration

On the TFS-DC01 Domain Controller, create the following CNAME records pointing to the TFS-CA01 server using the DNS Manager console:

1. Open the **DNS Manager** console (dnsmgmt.msc) on the **TFS-DC01** server:

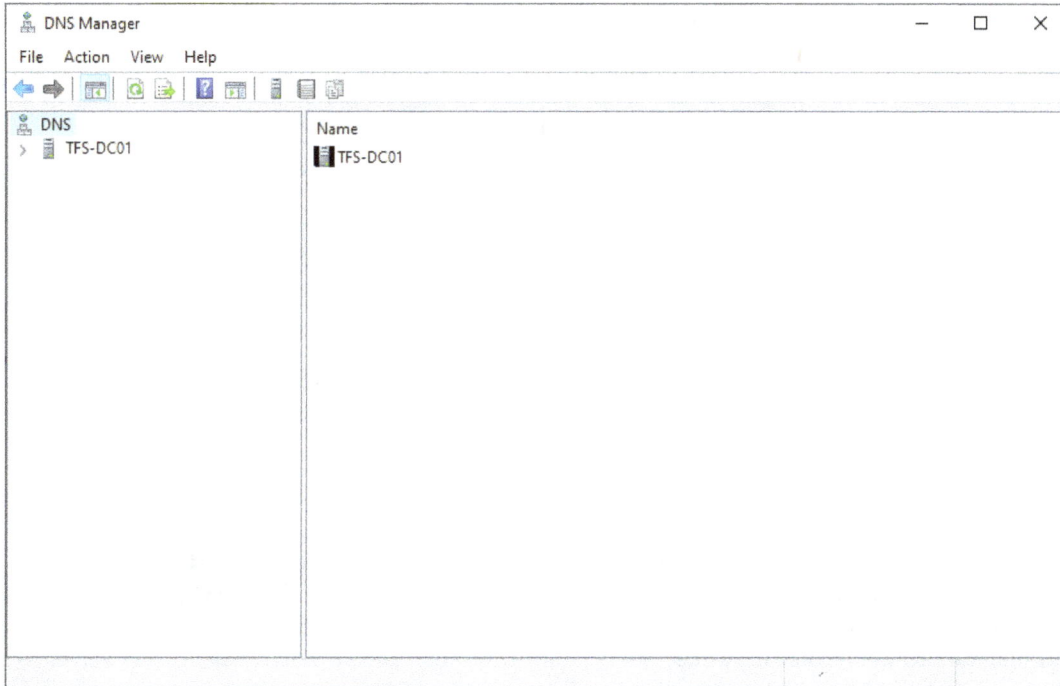

2. Under the **DNS** node in the **DNS Manager** console, expand the **TFS-DC01** server and then expand **Forward Lookup Zones**. Select the **corp.tfslabs.com** Zone:

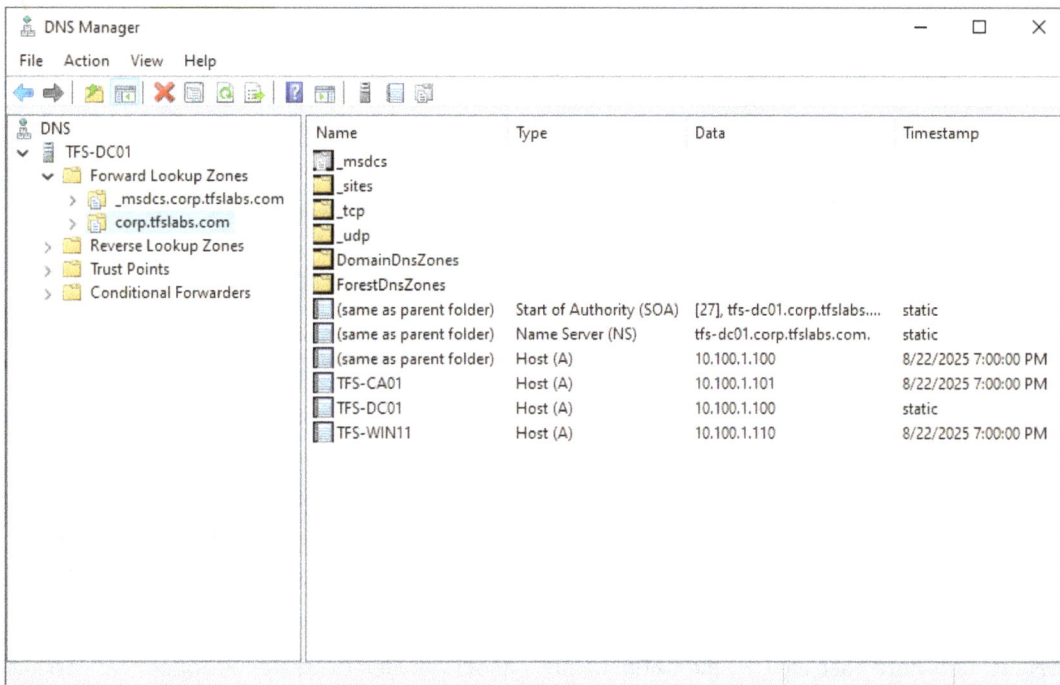

3. Right-click on the **corp.tfslabs.com** DSN zone and select the option for **New Alias (CNAME)....**
4. On the **New Resource Record** window, in **Alias name (uses parent domain if left blank)**, enter **OCSP** as the name. In the **Fully qualified domain name (FQDN)** field, enter **tfs-ca01.corp.tfslabs.com.** and then click **OK**:

5. Right-click on the **corp.tfslabs.com** DNS Zone and select the option for **New Alias (CNAME)....**
6. On the **New Resource Record** window, in **Alias name (uses parent domain if left blank)**, enter **PKI** as the name. In the **Fully qualified domain name (FQDN)** field, enter **tfs-ca01.corp.tfslabs.com.** and then click **OK**.
7. Verify that the **CNAME** records have been added to the DNS Zone and point to the **TFS-CA01** server:

8. Close the **DNS Manager** console.

Once the DNS records have been created, the CAPolicy.inf file that is needed to create the Subordinate certificate can be configured in the next section.

Subordinate CA Setup - Create DNS Records - Validation

Once the CNAME records have been created on the TFS-DC01 server, the records can be validated by opening a Command Prompt on any TFS Labs domain servers or workstations, and pinging the FQDN entries that were created in the previous steps. The CNAME records should resolve to the correct hostname and IP address, which both point to the TFS-CA01 server.

If the ping attempt fails with a timeout, but still resolves to the correct IP address for the TFS-CA01 server, that does not necessarily mean that there is an issue with the DNS records. If the Windows Defender Firewall on the server is blocking ping requests, then the ping responses will fail to send a reply. A step that is performed later in this chapter will correct any issues with ping requests to the TFS-CA01 server. Once the DNS records have been created and validated, the CAPolicy.inf file that is needed for the Subordinate certificate can be configured.

Subordinate CA Setup - CAPolicy.inf Installation

The CAPolicy.inf file is used to add configuration details to the Certificate Authority at the time when the Subordinate certificate is created. On the TFS-CA01 server, create a file in the C:\Windows folder called CAPolicy.inf (ensure that the file is saved with the correct file extension otherwise these settings will be ignored).

Copy the following contents into the CAPolicy.inf file and save the file before continuing:

```
C:\Windows\CAPolicy.inf

[Version]
Signature = "$Windows NT$"

[PolicyStatementExtension]
Policies = AllIssuancePolicy, InternalPolicy
Critical = FALSE

[AllIssuancePolicy]
; Enables all Certificate Templates.
OID = 2.5.29.32.0

[InternalPolicy]
OID = 1.2.3.4.1455.67.89.5
; Certification Practice Statement
Notice = "The TFS Labs Certification Authority is an internal only resource."
URL = http://pki.corp.tfslabs.com/cps.html

[Certsrv_Server]
; Renewal information for the Subordinate CA.
RenewalKeyLength = 4096
RenewalValidityPeriod = Years
RenewalValidityPeriodUnits = 5

; Disable support for issuing certificates using RSASSA-PSS.
AlternateSignatureAlgorithm = 0

; Load all certificate templates by default.
LoadDefaultTemplates = 1
```

Once the CAPolicy.inf file has been created and saved, proceed to installing the AD CS role on the TFS-CA01 server.

CAPolicy.inf Customization Options

The settings that are contained within the CAPolicy.inf file are used to create the Root or Subordinate certificates for a Certificate Authority. There are some configuration items that should be customized before the certificates are created, as modifying those items later is not always possible, which is why it is important to ensure that the settings are correct. In the case of the CAPolicy.inf file being used for the Subordinate CA in this example, items that should be modified include the **OID**, **Notice** and **URL** for the Certification Practice Statement (CPS).

Certificate Authority OID Number

The OID number that is defined in the **InternalPolicy** section of the CAPolicy.inf file can be modified if necessary for an organization. The OID number in this example is used in Microsoft technical documentation, but it should work for any organization if it is only ever going to be used internally. If a customized OID number is required for a Certificate Authority, a Private Enterprise Number can be registered through the IANA.

If a custom OID number is required for the Certificate Authority, modify the OID line in the **InternalPolicy** section to **OID = 1.3.6.1.4.1.X** (replace the X with the PEN number that was previously registered).

Ensure that if a custom OID was configured for the Root certificate that the same OID number is used when creating the CAPolicy.inf file for the Subordinate certificate. If these numbers do not match, there could be issues with certificates that are issued by the Certificate Authority.

Delta CRL with Subordinate Certificate Authorities

A Delta CRL is not normally required for a Root Certificate Authority, especially one that is offline since it is not normally handling certificate revocations in a PKI. The Root CA is only ever used to issue a Base CRL when there are Subordinate Certificate Authorities present in the PKI. The only certificates that are typically revoked by a Root CA is a Subordinate certificate, so that would necessitate the deployment of a new Base CRL instead of a Delta CRL if that occurs.

Since this is a Subordinate CA that is always online and used for handling all regular Certificate Authority tasks, a Delta CRL is needed to revoke certificates much more frequently. A Delta CRL can also be used in parallel with OCSP, which is optionally configured in a later chapter of this book.

Signature Algorithm Support Issues

The **AlternateSignatureAlgorithm = 0** flag in the CAPolicy.inf file explicitly uses SHA256 for the algorithm instead of the legacy RSASSA-PSS algorithm. This can cause issues with some devices (especially iOS) and by ensuring that it is disabled there should be no issues with certificates issued by the Certificate Authority.

CAPolicy.inf File Name and Locations

Ensure that the CAPolicy.inf file has been properly saved in the C:\Windows folder (%WINDIR%). Also make sure that the file extension is set to INF and not TXT. A common mistake is to accidentally save the file as CAPolicy.inf.txt which is not valid.

If the CAPolicy.inf file is not saved in the correct directory and without the correct file extension, all settings in the file will be ignored at the time when the Certificate Authority is created.

Subordinate CA Setup - AD CS Role Installation

Once the TFS-CA01 server has been configured properly and the CAPolicy.inf file has been created, the Active Directory Certificate Services role needs to be installed. The Active Directory Certificate Services role can be installed using PowerShell or with the Server Manager console. Either method for installing the Active Directory Certificate Services role can be used, and there is no need to use both methods for the installation.

> **Certificate Authority Web Enrollment**
>
> The Certificate Authority Web Enrollment feature in Active Directory Certificate Services is an optional feature that allows authorized users the ability manage certain certificate requests through a web interface, such as submitting CSR requests and downloading certificates. It is a legacy feature of AD CS, and has not seen major updates in several Windows Server releases. Despite this, the feature still works correctly when it is used for issuing certificates and is helpful for testing AD CS deployments.

Subordinate CA Setup - AD CS Role Installation - CLI Installation

The Active Directory Certificate Services installation can be performed using PowerShell, which requires much fewer steps to accomplish. Perform the following steps on the TFS-CA01 server to install the Active Directory Certificate Services role and associated management features:

1. Open an **elevated PowerShell prompt**.
2. Run the following command to install the **Active Directory Certificate Services** role, the **Certification Authority Web Enrollment** role, and the necessary **Administration Tools**:

```
Windows PowerShell (Elevated)

Add-WindowsFeature `
-Name ADCS-Cert-Authority, ADCS-Web-Enrollment, Web-Mgmt-Service `
-IncludeManagementTools
```

3. The command will automatically install the **Active Directory Certificate Services** role and output a **Success** status of **True** if there were no issues:

4. Once the installation for **Active Directory Certificate Services** has completed, close the **PowerShell prompt**.

Once the Active Directory Certificate Services role has been installed, the role can now be configured and the Subordinate certificate for the TFS Labs domain can be created.

Subordinate CA Setup - AD CS Role Installation - GUI Installation

To perform the Active Directory Certificate Services role installation using the Server Manager console, perform the following steps on the TFS-CA01 server to install the AD CS role and associated management features:

1. Open the **Server Manager** console (servermanager.exe), click on the **Manage** menu, and click on **Add Roles and Features** to start the installation wizard:

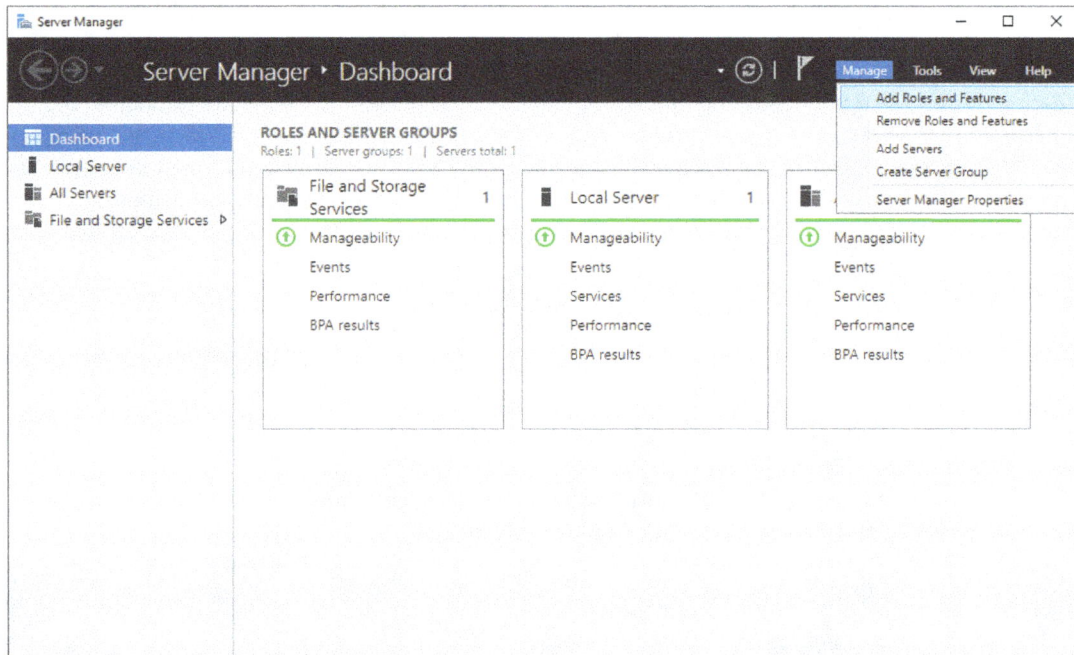

2. On the **Before you begin** screen, click the **Next** button to continue:

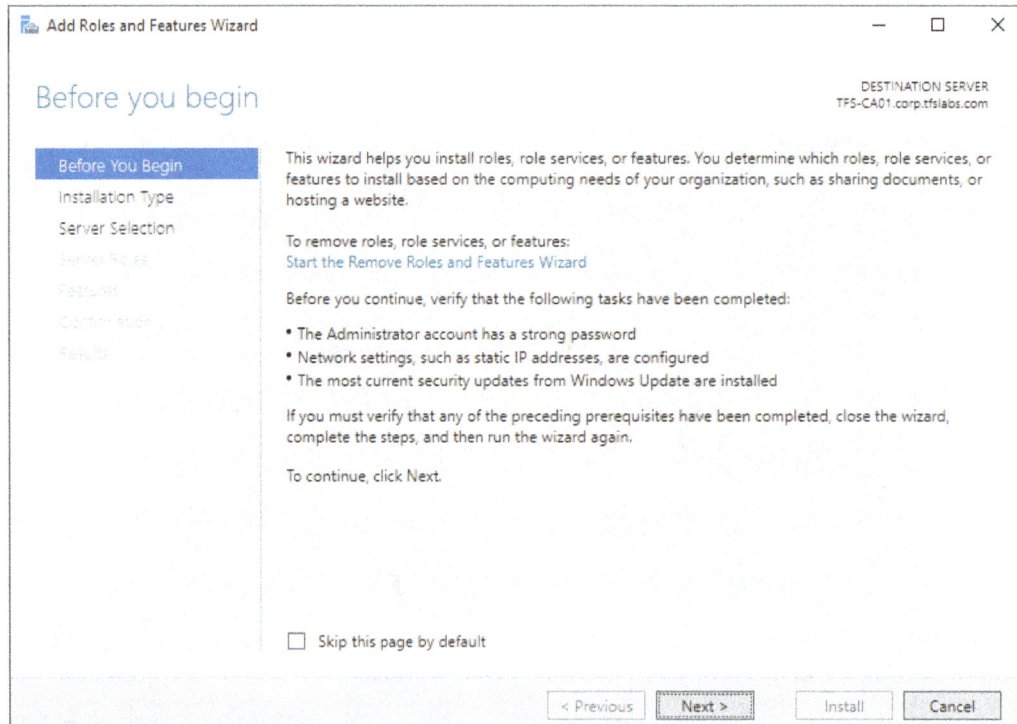

3. On the **Select installation type** screen, select the option for **Role-based or feature-based installation** and click the **Next** button to continue:

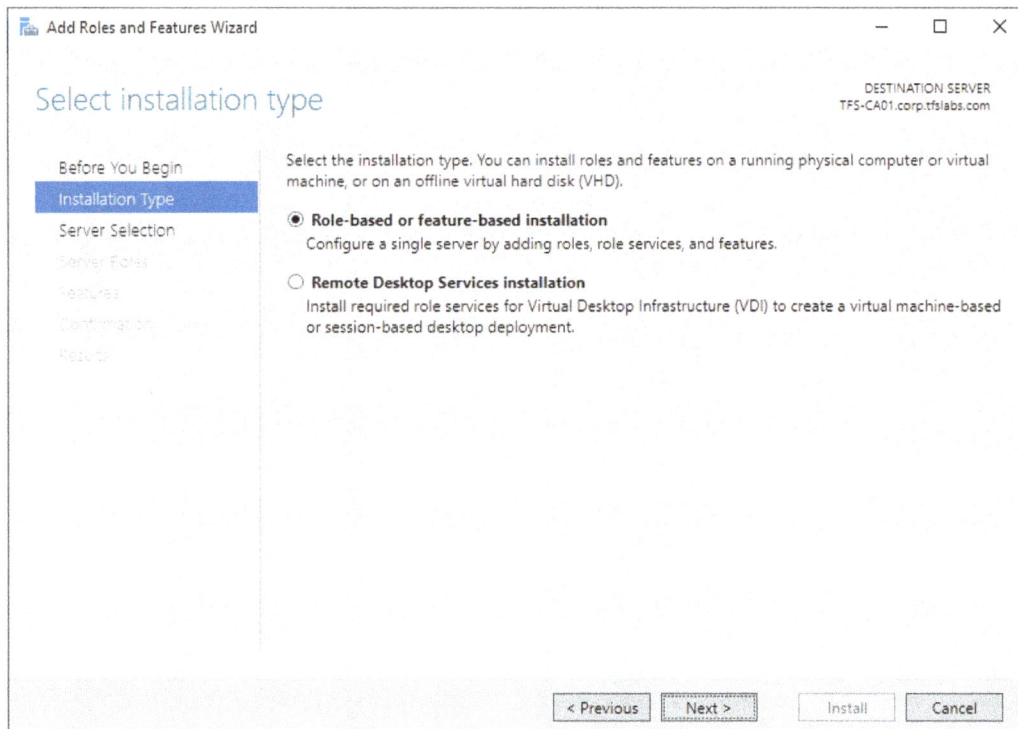

4. On the **Select destination server** screen, verify that the **TFS-CA01.corp.tfslabs.com** server is selected and click **Next** to continue:

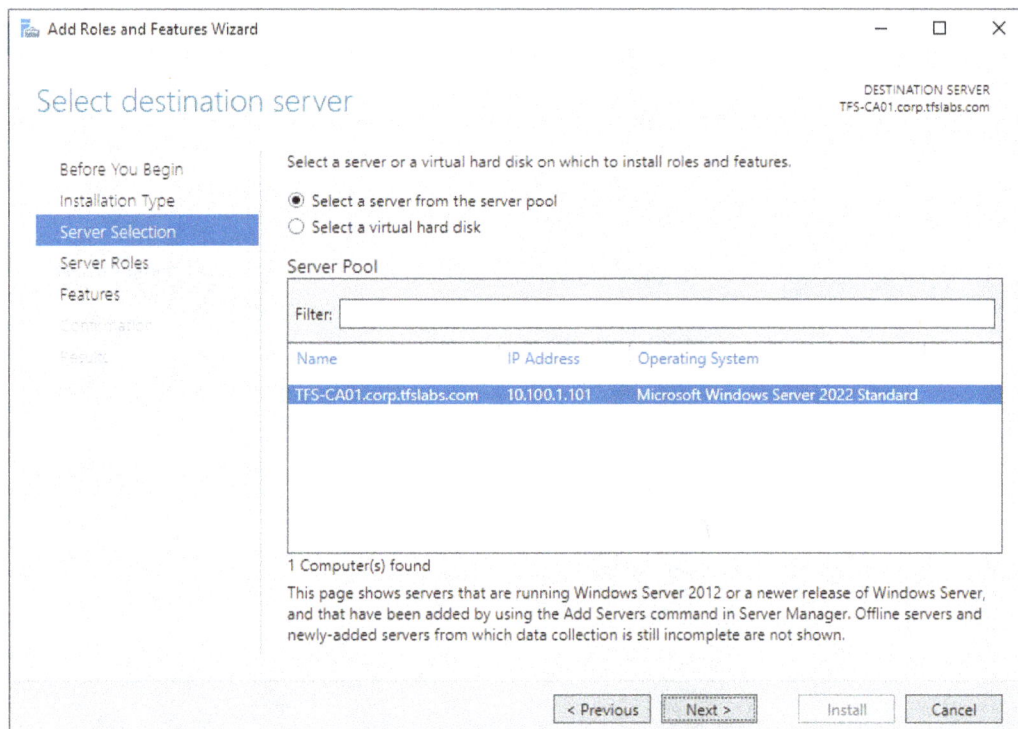

5. On the **Select server roles** screen, select the **Active Directory Certificate Services** option:

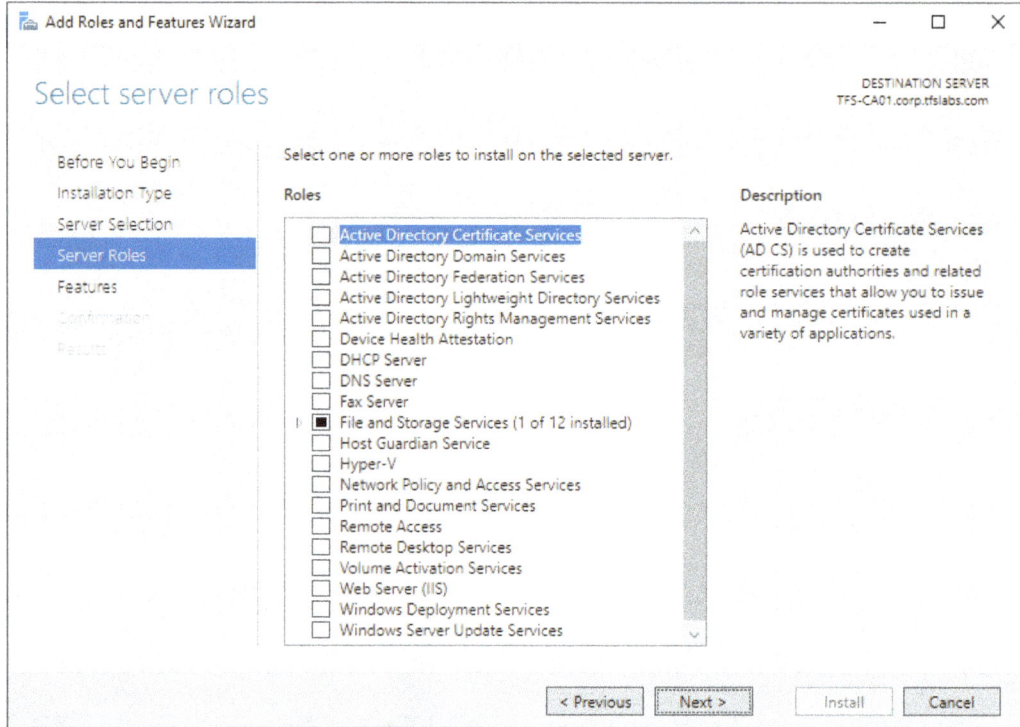

6. The installation wizard will ask to install any additional features required for the **Active Directory Certificate Services** role. Select the option to **Include management tools (if applicable)** to install the management tools for the role. Click the **Add Features** button to continue.
7. On the **Select server roles** screen, click the **Next** button to continue:

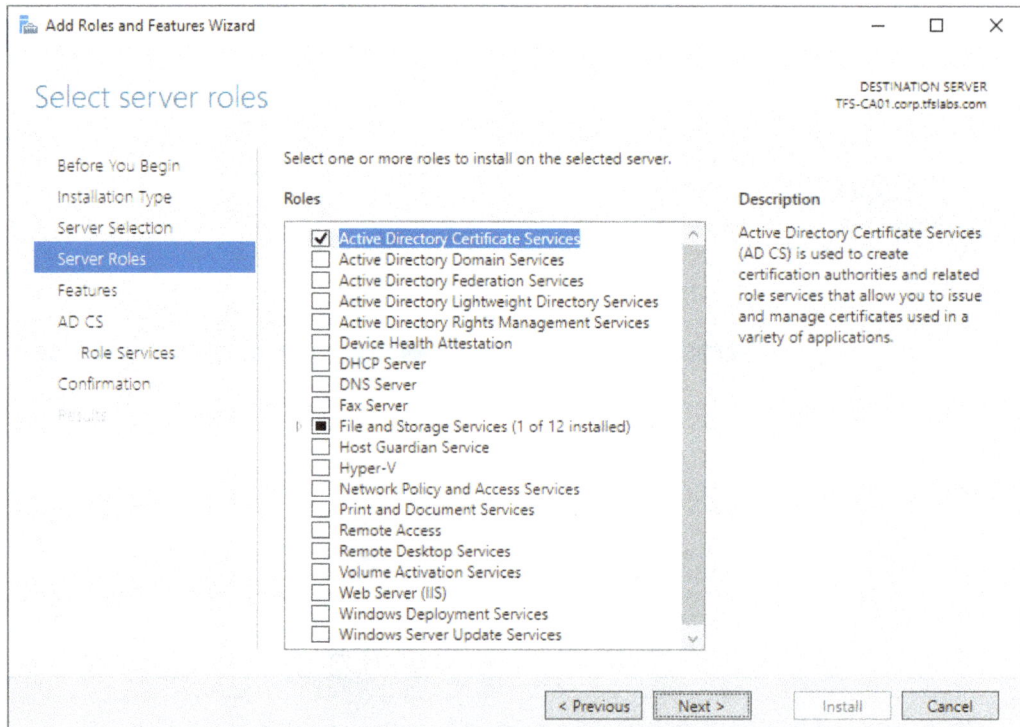

8. On the **Select features** screen, click the **Next** button to continue:

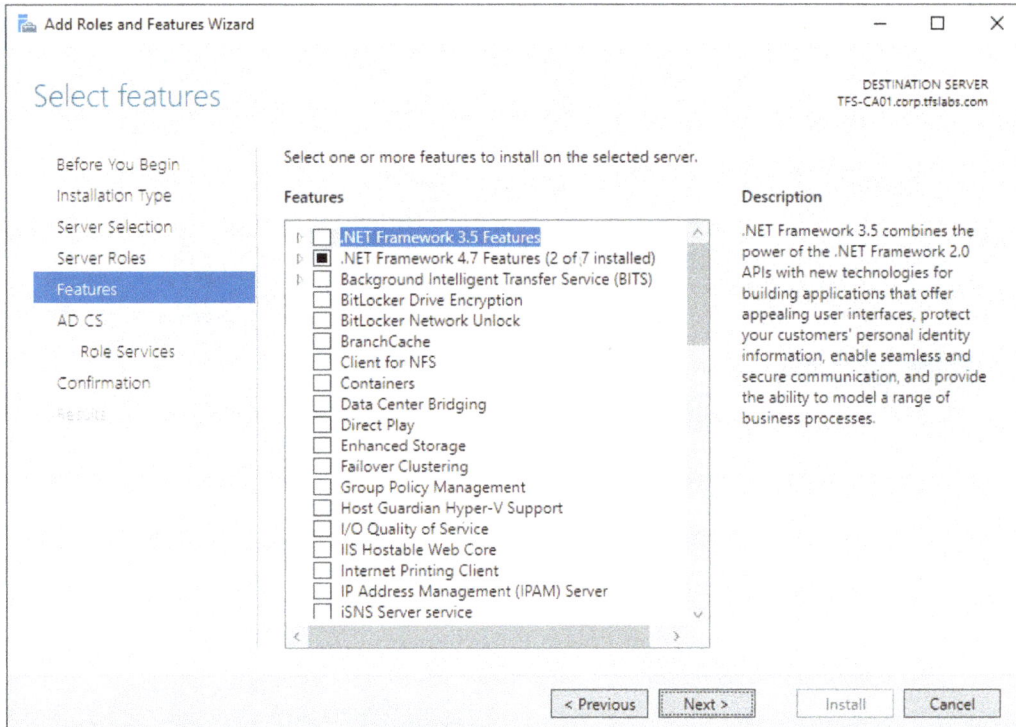

9. On the **Active Directory Certificate Services** screen, click the **Next** button to continue:

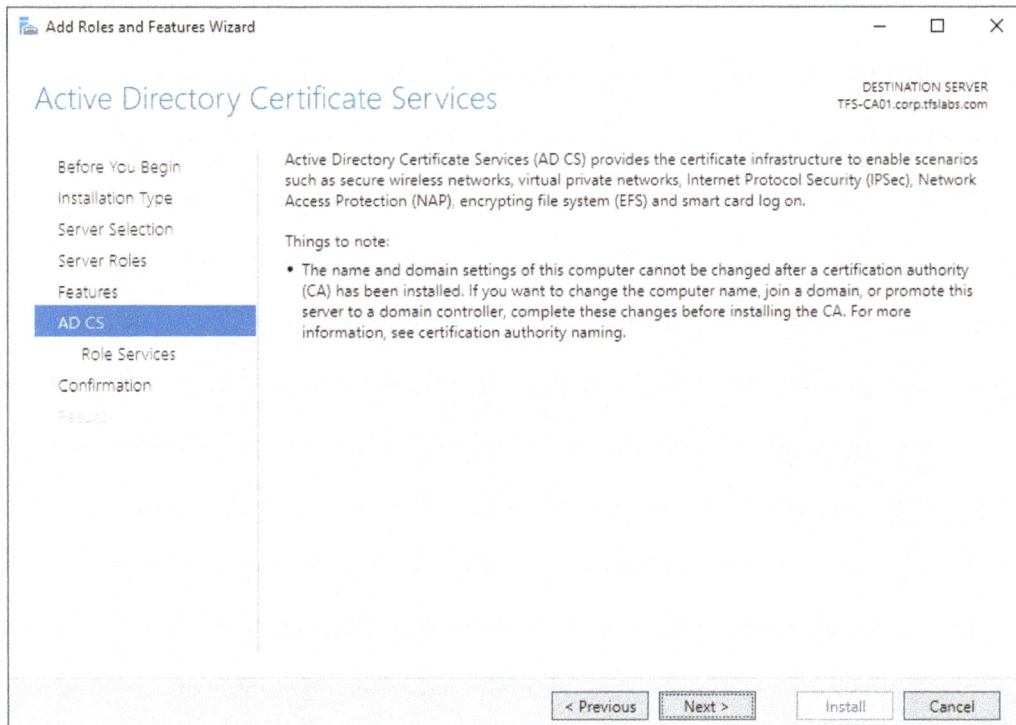

10. On the **Select role services** screen, select the option for **Certification Authority** and **Certificate Authority Web Enrollment**:

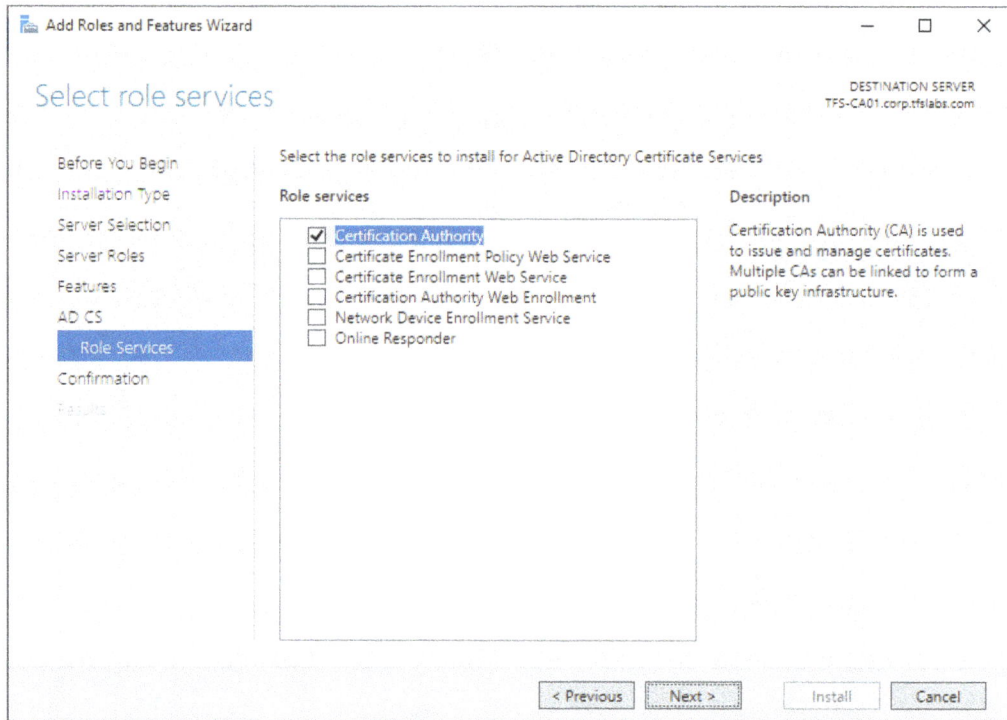

11. The installation wizard will ask to install any additional features required for **Certification Authority Web Enrollment**. Select the option to **Include management tools (if applicable)** to install the management tools for the role. Click the **Add Features** button to continue.

12. On the **Select role services** screen, click **Next** to continue:

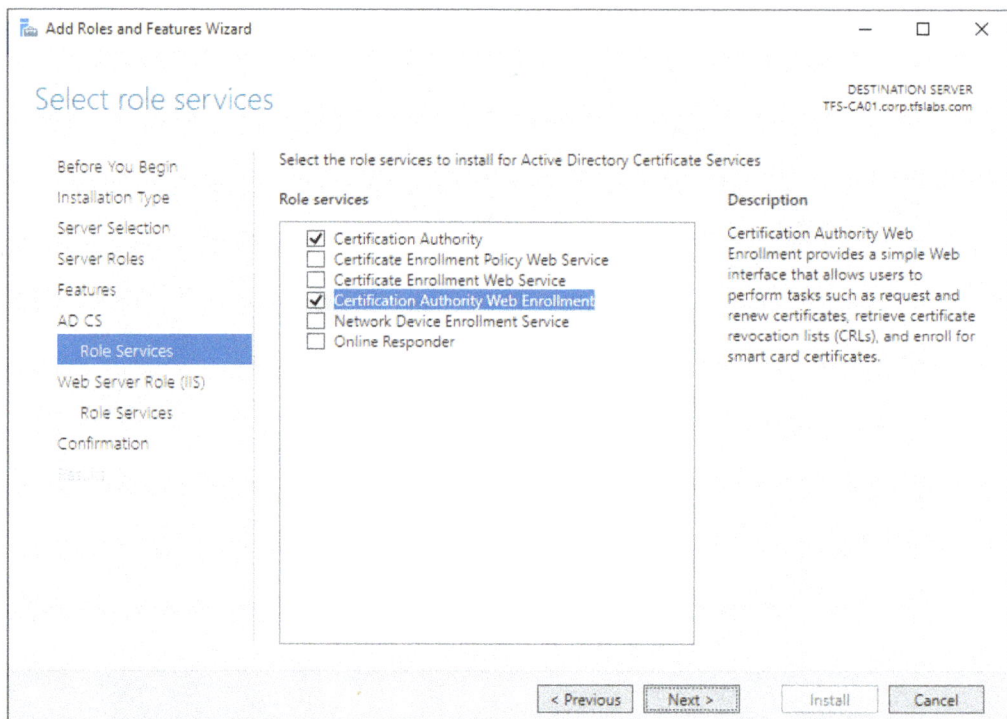

13. On the **Web Server Role (IIS)** screen, click the **Next** button to continue:

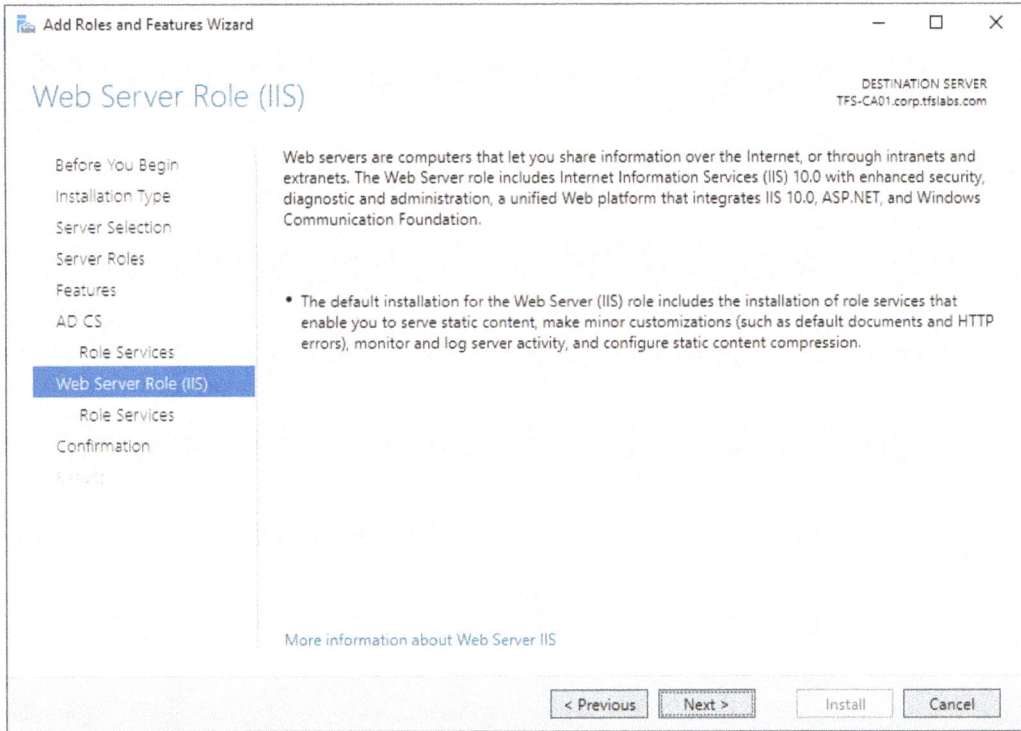

14. On the **Select role services** screen, click the **Next** button to continue:

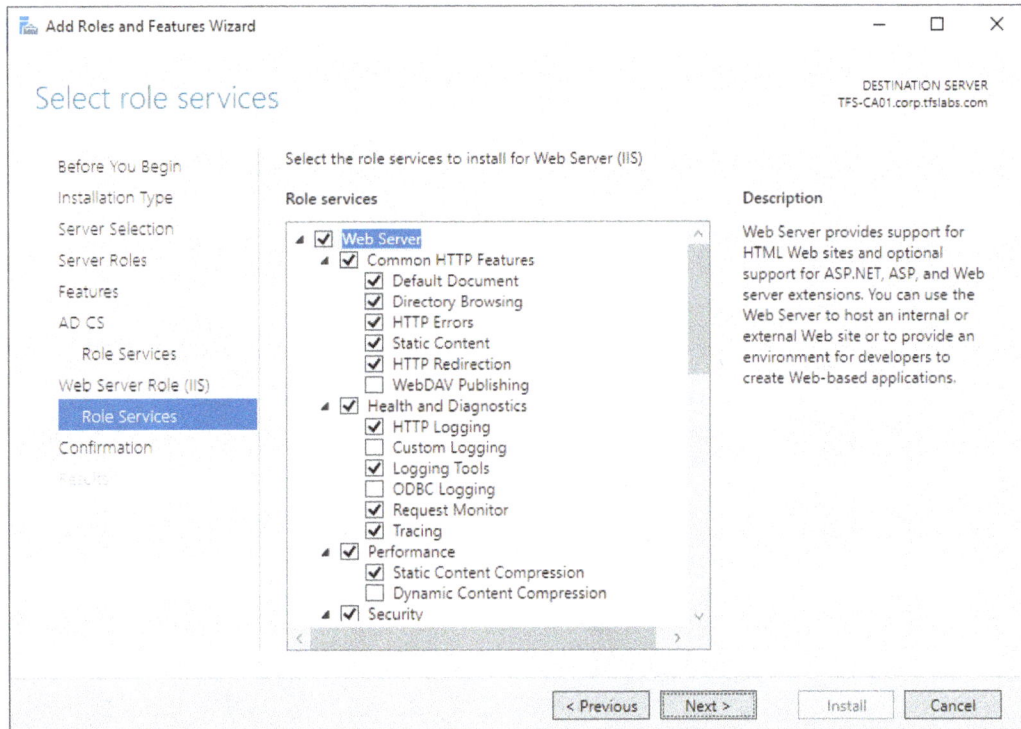

15. On the **Confirm installation selections** screen, select the option to **Restart the destination server automatically if required**:

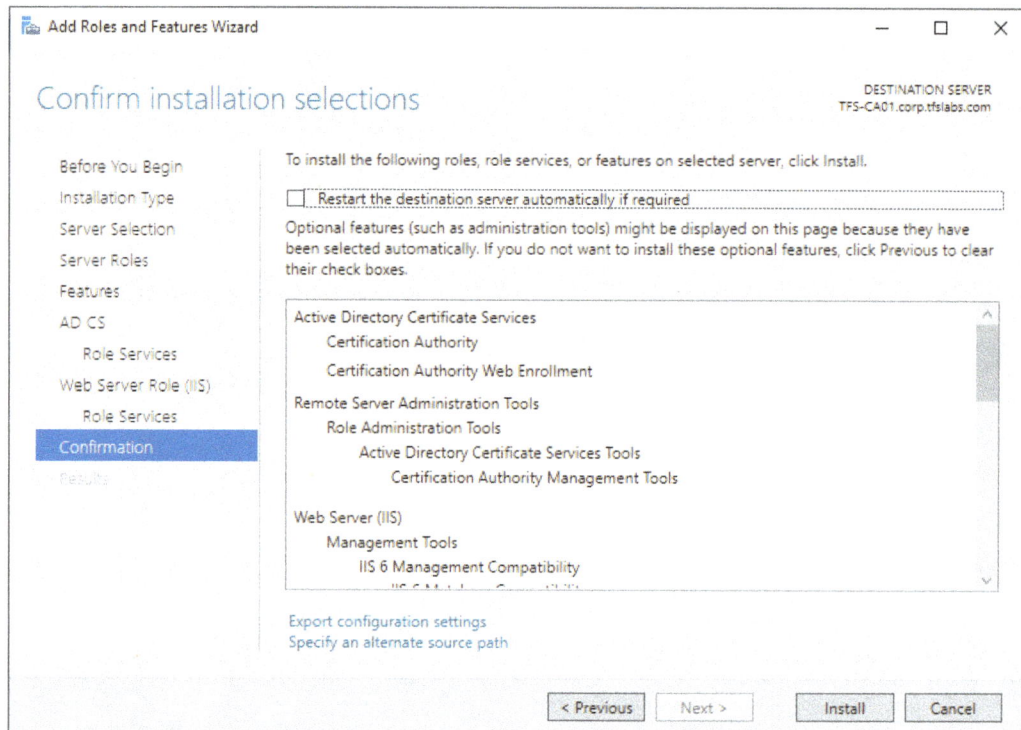

16. When prompted with a warning about restarting the server, click the **Yes** button.
17. On the **Confirm installation selections** screen, click the **Install** button to continue:

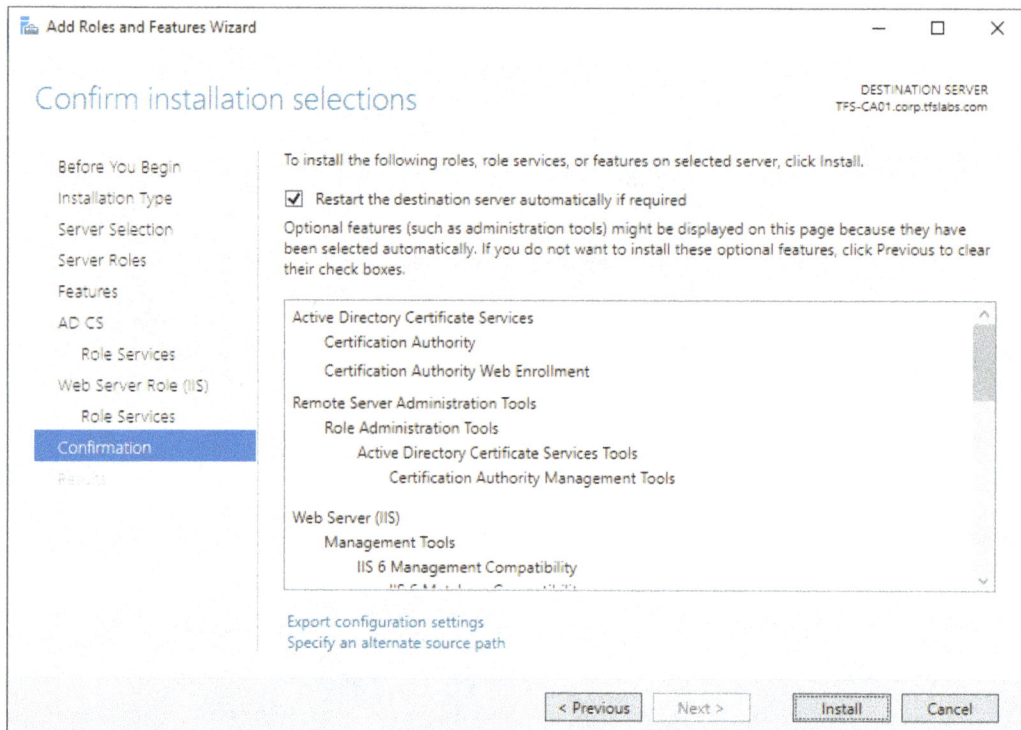

18. Once the installation is completed, click the **Close** button:

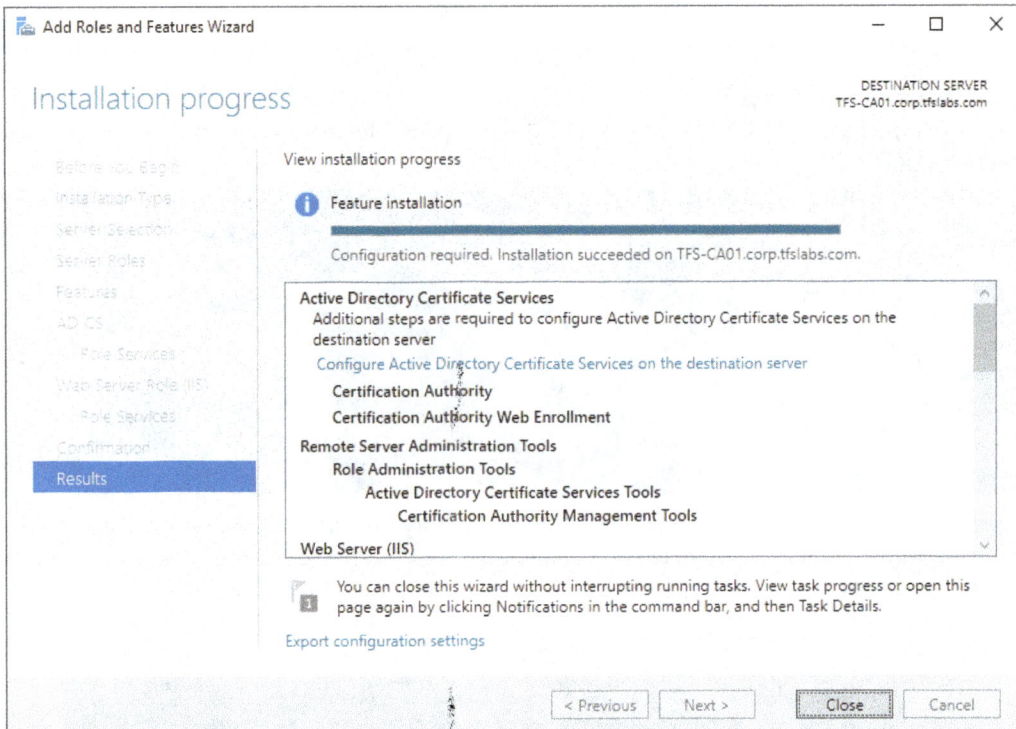

Once the Active Directory Certificate Services role has been installed, the role can be configured and the Subordinate certificate for the TFS Labs domain can be created.

Subordinate CA Setup - AD CS Role Configuration

The Active Directory Certificate Services role has been installed, but it will need to be configured to work as the Subordinate Certificate Authority. In the process of configuring the Active Directory Certificate Services role for the TFS Labs domain, the following Subordinate certificate will be created:

Root Certificate	TFS Labs Certificate Authority
Certificate Authority Setup Type	Enterprise CA
Certificate Authority Type	Subordinate CA
Cryptographic Provider	RSA#Microsoft Software Key Storage Provider
Key Length	4096 Bits
Signature Hash Algorithm	SHA256
CA Common Name	TFS Labs Enterprise CA
Validity Period	5 years

Table 7.6.1: Active Directory Certificate Services configuration for the Subordinate Certificate Authority.

The Active Directory Certificate Services role can be configured through the command line with PowerShell, or by using the Server Manager console. Only one method is needed to configure the Active Directory Certificate Services role, there is no need to perform the configuration twice. Once this section has been completed and the AD CS role has been configured, there are still several important configuration items to complete before it is usable.

Subordinate CA Setup - AD CS Role Configuration - CLI Configuration

The Active Directory Certificate Services configuration can be completed using PowerShell by performing the following steps on the TFS-CA01 server:

1. Open an **elevated PowerShell prompt**.
2. Run the following command to configure the **Active Directory Certificate Services** role and create the **Subordinate Certificate Authority**:

```
Windows PowerShell (Elevated)

Install-AdcsCertificationAuthority `
-CAType EnterpriseSubordinateCA `
-CACommonName "TFS Labs Enterprise CA" `
-KeyLength 4096 `
-HashAlgorithm SHA256 `
-CryptoProviderName "RSA#Microsoft Software Key Storage Provider" `
-Force
```

3. The command will automatically configure the **Active Directory Certificate Services** role, and output a warning that the installation can only be completed by submitting the CSR file to the Root Certificate Authority (this is normal, and will be completed later in this chapter):

4. When the **Subordinate Certificate Authority** has been created, run the following command to configure the **Certification Authority Web Enrollment** role:

```
Windows PowerShell (Elevated)

Install-AdcsWebEnrollment -Force
```

5. The command will automatically configure the **Certification Authority Web Enrollment** role, and output an **ErrorID** status of **0** if there were no issues.
6. Once the configuration for **Active Directory Certificate Services** has completed, close the **PowerShell prompt**.

At this point the Subordinate Certificate Authority for the TFS Labs domain has been created, but the Subordinate certificate still needs to be issued from the Root Certificate Authority. This will be completed in a section later in this chapter, and it will require transferring files to and from the Root CA server to complete the process. There are steps that can be performed to validate that the Certificate Authority has been successfully created before configuring the Subordinate certificate. Proceed to validating the AD CS service on the TFS-CA01 server in the next section.

Subordinate CA Setup - AD CS Role Configuration - GUI Configuration

To perform the Active Directory Certificate Services role configuration using the Server Manager console, perform the following steps on the TFS-CA01 server:

1. To begin the configuration of **Active Directory Certificate Services**, open the **Server Manager** console (servermanager.exe). Click the **Notifications** icon in the upper-right hand corner and click the **Configure Active Directory Certificate Services on the destination server** link in the **Post-deployment Configuration** box:

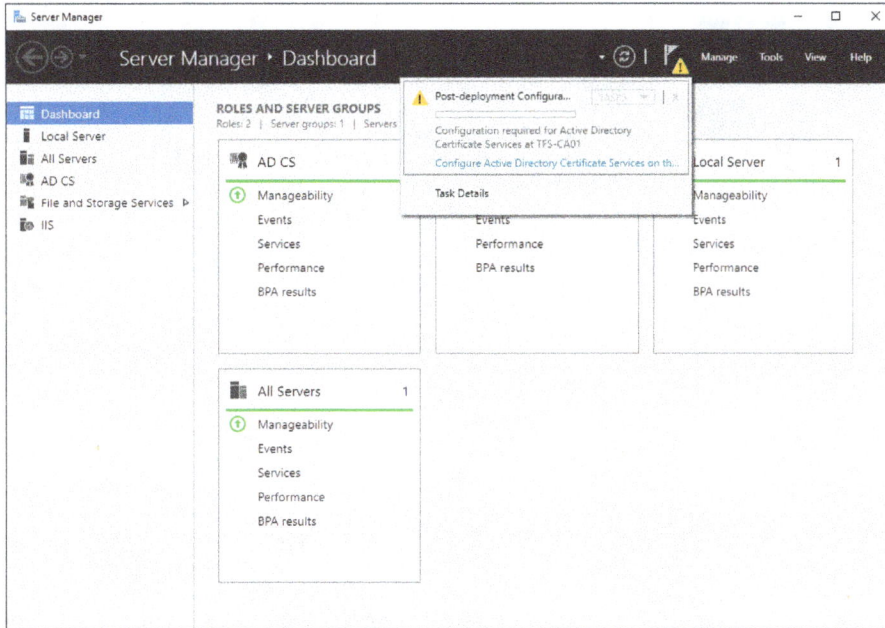

2. On the **Credentials** screen, verify that the credentials are set to a **Domain Administrator** account and click the **Next** button to continue:

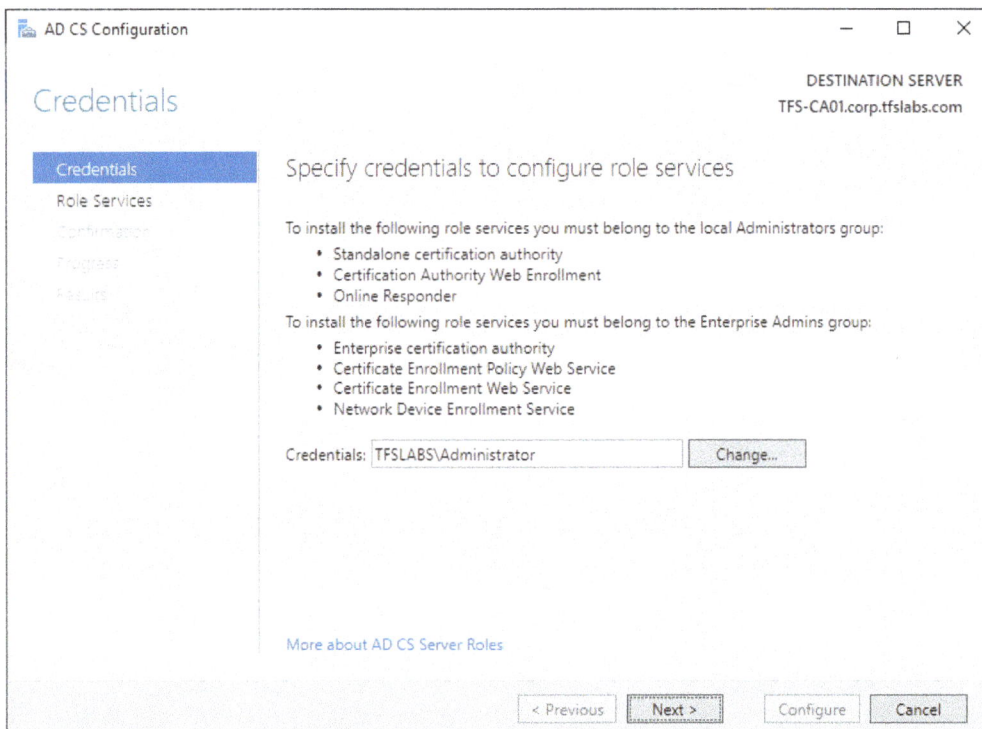

3. On the **Role Services** screen, select the options for **Certification Authority** and **Certification Authority Web Enrollment** and click **Next** to continue:

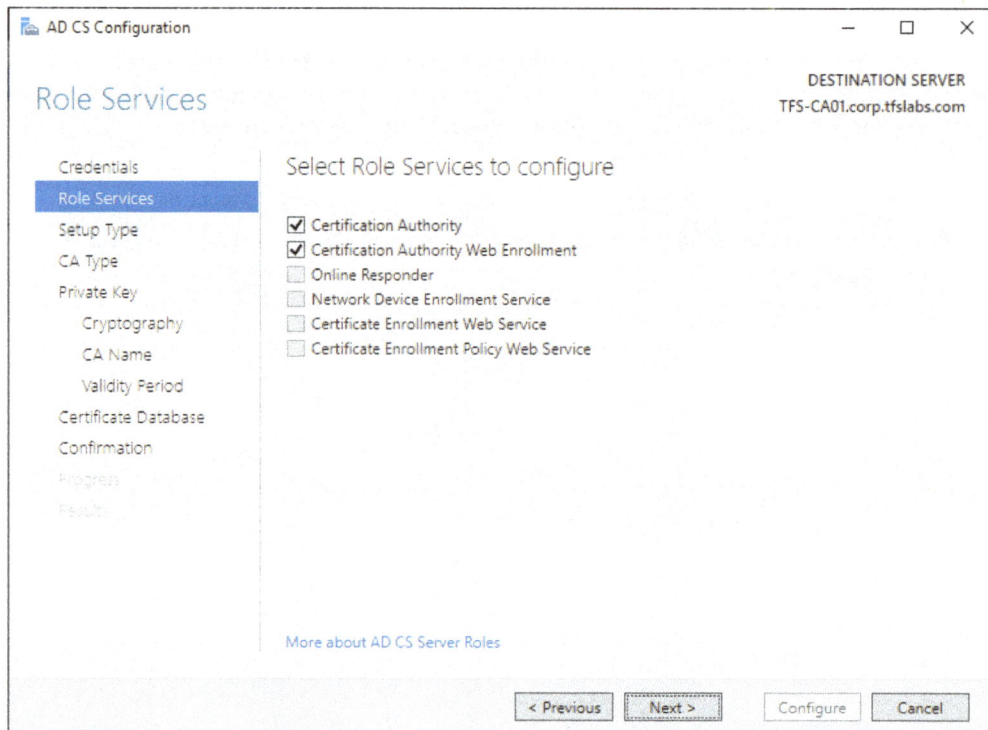

4. On the **Setup Type** screen, select the option for **Enterprise CA** and click the **Next** button to continue:

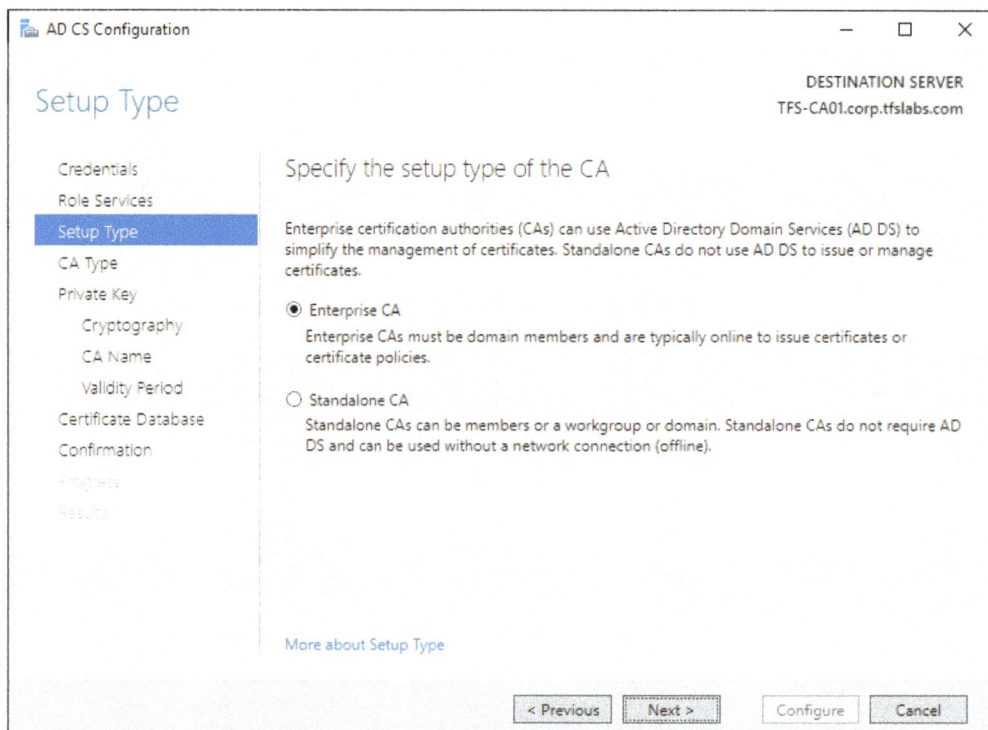

5. On the **CA Type** screen, ensure that the **Subordinate CA** option is selected and click the **Next** button to continue:

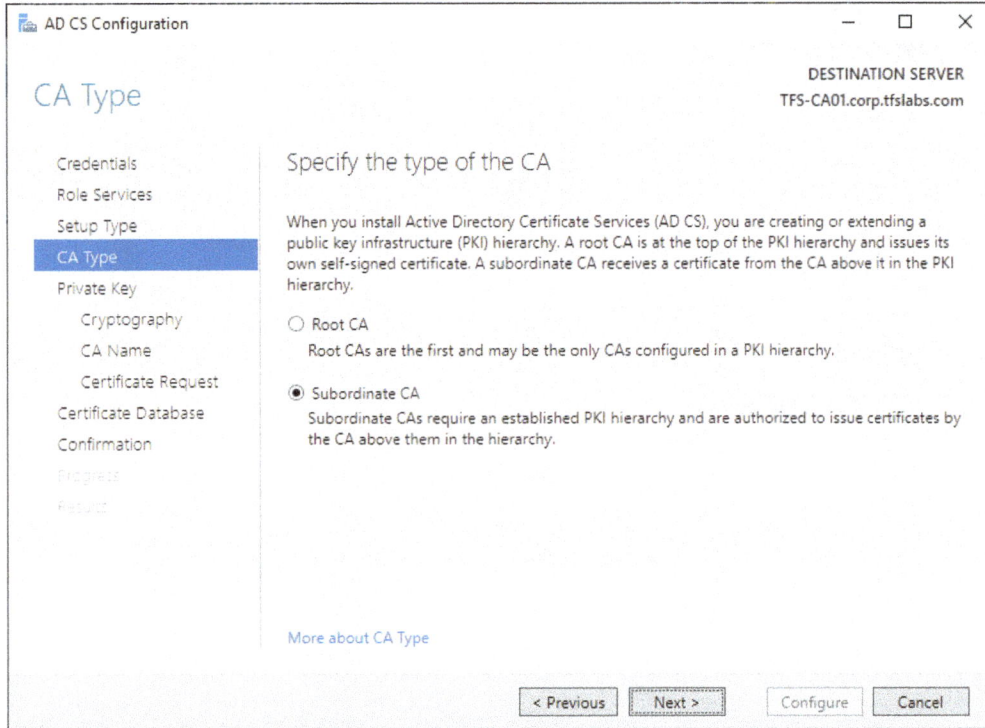

6. On the **Private Key** screen, verify that the **Create a new private key** option is selected. This is because this a new CA installation and the private key is not being restored from a previous server. Click the **Next** button to continue:

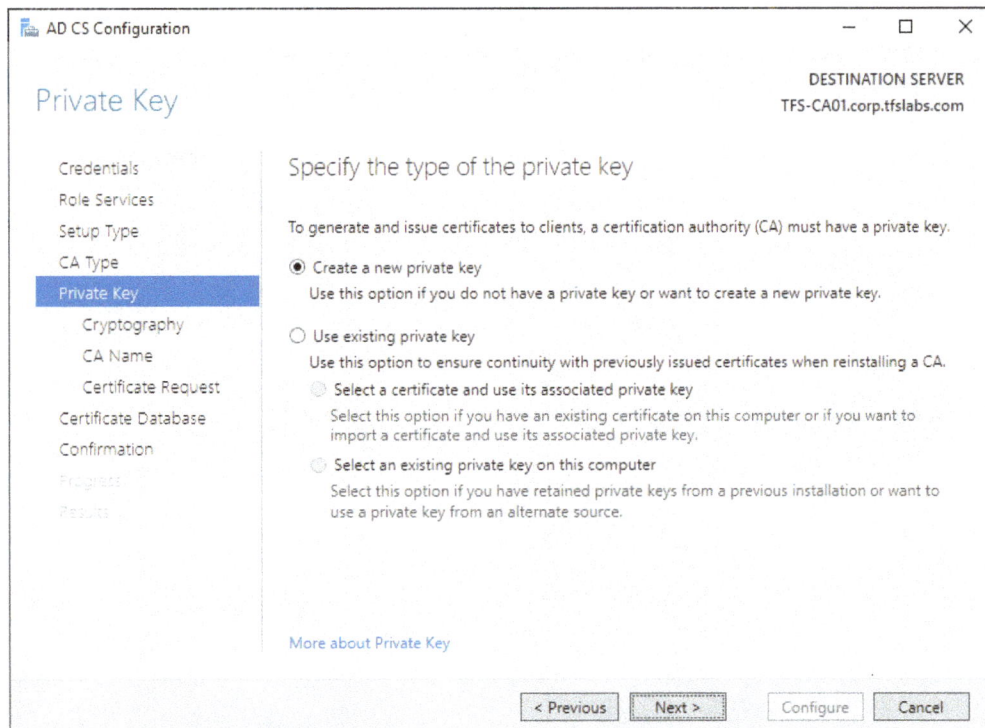

7. On the **Cryptography for CA** screen, make the following changes and then click the **Next** button to continue:
   - **Cryptographic Provider:** RSA#Microsoft Software Key Storage Provider
   - **Key Length:** 4096
   - **Hash Algorithm:** SHA256

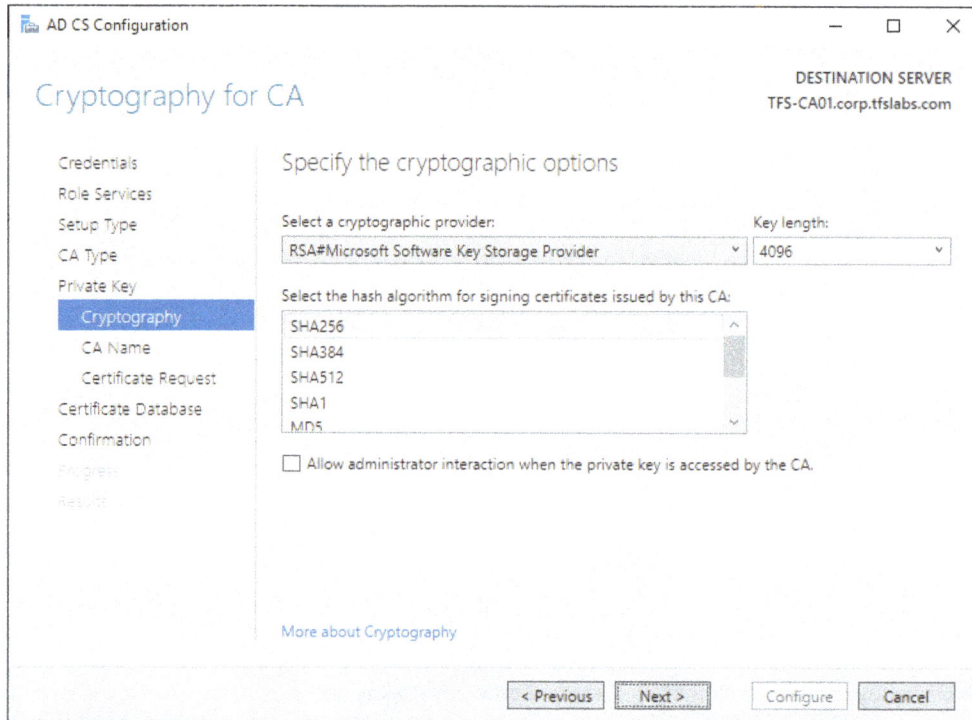

8. On the **CA Name** screen, set the **Common Name (CN)** for the CA to **TFS Labs Enterprise CA** and click the **Next** button to continue:

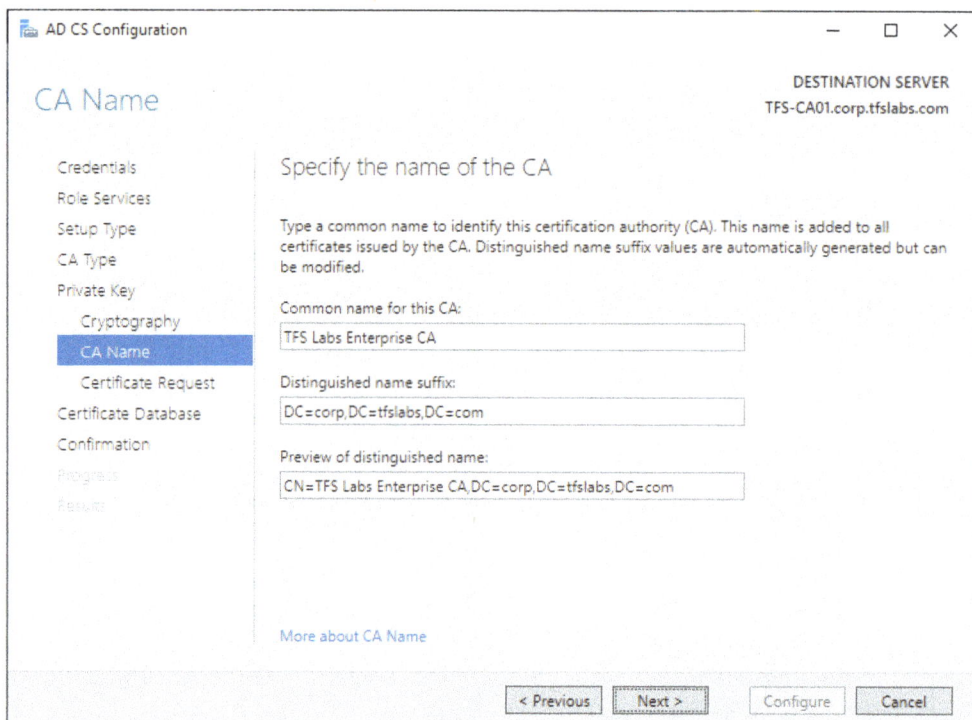

9. On the **Certificate Request** screen, accept the default location for saving the **Certificate Request** file. The file will be saved as **C:\TFS-CA01.corp.tfslabs.com_corp-TFS-CA01-CA.req**. Click the **Next** button to continue:

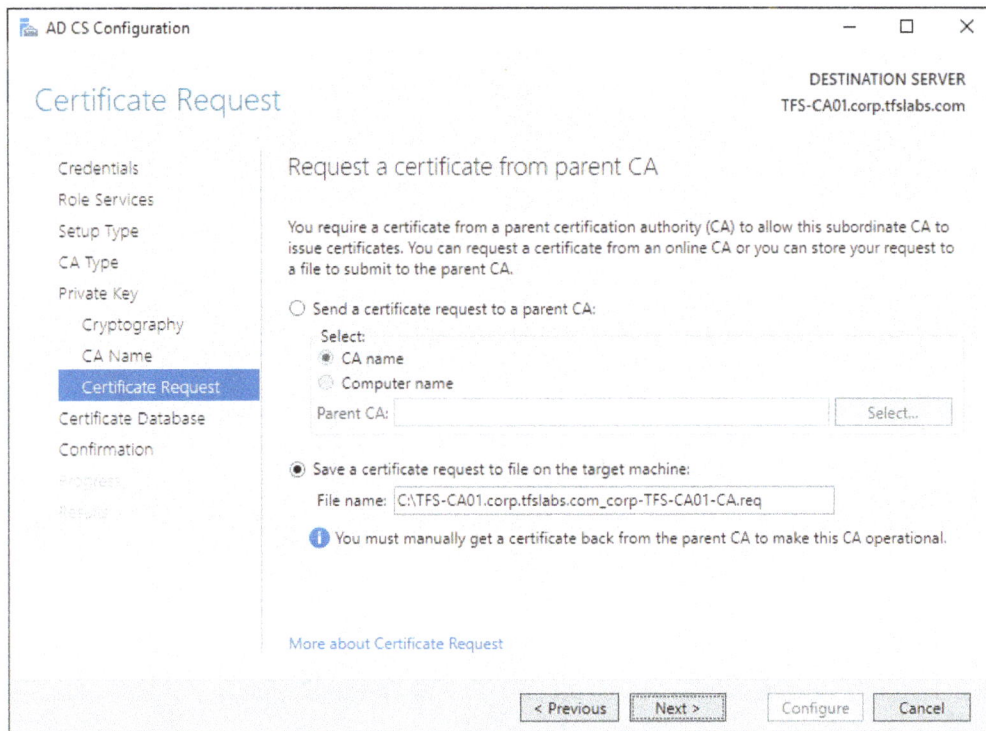

10. On the **CA Database** screen, make no changes to the database location and click the **Next** button to continue:

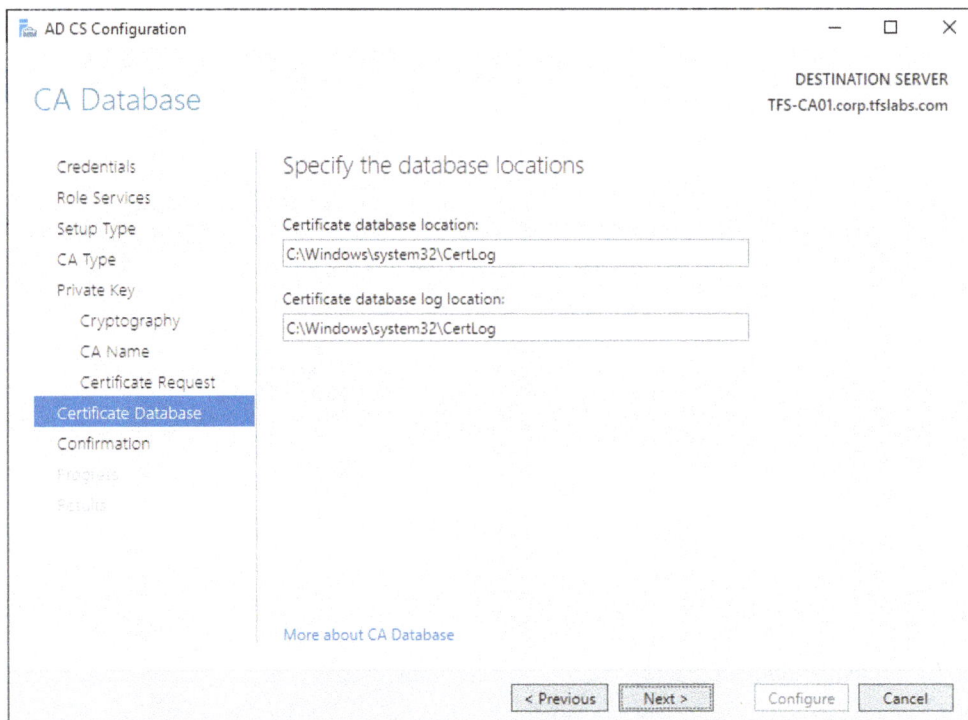

11. On the **Confirmation** screen, verify that the options are correct and click the **Configure** button:

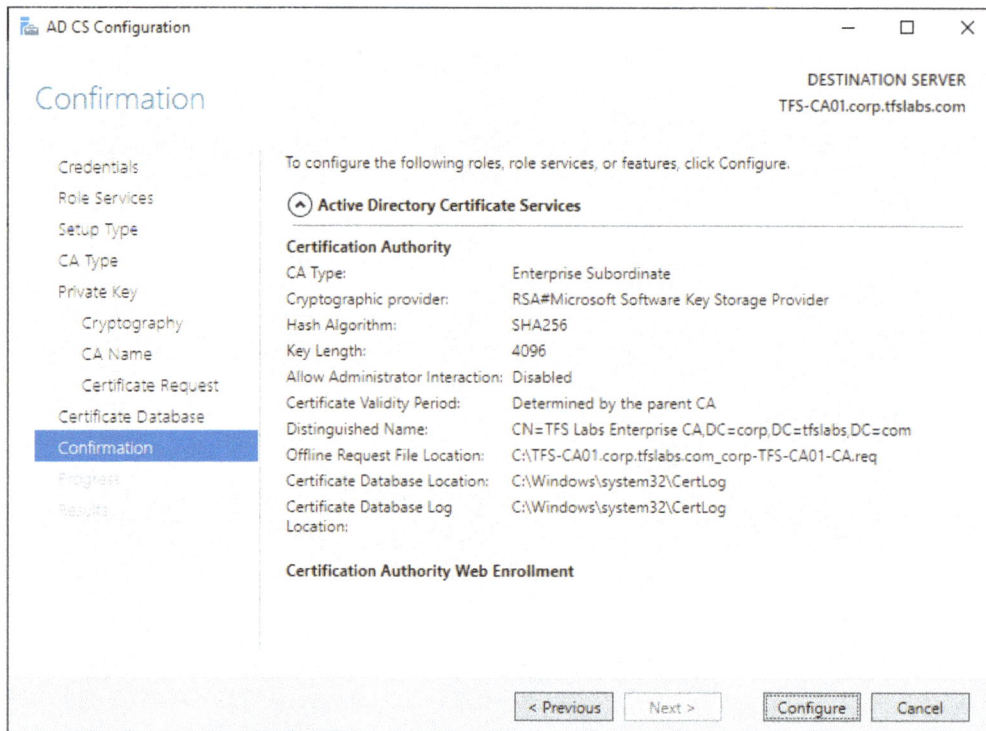

12. On the **Results** screen, click the **Close** button:

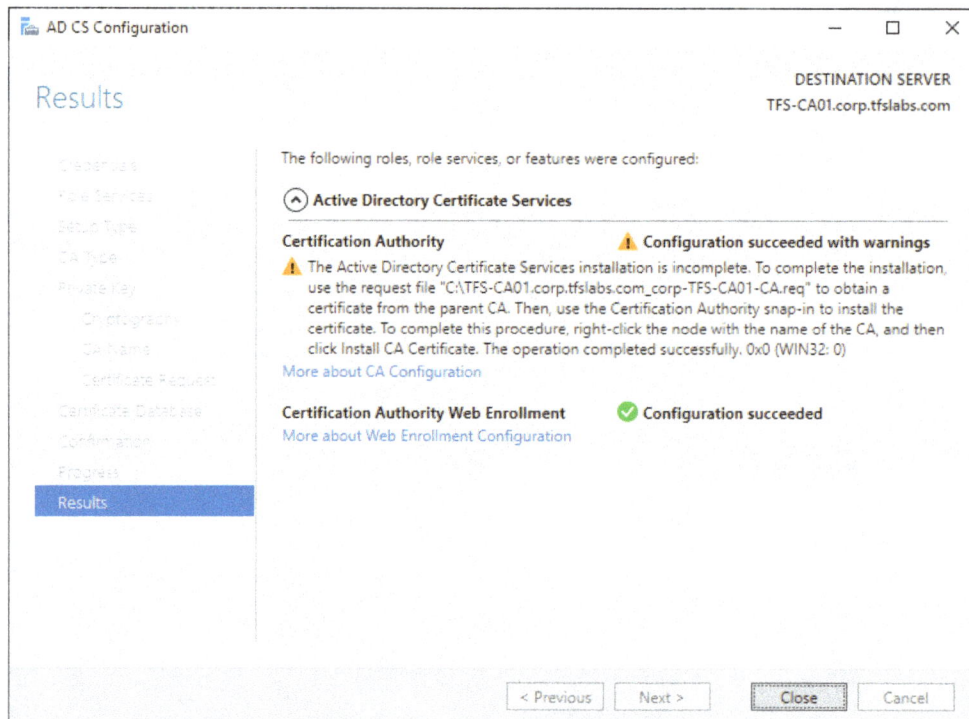

At this point the Subordinate Certificate Authority for the TFS Labs domain has been created, but the Subordinate certificate still needs to be issued from the Root Certificate Authority. There are steps that can be performed to validate that the Certificate Authority has been successfully created before configuring the Subordinate certificate.

Subordinate CA Setup - AD CS Role Validation

The Subordinate Certificate Authority for the TFS Labs domain has been created, so there is now an Enterprise CA available which can be validated. The Certificate Request for the Subordinate certificate has been created, which means it will need to be submitted to the Root Certificate Authority to complete the request. Until this CSR is submitted and completed, the Enterprise CA will not function correctly as there is no valid Subordinate certificate present yet.

Even though the Active Directory Certificate Services role was configured, it is not currently running as there is no valid certificate present on the server. Open the Certification Authority console (certsrv.msc) on the TFS-CA01 server:

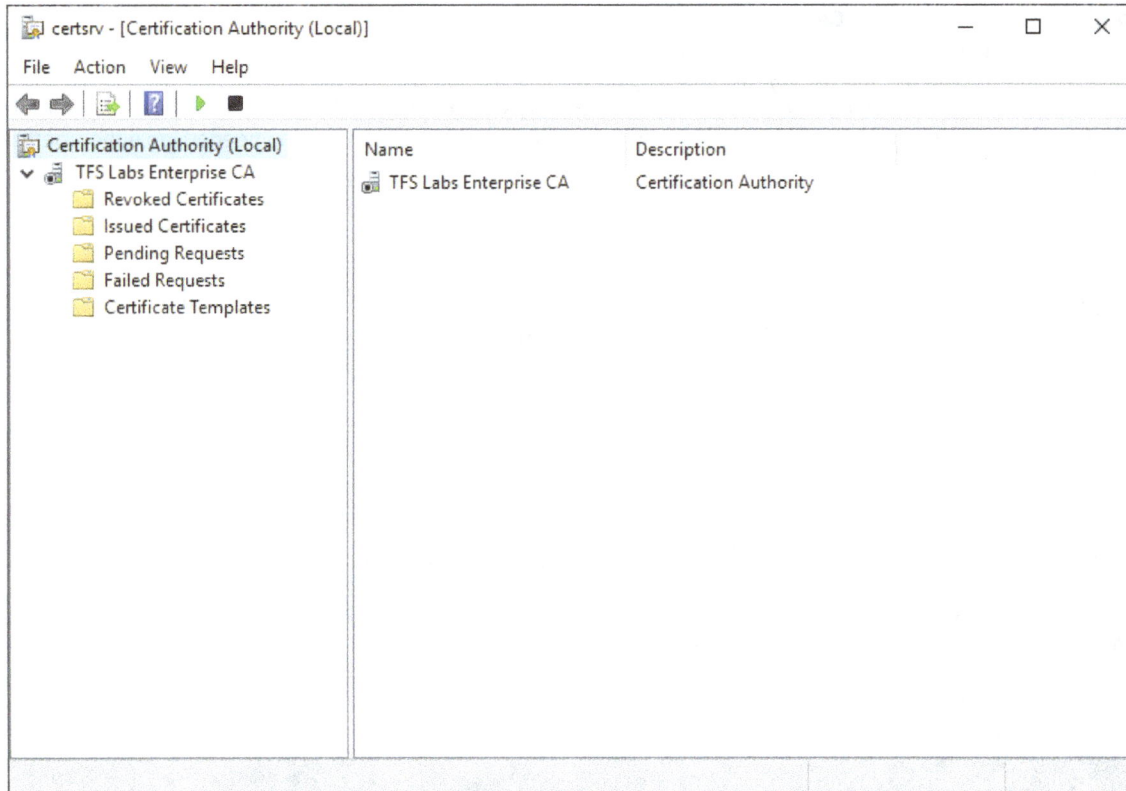

Figure 7.7.1: The Certification Authority console is used to manage the CA and allows administrators to issue and revoke certificates. This console also allows further customization of the CA, and several important components related to AD CS are managed with it. At this point in the configuration, the Enterprise CA is setup but the associated services are stopped as the certificate is not yet complete, so this is expected behaviour.

The Certificate Request file has been successfully generated in the previous section when the Active Directory Certificate Services role was configured, and it will need to be copied to the Root CA server to complete the request. The **RootCAFiles.vfd** virtual floppy disk that was created in the previous chapter can be used to transfer the CSR file to the TFS-ROOT-CA server. The same virtual floppy disk will also be used to transfer the associated files back to the TFS-CA01 server. To copy the Certificate Request file to the virtual floppy disk, perform the following steps on the TFS-CA01 server:

1. Add the **RootCAFiles.vfd** virtual floppy disk to the **TFS-CA01** virtual machine.
2. Browse to the **C:\ drive** and copy the **TFS-CA01.corp.tfslabs.com_corp-TFS-CA01-CA.req** to the **A:\ drive**.
3. Eject the **RootCAFiles.vfd** virtual floppy disk.

Once the Certificate Request has been successfully copied to the virtual floppy disk, proceed to creating the CertData directory in IIS on the TFS-CA01 server. This directory is required to host files needed for the Root CA server, and it needs to be accessible to all devices in the TFS Labs domain.

Subordinate CA Setup - CertData Virtual Directory Creation

In the previous chapter when the Root CA was configured, the *http://pki.corp.tfslabs.com/CertData/* address was referenced as the location where the Root CRL and other Root CA files were located. This location will be setup on the Subordinate CA server, as it is online and able to host those files.

Create the folder and copy the associated files by performing the following steps on the TFS-CA01 server:

1. On the root of the **C:\ drive**, create a folder called **CertData** (C:\CertData).
2. Add the **RootCAFiles.vfd** virtual floppy disk to the **TFS-CA01** virtual machine.
3. Open the **A:\ drive** and copy the **TFS Labs Certificate Authority.crl** and **TFS-ROOT-CA_TFS Labs Certificate Authority.crt** files to the **C:\CertData** folder.
4. Eject the **RootCAFiles.vfd** virtual floppy disk.

There are two methods for creating the CertData virtual directory on the TFS-CA01 server, one using the command line and the other using the IIS Manager. Only one method for creating the CertData folder is needed, as either method will have the same result.

> **ℹ** **Offline Root Certificate Authority Files**
>
> The Root CA was configured using the *http://pki.corp.tfslabs.com/CertData/* address in the previous chapter. This is the path that was used for the CDP and AIA locations, and issued certificates will expect these locations to be accessible.
>
> Ensure that this address and folder matches what was previously configured, otherwise there will be validation issues with the PKI in other environments.

Subordinate CA Setup - CertData Virtual Directory Creation - CLI Configuration

The CertData virtual directory can be created and directory browsing can be enabled using the command line by performing the following steps on the TFS-CA01 server:

1. Open an **elevated Command Prompt**.
2. Change to the IIS directory by entering the following command:

```
Command Prompt (Elevated)

cd C:\Windows\System32\inetsrv\
```

3. Run the following command to create the **CertData** virtual directory in **IIS**:

```
Command Prompt (Elevated)

appcmd.exe add vdir /app.name:"Default Web Site/" ^
/path:/CertData /physicalPath:C:\CertData
```

4. Run the following command to enable **Directory Browsing** on the **CertData** virtual directory:

```
Command Prompt (Elevated)

appcmd.exe set config "Default Web Site/CertData" ^
/section:directoryBrowse /enabled:true
```

5. Close the **Command Prompt**.

Once the CertData directory has been enabled and configured, proceed to validating that the directory is accessible on the TFS Labs domain.

Subordinate CA Setup - CertData Virtual Directory Creation - GUI Configuration

To add the CertData directory to IIS using the Internet Information Services (IIS) Manager, perform the following steps on the TFS-CA01 server:

1. Open the **Internet Information Services (IIS) Manager** (inetmgr.exe) console:

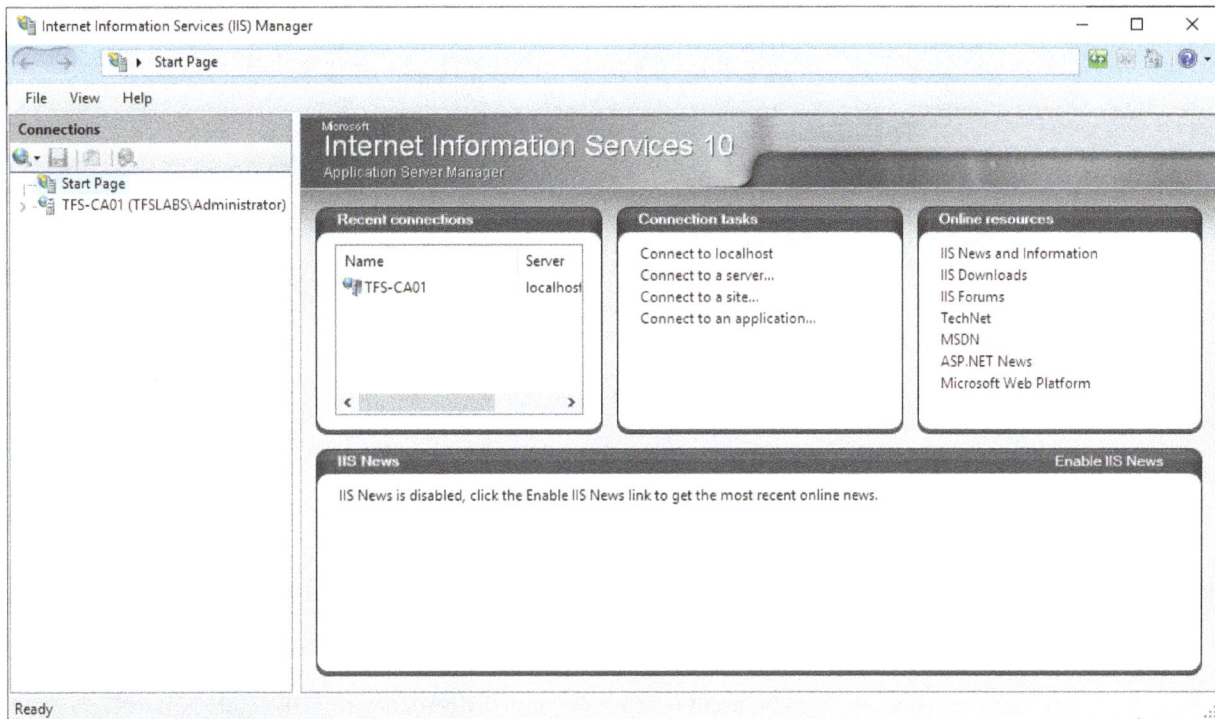

2. On the **Connections** pane, expand the **TFS-CA01** server, and then expand **Sites**:

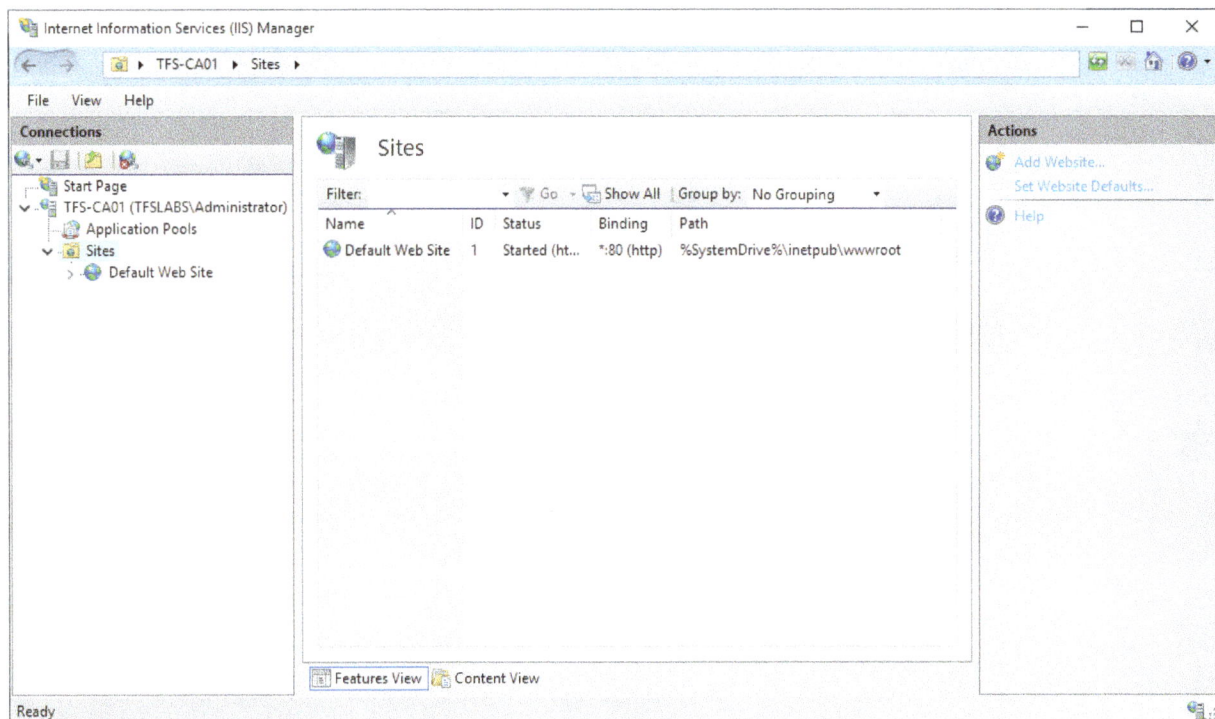

3. Right-click on **Default Web Site** and select the **Add Virtual Directory** option:

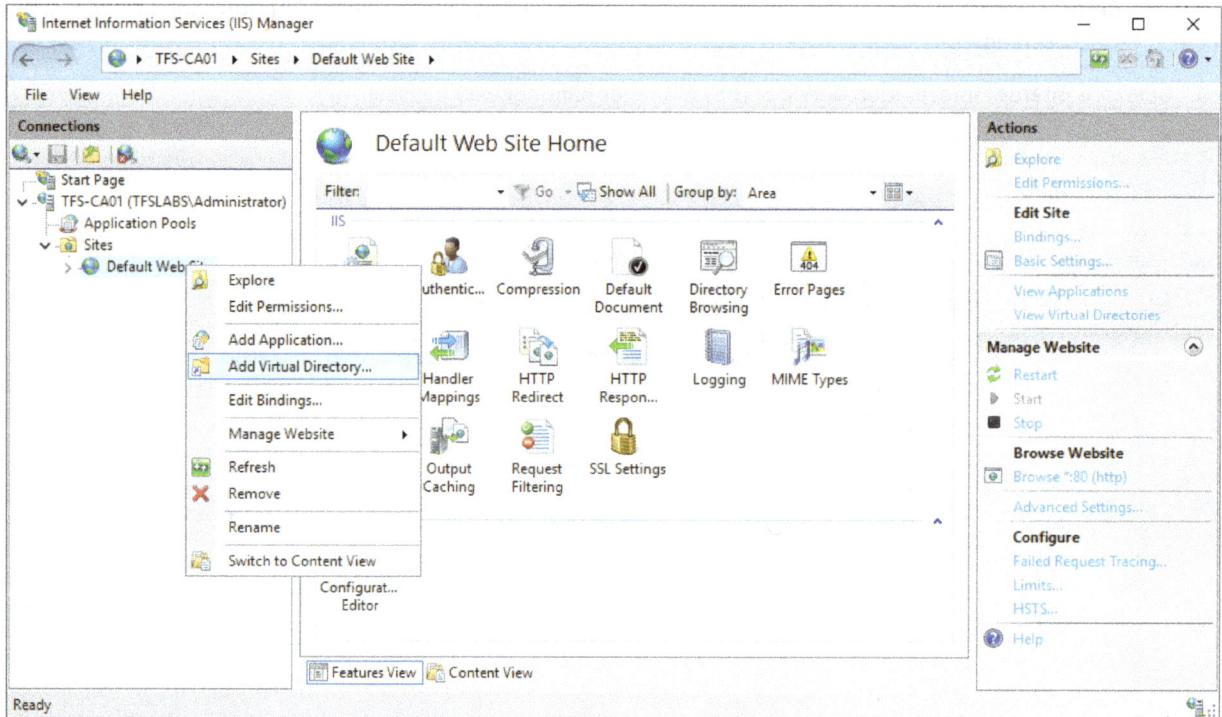

4. On the **Add Virtual Directory** screen, in the **Alias** field, enter **CertData**. For the **Physical path**, enter **C:\CertData** and then click **OK**.

5. In the **Connections** screen, under the **Default Web Site**, ensure the **CertData** virtual directory is selected:

6. In the **CertData Home** pane, double-click on the **Directory Browsing** option:

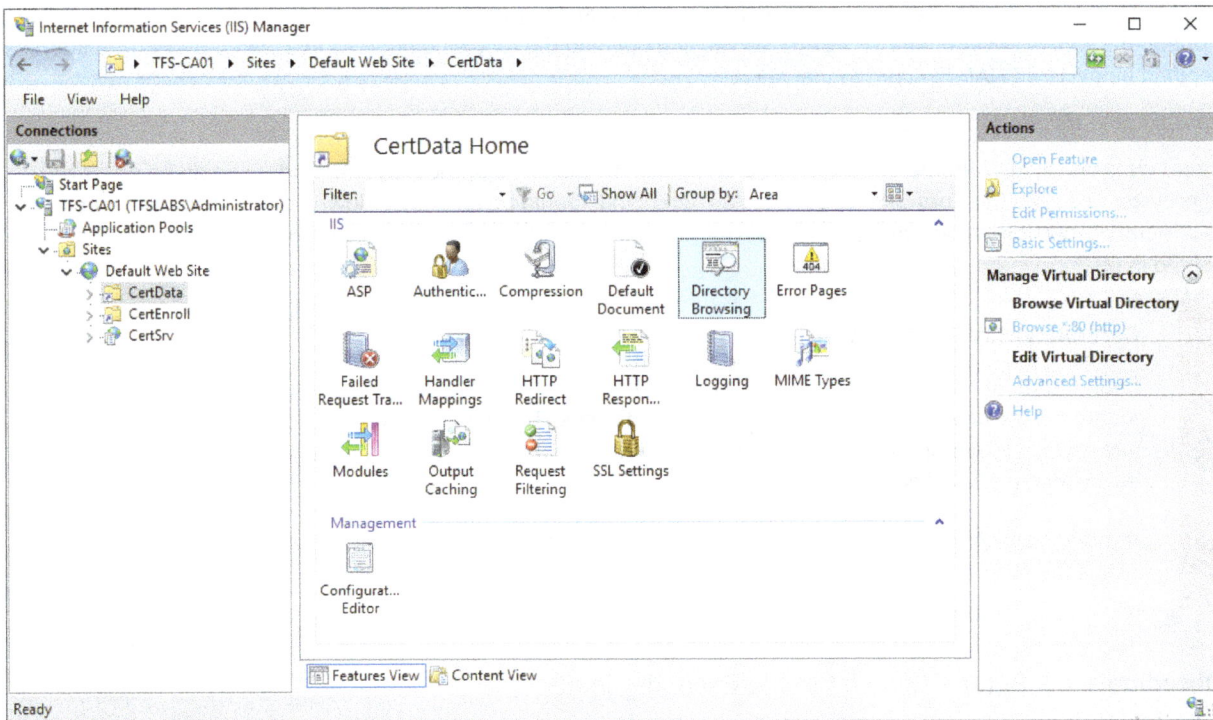

7. In the **Actions** pane on the right-side of the window, click the **Enable** option:

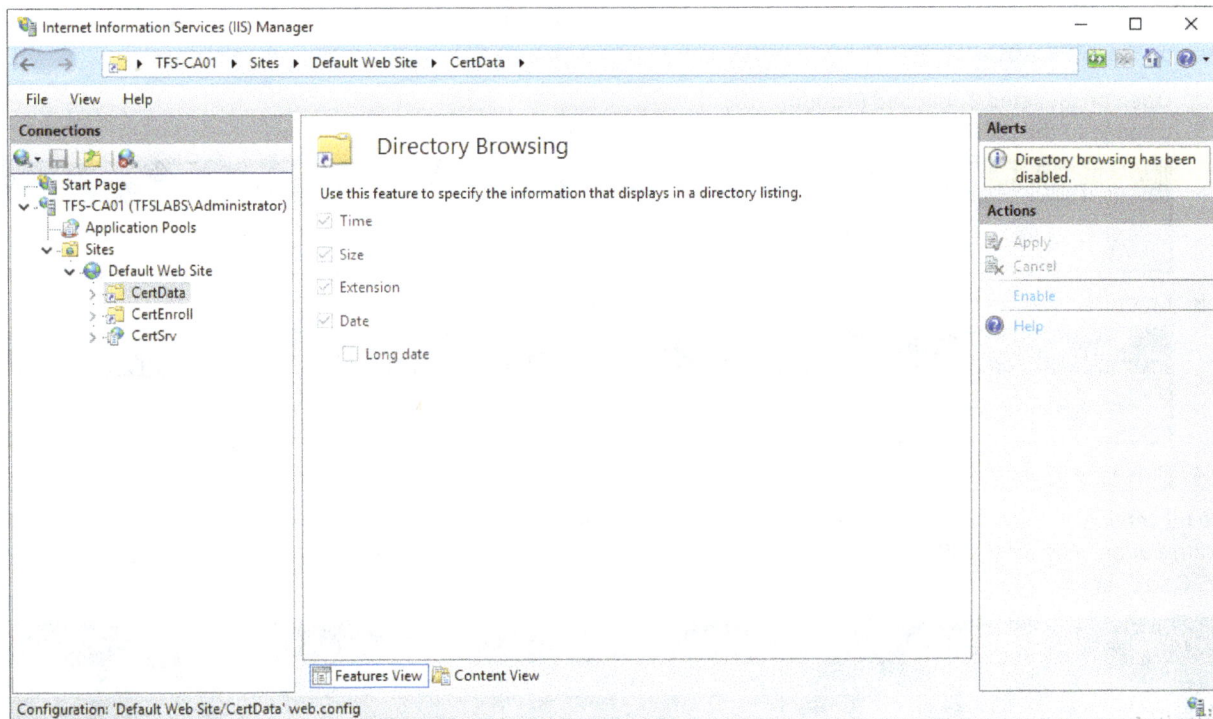

8. Close the **Internet Information Services (IIS) Manager** console.

Once the CertData directory has been enabled and configured, proceed to validating that the directory is accessible on the TFS Labs domain.

Subordinate CA Setup - CertData Virtual Directory Creation - Validation

Once the CertData directory has been created, it can now be tested that the directory is accessible. This can be done by opening a web browser on the TFS-CA01 server, and opening the following address in a web browser (the address specified below is a CNAME record to that server):

http://pki.corp.tfslabs.com/CertData/

If there were no issues with the CertData virtual directory, the contents of the CertData folder should be displayed in the browser window. The Root CRL files should be listed and should be able to be downloaded. Once the directory and the directory browsing option has been successfully enabled on the CertData directory, double escaping can now be enabled in IIS.

> **CertData Virtual Directory Validation**
>
> Ensure that the CertData virtual directory is configured correctly, and that the Root CRL files that are located in the directory are accessible on other devices. The files that are located in this directory are vital to the regular operation of the Certificate Authority, as there are dependencies for the Root CRL files embedded in issued certificates.
>
> If there is an issue with the CertData virtual directory, then there will be issues with validating the integrity of the Certificate Authority when the Subordinate Certificate is created.

Subordinate CA Setup - Enable Double Escaping in IIS

On the TFS-CA01 server, enable double escaping within Internet Information Services to allow for proper CRL publication on the TFS Labs domain. This applies specifically to the Delta CRL which requires this functionality. The Delta CRL has a plus (+) symbol in the name, and this can cause issues with some versions of IIS. This can sometimes be an issue with legacy configurations in some environments. To enable double escaping in IIS, perform the following steps on the TFS-CA01 server:

1. Open an **elevated Command Prompt**.
2. Change to the IIS directory by entering the following command:

```
Command Prompt (Elevated)

cd C:\Windows\System32\inetsrv\
```

3. Enter the following command to apply the change to the **IIS** server:

```
Command Prompt (Elevated)

appcmd.exe set config /section:requestfiltering /allowdoubleescaping:true
```

4. Close the **Command Prompt**.

The IIS service will need to be restarted afterwards when these commands are run to apply the changes to the configuration. Restart the IIS service by running the following command in an **elevated PowerShell prompt** on the TFS-CA01 server:

```
Windows PowerShell (Elevated)

Restart-Service W3SVC
```

After enabling double escaping in IIS, it will now be possible to properly distribute the Delta CRL files in the TFS Labs domain. In the next section, the Subordinate CA will be created and installed on the TFS-CA01 server, and this will involve the TFS-ROOT-CA server for that task as it is needed to create the certificate.

IIS Double Escaping Validation

If double escaping is not enabled correctly then there could potentially be issues with deploying the Delta CRL, and with the validation of the PKI. This issue will occur since the Delta CRL files are not able to be accessed over HTTP, and that is the way that they are distributed with the Enterprise CA in this book. If an issue arises with accessing the Delta CRL files, it is easy to correct by checking IIS to verify that double escaping has been enabled. This can also be verified in a later section in this chapter.

Subordinate CA Setup - Subordinate Certificate Creation

Once the Subordinate CA server has been configured and the Certificate Request successfully generated, it is now time to complete the Subordinate CA certificate request by using the TFS-ROOT-CA server.

Creating the Subordinate certificate requires multiple steps using both the Root CA and the Subordinate CA servers. These steps are not complicated, but they must be completed in the correct order and none of the steps can be skipped.

On a high-level, the workflow for creating the Subordinate certificate is as follows:

- Insert the virtual floppy disk on the TFS-ROOT-CA server.
- Submit the CSR for the Subordinate CA to the Root CA and issue it.
- Export the Subordinate certificate from the Root CA.
- Copy the Subordinate certificate to the virtual floppy disk.
- Insert the virtual floppy disk on the TFS-CA01 server.
- Install the Subordinate certificate on the Subordinate CA.
- Start Active Directory Certificate Services on the TFS-CA01 server.

To create the Subordinate CA certificate, perform the following steps on the TFS-ROOT-CA server:

1. Add the **RootCAFiles.vfd** virtual floppy disk to the **TFS-ROOT-CA** virtual machine.
2. Copy the **A:\TFS-CA01.corp.tfslabs.com_corp-TFS-CA01-CA.req** file to the **C:\RootCA** folder.
3. On the **TFS-ROOT-CA** server open **Certification Authority** console (certsrv.msc).
4. Right-click on the **TFS Labs Certificate Authority** server, select **All Tasks** and click on **Submit new request...**:

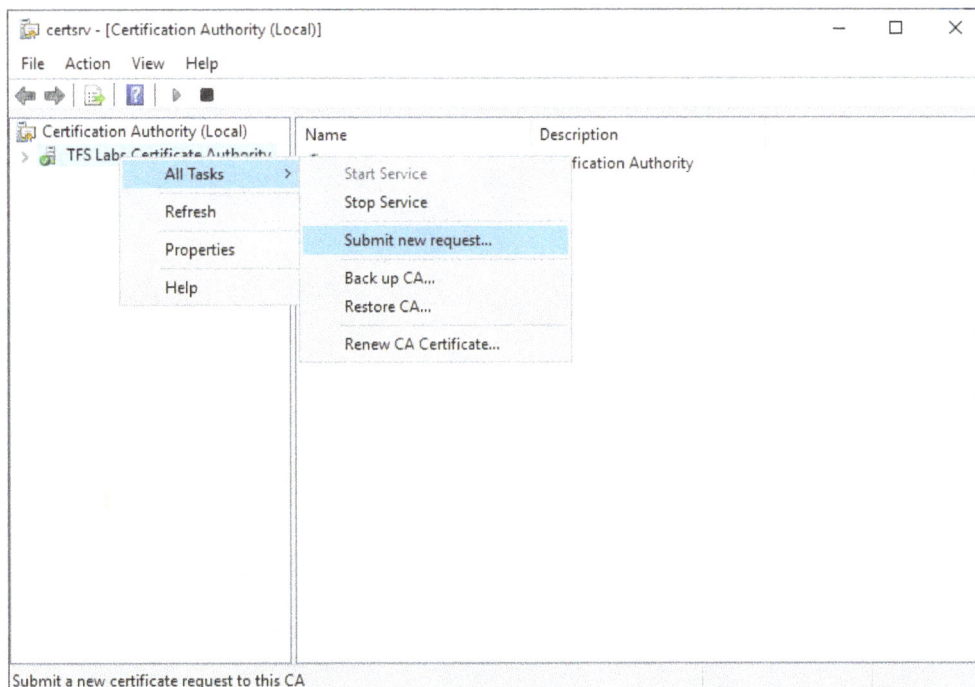

5. On the **Open Request File** window, browse to the **C:\RootCA** folder, and select the certificate request file (**TFS-CA01.corp.tfslabs.com_corp-TFS-CA01-CA.req**) that was previously copied from the **TFS-CA01** server. Click the **Open** button to continue.

6. Once the Certificate Request has been submitted to the Root Certificate Authority, go to the **Pending Requests** folder in the **TFS Labs Certificate Authority** to see the pending Certificate Request. In most cases, the request for the Subordinate certificate should be identified as **Request ID 2** for a new Certificate Authority server:

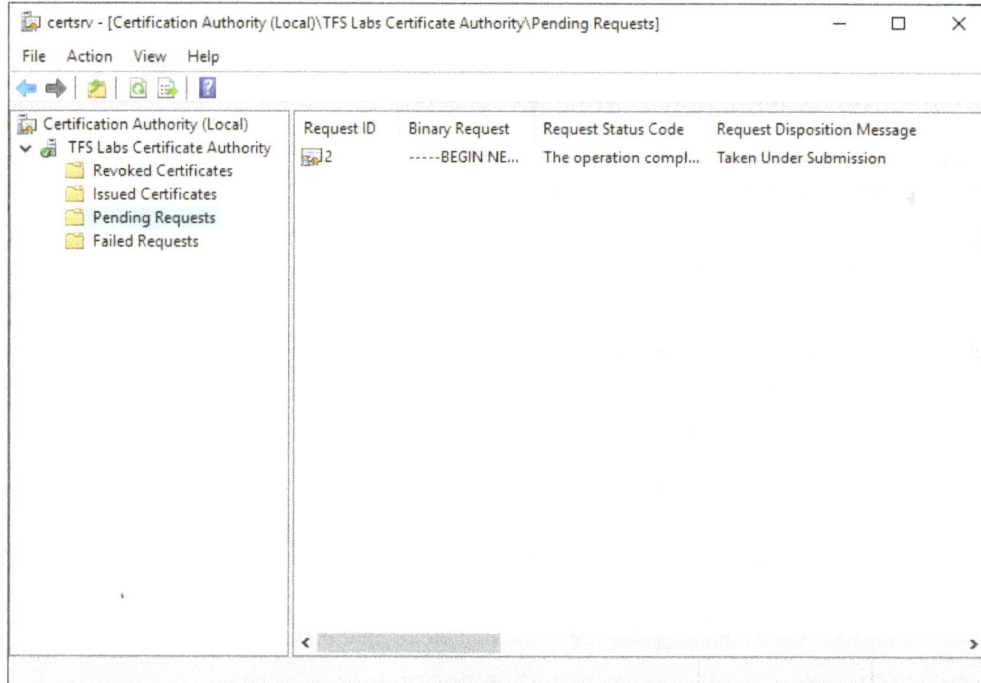

7. To issue the Subordinate certificate, right-click on the **Request ID 2**, select **All Tasks** and click on **Issue**:

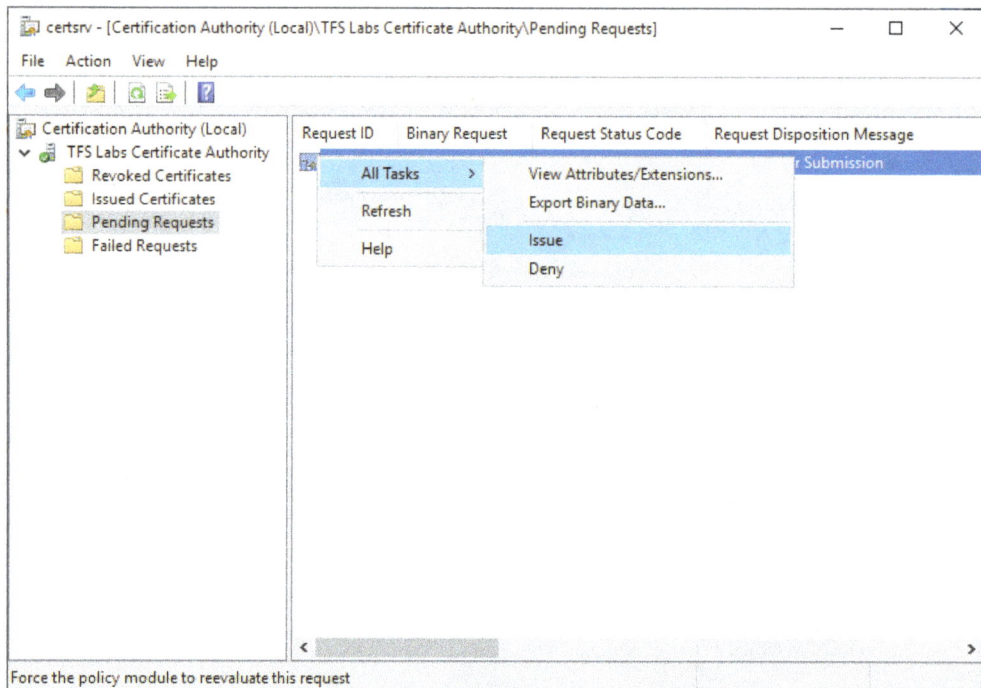

8. Once the certificate has been issued by the Certificate Authority, go to the **Issued Certificates** folder to see the certificate. It should still identified as **Request ID 2**:

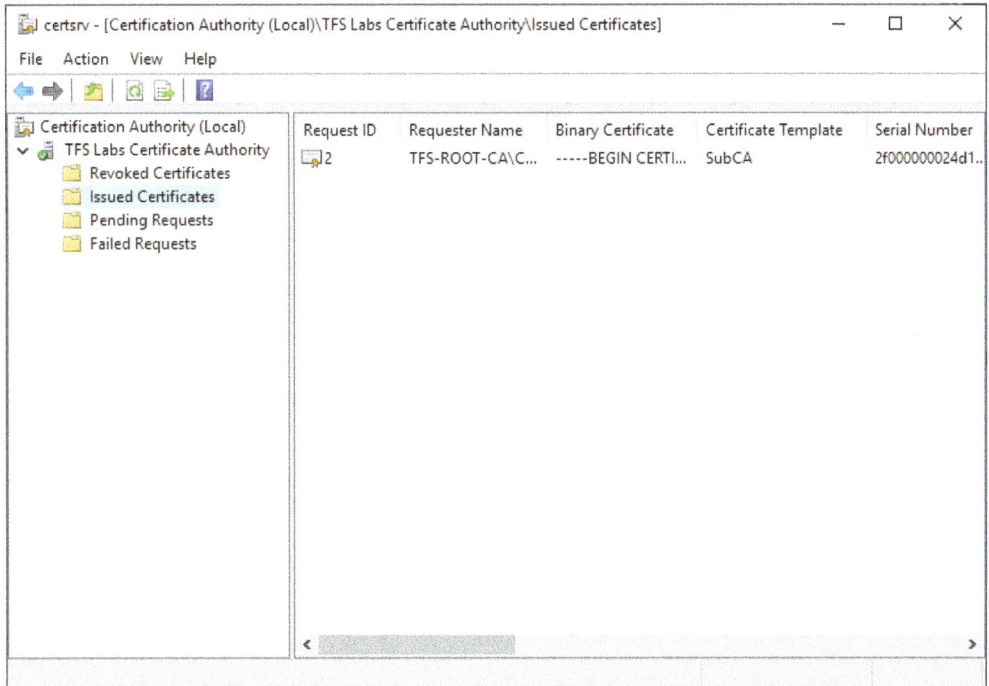

9. Double-click on the **Request ID 2** certificate to open the **Certificate** properties window:

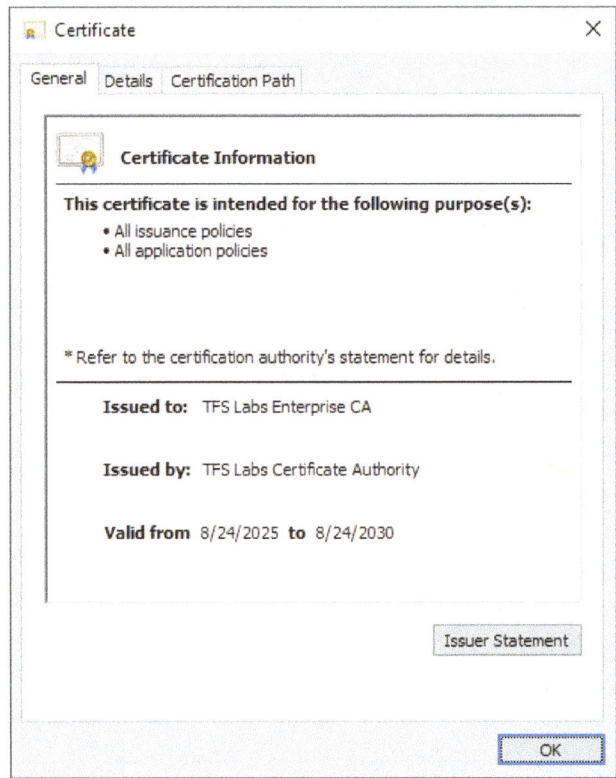

10. Go to the **Details** tab and click on the **Copy to File...** button:

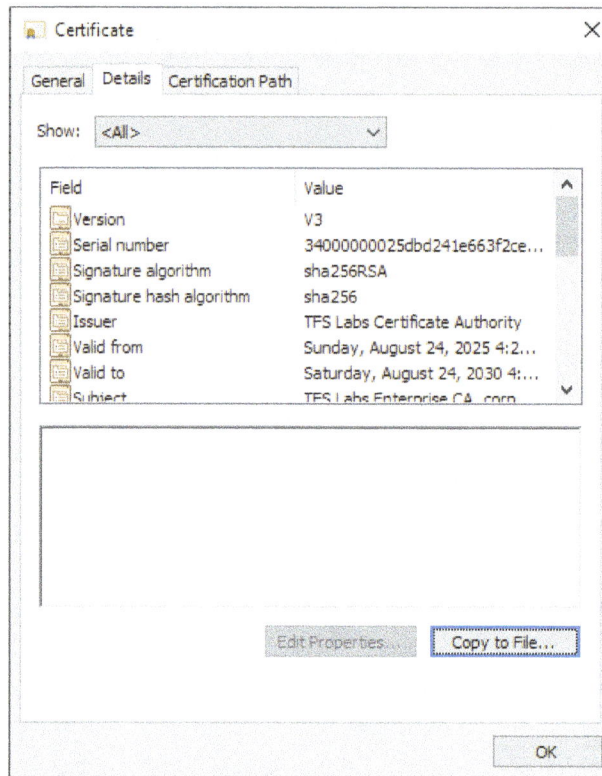

11. On the first screen of the **Certificate Export Wizard**, click the **Next** button to continue:

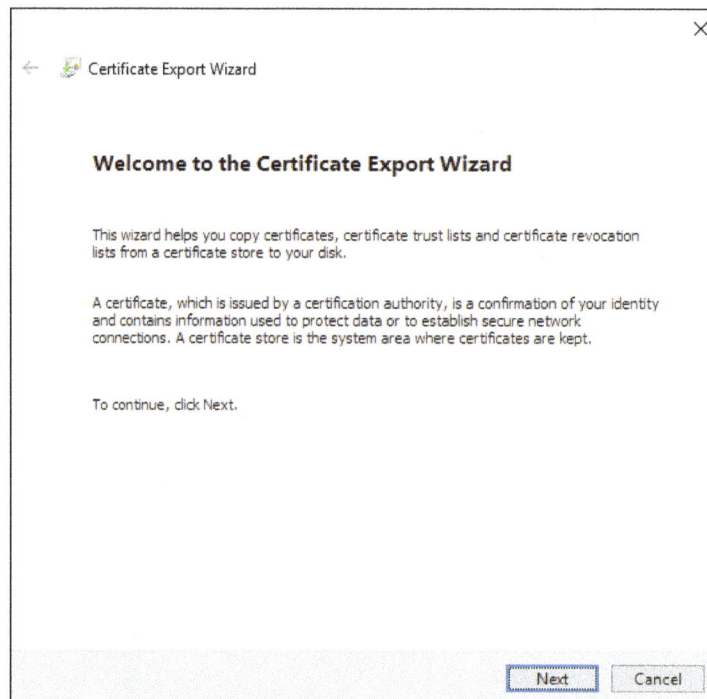

12. On the **Export File Format** screen, select the **Cryptographic Message Syntax Standard - PKCS #7 Certificate (.P7B)** format. Select the option to **Include all certificates in the certification path if possible** and click the **Next** button:

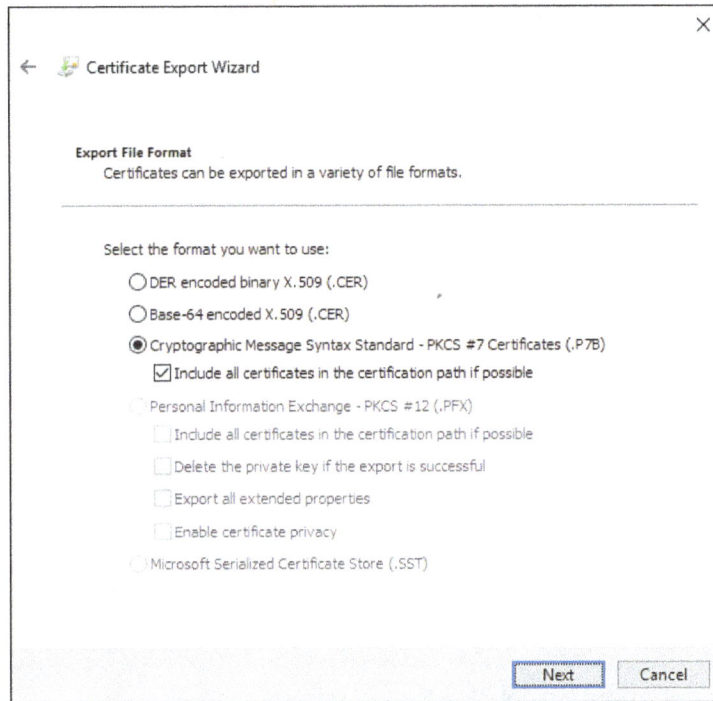

13. On the **File to Export** screen, enter **C:\RootCA\TFS Labs Enterprise CA.p7b** as the file name and click **Next** to continue:

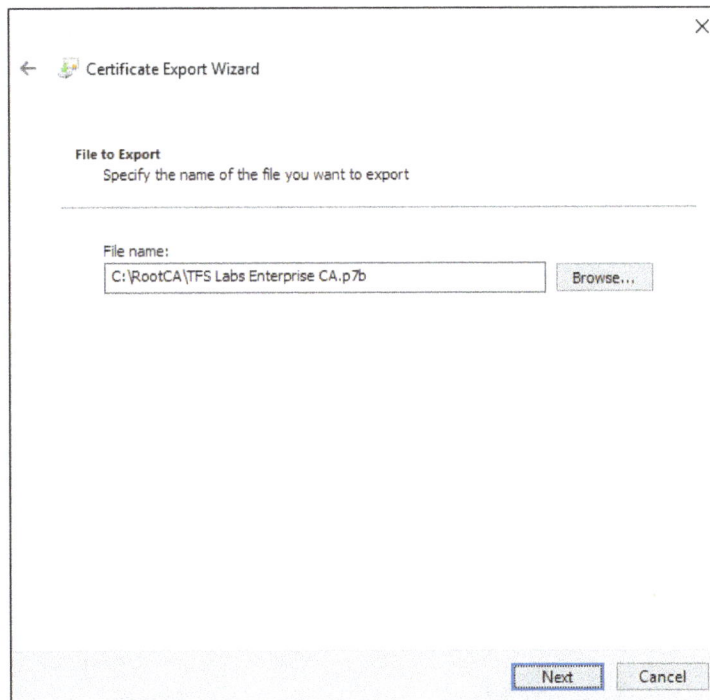

14. On the **Completing the Certificate Export Wizard** screen, click the **Finish** button to complete the wizard:

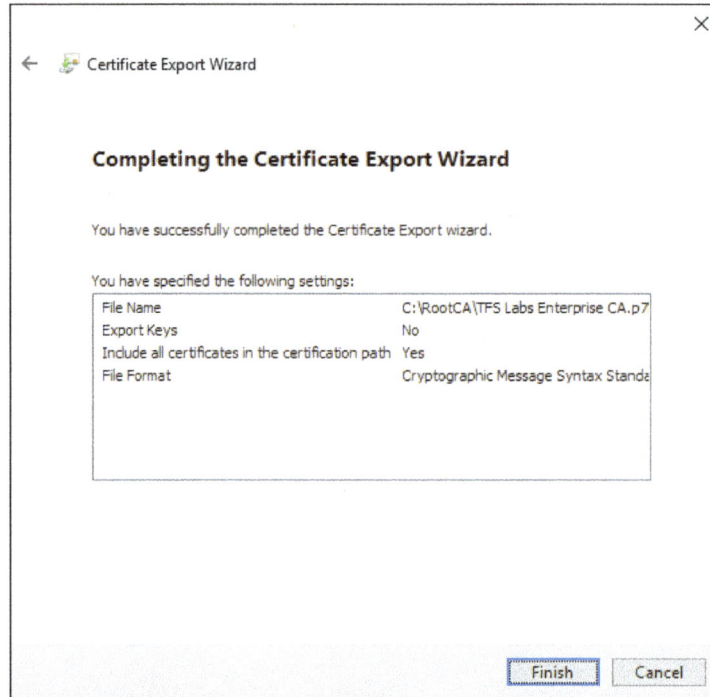

15. On the **Certificate Export Wizard** prompt, click the **OK** button to continue.
16. Copy the **C:\RootCA\TFS Labs Enterprise CA.p7b** file to the **A:\ drive**.
17. Eject the **RootCAFiles.vfd** virtual floppy disk.

To import the Subordinate CA certificate, perform the following steps on the TFS-CA01 server:

1. On the **TFS-CA01** server insert the **RootCAFiles.vfd** virtual floppy disk. Copy the **A:\TFS Labs Enterprise CA.p7b** file to the root of the **C:\ drive**.
2. On the **TFS-CA01** server, open the **Certification Authority** console (certsrv.msc):

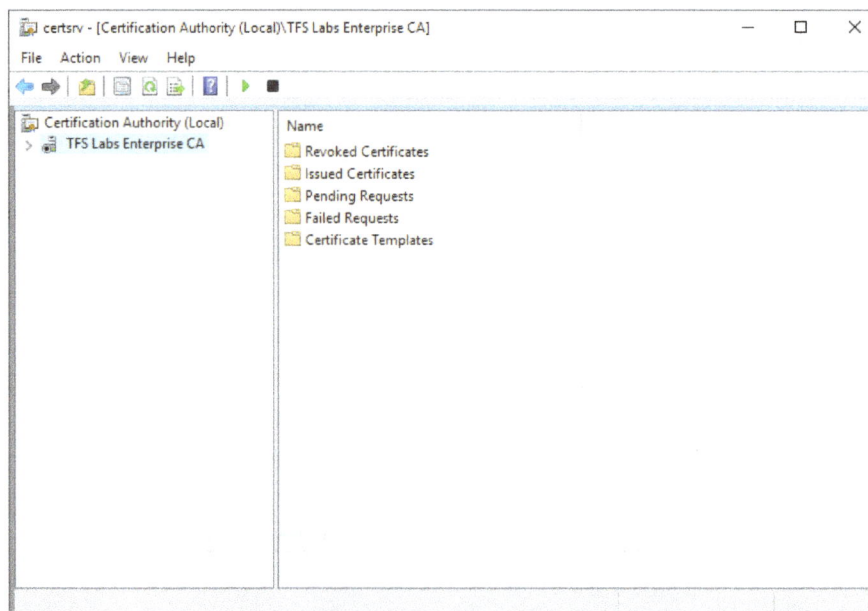

3. In the **Certification Authority** console, right-click on the **TFS Labs Enterprise CA** server, go to **All Tasks** and select the option to **Install CA Certificate...**:

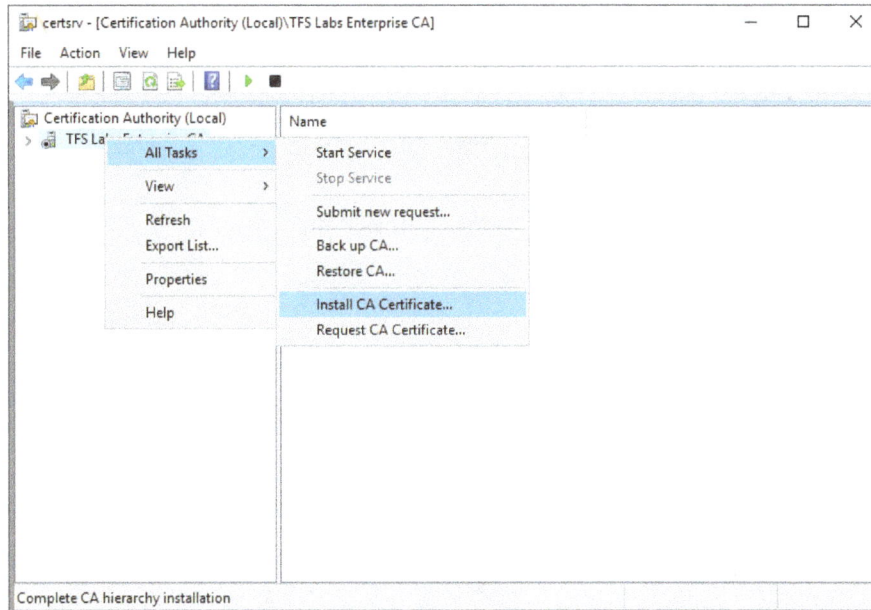

4. On the **Select file to complete CA installation** window, browse to the **C:\ drive**, select the **TFS Labs Enterprise CA.p7b** file and click **Open** to continue.

> ⚠️ **Untrusted Root Certificate Error**
>
> If a warning message about installing an untrusted Root certificate appears, click the **OK** button to continue with the installation. The error message is due to the Root certificate being untrusted, and should be referenced by the **CERT_E_UNTRUSTEDROOT** error message.

5. If there were no errors with installing the certificate, right-click on the **TFS Labs Enterprise CA** server, select the **All Tasks** option, and click the **Start Service** option:

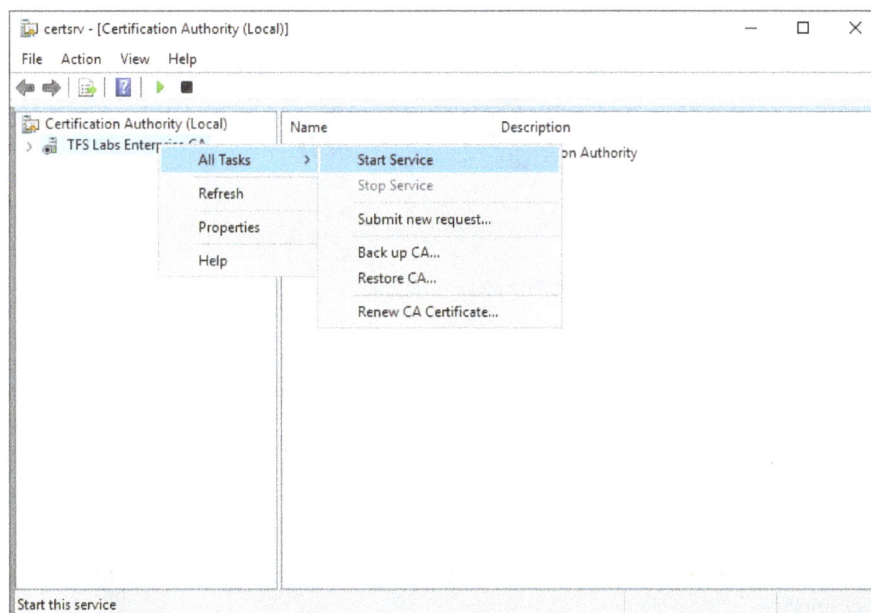

6. The **Subordinate Certificate** has now been installed successfully, and the **Subordinate Certificate Authority** is now running:

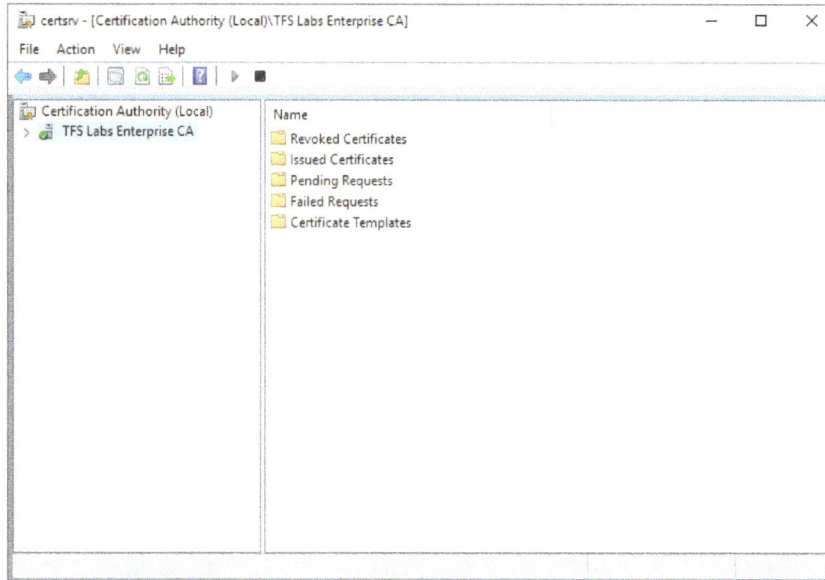

7. Eject the **RootCAFiles.vfd** virtual floppy disk.

Once installed, the Subordinate certificate can now be viewed and verified that it was created with the correct values that was setup during the initial configuration of the Certificate Authority:

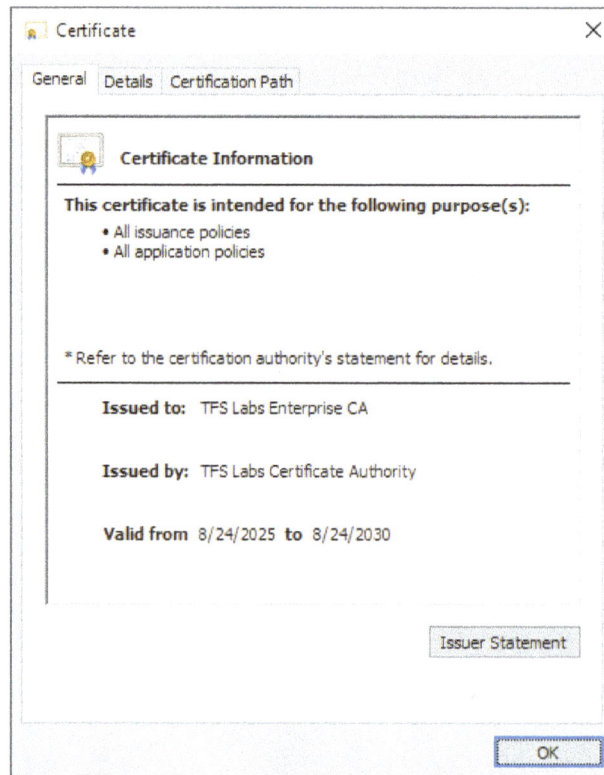

Figure 7.10.1: The TFS Labs Enterprise CA certificate has been signed by the TFS Labs Certificate Authority certificate, with a 5 year validity period.

If there were no issues with creating the Subordinate certificate, delete the following files from the TFS-CA01 server as they are no longer required as part of the Certificate Authority implementation:

- **C:\TFS-CA01.corp.tfslabs.com_corp-TFS-CA01-CA.req**
- **C:\TFS Labs Enterprise CA.p7b**

These files should be deleted as they should not remain on a server that has active network connections for security purposes. The files can remain on the TFS-ROOT-CA server as it is offline, and the files cannot be accessed.

> **Subordinate Certificate Issuing Error**
>
> **If the Subordinate certificate was successfully issued in the previous steps, skip this notice.**
>
> There may be instances where the installation and configuration of the Subordinate certificate may fail for several reasons. One of the common issues that can occur is when the Subordinate CA has issues with the Root CA CRL configuration, which is offline at the time of issuance of the Subordinate certificate. To correct this issue, run the following command in an **elevated PowerShell prompt**:
>
> ```
> Windows PowerShell (Elevated)
>
> certutil.exe -setreg ca\CRLFlags +CRLF_REVCHECK_IGNORE_OFFLINE
> ```
>
> Once the command is issued, the Active Directory Certificate Services role will need to be restarted. Run the following commands to restart the service:
>
> ```
> Windows PowerShell (Elevated)
>
> net stop CertSvc
> net start CertSvc
> ```
>
> At this point, try to install the Subordinate certificate again and restart Active Directory Certificate Services to complete the configuration.

Once the Subordinate certificate has been issued, proceed to setting the maximum age for certificates that are issued by the Certificate Authority in the next section.

Subordinate CA Setup - Set Maximum Certificate Age

As per the design of the TFS Labs Certificate Authority, all certificates that will be issued by the Subordinate CA will only be valid for 1 year. This setting can be forced so that a Certificate Template does not attempt to sign a certificate for a longer period of time, even if the settings are different from expected.

To configure the maximum certificate age for issued certificates on the Subordinate CA, run the following commands on the TFS-CA01 server:

1. Open an **elevated PowerShell prompt**.
2. To define the maximum age of any certificate that the **Subordinate CA** is capable of issuing, run the following commands:

```
Windows PowerShell (Elevated)

certutil.exe -setreg CA\ValidityPeriodUnits 1
certutil.exe -setreg CA\ValidityPeriod "Years"
```

3. Restart the **Active Directory Certificate Services** service to apply the configuration changes:

```
Windows PowerShell (Elevated)

net stop CertSvc
net start CertSvc
```

4. Close the **PowerShell prompt**.

Once the maximum age for certificates has been configured on the Subordinate Certificate Authority, proceed to modifying the CertEnroll virtual directory settings, which is used for certificate deployment for the PKI.

Subordinate CA Setup - CertEnroll Virtual Directory Modifications

Before the Subordinate CA CDP and AIA configuration can be added to the Subordinate certificate, the CertEnroll folder in IIS will need to have directory browsing enabled to allow for proper certificate file distribution. This setting is not enabled by default when the directory is created during the Active Directory Certificate Services configuration. This requirement is similar to the CertData virtual directory that was created earlier, and if access to the CertEnroll directory is restricted, there will be issues with accessing the Base CRL and Delta CRL files. This can cause issues with validating the overall status of the PKI, and users will not be able to access the necessary CRL information.

There are two methods for modifying the CertEnroll virtual directory on the TFS-CA01 server, one using the command line, and the other using the IIS Manager. Only one method for modifying the CertEnroll folder is needed.

> **Certificate File Network Locations**
>
> In large organizations it is not uncommon to place certificate files on network shares, or in some cases on DFS locations. For scalability purposes, this allows for greater options in allowing access to those files without putting too much overhead on an existing server.
>
> This is also why the OCSP (Online Responder) role within Active Directory Certificate Services is a crucial function, as it is designed to alleviate these issues as part of the architecture of the OCSP service.

Subordinate CA Setup - CertEnroll Virtual Directory Modifications - CLI Configuration

Directory browsing can be enabled on the CertEnroll virtual directory using the command line instead of using the Internet Information Services (IIS) Manager:

1. Open an **elevated Command Prompt**.
2. Change to the correct directory by entering the following command:

```
Command Prompt (Elevated)

cd C:\Windows\System32\inetsrv\
```

3. Run the following command to enable **Directory Browsing** on the **CertEnroll** virtual directory:

```
Command Prompt (Elevated)

appcmd.exe set config "Default Web Site/CertEnroll" ^
/section:directoryBrowse /enabled:true
```

4. Close the **Command Prompt**.

Once the directory browsing option has been enabled on the CertEnroll directory, proceed to validating the directory access, and then configuring auditing on the Subordinate CA.

Subordinate CA Setup - CertEnroll Virtual Directory Modifications - GUI Configuration

To modify the CertEnroll directory in IIS, perform the following steps on the TFS-CA01 server using the Internet Information Services (IIS) Manager:

1. Open the **Internet Information Services (IIS) Manager** (inetmgr.exe) console:

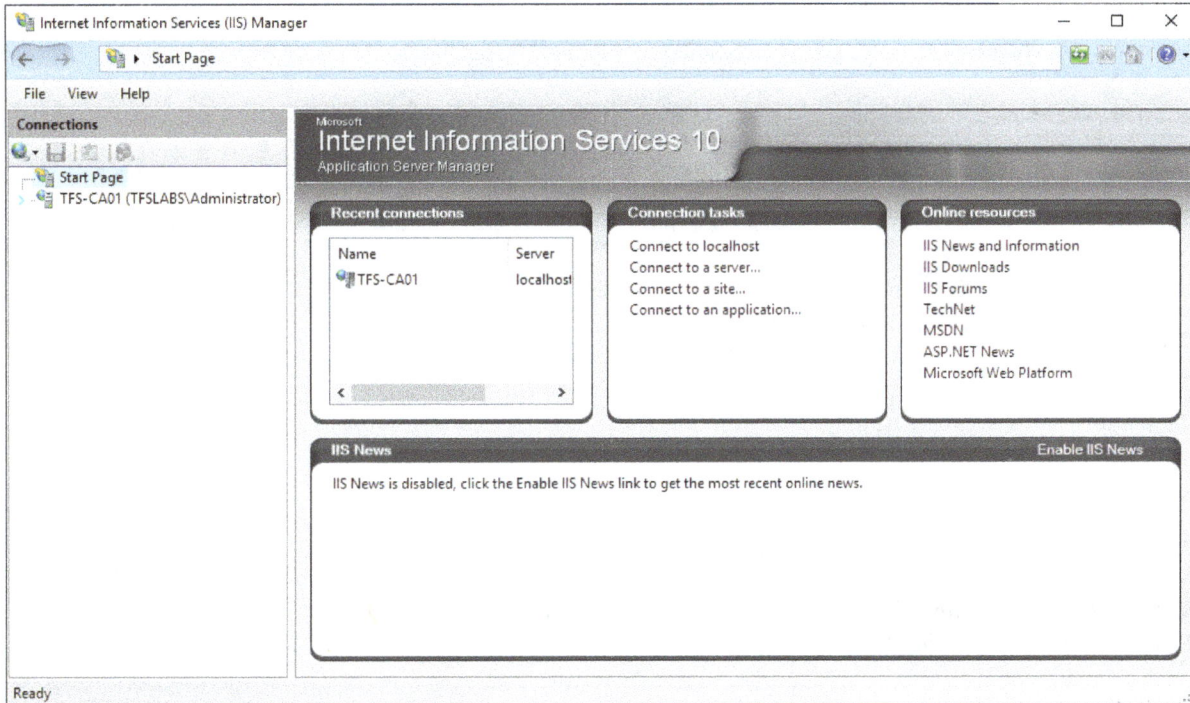

2. On the **Connections** pane, expand the **TFS-CA01** server, expand **Sites**, and then expand **Default Web Site**:

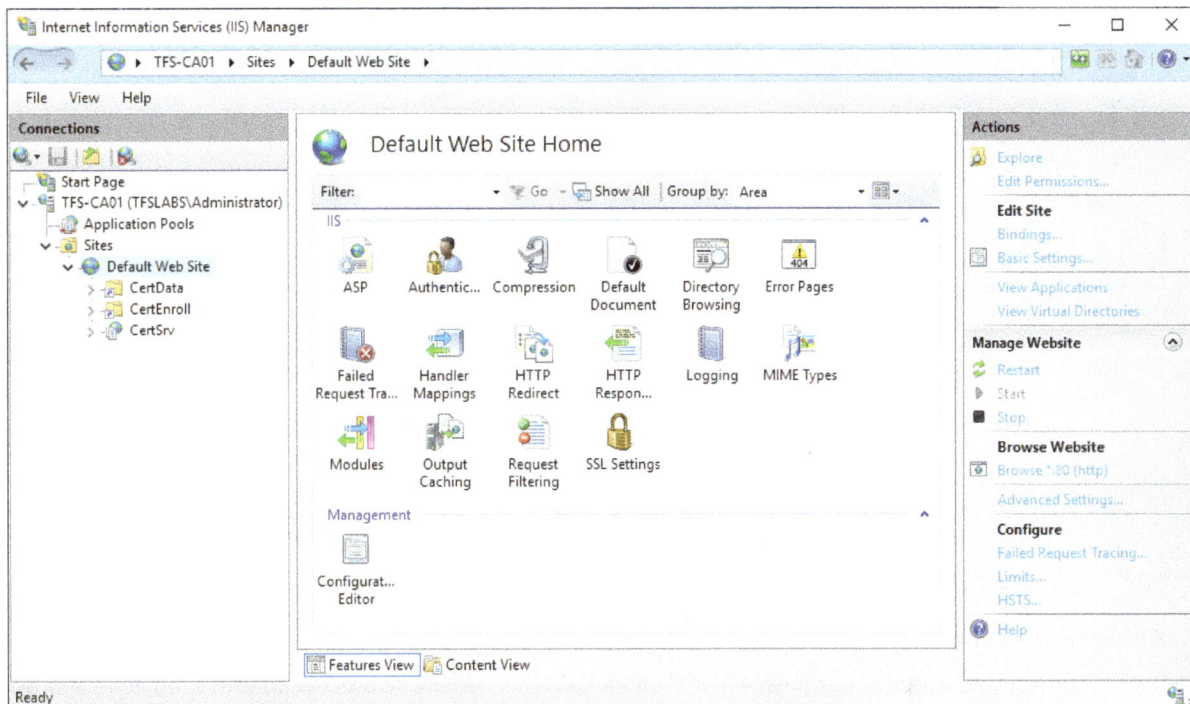

3. In the **Connections** pane, under the **Default Web Site**, ensure the **CertEnroll** virtual directory is selected:

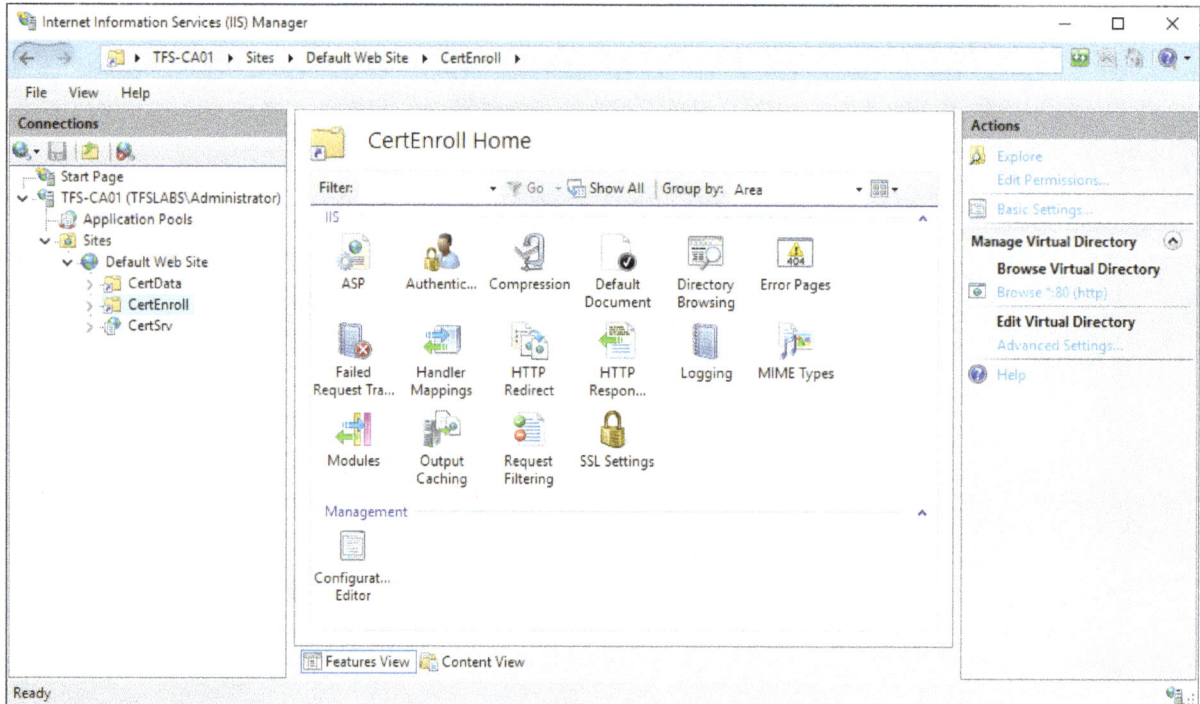

4. In the **CertEnroll Home** pane, double-click on **Directory Browsing**.
5. In the **Actions** pane, click **Enable**:

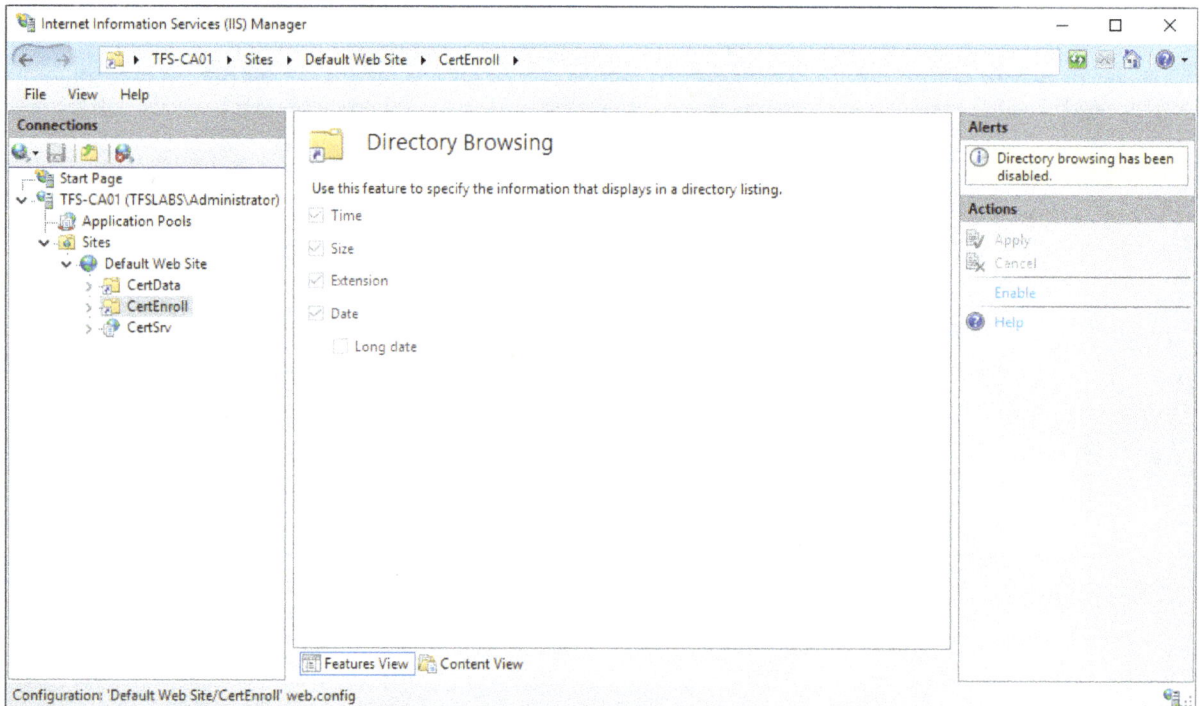

6. Close the **Internet Information Services (IIS) Manager** console.

Once the directory browsing option has been enabled on the CertEnroll directory, proceed to validating the directory access, and then configuring auditing on the Subordinate CA.

Subordinate CA Setup - CertEnroll Virtual Directory Modifications - Validation

Once the CertEnroll directory has been modified, it can now be tested that the directory is accessible to clients. This can be done by opening a web browser on the TFS-CA01 server, and opening the following address in a web browser (the address specified below is a CNAME record to that server):

http://pki.corp.tfslabs.com/CertEnroll/

If there were no issues, the contents of the CertEnroll folder should be displayed in the browser:

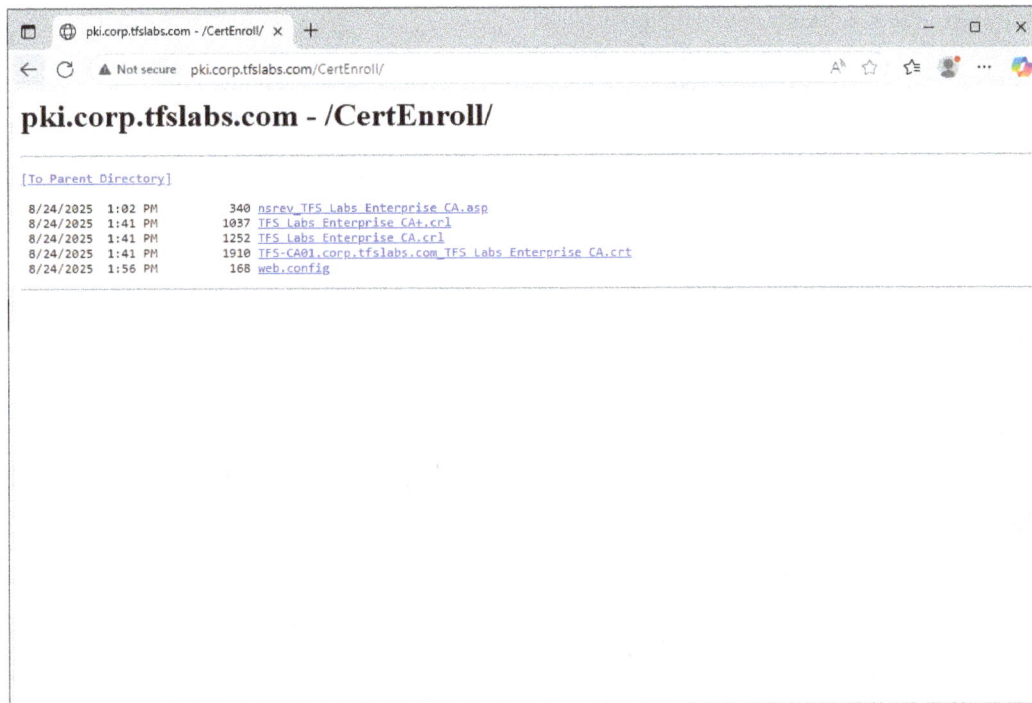

Figure 7.12.3.1: The CertEnroll folder on the TFS-CA01 server contains the Subordinate CA certificate, as well as the Subordinate CRL files. This includes the Base CRL and Delta CRL files for the Subordinate CA.

Once the directory browsing option has been enabled on the CertEnroll directory, proceed to configuring auditing on the Subordinate CA.

Root and Subordinate Certificate Authority CRL Files

The contents of the CertEnroll folder are automatically updated whenever there are updates to the Subordinate CA CRL through AD CS. There is no need to manually update the contents of the CertEnroll folder, as it is completely managed through Active Directory Certificate Services whenever a certificate needs to be revoked. This differs from the Root CA, where these files are manually managed and distributed through a different folder.

IIS Double Escaping

To ensure that double escaping has been correctly enabled on the IIS server, all files that are listed in the CertEnroll directory should be able to be downloaded. If any of the files are not able to be downloaded, especially the **TFS Labs Enterprise CA+.crl** file, that means that double escaping was not correctly enabled on the IIS server. Ensure that issues with double escaping are resolved at this stage in the Subordinate CA configuration, as this can cause issues in later steps in this book.

Subordinate CA Setup - Enable Advanced Auditing

Auditing is not necessary on servers that are running Active Directory Certificate Services, but it is highly recommended for best practices. Auditing is often required for compliance purposes, and it is important to know when certificates have been issued or revoked. When Active Directory Certificate Services has auditing enabled, it will create log entries in the Windows Event Log on the local server under the following circumstances:

- When a certificate is issued.
- When a certificate is revoked.
- When the CRL is updated.
- When the Certificate Authority configuration is modified.
- When the certificate archive keys are created and retrieved.
- When the Certificate Authority is backed up using the available methods within Active Directory Certificate Services.
- When administrative tasks are performed on the server, such as starting and stopping the AD CS service.

Even if the more advanced auditing options are not enabled for the Certificate Authority, there will always be Active Directory Certificate Services events written to the Windows Event Log. The settings configured in this section will enable the advanced auditing features for the service, which can be useful for troubleshooting purposes.

To configure auditing on the Subordinate Certificate Authority, perform the following steps on the TFS-CA01 server:

1. Open an **elevated PowerShell prompt**.
2. Enable the options to audit **Success** and **Failure** attempts on the **Audit object access** setting. This change is made in the **Local Security Policy** with the following command:

```
Windows PowerShell (Elevated)

auditpol.exe /set /category:"Object Access" /failure:enable /success:enable
```

3. Enable auditing for all events on the Certificate Authority by running the following command:

```
Windows PowerShell (Elevated)

certutil.exe -setreg CA\AuditFilter 127
```

4. Restart the **Active Directory Certificate Services** service to apply the changes:

```
Windows PowerShell (Elevated)

net stop CertSvc
net start CertSvc
```

5. Close the **PowerShell prompt**.

If the AD CS service is not restarted after auditing has been enabled, there will be no events written to the Windows Event Log until the service is restarted on the TFS-CA01 server. Auditing options can be verified by opening the Certification Authority console (certsrv.msc) and checking the properties of the TFS Labs Certificate Authority.

> **Active Directory Certificate Services Auditing**
>
> With auditing enabled for Active Directory Certificate Services, events that are enabled for auditing will be logged to the Windows Event Viewer. These events can be viewed through the Event Viewer Console (eventvwr.msc). There are 30 Active Directory Certificate Services related events that can be logged in the Windows Event Viewer with an Event ID between 4868 and 4898.

Once auditing has been enabled on the Subordinate Certificate Authority, the CDP and AIA settings on the Subordinate Certificate Authority can be configured.

Subordinate CA Setup - CDP and AIA Configuration

Before the Subordinate Certificate Authority can be utilized and begin issuing certificates, the Certificate Revocation List needs to be configured on the Subordinate CA. The CRL files that are provided by the Root CA are distributed with the Subordinate CA. This is because the Root CA is not available on the network since it is always offline, so there is no way for clients to access the files needed for the TFS Labs domain. This is not needed for the Subordinate CA as it is always online, so those workarounds are not required and the process is entirely automated.

There are multiple options where the CRL Distribution Point (CDP) and Authority Information Access (AIA) locations can be configured for the Subordinate Certificate Authority, and there are four locations that are configured by default when the Subordinate certificate is created with Active Directory Certificate Services:

- Local File System
- LDAP
- HTTP
- SMB

To complete the CDP and AIA configuration for the Subordinate Certificate Authority, several of the locations will be deleted as they are not required, and a new location will be added that will point to the Subordinate Certificate Authority. This location will be found on the TFS-CA01 server using the *http://pki.corp.tfslabs.com/CertEnroll/* address, which was created and configured earlier in this chapter.

The CDP and AIA configuration on the Subordinate Certificate Authority can be performed through the command line using PowerShell, or by using the Certification Authority console.

DNS for CDP and AIA Locations

Ensure that in this section the URL for the CDP and AIA location is correct. This URL relies on a CNAME entry that points to the TFS-CA01 server (Subordinate CA). The reason that a CNAME entry is used instead of the hostname of the TFS-CA01 server is to provide flexibility in the future should the PKI structure need to be modified, or servers are added.

Any *http://pki.corp.tfslabs.com/CertEnroll/* entries in this section should be modified to fit an existing Active Directory environment. Replace any references to this URL in the CLI and GUI sections with the correct URL in this section.

DNS for CDP and AIA Locations

For the purposes of the Subordinate Certificate Authority, most of the default options for CDP and AIA are not valid or even required in most environments. The only location that cannot be removed or modified is the location on the local file system, as it is required for normal operation:

- The local file system location is always required so the Certificate Authority server can access the CDP and AIA data. If this location is missing, the Subordinate CA will not be able to issue any CRL files to the domain.
- The LDAP location entry is not required as this is method is not recommended by Microsoft for distributing CRL files with newer versions of Active Directory Certificate Services.
- The HTTP location which is using the DNS name of the Subordinate CA server is not valid as it cannot be moved to another server. This is why CNAME records should be used, as it allows the files to be relocated in the future.
- The SMB location is not required as distribution through a web server is the preferred method for distribution of CRL files for Active Directory Certificate Services.

In any case, it is always important to validate the CDP and AIA locations as it can cause issues with the PKI if there are invalid entries present. Invalid entries can also introduce latency into the PKI if invalid entries are referenced by clients and are forced to time out.

Subordinate CA Setup - CDP and AIA Configuration - CLI Configuration

The CDP and AIA location settings for the Subordinate CA can be configured using the command line with PowerShell by performing the following steps on the TFS-CA01 server:

1. Open an **elevated PowerShell prompt**.
2. Run the following command to configure the **CDP** settings for the Subordinate certificate (execute this command as a single line with no breaks):

   Windows PowerShell (Elevated)
   ```
   certutil.exe -setreg CA\CRLPublicationURLs "65:C:\Windows\system32\CertSrv\
   CertEnroll\%3%8%9.crl\n6:http://pki.corp.tfslabs.com/CertEnroll/%3%8%9.crl"
   ```

3. Run the following command to configure the **AIA** settings for the Subordinate certificate (execute this command as a single line with no breaks):

   Windows PowerShell (Elevated)
   ```
   certutil.exe -setreg CA\CACertPublicationURLs "1:C:\Windows\system32\CertSrv\
   CertEnroll\%1_%3%4.crt\n2:http://pki.corp.tfslabs.com/CertEnroll/%1_%3%4.crt"
   ```

4. Restart the **Active Directory Certificate Services** service to apply the changes:

   Windows PowerShell (Elevated)
   ```
   net stop CertSvc
   net start CertSvc
   ```

5. Close the **elevated PowerShell prompt**.

Now that the CDP and AIA location settings have been successfully configured on the TFS-CA01 server, the settings should be validated to ensure that there are no issues. Once the settings have been confirmed, the CRL for the Subordinate CA can be published to the TFS Labs domain.

DNS Entries for CDP and AIA

Ensure that the URL for the CDP and AIA path locations is correct. The URL for both entries relies on a CNAME entry that is configured to point to the TFS-CA01 server (Subordinate CA). A CNAME entry is used instead of the hostname of the TFS-CA01 server is to provide flexibility in the future should the PKI structure need to be modified for whatever reason.

The *http://pki.corp.tfslabs.com/CertEnroll/* configuration was already configured in this chapter. The DNS records have already been created, and the folder has been configured using IIS. These files will be accessible to users and devices in the TFS Labs domain.

Command Line Entry for CDP and AIA Locations

In this section there are two commands (step 2 and step 3) that are used to modify the CDP and AIA locations for the Subordinate CA. These commands need to be executed as a single line, with no line breaks at all. They are shown with line breaks so that the entire command is visible, but they cannot be executed as they are displayed. Copy the entire command first, remove the line breaks while preserving the existing characters, and then execute the commands in each step.

If there is an error with the configuration in this section, it can cause unexpected issues with the Certificate Authority. Ensure that before proceeding to the next section in this chapter that all issues with the CDP and AIA entries and correct.

Subordinate CA Setup - CDP and AIA Configuration - GUI Configuration

To configure the CDP and AIA locations on the Subordinate Certificate Authority using the Certification Authority console, perform the following steps on the TFS-CA01 server:

1. Open the **Certification Authority** console (certsrv.msc) on the **TFS-CA01** server:

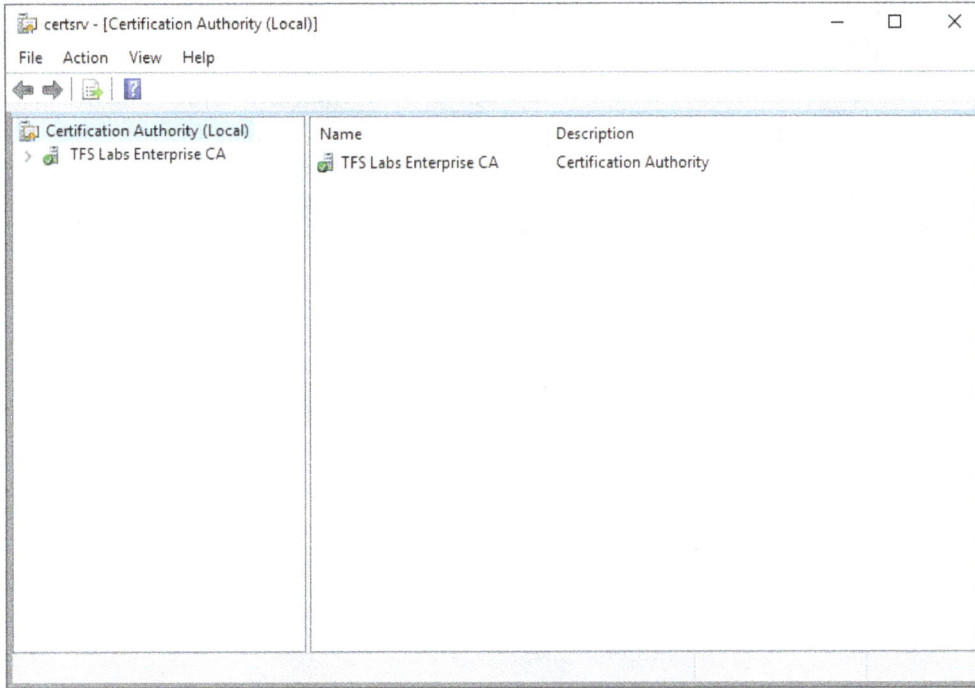

2. Right-click on **TFS Labs Enterprise CA** server and select **Properties**.
3. Select the **Extensions** tab, verify that the **CRL Distribution Point (CDP)** extension is selected under the **Select extension** field, and click the **Add** button:

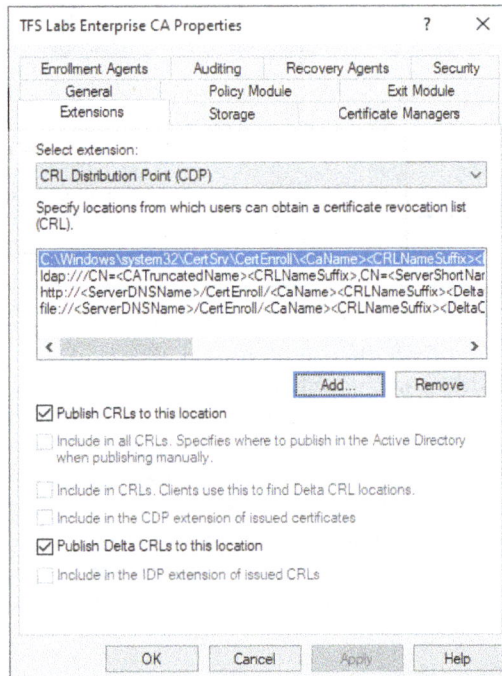

4. In the **Add Location** window, under the **Location** field, enter the following address and click the **OK** button:

```
http://pki.corp.tfslabs.com/CertEnroll/<CaName><CRLNameSuffix><DeltaCRLAllowed>.crl
```

5. On the **Extensions** tab, verify that the **Include in CRLs. Clients use this to find Delta CRL locations.** and **Include in the CDP extension of issued certificates** options are selected for the location that was just entered.
6. Select **ldap:///CN=<CATruncatedName><CRLNameSuffix>,CN=<ServerShortName>,CN=CDP,CN=Public Key Services,CN=Services,<ConfigurationContainer><CDPObjectClass>** from the list and click the **Remove** button. Click the **Yes** button to confirm the location removal.
7. Select **http://<ServerDNSName>/CertEnroll/<CaName><CRLNameSuffix><DeltaCRLAllowed>.crl** from the list and click the **Remove** button. Click the **Yes** button to confirm the location removal.
8. Select **file://<ServerDNSName>/CertEnroll/<CaName><CRLNameSuffix><DeltaCRLAllowed>.crl** from the list and click the **Remove** button. Click the **Yes** button to confirm the location removal.
9. On the **Extensions** tab, verify that under the **Selection extension** field, the **Authority Information Access (AIA)** extension is selected, and click the **Add** button:

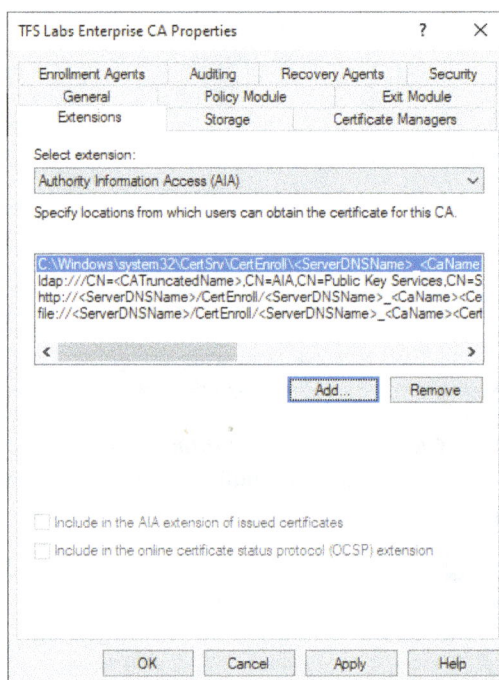

10. In the **Add Location** window, under the **Location** field, enter the following address and click the **OK** button:

```
http://pki.corp.tfslabs.com/CertEnroll/<ServerDNSName>_<CaName><CertificateName>.crt
```

11. On the **Extensions** tab, verify that the **Include in the AIA extension of issued certificates** option is selected for the location that was just entered.
12. Select **ldap:///CN=<CATruncatedName>,CN=AIA,CN=Public Key Services,CN=Services,<ConfigurationContainer><CDPObjectClass>** from the list and click the **Remove** button. Click the **Yes** button to confirm the location removal.
13. Select **http://<ServerDNSName>/CertEnroll/<ServerDNSName>_<CaName><CertificateName>.crt** from the list and click the **Remove** button. Click the **Yes** button to confirm the location removal.
14. Select **file://<ServerDNSName>/CertEnroll/<ServerDNSName>_<CaName><CertificateName>.crt** from the list and click the **Remove** button. Click the **Yes** button to confirm the location removal.
15. Once the CDP and AIA extensions have been configured, click the **OK** button to commit the changes.
16. On the **Certification Authority** window, when prompted to restart **Active Directory Certificate Services**, click the **Yes** button.
17. Close the **Certification Authority** console.

Now that the CDP and AIA location settings have been successfully configured on the TFS-CA01 server, the settings should be validated to ensure that there are no issues. Once the settings have been confirmed, the CRL for the Subordinate CA can be published.

Subordinate CA Setup - CDP and AIA Configuration - Validation

There is a simple way to validate that the CDP and AIA location settings have been applied correctly to the Subordinate CA by using the **certutil.exe** command. From an **elevated PowerShell prompt** on the TFS-CA01 server, run the following command to verify the CDP locations:

Windows PowerShell (Elevated)

```
certutil.exe -getreg CA\CRLPublicationURLs
```

From the same **elevated PowerShell prompt**, run the following command to verify the AIA locations:

Windows PowerShell (Elevated)

```
certutil.exe -getreg CA\CACertPublicationURLs
```

If there are no issues with the CDP and AIA locations for the Subordinate certificate, then the CRL for the Subordinate Certificate Authority can be published to the TFS Labs domain. This task can be performed in the next section.

Subordinate CA Setup - Publish CRL

Once the CRL configuration has been successfully completed for the Subordinate Certificate Authority, the CRL can be published. Unlike the CRL for the Root CA, the Subordinate CA is online at all times and is automatically updated. The CRL can be published using the command line, or through the Certificate Authority console. Either method produces the same result, and there is no need perform the procedure twice.

Unlike the Root CA CRL, the Subordinate CA CRL does not require any files to be copied to and from other servers for it to be accessible. The CRL file is managed by Active Directory Certificate Services, and there is usually no reason to manually update and publish a CRL. In a later chapter of this book, the Online Responder role is installed and configured, which can be used to provide more rapid certificate revocations to a domain without relying on slower updates from a normal CRL.

Subordinate CA Setup - Publish CRL - CLI Method

The CRL can be published using the **certutil.exe** command. From an **elevated PowerShell prompt** on the TFS-CA01 server, run the following command to publish the CRL:

Windows PowerShell (Elevated)

```
certutil.exe -crl
```

Once the CRL has been published for the Subordinate CA, the Certification Practice Statement (CPS) document can be configured for the TFS Labs domain.

Subordinate CA Setup - Publish CRL - GUI Method

The CRL can also be published using the Certificate Authority console by performing the following steps on the TFS-CA01 server:

1. Open the **Certification Authority** console (certsrv.msc).
2. In the **Certification Authority** Console, expand the **TFS Labs Enterprise CA**, right-click on **Revoked Certificates** under **TFS Labs Enterprise CA** and select **All Tasks > Publish**:

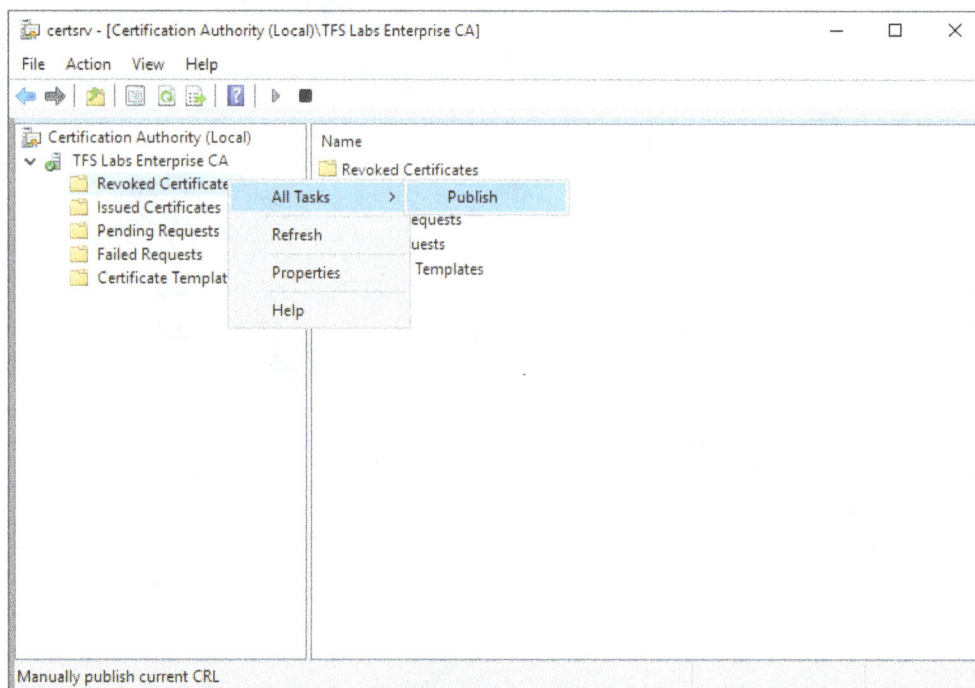

3. On the **Publish CRL** window, verify that **New CRL** is selected and click the **OK** button:

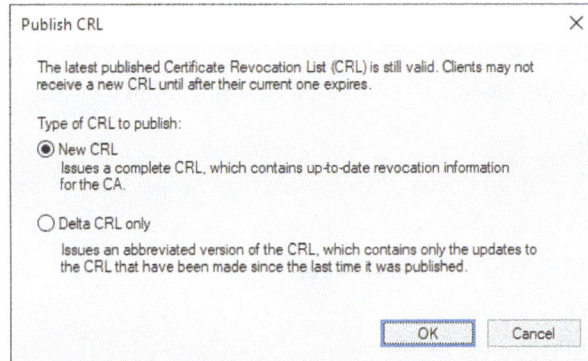

Publish CRL ✕

The latest published Certificate Revocation List (CRL) is still valid. Clients may not receive a new CRL until after their current one expires.

Type of CRL to publish:

⦿ New CRL
Issues a complete CRL, which contains up-to-date revocation information for the CA.

◯ Delta CRL only
Issues an abbreviated version of the CRL, which contains only the updates to the CRL that have been made since the last time it was published.

OK   Cancel

4. Close the **Certification Authority** console.

Once the CRL has been published for the Subordinate CA, the Certification Practice Statement (CPS) document can be configured for the TFS Labs domain.

Subordinate CA Setup - Certification Practice Statement Placeholder Document

During the Active Directory Certificate Services role configuration for the TFS Labs Certificate Authority, the CAPolicy.inf files for the Root and Subordinate CA specified a location for a Certification Practice Statement (CPS) document. The CPS is a document that is available to users who are using the Certificate Authority to inform them of important policies regarding the Certificate Authority. There are several ways that the CPS document can be displayed to users, but through a web browser using HTTP is the most common.

To create the CPS document for the TFS Labs domain, perform the following steps on the TFS-CA01 server:

1. Open the **C:\inetpub\wwwroot** folder on the **TFS-CA01** server using **Windows File Explorer** (explorer.exe).
2. Create a new file named **cps.html** (ensure the file extension is correct).
3. Copy the following text into the **cps.html** file, save it, and close the file:

```
C:\inetpub\wwwroot\cps.html

<!DOCTYPE html>
<html>
<head>
    <meta charset="utf-8">
    <title>TFS Labs Certification Practice Statement</title>
</head>
<body>

<h1>TFS Labs Certification Practice Statement</h1>

<p>The TFS Labs Certificate Authority is an internal only resource.</p>

<p>Issued certificates from this Certificate Authority are for internal use only.</p>

</body>
</html>
```

4. Close **Windows File Explorer**.

The CPS document can be tested that it is accessible by opening the web browser on the TFS-CA01 server, and going to the following address:

http://pki.corp.tfslabs.com/cps.html

If there are no issues, the CPS placeholder document should be displayed in the web browser:

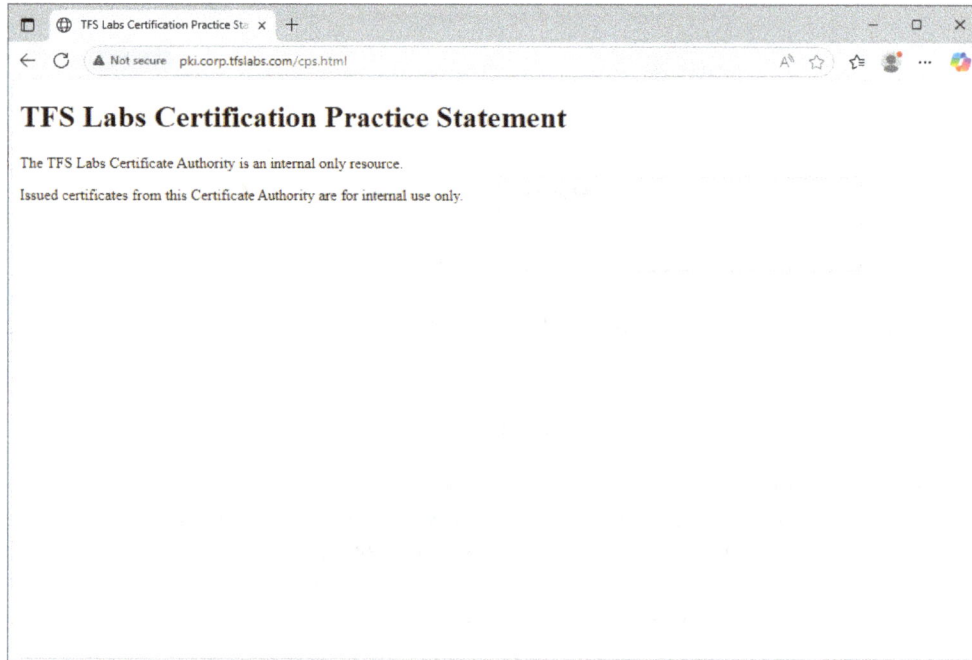

Figure 7.16.1: The CPS placeholder document can be modified at any time to fit the needs of an organization. This placeholder can be accessed from any certificate that is issued by the TFS Labs Certificate Authority.

The CPS document can also be accessed by checking the properties for any certificate issued by the TFS Labs Certificate Authority. Any certificate that was issued by the TFS Labs Certificate Authority will have a button called Issuer Statement, which will provide a direct link to the CPS document. In the future, should a different URL be required for accessing the CPS document, a redirect within IIS can be used to handle the request. If there is an issue with the CPS document, it will not affect the normal operation of a Certificate Authority. Keeping the CPS accessible and up to date should be a priority, as users are able to access it so it should always be available.

Once the CPS document has been created and validated, proceed to configuring the Windows Defender Firewall on the TFS-CA01 server.

> **CPS Document Availability**
>
> The CPS document varies for every organization, so the placeholder which has been put in place can be updated later to ensure that the Certificate Authority meets any compliance standards that may be required. This is especially important in industries with strict requirements (such as financial services), so having a CPS in place from day one can avoid a lot of issues in the future. There are several important items that should be defined in a CPS document, and the IETF has published RFC 3647 which is used to set the standards for a Certification Policy Statement.
>
> When the TFS Labs Certificate Authority on both the Root CA and the Subordinate CA were created, the path to the CPS document was set. This path will be displayed whenever any certificate that was issued by the TFS Labs Certificate Authority is displayed. In the future, should a more detailed CPS document be required, this can be remapped with IIS to go to another location.

Subordinate CA Setup - Windows Defender Firewall Configuration

The Windows Defender Firewall is always enabled in Windows Server by default, and there are many rules that are enabled by default. To allow for the necessary access to Certificate Authority related services on the TFS-CA01 server, there are several firewall rules that need to be enabled to allow for connections to the server. There are a few ports that are used for Active Directory Certificate Services on the TFS-CA01 server that need to be open for everything to work correctly.

The correct firewall rules should be automatically enabled when the Active Directory Certificate Services role is configured, but the rules should be checked to ensure that they are open before proceeding. Quickly validating the firewall rules now can save a lot of time later should there be an issue with the Certificate Authority. There are three specific firewall rules that need to be enabled on the TFS-CA01 server for Active Directory Certificate Services to function correctly:

Firewall Rule Name	Protocol	Ports	Profile
File and Printer Sharing (Echo Request - ICMPv4-In)	ICMP	N/A	All
World Wide Web Services (HTTP Traffic-In)	TCP	80	All
World Wide Web Services (HTTPS Traffic-In)	TCP	443	All

Table 7.17.1: Firewall rules for the TFS-CA01 server that are required for Active Directory Certificate Services. The first rule allows for ping requests to the server, and the second and third rules allow access to the IIS instance running on the server which hosts necessary certificate files for the Certificate Authority.

The firewall configuration on the Subordinate Certificate Authority can be performed through the command line using PowerShell, or by using Windows Defender Firewall with Advanced Security console.

> ### Disabling the Windows Defender Firewall
>
> It is extremely bad practice to disable the Windows Defender Firewall, even within an internal network. Disabling a host firewall will increase the attack surface on any server, and for best practices the Windows Defender Firewall should always enabled. Never assume that because a server is internal with no externally facing ports that is completely safe from threats.
>
> If a third-party firewall solution is being used for the server, then it is possible for the Windows Defender Firewall to be automatically disabled as a result.

Subordinate CA Setup - Windows Defender Firewall Configuration - CLI Configuration

To enable the firewall rules on the Subordinate CA using the command line with PowerShell, perform the following steps on the TFS-CA01 server:

1. Open an **elevated PowerShell prompt**.
2. Using the **Enable-NetFirewallRule** Cmdlet, enable the rule to allow for ping requests to the **TFS-CA01** server:

```
Windows PowerShell (Elevated)

Enable-NetFirewallRule `
-DisplayName "File and Printer Sharing (Echo Request - ICMPv4-In)"
```

3. Using the **Enable-NetFirewallRule** Cmdlet, enable the rule to allow for HTTP requests to the **TFS-CA01** server:

```
Windows PowerShell (Elevated)

Enable-NetFirewallRule -DisplayName "World Wide Web Services (HTTP Traffic-In)"
```

4. Using the **Enable-NetFirewallRule** Cmdlet, enable the rule to allow for HTTPS requests to the **TFS-CA01** server:

```
Windows PowerShell (Elevated)

Enable-NetFirewallRule -DisplayName "World Wide Web Services (HTTPS Traffic-In)"
```

5. Close the **PowerShell prompt**.

Once the Windows Defender Firewall has been correctly configured, proceed to validating the Certificate Authority.

Subordinate CA Setup - Windows Defender Firewall Configuration - GUI Configuration

To check if the firewall rules are enabled on the TFS-CA01 server, and modify any of those rules if, necessary, perform the following steps:

1. Open the **Windows Defender Firewall with Advanced Security** console (wf.msc) on the **TFS-CA01** server:

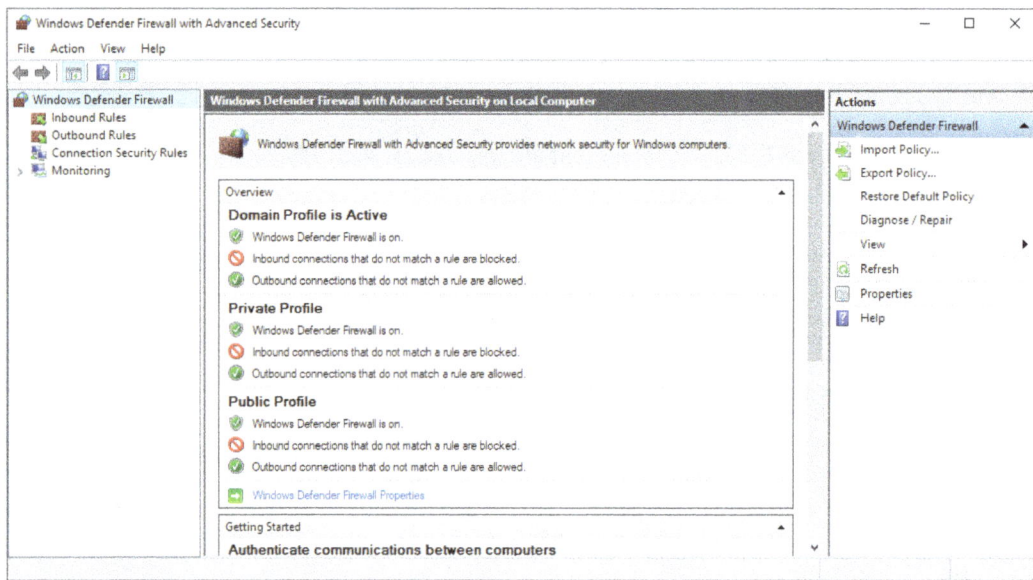

2. Under the **Windows Defender Firewall with Advanced Security on Local Computer**, click on **Inbound Rules**.

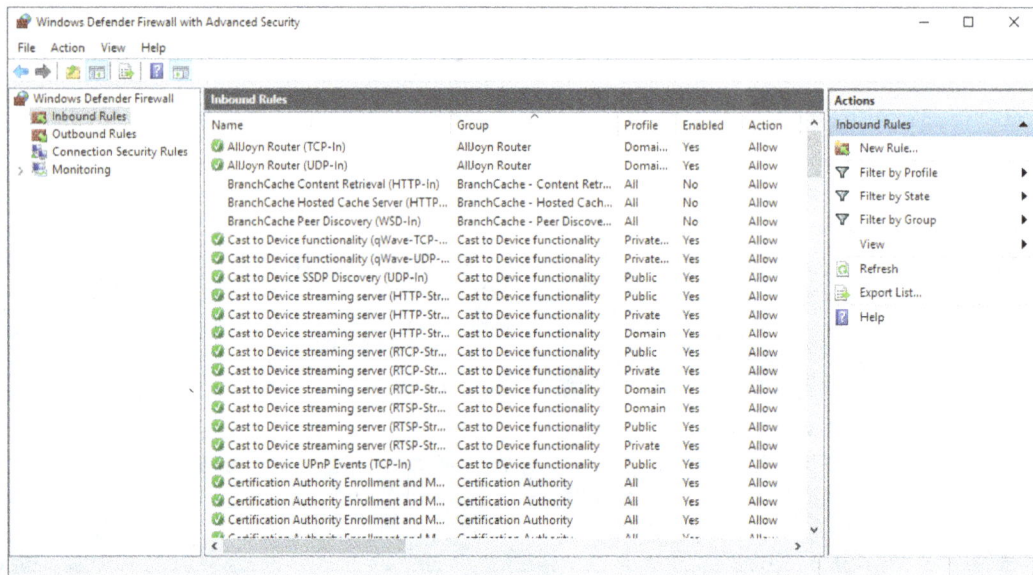

3. For each of the firewall rules listed in **Table 7.17.1** earlier in this section, perform the following steps:
   (a) Right-click on the firewall rule, and select the **Properties** option to open the **Rule Properties** window.
   (b) On the **General** tab, select the option for **Enabled**.
   (c) On the **Advanced** tab, ensure that the options for **Domain**, **Private** and **Public** are selected.
   (d) Click on the **Apply** button to apply the changes to the firewall rule.
   (e) Click the **OK** button to close the **Rule Properties** window.
4. Close the **Windows Defender Firewall with Advanced Security** console.

Once the Windows Defender Firewall has been correctly configured, proceed to validating the Certificate Authority.

Subordinate CA Setup - Verify PKI Infrastructure

Before continuing with the deployment of the Root and Subordinate certificates on the TFS Labs domain, it is important to verify that there are no issues with the Active Directory Certificate Services role on the TFS-CA01 server. There is a tool available for Active Directory Certificate Services called Enterprise PKI, which is used to validate a PKI in Windows Server. To validate the PKI configuration for the TFS Labs Certificate Authority, perform the following steps on the TFS-CA01 server:

1. On the **TFS-CA01** server, open the **Enterprise PKI** console (pkiview.msc).
2. On the default window for the **Enterprise PKI** console, it should state that the status of the **TFS Labs Certificate Authority (V0.0)** server is **OK**:

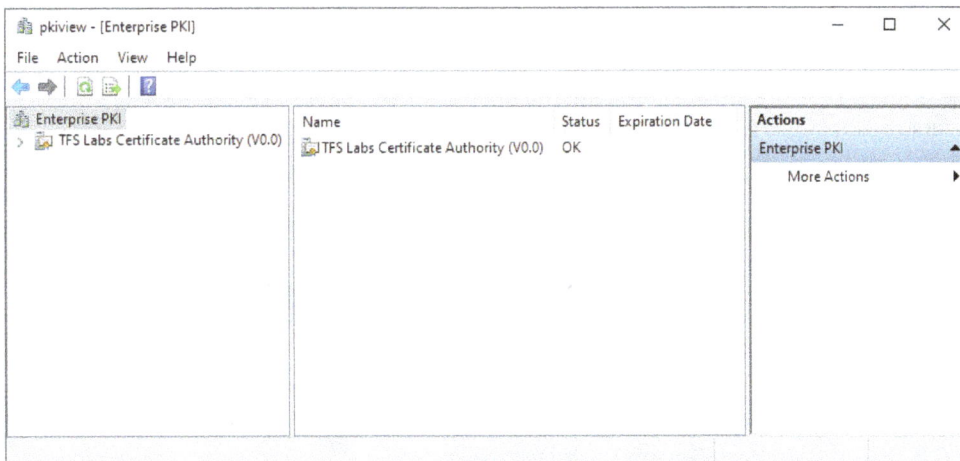

3. Under the **Enterprise PKI** node, click on the **TFS Labs Certificate Authority (V0.0)** server. Check that the status of the **CA Certificate**, **AIA Location #1** and **CDP Location #1** have the status of **OK**:

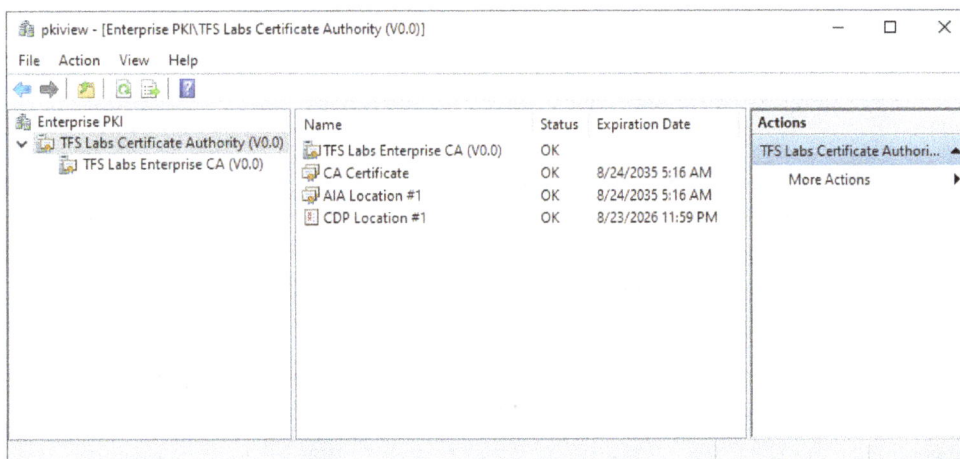

4. Under the **Enterprise PKI** node, click on the **TFS Labs Enterprise CA (V0.0)** server. Check that the status of the **CA Certificate, DeltaCRL Locations, AIA Locations** and **CDP Locations** have the status of **OK**:

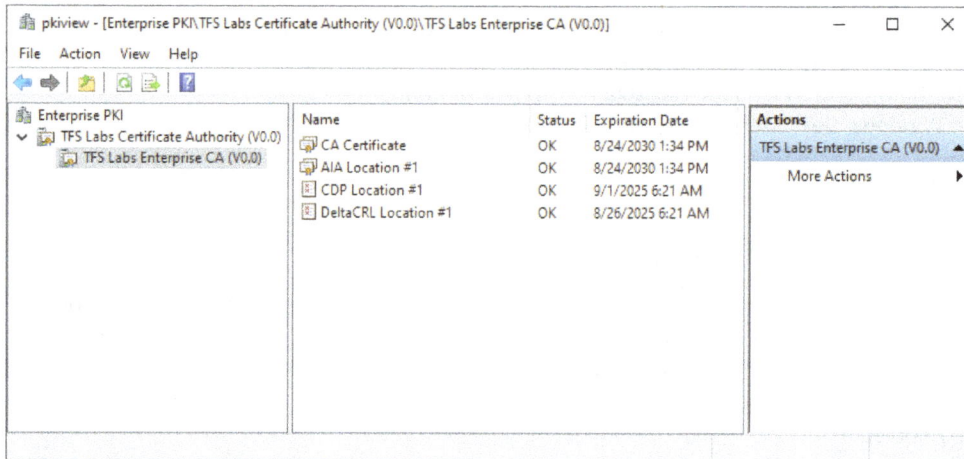

5. Close the **Enterprise PKI** console.

There are still additional items to be configured for the TFS Labs Certificate Authority, but checking the overall status of the PKI at this stage can determine if there are any obvious issues with the Certificate Authority. It will quickly determine if there are issues with the CDP and AIA configurations, as well as the CRL files that have been published. At this point in the overall configuration of the PKI, issues like this are much easier to correct before more complex configurations are introduced. If there are no issues with the PKI infrastructure configuration on the TFS Labs domain, then the initial deployment of the TFS Labs Certificate Authority is now complete. With an Enterprise CA, the TFS Labs Enterprise CA certificate should start to automatically deploy to all Active Directory devices in the TFS Labs domain.

Subordinate CA Setup - Server Restart

It is advisable to restart the Subordinate CA server before continuing with any additional configuration of the TFS Labs Certificate Authority. This will ensure that all changes to the Subordinate CA have been successfully committed and applied to the TFS Labs domain. Since the Subordinate CA is the Enterprise CA for the TFS Labs domain, it must remain online at all times to ensure that certificates can be issued and managed for all affected endpoints.

Subordinate CA Setup - Virtual Floppy Disk Deletion

Once the Certificate Authority has been successfully implemented and tested, the virtual floppy disk should be deleted as it is no longer required. The virtual floppy disk contains important files that are not needed after the implementation, and by keeping the virtual floppy disk can introduce an unnecessary security risk. Should the virtual floppy disk be required in the future, specifically for updating the Root CA CRL files, it can be easily recreated.

> ❌ **Additional Files on the Virtual Floppy Disk**
>
> Prior to deleting the virtual floppy disk, check if there are any BitLocker Recovery Keys present and back them up first. All of the other files should already be located on the TFS-ROOT-CA and TFS-CA01 servers.

Subordinate CA Setup - Checkpoint Deletion

If Checkpoints have been used for the deployment of the Certificate Authority up to this point, then they are no longer required. The major steps in this process are completed, and any changes in future chapters of this book will not adversely affect the configuration of Active Directory Certificate Services.

Delete any Checkpoints on the TFS-CA01, TFS-DC01, TFS-ROOT-CA and TFS-WIN11 virtual machines if they exist.

Subordinate CA Setup - Root CA Shut Down

Once the Certificate Authority has been successfully implemented, the Root CA can be powered off as it is no longer needed once the Subordinate CA is online and operating correctly. For security purposes it is important to keep the Root CA offline and protected. The TFS-ROOT-CA virtual machine will need to be powered on at least once every 52 weeks to update the Base CRL as per the configuration that was set with that CA.

> ⊗ **Root Certificate Authority Virtual Machine**
>
> Ensure that this virtual machine is never deleted. If this virtual machine is deleted, it will break the entire PKI and there will be no way of recovering from it unless a backup exists for the Root CA server.

Subordinate CA Setup - Windows Update

While it is not necessary to run Windows Update on any of the servers of workstations in this book, now would be a good time to run those updates if it is required. Since the TFS-CA01 server is a domain member, it will likely receive updates as part of policies applied to an organization, and would not be manually managed.

Windows Update can be accessed through the Settings app, or through the command line by opening an **elevated PowerShell prompt** and running the following command:

```
Windows PowerShell (Elevated)

Start-Process ms-settings:windowsupdate
```

Installing all available updates will take time to complete and will require several restarts of the server. Once completed, further configuration of the TFS-CA01 server can be completed in later chapters.

Subordinate CA Setup - Chapter Summary

Now that the Subordinate certificate has been successfully created, it is now time to deploy the Root and Subordinate certificates to the TFS Labs domain. The next chapter will demonstrate how to use Group Policy to automatically deploy the certificates to the TFS Labs domain.

Chapter 8 - Deploy CA Certificates

Once the Root and Subordinate certificates have been created, and the Certificate Authority has been setup correctly, those certificates will need to be deployed to the TFS Labs domain for those certificates to be utilized. With an Enterprise CA running with Active Directory Certificate Services, any Subordinate certificates should automatically deploy to any server or workstation within the Active Directory domain.

Since the TFS Labs Certificate Authority uses an Offline CA for the Root certificate, this means that the Root certificate will not be automatically deployed to the domain, since there is no network connection on that server and it is not an Enterprise CA. Fortunately, deploying the Root certificate is a trivial process since the use of Active Directory and Group Policy makes certificate deployment easy to perform.

Optionally, the Group Policy Objects that are created in this chapter will be used in later sections for certificate auto-enrollment and for deploying the OCSP settings to the TFS Labs domain.

There are several steps required for deploying the Root and Subordinate certificates to the TFS Labs domain:

- Organize the Root and Subordinate certificates into a more convenient location for deployment.
- Create a Group Policy Object for deploying the Root and Subordinate certificates to the TFS Labs domain.
- Apply the Group Policy Object to the TFS Labs domain, specifically to the correct OU structure.
- **Optional:** Create a virtual directory in IIS for deploying the Root and Subordinate certificates.
- **Optional:** Enable LDAP over SSL for the Domain Controller for the TFS Labs domain.

This chapter will focus on the deployment of the Root and Subordinate certificates to the TFS Labs domain. This deployment will be automated using Group Policy which will allow for rapid deployment to domain servers and workstations, and offers greater flexibility for deployment options.

> **Group Policy Object for Certificate Deployment**
>
> The Group Policy Object that is created in this chapter is used for deploying several different configurations that are related to the TFS Labs Certificate Authority. This GPO is used in the remaining chapters in this book, specifically with the Online Responder role and for certificate auto-enrollment.

Deploy CA Certificates - Prepare the Root and Subordinate Certificates

The easiest method that can be used to deploy the Root and Subordinate certificates in an organization is to use Group Policy for automatic deployment. In the case of the TFS Labs domain, this will automatically deploy the certificates to workstations and servers that are members of the domain, and in the correct Organizational Unit.

As a result of the Certificate Authority deployment that has already been completed so far in this book, the Root and Subordinate certificates for the TFS Labs domain are already located on the TFS-CA01 server and can be utilized immediately for deployment.

The Root certificate can be found in the following location on the TFS-CA01 server:

C:\CertData\TFS-ROOT-CA_TFS Labs Certificate Authority.crt

The Subordinate certificate can be found in the following location on the TFS-CA01 server:

C:\Windows\System32\certsrv\CertEnroll\TFS-CA01.corp.tfslabs.com_TFS Labs Enterprise CA.crt

Both certificates are DER encoded, and can be installed through Active Directory using Group Policy. The certificates can also be manually installed if required, or can be deployed using other methods (such as an MDM solution).

To prepare the Root and Subordinate certificate files for distribution on the TFS Labs domain, perform the following steps on the TFS-CA01 and TFS-DC01 servers:

1. On the **C:\ drive** on the **TFS-CA01** server, create a folder called **Certificates** (C:\Certificates).
2. On the **TFS-CA01** server, copy the following certificate files to the **C:\Certificates** folder:
    - **C:\CertData\TFS-ROOT-CA_TFS Labs Certificate Authority.crt**
    - **C:\Windows\System32\certsrv\CertEnroll\TFS-CA01.corp.tfslabs.com_TFS Labs Enterprise CA.crt**
3. Rename the certificate files to the following on the **TFS-CA01** server in the **C:\Certificates** folder:
    - **TFS-ROOT-CA_TFS Labs Certificate Authority.crt** to **TFS Labs Certificate Authority.crt**
    - **TFS-CA01.corp.tfslabs.com_TFS Labs Enterprise CA.crt** to **TFS Labs Enterprise CA.crt**
4. On the **C:\ drive** on the **TFS-DC01** server, create a folder called **Certificates** (C:\Certificates).
5. Copy the two certificates in the **C:\Certificates** folder on the **TFS-CA01** server to the **C:\Certificates** folder on the **TFS-DC01** server.

After the Root and Subordinate certificates have been successfully copied and renamed, they can now be deployed to the TFS Labs domain using Group Policy.

> **ⓘ Root and Subordinate Certificates**
>
> The names of the Root and Subordinate certificates will vary based on the name of the Active Directory domain that is being used. Factor these names in when proceeding with further steps in this chapter, as the names will need to match for the deployment to be successful in other environments.

Deploy CA Certificates - Deploy the Root and Subordinate Certificates

For the deployment of the Root and Subordinate certificates to the TFS Labs domain, a GPO will be applied to the root of TFS Labs OU in the TFS Labs Active Directory domain that was created in an earlier chapter. This is to ensure that best practices are being applied for Group Policy in an Active Directory domain for certificate deployment.

There are default Group Policy Objects available in an Active Directory domain, but it is advised to create a new GPO for specific purposes, and not modify the **Default Domain Policy** object. This way there will be complete control over the Group Policy Objects that are being assigned to the domain, and prevent issues with default policies.

When Active Directory Certificate Services is utilized in an Active Directory domain, the Subordinate certificate is already deployed to all the workstations and servers in the domain since the Subordinate CA is an Enterprise CA.

To deploy the Root and Subordinate certificates to the TFS Labs domain using Group Policy, perform the following steps on the TFS-DC01 server:

1. Open the **Group Policy Management** console (gpmc.msc) on the **TFS-DC01** server:

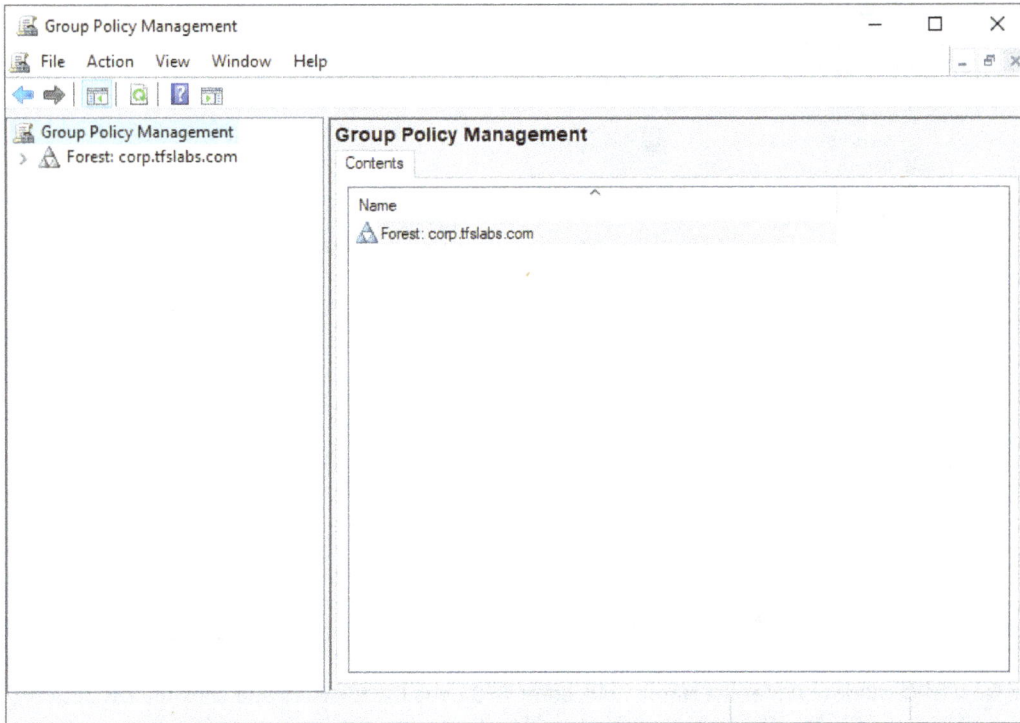

2. In the **Group Policy Management** console tree, expand the **Forest: corp.tfslabs.com** folder, expand **Domains**, and then expand the **corp.tfslabs.com** domain and then select the **TFS Labs** OU:

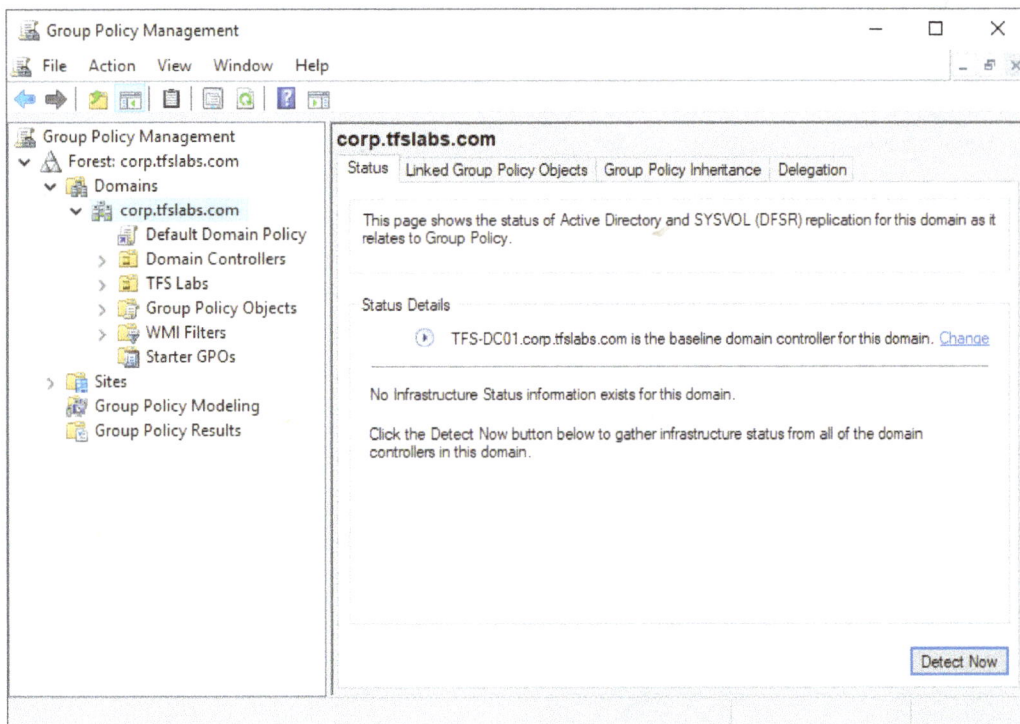

3. Right-click on the **TFS Labs** OU and select the option for **Create a GPO in this domain, and Link it here...**:

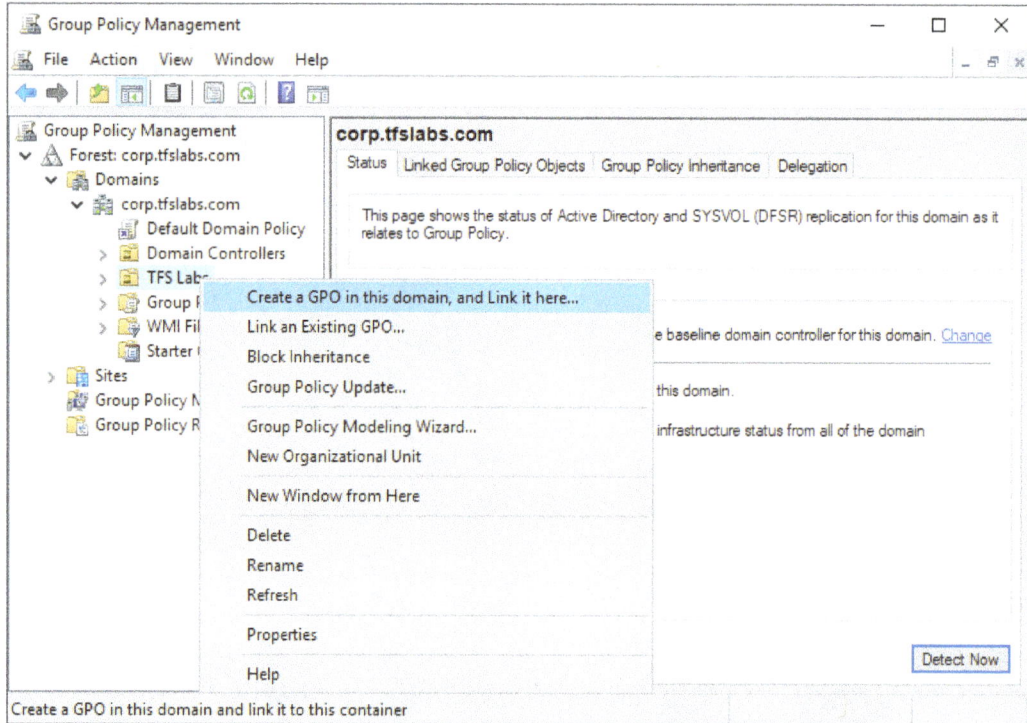

4. On the **New GPO** window, under the **Name** field, enter **TFS Labs Certificates** and click the **OK** button.
5. Under the **TFS Labs** OU, the **TFS Labs Certificates** OU will now be listed:

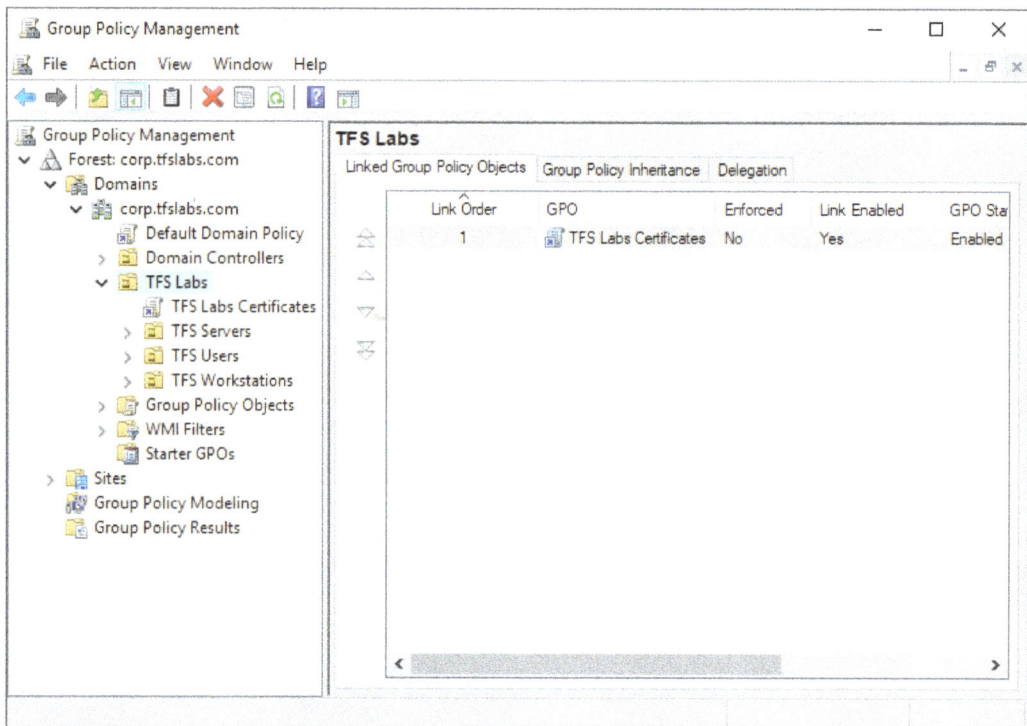

6. Right-click on the **TFS Labs Certificates** GPO and select the **Edit** option:

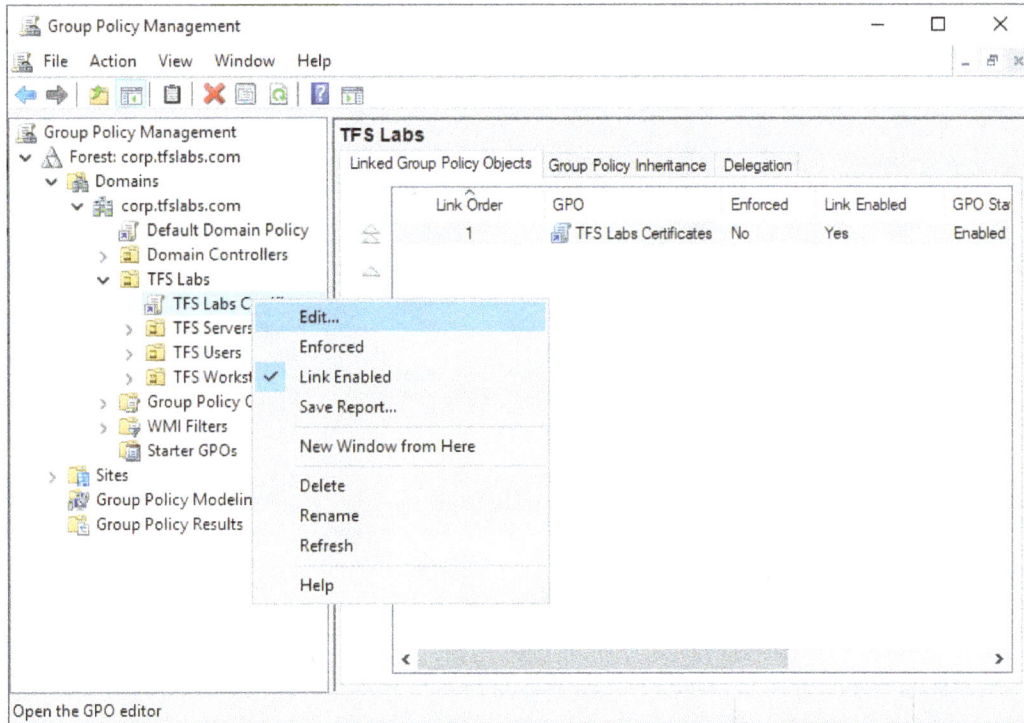

7. The **Group Policy Management Editor** window for the **TFS Labs Certificates** GPO should open:

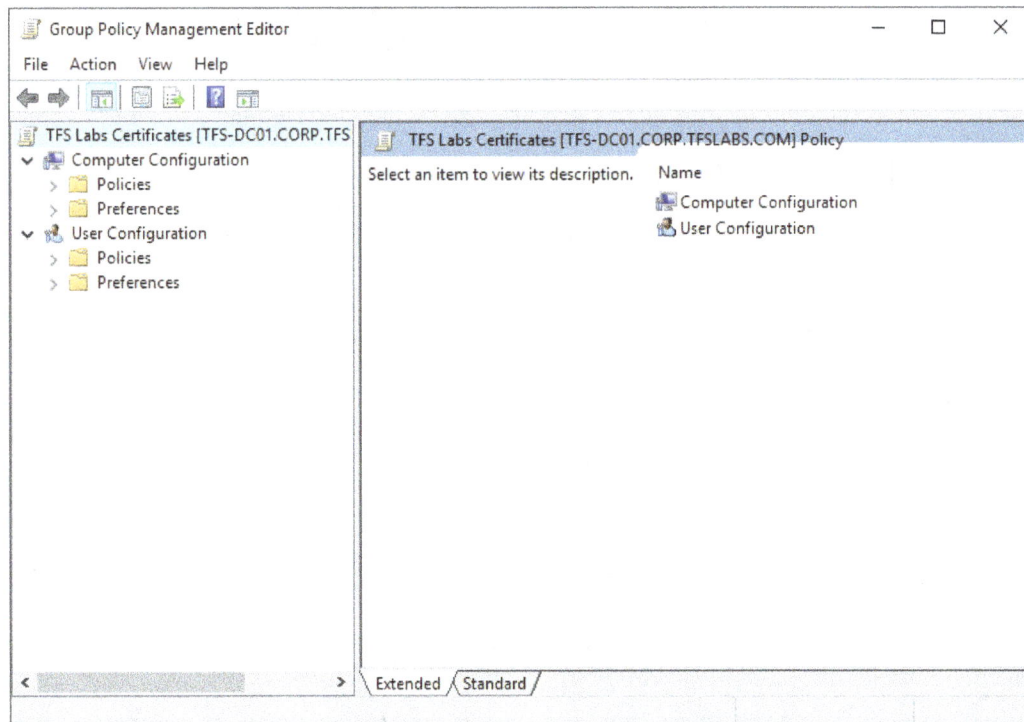

8. In the **Group Policy Management Editor** window, open the **Computer Configuration > Policies > Windows Settings > Security Settings > Public Key Policies** node:

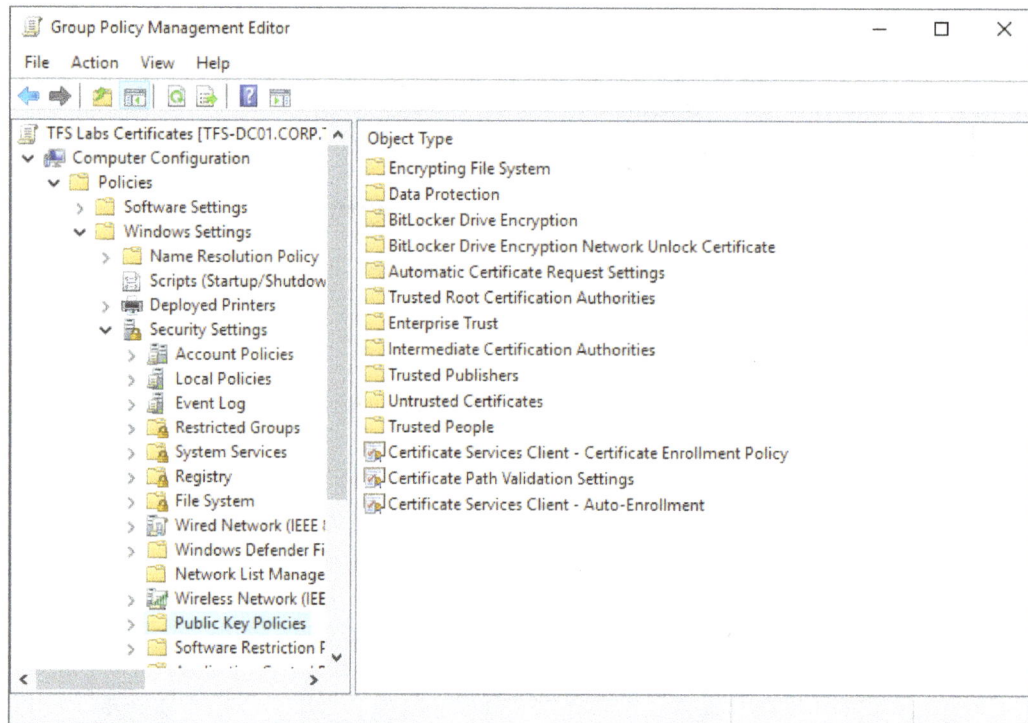

9. Right-click on the **Trusted Root Certification Authorities** folder and select the **Import...** option:
   (a) On the **Welcome to the Certificate Import Wizard** window, click the **Next** button to continue.
   (b) On the **File to Import** window, enter **C:\Certificates\TFS Labs Certificate Authority.crt** as the **File name** and click the **Next** button to continue.
   (c) On the **Certificate Store** window, ensure that the **Trusted Root Certification Authorities** store is selected and click the **Next** button to continue.
   (d) On the **Completing the Certificate Import Wizard** screen, click the **Finish** button.
   (e) On the **Certificate Import Wizard** prompt, click the **OK** button to complete the import of the Root certificate.
10. Right-click on the **Intermediate Certification Authorities** folder and select the **Import...** option:
   (a) On the **Welcome to the Certificate Import Wizard** window, click the **Next** button to continue.
   (b) On the **File to Import** window, enter **C:\Certificates\TFS Labs Enterprise CA.crt** as the **File name** and click the **Next** button to continue.
   (c) On the **Certificate Store** window, ensure that the **Intermediate Certification Authorities** store is selected and click the **Next** button to continue.
   (d) On the **Completing the Certificate Import Wizard** screen, click the **Finish** button.
   (e) On the **Certificate Import Wizard** prompt, click the **OK** button to complete the import of the Subordinate certificate.
11. Close the **Group Policy Management** console.

Once the Root and Subordinate certificates have been added to Group Policy, it will now be automatically applied to the workstations and servers in the TFS Labs domain. It may take some time for the Group Policy Object to be applied to the workstations and servers in the TFS Labs domain, but to test it immediately, open an **elevated Command Prompt** on any Windows device on the TFS Labs domain and run the following command:

```
Command Prompt (Elevated)

gpupdate.exe /force
```

Once the certificates have been deployed, check the Local Machine Certificate Store on any workstation or server in the TFS Labs domain to ensure that the Root and Subordinate certificates are now present on those devices.

Group Policy Object Naming Conventions

Ensure that when creating Group Policy Objects that the names of those objects make sense and are able to convey the purpose of the object. The Group Policy Objects that are created in this chapter are referenced in later steps and in later chapters of this book. This is important to consider when customizing the steps in this book for other Active Directory domains.

Duplicate Certificates

When deploying certificates to the domain using Group Policy it is entirely possible that duplicate certificates will be found in the Certificate Store. This is due to the way that Windows manages the Certificate Store, and the way that it displays certificates. Normally it lists the certificates stored on the device and puts all that information into the Certificate Store, which is why duplicates can appear.

Default Domain Policy GPO

The **TFS Labs Certificates** GPO was created to prevent modifications to the **Default Domain Policy** GPO, which is created at the time of any Active Directory domain creation. It is bad practice to add anything to the Default Domain Policy, as this GPO should only be used for essential account policies (such as passwords and account lockouts). The Default Domain Policy is applied to the root of the Active Directory domain to ensure that all users and computers receive the policy.

Creating Group Policy Objects and applying them to specific OUs is preferred, as it ensures that an administrator is aware of everything that is being applied to an Active Directory domain. It also ensures that Group Policy Objects are being correctly targeted to the correct users and workstations in the domain.

Root Certificate Deployment

Ensure that in a production network the certificates folder that is created on the Domain Controller is present on all Domain Controllers. Group Policy will require access to this folder and the contents of it, and if it is missing on a Domain Controller the Root certificate will not be deployed correctly. A way to prevent this is to put the folder on a network share that is accessible to the entire domain.

Once the new Group Policy Object has been created, proceed to deploying the Root certificate to the TFS-CA01 Domain Controller.

Deploy CA Certificates - Deploy the Root Certificate to the Domain Controller

As part of deploying the Root and Subordinate certificates to the TFS Labs domain, there is an exception for any of the Domain Controllers that are present in the Active Directory domain. By default, all Domain Controllers are placed in their own OU when they are promoted to a Domain Controller. An Enterprise CA will automatically deploy the Subordinate certificate to all devices in an Active Directory domain, but not the Root certificate. Since the TFS-ROOT-CA server is offline, there is no way to automatically deploy the certificate to the domain.

There are two options to deploy the Root certificate to the Domain Controllers in a domain:

- Automatic deployment of the Root certificate using Group Policy.
- Manual installation of the Root certificate on each Domain Controller in the domain.

Both options will produce the same result, and only one method is required to deploy the Root certificate to any Domain Controller in the domain. To deploy the Root certificate to the Domain Controllers using Group Policy, perform the following steps on the TFS-DC01 server:

1. Open the **Group Policy Management** console (gpmc.msc) on the **TFS-DC01** server.
2. In the **Group Policy Management** console tree, expand the **Forest: corp.tfslabs.com** folder, expand **Domains**, expand the **corp.tfslabs.com** domain, and then select the **Domain Controllers** OU.
3. Right-click on the **Domain Controllers** OU and select the option for **Link an Existing GPO....**
4. On the **Select GPO** window, select the **TFS Labs Certificates** GPO and click the **OK** button.

To deploy the Root certificate to the Domain Controllers manually, perform the following steps on the TFS-DC01 server:

1. Open **Windows File Explorer** (explorer.exe) on the **TFS-DC01** server.
2. Go to **This PC** and open the **C:** drive.
3. Open the **Certificates** folder, right-click on the **TFS Labs Certificate Authority.crt** certificate, and select the **Install Certificate** option.
4. On the **Welcome to the Certificate Import Wizard** window, ensure that the **Store Location** is set to **Local Machine** and click the **Next** button to continue.
5. On the **Certificate Store** window, select the option for **Certificate store** and click the **Browse...** button.
6. On the **Select Certificate Store** window, select the **Trusted Root Certification Authorities** Store, and click the **OK** button.
7. On the **Certificate Store** window, click the **Next** button.
8. On the **Completing the Certificate Import Wizard** window, click the **Finish** button.
9. On the **Certificate Import Wizard** prompt, click the **OK** button to complete the import of the certificate.

Once the Root certificate has been deployed to the TFS-DC01 server, the certificate chain on that server will be complete. At this point, the TFS-DC01 server will be enabled for LDAPS as it now has valid certificates to accommodate that feature. Proceed to the internal certificate deployment in the next section.

> **Default Domain Controllers Policy GPO**
>
> It is best practice to never modify the **Default Domain Controller Policy** GPO as this object contains important security information for the Domain Controllers. These settings are critical to ensure that proper audit, security, and user settings are correctly applied, and if this is modified incorrectly it can cause login failures within an Active Directory domain. Because of the importance of the Default Domain Controllers Policy, any changes that should be made to a Domain Controller should always be done in a separate Group Policy Object to reduce the risks with using it.

Deploy CA Certificates - Internal Certificate Deployment

It is possible to have non-Windows clients on a network that may require access to the Root and Subordinate certificates for the TFS Labs domain. A common scenario is Linux servers that are running a web server that requires SSL, and will need the Root and Subordinate certificates to apply their web certificates correctly. Another scenario is with Android and iOS devices that require the certificates to access internal services. Typically, these devices will receive the certificates using a Mobile Device Management solution, but that is not always available in some organizations. To create an internal website for deploying the Root and Subordinate certificates for the TFS Labs domain all that is needed is to add a new virtual directory in IIS, as a folder on the TFS-CA01 server was created earlier that can be used for this purpose. This configuration can be completed using the command line or with IIS Manager.

> **Internal Certificate Deployment**
>
> This step is entirely optional, and not completing this does not affect the deployment of Active Directory Certificate Services for the remainder of this book. This step allows for additional certificate deployment options, and operates independently of the other steps configured previously in this chapter.

> **MDM Solutions for Certificate Deployment**
>
> In organizations with extensive mobile device deployments, it is typical to have an MDM solution in place to manage tasks such as certificate deployment. In this case, the domain is too small to warrant such a solution, so it is being performed manually. The reason that a dedicated folder on the Subordinate CA was created earlier was to facilitate such scenarios where an MDM solution was not available.

> **Certificate Private Keys and Security**
>
> Ensure that any certificates that are included in this folder do not include any private keys. If the private keys for these certificates are accidentally included, it will compromise the integrity of the Certificate Authority. If the private key for a certificate is accidentally published, the certificate should be revoked immediately as it can no longer be trusted.

Deploy CA Certificates - Internal Certificate Deployment - CLI Configuration

The IIS virtual directory can be created using the command line on the TFS-CA01 by performing the following steps:

1. Open an **elevated Command Prompt** on the **TFS-CA01** server.
2. Change to the correct directory by entering the following command:

```
Command Prompt (Elevated)

cd C:\Windows\System32\inetsrv\
```

3. Run the following command to create the **Certificates** virtual directory in **IIS**:

```
Command Prompt (Elevated)

appcmd.exe add vdir /app.name:"Default Web Site/" ^
/path:/Certificates /physicalPath:C:\Certificates
```

4. Run the following command to enable **Directory Browsing** on the **CertData** Virtual Directory:

```
Command Prompt (Elevated)

appcmd.exe set config "Default Web Site/Certificates" ^
/section:directoryBrowse /enabled:true
```

5. Close the **Command Prompt**.

Once the virtual directory has been successfully configured, proceed to validating that the virtual directory is working correctly on the TFS-CA01 server.

Deploy CA Certificates - Internal Certificate Deployment - GUI Configuration

The IIS virtual directory can be created using Internet Information Services (IIS) by performing the following steps on the TFS-CA01 server:

1. Open the **Internet Information Services (IIS) Manager** (inetmgr.exe) console on the **TFS-CA01** server.
2. On the **Connections** pane, expand **TFS-CA01**, then expand **Sites** and then select **Default Web Site**.
3. Right-click on **Default Web Site** and select **Add Virtual Directory...**.
4. On the **Add Virtual Directory** window, in the **Alias** field, enter **Certificates**. For the **Physical path**, enter **C:\Certificates** and then click **OK**.
5. In the **Connections** pane, under the **Default Web Site**, ensure the **Certificates** virtual directory is selected.

6. In the **Certificates Home** pane, double-click on **Directory Browsing**.
7. In the **Actions** pane, click the **Enable** button.
8. Close the **Internet Information Services (IIS) Manager** console.

Once the certificates virtual directory has been successfully configured, proceed to validating that the virtual directory is working correctly on the TFS-CA01 server.

Deploy CA Certificates - Internal Certificate Deployment - Validation

The Certificates virtual directory can be tested by opening the web browser on the TFS-CA01 server and going to the following address:

http://pki.corp.tfslabs.com/Certificates/

The contents of the Certificates folder should be displayed in the browser:

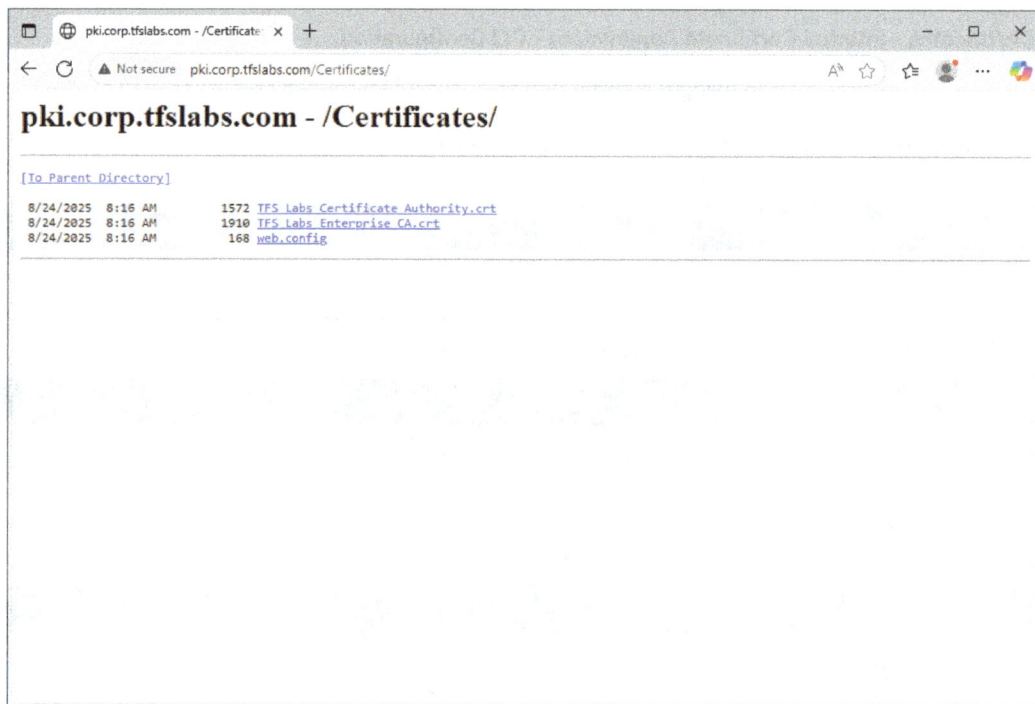

Figure 8.4.3.1: The Certificates folder contains the Root and Subordinate certificates in a format that can be easily deployed across multiple platforms. SSL encryption is not enabled on this virtual directory, as it is assumed that clients are missing the correct certificates to access it.

Once the virtual directory has been successfully configured and tested, certificate deployment has been completed for the TFS Labs domain. Proceed to testing LDAPS on the TFS Labs domain in the next section.

> **Internal Certificate Deployment Options**
>
> There are multiple options for securely deploying the Root and Subordinate certificates that are created using Active Directory Certificate Services to non-domain devices in an organization. The steps that were used in this section demonstrated how to deploy those certificates using a basic website in IIS, which was already being used on the Subordinate CA server. In large organizations, this would probably never be used, and an MDM solution would be used instead as it is more secure and easier to manage.

Converting Certificate Types

The certificates that are currently being deployed to the TFS Labs domain are in the DER Encoded format by default, but there are other formats such as Base-64 Encoded format that are supported. There is an option of exporting those certificates in that format, but there is a faster method to convert certificates using the **certutil.exe** utility. To convert from DER Encoded format to Base-64 Encoded format, run the following command from a Command Prompt:

```
Command Prompt

certutil.exe -encode der-certificate.cer base64-certificate.cer
```

To convert from Base-64 Encoded format to DER Encoded format, run the following command:

```
Command Prompt

certutil.exe -decode base64-certificate.cer der-certificate.cer
```

There should not be any issues with converting between certificate formats using the **certutil.exe** utility. If they are converted from one format to another, and then back again, the certificate contents and file sizes will be identical.

Deploy CA Certificates - LDAP over SSL for Active Directory

For Active Directory, LDAP traffic by default is transmitted over the network in a non-encrypted and unsecured manner on TCP port 389. LDAP over SSL, or LDAPS, is used to secure LDAP traffic to ensure that it is encrypted using a certificate. When it is being used, LDAPS operates on TCP port 636 for traffic. Active Directory natively supports LDAPS, either through Active Directory Certificate Services or through a third-party Certificate Authority.

LDAPS is not enabled on an Active Directory level, it is enabled on individual Domain Controllers in an environment. Because of this, it is important to ensure that all Domain Controllers are correctly configured with Active Directory Certificate Services to ensure that LDAPS operates correctly. A Certificate Authority that was created using Active Directory Certificate Services makes this easy to enable in Active Directory, and usually requires no actions to be taken as long as certificates are deployed to the Domain Controllers.

> **LDAP over SSL for Active Directory**
>
> Using LDAP over SSL is an optional feature that is available for Active Directory and there is no requirement to use the feature if it is not needed. If there is no requirement for utilizing this feature, then this section can be skipped.

The requirements for enabling LDAPS for Active Directory are quite simple, assuming there is already an existing Active Directory Certificate Services deployment in an Active Directory domain. The basic requirements that must be met for enabling LDAPS on a domain are:

- The certificate must contain the FQDN for the Domain Controller, and this can be found in either the Common Name (CN) field or the Alternative Name extension.
- The certificate must have the associated private key available on the server.
- The devices on the associated Active Directory domain must contain the complete certificate chain to ensure that the LDAPS certificate is valid.
- The Enhanced Key Usage extension must include the Server Authentication (1.3.6.1.5.5.7.3.1) OID in the certificate.
- The certificate uses the Schannel Cryptographic Service Provider (CSP) to generate the keys for the certificate.

There is no user interface in Active Directory Domain Services for enabling LDAPS. Installing a valid certificate and meeting the above requirements will permit a Domain Controller to utilize LDAP over SSL. The easiest method to enable LDAPS is to use a computer certificate that is already available in Active Directory Certificate Services and issue one of those certificates to the Domain Controllers in that environment. There are third-party utilities that can be used to verify that LDAPS is enabled on a Domain Controller, but there is a utility available in Windows Server (ldp.exe) that can quickly verify that LDAPS is enabled.

Deploy CA Certificates - LDAP over SSL for Active Directory - LDAPS Prerequisites

If there have been no issues with the deployment of the Certificate Authority so far, then the certificate needed to support LDAPS has likely already been created by Active Directory Certificate Services and deployed to Domain Controllers in the domain. There is a Certificate Template included by default that is meant for Domain Controllers, and this can be used for LDAPS. When the Enterprise CA was created and configured in the previous chapter, the certificate should have automatically been created and issued to the Domain Controller.

The certificate can be found in the Local Machine Certificate Store, under the Personal Store if it has been created on the Domain Controller:

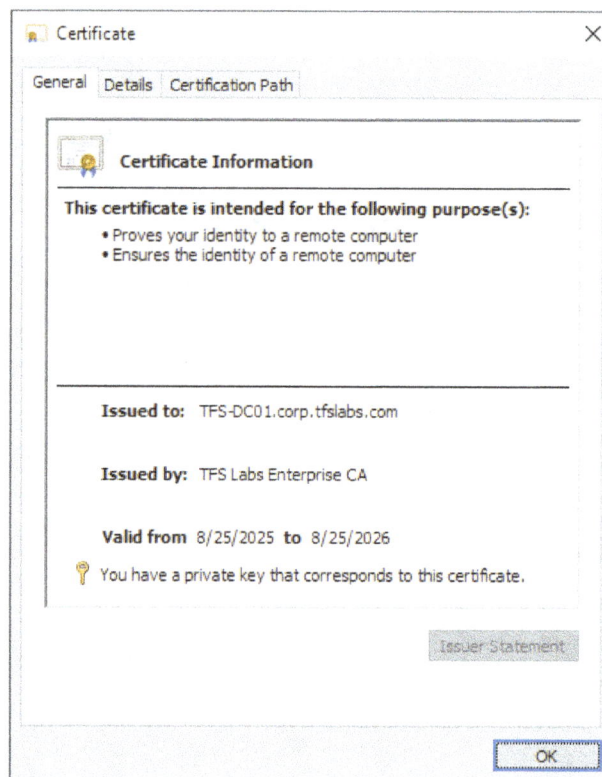

Figure 8.5.1.1: The certificate for the TFS-DC01 server as issued by the Subordinate CA. The certificate should only be valid for 1 year, as that is the maximum length of time that all certificates issued by the TFS-CA01 server should be.

If the certificate for the TFS-DC01 server is present, then proceed to the next section for validating that LDAPS is enabled on the Domain Controller. If there is an issue with the certificate, more information on Certificate Templates and how to deploy them can be found in chapter 11.

> **LDAPS and the Windows Defender Firewall**
>
> There should be no issues with the Windows Defender Firewall when using LDAPS, and TCP port 636 should be open by default. If it is not open, making the change on the TFS-DC01 server should be trivial.

Deploy CA Certificates - LDAP over SSL for Active Directory - Test LDAPS Connections

To check the current LDAP settings on a Domain Controller and check if LDAPS is enabled, perform the following steps on the TFS-DC01 server:

1. Open the **Ldp** application by running the **ldp.exe** command from the **Run** prompt.
2. The **Ldp** window will appear, which can be used to test LDAP and LDAPS connections:

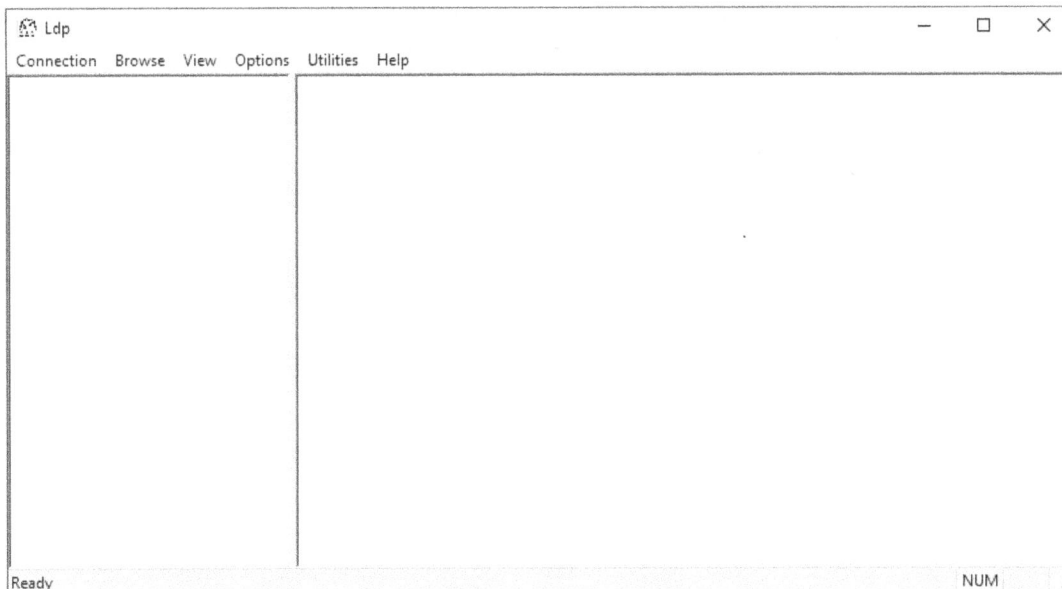

3. To test **LDAP** connections, click on the **Connection** menu and select the **Connect...** option.
4. In the **Connect** window, enter the following details:
   - **Server** - TFS-DC01.corp.tfslabs.com
   - **Port** - 389
   - **Connectionless** - Disabled
   - **SSL** - Disabled
5. The **LDAP** information for the **TFS Labs** domain should be displayed in the window, and the full **LDAP** entry for the domain (**ldap://TFS-DC01.corp.tfslabs.com/DC=corp, DC=tfslabs,DC=com**) should be in the title of the window:

6. To close the current **LDAP** connection, click on the **Connection** menu and select the **Disconnect** option.
7. To test **LDAPS** connections, click on the **Connection** menu and select the **Connect...** option.
8. On the **Connect** window, enter the following details:
   - **Server** - TFS-DC01.corp.tfslabs.com
   - **Port** - 636
   - **Connectionless** - Disabled
   - **SSL** - Enabled
9. The **LDAP** information for the **TFS Labs** domain should be displayed in the window, and the full **LDAP** entry for the domain (**ldaps://TFS-DC01.corp.tfslabs.com/DC=corp, DC=tfslabs,DC=com**) should be in the title of the window:

10. Close the **Ldp** application.

The purpose of this book is to introduce extra security to an Active Directory domain using Active Directory Certificate Services, and not necessarily on enhancing the security of specific Windows services. Enabling LDAPS is quite simple once a valid Active Directory Certificate Services deployment is completed, and is an easy way to enhance security. As of the time of this writing, Microsoft is not enforcing LDAPS within an Active Directory domain, but that could always change in the future.

> ⚠️ **LDAPS Deployment**
>
> It is early in this book to enable LDAPS for the TFS Labs domain as there are still potentially some deployment options remaining to be configured. Return to this section after completing the steps in this book to verify that LDAPS was successfully enabled.

Deploy CA Certificates - Chapter Summary

Now that the Root and Subordinate certificates have been deployed within the Active Directory domain, the framework is now in place to setup OCSP for revoking certificates, and to deploy more complex Certificate Templates to the TFS Labs domain. In the next chapter, the Online Responder role will be installed and configured on the TFS Labs domain.

Chapter 9 - Online Responder Role

The ability to issue and manage certificates is the primary purpose of a Certificate Authority, but if the integrity of any of those certificates is ever compromised, then it is up to an administrator to revoke those certificates since they can no longer be trusted. Typically, a Certificate Revocation List is used to revoke certificates, but a CRL is not always updated often enough, and they only grow in size as a Certificate Authority ages. The Online Certificate Status Protocol (OCSP) is a service that is available that speeds up the revocation of certificates and reduces overhead on the CRL. In Active Directory Certificate Services, this feature is implemented as the Online Responder role.

For large environments using Active Directory Certificate Services, the Online Responder role is convenient because it allows for rapid revocation of certificates. In smaller environments where certificates are not as essential, the Online Responder role is not always needed, so this chapter is optional if it is not required for an organization. Fortunately, the Online Responder role can be added to Active Directory Certificate Services at any time in the future should it be required.

There are several steps that are required for adding the Online Responder role to the Subordinate CA server:

- Install the Online Responder role on the TFS-CA01 server.
- Configure the Online Responder role on the TFS-CA01 server.
- Add the OCSP URL to the Subordinate CA.
- Configure the revocation policies for the Subordinate CA.
- Create the certificate required for the Online Responder role.
- Enable auditing for the Online Responder role.

This chapter will focus on installing, configuring and validating the Online Responder role within Active Directory Certificate Services for the TFS Labs domain.

> **Online Responder Role**
>
> This chapter is completely optional and can be skipped if it is not required. The Online Responder role can be added in the future if the requirements for an organization changes and the functionality is needed. If the Online Responder is located on the same server as the Subordinate CA server, it can be relocated to a different server using the same steps in this chapter with minor modifications. These steps are beyond the scope of this book.

> **Online Responder Role CLI Utilities**
>
> There are not many command line management tools that can be used for the Online Responder role, as Microsoft never created them. As a result, there are few CLI options in this chapter, and it is not an omission.

Online Responder Role - Online Responder Role Installation

The Online Responder role is a component of Active Directory Certificate Services that can be added as an additional feature with the role. The feature can be added using the command line with PowerShell or with the Server Manager console. Only one method is required for adding the Online Responder role on the TFS-CA01 server.

Online Responder Role - Online Responder Role Installation - CLI Installation

To add the Online Responder role using PowerShell, perform the following steps on the TFS-CA01 server:

1. Open an **elevated PowerShell prompt**.
2. Run the following command to add the **Online Responder** role and the required **Remote Server Administration Tools**:

```
Windows PowerShell (Elevated)

Add-WindowsFeature Adcs-Online-Cert, RSAT-Online-Responder
```

3. Once the **Online Responder** role has been added, close the **PowerShell prompt**.

Once the Online Responder role has been added to the TFS-CA01 server, proceed to enabling the feature for the TFS Labs domain.

Online Responder Role - Online Responder Role Installation - GUI Installation

To add the Online Responder role on the TFS-CA01 server using the Server Manager console, perform the following steps:

1. Open the **Server Manager** console (servermanager.exe), click on the **Manage** menu, and click on **Add Roles and Features** to start the installation wizard:

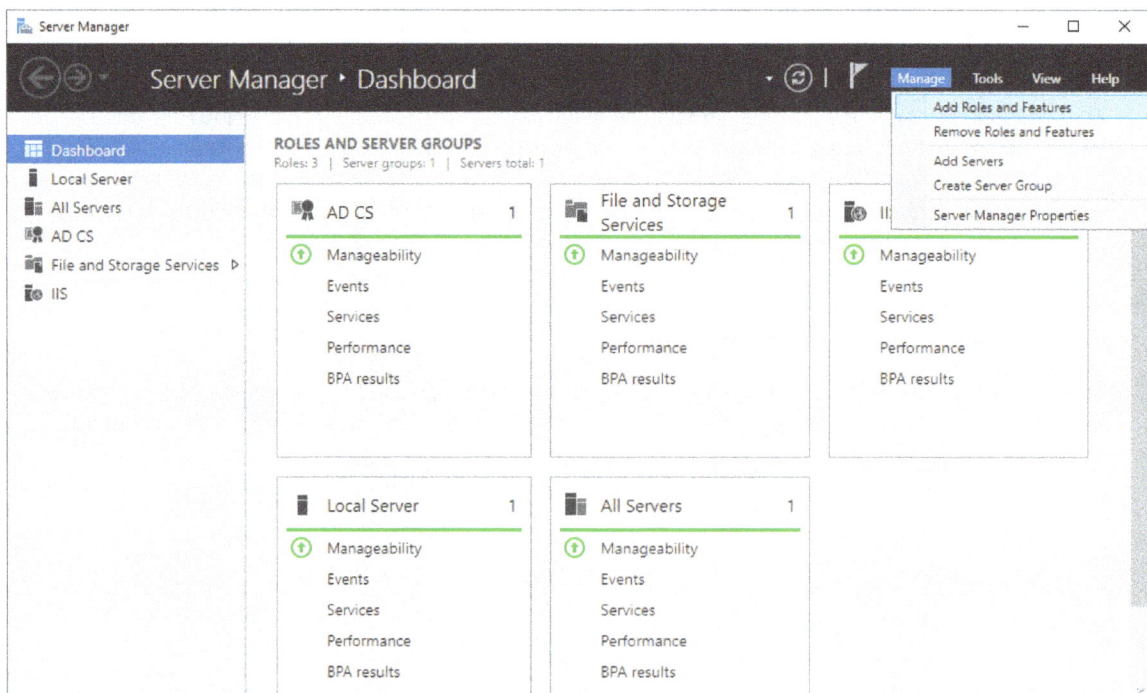

2. On the **Before you begin** screen, click the **Next** button to continue.
3. On the **Select installation type** screen, select the option for **Role-based or feature-based installation** and click the **Next** button to continue.

4. On the **Select destination server** screen, verify that the **TFS-CA01.corp.tfslabs.com** server is selected and click **Next** to continue.
5. On the **Select server roles** screen, expand the **Active Directory Certificate Services** option and select the **Online Responder** role:

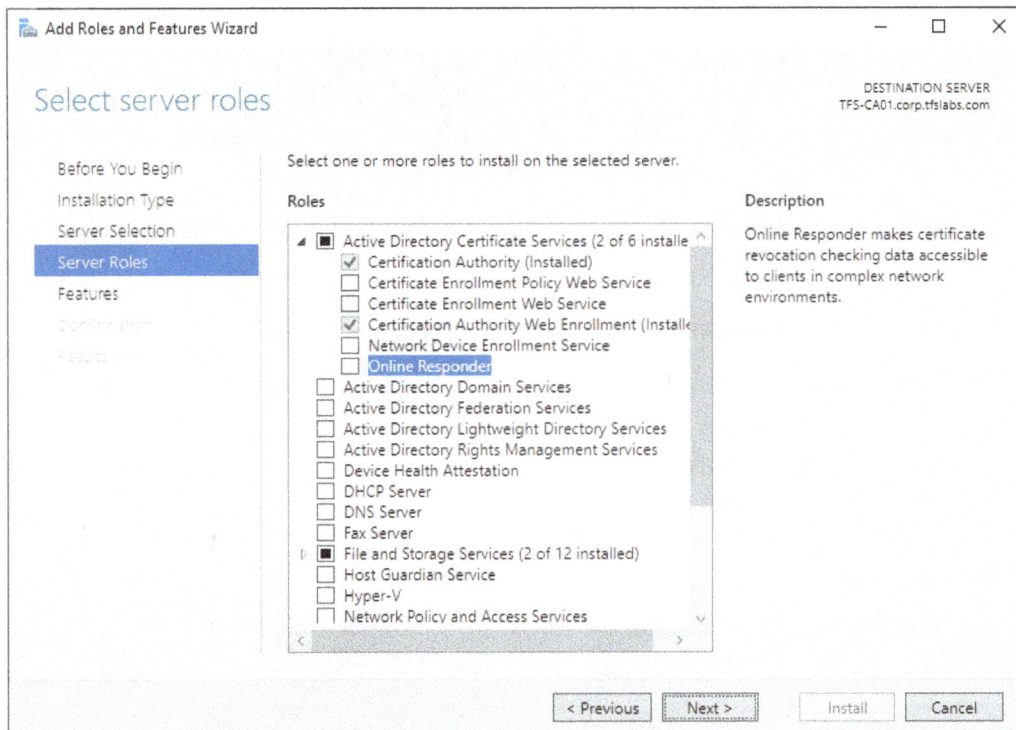

6. The installation wizard will ask to install any additional features required for the **Active Directory Certificate Services** role. Select the option to **Include management tools (if applicable)** to install the management tools for the role. Click the **Add Features** button to continue.
7. On the **Select server roles** screen, click the **Next** button to continue.
8. On the **Select features** screen, click the **Next** button to continue.
9. On the **Confirm installation selections** screen, select the option to **Restart the destination server automatically if required**.
10. When prompted with a warning about restarting the server, click the **Yes** button.
11. On the **Confirm installation selections** screen, click the **Install** button to continue.
12. Once the installation is completed, click the **Close** button.

Once the Online Responder role has been added to the TFS-CA01 server, proceed to enabling the feature for the TFS Labs domain.

Online Responder Role - Online Responder Role Configuration

When the Online Responder role has been successfully added to the TFS-CA01 server, it will need to be enabled before further options can be configured with the role. The Online Responder role can be enabled using the command line with PowerShell, or with the Server Manager console. Only one method is required for enabling the Online Responder role.

> ⚠️ **Online Responder Role Configuration**
>
> Once the Online Responder role configuration has been started, it is important to finish the configuration to allow for the role to be used. Do not leave the role in a partially configured state, as this can potentially cause issues with Active Directory Certificate Services.

Online Responder Role - Online Responder Role Configuration - CLI Configuration

The Online Responder role can be enabled using PowerShell by performing the following steps on the TFS-CA01 server:

1. Open an **elevated PowerShell prompt**.
2. Run the following command to enable the **Online Responder** role:

```
Windows PowerShell (Elevated)

Install-AdcsOnlineResponder -Force
```

3. Once the **Online Responder** role has been enabled, close the **PowerShell prompt**.

Once the Online Responder role has been enabled on the TFS-CA01 server, proceed to validating that the role was added correctly to the Subordinate CA.

Online Responder Role - Online Responder Role Configuration - GUI Configuration

To enable the Online Responder role on the TFS-CA01 server using the Server Manager console, perform the following steps:

1. To begin the configuration of the **Online Responder Service**, open the **Server Manager** console (servermanager.exe). Click the **Notifications** icon in the upper-right hand corner and click the **Configure Active Directory Certificate Services on the destination server** link in the **Post-deployment Configuration** box:

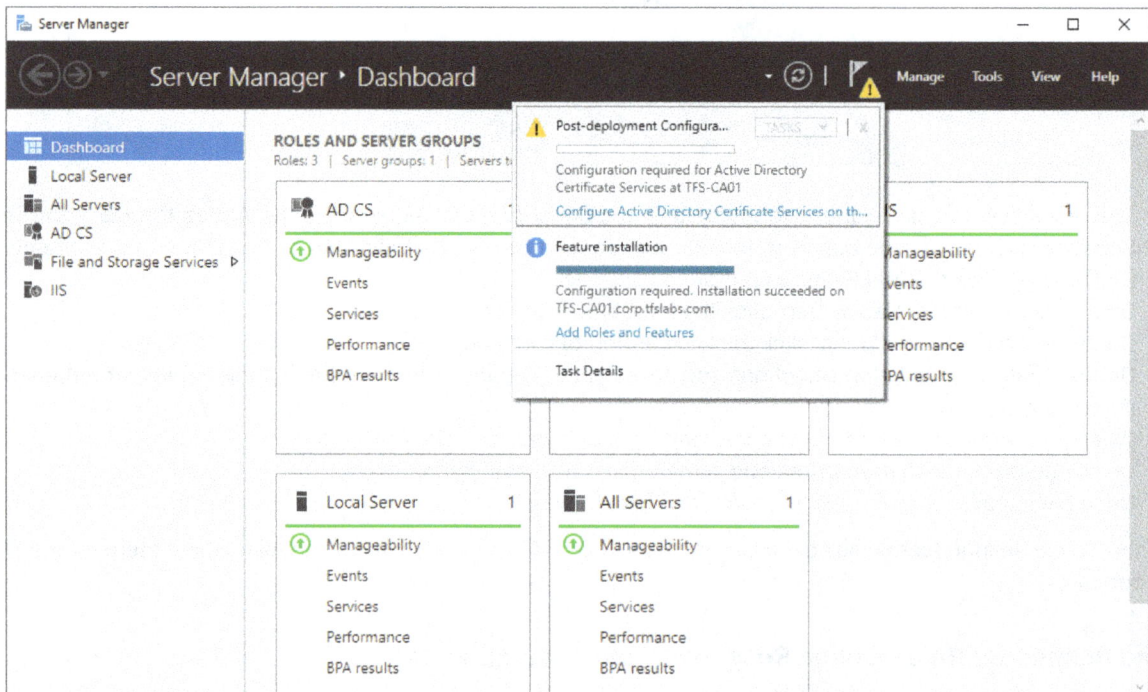

2. On the **Credentials** screen, verify that the Administrator credentials are set to a **Domain Administrator** account and click the **Next** button to continue. If a **Domain Administrator** account is not used, then the **Online Responder Role** installation will not complete correctly.
3. On the **Role Services** screen, select the option for **Online Responder** and click **Next** to continue.
4. On the **Confirmation** screen, click on the **Configure** button to continue.
5. Once the installation is completed, click the **Close** button.

Once the Online Responder role has been enabled on the TFS-CA01 server, proceed to validating that the role was added correctly to the Subordinate CA.

Online Responder Role - Online Responder Role Configuration - Validation

Once the Online Responder role has been enabled, it should be verified that the OCSP folder is present in the Internet Information Services Manager console. To verify that the directory is present, open the Internet Information Services (IIS) Manager console and expand the **TFS-CA01 > Sites > Default Web Site** folder. The **ocsp** folder should be listed as one of the available directories:

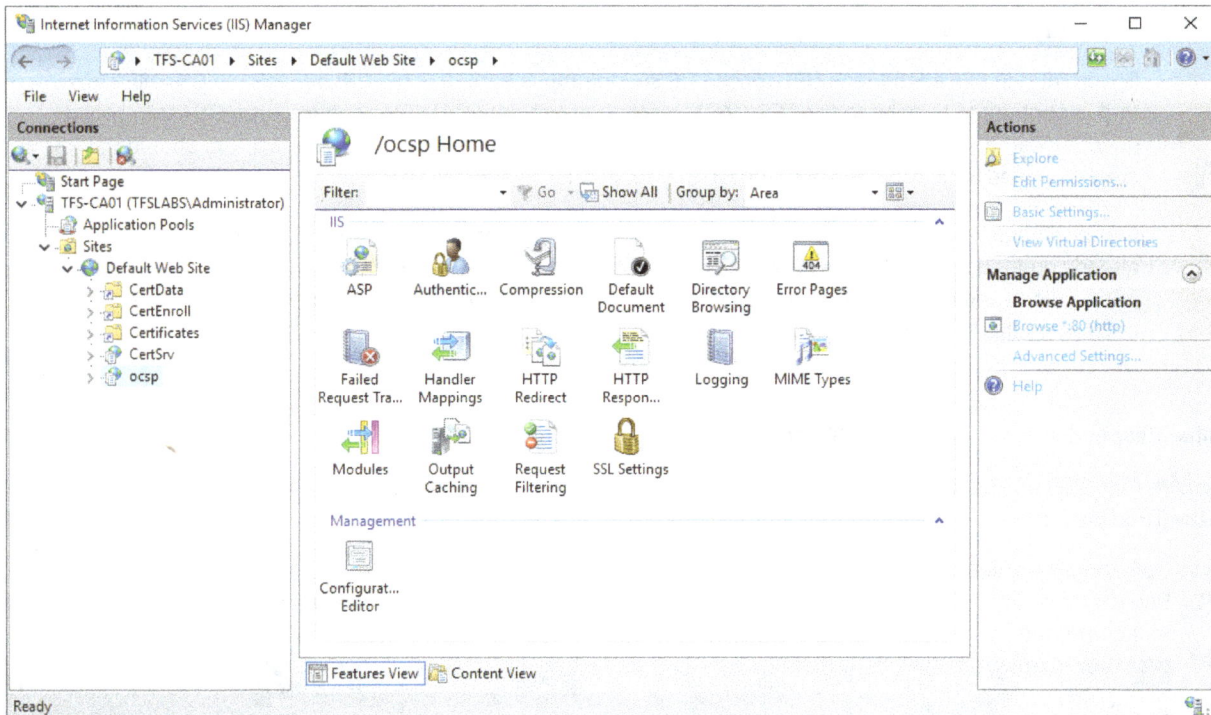

Figure 9.2.3.1: The **ocsp** folder should have automatically been created and added to the IIS configuration on the TFS-CA01 server. All necessary settings and permissions should have been added using the Online Responder role configuration.

Once the Online Responder role has been enabled on the TFS-CA01 server, proceed to adding the OCSP URL to the Subordinate CA configuration.

OCSP Folder Creation Issues

If the OCSP folder is not present for whatever reason after performing the steps in this section, run the following command in an **elevated PowerShell prompt** on the TFS-CA01 server to create the folder:

```
Windows PowerShell (Elevated)

certutil.exe -vocsproot
```

The IIS service will need to be restarted afterwards if this command is run to apply the changes. Restart the IIS service by running the following command in an **elevated PowerShell prompt** on the TFS-CA01 server:

```
Windows PowerShell (Elevated)

Restart-Service W3SVC
```

Once the commands have been executed, validate that the OCSP folder has been created.

Online Responder Role - Add the OCSP URL to the Subordinate CA

Once the Online Responder role has been installed and configured, the OCSP URL will need to be added to the AIA settings for the Subordinate CA. This can be configured using the command line with PowerShell, or through the Certification Authority console. Only one method is required to add the OCSP URL to the Subordinate CA, there is no need to use both methods.

> **DNS Entry for OCSP**
>
> Ensure that in this section the URL for the OCSP location is correct. This URL relies on a CNAME entry that is configured to point to the TFS-CA01 server (Subordinate CA). The reason that a CNAME entry is used instead of the hostname of the TFS-CA01 server is to provide flexibility in the future should the PKI structure need to be modified, and the Online Responder role needs to be moved to another server.
>
> For the Online Responder role configuration, the *http://ocsp.corp.tfslabs.com/ocsp/* configuration was already created in this chapter. The DNS records have already been created in an earlier chapter, and the folder has already been configured using IIS. The OCSP configuration will be accessible to users and devices on the TFS Labs domain.

Online Responder Role - Add the OCSP URL to the Subordinate CA - CLI Configuration

The URL for OCSP can be added to the Subordinate CA certificate by performing the following steps using PowerShell on the TFS-CA01 server:

1. Open an **elevated PowerShell prompt**.
2. Run the following command to add the **OCSP URL** to the **AIA** configuration on the **TFS Labs Enterprise CA** (execute this command as a single line with no breaks):

```
Windows PowerShell (Elevated)

certutil.exe -setreg CA\CACertPublicationURLs "1:C:\Windows\system32\CertSrv\
CertEnroll\%1_%3%4.crt\n2:http://pki.corp.tfslabs.com/CertEnroll/%1_%3%4.crt\n
32:http://ocsp.corp.tfslabs.com/ocsp"
```

3. Restart the **Active Directory Certificate Services** service to apply the changes:

```
Windows PowerShell (Elevated)

net stop CertSvc
net start CertSvc
```

4. Once the **Online Responder** role has been configured, close the **PowerShell prompt**.

Once the OCSP URL has been added to the Subordinate CA, proceed to validating that the OCSP location is valid.

> **Command Line Entry for AIA Locations**
>
> In this section there is a command (step 2) that is used to modify the AIA locations for the Subordinate CA. This command needs to be run as a single line, with no line breaks. This command is shown with line breaks so that the entire command is visible, but the command cannot be executed as it is displayed. Copy the entire command first, remove the line breaks while preserving the existing characters, and then execute the command.
>
> If there is an error with the configuration in this section, it can cause unexpected issues with the Certificate Authority. Ensure that before proceeding to the next section in this chapter that the AIA entries and correct for the TFS Labs domain.

Online Responder Role - Add the OCSP URL to the Subordinate CA - GUI Configuration

The URL for OCSP can be added to the Subordinate CA certificate by performing the following steps using the Certification Authority console on the TFS-CA01 server:

1. Open the **Certification Authority** console (certsrv.msc) on the **TFS-CA01** server.
2. In the console tree, right-click on **TFS Labs Enterprise CA**, and then select **Properties**.
3. On the **TFS Labs Enterprise CA** Properties window, click on the **Extensions** tab.
4. On the **Extensions** tab, under **Select extension**, select **Authority Information Access (AIA)**, and then click **Add...** button.
5. On the **Add Location** window, enter **http://ocsp.corp.tfslabs.com/ocsp** in the **Location** field and then click the **OK** button.
6. With the **http://ocsp.corp.tfslabs.com/ocsp** location selected, check the **Include in the online certificate status protocol (OCSP) extension** option and then click the **OK** button (ensure that the **Include in the AIA extension of issued certificates** option is not selected):

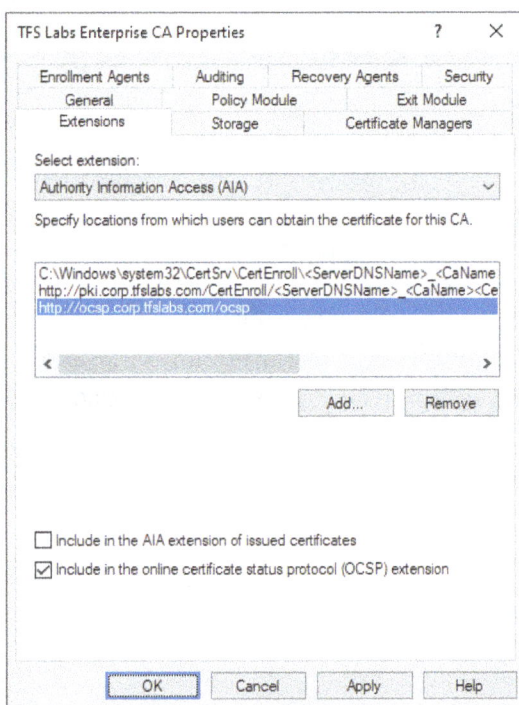

7. When prompted by the Certification Authority dialog box to restart **Active Directory Certificate Services**, click Yes.
8. Close the **Certification Authority** console.

Once the OCSP URL has been added to the Subordinate CA, proceed to validating that the OCSP location is valid and is accessible.

Online Responder Role - Add the OCSP URL to the Subordinate CA - Validation

There is a simple way to validate that the OCSP location settings have been applied correctly to the Subordinate CA by using the **certutil.exe** command. From an **elevated PowerShell prompt** on the TFS-CA01 server, run the following command to verify the OCSP location:

```
Windows PowerShell (Elevated)

certutil.exe -getreg CA\CACertPublicationURLs
```

The command will output the AIA and OCSP locations that have been configured on the Subordinate CA:

```
Administrator: Windows PowerShell                                    —  □  ×

PS C:\Users\Administrator.TFSLABS> certutil.exe -getreg CA\CACertPublicationURLs
HKEY_LOCAL_MACHINE\SYSTEM\CurrentControlSet\Services\CertSvc\Configuration\TFS Labs Enterprise CA\CA
CertPublicationURLs:

  CACertPublicationURLs REG_MULTI_SZ =
    0: 1:C:\Windows\system32\CertSrv\CertEnroll\%1_%3%4.crt
    CSURL_SERVERPUBLISH -- 1

    1: 2:http://pki.corp.tfslabs.com/CertEnroll/%1_%3%4.crt
    CSURL_ADDTOCERTCDP -- 2

    2: 32:http://ocsp.corp.tfslabs.com/ocsp
    CSURL_ADDTOCERTOCSP -- 20 (32)

CertUtil: -getreg command completed successfully.
PS C:\Users\Administrator.TFSLABS>
```

If there are no issues with the OCSP location for the Subordinate certificate, proceed to configuring and publishing the OCSP Response Signing certificate.

Online Responder Role - OCSP Response Signing Certificate Template Creation

The OCSP Response Signing Certificate Template will be used by the Online Responder role to manage the OCSP services for the TFS Labs domain. With Active Directory Certificate Services, all Certificate Templates are stored and managed by Active Directory, and one of those templates will be used for this purpose. This will need to be created before a certificate can be issued for the Online Responder role. To configure the OCSP Response Signing Certificate Template, perform the following steps on the TFS-CA01 server:

1. Open the **Certification Authority** console (certsrv.msc) on the **TFS-CA01** server:

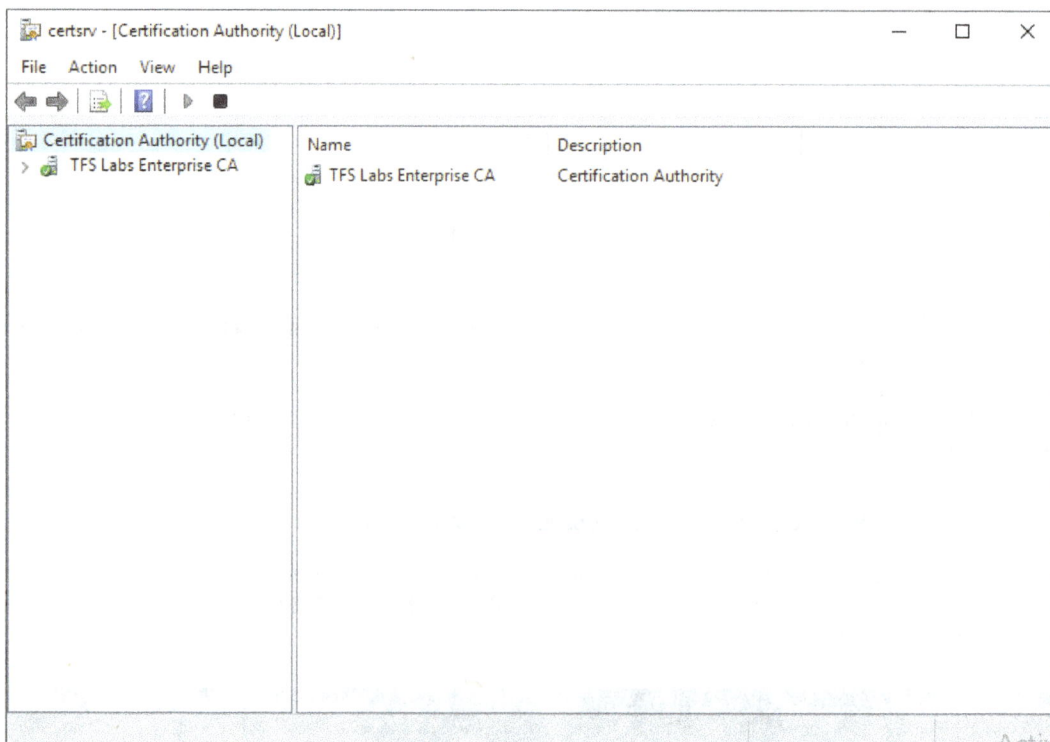

2. Ensure that the **TFS Labs Enterprise CA** server is expanded in the console tree.

3. Right-click on the **Certificate Templates** folder and then click **Manage**:

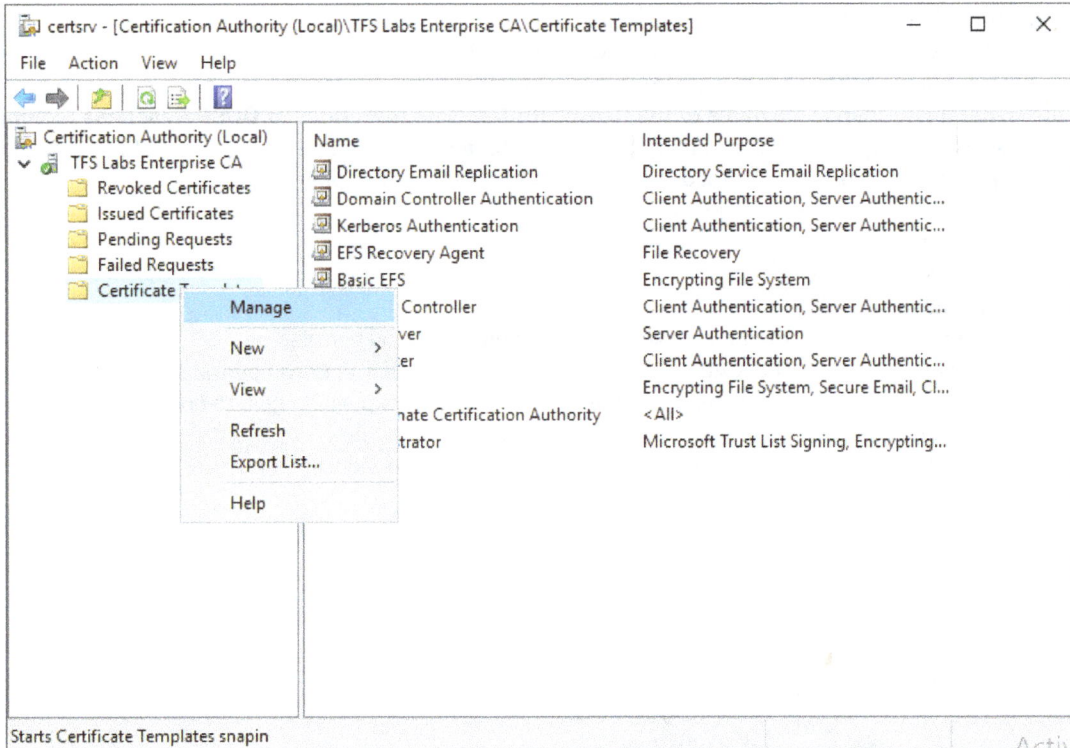

4. The **Certificate Templates** console window will open and display the current Certificate Templates that are stored in **Active Directory**.
5. In the main window, right-click on the **OCSP Response Signing** template and then click **Duplicate Template**:

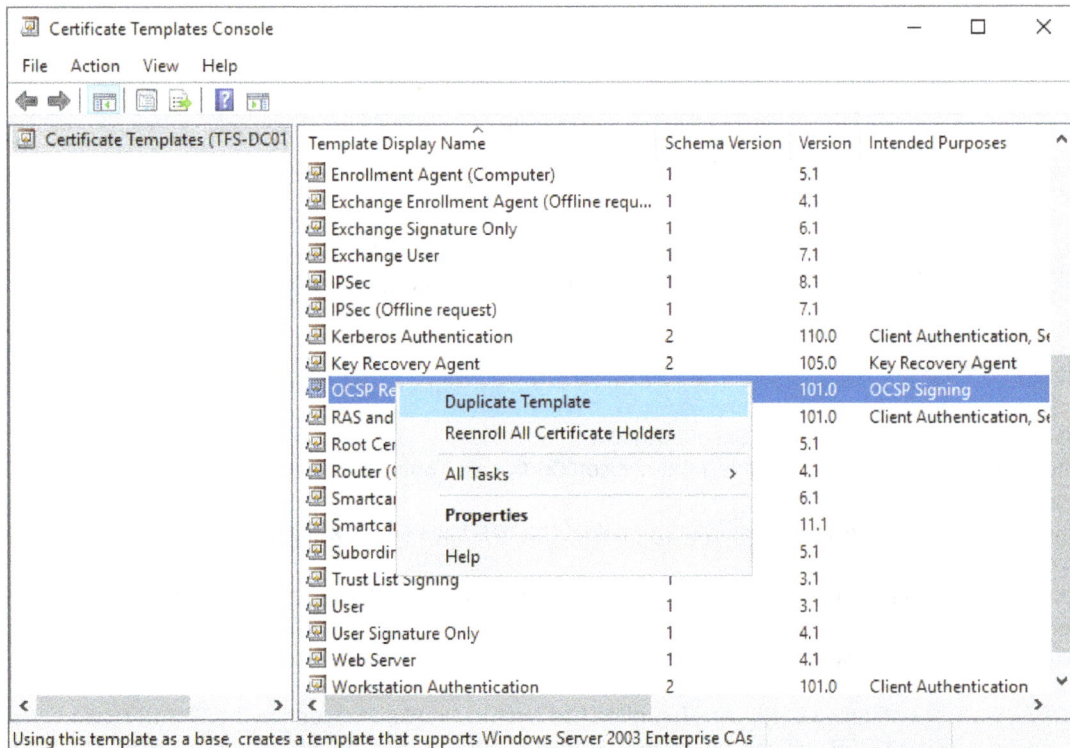

6. The **Properties of New Template** window will open for the **Duplicated Certificate**.
7. On the **Compatibility** tab, make the following changes in the **Compatibility Settings** pane:
   - **Certification Authority** - Windows Server 2016
   - **Certificate recipient** - Windows 10 / Windows Server 2016
8. When the **Resulting changes** window appears, click the **OK** button to continue.
9. On the **General** tab, change the name of the Certificate Template from **Copy of OCSP Response Signing** to **TFS Labs OCSP Response Signing**. The **Validity period** and **Renewal period** times can remain at the default values.
10. On the **Cryptography** tab, make the following changes for the **Cryptography** settings:
    - **Provider Category** - Key Storage Provider
    - **Algorithm name** - RSA
    - **Minimum key size** - 4096
    - **Request hash** - SHA256
11. On the **Security** tab, select **Authenticated Users** and enable the **Enroll** permission.
12. On the **Security** tab, add the **TFS-CA01** server and enable the **Read** and **Enroll** permissions. If there are issues with enabling this option, there are steps at the end of this section explaining how to configure this.
13. Click **OK** to close the **Properties of New Template** window.
14. In the **Certificate Templates** console, the **TFS Labs OCSP Response Signing** Certificate Template should now be listed as a certificate template:

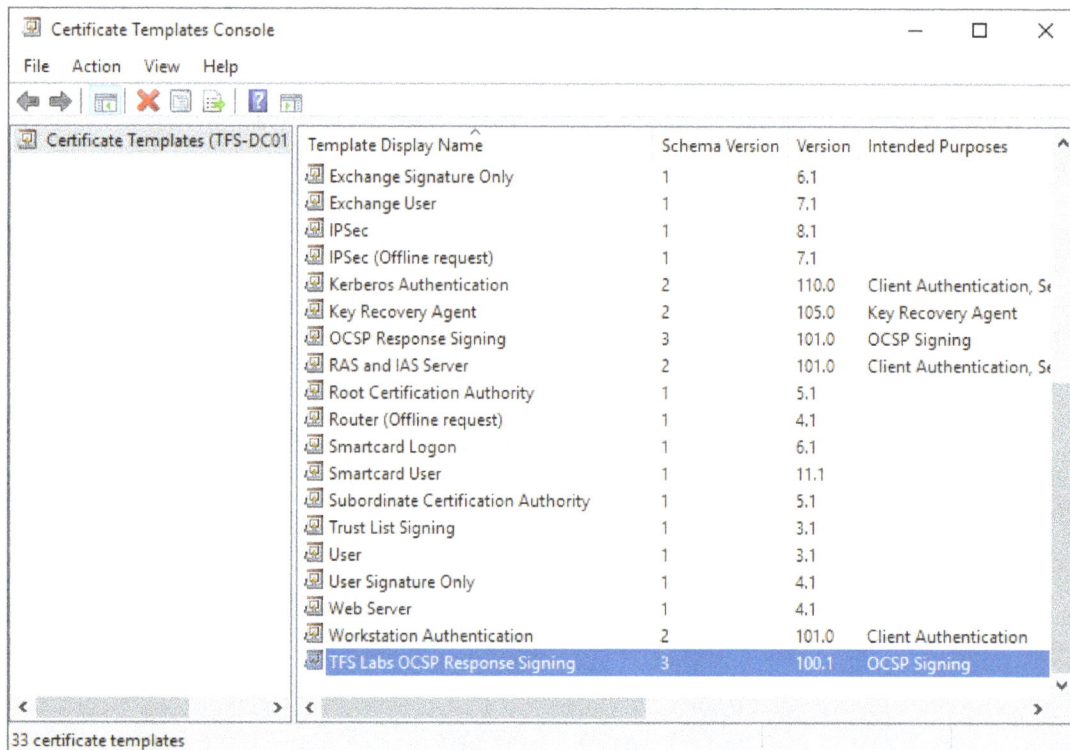

15. Close the **Certificate Templates** console window.
16. In the **Certification Authority** console, right-click on **Certificate Templates**, then select **New > Certificate Template to Issue**.
17. In the **Enable Certificate Templates** window, select the **TFS Labs OCSP Response Signing** Certificate Template, and click **OK**.
18. In the **Certificate Templates** folder, the **TFS Labs OCSP Response Signing** Certificate Template should now be listed.
19. Close the **Certification Authority** console.

Once the OCSP Response Signing Certificate Template has been created and issued to the TFS-CA01 server, a certificate that is used for OCSP can now be created. Proceed to the revocation configuration on the TFS-CA01 server.

Server Object Security Permissions

There are a few extra steps required for adding server and computer objects to the security settings, as those objects are not searchable by default. To be able to add a server object, perform the following steps to be able to search for those objects:

1. On the **Security** tab, click the **Add...** button.
2. In the **Select Users, Computers, Service Accounts, or Groups** window, click the **Object Types...** button.
3. In the **Object Types** window, select the option for **Computers** and click the **OK** button.
4. In the **Enter the object names to select** field, enter the **TFS-CA01** server, and click the **Check Names** button.
5. Click the **OK** button to finish adding the server object.

Once these steps have been completed, the server object should be a configurable option in the Active Directory Certificate Services configuration for OCSP.

This extra step is required since these options are not enabled by default, and those options are configured every time a change is made to the security settings for server objects.

Online Responder Role - Revocation Configuration

Once the OCSP Response Signing Certificate Template has been created for the TFS Labs domain, the Online Responder role can now be configured on the TFS-CA01 server. A certificate is required for the Online Responder service, as it is used for securing communication and will be created automatically during the configuration.

To perform the revocation configuration for the TFS Labs domain, complete the following steps on the TFS-CA01 server:

1. Open the **Online Responder Management** console (ocsp.msc) on the **TFS-CA01** server:

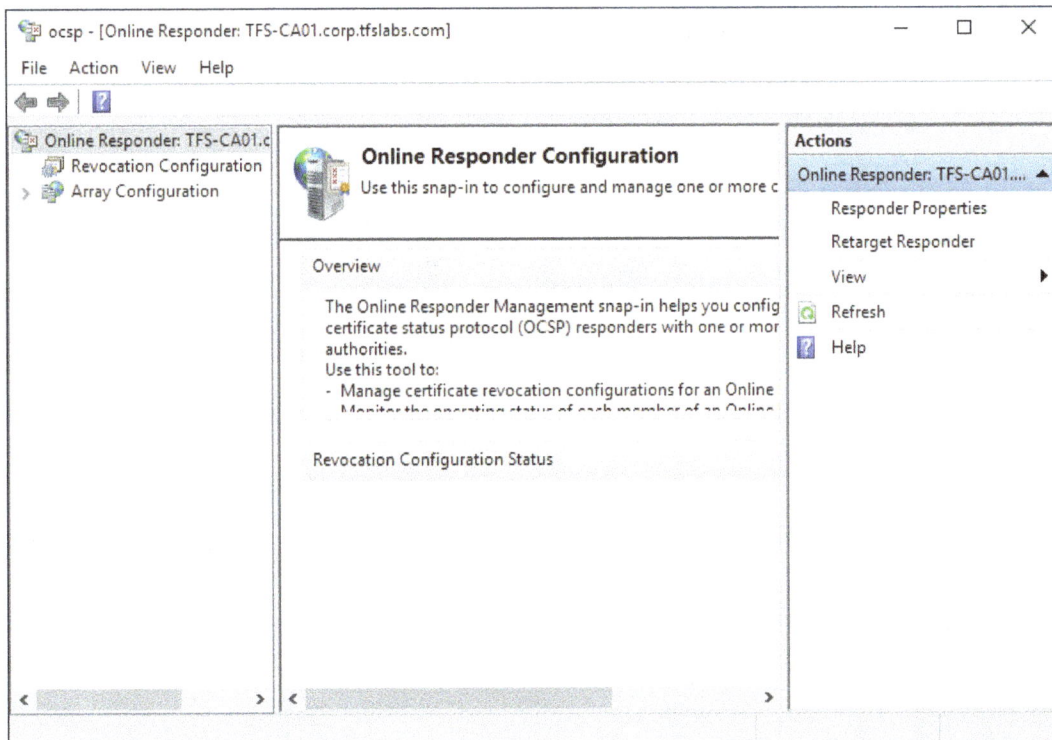

2. Right-click on **Revocation Configuration** and then click **Add Revocation Configuration**:

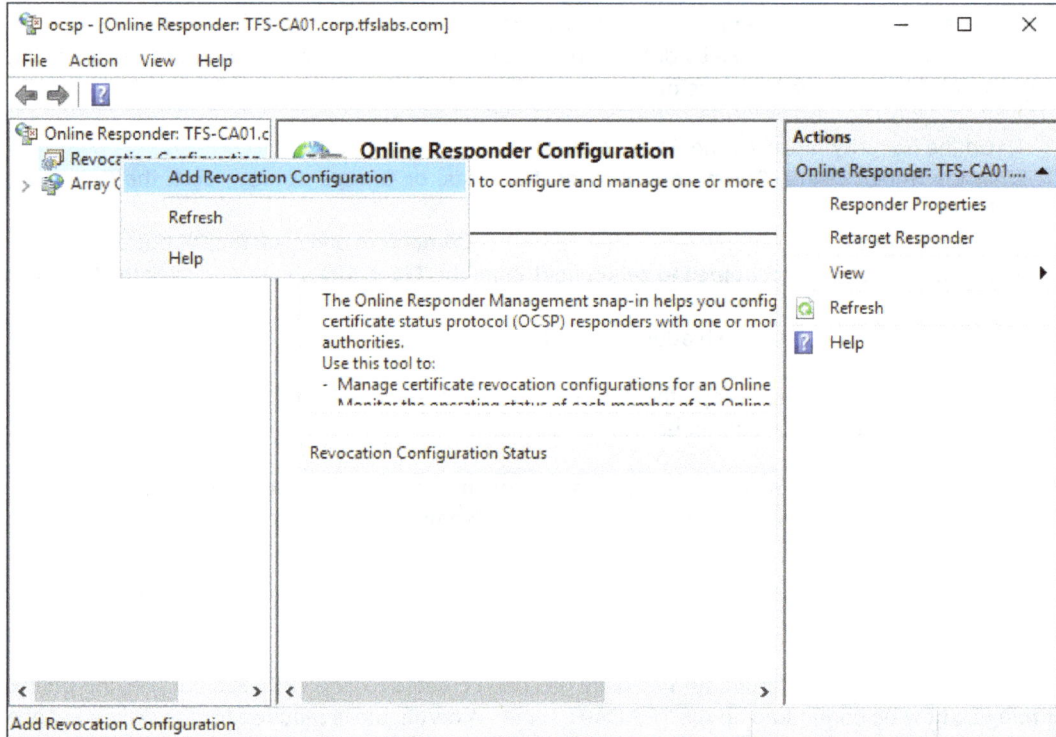

3. On the **Getting started with adding a revocation configuration** screen, click **Next** to continue:

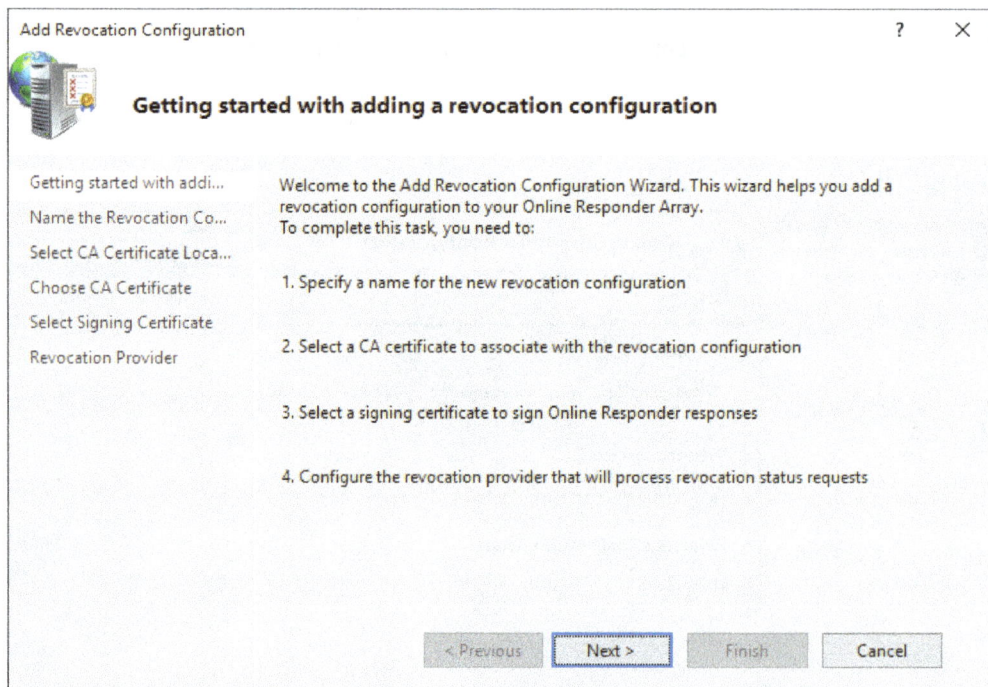

4. On the **Name the Revocation Configuration** screen, enter **TFS Labs Enterprise CA OCSP** in the **Name** field, and then click **Next** to continue:

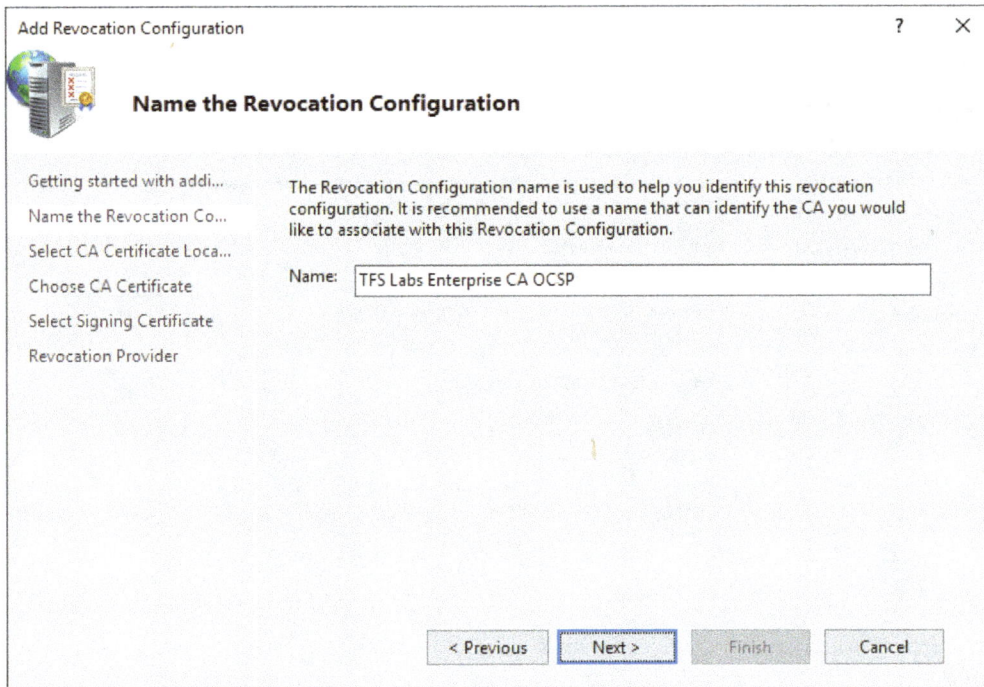

Add Revocation Configuration   ?   ✕

Name the Revocation Configuration

Getting started with addi...

Name the Revocation Co...   The Revocation Configuration name is used to help you identify this revocation
                                   configuration. It is recommended to use a name that can identify the CA you would
Select CA Certificate Loca...   like to associate with this Revocation Configuration.

Choose CA Certificate   Name: TFS Labs Enterprise CA OCSP

Select Signing Certificate

Revocation Provider

                                          < Previous   Next >   Finish   Cancel

5. On the **Select CA Certificate Location** screen, ensure that **Select a certificate for an Existing enterprise CA** is selected, then click **Next** to continue:

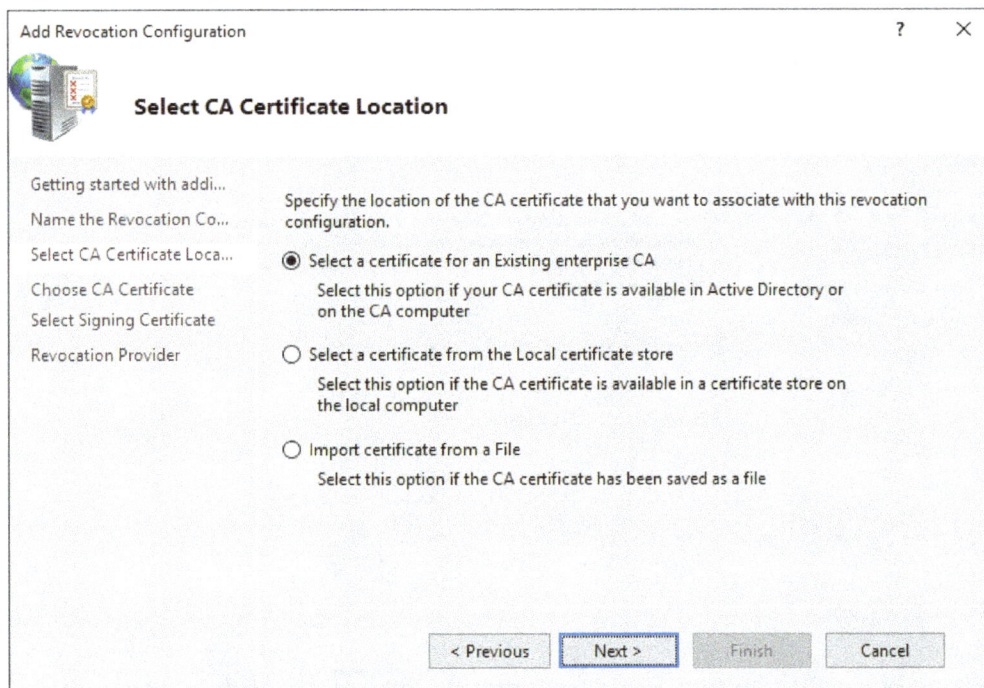

Add Revocation Configuration   ?   ✕

Select CA Certificate Location

Getting started with addi...

Name the Revocation Co...   Specify the location of the CA certificate that you want to associate with this revocation
                                   configuration.
Select CA Certificate Loca...
                                   ◉ Select a certificate for an Existing enterprise CA
Choose CA Certificate
                                        Select this option if your CA certificate is available in Active Directory or
Select Signing Certificate   on the CA computer

Revocation Provider   ○ Select a certificate from the Local certificate store

                                        Select this option if the CA certificate is available in a certificate store on
                                        the local computer

                                   ○ Import certificate from a File

                                        Select this option if the CA certificate has been saved as a file

                                          < Previous   Next >   Finish   Cancel

6. On the **Choose CA Certificate** screen, ensure that **Browse CA certificates published in Active Directory** is selected, and then click the **Browse** button:

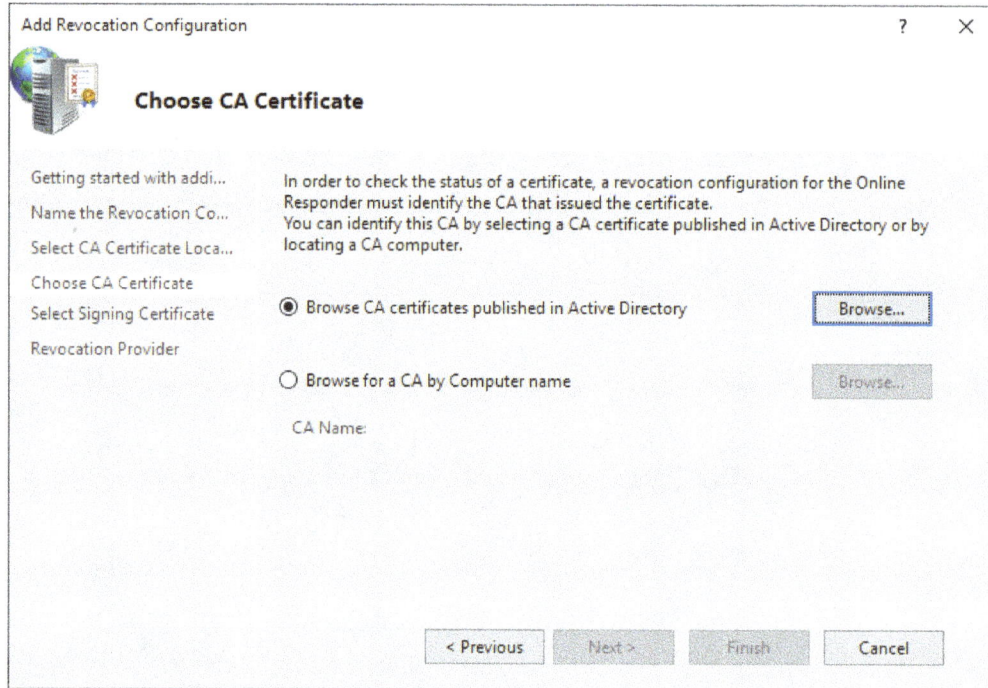

7. On the **Select Certification Authority** dialog box, ensure that the **TFS Labs Enterprise CA** Certificate Authority is selected, and then click **OK**.
8. On the **Choose CA Certificate** screen, click the **Next** button to continue:

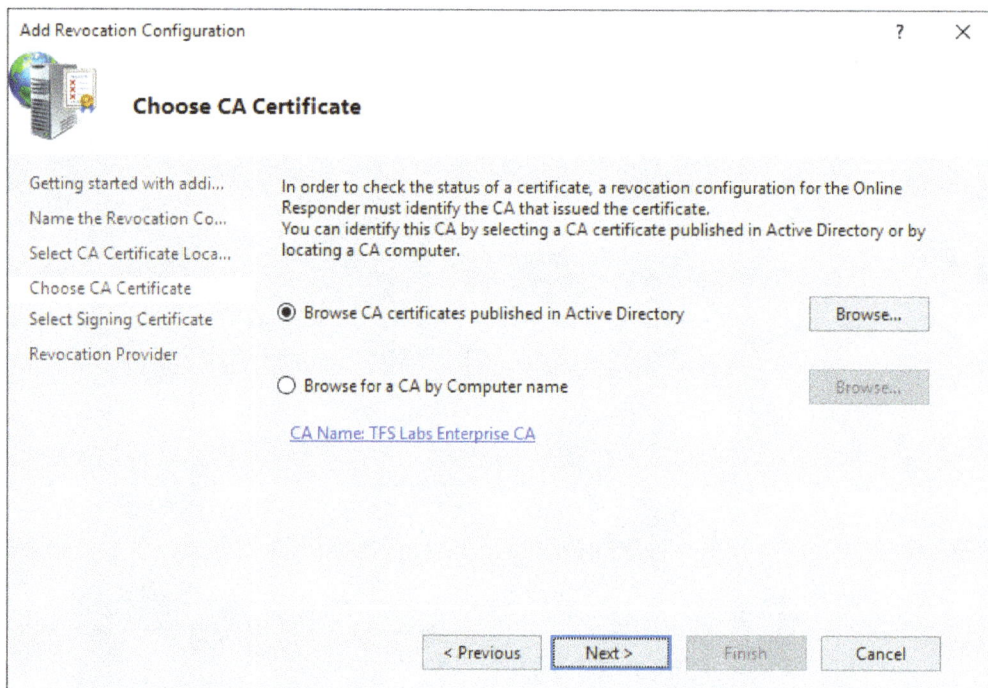

9. On the **Select Signing Certificate** screen, use the default options and then click **Next** to continue. The **TFS Labs OCSP Response Signing** Certificate Template should automatically be selected as the default option:

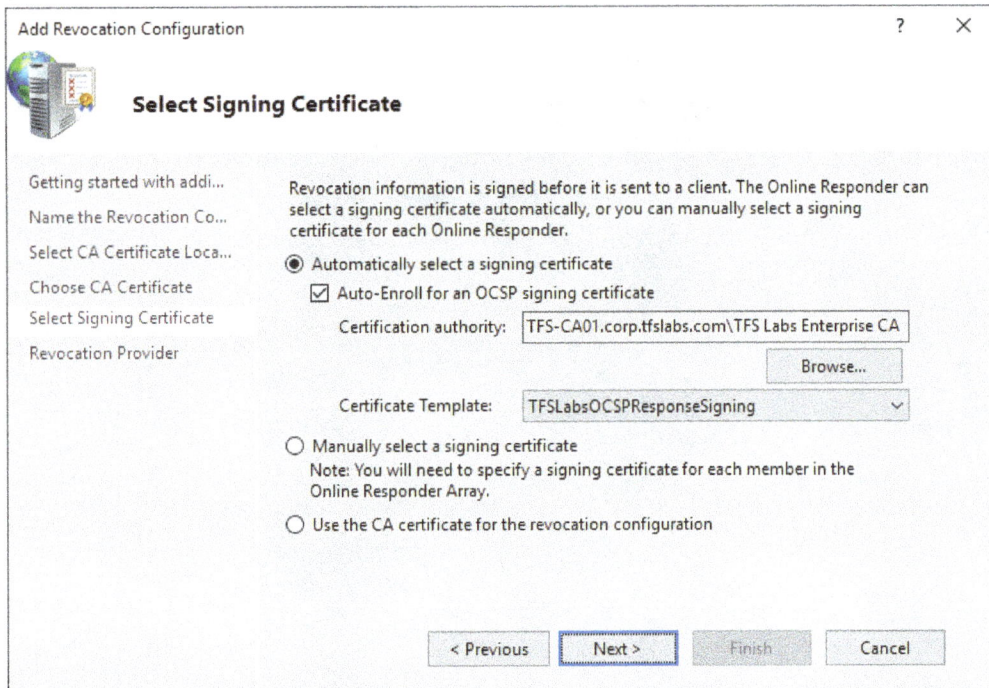

10. On the **Revocation Provider** screen, click the **Provider...** button:

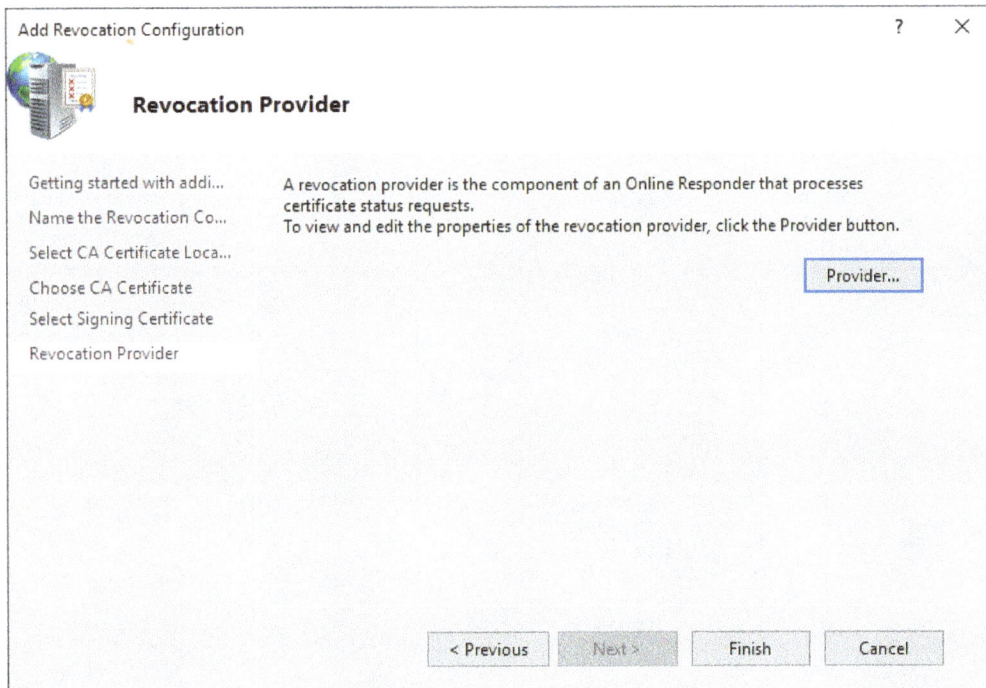

11. On the **Revocation Provider Properties** window, for the **HTTP** location in the **Base CRLs** pane, clear the **Refresh CRLs based on their validity periods** option. In the **Update CRLs at this refresh interval (min)** field, enter **15** as the value, and then click **OK** to close the window:

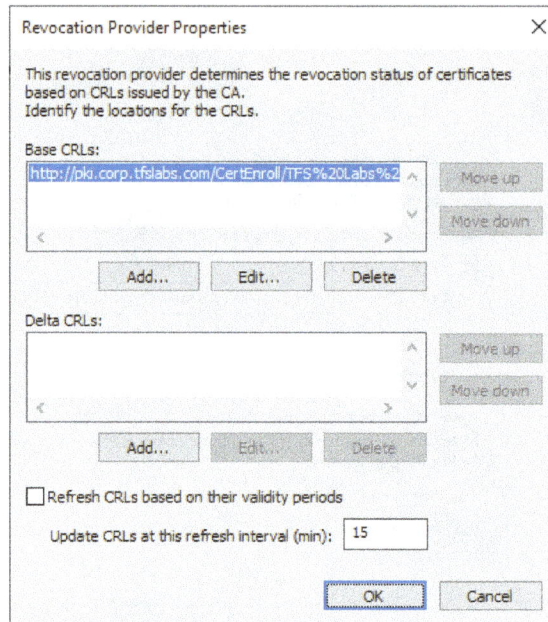

12. Click **Finish** to close the window and complete the configuration.
13. In the **Online Responder Management** console, expand the **Array Configuration** node, and then click on the **TFS-CA01.corp.tfslabs.com** configuration. Review the **Revocation Configuration Status** in the middle pane to ensure there is a valid OCSP Response Signing certificate present and the status reports as **Ok**:

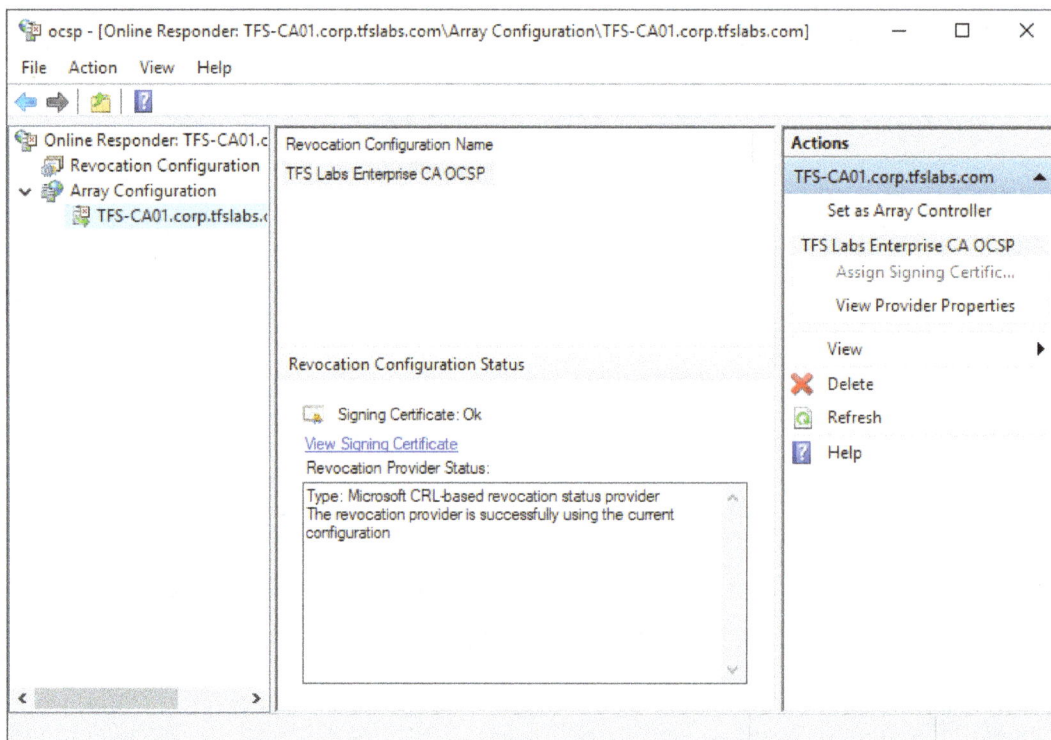

14. Click on the **View Signing Certificate** link to view the OCSP Certificate and verify that the certificate is only valid for **2 weeks** only. Click **OK** to close the certificate:

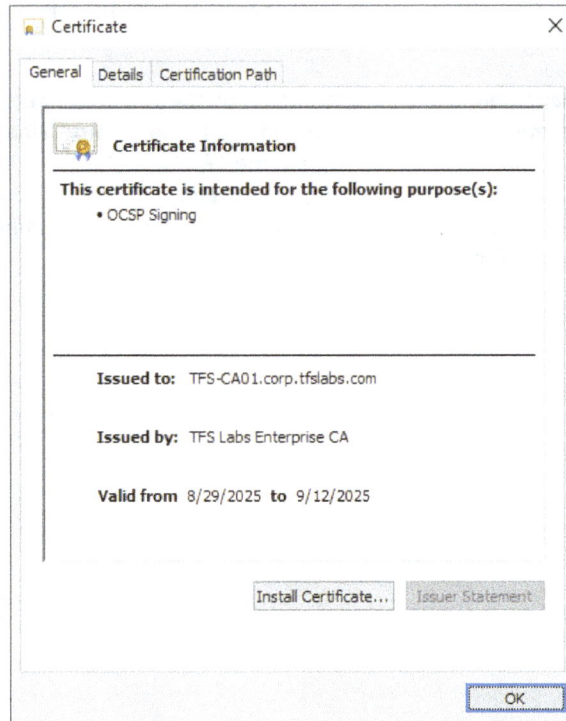

15. Close the **Online Responder Management** console.

Once the revocation configuration has been completed for the Online Responder role, proceed to configure auditing for the Online Responder role.

Online Responder Role - Enable OCSP Auditing

Auditing is not necessary on servers that are running the Online Responder role to function correctly, but it is highly recommended for best practices and to have visibility on issues with the Certificate Authority. In some cases, there are compliance and external auditing requirements depending on the organization, so enabling these features will assist with that.

Just like with Active Directory Certificate Services, auditing on servers that are running the Online Responder role will write to the Windows Event Log on the local server under the following circumstances:

- When the Online Responder configuration, or associated security settings are changed.
- When a request is made to the Online Responder.
- When administrative tasks such as starting or stopping the Online Responder service is initiated.

To configure auditing for the Online Responder role, perform the following steps on the TFS-CA01 server:

1. Open the **Online Responder Management** console (ocsp.msc).
2. In the **Actions** Pane, select the **Responder Properties** option.
3. In the **Online Responder Properties** window, click on the **Audit** tab.
4. On the **Audit** tab, select all the auditing options and click the **OK** button.
5. Close the **Online Responder Management** console.
6. Restart the **Active Directory Certificate Services** service to apply the changes.

Once auditing has been enabled for the Online Responder role, proceed to adding the OCSP URL to Group Policy for the TFS Labs domain.

Online Responder Role - Add the OCSP URL to Group Policy

Once the Online Responder role has been installed and configured, the URL for OCSP can now be added to the Subordinate CA certificate in Group Policy to ensure that it is deployed to the TFS Labs domain. To add the OCSP URL to Group Policy, perform the following steps on the TFS-DC01 server:

1. Open the **Group Policy Management** console (gpmc.msc) on the **TFS-DC01** server.
2. In the **Group Policy Management** console tree, expand the **Forest: corp.tfslabs.com** folder, expand **Domains**, expand the **corp.tfslabs.com** domain, and then expand the **TFS Labs** OU.
3. Right-click on the **TFS Labs Certificates** GPO and select the **Edit...** option.
4. In the **Group Policy Management Editor** window, open the **Computer Configuration > Policies > Windows Settings > Security Settings > Public Key Policies** node:

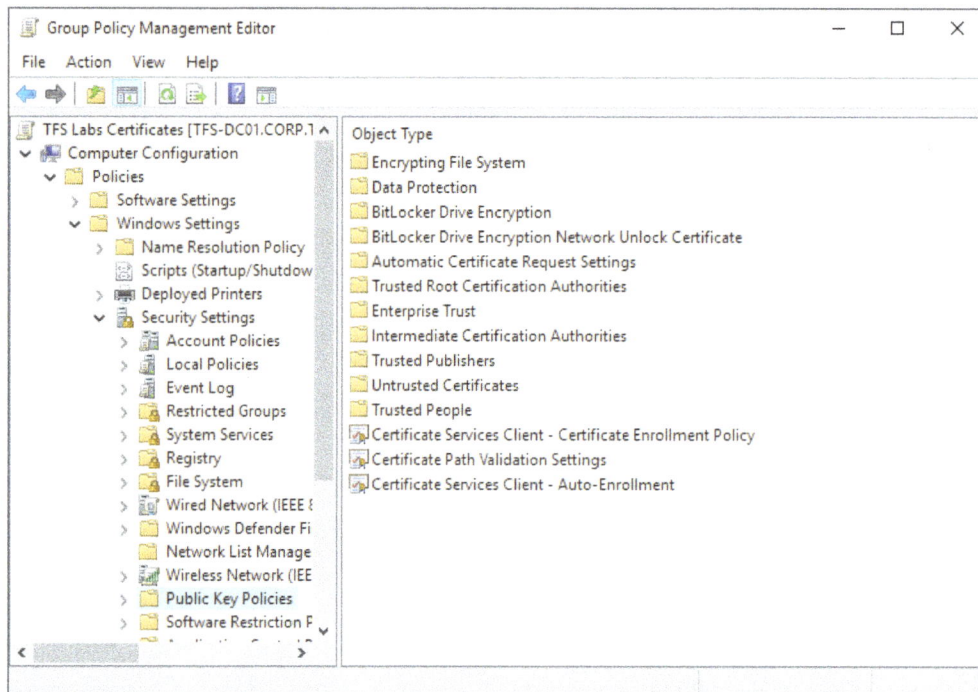

5. Open the **Intermediate Certification Authorities** folder, right-click on the **TFS Labs Enterprise CA** certificate and select **Properties**.
6. In the **TFS Labs Enterprise CA** properties window, click on the **OCSP** tab and in the text field to the right of the **Add URL** button, enter **http://ocsp.corp.tfslabs.com/ocsp** and click the **Add URL** button. Click the **OK** button.
7. Close the **Group Policy Management** console.
8. Restart the **Active Directory Certificate Services** service on the **TFS-CA01** server to apply the changes.

When the OCSP URL has been added to Group Policy, allow up to 90 minutes for the OCSP URL to be deployed to the entire Active Directory domain. Proceed to validating the OCSP configuration on the TFS-CA01 server.

> ### OCSP URL Modifications and Group Policy
>
> The URL for the Online Responder role will differ for every organization. The URL will also rely on internal DNS entries and resolution to ensure that the OCSP services are available. Ensure that this URL is correct when configuring the Group Policy options for the Subordinate CA, and that it is not using HTTPS.
>
> If the Online Responder role is modified in the future, and the same CNAME records are used, then there are no updates required for this section if the role is moved to another server.

Online Responder Role - Verify OCSP Status

Once the Online Responder role has been configured, it is important to verify it is working correctly within the PKI infrastructure for the TFS Labs domain. This can be done by checking the Enterprise PKI console on the TFS-CA01 server:

1. On the **TFS-CA01** server, open the **Enterprise PKI** console (pkiview.msc).
2. Under the **Enterprise PKI** node, click on the **TFS Labs Certificate Authority** server, click on the **TFS Labs Enterprise CA** server and check that the status of **OCSP** is **OK**:

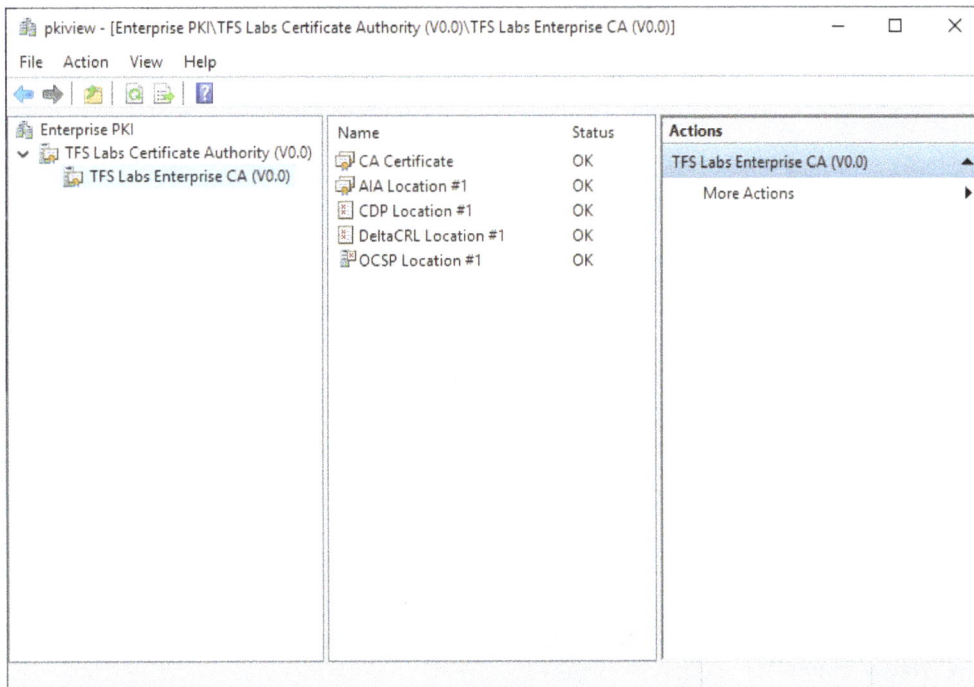

3. Close the **Enterprise PKI** console.

Once the OCSP status has been verified and there are no errors with the Certificate Authority configuration, proceed to checking that there are no issues with the Windows Defender Firewall and connections to OCSP.

OCSP Location Issues

If there is an issue with the OCSP location due to an issue with the **CA Exchange Certificate**, the error would look like this while viewing the Enterprise PKI console for the Subordinate CA:

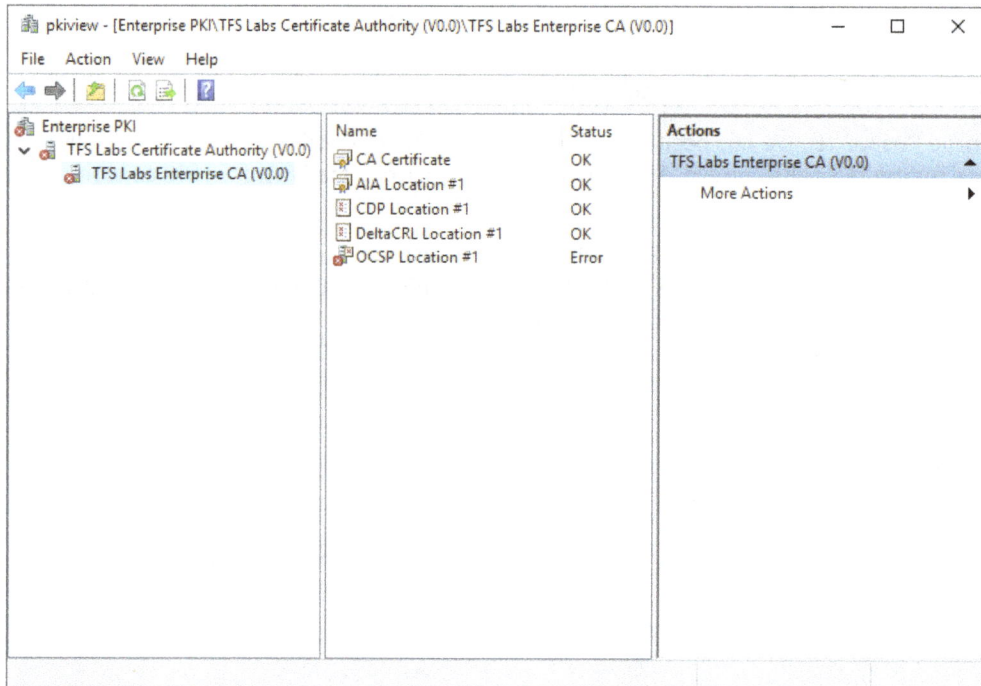

Figure 9.8.1: In this example, the OCSP location is invalid since the Online Responder role was added after several certificates were created. This can be corrected by revoking a certificate and recreating it, as the new certificate will be aware of the correct OCSP location.

To fix the error with the OCSP location, perform the following steps:

1. Open the **Certification Authority** console (certsrv.msc) on the **TFS-CA01** server.
2. Expand the **TFS Labs Enterprise CA** server in the console tree.
3. Under the **Issued Certificates** folder, look for a certificate using the **CA Exchange (CAExchange)** Certificate Template.
4. Right-click on the certificate and select the **All Tasks > Revoke Certificate** option.
5. On the **Certificate Revocation** window, leave the **Reason code** as **Unspecified** and click the **Yes** button to revoke the certificate.
6. Open an **elevated PowerShell prompt** and run the following command request a new certificate:

```
Windows PowerShell (Elevated)

certutil.exe -cainfo xchg
```

7. On the **TFS-CA01** server, open the **Enterprise PKI** console (pkiview.msc). Under the **Enterprise PKI** node, click on the **TFS Labs Certificate Authority**, and then click on the **TFS Labs Enterprise CA** server. The status of **OCSP** should be **OK**.
8. Close the **Enterprise PKI** console.

At this point, the Online Responder role should function correctly when the invalid certificate has been issued, and is in use for OCSP for the domain.

Online Responder Role - Windows Defender Firewall Configuration

The Windows Defender Firewall is always enabled in Windows Server by default, and there are many rules that are enabled by default. The Online Responder role requires certain ports to be open for it to function correctly, and those ports should already be open if steps in previous chapters have been followed. Unlike the configuration of the appropriate rules when the Active Directory Certificate Services role is configured, the Online Responder is an optional role and those rules may be disabled. This is also a factor if the Online Responder role is added to a separate server.

There is only one firewall rule that needs to be enabled on the TFS-CA01 server for the Online Responder role to function correctly:

Firewall Rule Name	Protocol	Ports	Profile
World Wide Web Services (HTTP Traffic-In)	TCP	80	All

Table 9.10.1: Firewall rules that is required for the Online Responder role to function correctly. HTTPS is not required for this role to function, as HTTP is only used for OCSP traffic.

Open an **elevated PowerShell prompt** on the **TFS-CA01** server, and use the **Enable-NetFirewallRule** Cmdlet to enable the appropriate rule to allow for HTTP requests needed for the OCSP role:

```
Windows PowerShell (Elevated)

Enable-NetFirewallRule -DisplayName "World Wide Web Services (HTTP Traffic-In)"
```

Once the Windows Defender Firewall has been correctly configured for the Online Responder role, the configuration for the role has been completed.

Online Responder Role - Test OCSP Connectivity

To verify that the Online Responder role can communicate properly with devices on the TFS Labs domain, a certificate will need to be exported and analyzed through the URL Retrieval Tool. At the same time, the Enterprise CA and CRLs locations can also be verified to ensure that they are accessible for issued certificates on the TFS Labs domain.

> ⚠️ **OCSP Status Result Delay**
>
> This section may not immediately return a positive result, and that is nothing to be concerned about during the deployment of the Certificate Authority. A certificate needs to be issued after the Online Responder role has been configured for the test to work correctly. If this test is performed now, nothing will likely be returned for OCSP. Even though this section is present in this chapter, wait until later in the Certificate Authority deployment to go through these steps. Run this test using the TFS-WIN11 workstation certificate, or with a user certificate once the Active Directory Certificate Services deployment has been completed.

To test the OCSP connectivity, perform the following steps on the TFS-CA01 server:

1. On the **TFS-CA01** server, export the **TFS-WIN11** computer certificate as a **DER Encoded Binary** to the root of the **C:\ drive** (C:\TFS-WIN11.cer).
2. Run the following command in an **elevated PowerShell prompt** to launch the **URL Retrieval Tool**, and load the certificate to be checked:

```
Windows PowerShell (Elevated)

certutil.exe -URL "C:\TFS-WIN11.cer"
```

3. The **URL Retrieval Tool** window will open with the **C:\TFS Labs Enterprise CA.cer** already loaded:

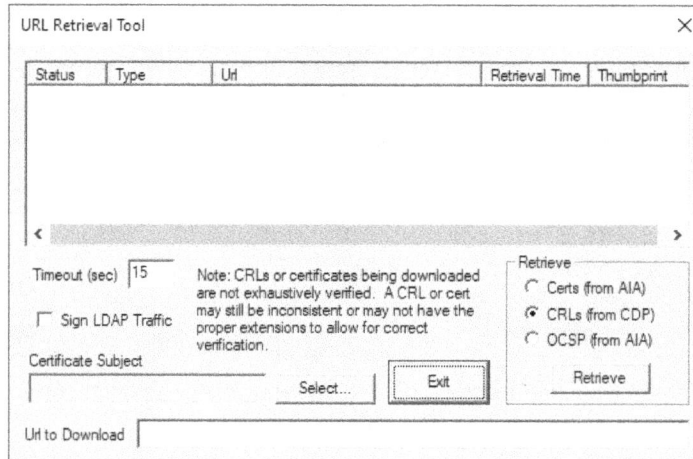

4. In the **Retrieve** pane, select the option for **Certs (from AIA)** and then click the **Retrieve** button. The results that are returned should include the **Enterprise CA** locations with a **Verified** status:

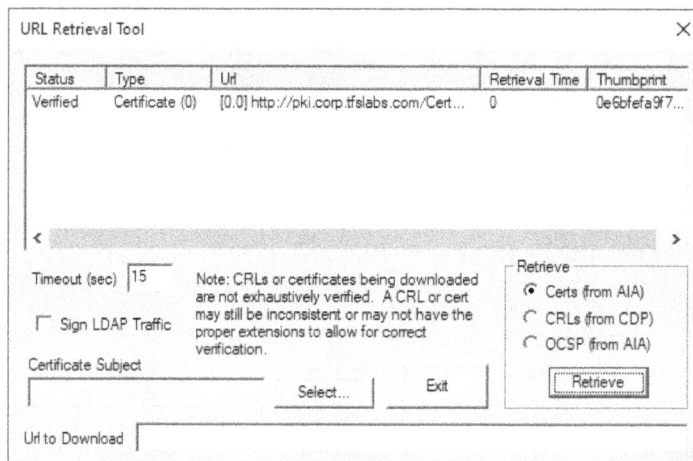

5. In the **Retrieve** pane, select the option for **CRLs (from CDP)** and then click the **Retrieve** button. The results that are returned should include the **Base CRL** and **Delta CRL** locations with a **Verified** status:

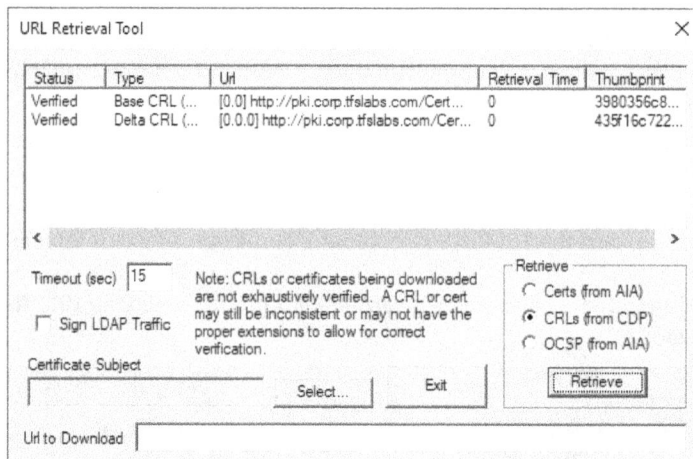

6. In the **Retrieve** pane, select the option for **OCSP (from AIA)** and then click the **Retrieve** button. The result returned should be **(0.0) http://ocsp.corp.tfslabs.com/ocsp** with a **Verified** status:

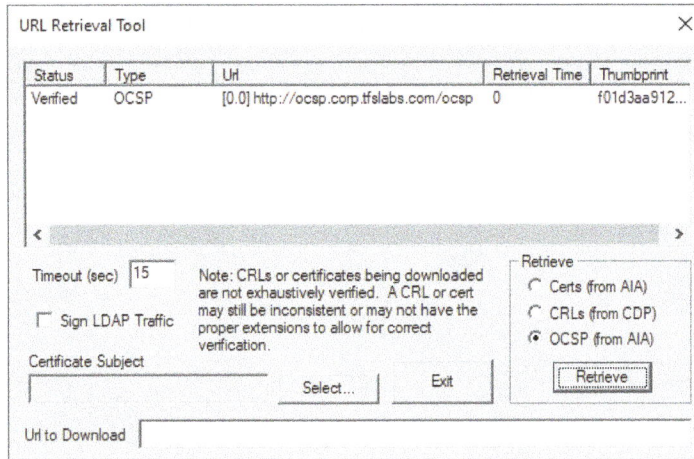

7. Close the **URL Retrieval Tool** window.
8. Delete the **C:\TFS-WIN11.cer** certificate, as it is no longer needed since the test is complete.

Once the test of OCSP connectivity has been completed, the Online Responder role is now functioning correctly for the TFS Labs domain.

Online Responder Role - Chapter Summary

Now that the Online Responder role has been installed and configured, the next step is to configure the Certificate Authority for Private Key Archival in the next chapter.

> **Online Responder Role Limitations**
>
> The Online Responder role does have some limitations and potential issues when it is used within an environment that should be noted. It is important to maintain the Online Responder role to ensure that there are no issues with any services. This means keeping the revocation certificate current and not letting it expire. Having a misconfigured OCSP server can cause several unintended consequences with a Certificate Authority, so always ensure that the server holding the Online Responder role is healthy and functioning properly.

Chapter 10 - Private Key Archive and Recovery

With the use of Active Directory Certificate Services in an Active Directory domain, a lot of enhanced functionality can be utilized that relies on issued certificates for multiple purposes. This enhanced functionality relies on public and private keys always being available for issued certificates, and it is important to ensure the integrity of those keys. If any of the keys are compromised it is an entirely different issue, but losing those keys can cause serious issues.

An important issue to factor in with certificates is to ensure that the private keys are backed up correctly, which most users would typically not understand how to do. It is also not the best policy to have something as important as private key backups managed by a user, as compromising the key can happen easily. Fortunately, this is a straightforward process to automate with Active Directory, and can be performed natively with no third-party software or utilities required in Windows Server.

There are several steps that are required for adding the appropriate Certificate Templates and configurations to the Subordinate CA server to support private key archival:

- Create the Private Key Recovery Agent Certificate Template.
- Deploy the Private Key Recovery Agent Certificate Template.
- Configure the Certificate Authority for private key archival.

This chapter will focus on the setup and deployment of the Certificate Templates needed to enable private key archival. This will allow for the recovery of the private keys for a user if their private key is lost and needs to be recovered.

> **Private Key Archive and Recovery with Active Directory Certificate Services**
>
> This chapter is entirely optional and is not required in every organization. Private key archival is not a critical function to enable for testing purposes, but it is important that private keys for certificates are properly backed in a production environment. Ensure that critical services that depend on certificates have proper backups in place to prevent data loss and downtime.

> **Private Key Archive and Recovery with Third-Party Solutions**
>
> There are third-party solutions that can be used for archiving private keys from Active Directory Certificate Services. There may be differing requirements on how those keys are archived and backed up, and the solution that is present in AD CS may not be sufficient for some organizations. Those solutions and how to use them are beyond the scope of this book.

Private Key Archive and Recovery - Create the Key Recovery Agent Certificate Template

The Key Recovery Agent feature of Active Directory Certificate Services allows for the archival of private keys that are generated by the Certificate Authority. This is specific to the Subordinate CA as it is an Enterprise CA, and this does not apply to the Root CA as it is a Standalone CA. There is a Certificate Template needed to activate the required archival features, and that task can be completed by performing the following steps on the TFS-CA01 server:

1. Open the **Certification Authority** console (certsrv.msc):

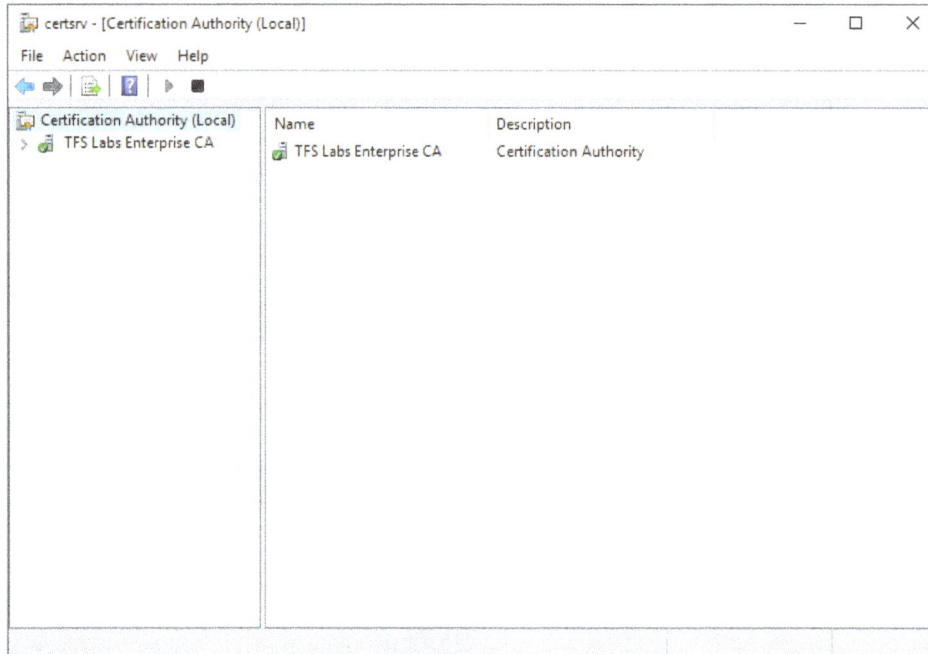

2. Expand the **TFS Labs Enterprise CA** server in the console tree.
3. Right-click on **Certificate Templates** and then click the **Manage** option. The **Certificate Templates** console will open and display the Certificate Templates stored in **Active Directory**:

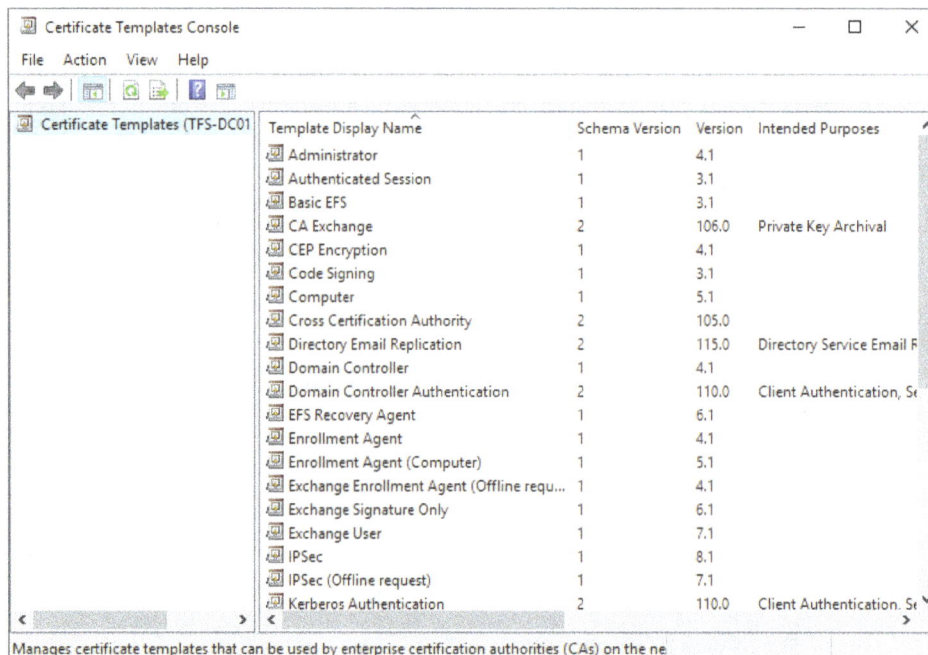

4. In the details pane, search for and then right-click on the **Key Recovery Agent** Certificate Template, and then click **Duplicate Template**:

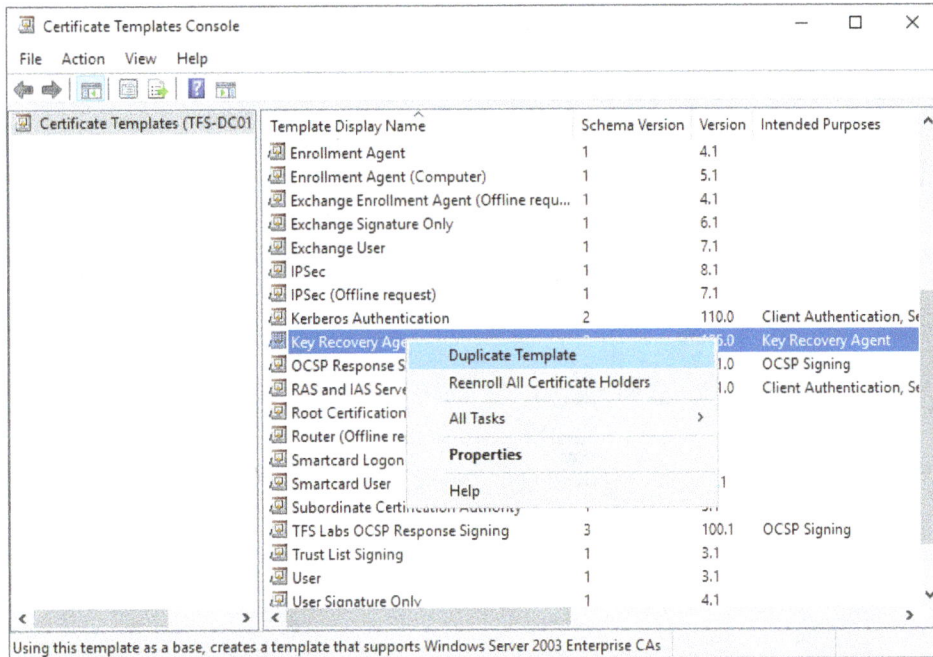

5. The **Properties of New Template** window will open for the **Duplicated Certificate**.
6. On the **Compatibility** tab, make the following changes in the **Compatibility Settings** pane (when the **Resulting changes** window appears for both selections, click the **OK** button to continue):
   - **Certification Authority** - Windows Server 2016
   - **Certificate recipient** - Windows 10 / Windows Server 2016

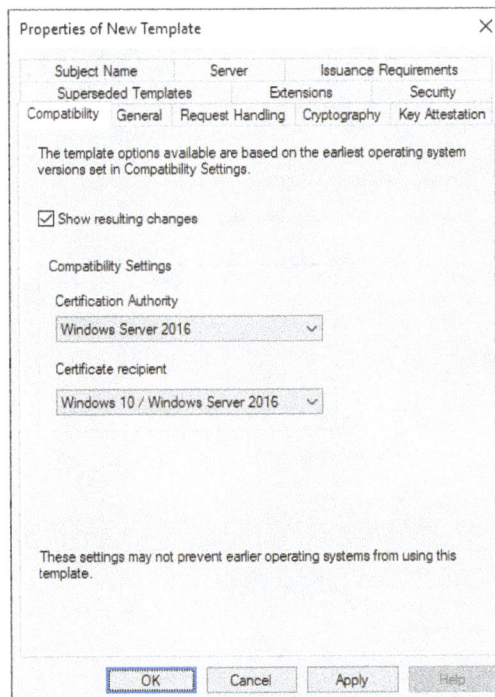

7. On the **Properties of New Template** window, click on the **General** tab. Change the name of the template from **Copy of Key Recovery Agent** to **TFS Labs Key Recovery Agent**. Ensure that the **Validity Period** is set to **1 year**. Also ensure that the option to **Publish certificate in Active Directory** is selected:

8. On the **Issuance Requirements** tab, uncheck the option for **CA certificate manager approval** and ensure that the **The number of authorized signatures** is set to **0**:

9. On the **Cryptography** tab, make the following changes for the **Cryptography** settings:
   - **Provider Category** - Key Storage Provider
   - **Algorithm name** - RSA
   - **Minimum key size** - 4096
   - **Requests can use any provider available on the subject's computer** - Enabled
   - **Request hash** - SHA256

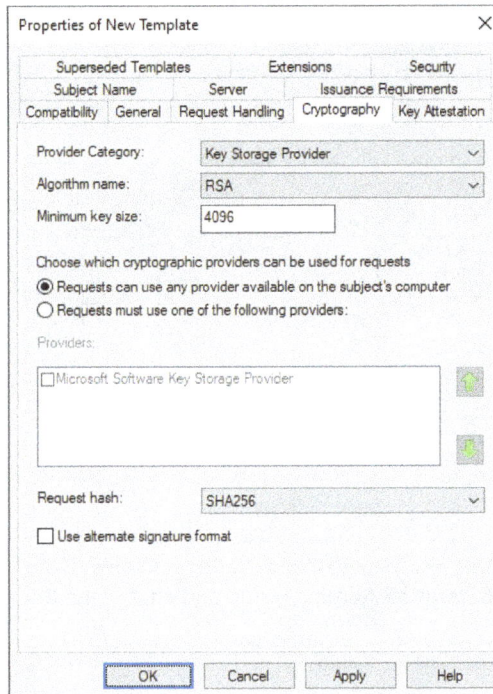

10. On the **Security** tab, verify that **Authenticated Users** group only has the **Read** permission enabled:

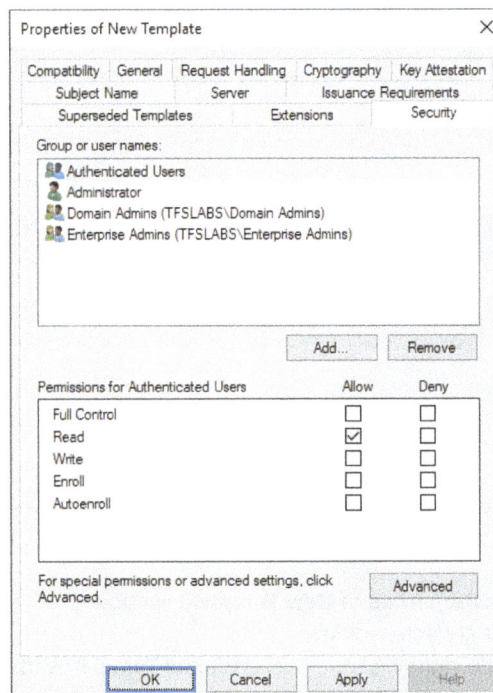

11. On the **Security** tab, select the **Domain Admins** group and enable the **Read**, **Write** and **Enroll** permissions:

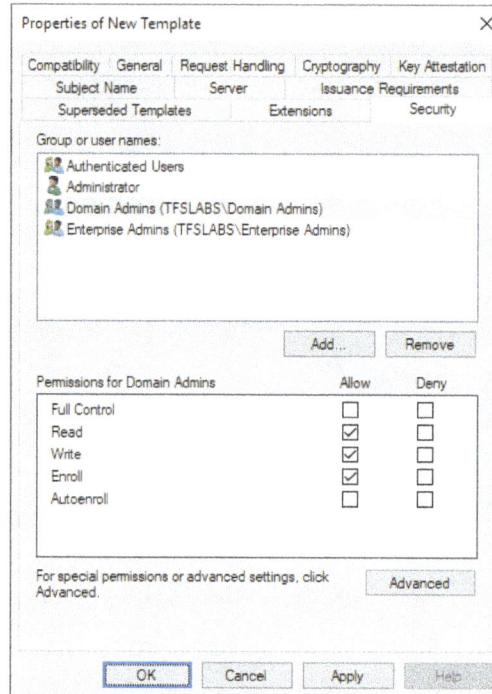

12. On the **Security** tab, select the **Enterprise Admins** group and enable the **Read**, **Write** and **Enroll** permissions:

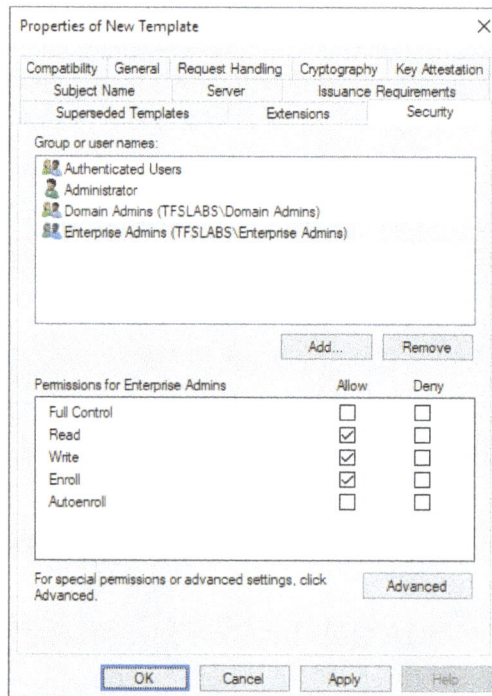

13. Click the **OK** button to close the **Properties of New Template** window.
14. Close the **Certificate Templates** console window.
15. In **Certification Authority** console, right-click on the **Certificate Templates** folder, then select **New** and then select **Certificate Template to Issue**.

16. On the **Enable Certificate Templates** window, select **TFS Labs Key Recovery Agent** and then click **OK**:

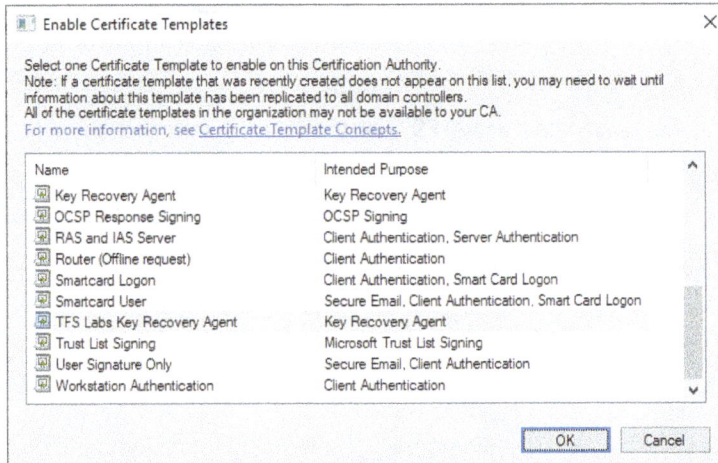

17. The **TFS Labs Key Recovery Agent** Certificate Template should now appear in the **Certificate Templates** folder:

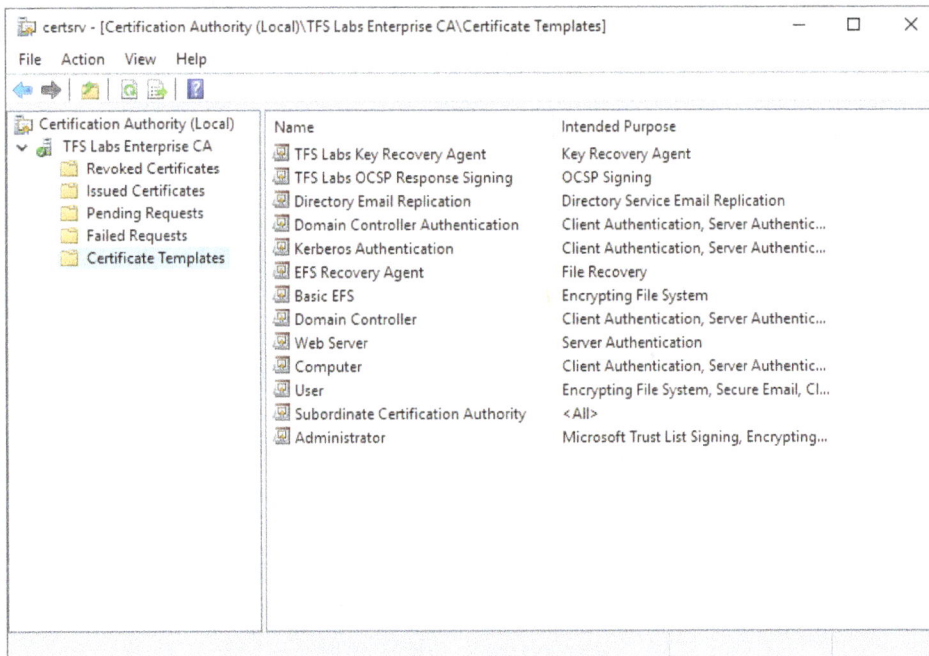

18. Close the **Certification Authority** console.

Once the Key Recovery Agent Certificate Template has been created, it can now be used to create the Key Recovery Agent certificate for the domain. Proceed to the next section for issuing the necessary certificate to the Domain Administrator account for the TFS Labs domain.

Key Recovery Agent Certificate Template Permissions

The Key Recovery Agent Certificate Template is setup with the necessary permissions to allow for Domain Administrator accounts to create and manage the certificate that is used for private key archival. There is no reason for a normal user to ever issue, or need to manage this particular certificate under normal operation. It is also advised in a production Active Directory environment to have a dedicated account for private key recovery tasks, as using the Domain Administrator account is not best practice.

Private Key Archive and Recovery - Deploy the Key Recovery Agent Certificate

Once the Key Recovery Agent Certificate Template has been created, the Key Recovery Agent certificate can now be requested for the Domain Administrator account. This certificate will be used for the private key archival process with Active Directory Certificate Services and Active Directory.

To request a Key Recovery Agent certificate for the TFS Labs Domain Administrator account, perform the following steps on the TFS-CA01 server:

1. On the **TFS-CA01** server, open the **Certificates** console (certmgr.msc) for the **Current User Account**, which should be the **Domain Administrator** account:

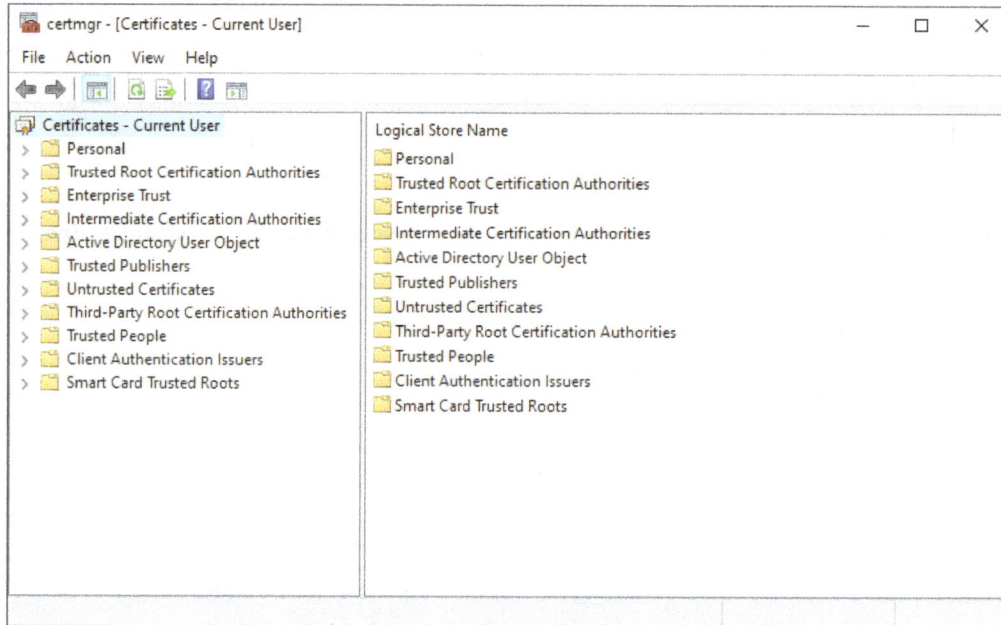

2. Right-click on the **Personal** folder and select the **All Tasks > Request New Certificate** option:

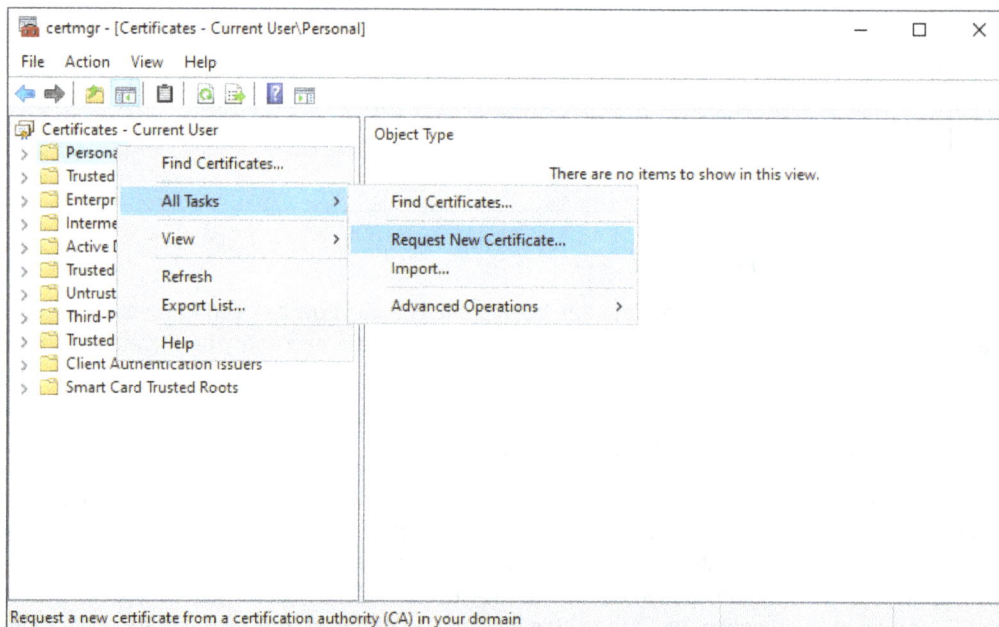

3. On the **Before You Begin** screen, click the **Next** button to continue.
4. On the **Select Certificate Enrollment Policy** screen, the **Active Directory Enrollment Policy** will be automatically selected. Click the **Next** button to continue.
5. On the **Request Certificates** screen, check the box beside the **TFS Labs Key Recovery Agent** certificate and click the **Enroll** button:

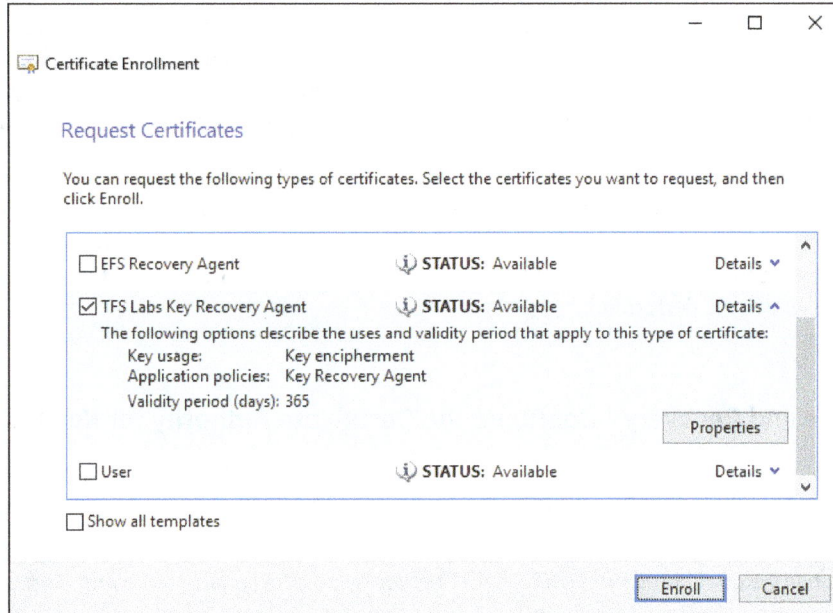

6. On the **Certificate Installation Results** screen, click the **Finish** button.
7. In the **Certificates** console, expand the **Personal** folder and expand the **Certificates** folder. The new **Key Recovery Agent** certificate should be listed in the issued Certificates for the **TFSLABS\Administrator** user:

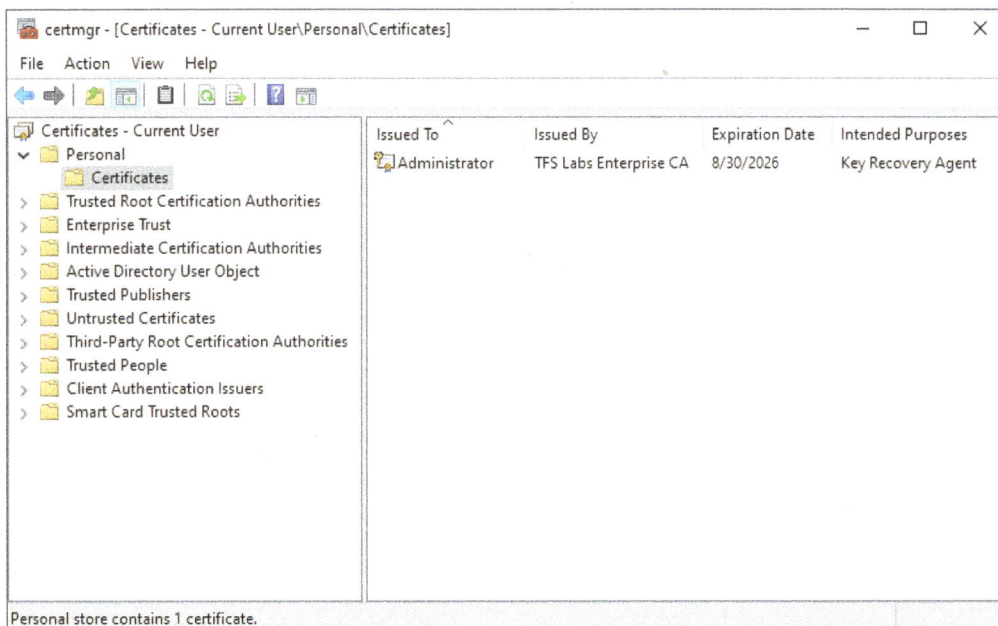

8. Close the **Certificates** console.

Once the Key Recovery Agent certificate has been issued for the Domain Administrator account, proceed to configuring the Certificate Authority to use Key Recovery.

Alternate Account for Key Recovery

It is not advised to setup the Domain Administrator account for the Key Recovery Agent for large organizations, and it is better to use a dedicated account for key recovery if the task of restoring certificates has been delegated to other users in the organization.

Using an alternate administrator account with the correct privileges specifically for this purpose adds an additional layer of security to the Certificate Authority. It also reduces dependency on Domain Administrator accounts, which should not be used for specific tasks such as key recovery. The fewer services that are linked to Domain Administrator accounts reduces dependency on those accounts, as they should not be used for day-to-day activities.

Since key recovery is a critical function of the Certificate Authority, and can be used to retrieve private keys for user accounts, it is advised to provide this capability to as few users as possible. This is also why it is important to enable auditing on the Certificate Authority, as there should be logs present for whenever this activity is performed.

Private Key Archive and Recovery - Configure the Certificate Authority for Key Recovery

The option to archive private keys that are generated by the Subordinate CA will need to be explicitly activated for it work correctly on the Certificate Authority. This requires several configuration changes to the TFS-CA01 server to enable the options.

This recovery options can be configured on the TFS-CA01 server by performing the following steps:

1. Open the **Certification Authority** console (certsrv.msc) on the **TFS-CA01** server.
2. Right-click on the **TFS Labs Enterprise CA** server and select the **Properties** option.
3. In the **TFS Labs Enterprise CA Properties** window, click on the **Recovery Agents** tab.
4. On the **Recovery Agents** tab, select the option to **Archive the Key**. Leave the **Number of recovery agents to use** number set to **1**:

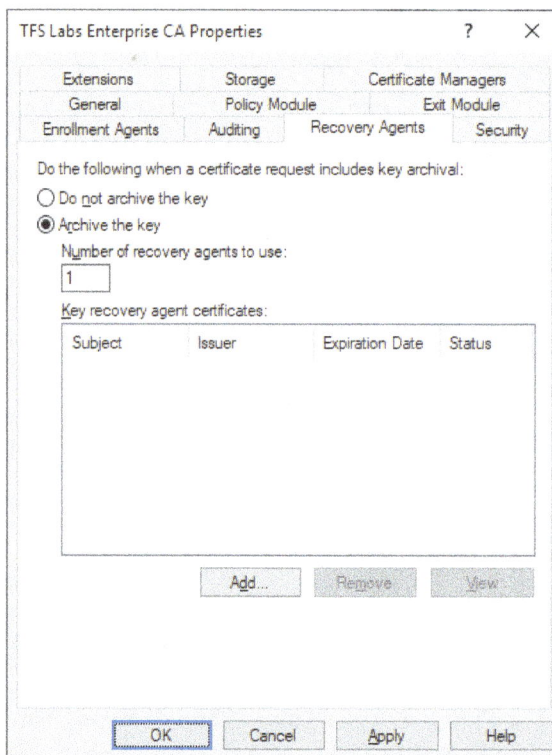

5. On the **Recovery Agents** tab, under the **Key recovery agent certificates** pane, click the **Add...** button and select the **Key Recovery Agent Certificate** that was just requested by clicking the **OK** button:

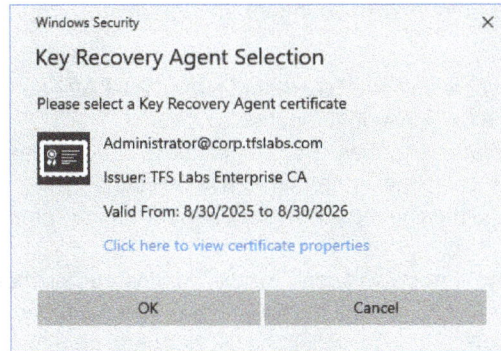

6. On the **Recovery Agents** tab, the **Key recovery agent certificates** pane should now list the **Key Recovery Agent** Certificate (the status will be shown as **Not loaded** until the **Active Directory Certificate Services** service is restarted):

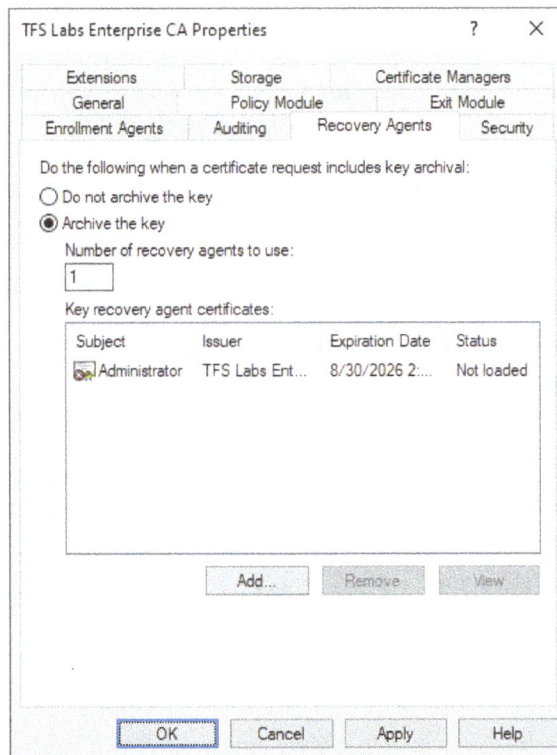

7. Click the **OK** button. When prompted to restart **Active Directory Certificate Services**, click the **Yes** button.
8. Close the **Certification Authority** console.

Once the Certificate Authority has been configured to allow for key archival and recovery, the task of archiving private keys for issued certificates has been completed.

> ⚠️ **Valid Key Recovery Agent Certificate**
>
> It is important to ensure that the Key Recovery Agent certificate remains valid to ensure that there are no issues with private key archival. Ensure that this certificate is kept active and that if it expires, it is immediately renewed to allow key archival to continue.

Private Key Archive and Recovery - Configure the Certificate Template for Key Archival

Now that the Certificate Authority has been configured for key archival, the required certificate can now be published to Active Directory and the Certificate Authority. To configure the Certificate Template for key archival, perform the following steps on the TFS-CA01 server:

1. Open the **Certification Authority** console (certsrv.msc) on the **TFS-CA01** server.
2. Expand the **TFS Labs Enterprise CA** server in the console tree.
3. Right-click on **Certificate Templates** and then click the **Manage** option. The **Certificate Templates** console will open and display the Certificate Templates stored in **Active Directory**.
4. In the details pane, search for and then right-click on the **User** Certificate Template, and then click on the **Duplicate Template** option.
5. The **Properties of New Template** window will open for the **Duplicated Certificate**.
6. On the **Compatibility** tab, make the following changes in the **Compatibility Settings** pane (when the **Resulting changes** window appears for both selections, click the **OK** button to continue):
   - **Certification Authority** - Windows Server 2016
   - **Certificate recipient** - Windows 10 / Windows Server 2016
7. On the **Properties of New Template** window, click on the **General** tab. Change the name of the template from **Copy of User** to **TFS Labs Key Archive**. Ensure that the **Validity Period** is set to **1 year**. Also ensure that the option to **Publish certificate in Active Directory** is selected.
8. On the **Subject Name** tab, uncheck the options for **Include e-mail name in the subject name** and the **E-mail name** from the Active Directory settings.
9. On the **Request Handling** tab, select the option for **Archive subject's encryption private key**. When the **Changing Key Archival Property** box opens, click the **OK** button to continue.
10. On the **Cryptography** tab, make the following changes for the **Cryptography** settings:
    - **Provider Category** - Key Storage Provider
    - **Algorithm name** - RSA
    - **Minimum key size** - 4096
    - **Requests can use any provider available on the subject's computer** - Enabled
    - **Request hash** - SHA256
11. Click the **OK** button to close the Certificate Template window.
12. Close the **Certificate Templates** console window.
13. In **Certification Authority** console, right-click on the **Certificate Templates** folder, then select **New** and then select **Certificate Template to Issue**.
14. On the **Enable Certificate Templates** window, select **TFS Labs Key Archive** and then click **OK**.
15. The **TFS Labs Key Recovery Agent** Certificate Template should now appear in the **Certificate Templates** folder.
16. Close the **Certification Authority** console.

Now that the necessary Certificate Templates have been created for key archival purposes, and the certificate has been deployed to the TFS Labs domain, restoring a private key can now be tested on the domain.

Private Key Archive and Recovery - Restore a Private Key

It is entirely possible that a user will lose their private key at some point after it has been issued, and it not necessarily their fault. The private key can be lost when a user's workstation is replaced or re-imaged, and the key is not always backed up prior to this. In most cases it should not be the responsibility of the user to manage their private key, and it should be automated when possible using Active Directory Certificate Services. Most of the time, a user could just request a new user certificate from the Certificate Authority, but that could cause the following issues when existing items have already been attached to that private key:

- Encrypted email could be lost.
- Encrypted files could become inaccessible.
- VPN authentication could be interrupted.

By setting up private key archive and private key recovery in this previous chapter, Certificate Templates that are configured with the archive option will have their private keys automatically archived. It is a straightforward process to recover a private key should it ever need to be restored for a user account.

> **⚠ Restore a User Account Private Key**
>
> At this stage of the Certificate Authority implementation, there should not be any certificates issued to any users in the TFS Labs domain. The next few chapters focuses on creating Certificate Templates for this purpose, and deploying those templates for users. When a certificate has been issued for a user, return to this section to test the process for recovering a private key for a user account.

In this example, the private key for the **Mary Smith** account that was created in an earlier chapter will be retrieved from the private key archive. As a prerequisite, the account will need to login to the TFS-WIN11 workstation to create the certificate after the appropriate Certificate Template has been created.

To restore a private key for a user account, perform the following steps on the TFS-CA01 server:

1. On the root of the **C:\ drive**, create a folder called **CertRecovery** (C:\CertRecovery).
2. Open **Certification Authority** console (certsrv.msc).
3. Expand the **TFS Labs Enterprise CA** console tree and select the **Issued Certificates** folder.
4. Find the **User Certificate** that the private key is going to be recovered from (**TFSLABS\msmith**), right-click on it, and select **Open**.
5. On the **Certificate** window, go to the **Details** tab.
6. Find the **Serial number** field, which contains the 38-digit alphanumeric serial number for the certificate:

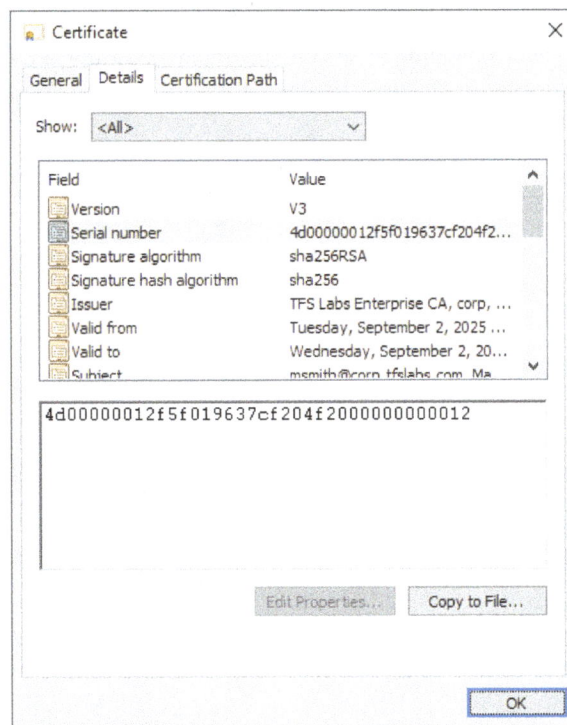

7. Open an **elevated PowerShell prompt**.
8. Change to the **C:\CertRecovery** directory.
9. Run the following command to retrieve the user certificate and private key (insert the correct serial number and the outputted file name):

```
Windows PowerShell (Elevated)

certutil.exe -getkey 4d00000012f5f019637cf204f2000000000012 msmith
```

10. Run the following command to recover the private key for the certificate (insert the file name with a **.PFX** extension). A prompt will ask to enter a password which will be used to import the certificate:

```
Windows PowerShell (Elevated)

certutil.exe -recoverkey .\msmith msmith.pfx
```

11. Once the certificate has been exported, close the **PowerShell prompt**.

The outputted PFX file will contain the public and private keys for the user's certificate, as well as the Root and Subordinate certificates for the domain. A user can install the certificate in the Personal Store for their user account to make their private key available again for usage. Once this task has been completed, there should be no issues with the private key.

> ⚠️ **User Private Key Security**
>
> Ensure that outputted certificates are kept safe and secure as it contains the private key for the user account that was recovered. If possible, try and avoid sending the recovered certificate through email and use more secure manners for transmission.

Private Key Archive and Recovery - Chapter Summary

Now that the key archival and recovery configuration has been completed for the TFS Labs domain, proceed to configuring custom Certificate Templates in the next chapter.

Chapter 11 - Certificate Templates

Active Directory Certificate Services provides multiple default Certificate Templates that are available for use within a domain. Most of these default Certificate Templates are completely adequate and would work well in most organizations, but they can sometimes require some additional customization from the default settings to ensure the greatest compatibility in an environment.

By creating custom Certificate Templates for an Active Directory domain, this will ensure that the security settings for issued certificates are correct, and that the correct servers can manage those certificates. There are also additional Certificate Templates present by default which can be deleted if they are not required as it is good practice to delete them.

This chapter will focus on the modification and deployment of various Certificate Templates for AD CS. There will also be a focus on how to modify those Certificate Templates to follow the best security practices, as well and modifying them to work with automatic deployment of certificates.

> **Certificate Template Customizations**
>
> This chapter is entirely optional and is not required in every organization. Creating custom Certificate Templates for an organization does have some advantages over the default ones that are provided with a default Active Directory Certificate Services installation. Unless an organization is going to take advantage of any certificate customizations, there is no reason to create them if it is not necessary.

> **Certificate Templates and Active Directory Security Issues**
>
> There are several things to consider when creating Certificate Templates with Active Directory Certificate Services. While Certificate Templates are convenient, if they are improperly configured they can introduce security issues into a domain.
>
> For example, incorrect permissions on a Certificate Template could allow a certificate meant for administrative tasks to be issued to a regular user account. While this may not seem like a major issue, it could compromise the integrity of the Certificate Authority if a Subordinate CA certificate is accidentally issued to a device that does not support it or is not directly controlled by the administrators of the Active Directory domain.

Certificate Templates - Active Directory Certificate Templates

Active Directory Certificate Services provides over 30 Certificate Templates which are available for use within an environment.

These are the Certificate Templates that are available by default with Windows Server 2022, all with different purposes:

Administrator	EFS Recovery Agent	RAS and IAS Server
Authenticated Session	Enrollment Agent	Root Certification Authority
Basic EFS	Enrollment Agent (Computer)	Router
CA Exchange	Exchange Enrollment Agent	Smartcard Logon
CEP Encryption	Exchange Signature Only	Smartcard User
Code Signing	Exchange User	Subordinate Certification Authority
Computer	IPSec	Trust List Signing
Cross Certification Authority	IPSec	**User**
Directory Email Replication	Kerberos Authentication	User Signature Only
Domain Controller	Key Recovery Agent	**Web Server**
Domain Controller Authentication	OCSP Response Signing	Workstation Authentication

Table 11.1.1: Certificate Templates that are available by default with Active Directory Certificate Services. These templates can all be duplicated and modified as required for an organization. The highlighted Certificate Templates will be optionally configured later in this chapter.

The default Certificate Templates are available for usage and can be customized to fit the needs of an organization. Certificate Templates are published in Active Directory, which allows for greater ease of certificate deployment within an organization, which is one of the key benefits of Active Directory Certificate Services. Even though these are the default Certificate Templates, there is no reason why custom Certificate Templates cannot be created.

There are a several best practices that should be followed when dealing with Certificate Templates, which includes :

- Always duplicate existing Certificate Templates and then modify the duplicate Certificate Template accordingly. Some of the default templates can be modified without duplicating them, but this is not a recommended way to modify Certificate Templates.
- Always use descriptive names for custom Certificate Templates and ensure that it is different from the Certificate Template that was duplicated. If the name is too similar to the default Certificate Template, it can be easy to confuse which templates are default, and which ones are duplicated.
- Always confirm the security settings when configuring a Certificate Template. Ensure that the correct permissions are assigned to the Certificate Template, and that the intended behaviour will be correct once it has been published and used in the organization.
- When publishing a Certificate Template to Active Directory, ensure that the correct users or groups have access to that Certificate Template. Do not allow anyone in an organization to request a certificate if they should not be allowed to.
- For important Certificates Templates, do not allow those templates to be enrolled automatically. Important certificates should require an administrator to request and issue them. Those certificates should then be validated after they are issued to ensure they are valid.
- Only ever publish Certificate Templates that intend to be used within an organization. Never publish Certificate Templates if there is no intention of using them. This also applies to any of the default Certificate Templates that are present, and they should be removed if they are not going to be used.
- When a Certificate Template is no longer required, it should be deleted from the list of available templates. Never keep Certificate Templates available to be issued if they are obsolete.

For the TFS Labs domain, the following Certificate Templates will be created and published so that they can be utilized by users, workstations, and servers on the domain:

Certificate Template Name	Default Certificate Template	Security Options
TFS Labs User Certificate	User	TFS-CA01 (Read, Enroll) Domain Users (Read, Enroll, Autoenroll)
TFS Labs Computer Certificate	Computer	TFS-CA01 (Read, Enroll) Domain Computers (Read, Enroll, Autoenroll)
TFS Labs Web Server Certificate	Web Server	TFS-CA01 (Read, Enroll) Domain Admins (Read, Enroll, Autoenroll)

Table 11.1.2: TFS Labs Certificate Templates that will be created using the default Certificate Templates and customized to ensure that they have the correct security options for the domain.

These Certificate Templates will be used to issue certificates to the TFS Labs domain. Some of these certificates will be issued automatically using Group Policy, and the other certificates can be requested by users as needed. The procedure for creating these Certificate Templates is mostly the same, and only requires slight modifications from the default settings for them to work for the TFS Labs domain.

When working with Certificate Templates there are several compatibility settings that need to be factored in for an environment. In Active Directory Certificate Services there are two types of compatibility settings that can be modified, and that is the certificate authority and the certificate recipient settings.

For the Certification Authority settings, there are six options for what the minimum level of support is:

- Windows Server 2003
- Windows Server 2008
- Windows Server 2008 R2
- Windows Server 2012
- Windows Server 2012 R2
- Windows Server 2016

For the certificate recipient settings, there are six options for what the minimum level of support is:

- Windows XP / Server 2003
- Windows Vista / Server 2008
- Windows 7 / Server 2008 R2
- Windows 8 / Windows Server 2012
- Windows 8.1 / Windows Server 2012 R2
- Windows 10 / Windows Server 2016

Now that the options for creating custom Certificate Templates have been reviewed, proceed to creating the custom Certificate Template for user accounts for the TFS Labs domain.

Certificate Templates and Windows Compatibility

Typically, it is best practice to support the previous major operating system version to ensure that there are no issues within an environment. For example, if an Active Directory environment is primarily using Windows Server 2022 and Windows 11, then Windows Server 2019 and Windows 10 (or equivalent) should also be supported to ensure the greatest compatibility in the network.

Since this book only focuses on the latest versions of Windows Server, and is just for demonstration purposes, only the highest compatibility settings are used.

Certificate Templates - User Certificate Template Creation

The purpose of the user Certificate Template is primarily to provide signature and encryption capabilities on a user level that is not necessarily tied to a particular workstation. Some of the main uses of a user Certificate Template include:

- 802.1X authentication
- Email signing
- File encryption
- VPN authentication

Since user certificates are used for critical purposes that can effectively lock a user out of important data, it is strongly advised that these certificates utilize a Key Recovery Agent that was setup in the previous chapter. To create the user Certificate Template, which can be automatically issued later and enrolled, perform the following steps on the TFS-CA01 server:

1. Open the **Certification Authority** console (certsrv.msc) on the **TFS-CA01** server.
2. Expand the **TFS Labs Enterprise CA** console tree and select the **Certificate Templates** folder.
3. Right-click on the **Certificate Templates** and select the **Manage** option.
4. In the **Certificate Templates** window, right-click on the **User** Certificate Template and then click **Duplicate Template**.
5. The **Properties of New Template** window will open for the **Duplicated Certificate**.
6. On the **Compatibility** tab, make the following changes in the **Compatibility Settings** pane (when the **Resulting changes** window appears, click the **OK** button to continue):
    - **Certification Authority** - Windows Server 2016
    - **Certificate recipient** - Windows 10 / Windows Server 2016
7. On the **Properties of New Template** window, click on the **General** tab. Make the following changes to the **Certificate Template** if needed:
    - **Template display name** - TFS Labs User Certificate
    - **Validity period** - 1 Year
    - **Renewal period** - 6 Weeks
    - **Publish certificate in Active Directory** - Enabled
    - **Do not automatically reenroll if a duplicate certificate exists in Active Directory** - Enabled
8. On the **Request Handling** tab, make the following changes for the request handling settings (if prompted, click **OK** to continue):
    - **Purpose** - Signature and encryption
    - **Include symmetric algorithms allowed by the subject** - Enabled
    - **Archive subject's encryption private key** - Enabled
    - **Allow private key to be exported** - Enabled
    - **Renew with the same key** - Enabled
9. On the **Cryptography** tab, make the following changes for the **Cryptography** settings:
    - **Provider Category** - Key Storage Provider
    - **Algorithm name** - RSA
    - **Minimum key size** - 4096
    - **Request hash** - SHA256
10. On the **Security** tab, click the **Add...** button, and then add the **TFS-CA01** server. Assign the **Read** and the **Enroll** permissions.
11. On the **Security** tab, select the **Domain Users** group and assign the **Read**, **Enroll** and **Autoenroll** permissions.
12. Click the **OK** button to close the **Properties of New Template** window.
13. Close the **Certificate Templates** console window.
14. In the **Certification Authority** console, right-click on **Certificate Templates**, then select **New** and then select **Certificate Template to Issue**.
15. In the **Enable Certificate Templates** dialog box, click **TFS Labs User Certificate** and then click **OK**.
16. The **TFS Labs User Certificate** should now be listed in the available Certificates for the **TFS Labs** domain.
17. Close the **Certification Authority** console.

The user Certificate Template is now ready to be utilized on the TFS Labs domain and can be requested manually by users, or enrolled automatically if that option is enabled in Group Policy.

Server Object Security Permissions

There are a few extra steps required for adding server and computer objects to the security settings, as those objects are not searchable by default. To be able to add a server object, perform the following steps to be able to search for those objects:

1. On the **Security** tab, click the **Add...** button.
2. In the **Select Users, Computers, Service Accounts, or Groups** window, click the **Object Types...** button.
3. In the **Object Types** window, select the option for **Computers** and click the **OK** button.
4. In the **Enter the object names to select** field, enter the **TFS-CA01** server, and click the **Check Names** button.
5. Click the **OK** button to finish adding the server object.

Once these steps have been completed, the server object should be a configurable option while configuring the security options for Certificate Templates.

This extra step is required since these options are not enabled by default, and those options are configured every time a change is made to the security settings for server objects.

User Certificate Template Limitations

Ensure that the user has their email address entered into their user account details in Active Directory, otherwise this certificate will not deploy correctly to their account.

If the email address is missing in the Active Directory user object, this error will appear when attempting to issue the certificate:

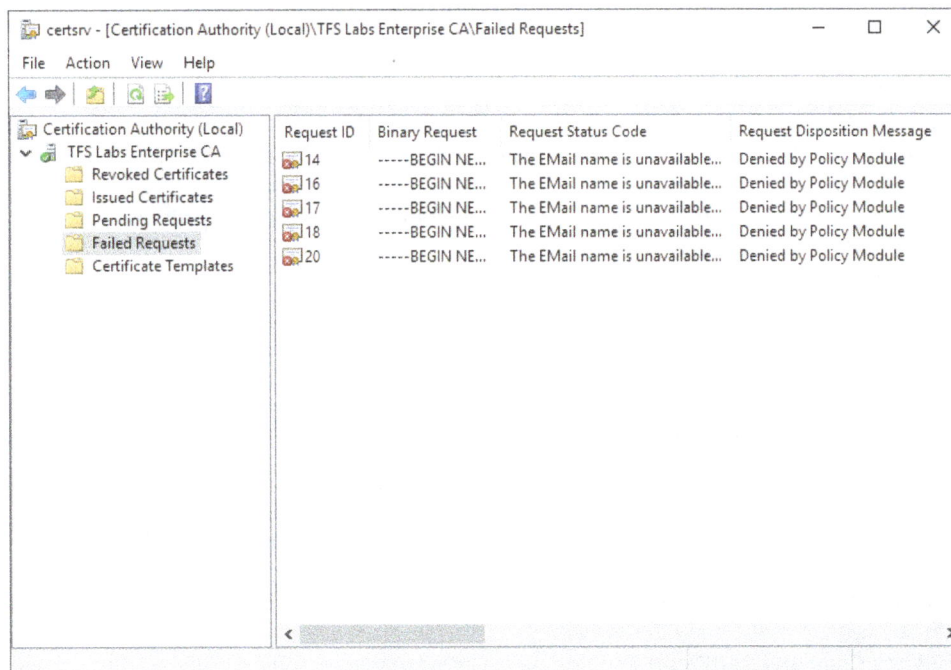

Once the email address is entered for the affected user accounts, the certificate should then be able to be issued correctly by re-requesting the certificate.

Certificate Templates - Computer Certificate Template Creation

The purpose of the computer Certificate Template is like the user Certificate Template, but it is primarily used to provide authentication capabilities to the workstation. Some of the main uses of a computer Certificate Template include:

- 802.1X authentication
- Authentication for MDM or workstation management
- Full disk encryption
- Pre-logon VPN authentication

The computer Certificate Template typically works independently of the user Certificate Template, and the user on a particular workstation is usually unaware that it is being used. There are some features within the Windows operating system which work without requiring any information or input from the user, and this is usually the case with Active Directory domains with advanced security or authentication features. To create the computer Certificate Template, which can be automatically issued later and enrolled using Group Policy, perform the following steps on the TFS-CA01 server:

1. Open the **Certification Authority** console (certsrv.msc) on the **TFS-CA01** server.
2. Expand the **TFS Labs Enterprise CA** console tree and select the **Certificate Templates** folder.
3. Right-click on the **Certificate Templates** and select the **Manage** option.
4. In the **Certificate Templates** window, right-click on the **Computer** Certificate Template and then click **Duplicate Template**.
5. The **Properties of New Template** window will open for the **Duplicated Certificate**.
6. On the **Compatibility** tab, make the following changes in the **Compatibility Settings** pane (when the **Resulting changes** window appears, click the **OK** button to continue):
   - **Certification Authority** - Windows Server 2016
   - **Certificate recipient** - Windows 10 / Windows Server 2016
7. On the **Properties of New Template** window, click on the **General** tab. Make the following changes to the **Certificate Template** if needed:
   - **Template display name** - TFS Labs Computer Certificate
   - **Validity period** - 1 Year
   - **Renewal period** - 6 Weeks
   - **Publish certificate in Active Directory** - Enabled
   - **Do not automatically reenroll if a duplicate certificate exists** - Disabled
8. On the **Request Handling** tab, make the following changes for the request handling settings:
   - **Purpose** - Signature and encryption
9. On the **Cryptography** tab, make the following changes for the **Cryptography** settings:
   - **Provider Category** - Key Storage Provider
   - **Algorithm name** - RSA
   - **Minimum key size** - 4096
   - **Request hash** - SHA256
10. On the **Security** tab, click the **Add...** button, and then add the **TFS-CA01** server. Assign the **Read** and the **Enroll** permissions.
11. On the **Security** tab, select the **Domain Computers** group and assign the **Read, Enroll** and **Autoenroll** permissions.
12. Click the **OK** button to close the **Properties of New Template** window.
13. Close the **Certificate Templates** console window.
14. In the **Certification Authority** console, right-click on **Certificate Templates**, then select **New** and then select **Certificate Template to Issue**.
15. In the **Enable Certificate Templates** dialog box, click **TFS Labs Computer Certificate**, and then click the **OK** button to continue.
16. The **TFS Labs Computer Certificate** should now be listed in the available Certificate Templates for the **TFS Labs** domain.
17. Close the **Certification Authority** console.

The computer Certificate Template is now ready to be utilized on the TFS Labs domain, and can be requested manually or enrolled automatically for workstations or servers using Group Policy.

Certificate Templates - Web Server Certificate Template Creation

The web server Certificate Template only requires minor changes to make it deployable in the TFS Labs domain, and most of those changes are related to the security settings of the Certificate Template. This Certificate Template will be available on the Active Directory Certificate Services Web Enrollment website and in the Certificate Authority, which will allow users to submit a Certificate Request to the Enterprise CA to have it issued. To create the web server Certificate Template for the TFS Labs domain, perform the following steps on the TFS-CA01 server:

1. Open the **Certification Authority** console (certsrv.msc) on the **TFS-CA01** server.
2. Expand the **TFS Labs Enterprise CA** console tree and select the **Certificate Templates** folder.
3. Right-click on the **Certificate Templates** and select the **Manage** option.
4. In the **Certificate Templates** window, right-click on the **Web Server** Certificate Template and then click **Duplicate Template**.
5. The **Properties of New Template** window will open for the **Duplicated Certificate**.
6. On the **Compatibility** tab, make the following changes in the **Compatibility Settings** pane (when the **Resulting changes** window appears, click the **OK** button to continue):
   - **Certification Authority** - Windows Server 2016
   - **Certificate recipient** - Windows 7 / Windows Server 2008 R2
7. On the **Properties of New Template** window, click on the **General** tab. Make the following changes to the **Certificate Template** if needed:
   - **Template display name** - TFS Labs Web Server Certificate
   - **Validity period** - 1 Year
   - **Renewal period** - 6 Weeks
   - **Publish certificate in Active Directory** - Disabled
   - **Do not automatically reenroll if a duplicate certificate exists in Active Directory** - Disabled
8. On the **Request Handling** tab, make these changes for the request handling settings:
   - **Purpose** - Signature and encryption
9. On the **Cryptography** tab, make the following changes for the **Cryptography** settings:
   - **Provider Category** - Legacy Cryptographic Service Provider
   - **Algorithm name** - Determined by CSP
   - **Minimum key size** - 2048
10. On the **Security** tab, click the **Add...** button, and then add the **TFS-CA01** server. Assign the **Read** and the **Enroll** permissions for the certificate.
11. On the **Security** tab, select the **Domain Admins** group and assign the **Read, Write, Enroll** and **Autoenroll** permissions.
12. Click the **OK** button to close the **Properties of New Template** window.
13. Close the **Certificate Templates** console window.
14. In the **Certification Authority** console, right-click on **Certificate Templates**, then select **New** and then select **Certificate Template to Issue**.
15. In the **Enable Certificate Templates** dialog box, click on the **TFS Labs Web Server Certificate**, and then click **OK** to continue.
16. The **TFS Labs Web Server Certificate** should now be listed in the available certificates that are available for the **TFS Labs** domain.
17. Close the **Certification Authority** console.

The web server Certificate Template is now ready to be utilized on the TFS Labs domain, and can be requested by authenticated users when it is required.

Web Server Certificate Template Cryptography Options

The settings for a web server Certificate Template are slightly different from the previously configured certificates, and this is due to those certificates being used primarily in a Windows environment. A web server certificate requires less strict settings to maximize the compatibility between the most devices where the website will be used, and which web browsers are used to access websites that use the certificates. Some settings are intentionally relaxed to ensure the maximum compatibility with other devices that may be using the certificate.

Certificate Templates - Delete Unnecessary Certificate Templates

There are several Certificate Templates that are present in the Certificate Templates folder that should be removed prior to a Certificate Authority going into production. These Certificate Templates are not necessarily needed as they were included by default with Active Directory Certificate Services and may not be needed for all Active Directory environments. For example, the Subordinate Certification Authority Certificate Template should never be available on a production Certificate Authority since it can potentially cause security issues. Other Certificate Templates provide some overlap with the customized Certificate Templates that were previously configured and can cause support issues should users utilize the incorrect Certificate Templates.

The Certificate Templates that were present at the beginning of the TFS Labs Certificate Authority deployment and at the end of the deployment are listed below:

Certificate Template	AD CS Default	TFS Labs Domain
Administrator	Yes	Yes
Basic EFS	Yes	No
Computer	Yes	No
Directory E-mail Replication	Yes	Yes
Domain Controller	Yes	Yes
Domain Controller Authentication	Yes	Yes
EFS Recovery Agent	Yes	No
Kerberos Authentication	Yes	Yes
User	Yes	No
Web Server	Yes	No
Subordinate Certification Authority	Yes	No
TFS Labs Computer Certificate	No	Yes
TFS Labs Key Archive	No	Yes
TFS Labs Key Recovery Agent	No	Yes
TFS Labs OCSP Response Signing	No	Yes
TFS Labs User Certificate	No	Yes
TFS Labs Web Server Certificate	No	Yes

Table 11.5.1: Certificate Templates that are available in the TFS Labs domain at the end of the steps completed so far in this chapter. There are several Certificate Templates that are not required for normal operation of the Certificate Authority and can be safely removed.

Some of the default Certificate Templates, such as Domain Controller or Kerberos Authentication, should not be modified unless there is a good reason to make modifications to those Certificate Templates. These Certificate Templates are needed for secure information exchange between workstations and servers to Domain Controllers, so they must be present for that functionality to operate correctly. To remove the unnecessary Certificate Templates that are present in the TFS Labs domain, perform the following steps on the TFS-CA01 server:

1. Open the **Certification Authority** console (certsrv.msc).
2. Expand the **TFS Labs Enterprise CA** console tree and select the **Certificate Templates** folder.
3. Right-click on the following **Certificate Templates** and select the **Delete** option (if they exist). When prompted in the **Disable certificate templates** dialog box, select the **Yes** option.
   - **Basic EFS**
   - **Computer**
   - **EFS Recovery Agent**
   - **Subordinate Certification Authority**
   - **User**
   - **Web Server**
4. The deleted **Certificate Templates** should no longer be listed in the available certificates for the **TFS Labs** domain, and the **TFS Labs Certificate Templates** that have been created should all be listed:

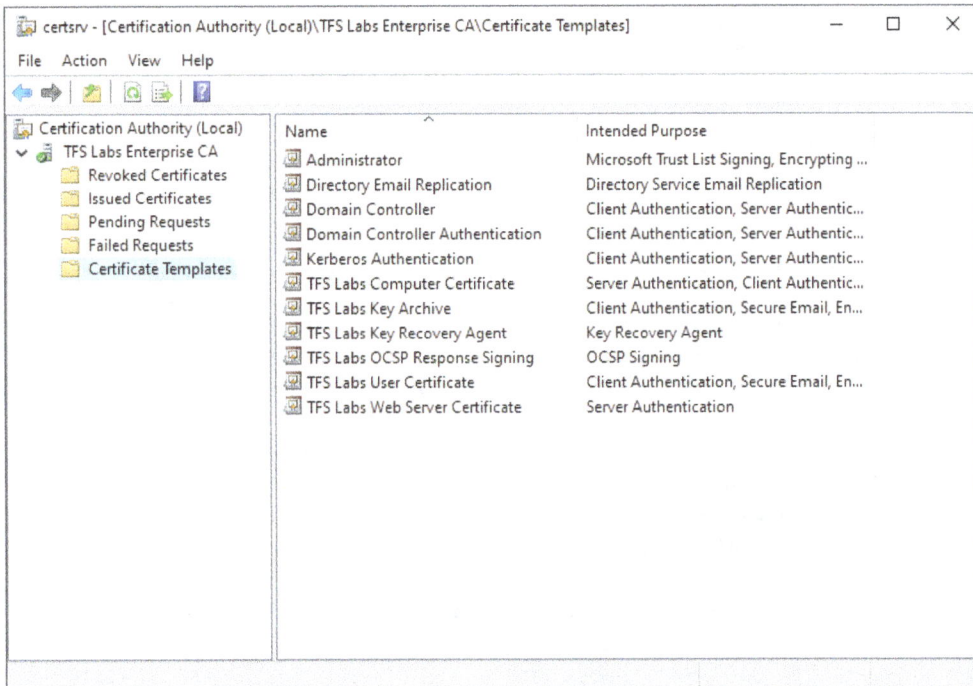

5. Close the **Certification Authority** console.

Once the unnecessary Certificate Templates have been removed, there are no longer any additional changes needed to be made to the Certificate Templates on the TFS Labs domain.

> **Unnecessary Certificate Templates**
>
> It does not affect the operation of the Certificate Authority to keep extra Certificate Templates available, but Certificate Templates that are not required should be removed if they are not required. This can reduce the complexity of the Certificate Authority, and make it easier for troubleshooting and upgrades in the future. It will also make it easier to select the correct templates as there will be fewer choices for users.

Certificate Templates - Active Directory Certificate Services Web Enrollment

> **Active Directory Certificate Services Web Enrollment Feature**
>
> The Active Directory Certificate Services Web Enrollment feature is optional and is not required for the normal operation of the Certificate Authority. If there is no need to deploy this feature, then this section can be skipped.

Active Directory Certificate Services Web Enrollment is a feature that allows authenticated users in the organization the ability to submit Certificate Requests and download the completed certificates through a web interface. It also gives the option of downloading the Certificate Authority certificate chain and the CRL files. By default, any user that is a member of the Domain Admins group can login and request certificates, but additional groups can be added if needed (and is recommended in a production environment). The Active Directory Certificate Services Web Enrollment website can be accessed by going to the following URL on the TFS Labs domain:

http://pki.corp.tfslabs.com/CertSrv/

The only issue is that SSL should be enabled on this site to enhance the security for it, so an SSL certificate will be needed for it. Fortunately, the Certificate Authority is now able to issue certificates and a proper certificate can now be requested and applied to this site. Since there are multiple sites linked to the TFS-CA01 server, a SAN certificate is needed to add the other names to the certificate (if applicable):

- **TFS-CA01.corp.tfslabs.com**
- **OCSP.corp.tfslabs.com**
- **PKI.corp.tfslabs.com**

To add a certificate to the web server to allow for SSL encryption, perform the following steps on the TFS-CA01 server:

1. Open the **Certificates** console (certlm.msc), which lists the certificates on the **Local Computer Account**.
2. Open the **Certificates > Personal > Certificates** store.
3. Right-click on the **Certificates** folder, go to **All Tasks** and select the **Request New Certificate...** option.
4. On the **Before you begin** screen, click the **Next** button to continue.
5. On the **Select Certificate Enrollment Policy** screen, the **Active Directory Enrollment Policy** option should be pre-selected. Click the **Next** button to continue.
6. On the **Request Certificates** screen, select the **TFS Labs Web Server Certificate** and click the **More information is required to enroll for this certificate. Click here to configure settings** link below it.
7. On the **Certificate Properties** window, enter the details for the certificate.
8. On the **Subject** tab, add the following details for the **Subject name**. Select the **Type**, enter the **Value** and click the **Add >** button to add the fields to the certificate:
   - **Common name** - TFS-CA01.corp.tfslabs.com
   - **Country** - CA
   - **Email** - administrator@corp.tfslabs.com
   - **Locality** - Toronto
   - **Organization** - TFS Labs
   - **Organizational Unit** - IT
   - **State** - Ontario
9. On the **Subject** tab, add the following details for the **Alternative name**. Select the **Type**, enter the **Value** and click the **Add >** button to add the fields to the certificate:
   - **DNS** - OCSP.corp.tfslabs.com
   - **DNS** - PKI.corp.tfslabs.com
10. On the **General** tab, set the **Friendly name** to **TFS-CA01.corp.tfslabs.com**.
11. Click the **OK** button to close **Certificate Properties** window.
12. On the **Request Certificates** screen, click the **Enroll** button to continue.
13. On the **Certificate Installation Results** screen, click the **Finish** button to close the wizard.

14. The new certificate should now be listed in the **Certificates > Personal > Certificates** store and should be labelled **TFS-CA01.corp.tfslabs.com**.
15. Close the **Certificates** console.

Once the SSL certificate has been created, it will need to be applied to the IIS server to ensure that it is used, and to ensure that SSL is enforced on the Active Directory Certificate Services Web Enrollment website. Perform the following steps on the TFS-CA01 server to apply the SSL certificate to IIS:

1. Open the **Internet Information Services (IIS) Manager** (inetmgr.exe) console on the **TFS-CA01** server.
2. In the **Connections** pane, select the **TFS-CA01** server and expand **Sites**.
3. Select the **Default Web Site** and in the **Actions** pane, select **Bindings....**
4. In the **Site Bindings** window, click the **Add...** button.
5. On the **Add Site Binding** window, use the following settings and then click the **OK** button:
   - **Type:** https
   - **IP Address:** All Unassigned
   - **Port:** 443
   - **SSL Certificate:** TFS-CA01.corp.tfslabs.com
6. Click the **Close** button to close the **Site Binding** window.
7. Expand **Default Web Site** and select the **CertSrv** folder.
8. In the **/CertSrv Home** pane, double-click on the **SSL Settings** icon.
9. In the **SSL Settings** window, select the option for **Require SSL** and then click the **Apply** button in the **Actions** pane.
10. Close the **Internet Information Services (IIS) Manager** console.

To ensure that the changes to the SSL settings were applied correctly to the TFS-CA01 server, restart the Internet Information Services service. Perform this action by opening an **elevated PowerShell prompt** and running the following command on the TFS-CA01 server:

```
Windows PowerShell (Elevated)

Restart-Service W3SVC
```

Since there is a SAN certificate in use on the IIS server, the *https://tfs-ca01.corp.tfslabs.com/CertSrv/* and *https://ocsp.corp.tfslabs.com/CertSrv/* links will also work for accessing the website should that URL be used instead. If an attempt to go to the site without specifying HTTPS in the URL, the connection will not be successful and it will display an error and the connection will be unsuccessful.

Once the Active Directory Certificate Services Web Enrollment website is working correctly with SSL, the site can be used for purposes such as requesting a web server certificate for a Linux server running Apache or Nginx. Depending on the needs of an organization, custom Certificate Templates can also be added that users can request from the Active Directory Certificate Services Web Enrollment website.

> **Active Directory Certificate Services Web Enrollment Alternate URL**
>
> Since there are CNAME records that are in place for accessing services on the Subordinate CA, there are several URLs that are not available since there are no SSL certificates in place for those CNAME records. To allow for proper SSL access to URLs such as *https://pki.corp.tfslabs.com/*, ensure that a proper SAN certificate has been issued to the TFS-CA01 server. Without a proper SAN certificate in place, those URLs will not be secured properly.

Verify that SSL is working correctly on the Active Directory Certificate Services Web Enrollment website by opening the Active Directory Certificate Services Web Enrollment (*https://pki.corp.tfslabs.com/CertSrv/*) website. Login with a Domain Administrator account to test access to the website.

The Active Directory Certificate Services Web Enrollment website should now be properly secured with SSL:

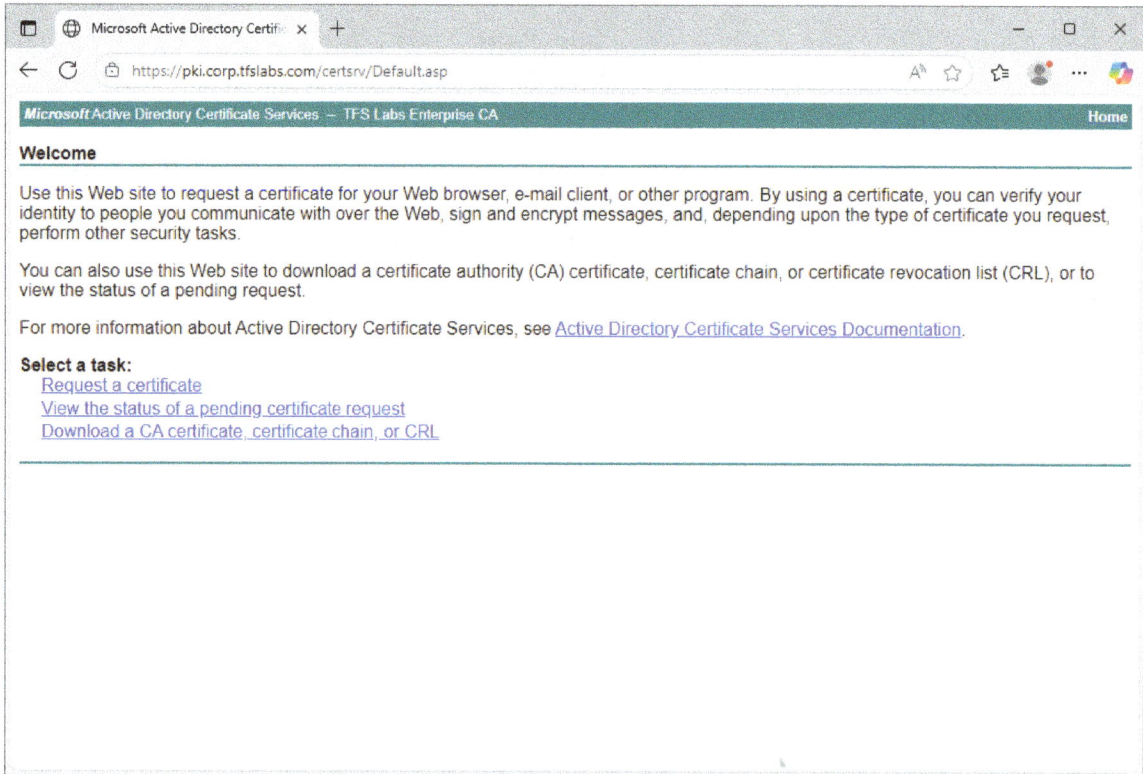

Figure 11.6.1: The Active Directory Certificate Services Web Enrollment website allows users to submit certificate requests and request other certificates that are available with Active Directory Certificate Services.

At this point, the TFS-CA01 server is ready to deploy certificates to the TFS Labs domain, as well as other devices that connect to it for certificates.

Certificate Templates - Chapter Summary

Now that the Certificate Templates have been modified from the default settings and customized for the TFS Labs domain, they can now be configured for automatic deployment using Group Policy. The next chapter will focus of the methods for manual and automatic certificate enrollment on the TFS Labs domain.

Chapter 12 - Certificate Enrollment

Requesting and issuing certificates using Active Directory Certificate Services is an easy process by design, but the ability to rapidly deploy certificates within a domain is critical in large organizations. Most users do not understand how a PKI works, so it would be a large burden on them to have them manually go through the process of requesting certificates on their own. Fortunately, with Active Directory and Group Policy, deploying certificates with no interaction is easy to configure.

There are several ways to create certificates through automatic means, or created manually as required. There are also multiple platforms that can utilize certificates that are issued by Active Directory Certificate Services, and it is not restricted to the Windows operating system. Certificates that can be deployed using Active Directory Certificate Services can include:

- Windows user certificates with auto-enrollment using Group Policy.
- Windows computer or server certificates with auto-enrollment using Group Policy.
- Apache web server certificates on Linux.
- Nginx web server certificates on Linux.
- Network appliances and firewalls.

For unmanaged Windows and non-Windows operating systems, the Root and Subordinate certificates will need to be deployed to allow for issued certificates to work correctly from the TFS Labs Certificate Authority. Normally this can be accomplished using an MDM solution, but it is a trivial process to deploy those certificates to the following operating systems:

- Android and chromeOS
- iOS and iPadOS
- Linux
- macOS

This chapter will focus on the automatic deployment of certificates within an Active Directory domain using Group Policy. It will also demonstrate how to deploy the Root and Subordinate certificates on a Linux server, as well as demonstrating how to create a CSR for that operating system.

> **Certificate Enrollment Options**
>
> Much of this chapter is optional and is not required for every organization. This chapter can be skipped if it is not relevant or needed, but there are some sections that can be applied to devices in an organization in the future should it be required.

> **Certificate Deployment on Other Operating Systems**
>
> Deploying the Root and Subordinate certificates for other operating systems such as Android, chromeOS, iOS, iPadOS and macOS are beyond the scope of this book. These deployments are supported with Active Directory Certificate Services, but requires additional configurations.

Certificate Enrollment - User Certificate Auto-Enrollment

Enabling the user certificate auto-enrollment feature will allow users within the TFS Labs domain the ability to automatically receive a certificate from Active Directory Certificate Services. This certificate will be the **TFS Labs User Certificate** that was created in the previous chapter. To enable this functionality, perform the following steps on the TFS-DC01 server:

1. Open the **Group Policy Management** console (gpmc.msc) on the **TFS-DC01** server.
2. In the **Group Policy Management** console tree, expand the **Forest: corp.tfslabs.com** folder, expand **Domains**, expand the **corp.tfslabs.com** domain, and select the **TFS Labs** OU.
3. Right-click on the **TFS Labs Certificates** GPO, and select the **Edit...** option.
4. In the **Group Policy Management Editor** window, open the **User Configuration > Policies > Windows Settings > Security Settings > Public Key Policies** node.
5. Right-click on the **Certificate Services Client - Certificate Enrollment Policy** object and select **Properties**.
6. In the **Certificate Services Client - Certificate Enrollment Policy** window, change the **Configuration Model** option to **Enabled**. Click the **OK** button to close the window.
7. Right-click on the **Certificate Services Client - Auto-Enrollment** object, and select the **Properties** option to modify the configuration.
8. In the **Certificate Services Client - Auto-Enrollment** window, change the **Configuration Model** option to **Enabled**. Select the options for **Renew expired certificates, update pending certificates, and remove revoked certificates** and **Update certificate that use certificate templates** options. Click the **OK** button to close the window:

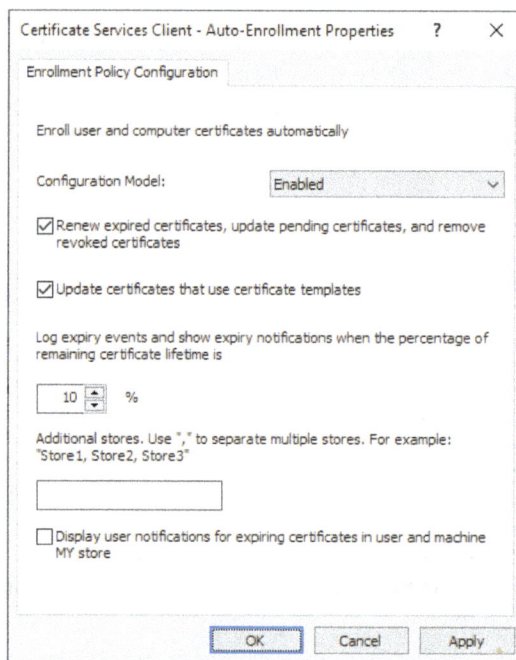

9. Close the **Group Policy Management Editor** window.

Confirm that the auto-enrollment of the TFS Labs User Certificate is working correctly by logging in with a regular user account on the TFS-WIN11 workstation, and checking the Certificate Store for the issued certificate.

> **Group Policy Object Propagation Time**
>
> Once the auto-enrollment options have been added to Group Policy for the user certificate, allow up to 90 minutes for the update to be propagated to the entire Active Directory Forest. This process can be expedited manually by using the **gpupdate.exe /force** command on the workstation where the user is logged into, or by restarting the workstation to update the Group Policy Objects from the domain. Either method will ensure that the Group Policy settings are updated for the user accounts.

Certificate Enrollment - Computer Certificate Auto-Enrollment

Enabling the computer auto-enrollment feature will allow workstations and servers within the TFS Labs domain the ability to automatically receive a certificate from Active Directory Certificate Services. This certificate will be the **TFS Labs Computer Certificate** that was created in the previous chapter. To enable this functionality, perform the following steps on the TFS-DC01 server:

1. Open the **Group Policy Management** console (gpmc.msc) on the **TFS-DC01** server.
2. In the **Group Policy Management** console tree, expand the **Forest: corp.tfslabs.com** folder, expand **Domains**, expand the **corp.tfslabs.com** domain, and select the **TFS Labs** OU.
3. Right-click on the **TFS Labs Certificates** GPO and select the **Edit...** option.
4. In the **Group Policy Management Editor** window, open the **Computer Configuration > Policies > Windows Settings > Security Settings > Public Key Policies** node.
5. Right-click on the **Certificate Services Client - Certificate Enrollment Policy** object and select **Properties**.
6. In the **Certificate Services Client - Certificate Enrollment Policy** window, change the **Configuration Model** option to **Enabled**. Click the **OK** button to close the window.
7. Right-click on the **Certificate Services Client - Auto-Enrollment** object and select the **Properties** option.
8. In the **Certificate Services Client - Auto-Enrollment** window, change the **Configuration Model** option to **Enabled**. Select the options for **Renew expired certificates, update pending certificates, and remove revoked certificates** and **Update certificate that use certificate templates** options. Click the **OK** button to close the window:

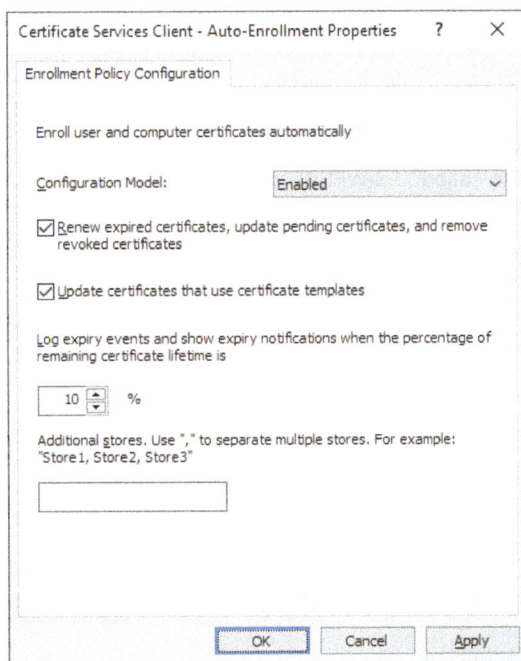

9. Close the **Group Policy Management Editor** window.

Confirm that the auto-enrollment of the **TFS Labs Computer Certificate** is working correctly by logging in on the TFS-WIN11 workstation and checking the Certificate Store for the certificate after Group Policy has taken enough time to update and apply the settings.

> **Group Policy Object Propagation Time**
>
> Once the auto-enrollment options have been added to Group Policy for the computer certificate, allow up to 90 minutes for the update to be propagated to the entire Active Directory Forest. This process can be expedited manually by using the **gpupdate.exe /force** command on the workstation, or by restarting the workstation to update the Group Policy Objects from the domain. Either method will ensure that the Group Policy settings are updated on the workstation.

Certificate Enrollment - Deploy Certificates to a Linux Server

In this example, a certificate will be requested from the Active Directory Certificate Services Web Enrollment website for use with the Apache web server and Nginx web server running on a Linux server. Typically, only one web server is used at a time, so there is no need to configure both applications. To request the SSL certificate, OpenSSL will be used to create the CSR Request that will be submitted to the Enterprise CA. The certificate will then be applied to both web servers to demonstrate how each is configured with the certificate and tested.

> **Linux Server Certificate Deployment**
>
> This section is completely optional and can be skipped if deploying SSL certificates to a Linux server is not required. These steps were tested with AlmaLinux 10.0, but they should work with other recent Linux distributions as well without major changes to the steps.
>
> Installing and configuring a Linux server is beyond the scope of this book. This includes the installation of the Linux distribution, the configuration of the network settings, and modifying firewall configurations to allow web servers to operate on the correct port for SSL.
>
> Installing and configuring the Apache and Nginx web servers are also beyond the scope of this book. The only configurations that are included in this section are for enabling SSL on default sites. This is sufficient for demonstration purposes, but more advanced deployments will require different configuration steps.

Certificate Enrollment - Deploy Certificates to a Linux Server - Server Setup

In this example, a new virtual machine called TFS-WEB01 was provisioned, and AlmaLinux 10.0 was installed in Hyper-V using the following network settings:

IP Address	10.100.1.120
Netmask	255.255.255.0
Gateway	10.100.1.1
DNS Server 1	10.100.1.100

Table 12.3.1.1: Network configuration settings for the TFS-WEB01 server.

For the DNS settings, there is one A record and one CNAME record that was created in the TFS Labs DNS Zone to support the TFS-WEB01 virtual machine, and to facilitate testing of the issued SSL certificate:

- **A record** - TFS-WEB01.corp.tfslabs.com
- **CNAME record** - WWW.corp.tfslabs.com

The TFS-WEB01 server will resolve to the *https://tfs-web01.corp.tfslabs.com/* and *https://www.corp.tfslabs.com/* addresses, so a SAN or a UCC certificate will be required for the TFS-WEB01 server to accommodate that requirement. This functionality is available with Active Directory Certificate Services and can be added to the CSR request. In the next section, create the CSR request for the Linux server containing the two DNS entries needed for the SSL certificate.

Certificate Enrollment - Deploy Certificates to a Linux Server - CSR Request

Creating a CSR request on the TFS-WEB01 server is not difficult, and only requires minimal configuration tasks to be completed. Since this is a Linux server, there is no easy way to automatically submit a request to the Certificate Authority, so the Active Directory Certificate Services Web Enrollment website can be used to submit the CSR request and download the issued certificate. OpenSSL is used to create the CSR request for the TFS-WEB01 server, so it will need to be installed for the request to be created successfully if it is not already present.

There is also an additional step that it is required to make the process of creating the CSR request easier with OpenSSL, which is less prone to errors when using the command line for this type of request.

OpenSSL Configuration File

The use of a configuration file for creating a CSR request using OpenSSL is optional. The request can be completed without one, but it requires manually inputting all configuration items at the time of the CSR request.

To create the CSR request for the TFS-WEB01 server and submit the request, perform the following steps on the TFS-WEB01 and TFS-CA01 servers:

1. On the **TFS-WEB01** server, create a folder in the **/etc/ssl** directory called **TFS-WEB01** (/etc/ssl/TFS-WEB01). This folder will be used to store the SSL files for the **TFS-WEB01** server.
2. Go to the **/etc/ssl/TFS-WEB01** directory.
3. Create a file to store the additional CSR request information called **tfs-web01.cnf** and copy the contents below into the file:

```
/etc/ssl/TFS-WEB01/tfs-web01.cnf

[req]
default_bits            = 2048
prompt                  = no
distinguished_name      = req_distinguished_name
req_extensions          = req_ext

[req_distinguished_name]
commonName              = TFS-WEB01.corp.tfslabs.com
countryName             = CA
stateOrProvinceName     = Ontario
localityName            = Toronto
organizationName        = TFS Labs
organizationalUnitName  = IT
emailAddress            = administrator@corp.tfslabs.com

[req_ext]
subjectAltName          = @alt_names

[alt_names]
DNS.1                   = TFS-WEB01.corp.tfslabs.com
DNS.2                   = WWW.corp.tfslabs.com
```

4. Run the following command to create the **CSR** request file and the **private key** file for the **TFS-WEB01** server:

```
Linux Terminal

openssl req \
-out tfs-web01.csr \
-newkey rsa:2048 \
-nodes \
-keyout tfs-web01.key \
-config tfs-web01.cnf
```

5. Copy the **tfs-web01.csr** file to the **TFS-CA01** server and place it in a location that is accessible as it is required to complete the certificate request.

6. On the **TFS-CA01** server, open the **Active Directory Certificate Services Web Enrollment** website by going to the **https://pki.corp.tfslabs.com/CertSrv/** address using the web browser (if prompted, login with the **Domain Administrator** account to access it):

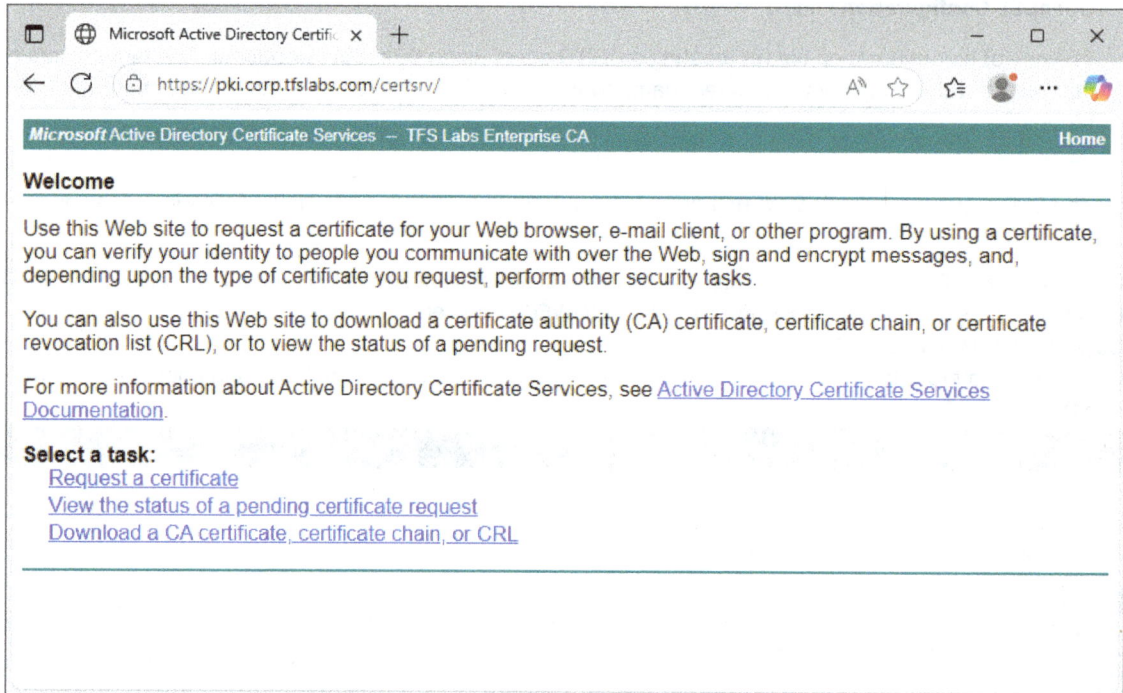

7. To submit the **CSR** file for the TFS-WEB01 server, click on the **Request a certificate** link which is listed under **Select a task** on the **Welcome** page.

8. On the **Advanced Certificate Request** page, click on the **Submit a certificate request by using a base-64-encoded CMC or PKCS #10 file, or submit a renewal request by using a base-64-encoded PKCS #7 file** link to continue:

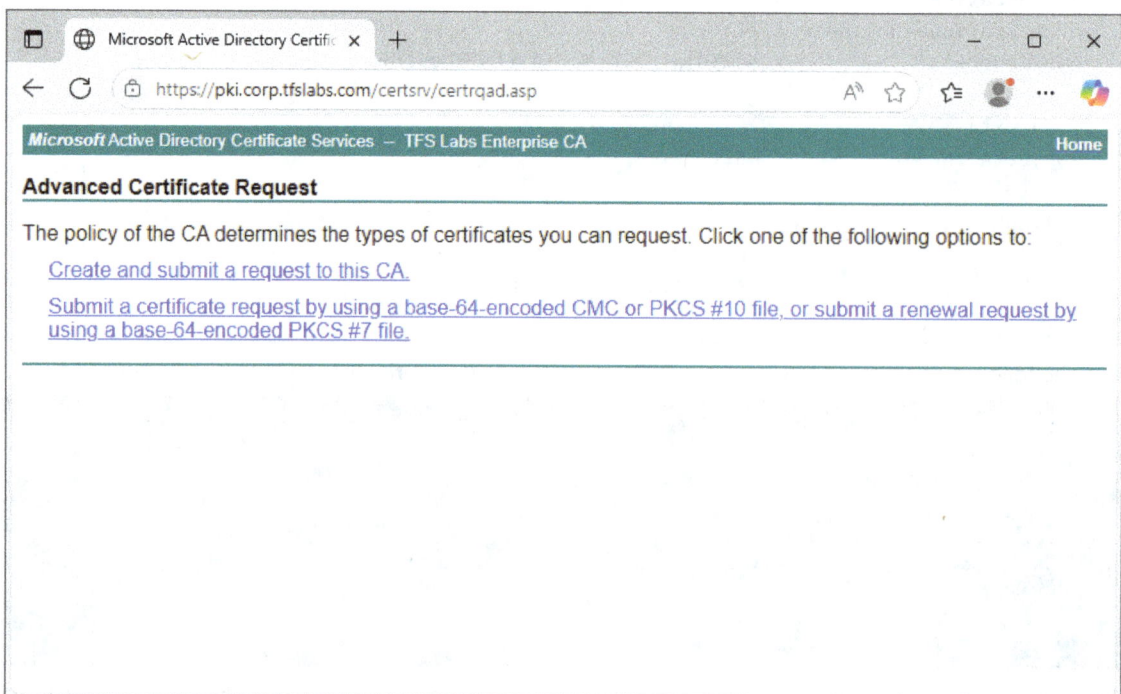

9. On the **Submit a Certificate Request or Renewal Request** page, copy the contents of the **tfs-web01.csr** file into the **Saved Request** box. Under the **Certificate Template** list, select the **TFS Labs Web Server Certificate** template. Click the **Submit** button to continue:

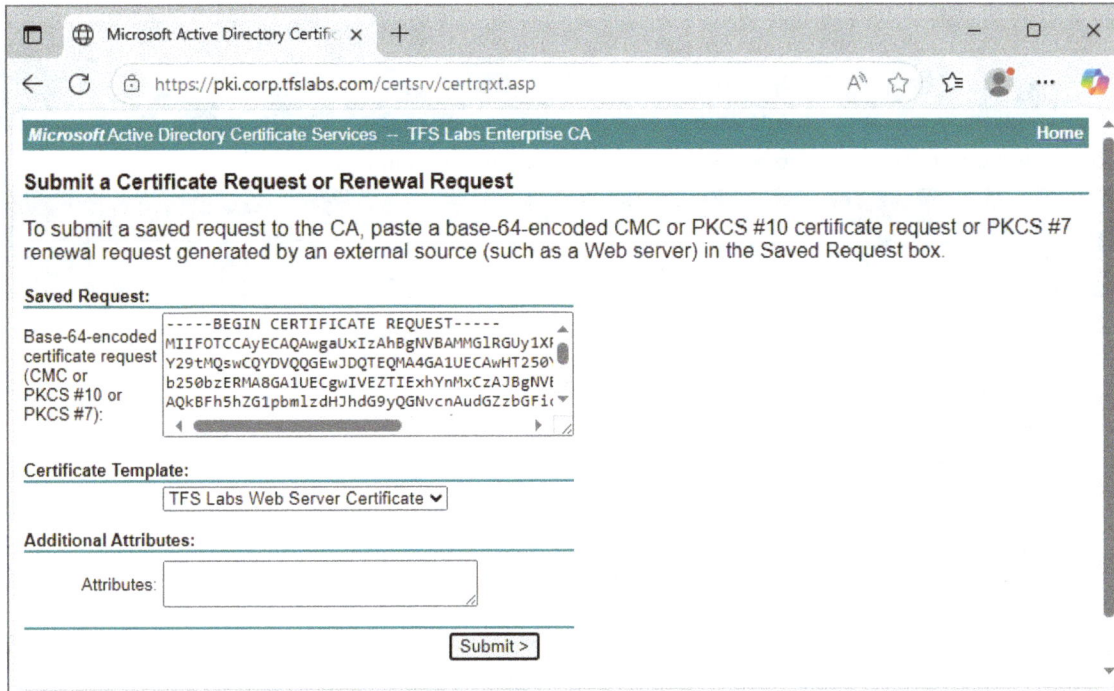

10. On the **Certificate Issued** page, select the option for **Base 64 encoded** and download both the **Certificate** and **Certificate Chain** files. These files should be saved as the **certnew.cer** and **certnew.p7b** files:

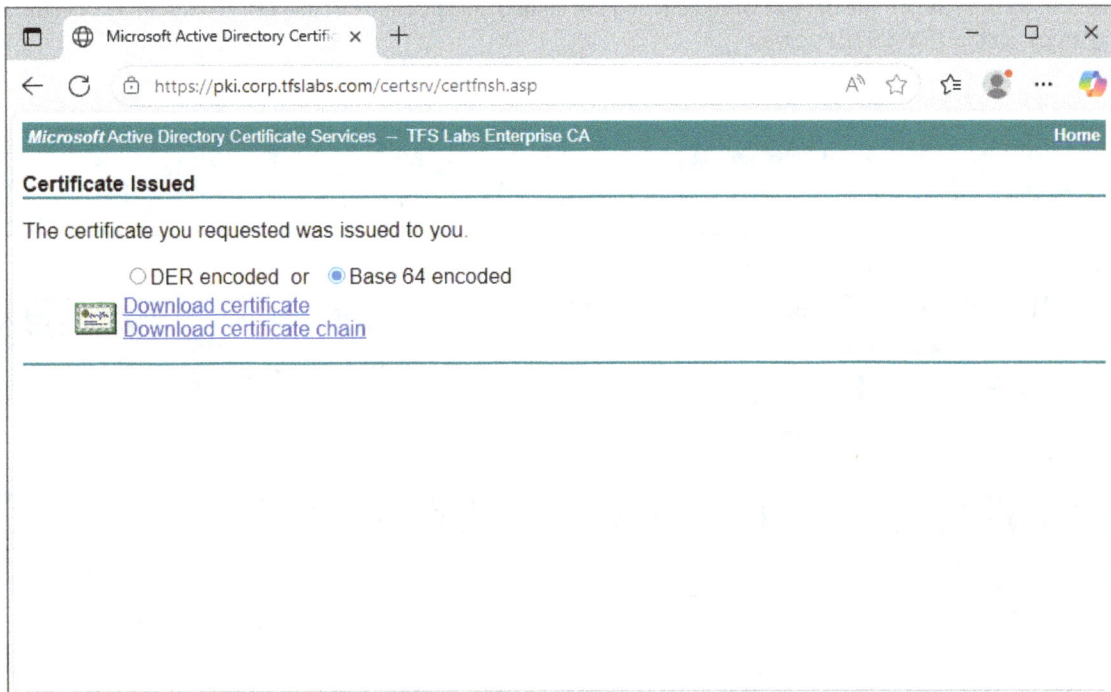

11. Close the **Active Directory Certificate Services Web Enrollment** website.

12. Copy the **certnew.cer** and **certnew.p7b** files that were downloaded from the **Active Directory Certificate Services Web Enrollment** website to the **TFS-WEB01** server, and place them in the **/etc/ssl/TFS-WEB01** folder.
13. On the **TFS-WEB01** server, switch to the **/etc/ssl/TFS-WEB01** directory.
14. Convert the **Certificate Chain** file to the correct format by running the following command:

```
Linux Terminal

openssl pkcs7 -print_certs -in certnew.p7b -out tfs-labs-ca
```

15. Rename the **Certificate** file to the correct name by running the following command:

```
Linux Terminal

cp certnew.cer tfs-web01.cer
```

16. There should now be the following certificate files located in the **/etc/ssl/TFS-WEB01** directory:
    - **certnew.cer**
    - **certnew.p7b**
    - **tfs-labs-ca**
    - **tfs-web01.cer**
    - **tfs-web01.cnf**
    - **tfs-web01.csr**
    - **tfs-web01.key**
17. Delete the **certnew.cer**, **certnew.p7b**, and **tfs-web01.csr** files as they are no longer required on the server.

Once the SSL certificate has been successfully installed on the TFS-WEB01 server, the Apache or Nginx web servers can be configured to use it. Other applications can also use the same certificate, as it is not specific to either web server.

Certificate Enrollment - Deploy Certificates to a Linux Server - Apache Setup

To enable SSL for Apache on the default website using the issued certificate from the TFS Labs domain, perform the following steps on the TFS-WEB01 server:

1. If it is not already installed on the server, install the **Apache web server** using the following command:

```
Linux Terminal

sudo yum install httpd
```

2. Enable the **SSL** module in **Apache** by running the following command:

```
Linux Terminal

sudo yum install mod_ssl
```

3. Edit the **/etc/httpd/conf.d/ssl.conf** file and make following changes. Add or edit the existing configuration file for the SSL certificate information:

```
/etc/httpd/conf.d/ssl.conf

ServerName TFS-WEB01.corp.tfslabs.com

SSLCertificateFile /etc/ssl/TFS-WEB01/tfs-web01.cer
SSLCertificateKeyFile /etc/ssl/TFS-WEB01/tfs-web01.key
SSLCertificateChainFile /etc/ssl/TFS-WEB01/tfs-labs-ca
```

4. Run the following command to restart the **Apache** service to apply the SSL changes:

```
Linux Terminal

sudo systemctl restart httpd
```

5. Run the following command to enable the **Apache** service to start automatically when the server is booted:

```
Linux Terminal

sudo systemctl enable httpd
```

6. If there were no errors with the **Apache** service, the configuration is now complete.

If there were no issues with configuring SSL on Apache, test that SSL is working correctly by going to the following website on the TFS-CA01 server:

https://tfs-web01.corp.tfslabs.com/

The Apache placeholder website should be displayed in the web browser:

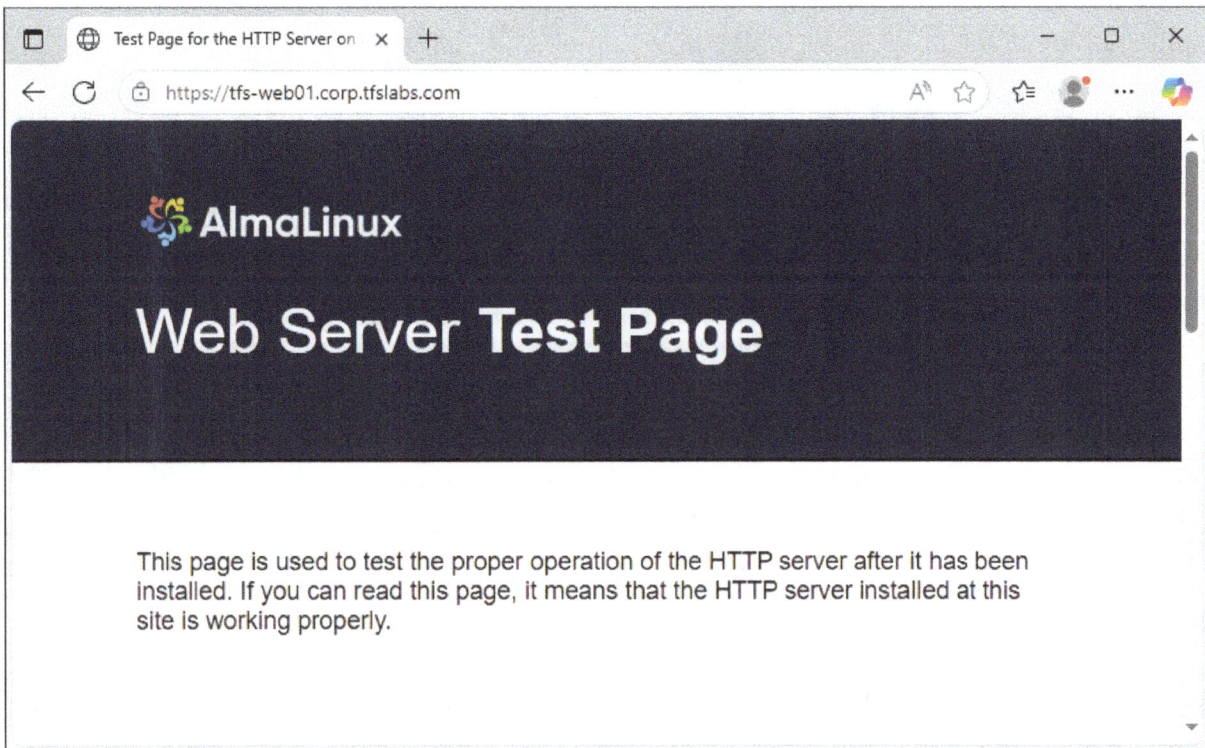

Figure 12.3.3.1: The Apache test website is installed by default on an AlmaLinux server. The A record for the TFS-WEB01 server is being used to access the page. SSL is being used on the website, based on the lock icon to the left of the URL.

Since the certificate for the TFS-WEB01 server was setup using a SAN certificate, the website can also be reached using the CNAME record as well:

https://www.corp.tfslabs.com/

Once the Apache web server has been confirmed to be working correctly with SSL using the issued certificate, there are no additional steps to complete.

Certificate Enrollment - Deploy Certificates to a Linux Server - Nginx Setup

Adding the SSL certificate to the Nginx web server is not complicated, and only requires modifying one configuration file to enable SSL. To enable SSL on Nginx for the default website, perform the following steps on the TFS-WEB01 server:

1. If it is not already installed on the server, install the **Nginx web server** using the following command:

    Linux Terminal
    ```
    sudo yum install nginx
    ```

2. Edit the **/etc/nginx/nginx.conf** file and make following changes. Add or edit the existing configuration file for the SSL certificate information:

    /etc/nginx/nginx.conf
    ```
    server {
        listen 443 ssl default_server;
        listen [::]:443 ssl default_server;

        ssl_certificate /etc/ssl/TFS-WEB01/tfs-web01.cer;
        ssl_certificate_key /etc/ssl/TFS-WEB01/tfs-web01.key;
    }
    ```

3. Run the following command to restart the **Nginx** service to apply the SSL changes:

    Linux Terminal
    ```
    sudo systemctl restart nginx
    ```

4. Run the following command to enable the **Nginx** service to start when the server is booted:

    Linux Terminal
    ```
    sudo systemctl enable nginx
    ```

5. If there were no errors with the **Nginx** web server, the configuration is now complete.

If there were no issues with configuring SSL on Nginx, test that SSL is working by going to the following website on the TFS-CA01 server:

http://tfs-web01.corp.tfslabs.com/

The Nginx placeholder website should be displayed in the web browser if there are no issues. Since the certificate for the TFS-WEB01 server was setup using a SAN certificate, the website can also be reached using the CNAME record as well:

http://www.corp.tfslabs.com/

Once the Nginx web server has been confirmed to be working correctly with SSL, there are no additional steps to complete.

Certificate Enrollment - Chapter Summary

Now that certificate auto-enrollment has been configured, and certificates are being automatically generated and deployed within the Active Directory domain, the Certificate Authority is now functionally complete. The next chapter will focus on ongoing maintenance tasks that are required for Active Directory Certificate Services.

Chapter 13 - AD CS Maintenance Tasks

If the steps in this book have been followed correctly up to this point, there should now be a complete and functioning Certificate Authority using Active Directory Certificate Services for the TFS Labs domain. There are no steps remaining in setting up the Certificate Authority, and only maintenance tasks are required for day-to-day operation.

This chapter will focus on the process for renewing the Root CA CRL, and the process for manually backing up and restoring the Certificate Authority.

> **Recurring Certificate Authority Maintenance Tasks**
>
> The tasks that are discussed in this chapter do not need to be performed at this point, but are tasks that should be performed at some point in the future. The process for renewing the Root CA CRL only needs to be performed when it is about to expire, which is once every 52 weeks as per the configuration in this book.
>
> Backing up the Certificate Authority can be performed at any time. Typically, there are full virtual machine backup solutions and other third-party solutions that offer this functionality, so using the native backup features within Windows Server is optional.

> **Certificate Authority Backup Solutions**
>
> The steps in this section related to backup and restoration of a Certificate Authority is not a complete solution. It is only present for demonstration purposes, and in a production environment there should be a more robust and capable backup solution in place to ensure that the Certificate Authority is being properly backed up and restored.
>
> For example, the backup and restoration process only demonstrates how to manage local backups on the associated servers. This is not an issue for backups, but there is usually no reason to restore a backup on the same server. This would usually occur on a different server, assuming that the original server was not available.
>
> The steps for backing up and restoring the Certificate Authority are optional and do not need to be completed at this time. Restoring a Certificate Authority is only required under specific circumstances, and there are several factors to consider before attempting to restore the configuration on a server. The instructions are provided for reference purposes.

AD CS Maintenance Tasks - Renewing the Root CA CRL

The only major task that should need to performed on a PKI is the renewal of the Base CRL on the Root CA at least once a year (or as configured on the Root CA). Once the Certificate Authority implementation is completed, consider setting a yearly recurring task to make sure this task is not forgotten, and the renewal of the CRL happens in time. Renewing a CRL before it expires is perfectly fine, and will not affect the operation of a Certificate Authority. Since the Root CA is an Offline CA, renewing the CRL file is the only time the TFS-ROOT-CA server will need to be powered on, as there are no other tasks that need to be performed on the server on a regular basis. The server needs to be powered on while the CRL is renewed, and it can be shut down immediately afterwards.

To renew the Root CA CRL using PowerShell, perform the following steps on the TFS-ROOT-CA server:

1. Open an **elevated PowerShell prompt**.
2. Publish the **CRL** by running the following command:

```
Windows PowerShell (Elevated)

certutil.exe -crl
```

3. Close the **elevated PowerShell prompt**.

Alternatively, to renew the CRL on the Root CA server using the Certification Authority console, perform the following steps on the TFS-ROOT-CA server:

1. Open the **Certification Authority** console (certsrv.msc).
2. In the **Certification Authority** console, expand the **TFS Labs Certificate Authority**, right-click on **Revoked Certificates** under **TFS Labs Certificate Authority** and select **All Tasks > Publish**.
3. On the **Publish CRL** window, verify that **New CRL** is selected and click the **OK** button.
4. Close the **Certification Authority** console.

Once the CRL file has been renewed, use a virtual floppy disk to copy the file to the TFS-CA01 server. If required, create a new virtual floppy disk to move the file, which will also need to be formatted before it can be used. To copy the CRL file to the TFS-CA01 server, perform the following steps on the TFS-ROOT-CA server:

1. Add the virtual floppy disk to the **TFS-ROOT-CA** virtual machine. Format the virtual floppy disk if necessary.
2. Copy the **C:\Windows\System32\CertSrv\CertEnroll\TFS Labs Certificate Authority.crl** file to the **C:\RootCA** folder. Overwrite the existing file that is already in that directory as it is obsolete.
3. Copy the **C:\RootCA\TFS Labs Certificate Authority.crl** file to the **A:\ drive**.
4. Eject the virtual floppy disk.
5. Shut down the **TFS-ROOT-CA** server as it is no longer required.

Once the Root CA CRL file has been copied from the Root CA server, it can then be placed on the TFS-CA01 server:

1. Add the virtual floppy disk to the **TFS-CA01** virtual machine.
2. Copy the **A:\TFS Labs Certificate Authority.crl** file to the **C:\CertData** folder. Overwrite the existing file that is already in that directory as it is obsolete.
3. Eject the virtual floppy disk.

Now that the CRL file has been copied to the TFS-CA01 server, the virtual floppy disk can be deleted as it is no longer required. The final task is to publish the renewed Root CA CRL to Active Directory. This can be completed by running the following command from an **elevated PowerShell prompt** on the TFS-CA01 server:

```
Windows PowerShell (Elevated)

certutil.exe -addstore -f root "C:\CertData\TFS Labs Certificate Authority.crl"
```

Renewing the Root CA CRL file is a trivial process, and the most difficult step is ensuring that the CRL is renewed before it expires. Not renewing the CRL can cause issues with the entire PKI, and renewing it before it expires can save a lot of trouble.

AD CS Maintenance Tasks - Manual Backup of the Certificate Authority

When a Certificate Authority is deployed in a production environment, it is usually backed up as part of the regular backups that are maintained by an organization. Like other components of Windows Server, it is possible to manually create a backup of a Certificate Authority without requiring any third-party tools. Since the Certificate Authority for TFS Labs is a Two-Tier Certificate Authority, this means both servers would need to be backed up to ensure that the Certificate Authority would function correctly if it needed to be restored in this manner. There is the option of using the native Windows Server Backup tool that is included with Windows Server to backup the entire server, or the tools included with Active Directory Certificate Services can be used to backup only the Certificate Authority. In this section, the tools included with AD CS will be used for backing up the CA servers, and it can be used with the command line with PowerShell, or with the Certification Authority console. Either method will produce the same result, and only one method needs to be used.

> ⚠️ **Certificate Authority Server Backups**
>
> The steps for backing up the Certificate Authority applies to both of the servers in the PKI. Once the backups are completed, ensure that the backups are kept in a secure location. Do not leave backups on either of the servers. Always use a secure and complex password for any CA backup files.

AD CS Maintenance Tasks - Manual Backup of the Certificate Authority - CLI Method

To create a complete backup of the Certificate Authority of the TFS-CA01 server using the command line, perform the following steps:

1. On the **TFS-CA01** server, create a folder called **CA-Backup** (C:\CA-Backup) on the root of the **C:\ drive**.
2. Open an **elevated PowerShell prompt**.
3. Using the **Backup-CARoleService** Cmdlet, run the following command to backup the Certificate Authority (enter a secure password when prompted):

```
Windows PowerShell (Elevated)

Backup-CARoleService `
-Path "C:\CA-Backup" `
-Password (Read-Host -prompt "CA Backup Password" -AsSecureString)
```

4. Close the **PowerShell prompt**.

Once the backup has been completed, the associated Registry Keys for the Certificate Authority should also be backed up. On the TFS-CA01 server, run the following command from an **elevated PowerShell prompt**:

```
Windows PowerShell (Elevated)

reg export HKLM\SYSTEM\CurrentControlSet\Services\CertSvc "C:\CA-Backup\TFS-CA01.reg"
```

At this point the backup of the Certificate Authority is completed. The contents of the **CA-Backup** folder can be moved to another location for securely storing the backup files.

> 🗄 **Root and Subordinate Server Backups**
>
> Repeat the steps in this section for the TFS-ROOT-CA server. Replace all instances of the TFS-CA01 server name with the TFS-ROOT-CA server. The TFS-ROOT-CA server will need to be powered on for the backup to be made, and can be powered down immediately upon completing the backup of the Certificate Authority.

AD CS Maintenance Tasks - Manual Backup of the Certificate Authority - GUI Method

To create a complete backup of the Certificate Authority on the TFS-CA01 server using the Certification Authority console, perform the following steps:

1. On the **TFS-CA01** server, create a folder called **CA-Backup** (C:\CA-Backup) on the root of the **C:\ drive**.
2. Open the **Certification Authority** console (certsrv.msc) on the **TFS-CA01** server.
3. Right-click on **TFS Labs Enterprise CA** server, select the **All Tasks** option, and select **Back up CA...**:

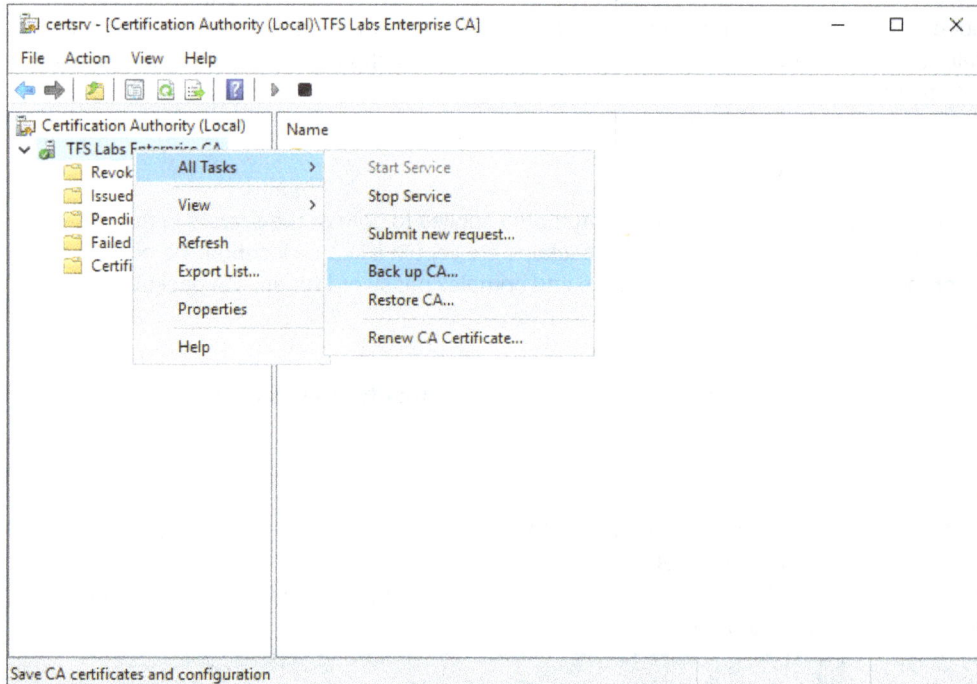

4. On the **Welcome to the Certification Authority Backup Wizard** window, click the **Next** button to continue.
5. On the **Items to Back Up** window, select the following options and click the **Next** button to continue:
   - **Private key and CA certificate** - Enabled
   - **Certificate database and certificate database log** - Enabled
   - **Back up to this location** - C:\CA-Backup

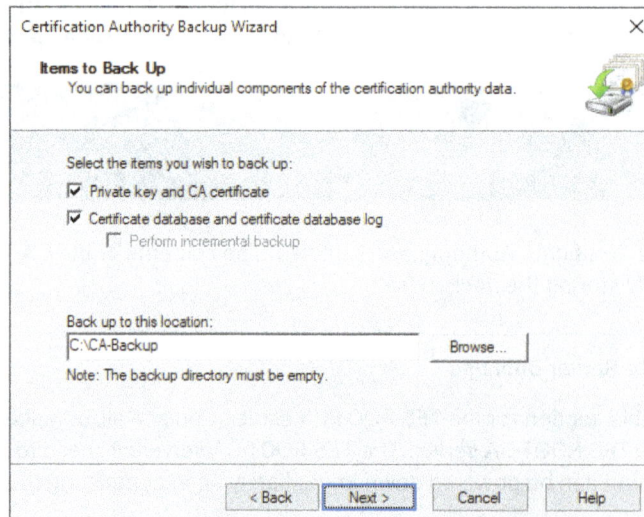

6. On the **Select a Password** window, enter a complex password for the backup in both fields and click the **Next** button to continue.
7. On the **Completing the Certification Authority Backup Wizard** window, click the **Finish** button to close the wizard.
8. On the **TFS-CA01** server, open the **Registry Editor** (regedit.exe).
9. Browse to the **HKLM\SYSTEM\CurrentControlSet\Services\CertSvc** Registry Key.
10. Right-click on the **CertSvc** Registry Key and select the **Export** option:

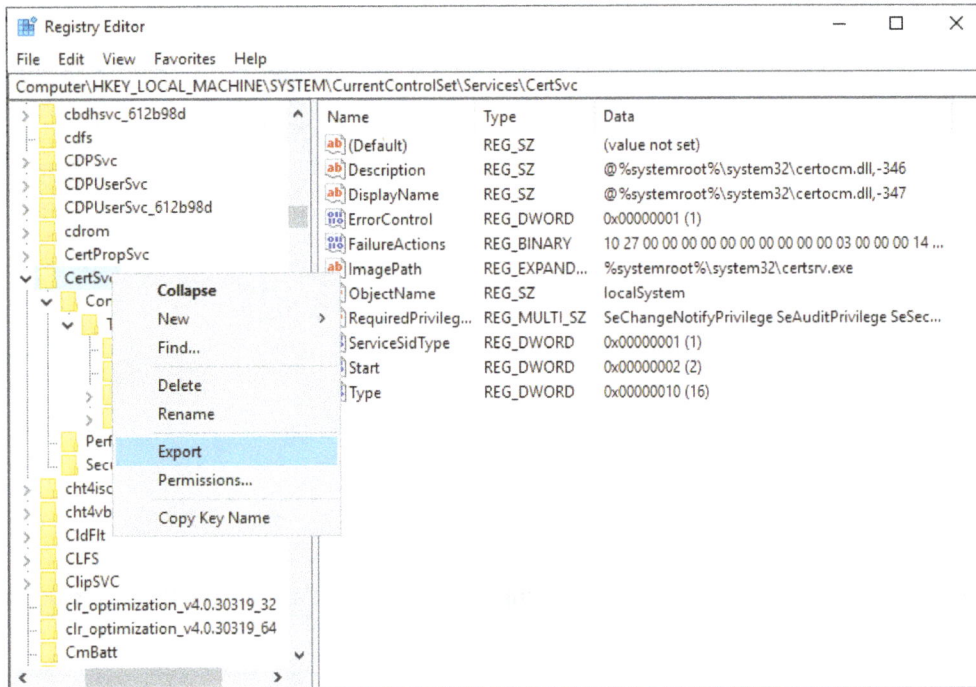

11. On the **Export Registry File** window, select the **C:\CA-Backup** folder, enter **TFS-CA01.reg** in the **File name** field, and then click the **Save** button to continue:

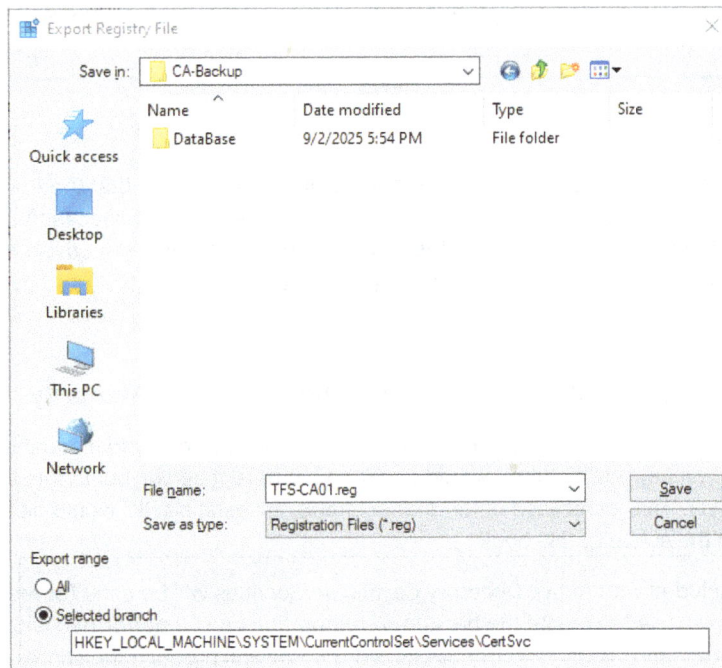

12. Close the **Registry Editor**.
13. Browse to the **C:\CA-Backup** folder on the server, and it should list the Certificate Authority files that have been backed up so far:

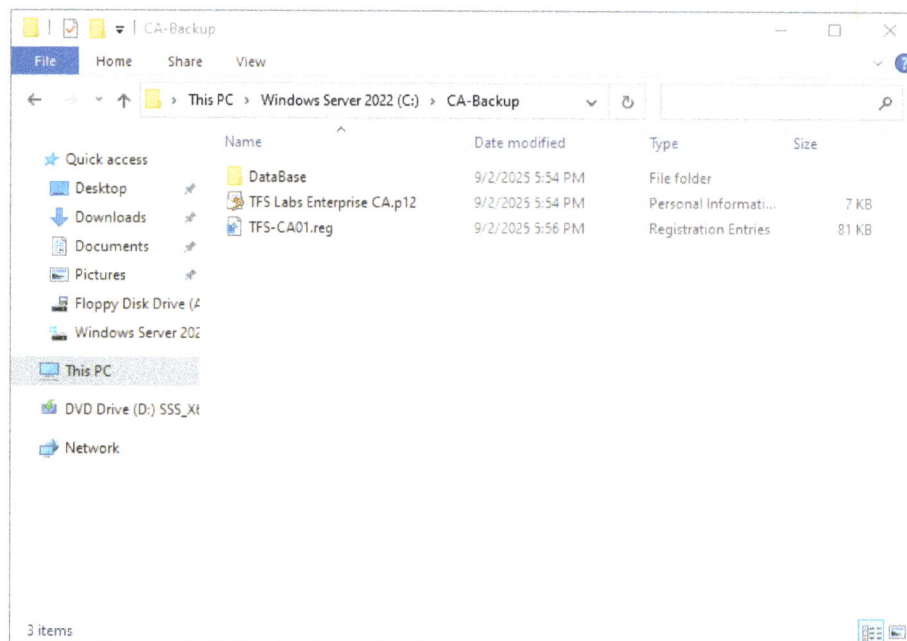

At this point the backup of the Certificate Authority is completed. The contents of the **CA-Backup** folder can be moved to another location for securely storing the backup files.

> **Root and Subordinate Server Backups**
>
> Repeat the steps in this section for the TFS-ROOT-CA server. Replace all instances of the TFS-CA01 server name with the TFS-ROOT-CA server. The TFS-ROOT-CA server will need to be powered on for the backup to be made, and can be powered down immediately upon completing the backup of the Certificate Authority.

> **Certificate Authority Backups**
>
> Just like every important infrastructure server in an environment, ensure that the Root and Subordinate Certificate Authority servers are backed up regularly and can be restored successfully. If there is an issue with backups and the Root CA is lost, then the PKI for an environment is effectively broken. The only way to fix it is to create a new PKI, and then re-issue all certificates.

AD CS Maintenance Tasks - Manual Restoration of the Certificate Authority

There are several reasons why a Certificate Authority would need to be restored, and it usually is related to some type of data corruption issue. Typically, a restoration would occur on a different server, but in this section the restoration will occur on the same server. This is because under that scenario, the existing PKI would be rebuilt on different servers and that is beyond the scope of this book.

In this section, the tools included with Active Directory Certificate Services will be used for restoring a backup for the Certificate Authority, as it was used to create the backup. A restoration can be performed with the command line with PowerShell, or with the Certification Authority console. Either method will produce the same result, and only one method needs to be used for the restoration of the Certificate Authority.

Certificate Authority Restoration and Existing Certificates

It is important to factor in that Certificate Authority backups are a point in time snapshot of what the configuration was when the backup was created. This also includes any certificates that were issued by the Certificate Authority. If a certificate was issued after the backup was created, then a restored Certificate Authority will not know about any certificate that was issued later.

AD CS Maintenance Tasks - Manual Restoration of the Certificate Authority - CLI Method

To restore a backup of the Certificate Authority on the TFS-CA01 server using the command line, perform the following steps:

1. Open an **elevated PowerShell prompt**.
2. Stop the **Active Directory Certificate Services** service prior to restoring the backup:

```
Windows PowerShell (Elevated)

net stop CertSvc
```

3. Using the **Restore-CARoleService** Cmdlet, run the following command to restore the Certificate Authority (enter the secure password when prompted):

```
Windows PowerShell (Elevated)

Restore-CARoleService `
-Path C:\CA-Backup\ `
-Password (Read-Host -prompt "CA Restore Password" -AsSecureString) `
-Force
```

4. Start the **Active Directory Certificate Services** service after the backup has been restored:

```
Windows PowerShell (Elevated)

net start CertSvc
```

5. Close the **PowerShell prompt**.

If there were no errors during the restoration of the Certificate Authority, then the restoration of the Certificate Authority has been completed. Validate that the restoration was successful by opening the Certification Authority console and checking that the services are running correctly.

Root and Subordinate Server Restoration

Repeat the steps in this section for the TFS-ROOT-CA server. Replace all instances of the TFS-CA01 server name with the TFS-ROOT-CA server. The server will need to be powered on for the restoration to be made, and can be powered down immediately upon completing the restoration of the Certificate Authority.

Certificate Authority Registry Backup

In the previous section a backup of the Registry Keys were created that contained additional configuration for the Certificate Authority. In this example these keys were not used for the restoration of the Certificate Authority as they were not needed. It is usually only in scenarios where the Certificate Authority needs to be recreated on new servers where the Registry Keys are used for that purpose.

AD CS Maintenance Tasks - Manual Restoration of the Certificate Authority - GUI Method

To restore a backup of the Certificate Authority on the TFS-CA01 server using the Certification Authority console, perform the following steps:

1. Open the **Certification Authority** console (certsrv.msc) on the **TFS-CA01** server.
2. Right-click on **TFS Labs Enterprise CA** server, select the **All Tasks** option, and select **Restore CA...**:

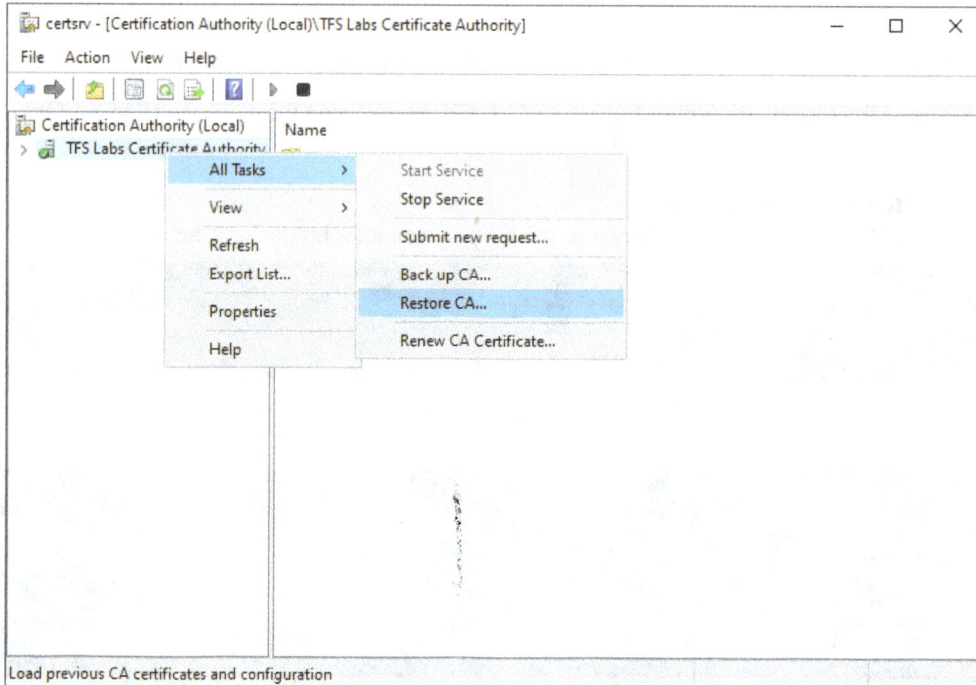

3. When the prompt stating that Active Directory Certificate Services must be stopped prior to restoring a backup, click the **OK** button to continue.
4. On the **Welcome to the Certification Authority Restore Wizard** window, click the **Next** button to continue.
5. On the **Items to Restore** window, select the following restore options and click the **Next** button to continue:
   - **Private key and CA certificate** - Enabled
   - **Certificate database and certificate database log** - Enabled
   - **Restore from this location** - C:\CA-Backup

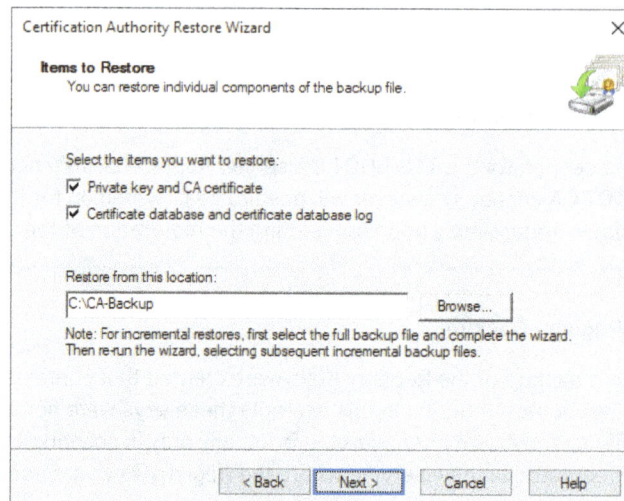

6. On the **Provide Password** window, enter the password for the backup and click the **Next** button to continue.
7. On the **Completing the Certification Authority Restore Wizard** window, click the **Finish** button to close the wizard:

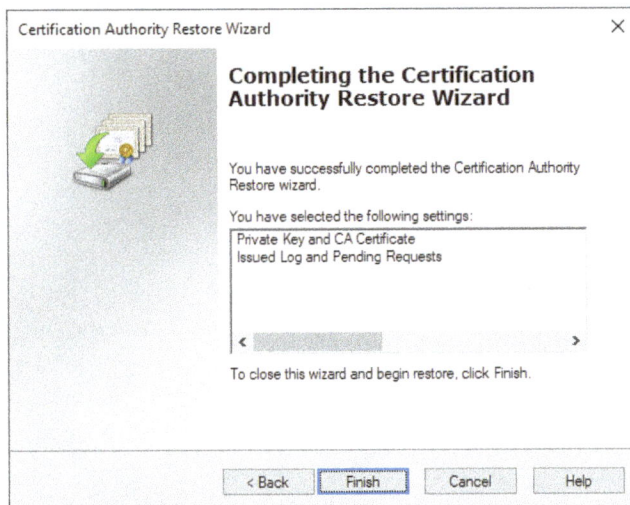

Certification Authority Restore Wizard

Completing the Certification Authority Restore Wizard

You have successfully completed the Certification Authority Restore wizard.

You have selected the following settings:

Private Key and CA Certificate
Issued Log and Pending Requests

To close this wizard and begin restore, click Finish.

< Back   Finish   Cancel   Help

8. If there were no issues, a prompt will appear stating that the restoration is complete and Active Directory Certificate Services needs to be started. Click the **Yes** button to continue.

If there were no errors during the restoration of the Certificate Authority, then the restoration of the Certificate Authority has been completed. Validate that the restoration was successful by opening the Certification Authority console and checking that the services are running correctly.

> **Root and Subordinate Server Restoration**
>
> Repeat the steps in this section for the TFS-ROOT-CA server. Replace all instances of the TFS-CA01 server name with the TFS-ROOT-CA server. The server will need to be powered on for the restoration to be made, and can be powered down immediately upon completing the restoration of the Certificate Authority.

AD CS Post-Implementation Tasks - Chapter Summary

The method for renewing the Root CA CRL is an important task that will need to be completed on a regular basis, and the process is critical for the operation of the Certificate Authority. The process for creating backups will always required for the CA, regardless of the method that is used. Both of these tasks are required to maintain a healthy PKI. The next chapter will focus on how to test Active Directory Certificate Services on an existing Active Directory domain.

Chapter 14 - AD CS on an Existing Domain

An important step to perform before deploying a Certificate Authority using Active Directory Certificate Services to an existing domain is to ensure that there are no potential issues with the existing domain. There are several reasons why deploying Active Directory Certificate Services can fail on an existing domain, or not work as intended, and it is important to identify issues before deploying the Certificate Authority to a production Active Directory domain.

The steps in this book involve the deployment of Active Directory Certificate Services to an Active Directory domain that was setup specifically for demonstration purposes. In a production environment this will almost never be the case as it is not practical to create a separate domain for a Certificate Authority. This would make the deployment of an Enterprise CA difficult to deploy and manage, and the benefits of using AD CS would not be fully utilized for an environment that is configured in this manner.

This chapter will focus of the steps that are needed to safely test the deployment of Active Directory Certificate Services on an existing domain. The major steps that are required to complete the testing are:

- Create a plan for how the Certificate Authority will be deployed.
- Check for any existing Active Directory Certificate Services deployments.
- Remove any existing Active Directory Certificate Services configurations if necessary.
- Create an isolated virtualization environment that is dedicated to the test environment.
- Clone a Domain Controller that is a member of the domain to be tested.
- Create the Root and Subordinate Certificate Authorities and test the deployment.

Once the steps in this chapter have been completed, and there are no issues with the deployment of Active Directory Certificate Services, then a Certificate Authority can be deployed on an existing domain.

Active Directory Domain and Test Environments

The steps that are found in this chapter are subjective, and may or may not apply to an environment that Active Directory Certificate Services will be deployed to. Active Directory domains are complex, and due to the age of a domain there can potentially be legacy issues that cause deployment problems. This is why it is important to test the deployment of the Certificate Authority in a controlled and non-destructive manner before attempting it on a production environment.

Similar to the previous chapters, the steps that are included in this chapter are not dependent on any particular virtualization platform. The only requirement is the ability to isolate a virtual machine from the same network as the production Active Directory domain to ensure that there is no interaction.

New and Old Active Directory Domains with Active Directory Certificate Services

The steps in this chapter are provided on the assumption that a Certificate Authority is being deployed to a legacy Active Directory domain that has been in use for a long period of time. If this is for a new domain, then the steps in this chapter are not necessary.

Test Environment Risks with Active Directory Domain Services

Ensure that while testing the steps in this chapter that the test environment is properly isolated from the production network. If a Domain Controller involved in this test is able to communicate with the production network, it could cause unintended issues if configuration settings are modified unintentionally.

AD CS on an Existing Domain - Prerequisites

Before beginning with a test of Active Directory Certificate Services on an existing domain, there are several tasks that should be performed first. At a minimum, the following items should be available prior to testing the deployment on an existing Active Directory domain:

- A virtualization environment that is able to be segmented from the production network.
- A Domain Administrator account (or equivalent) on the domain that is being tested.
- Access to a Domain Controller that is part of the domain where Active Directory Certificate Services will be tested.

There are two methods that can be used for creating a Domain Controller that can be used for testing Active Directory Certificate Services on an existing domain:

- Clone an existing Domain Controller that is already a member of the domain. Isolate the cloned Domain Controller once it has been cloned, and keep a copy of the virtual machine until testing has been completed.
- Create a new Domain Controller on the domain. Once created, remove the newly created Domain Controller from the production network, and leave the cloned Domain Controller for testing purposes. Keep a copy of the virtual machine until testing has been completed.

Either method for creating a Domain Controller will have the same result when testing Active Directory Certificate Services with minor modifications. In the next section, the steps that are required for testing a domain will be reviewed.

> ⚠️ **Domain Controller FSMO Roles**
>
> Ensure that the test Domain Controller that is used for testing Active Directory Certificate Servers has a healthy Active Directory configuration with a properly configured DNS server. This will ensure that the test is performed correctly, and that there are no potential issues with the implementation.
>
> As part of ensuring that the Domain Controller operates correctly, it may require seizing FSMO roles for the test domain which is beyond the scope of this book.

AD CS on an Existing Domain - Test Active Directory Certificate Services

There are a few ways to test an Active Directory Certificate Services deployment on an existing Active Directory domain without making changes to the production network. Since Active Directory Certificate Services makes changes to Active Directory, it is good practice to test the deployment prior to putting it into production. All that is needed for testing purposes is a Domain Controller that is a member of an existing Active Directory Domain. As specified in the previous section, there are different ways to get access to a Domain Controller that can be used for this purpose.

Regardless of which method is chosen for getting a Domain Controller for an existing Active Directory domain, ensure that the following steps are completed prior to attempting to deploy Active Directory Certificate Services:

1. Place the Domain Controller on a network segment that has no connections to the production network.
2. Test that an account with Domain Administrator privileges (or equivalent) are available, as it will be required for all tasks related to installing and configuring the Active Directory Certificate Services roles.
3. Update the DNS records on the Domain Controller to allow it to handle DNS resolution. This is also required if the IP addresses are changed for testing purposes.
4. If the Domain Controller does not have all FSMO roles available, seize those roles to ensure that all FSMO roles are on the test Domain Controller. This avoids Active Directory issues, so fixing this issue now save time with testing.

Once the Domain Controller has been properly isolated and setup for proper authentication and DNS resolution, proceed to testing the deployment of Active Directory Certificate Services on the domain. This book uses the fictional TFS Labs domain as an example for deploying a Certificate Authority using Active Directory Certificate Services, and the deployment steps in all chapters can be easily modified to fit with an existing Active Directory domain without too many changes required.

For example, if the fictional MJCB Active Directory domain was being used for testing the deployment of a Certificate Authority, the environment might look something like this:

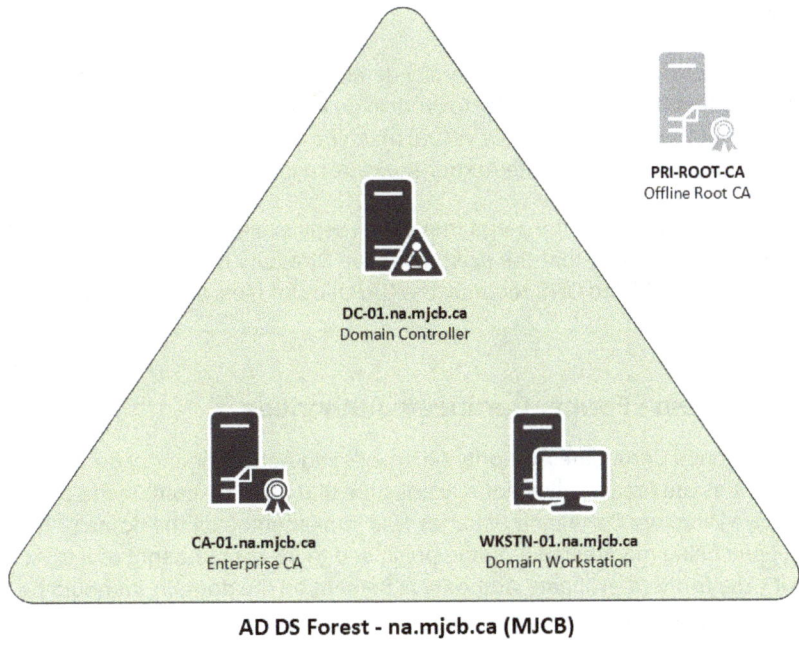

AD DS Forest - na.mjcb.ca (MJCB)

Figure 14.2.1: The MJCB Certificate Authority is a Two-Tier Certificate Authority consisting of a Root and Subordinate Certificate Authority. The Root CA server is offline and not a domain member.

The Certificate Authority hierarchy for the MJCB domain might look like this:

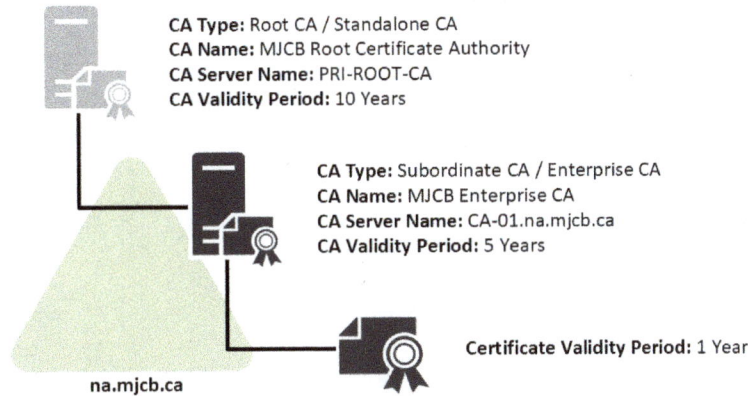

Figure 14.2.2: The MJCB Certificate Authority and MJCB Enterprise CA certificate can be viewed in the completed certificates for the MJCB domain. These two certificates make up the Two-Tier Certificate Authority, and make up the foundation of the PKI for the domain.

Testing the deployment of Active Directory Certificate Services in a controlled manner is strongly recommended prior to putting it into production. Active Directory domains that have been in production for extended periods of time tend to accumulate technical issues as they are upgraded and migrated over time, which can cause issues with complex services such as a Certificate Authority. Testing the deployment of Active Directory Certificate Services in a controlled manner on a copy of a Domain Controller is something that should seriously be considered prior to deploying it in production.

> **Testing Active Directory Certificate Services on an Existing Domain**
>
> On a high-level, testing the deployment of Active Directory Certificate Services on an existing domain should be performed in the following order:
>
> 1. Establish the Certificate Authority hierarchy details for the existing domain.
> 2. Configure the test Domain Controller to work in an isolated environment.
> 3. Create the Root Certificate Authority virtual machine and configure it as a Standalone CA.
> 4. Create the Subordinate Certificate Authority virtual machine and configure it as an Enterprise CA.
>
> This process more or less follows the steps that are already explained in this book. This will require customizing each step to ensure that the existing Active Directory domain works with the Certificate Authority. This means modifying DNS records, the CAPolicy.inf files, and any references to TFS Labs.

AD CS on an Existing Domain - Former Certificate Authorities

Before attempting to implement a Certificate Authority on an existing Active Directory domain, it is important to check if former Certificate Authorities are present. It is entirely possible that at some point in the past, a Certificate Authority on an older version of Active Directory Certificate Services was implemented on the domain. It is also possible that the Certificate Authority stopped being maintained at some point, and there are remnants of it in Active Directory. Regardless of how or why the former Certificate Authority is present on the domain, it should be safely removed prior to putting a new Certificate Authority in production. There are several ways that a former Certificate Authority can cause issues with a new Active Directory Certificate Services deployment:

- Cause conflicts with the CDP and AIA settings.
- Cause issues with Enterprise CA deployments.
- Cause issues with Certificate Templates that are stored in Active Directory.

The first step should be to check Active Directory to see if there was a former Certificate Authority in the domain. On any of the Domain Controllers in the domain, perform the following steps:

1. Open the **Active Directory Sites and Services** (dssite.msc) console on a Domain Controller in the domain:

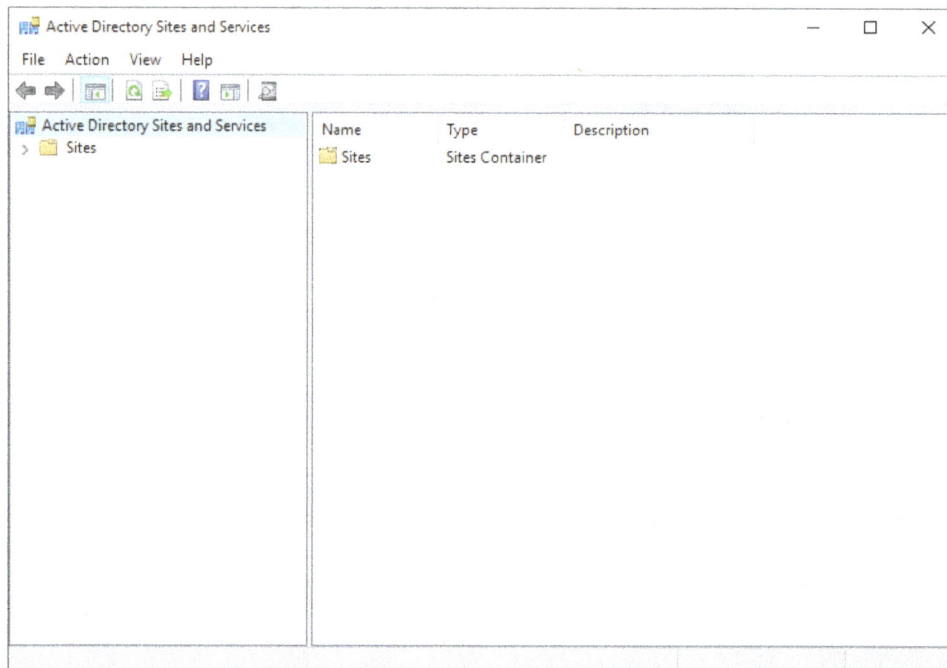

2. Ensure that the **Active Directory Sites and Services** node is selected, click on the **View** menu and select the **Show Services Node** option:

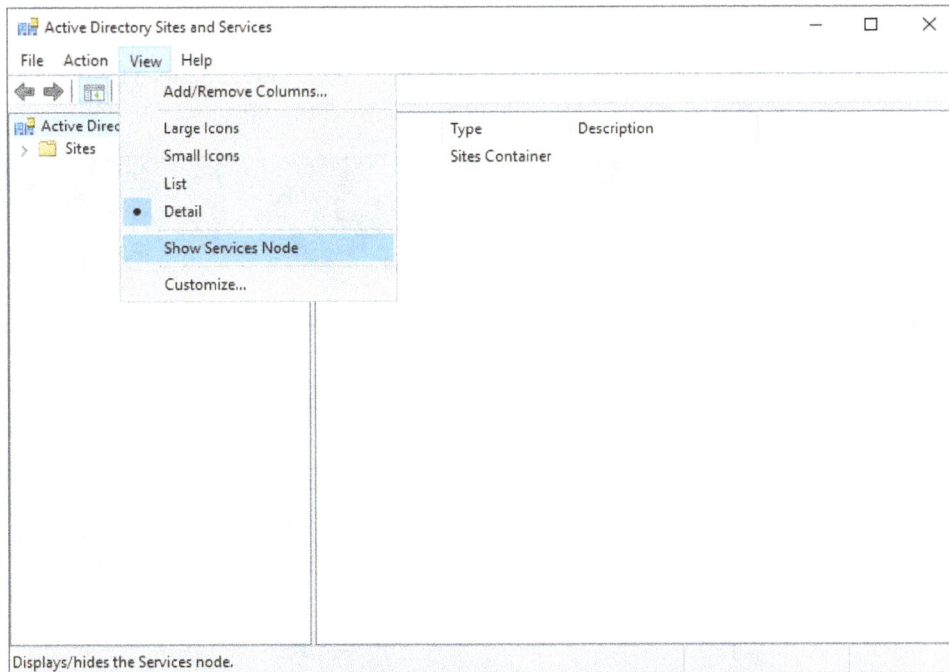

3. Expand the **Active Directory Sites and Services > Services > Public Key Services** node:

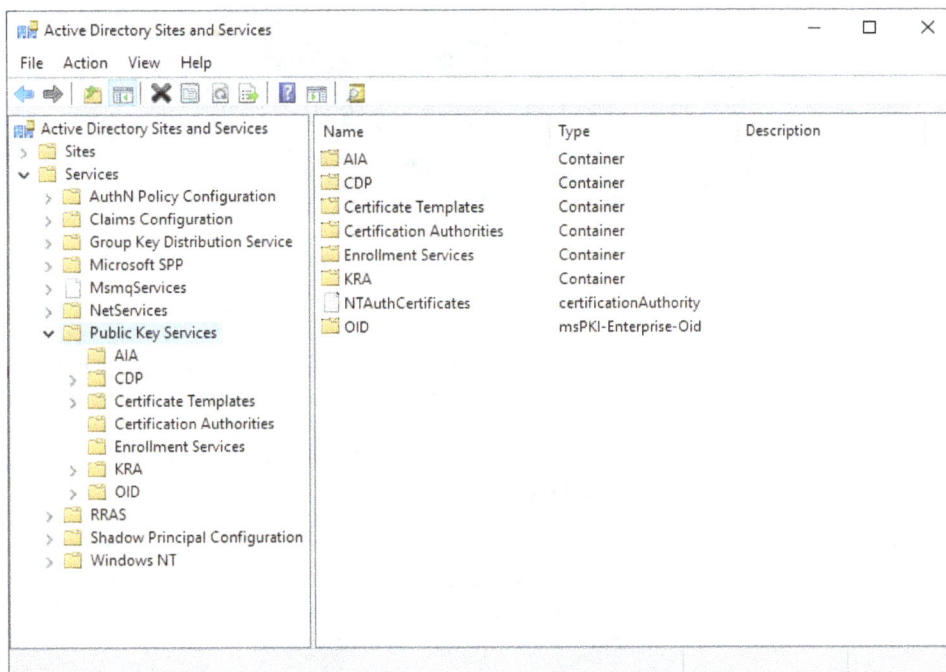

4. There are three nodes to check to verify that there was not previously an **Enterprise CA** or **Root CA** present on the domain:
   - **AIA**
   - **CDP**
   - **Certification Authorities**

5. If there was previously an **Enterprise CA** or **Root CA** present on the domain, any of those nodes will contain references to servers that hosted the **Active Directory Certificate Services** role. Check those servers to determine if they are still in use on the domain.
6. Close the **Active Directory Sites and Services** console.

There is an alternative method to checking Active Directory for former Certificate Authorities that may have been present. Open an **elevated PowerShell prompt** and run the following command on a Domain Controller:

Windows PowerShell (Elevated)

```
certutil.exe -dump
```

The output of the command will display all known Enterprise CA servers that are configured in Active Directory:

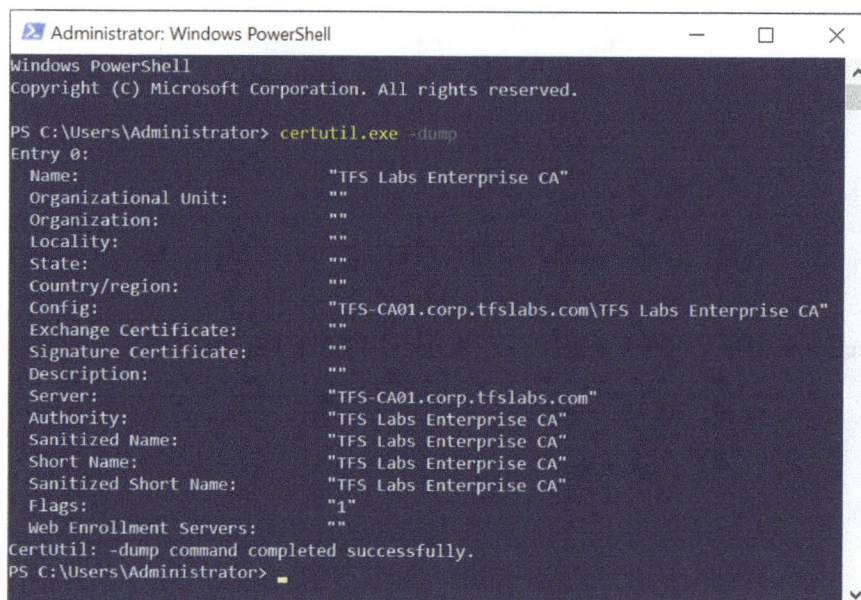

Figure 14.3.1: The certutil.exe tool will list the Enterprise CA servers that are registered and available within the Active Directory domain.

At the same time, check Group Policy on the domain to see if there are any Group Policy Objects that are being used to deploy certificates. Also check the Certificate Store on servers and workstations to see if there are any certificates in the **Trusted Root Certification Authorities** or **Intermediate Certification Authority** Stores that would have come from an Enterprise CA. Typically, these certificates are easy to find because the Root Certificate is usually missing since it is not deployed automatically by the Enterprise CA if there is a misconfiguration or the certificates are expired.

Removing former Certificate Authorities is easier to do before adding a new one to the environment, and leaving an old Certificate Authority in place can cause unexpected issues later that are not immediately apparent with a new Active Directory Certificate Services deployment. The process of removing a former Certificate Authority is beyond the scope of this book, but Microsoft does provide excellent documentation on how to do this properly.

AD CS on an Existing Domain - Chapter Summary

Now that the steps have been reviewed for how to test Active Directory Certificate Services on an existing domain, there are no additional tasks remaining for creating a Certificate Authority. The next chapter is optional, and it focuses on how to rapidly deploy a basic Two-Tier Certificate Authority.

Chapter 15 - AD CS Quick Start

This chapter will focus on quickly deploying a Two-Tier Certificate Authority using Active Directory Certificate Services. A subset of the instructions that were provided in the previous chapters of this book will be used for this task. This chapter uses a simplified and more basic Active Directory environment for demonstration purposes, which represents the bare minimum that is required for Active Directory Certificate Services to operate correctly. To make the deployment of Active Directory Certificate Services faster, all configurations will be done using the CLI instead of the GUI, whenever possible.

There are several items that are intentionally omitted from this chapter to make the deployment of the Certificate Authority faster, and those items include:

- A Windows 11 workstation for testing purposes.
- Group Policy and Security Policy changes to the Root CA server.
- BitLocker encryption of the Root CA server.
- Auditing in Active Directory Certificate Services.
- Deployment of certificates using Group Policy.
- Online Responder role deployment and configuration.
- Private key archival and recovery.
- Certificate Template customization.
- Certificate auto-enrollment options.

Even though this chapter focuses on quickly deploying a Certificate Authority using Active Directory Certificate Services using all available CLI commands, it does not offer an automated or scripted method.

This chapter will focus on setting up a basic Two-Tier Certificate Authority, with the option to add any additional features to the Certificate Authority at any given time after it has been created.

> **Active Directory Certificate Services Quick Start**
>
> This chapter is optional, and if the Certificate Authority has already been successfully created using the steps in previous chapters, skip this chapter as it is not necessary.

AD CS Quick Start - Environment Setup

The Active Directory domain that is going to be used in this chapter is the TFS Labs domain (corp.tfslabs.com), which is being used by a small IT Company that is based in Toronto, Ontario, Canada. In total, there are three Windows servers that will be used to build and test the TFS Labs environment:

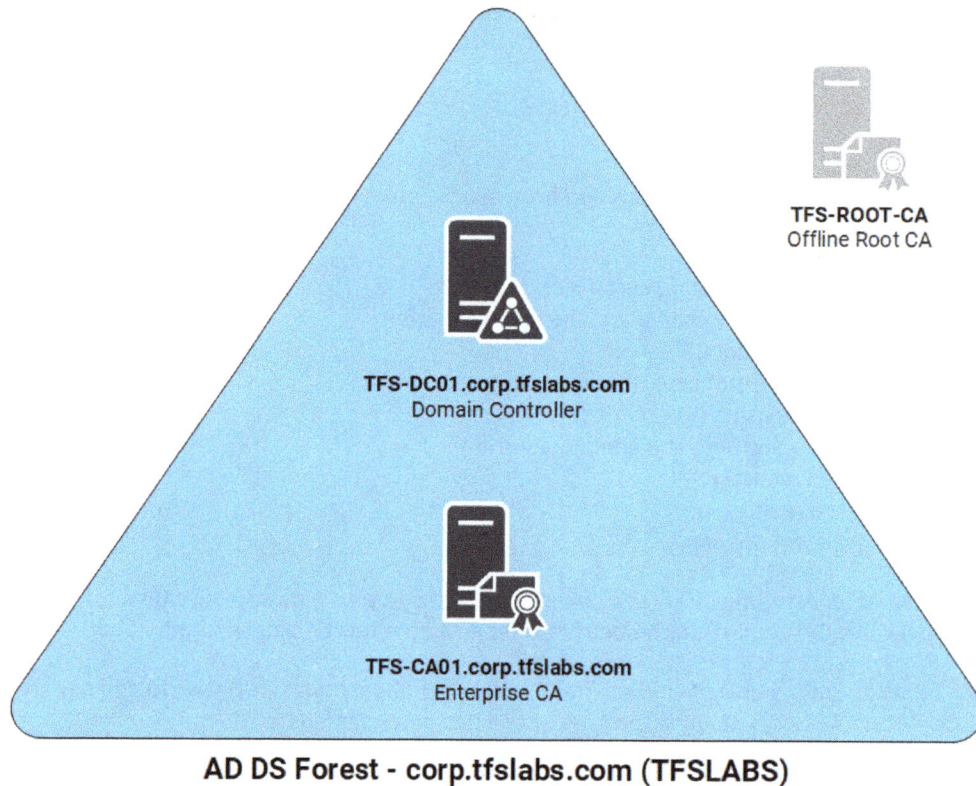

Figure 15.1.1: The TFS Labs Active Directory domain consists of three servers and no workstations. This domain represents the bare minimum environment required to test Active Directory Certificate Services.

The virtual machines that are being used in this chapter for the test environment are using the following specifications:

VM	Operating System	CPU	Memory	Disk	IP Address	Hyper-V Generation
TFS-CA01	Windows Server 2022	2	4096 MB	40 GB	10.100.1.101	1
TFS-DC01	Windows Server 2022	2	4096 MB	40 GB	10.100.1.100	2
TFS-ROOT-CA	Windows Server 2022	2	4096 MB	40 GB	N/A	1

Table 15.1.1: TFS Labs domain virtual machine specifications and network configurations.

Here is a breakdown of the servers that are being used in the TFS Labs test environment:

- **TFS-CA01** is the Subordinate Certificate Authority in the TFS Labs domain. It is an Enterprise CA that is using the Active Directory Certificate Services role. It is used to issue all certificates within the domain, except for the Root certificate that is issued by the Root Certificate Authority that is located on the TFS-ROOT-CA server. It is also used to handle CRL distribution that is needed for certificate revocation. It is a TFS Labs domain member server.
- **TFS-DC01** is the Domain Controller for the TFS Labs Active Directory domain. The Active Directory Forest and Domain Functional Levels are set to Windows Server 2016 Functional Levels.

- **TFS-ROOT-CA** is the Root Certificate Authority for the TFS Labs domain, which is a Standalone Certificate Authority that is using the Active Directory Certificate Services role. It is used to create the Root certificate, and is also used to sign the certificate for the Subordinate Certificate Authority. It is left in an offline state unless there is an issue with the Subordinate Certificate Authority, or the CRL needs to be updated (which occurs at least once a year). It is not a member of the TFS Labs domain, and is technically just a workgroup server. Once the implementation of the Certificate Authority is complete, this server can be shut down, but not deleted. This server has no network access to keep the server secured.

For networking purposes all devices in this test environment are using the 10.100.1.0/24 network. Since there is only a handful of devices involved, all the IP addresses are set to static and there is no DHCP server present to automatically distribute IP addresses.

For the certificates that will be issued for the TFS Labs domain, there will be one Root and one Subordinate certificate in a Two-Tier Certificate Authority. Here is an overview of what that certificate hierarchy will look like after the implementation of the Certificate Authority has been completed:

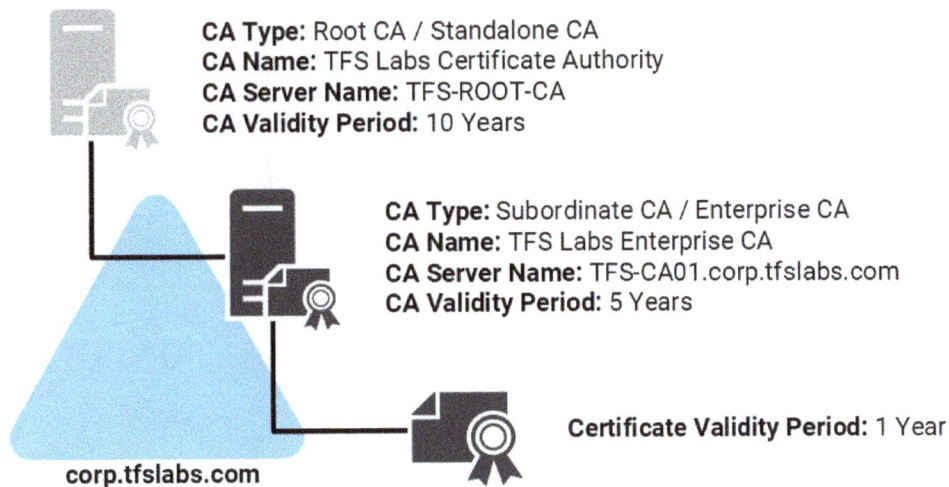

CA Type: Root CA / Standalone CA
CA Name: TFS Labs Certificate Authority
CA Server Name: TFS-ROOT-CA
CA Validity Period: 10 Years

CA Type: Subordinate CA / Enterprise CA
CA Name: TFS Labs Enterprise CA
CA Server Name: TFS-CA01.corp.tfslabs.com
CA Validity Period: 5 Years

Certificate Validity Period: 1 Year

corp.tfslabs.com

Figure 15.1.2: The TFS Labs Certificate Authority is a Two-Tier Certificate Authority consisting of a Root and Subordinate Certificate Authority.

The certificate structure and associated servers for TFS Labs Certificate Authority will be as follows:

Certificate Name	Certificate Type	Validity	Virtual Machine
TFS Labs Certificate Authority	Root Certificate	10 years	TFS-ROOT-CA
TFS Labs Enterprise CA	Subordinate Certificate	5 years	TFS-CA01
N/A	Issued Certificate	1 year	N/A

Table 15.1.2: TFS Labs Certificate Authority structure and validity periods for issued certificates.

Now that the TFS Labs domain has been explained, including the required virtual machines and the format of the certificate structure, proceed to provisioning the Domain Controller for the TFS Labs domain.

> **TFS Labs Test Workstation**
>
> There is no test workstation in this chapter as it is not necessary, but one can be added at any point after the Domain Controller is created and configured if the need for one arises.

AD CS Quick Start - AD DS Setup

Using Hyper-V, provision and configure a new virtual machine called TFS-DC01, and install Windows Server 2022 Standard (Desktop Experience) using the following specifications:

Virtual Machine Generation	2
Virtual Processors	2
Virtual Memory	4 GB (4096 MB)
Virtual Hard Disk	40 GB
Virtual Network Adapters	1

Table 15.2.1: Virtual machine specifications for the TFS-DC01 server.

Once the TFS-DC01 virtual machine has been created and the operating system has been installed, there are a few tasks that need to be completed:

- Set the password for the local administrator account (ensure that a complex password is used).
- Set the hostname of the server to TFS-DC01 (restart the server to apply the change).

Once the local Administrator account and the hostname have been setup, the network settings for the virtual machine will also need to be configured:

IP Address	10.100.1.100
Netmask	255.255.255.0
Gateway	10.100.1.1
DNS Server 1	1.1.1.1

Table 15.2.2: Network configuration and DNS settings for the TFS-DC01 server.

Once the network has been setup correctly, proceed to setting up the TFS-DC01 server as a Domain Controller.

TFS Labs External DNS Servers

Once the TFS-DC01 server has been successfully promoted to a Domain Controller, the DNS settings will be automatically updated to utilize the DNS server that has been added as part of the installation. The TFS-DC01 server will be added as the first DNS server in the network settings, and the original DNS entry will be automatically moved to the second DNS server. If there are any DNS resolution issues after the Domain Controller promotion, check the DNS settings on the TFS-DC01 server to ensure that there is a forwarding DNS server listed to allow for DNS resolution.

TFS Labs Domain Administrator Account Password

The password that is set for the local administrator account during the initial setup of the TFS-DC01 server will become the password for the Domain Administrator account for the TFS Labs domain once the server has been promoted to a Domain Controller. Ensure that this is a strong password since it is going to be the most privileged account in the TFS Labs domain. Once the Active Directory installation has been completed, the local administrator account that is on the TFS-DC01 server will become the **TFSLABS\Administrator** account, which is the Domain Administrator account for the TFS Labs domain. This Domain Administrator account will be used for the remainder of the Certificate Authority implementation, except for any configurations made on the Offline Root CA server.

AD CS Quick Start - AD DS Setup - AD DS Installation

To install the Active Directory Domain Services role on the TFS-DC01 server, perform the following steps:

1. Open an **elevated PowerShell prompt**.
2. Run the following command to install the **Active Directory Domain Services** role and the necessary **Remote Server Administration Tools**:

```
Windows PowerShell (Elevated)

Install-WindowsFeature AD-Domain-Services, RSAT-ADDS
```

3. Once the installation for **Active Directory Domain Services** has completed, close the **PowerShell prompt**.

Once the Active Directory Domain Services role has been installed on the TFS-DC01 server, proceed to configuring the AD DS role to create the Domain Controller for the domain.

AD CS Quick Start - AD DS Setup - AD DS Configuration

Once the Active Directory Domain Services role has been installed on the TFS-DC01 server, it will need to be properly configured to become a Domain Controller for the TFS Labs domain. In the process of configuring the TFS Labs domain, the following Active Directory Domain settings will be configured on the TFS-DC01 server:

Forest Name	corp.tfslabs.com
NetBIOS Domain Name	TFSLABS
Forest Functional Level	Windows Server 2016
Domain Functional Level	Windows Server 2016

Table 15.2.2.1: Active Directory domain configuration options for the TFS Labs domain.

To configure the TFS-DC01 server as a Domain Controller for the TFS Labs domain, perform the following steps:

1. Open an **elevated PowerShell prompt**.
2. Run the following command to import the **ADDSDeployment** PowerShell module which is needed to configure **Active Directory Domain Services**:

```
Windows PowerShell (Elevated)

Import-Module ADDSDeployment
```

3. Run the following command to configure **Active Directory Domain Services**:

```
Windows PowerShell (Elevated)

Install-ADDSForest `
-CreateDnsDelegation:$false `
-DatabasePath "C:\Windows\NTDS" `
-DomainMode "WinThreshold" `
-DomainName "corp.tfslabs.com" `
-DomainNetbiosName "TFSLABS" `
-ForestMode "WinThreshold" `
-InstallDns:$true `
-LogPath "C:\Windows\NTDS" `
-NoRebootOnCompletion:$false `
-SysvolPath "C:\Windows\SYSVOL" `
-Force:$true
```

4. The command will prompt for setting the **SafeModeAdministratorPassword**, which is the **Directory Services Restore Mode (DSRM)** password. Enter a complex password for this, and the command will prompt to confirm the password before proceeding (ensure that this password is recorded in case it is needed).
5. The **Active Directory Domain Services** configuration will take several minutes to complete.
6. The **TFS-DC01** server will automatically restart when the configuration has completed.

Once the TFS-DC01 server has restarted, there is now a functioning Domain Controller for the TFS Labs domain. Proceed to the OU configuration for the TFS Labs domain.

AD CS Quick Start - AD DS Setup - OU Structure Configuration

It is optional to create an Organizational Unit (OU) structure for organizing the objects in the Active Directory domain, and the Certificate Authority deployment will function without it. The OU structure for the TFS Labs domain is not complex, and consists of the following structure:

- TFS Labs
- TFS Labs\TFS Servers
- TFS Labs\TFS Users

To create a basic OU structure using PowerShell, perform the following steps on the TFS-DC01 server:

1. Open an **elevated PowerShell prompt**.
2. Run the following commands to create the **OU structure**:

```
Windows PowerShell (Elevated)

New-ADOrganizationalUnit `
-Name "TFS Labs" `
-Path "DC=corp,DC=tfslabs,DC=com"

New-ADOrganizationalUnit `
-Name "TFS Servers" `
-Path "OU=TFS Labs,DC=corp,DC=tfslabs,DC=com"

New-ADOrganizationalUnit `
-Name "TFS Users" `
-Path "OU=TFS Labs,DC=corp,DC=tfslabs,DC=com"
```

3. Close the **PowerShell prompt**.

Once the OU structure has been created for the TFS Labs domain, the Domain Administrator account needs to have the email address field set to ensure that there are no issues with certificates being issued to the account.

AD CS Quick Start - AD DS Setup - Administrator Configuration

Before moving on from setting up the TFS Labs domain, the Domain Administrator account should have the email address field set as well. The Domain Administrator account can be found in the Users OU in the TFS Labs domain (this account is not moved at all in this chapter, so it should be found there by default). The change can be made from an **elevated PowerShell prompt** with the following command on the TFS-DC01 server:

```
Windows PowerShell (Elevated)

Set-ADUser `
-Identity Administrator `
-EmailAddress "administrator@corp.tfslabs.com"
```

Now that the email field has been set for the Domain Administrator account, there should be no problems with issuing certificates for that account. Proceed to creating the Root CA server for the TFS Labs domain.

AD CS Quick Start - Root CA Setup

Using Hyper-V, provision and configure a new virtual machine called TFS-ROOT-CA and install Windows Server 2022 Standard (Desktop Experience) using the following specifications:

Virtual Machine Generation	1
Virtual Processors	2
Virtual Memory	4 GB (4096 MB)
Virtual Hard Disk	40 GB
Virtual Network Adapters	0

Table 15.3.1: Virtual machine specifications for the TFS-ROOT-CA server.

Once the TFS-ROOT-CA virtual machine has been created and the operating system has been installed, there are a few tasks that need to be completed before proceeding to configure the Root Certificate Authority. Several of these steps will require the TFS-ROOT-CA server to be restarted for the settings to be applied correctly:

1. Set the local Administrator account on the **TFS-ROOT-CA** server to a complex password that is at least 14 characters and store the password securely. Ensure that there are no additional user accounts present on the server (this can be verified in the Computer Management console). The Guest account that is created by default should already be disabled as part of the installation of Windows Server.
2. Set the hostname of the server to **TFS-ROOT-CA** (restart the server to apply the change).
3. Set the **TFS-ROOT-CA** server to be a member of the **TFS-CA** workgroup (restart the server to apply the change).
4. On the root of the **C:\ drive** create a folder called **RootCA** (C:\RootCA). This folder will store the Root certificate, Subordinate certificate, CRL files and any other certificate files that are needed during the entire Certificate Authority implementation process.
5. Create a virtual floppy disk on the Hyper-V host named **RootCAFiles.vfd** and then insert the **RootCAFiles.vfd** virtual floppy disk into the virtual floppy drive. Format the floppy disk using the default settings using Windows File Explorer. Eject the virtual floppy disk when the formatting has been completed.

Once the TFS-ROOT-CA server has been initially configured, the server can now be configured with Active Directory Certificate Services.

> ℹ️ **Virtual Floppy Disk Location**
>
> If the virtual floppy disk is being created using Hyper-V, ensure that the location is accessible by both the TFS-ROOT-CA and TFS-CA01 servers. This virtual floppy disk will be deleted at the end of this chapter.

AD CS Quick Start - Root CA Setup - Local Policies

Once the TFS-ROOT-CA server has been setup, the Local Group Policy settings and Local Security Policies can now be configured to increase the security of the local administrator account on the server. Normally these changes are made with Group Policy on an Active Directory domain, but since the TFS-ROOT-CA server is not a domain member the changes need to be made locally. If these policy changes are required, the steps are thoroughly documented in an earlier chapter. If the policy changes are not needed, proceed to configuring the CAPolicy.inf file for the Root CA.

AD CS Quick Start - Root CA Setup - CAPolicy.inf Installation

The CAPolicy.inf file is used to add configuration details to the Certificate Authority at the time when the Root certificate is created. On the TFS-ROOT-CA server, create a file in the C:\Windows folder called CAPolicy.inf (ensure that the file is saved with the correct file extension otherwise these settings will be ignored).

Copy the following contents into the CAPolicy.inf file and save the file before continuing:

```
C:\Windows\CAPolicy.inf

[Version]
Signature = "$Windows NT$"

[PolicyStatementExtension]
Policies = AllIssuancePolicy, InternalPolicy
Critical = FALSE

[AllIssuancePolicy]
; Enables all Certificate Templates.
OID = 2.5.29.32.0

[InternalPolicy]
OID = 1.2.3.4.1455.67.89.5
Notice = "The TFS Labs Certification Authority is an internal only resource."
URL = http://pki.corp.tfslabs.com/cps.html

[Certsrv_Server]
; Renewal information for the Root CA.
RenewalKeyLength = 4096
RenewalValidityPeriod = Years
RenewalValidityPeriodUnits = 10

; Disable support for issuing certificates using RSASSA-PSS.
AlternateSignatureAlgorithm = 0

; The CRL publication period is the lifetime of the Root CA.
CRLPeriod = Years
CRLPeriodUnits = 10

; The option for Delta CRL is disabled since this is a Root CA.
CRLDeltaPeriod = Days
CRLDeltaPeriodUnits = 0
```

Once the CAPolicy.inf file has been saved, proceed to installing the AD CS role on the TFS-ROOT-CA server.

Certificate Authority OID Number

The OID number that is defined in the **InternalPolicy** section of the CAPolicy.inf file can be modified if necessary for an organization. The OID number in this example is used in Microsoft technical documentation, but it should work for any organization if it is only ever going to be used internally. If a customized OID number is required for a Certificate Authority, a Private Enterprise Number can be registered through the IANA.

If a custom OID number is required for the Certificate Authority, modify the OID line in the **InternalPolicy** section to **OID = 1.3.6.1.4.1.X** (replace the X with the PEN number that was previously registered).

Ensure that if a custom OID is configured for the Root certificate that the same OID number is used when creating the CAPolicy.inf file for the Subordinate certificate. If these numbers do not match, there could be issues with certificates that are issued.

Delta CRL with Root Certificate Authorities

A Delta CRL is not normally required for a Root Certificate Authority, especially one that is offline since it is not normally handling certificate revocations in a PKI. The Root CA is only ever used to issue a Base CRL when there are Subordinate Certificate Authorities present in the PKI.

The Base CRL is updated on a yearly basis as per the configuration of the CAPolicy.inf file that is used in this example, and that file is copied to an online Certificate Authority (typically the Subordinate CA) whenever it is updated.

The only certificates that are typically revoked by a Root CA are Subordinate certificates, and that would necessitate the deployment of a new Base CRL instead of a Delta CRL when the certificate is revoked and a new one is issued.

Signature Algorithm Support Issues

The **AlternateSignatureAlgorithm = 0** flag in the CAPolicy.inf file explicitly uses SHA256 for the algorithm instead of the legacy RSASSA-PSS algorithm. This can cause issues with some devices (especially iOS) and by ensuring that it is disabled there should be no issues with certificates issued by the Certificate Authority.

CAPolicy.inf File Name and Locations

Ensure that the CAPolicy.inf file has been properly saved in the C:\Windows folder (%WINDIR%). Also make sure that the file extension is set to INF and not TXT. A common mistake is to accidentally save the file as CAPolicy.inf.txt.

If the CAPolicy.inf file is not saved in the correct directory and without the correct file extension, all settings in the file will be ignored at the time when the Certificate Authority is created. An error message will not be displayed if the file is not named correctly, and the only way to verify that the settings are correct is to check the Root certificate after it has been created.

If there is an error with the settings in the CAPolicy.inf file, the Root certificate will not be created.

AD CS Quick Start - Root CA Setup - AD CS Role Installation

The Active Directory Certificate Services installation can be performed using PowerShell by running the following steps on the TFS-ROOT-CA server:

1. Open an **elevated PowerShell prompt**.
2. Run the following command to install the **Active Directory Certificate Services** role and the necessary **Administration Tools**:

```
Windows PowerShell (Elevated)

Add-WindowsFeature -Name ADCS-Cert-Authority -IncludeManagementTools
```

3. The command will automatically install the **Active Directory Certificate Services** role and output a **Success** status of **True**.
4. Once the installation for **Active Directory Certificate Services** has completed, close the **PowerShell prompt**.

Once the Active Directory Certificate Services role has been installed, proceed to configuring the role and creating the Root certificate for the TFS Labs domain.

AD CS Quick Start - Root CA Setup - AD CS Role Configuration

Once the Active Directory Certificate Services role has been installed it will need to be configured to work as the Root Certificate Authority. In the process of configuring the Active Directory Certificate Services role for the TFS Labs domain, the following Root Certificate will be created:

Certificate Authority Setup Type	Standalone CA
Certificate Authority Type	Root CA
Cryptographic Provider	RSA#Microsoft Software Key Storage Provider
Key Length	4096 Bits
Signature Hash Algorithm	SHA256
CA Common Name	TFS Labs Certificate Authority
Validity Period	10 years

Table 15.3.4.1: Active Directory Certificate Services configuration for the Root Certificate Authority.

The Active Directory Certificate Services configuration can be performed using PowerShell by running the following steps on the TFS-ROOT-CA server:

1. Open an **elevated PowerShell prompt**.
2. Run the following command to configure the **Active Directory Certificate Services** role and create the **Root Certificate**:

```
Windows PowerShell (Elevated)

Install-AdcsCertificationAuthority `
-CAType StandaloneRootCA `
-CACommonName "TFS Labs Certificate Authority" `
-KeyLength 4096 `
-HashAlgorithm SHA256 `
-CryptoProviderName "RSA#Microsoft Software Key Storage Provider" `
-ValidityPeriod Years `
-ValidityPeriodUnits 10 `
-DatabaseDirectory $(Join-Path $env:SystemRoot "System32\CertLog") `
-Force
```

3. The command will automatically configure the **Active Directory Certificate Services** role and output an **ErrorID** status of **0**.
4. Once the configuration for **Active Directory Certificate Services** has completed, close the **PowerShell prompt**.

At this point the Root Certificate for the TFS Labs domain has been created. Proceed to validating that the Certificate Authority has been successfully created in the next section.

> **Root Certificate Authority Private Key**
>
> Since this is a new CA installation and the private key is not being restored from a previous server, a new private key will be created. The private key for the Root certificate will reside on the TFS-ROOT-CA server.

AD CS Quick Start - Root CA Setup - Root CA Validation

To verify that the Active Directory Certificate Services role has been successfully configured and the Root certificate was created, open the Certification Authority console (certsrv.msc) on the TFS-ROOT-CA server to check the Certificate Authority status, which should be running.

The Root certificate can also be viewed to verify that it was created with the correct values that were setup during the Active Directory Certificate Services configuration:

Figure 15.3.5.1: The TFS Labs Certificate Authority issued the Root certificate to itself, as it is the root of the PKI for the TFS Labs domain. The validity period for the Root certificate is important, since that will affect any Subordinate certificates that are issued by the Certificate Authority.

When the Subordinate Certificate Authority is created on the TFS-CA01 server in the next chapter, it can also be validated that the Offline CA is functioning correctly when that certificate is created. The CDP and AIA settings still requires some customization to work correctly with the TFS Labs domain, and those settings will be configured on the Root Certificate Authority later in this chapter.

If everything has been setup correctly for the Root certificate, proceed to configuring the CRL for the Root CA and specifying the validity period for any signed certificates.

AD CS Quick Start - Root CA Setup - Root CA CRL Configuration

The CRL configuration for the Root CA is configured in this section to give greater control over when the CRL expires and needs to be renewed. The time is being extended to 52 weeks since the CRL does not need to be updated that often on the Root CA. The changes here also ensures that the Subordinate CA lifetime is extended from 1 year to 5 years.

All the commands in this section are just making changes to the Windows Registry using the certutil.exe command. The settings for the Certificate Authority can be viewed at any time by opening the Windows Registry (regedit.exe), and going to the following location:

HKLM\SYSTEM\CurrentControlSet\Services\CertSvc\Configuration

> **Active Directory Customization**
>
> During the configuration of the Root Certificate Authority in this section, the **Active Directory Configuration Partition Distinguished Name** is configured for the Certificate Revocation List. This is specific to the TFS Labs Active Directory domain, and this configuration is unique for every organization. Steps on how to determine the correct Active Directory information are provided in this section.

> **CRL Renewal Period**
>
> As defined in step 4 below, the CRL Period on the Root Certificate Authority is set to 52 weeks. This means that every 52 weeks there will be a need to power on the TFS-ROOT-CA server and renew the CRL. A reminder should be set to perform this task every 50 weeks to ensure that it is renewed on time and distributed to the rest of the PKI in the environment. Renewing the CRL early does not cause any issues, and it is advised to renew it ahead of time before it expires to avoid issues.

To configure the CRL settings for the Root CA, perform the following steps on the TFS-ROOT-CA server:

1. Open an **elevated PowerShell prompt**.
2. To define the **Active Directory Configuration Partition Distinguished Name**, run the following command (replace **DC=corp,DC=tfslabs,DC=com** with the distinguished name of the Active Directory domain):

```
Windows PowerShell (Elevated)

certutil.exe -setreg `
CA\DSConfigDN "CN=Configuration,DC=corp,DC=tfslabs,DC=com"
```

3. To define the **Validity Period Units** for all issued certificates by the Root Certificate Authority, run following commands:

```
Windows PowerShell (Elevated)

certutil.exe -setreg CA\ValidityPeriodUnits 5
certutil.exe -setreg CA\ValidityPeriod "Years"
```

4. To define the **CRL Period Units** and **CRL Period**, run the following commands:

```
Windows PowerShell (Elevated)

certutil.exe -setreg CA\CRLPeriodUnits 52
certutil.exe -setreg CA\CRLPeriod "Weeks"
```

5. To define the **CRL Overlap Period Units** and **CRL Overlap Period**, run the following commands:

```
Windows PowerShell (Elevated)

certutil.exe -setreg CA\CRLOverlapPeriodUnits 12
certutil.exe -setreg CA\CRLOverlapPeriod "Hours"
```

6. Restart the **Active Directory Certificate Services** service to apply the changes:

```
Windows PowerShell (Elevated)

net stop CertSvc
net start CertSvc
```

7. Close the **PowerShell prompt**.

Once the CRL settings have been configured on the Root Certificate Authority, proceed to configuring the CDP and AIA settings on the Root CA.

Determining the Active Directory Configuration Partition Distinguished Name

There are several ways to determine the Active Directory Configuration Partition Distinguished Name in an Active Directory domain. One of the easiest ways to determine the correct format of this name can be accomplished in only a few steps by using the Active Directory Users and Computers console on a Domain Controller.

Perform the following steps to determine the Active Directory Configuration Partition Distinguished Name for an Active Directory domain:

1. On the **TFS-DC01** server, open the **Active Directory Users and Computers** console (dsa.msc).
2. Go to the **View** menu and select **Advanced Features**.
3. Right-click on **corp.tfslabs.com** and select **Properties**.
4. Go to the **Attribute Editor** tab.
5. Scroll down and find the **distinguishedName** attribute field, and click the **View** button:

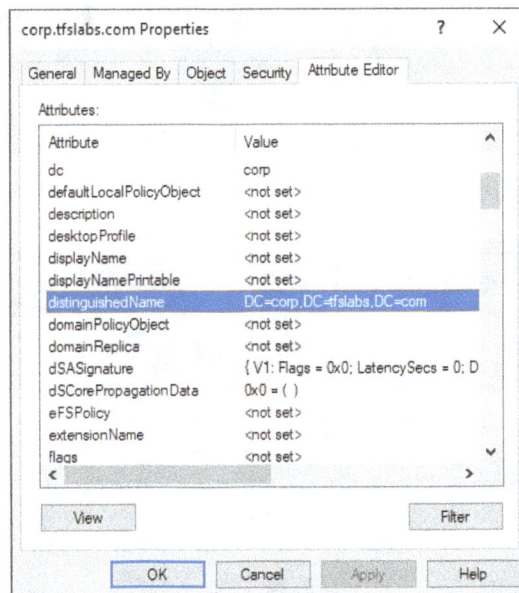

6. The **String Attribute Editor** window will appear for the **distinguishedName** attribute. Copy the value in the **Value** field, this is the information needed for configuring the CRL.

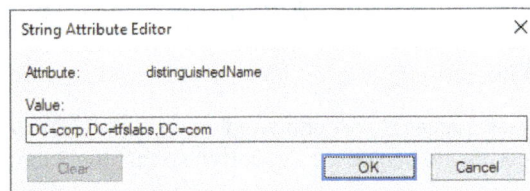

7. Close the **Active Directory Users and Computers** console.

Aside from using the Active Directory Users and Computers console to retrieve the Active Directory Configuration Partition Distinguished Name, the ADSI Edit (Active Directory Service Interface Editor) tool (adsiedit.msc) can also be used to obtain the same result.

AD CS Quick Start - Root CA Setup - CDP and AIA Configuration

The CRL files that are provided by the Root CA are distributed with the Subordinate CA, and this is because the Root CA is not available on the network so there is no way for devices to access the files on the TFS Labs domain. This is accomplished by configuring the CDP and AIA settings on the Root CA by specifying certain DNS records and pointing them to the TFS-CA01 server. The Base CRL will be configured and exported as part of this section, and the Delta CRL will be published on the Subordinate CA in the next chapter. There are multiple locations where the CDP and AIA locations are used for the Root Certificate Authority, but not all are needed:

- Local File System
- LDAP
- HTTP
- SMB

The CDP and AIA settings can be configured using the command line using PowerShell on the TFS-ROOT-CA server:

1. Open an **elevated PowerShell prompt**.
2. Run the following command to configure the **CDP** settings for the Root certificate (execute this command as a single line with no breaks):

```
Windows PowerShell (Elevated)

certutil.exe -setreg CA\CRLPublicationURLs "65:C:\Windows\system32\CertSrv\
CertEnroll\%3%8%9.crl\n6:http://pki.corp.tfslabs.com/CertData/%3%8%9.crl"
```

3. Run the following command to configure the **AIA** settings for the Root certificate (execute this command as a single line with no breaks):

```
Windows PowerShell (Elevated)

certutil.exe -setreg CA\CACertPublicationURLs "1:C:\Windows\system32\CertSrv\
CertEnroll\%1_%3%4.crt\n2:http://pki.corp.tfslabs.com/CertData/%1_%3%4.crt"
```

4. Restart the **Active Directory Certificate Services** service to apply the changes:

```
Windows PowerShell (Elevated)

net stop CertSvc
net start CertSvc
```

5. To publish the **CRL**, run the following command:

```
Windows PowerShell (Elevated)

certutil.exe -crl
```

6. Close the **PowerShell prompt**.

Now that the CRL settings have been successfully configured on the TFS-ROOT-CA server and the CRL has been published, the CRL and the Root certificate can now be exported so that the Subordinate CA server can host it for the TFS Labs domain.

AD CS Quick Start - Root CA Setup - Root CA Certificate and CRL Export

Exporting the Root certificate and the Root CRL is needed to make it available on the TFS-CA01 server and for the rest of the TFS Labs domain. The links to these files were referenced in the Root certificate configuration, so they will need to be copied to the Subordinate CA server for users to be able to access these files. To prepare the Root certificate and Root CRL files, perform the following steps on the TFS-ROOT-CA server:

1. Copy the contents of the **C:\Windows\System32\CertSrv\CertEnroll** folder to the **C:\RootCA** folder.
2. The following files should be present in the **C:\RootCA** folder:
   - C:\RootCA\TFS Labs Certificate Authority.crl
   - C:\RootCA\TFS-ROOT-CA_TFS Labs Certificate Authority.crt
3. Add the **RootCAFiles.vfd** virtual floppy disk to the **TFS-ROOT-CA** virtual machine.
4. Copy the contents of the **C:\RootCA** folder to the **A:\ drive**.
5. Eject the **RootCAFiles.vfd** virtual floppy disk.

Once the Root certificate and CRL files have been successfully copied to the virtual floppy disk, all the initial tasks for the TFS-ROOT-CA server are now complete. The Subordinate CA server can now be created and configured.

AD CS Quick Start - Subordinate CA Setup

Using Hyper-V, provision and configure a new virtual machine called TFS-CA01 and install Windows Server 2022 Standard (Desktop Experience) using the following specifications:

Virtual Machine Generation	1
Virtual Processors	2
Virtual Memory	4 GB (4096 MB)
Virtual Hard Disk	40 GB
Virtual Network Adapters	1

Table 15.4.1: Virtual machine specifications for the TFS-CA01 server.

Once the TFS-CA01 virtual machine has been created and the operating system has been installed, there are a few tasks that need to be completed:

- Set the local administrator account on the TFS-CA01 server to a complex password that is at least 14 characters.
- Set the hostname to TFS-CA01 (restart the server to apply the change).

Once the local administrator account and the hostname have been setup, the network settings for the virtual machine will also need to be configured:

IP Address	10.100.1.101
Netmask	255.255.255.0
Gateway	10.100.1.1
DNS Server 1	10.100.1.100

Table 15.4.2: Network configuration settings for the TFS-CA01 server.

Once the network settings have been configured for the server, join the TFS-CA01 server to the TFS Labs domain (restart the server to apply the change). If the Organizational Unit (OU) structure was created earlier in this chapter, move the TFS-CA01 computer object by running the following command from an **elevated PowerShell prompt** on the TFS-DC01 server:

```
Windows PowerShell (Elevated)

Get-ADComputer "TFS-CA01" | `
Move-ADObject -TargetPath "OU=TFS Servers,OU=TFS Labs,DC=corp,DC=tfslabs,DC=com"
```

Once the server has been setup and joined to the TFS Labs domain, proceed to the next steps on creating DNS records to support the Active Directory Certificate Services role.

AD CS Quick Start - Subordinate CA Setup - Create CNAME Records in DNS

The PKI.corp.tfslabs.com CNAME record needs to be added to the TFS Labs DNS Zone to support the PKI infrastructure in the TFS Labs domain, and the record can be added by performing the following steps on the TFS-DC01 server:

1. Open an **elevated PowerShell prompt**.
2. Enter the following command to create a **CNAME** record for **PKI.corp.tfslabs.com**:

```
Windows PowerShell (Elevated)

Add-DnsServerResourceRecordCName `
  -Name "PKI" -HostNameAlias "TFS-CA01.corp.tfslabs.com" -ZoneName "corp.tfslabs.com"
```

3. Close the **PowerShell prompt**.

Once the DNS record has been created, proceed to creating the CAPolicy.inf file for the Subordinate certificate.

AD CS Quick Start - Subordinate CA Setup - CAPolicy.inf Installation

On the TFS-ROOT-CA server, create a file in the C:\Windows folder called CAPolicy.inf (ensure that the file is saved with the correct file extension otherwise these settings will be ignored). Copy the following contents into this file:

```
C:\Windows\CAPolicy.inf

[Version]
Signature = "$Windows NT$"

[PolicyStatementExtension]
Policies = AllIssuancePolicy, InternalPolicy
Critical = FALSE

[AllIssuancePolicy]
; Enables all Certificate Templates.
OID = 2.5.29.32.0

[InternalPolicy]
OID = 1.2.3.4.1455.67.89.5
; Certification Practice Statement
Notice = "The TFS Labs Certification Authority is an internal only resource."
URL = http://pki.corp.tfslabs.com/cps.html

[Certsrv_Server]
; Renewal information for the Subordinate CA.
RenewalKeyLength = 4096
RenewalValidityPeriod = Years
RenewalValidityPeriodUnits = 5

; Disable support for issuing certificates using RSASSA-PSS.
AlternateSignatureAlgorithm = 0

; Load all certificate templates by default.
LoadDefaultTemplates = 1
```

Once the CAPolicy.inf file has been saved, proceed to installing the AD CS role on the TFS-CA01 server.

Certificate Authority OID Number

The OID number that is defined in the **InternalPolicy** section of the CAPolicy.inf file can be modified if necessary for an organization. The OID number in this example is used in Microsoft technical documentation, but it should work for any organization if it is only ever going to be used internally.

If a customized OID number is required for a Certificate Authority, a Private Enterprise Number can be registered through the IANA.

If a custom OID number is required for the Certificate Authority, modify the OID line in the **InternalPolicy** section to **OID = 1.3.6.1.4.1.X** (replace the X with the PEN number that was previously registered).

Ensure that if a custom OID is configured for the Root certificate that the same OID number is used when creating the CAPolicy.inf file for the Subordinate certificate. If these numbers do not match, there could be issues with certificates that are issued.

Delta CRL with Subordinate Certificate Authorities

A Delta CRL is not normally required for a Root Certificate Authority, especially one that is offline since it is not normally handling certificate revocations in a PKI. The Root CA is only ever used to issue a Base CRL when there are Subordinate Certificate Authorities present in the Certificate Authority.

The only certificates that are typically revoked by a Root CA is a Subordinate certificate, so that would necessitate the deployment of a new Base CRL instead of a Delta CRL.

Since this is a Subordinate CA that is always online and used for handling all regular Certificate Authority tasks, a Delta CRL is needed to revoke certificates much more frequently. A Delta CRL can also be used in parallel with OCSP, which is optionally configured in a later chapter of this book.

Signature Algorithm Support Issues

The **AlternateSignatureAlgorithm = 0** flag in the CAPolicy.inf file explicitly uses SHA256 for the algorithm instead of the legacy RSASSA-PSS algorithm. This can cause issues with some devices (especially iOS) and by ensuring that it is disabled there should be no issues with certificates issued by the Certificate Authority.

CAPolicy.inf File Name and Locations

Ensure that the CAPolicy.inf file has been properly saved in the C:\Windows folder (%WINDIR%). Also make sure that the file extension is set to INF and not TXT. A common mistake is to accidentally save the file as CAPolicy.inf.txt.

If the CAPolicy.inf file is not saved in the correct directory and without the correct file extension, all settings in the file will be ignored at the time when the Certificate Authority is created.

AD CS Quick Start - Subordinate CA Setup - AD CS Role Installation

The Active Directory Certificate Services installation can be performed using PowerShell by running the following steps on the TFS-CA01 server:

1. Open an **elevated PowerShell prompt**.

2. Run the following command to install the **Active Directory Certificate Services** role, as well as the **Certification Authority Web Enrollment** role, and the necessary **Administration Tools**:

```
Windows PowerShell (Elevated)

Add-WindowsFeature `
-Name ADCS-Cert-Authority, ADCS-Web-Enrollment, Web-Mgmt-Service `
-IncludeManagementTools
```

3. The command will automatically install the **Active Directory Certificate Services** role and output a **Success** status of **True**.
4. Once the installation for **Active Directory Certificate Services** has completed successfully, close the **PowerShell prompt**.

Once the Active Directory Certificate Services role has been installed, proceed to configuring the role and creating the Subordinate certificate for the TFS Labs domain.

AD CS Quick Start - Subordinate CA Setup - AD CS Role Configuration

Once the Active Directory Certificate Services role has been added, it will need to be properly configured as the Subordinate Certificate Authority. In the process of configuring the Active Directory Certificate Services role for the TFS Labs domain, the following Subordinate Certificate be configured:

Certificate Authority Setup Type	Enterprise CA
Certificate Authority Type	Subordinate CA
Cryptographic Provider	RSA#Microsoft Software Key Storage Provider
Key Length	4096 Bits
Signature Hash Algorithm	SHA256
CA Common Name	TFS Labs Enterprise CA
Validity Period	5 years

Table 15.4.4.1: Active Directory Certificate Services configuration for the Subordinate CA.

The Active Directory Certificate Services configuration can be performed using PowerShell by running the following steps on the TFS-CA01 server:

1. Open an **elevated PowerShell prompt**.
2. Run the following command to configure the **Active Directory Certificate Services** role and create the **Subordinate Certificate Authority**:

```
Windows PowerShell (Elevated)

Install-AdcsCertificationAuthority `
-CAType EnterpriseSubordinateCA `
-CACommonName "TFS Labs Enterprise CA" `
-KeyLength 4096 `
-HashAlgorithm SHA256 `
-CryptoProviderName "RSA#Microsoft Software Key Storage Provider" `
-Force
```

3. The command will automatically configure the **Active Directory Certificate Services** role and output a **Success** status of **True**.

---

4. Run the following command to configure the **Certification Authority Web Enrollment** role:

```
Windows PowerShell (Elevated)

Install-AdcsWebEnrollment -Force
```

5. The command will automatically configure the **Certification Authority Web Enrollment** role.
6. Once the configuration for **Active Directory Certificate Services** has completed, close the **PowerShell prompt**.

At this point the Subordinate Certificate Authority for the TFS Labs domain has been created, but the Subordinate certificate needs to be issued. Proceed to validating that the Certificate Authority has been successfully created.

AD CS Quick Start - Subordinate CA Setup - Subordinate CA Validation

At this point the Subordinate Certificate Authority for the TFS Labs domain has been created, so there is now an Enterprise CA available. The CSR for the Subordinate certificate has been created, which means it will need to be submitted to the Root Certificate Authority to complete the request. Until this CSR is submitted and completed, the Enterprise CA will not function correctly. Even though the Active Directory Certificate Services role was configured, it is not currently running as there is no valid certificate present. If the Certification Authority console (certsrv.msc) is opened, the service will not be not running:

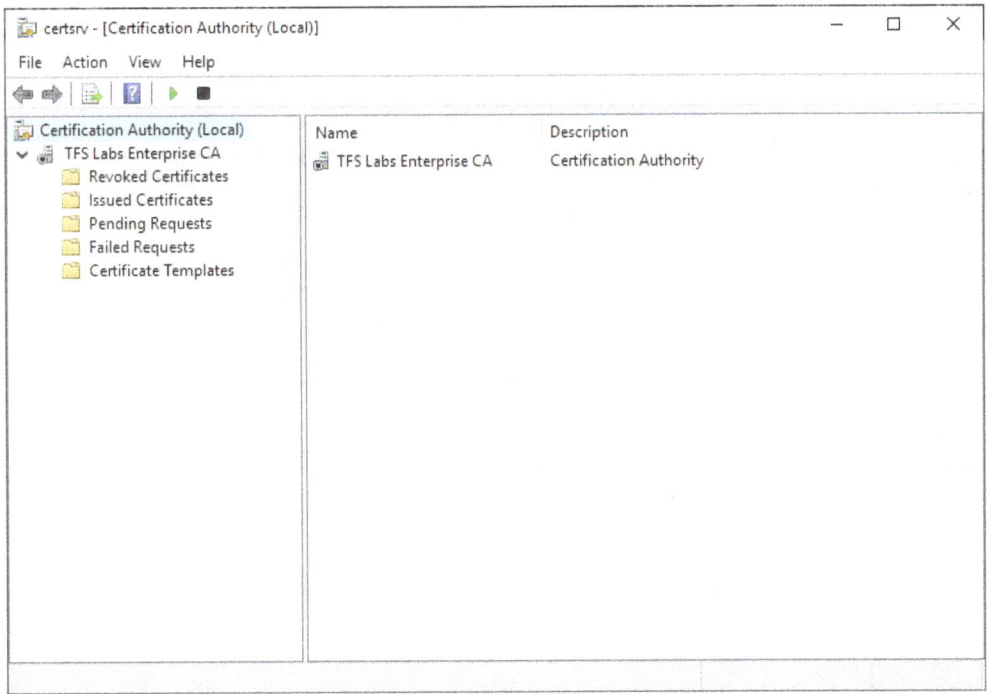

Figure 15.4.5.1: The Certification Authority console is used to manage the Certificate Authority and allows administrators to issue and revoke certificates. This console also allows further customization of the CA.

Once the CSR file has been successfully generated, it will need to be copied to the **RootCAFiles.vfd** virtual floppy disk since the Root CA on TFS-ROOT-CA needs the request file to issue the Subordinate Certificate.

To copy the Certificate Request file from the TFS-CA01 server to the TFS-ROOT-CA server, perform the following steps:

1. Add the **RootCAFiles.vfd** virtual floppy disk to the **TFS-CA01** virtual machine.
2. Browse to the **C:\ drive** and copy the **TFS-CA01.corp.tfslabs.com_corp-TFS-CA01-CA.req** to the **A:\ drive**.
3. Eject the **RootCAFiles.vfd** virtual floppy disk.

Once the Certificate Request has been successfully copied to the virtual floppy disk, proceed to creating the CertData directory in IIS on the TFS-CA01 server.

AD CS Quick Start - Subordinate CA Setup - Create the CertData Virtual Directory

On the TFS-CA01 server, create a folder that will be used to host important certificate files such as the Root certificate and the CRL files for the users, workstations, and servers in the TFS Labs domain. These are the necessary files from the Offline Root Certificate Authority, which need to be available to users and devices on the domain.

Before creating the CertData folder and virtual directory, there are several files that need to be copied to the TFS-CA01 server:

1. Add the **RootCAFiles.vfd** virtual floppy disk to the **TFS-CA01** virtual machine.
2. On the root of the **C:\ drive**, create a folder called **CertData** (C:\CertData).
3. Open the **A:\ drive** and copy the **TFS Labs Certificate Authority.crl** and **TFS-ROOT-CA_TFS Labs Certificate Authority.crt** files to the **C:\CertData** folder.
4. Eject the **RootCAFiles.vfd** virtual floppy disk.

Create the CertData virtual directory using the command line instead of using the Internet Information Services (IIS) Manager by performing the following steps on the TFS-CA01 server:

1. Open an **elevated Command Prompt**.
2. Change to the correct directory by entering the following command:

```
Command Prompt (Elevated)

cd C:\Windows\System32\inetsrv\
```

3. Run the following command to create the **CertData** virtual directory in **IIS**:

```
Command Prompt (Elevated)

appcmd.exe add vdir /app.name:"Default Web Site/" ^
/path:/CertData /physicalPath:C:\CertData
```

4. Run the following command to enable **Directory Browsing** on the **CertData** virtual directory:

```
Command Prompt (Elevated)

appcmd.exe set config "Default Web Site/CertData" ^
/section:directoryBrowse /enabled:true
```

5. Close the **Command Prompt**.

Once the directory and the directory browsing option has been enabled on the CertData directory, double escaping can now be enabled in IIS.

AD CS Quick Start - Subordinate CA Setup - Enable Double Escaping in IIS

On the TFS-CA01 server, enable double escaping within Internet Information Services to allow for proper CRL publication on the TFS Labs domain. This applies specifically to the Delta CRLs which require this functionality. The Delta CRL has a plus (+) symbol in the name, and this can cause issues with some versions of IIS.

To enable double escaping in IIS, perform the following steps on the TFS-CA01 server:

1. Open an **elevated Command Prompt**.
2. Change to the correct directory by entering the following command:

```
Command Prompt (Elevated)

cd C:\Windows\System32\inetsrv\
```

3. Enter the following command to apply the change to **IIS**:

```
Command Prompt (Elevated)

appcmd.exe set config "Default Web Site" ^
/section:system.webServer/Security/requestFiltering ^
-allowDoubleEscaping:True
```

4. Close the **Command Prompt**.

The final step is to restart the **IIS** service by opening an **elevated PowerShell prompt** and running the following command on the TFS-CA01 server:

```
Windows PowerShell (Elevated)

Restart-Service W3SVC
```

After enabling double escaping in IIS, it will now be possible to distribute the Delta CRL files in the TFS Labs domain. Proceed to creating the Subordinate certificate in the next section.

AD CS Quick Start - Subordinate CA Setup - Subordinate Certificate Creation

Once the Subordinate CA has been configured and the CSR successfully generated, it is now time to complete the Subordinate CA certificate by using the TFS-ROOT-CA server.

Creating the Subordinate certificate requires multiple steps using both the Root CA server and the Subordinate CA servers. These steps are not complicated, but they must be completed in the correct order and none of the steps can be skipped.

The workflow for creating the Subordinate certificate on the TFS-CA01 and TFS-ROOT-CA servers is as follows:

- Insert the virtual floppy disk on the TFS-ROOT-CA server.
- Submit the CSR for the Subordinate CA to the Root CA.
- Export the Subordinate certificate from the Root CA.
- Copy the Subordinate certificate to the virtual floppy disk.
- Insert the virtual floppy disk on the TFS-CA01 server.
- Install the Subordinate certificate on the Subordinate CA.
- Start Active Directory Certificate Services on the TFS-CA01 server.

To create the Subordinate CA certificate, perform the following steps on the TFS-ROOT-CA server:

1. Add the **RootCAFiles.vfd** virtual floppy disk to the **TFS-ROOT-CA** virtual machine.
2. Copy the **A:\TFS-CA01.corp.tfslabs.com_corp-TFS-CA01-CA.req** file to the **C:\RootCA** folder.
3. On the **TFS-ROOT-CA** server open **Certification Authority** console (certsrv.msc).
4. Right-click on the **TFS Labs Certificate Authority** server, select **All Tasks** and click on **Submit new request...**.
5. On the **Open Request File** window, browse to the **C:\RootCA** folder location, and then select the **TFS-CA01.corp.tfslabs.com_corp-TFS-CA01-CA.req** file that was copied from **TFS-CA01**. Click the **Open** button to continue.
6. Once the Certificate Request has been submitted to the Root Certificate Authority, go to the **Pending Requests** folder in the **TFS Labs Certificate Authority** to see the pending Certificate Request. It should be identified as **Request ID 2**, the first request being the self-signed Root certificate which has already been issued by the Certificate Authority.
7. To issue the Subordinate certificate, right-click on the **Request ID 2**, select **All Tasks** and click on **Issue**.
8. Go to the **Issued Certificates** folder to see the issued Subordinate certificate.
9. Double-click on the **Request ID 2** certificate to open the **Certificate** properties window.

10. Go to the **Details** tab and click on the **Copy to File...** button.
11. On the first screen of the **Certificate Export Wizard**, click the **Next** button to continue.
12. On the **Export File Format** screen, select the **Cryptographic Message Syntax Standard - PKCS #7 Certificate (.P7B)** format. Select the option to **Include all certificates in the certification path if possible** and click the **Next** button.
13. On the **File to Export** screen, enter **C:\RootCA\TFS Labs Enterprise CA.p7b** as the file name and click **Next** to continue.
14. On the **Completing the Certificate Export Wizard** screen, click the **Finish** button to complete the wizard.
15. On the **Certificate Export Wizard** prompt, click the **OK** button to continue.
16. Copy the **C:\RootCA\TFS Labs Enterprise CA.p7b** file to the **A:\ drive**.
17. Eject the **RootCAFiles.vfd** virtual floppy disk.

To import the Subordinate CA certificate and start the AD CS services, perform the following steps on the TFS-CA01 server:

1. On the **TFS-CA01** server insert the **RootCAFiles.vfd** virtual floppy disk. Copy the **A:\TFS Labs Enterprise CA.p7b** file to root of the **C:\ drive**.
2. On the **TFS-CA01** server, open the **Certification Authority** console (certsrv.msc).
3. Right-click on the **TFS Labs Enterprise CA** server, go to **All Tasks** and select the option to **Install CA Certificate...**.
4. On the **Select file to complete CA installation** window, browse to the **C:\ drive**, select the **TFS Labs Enterprise CA.p7b** file and click **Open**.
5. If there is a warning message about installing an untrusted Root certificate, click the **OK** button.
6. If there were no errors in installing the certificate, right-click on the **TFS Labs Enterprise CA** server, select the **All Tasks** option, and click the **Start Service** option.
7. The **Subordinate Certificate** has now been installed, and the **Subordinate Certificate Authority** is now running.
8. Eject the **RootCAFiles.vfd** virtual floppy disk.

The Subordinate certificate can also be viewed to verify that it was created with the correct values that were setup during the Active Directory Certificate Services configuration:

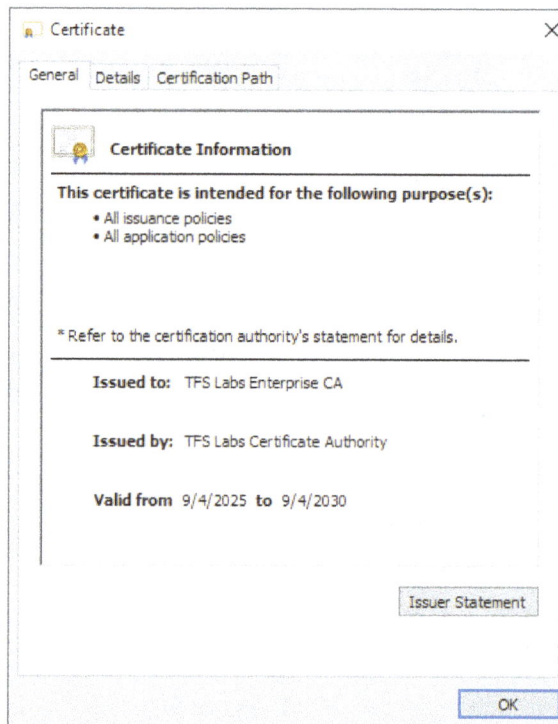

Figure 15.4.8.1: The TFS Labs Enterprise CA is signed by the TFS Labs Certificate Authority, with a 5 year validity period.

If there were no issues with creating the Subordinate certificate, delete the following files from the TFS-CA01 server as they are no longer needed for the implementation:

- **C:\TFS-CA01.corp.tfslabs.com_corp-TFS-CA01-CA.req**
- **C:\TFS Labs Enterprise CA.p7b**

These files should be deleted as they should not remain on a server that has active network connections for security purposes. Those files can remain on the TFS-ROOT-CA server as it is offline, and the files cannot be accessed. Proceed to setting the maximum age for any certificate that is issued by the Certificate Authority in the next section.

> **Active Directory Certificate Services Web Enrollment Alternate URL**
>
> There may be instances where the installation and configuration of the Subordinate certificate may fail for several reasons (if the Subordinate certificate was successfully issued, skip this step). This may occur when the Subordinate CA has issues with the Root CA CRL configuration, which is offline at the time of issuance of the Subordinate certificate. To correct this issue when attempting to issue the Subordinate CA, run the following command in an **elevated PowerShell prompt** on the TFS-CA01 server:
>
> Windows PowerShell (Elevated)
> ```
> certutil.exe -setreg ca\CRLFlags +CRLF_REVCHECK_IGNORE_OFFLINE
> ```
>
> Once the command is issued, the Active Directory Certificate Services role will need to be restarted:
>
> Windows PowerShell (Elevated)
> ```
> net stop CertSvc
> net start CertSvc
> ```
>
> At this point, try to install the Subordinate certificate again and restart Active Directory Certificate Services to complete the configuration.

AD CS Quick Start - Subordinate CA Setup - Set Maximum Certificate Age

All certificates that will be issued by the Subordinate CA will only be valid for 1 year, and the setting can be forced so that a Certificate Template does not attempt to issue a certificate for a longer period of time. To configure the certificate age for the Subordinate CA, run the following commands on the TFS-CA01 server from an **elevated PowerShell prompt**:

1. To define the maximum age of any certificate that the **Subordinate CA** can issue, run the following commands:

   Windows PowerShell (Elevated)
   ```
   certutil.exe -setreg CA\ValidityPeriodUnits 1
   certutil.exe -setreg CA\ValidityPeriod "Years"
   ```

2. Restart the **Active Directory Certificate Services** service to apply the configuration:

   Windows PowerShell (Elevated)
   ```
   net stop CertSvc
   net start CertSvc
   ```

3. Close the **PowerShell prompt**.

Once the maximum age for certificates has been specified on the Certificate Authority, proceed to modifying the CertEnroll virtual directory settings, which is used for certificate deployment.

AD CS Quick Start - Subordinate CA Setup - Modify the CertEnroll Virtual Directory

Directory browsing on the CertEnroll virtual directory needs to be enabled as it is disabled by default in IIS. This can be completed by performing the following steps on the TFS-CA01 server:

1. Open an **elevated Command Prompt**.
2. Change to the correct directory by entering the following command:

```
Command Prompt (Elevated)

cd C:\Windows\System32\inetsrv\
```

3. Run the following command to enable **Directory Browsing** on the **CertEnroll** virtual directory:

```
Command Prompt (Elevated)

appcmd.exe set config "Default Web Site/CertEnroll" ^
/section:directoryBrowse /enabled:true
```

4. Close the **Command Prompt**.

Once the directory browsing option has been enabled on the CertEnroll directory, proceed to configuring the CDP and AIA settings on the Subordinate CA.

AD CS Quick Start - Subordinate CA Setup - CDP and AIA Configuration

Before the Subordinate Certificate Authority can be properly configured, the Certificate Revocation List needs to be configured on the Subordinate Certificate Authority. The CRL files that are provided by the Root CA are distributed with the Subordinate CA. This is because the Root CA is not available on the network since it is always offline, so there is no way for clients to access the files needed for the TFS Labs domain. This is accomplished by configuring CDP and AIA on the Subordinate CA. There are multiple locations where the CDP and AIA locations are used for the Subordinate Certificate Authority:

- Local File System
- LDAP
- HTTP
- SMB

To configure CDP and AIA on the Subordinate CA, perform the following steps on the TFS-CA01 server:

1. Open an **elevated PowerShell prompt**.
2. Run the following command to configure the **CDP** settings for the Subordinate Certificate (execute this command as a single line with no breaks):

```
Windows PowerShell (Elevated)

certutil.exe -setreg CA\CRLPublicationURLs "65:C:\Windows\system32\CertSrv\
CertEnroll\%3%8%9.crl\n6:http://pki.corp.tfslabs.com/CertEnroll/%3%8%9.crl"
```

3. Run the following command to configure the **AIA** settings for the Subordinate Certificate (execute this command as a single line with no breaks):

```
Windows PowerShell (Elevated)

certutil.exe -setreg CA\CACertPublicationURLs "1:C:\Windows\system32\CertSrv\
CertEnroll\%1_%3%4.crt\n2:http://pki.corp.tfslabs.com/CertEnroll/%1_%3%4.crt"
```

4. Restart the **Active Directory Certificate Services** service to apply the changes:

```
Windows PowerShell (Elevated)

net stop CertSvc
net start CertSvc
```

5. To publish the **CRL**, run the following command:

```
Windows PowerShell (Elevated)

certutil.exe -crl
```

6. Close the **PowerShell prompt**.

Once the CRL settings for the Subordinate CA have been configured, proceed to configuring the CPS document for the Certificate Authority.

AD CS Quick Start - Subordinate CA Setup - CPS Document

At the time of the Active Directory Certificate Services role configuration for the Certificate Authority, the CAPolicy.inf files specified the location for a Certification Practice Statement (CPS). The CPS is a document that is available to users who are using the Certificate Authority to inform them of important policies regarding the Certificate Authority. The CPS varies for every organization, so a placeholder will be put in place which can be updated later to ensure that the Certificate Authority meets any compliance standards that may be required. This is especially important in industries with strict requirements (such as financial services), so having a CPS in place from day one can alleviate a lot of issues in the future.

To create the CPS document, perform the following steps on the TFS-CA01 server:

1. On the **TFS-CA01** server, open **Windows File Explorer** (explorer.exe), then go to **This PC** and then go to the **C:**.
2. Open the **C:\inetpub\wwwroot** folder.
3. Create a file named **cps.html** (ensure the file extension is correct).
4. Copy the following text into the **cps.html** file, save it and close the file:

```
C:\inetpub\wwwroot\cps.html

<!DOCTYPE html>
<html>
<head>
    <meta charset="utf-8">
    <title>TFS Labs Certification Practice Statement</title>
</head>
<body>

<h1>TFS Labs Certification Practice Statement</h1>

<p>The TFS Labs Certificate Authority is an internal only resource.</p>

<p>Issued certificates from this Certificate Authority are for internal use only.</p>

</body>
</html>
```

5. Close **Windows File Explorer**.

Test that the CPS document is accessible by opening the web browser on the TFS-CA01 server. Open the following address in a web browser on the TFS-CA01 server:

http://pki.corp.tfslabs.com/cps.html

Once the CPS document has been created, proceed to configuring the Windows Defender Firewall for the TFS-CA01 server.

AD CS Quick Start - Subordinate CA Setup - Windows Defender Firewall Configuration

Disabling the Windows Defender Firewall is extremely bad practice and can cause unexpected issues with the TFS-CA01 server if is not enabled. Active Directory Certificate Services utilizes HTTP and HTTPS connections to distribute and manage files needed to support the Certificate Authority. This includes all certificate files and CRL files that need to be distributed to users and workstations. For anything that is handled through Group Policy or LDAP, that is handled through the TFS-DC01 server which is the Domain Controller for the TFS Labs domain.

There are three firewall rules that need to be enabled on the TFS-CA01 server for Active Directory Certificate Services to function correctly:

Firewall Rule Name	Protocol	Port	Profile
File and Printer Sharing (Echo Request - ICMPv4-In)	ICMP	N/A	All
World Wide Web Services (HTTP Traffic-In)	TCP	80	All
World Wide Web Services (HTTPS Traffic-In)	TCP	443	All

Table 15.4.13.1: Windows Defender Firewall rules that are required for the TFS-CA01 server.

To check if the firewall rules are enabled on the TFS-CA01 server, perform the following steps:

1. Open the **Windows Defender Firewall with Advanced Security** console (wf.msc) on the **TFS-CA01** server.
2. Under the **Windows Defender Firewall with Advanced Security on Local Computer**, click on **Inbound Rules**.
3. For each of the firewall rules listed above, perform the following steps:
    (a) Right-click on the firewall rule and select the **Properties** option to open the **Rule Properties** window.
    (b) On the **General** tab, select the option for **Enabled**.
    (c) On the **Advanced** tab, ensure that the options for **Domain**, **Private** and **Public** are selected.
    (d) Click on the **Apply** button to apply the changes and then click the **OK** button to close the window.
4. Close the **Windows Defender Firewall with Advanced Security** console.

Once the Windows Defender Firewall has been correctly configured on the TFS-CA01 server, proceed to verifying the PKI infrastructure for the TFS Labs domain.

AD CS Quick Start - Subordinate CA Setup - Add the Root CA to Active Directory

Since the TFS-ROOT-CA server is an Offline CA and there are no network connections from Active Directory to that server, Active Directory is not aware that there is another Certificate Authority in the TFS Labs domain. The Enterprise CA automatically adds itself to Active Directory when it is configured, but there is a manual step that is required to add the Root Certificate Authority to Active Directory. The Root certificate and CRL are already located on the TFS-CA01 server and can be found in the **C:\CertData** folder. To add the Root CA and Root CRL to the TFS Labs domain, perform the following steps on the TFS-CA01 server:

1. Open an **elevated PowerShell prompt**.
2. Run the following command to add the **TFS Labs Certificate Authority** to **Active Directory**:

```
Windows PowerShell (Elevated)

certutil.exe -dspublish `
-f "C:\CertData\TFS-ROOT-CA_TFS Labs Certificate Authority.crt" RootCA
```

3. Run the following command to add the **Root CA** to the **Certificate Store** in **Active Directory**:

```
Windows PowerShell (Elevated)

certutil.exe -addstore `
-f root "C:\CertData\TFS-ROOT-CA_TFS Labs Certificate Authority.crt"
```

4. Run the following command to add the **Root CRL** to the **Certificate Store** in **Active Directory**:

```
Windows PowerShell (Elevated)

certutil.exe -addstore `
-f root "C:\CertData\TFS Labs Certificate Authority.crl"
```

5. Close the **PowerShell prompt**.

Now that the Root CA and CRL have been added to Active Directory, proceed to verifying the PKI infrastructure for the TFS Labs domain.

AD CS Quick Start - Subordinate CA Setup - Verify PKI Infrastructure

There is a tool available for Active Directory Certificate Services called Enterprise PKI, which is used to validate a PKI in Windows Server. It conveniently lists all the certificates and Certificate Revocation Lists that are part of the PKI, and specifies whether they are valid or not. To validate the PKI configuration for the TFS Labs domain, perform the following steps on the TFS-CA01 server:

1. On the **TFS-CA01** server, open the **Enterprise PKI** console (pkiview.msc).
2. On the default window for the **Enterprise PKI** console, it should state that the status of the **TFS Labs Certificate Authority (V0.0)** server is **OK**.
3. Under the **Enterprise PKI** node, click on the **TFS Labs Certificate Authority (V0.0)** server. Check that the status of the **CA Certificate**, **AIA Location #1** and **CDP Location #1** have the status of **OK**.
4. Under the **Enterprise PKI** node, click on the **TFS Labs Enterprise CA (V0.0)** server. Check that the status of the **CA Certificate**, **DeltaCRL Locations**, **AIA Locations** and **CDP Locations** have the status of **OK**:

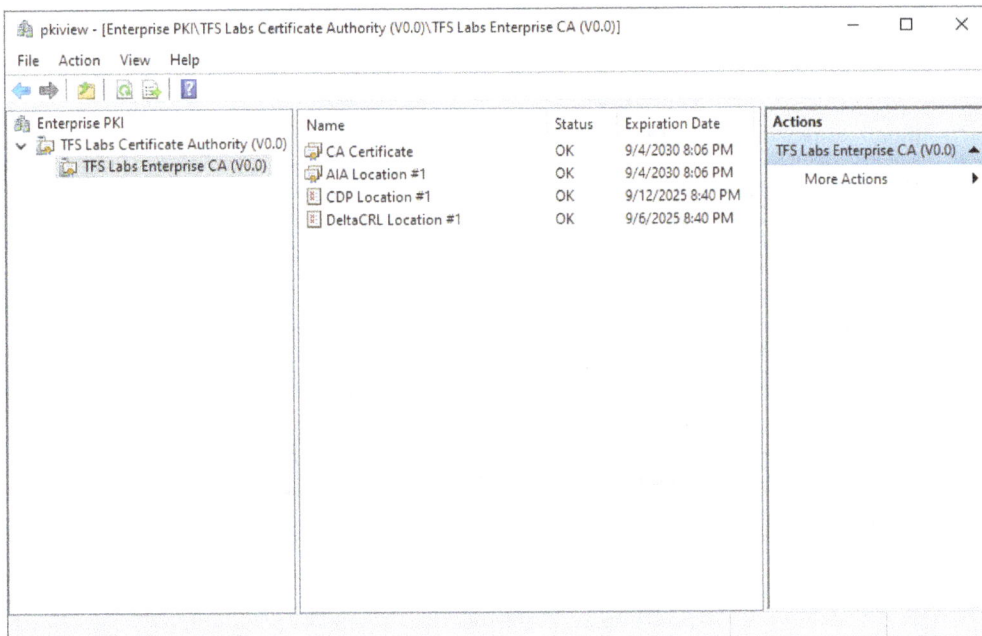

5. Close the **Enterprise PKI** console.

There are still additional items that can be configured for the TFS Labs Certificate Authority, but checking the overall status of the PKI at this stage can determine if there are any obvious issues with the Certificate Authority. It will quickly determine if there are issues with the CDP and AIA configurations, as well as the CRL files that have been published for the Certificate Authority. At this point in the overall configuration of the PKI, issues like this are much easier to correct before more complex configurations are introduced later on.

If there are no issues with the PKI infrastructure configuration, then the initial deployment of the TFS Labs Certificate Authority is now complete. With an Enterprise CA, the TFS Labs Enterprise CA certificate should start to automatically deploy to all Active Directory devices.

AD CS Quick Start - Post-Implementation Tasks

Once the implementation of the Certificate Authority has been completed, there are two tasks that need to be completed. It involves the deletion of the virtual floppy disk, and shutting down the Root CA server.

AD CS Quick Start - Post-Implementation Tasks - Virtual Floppy Disk Deletion

Once the Certificate Authority has been successfully implemented, completed, and tested, the virtual floppy disk should be deleted as it is no longer required. The virtual floppy disk contains important files that are not needed after the implementation, and by keeping the virtual floppy disk can introduce an unnecessary security risk.

> **Virtual Floppy Disk Deletion**
>
> Prior to deleting the virtual floppy disk, if there are any BitLocker Recovery Keys present, they should be backed up before deletion. Should the virtual floppy disk be required in the future, specifically for updating the Root CA CRL files, it can be easily recreated for that purpose.

AD CS Quick Start - Post-Implementation Tasks - Root CA Shut Down

Once the Certificate Authority has been successfully implemented, the Root CA can be powered off as it is no longer needed once the Subordinate CA is online and operating correctly. For security purposes it is important to keep the Root CA offline and protected. The TFS-ROOT-CA virtual machine will need to be powered on at least once every 52 weeks to update the Base CRL.

> **Root Certificate Authority Virtual Machine**
>
> Ensure that this virtual machine is never deleted. If this virtual machine is deleted, it will break the entire PKI and there will be no way of recovering from it unless a backup exists for the Root CA server.

AD CS Quick Start - Chapter Summary

Once the steps for creating the Certificate Authority have been completed, there is the option to go through the previous chapters in this book and add additional functionality, as well as complete further customizations. The major items that are missing from the include the Online Responder role configuration, Certificate Template customization and auto-enrollment of certificates in the TFS Labs domain. These items can be added at any time should they be required for an organization in the future.

Glossary of Terms

802.1X   802.1X is an open standard that is used for securing physical ports on a network. It provides authentication capabilities to devices that are connecting to a network.

A

A Record   An A record is a type of DNS record that returns a 32-bit IPv4 address, and is commonly used to map a hostname to an IP address.

Active Directory   Active Directory is a directory service application developed by Microsoft for managing, authenticating, and authorizing access to a domain.

AD CS   Active Directory Certificate Services is a server role available in Windows Server that allows for the creation and management of a Certificate Authority.

AD DS   Active Directory Domain Services is a server role available in Windows Server that allows for the creation of a Domain Controller for a domain. This allows for creating an Active Directory domain, or adding onto an existing one.

AIA   Authority Information Access is a feature in a Certificate Authority that publishes CRL information and the OCSP URL for issued certificates.

Air Gapped   An air gapped server has no network connections, and is isolated from the outside world.

Apache   The Apache HTTP Server is an open-source web server platform that is available on multiple operating systems.

ARM   ARM is a processor architecture that is typically used for low power computers. The architecture is considerably simpler than x86 or x64 architectures.

Azure   Azure is a cloud computing platform that is owned and operated by Microsoft.

Azure Stack HCI   Azure Stack HCI is an on-premise virtualization solution that uses Hyper-V and integrates with Azure.

B

Base CRL   A Base CRL is a large list of certificates that have been revoked previously by the Certificate Authority. It is a large file that is updated infrequently and is tied to the Delta CRL as it incorporates those revocations over time.

BDE   BitLocker Drive Encryption is a full disk encryption application developed and maintained by Microsoft for the Windows operating system.

C

CDP   A CRL Distribution Point is where clients can download a CRL to check the revocation status of certificates for a Certificate Authority.

Certificate Authority   A Certificate Authority is an entity that issues and manages certificates.

CLI   A Command Line Interface is a method of interacting with a computer that relies on inputting commands with text without a graphical interface.

Cmdlet	A Cmdlet is a PowerShell command which are useful for automation tasks within the operating system. They can be added with modules as required depending on what functionality is required.
CNAME Record	A Canonical Name record is a resource record for DNS that maps one DNS entry to another one. This allows for multiple DNS records for a single A record.
CRL	A Certificate Revocation List is a list of certificates that have been revoked before they are set to expire on their own. This occurs when a certificate is compromised or can no longer be trusted for multiple reasons.
CSR	A Certificate Signing Request is a digital application for a certificate. A CSR is received by a Certificate Authority and if approved, is issued back to the applicant as a valid certificate that can be utilized.

D

Daemon	A daemon is a program that runs in the background as a process and performs actions as required and is typically used with Linux.
Delta CRL	A Delta CRL is a small list of certificates that have been revoked since the last time a Base CRL was published and is typically used on a Subordinate CA.
DISM	The Deployment Image Servicing and Management is a command line tool that is used to mount and update Windows images. It can also be used to add or remove Windows features as needed on an active Windows operating system.
DER	Distinguished Encoding Rules is a certificate format that is stored in binary format.
DNS	The Domain Name System is a hierarchical naming system for devices or services that are connected to a private network or the public internet. It is critical for an Active Directory environment and is usually installed on a Domain Controller using the Active Directory integrated DNS feature. DNS relies on UDP port 53 for communication.
DNS Zone	A DNS Zone is a domain space that holds all records for a particular domain. This zone will contain all relevant records which can be used by clients who have access to it, whether it is public or private.

E

Enterprise CA	An Enterprise CA is a server that is a member of an Active Directory domain and is typically used as a Subordinate or Issuing Certificate Authority. An Enterprise CA will have the AD CS role installed and configured on it, and will always be online.

F

FAT	The File Allocation Table is a legacy file system format that is available for multiple operating systems. It is considered obsolete and not frequently used.
Firewall	A Firewall is a network security device that is used to control access to and from a network, as well as other functions such as Malware detection, and other malicious activity.
FDE	Full Disk Encryption is a method of encryption used on hard drives and other devices that fully encrypts the contents when the device is online or offline.
FQDN	A Fully Qualified Domain Name is the complete domain name for a specific host on a network which resolves to a specific IP address.

FSMO	The Flexible Single Master Operation are several roles within Active Directory (Schema Master, Domain Naming Master, RID Master, PDC Emulator and Infrastructure Master) that are responsible for critical AD DS functions. FSMO roles can be installed on a single or multiple Domain Controllers in an Active Directory domain as required.
Functional Level	Functional Levels are used to determine what capabilities an Active Directory domain has available to it. There are Forest and Domain Functional Levels that provide different capabilities to a domain. Raising a Functional Level can add additional functionality to an Active Directory domain depending on which version is used.

G

GPO	A Group Policy Object is a complete set of Group Policy configurations that can be applied in multiple ways to an Active Directory domain.
Group Policy	Group Policy is a feature in Windows Server that allows for the centralized management of Windows Settings within an Active Directory domain. It is also available locally on Windows devices if Active Directory is unavailable.
GUI	A Graphical User Interface is an interface that allows for interaction with an operating system using buttons, icons, and windows.

H

Hash Algorithm	A hash algorithm is a function that takes inputted data and outputs it into a fixed sized output. It is used extensively in cryptography to secure data.
HTTP	The Hypertext Transfer Protocol is an application layer protocol that is used on the internet for communication with webpages. All information that is transferred is in plain text and is not encrypted, and it typically uses TCP port 80. It was first defined in RFC 1945.
HTTPS	The Hypertext Transfer Protocol Secure is an extension of HTTP that utilizes certificates to allow for secure transfer of information over the internet, and typically uses TCP port 443.
Hyper-V	Hyper-V is a hypervisor that can run virtual machines on modern versions of Windows 64-bit operating systems. Hyper-V was developed by Microsoft and is an optional feature that is available at no additional cost with certain versions of Windows.
Hypervisor	A hypervisor is computer software that can emulate the hardware of a physical computer to allow for multiple operating systems to be run on the same physical hardware.

I

IANA	The Internet Assigned Numbers Authority is responsible for assigning and managing all public IP addresses, Root Zone management and Private Enterprise Numbers.
ICMP	The Internet Control Message Protocol is a network protocol that is typically used to determine if network devices are reachable on a network, and if there are any issues with connectivity.
IETF	The Internet Engineering Task Force is an organization that primarily develops and maintains internet standards.
IIS	Internet Information Services is a web server platform that is available for the Windows platform.

L

LAN Manager
LAN Manager is an obsolete networking technology and associated protocols that was used by Microsoft in early versions of Windows NT. For backwards compatibility reasons it is still included with modern versions of Windows, but can be safely disabled in most cases.

LDAP
The Lightweight Directory Access Protocol is an open protocol that is used for accessing a directory service such as Active Directory. LDAP typically operates on TCP port 389, and LDAP over SSL operates on TCP port 636.

LDAPS
Lightweight Directory Access Protocol over SSL is a secure form of LDAP that typically operates on TCP port 636.

M

Microsoft Account
A Microsoft Account is an account that is provided by Microsoft that is used to access various services and platforms.

MDM
Mobile Device Management is a platform that is used to manage mobile devices such a phones or tablets and ensures that they meet necessary compliance standards. An MDM can also be used to automatically distribute files and policies to mobile devices.

MMC
The Microsoft Management Console is a component of Windows that allows a single application the ability to manage and monitor the operating system using modules, called Snap-ins.

N

NAT
Network Address Translation is a method of mapping an IP address into another by changing the network address while the traffic is in transit. In practice, this allows for one WAN IP address to be mapped to multiple internal LAN IP addresses, or for one WAN IP address to be mapped to one internal LAN IP address for things like web servers.

NDES
The Network Device Enrollment Service is an AD CS feature that allows network devices such as routers or switches without proper Active Directory credentials to receive proper certificates in a network.

Nginx
Nginx is an open-source web server platform that is available for multiple operating systems.

O

OCSP
The Online Certificate Status Protocol is a protocol that is used to determine the revocation status of a certificate. It is like a CRL in nature but is updated more frequently.

Offline CA
An Offline Certificate Authority is a Certificate Authority that is not connected to a network and can only sign certificates manually.

OID
An Object Identifier is an identification method used to uniquely name an object or attribute and is used with certificates.

Operating System
An operating system is software that is used to manage the hardware of a computer. It allows software to be used, and for a user to interact with a computer.

OU
An Organizational Unit is a container in an Active Directory domain that is used to store objects based on their usage. It can be linked with Group Policy to enforce settings or push software to those objects, whether they be users or computers.

P

P7B
P7B is a PKCS #7 signed certificate that is stored in the Cryptographic Message Syntax Standard format, which is a binary format.

PEN
A Private Enterprise Number is a unique identifier that is maintained by the IANA in a public registry that can be used with an OID. A PEN number is free to acquire and use within an organization as needed.

PFX
PFX is a PKCS #12 signed certificate that is stored in the Personal Information Exchange format, which is a binary format. This format is commonly used on the Windows operating system and with IIS.

PKI
A Public Key Infrastructure is a set of roles and services that are needed to create and manage certificates using public key encryption.

PowerShell
PowerShell is a framework that provides a command line interface that is maintained by Microsoft. Administrative tasks are performed using Cmdlets, which simplify complex tasks.

Private Key
In cryptography, a private key is the key that is known only to the owner that is used to decrypt data that is signed using the public key.

Production Environment
A production environment is an IT term for the set of servers and computers where day-to-day business normally occurs. It usually consists of mission critical services that a business relies on.

Public Key
In cryptography, a public key is the key that is known to others that is used to digitally sign data, to be decrypted using the private key.

R

RDP
Remote Desktop Protocol is a method of remotely connecting to a Windows device over the network, and typically uses TCP port 3389 for connectivity.

RFC
Request for Comments is a publication that is used to develop standards for the internet and other networking services.

Root CA
A Root Certificate Authority is the top of a Certificate Authority and is used to sign all Subordinate certificates for a PKI hierarchy.

RSA
Rivest-Shamir-Adleman is a public key encryption system that is widely used for the secure transmission of data over networks.

RSAT
Remote Server Administration Tools are a set of management tools that are available for Windows devices.

S

S/MIME
Secure/Multipurpose Internet Mail Extensions is a method of encrypting and decrypting emails using digital signatures.

SAN
Subject Alternative Name is a type of certificate that allows for multiple DNS names to be used on a single certificate. Also known as a UCC certificate.

SSL
Secure Socket Layers is a method of public key encryption that is most used on the World Wide Web. Websites that are encrypted with SSL typically use HTTPS as the protocol for transmitting and receiving data. TLS is the successor to SSL.

Subordinate CA
A Subordinate CA is a Certificate Authority that is certified by another Certificate Authority, which is most often a Root Certificate Authority.

T

TCP   The Transmission Control Protocol is a transport protocol that is used to ensure a reliable transmission of packets over a network.

TCP/IP   The Transmission Control Protocol/Internet Protocol is a network protocol that is primarily used on the internet and on internal networks.

TLS   The Transport Layer Security is the successor to SSL that supports greater encryption capabilities.

TPM   A Trusted Platform Module is a standard for providing secure cryptographic functions to a computer through dedicated hardware on the device.

U

UCC   A Unified Communications Certificate is a type of certificate that allows for multiple DNS names to be used on a single certificate. Also known as a SAN certificate.

UDP   The User Datagram Protocol is a transport protocol that is used mostly in scenarios where loss is more generally accepted, but with the benefit of higher transfer speeds.

URL   A Uniform Resource Locator is a reference to a resource on a network that uses DNS. It can also be referred to as a Uniform Resource Identifier (URI).

V

VFD   A Virtual Floppy Disk is a virtual disk format that is used by Microsoft to emulate 1.44 MB floppy disks. They are compatible with all versions of Hyper-V and several other virtualization platforms.

VHD   A Virtual Hard Disk is a virtual disk format that is used by Microsoft to emulate a hard disk of varying sizes up to 2 TB. It can contain disk partitions and file systems that can be used by an operating system used for virtualization.

VHDX   A Virtual Hard Disk format that is used by Microsoft that is an enhanced version of a VHD that can support up to 64 TB of storage capacity. It also allows for enhanced capabilities with recent versions of Hyper-V.

Virtual Machine   A virtual machine is an emulation of a computer system and is most used to run multiple operating systems on a single computer.

W

Wildcard Certificate   A Wildcard Certificate is a type of certificate that is applied to a domain and all associated subdomains. A wildcard certificate is usually specified using an asterisk before the domain name (*.tfslabs.com).

Workgroup   A Workgroup is a collection of computers that are on the same network that can share files and resources without a centralized authentication system such as Active Directory or other LDAP providers.

X

X.509   X.509 is an open standard that is used in defining public key certificates and several other associated protocols that are needed for supporting certificates.

Commands Index

Cmdlets for Installing Active Directory Certificate Services

Cmdlet	Purpose
Install-AdcsCertificationAuthority	Installs and configures the AD CS role on Windows Server.
Install-AdcsOnlineResponder	Installs the Online Responder role.
Install-AdcsWebEnrollment	Installs the AD CS Web Enrollment role.
Uninstall-AdcsCertificationAuthority	Uninstalls the AD CS role and configuration files.
Uninstall-AdcsOnlineResponder	Uninstalls the Online Responder role from the Certificate Authority.
Uninstall-AdcsWebEnrollment	Uninstalls the AD CS Web Enrollment role from the Certificate Authority.

Table 16.1.1: Cmdlets that can be used for installing and uninstalling various Active Directory Certificate Services roles on Windows Server. These Cmdlets accept multiple options depending on how the role needs to be configured, and can be used instead of Server Manager for those roles.

Cmdlets for Managing Active Directory Certificate Services

Cmdlet	Purpose
Add-CAAuthorityInformationAccess	Configures the AIA or OCSP settings for a Certificate Authority using AD CS.
Add-CACrlDistributionPoint	Adds a CRL distribution point that AD CS uses to publish certificate revocations.
Add-CATemplate	Adds a Certificate Template to the Certificate Authority.
Backup-CARoleService	Backs up the Certificate Authority files, including the certificates, database, and private key.
Get-CAAuthorityInformationAccess	Returns the current AIA and OCSP settings for the Certificate Authority.
Get-CACrlDistributionPoint	Returns the current CDP extension settings for the Certificate Authority.
Get-CATemplate	Returns the currently configured Certificate Templates that are available on the Certificate Authority.
Remove-CAAuthorityInformationAccess	Removes AIA or OCSP settings on a Certificate Authority.
Remove-CACrlDistributionPoint	Removes a CRL distribution point from the Certificate Authority.
Remove-CATemplate	Removes Certificate Templates from the Certificate Authority.
Restore-CARoleService	Restores the Certificate Authority files, including the certificates, database, and private key.

Table 16.2.1: Cmdlets that can be used for managing Active Directory Certificate Services roles running on Windows Server. These Cmdlets accept multiple options depending on how the role needs to be configured, and can be used instead of Server Manager for those roles.

Cmdlets for Managing Windows Server

Cmdlet	Purpose
Add-DnsServerResourceRecordCName	Adds DNS records to a DNS Zone, specifically CNAME records.
Add-WindowsFeature	Adds optional features to a Windows workstation or server.
Enable-WindowsOptionalFeature	Enables optional features to a Windows workstation or server.
Get-ADComputer	Used to search for and retrieve computer objects within Active Directory.
Import-Module	Import a specific set of Cmdlets into a PowerShell session which are not present by default.
Install-AdcsCertificationAuthority.	Installs and configures an AD CS Certificate Authority once the AD CS role has been installed.
Install-AdcsWebEnrollment	Installs and configures the AD CS Web Enrollment role for AD CS, plus any additional required features.
Install-AdcsOnlineResponder	Installs and configures the AD CS Online Responder role for AD CS.
Install-ADDSForest	Installs and configures an AD DS Forest once the AD DS role has been installed.
Install-WindowsFeature	Enables optional features to a Windows workstation or server.
Move-ADObject	Moves objects within Active Directory.
New-ADOrganizationalUnit	Adds Organizational Units to Active Directory.
New-ADUser	Used to add users to Active Directory.
Set-ADUser	Modifies user properties in Active Directory.

Table 16.3.1: Cmdlets that can be used for managing various components of Windows Server.

Cmdlets for Managing Hyper-V Server

Cmdlet	Purpose
Add-VMDvdDrive	Adds a virtual DVD drive to a Hyper-V VM.
Add-VMNetworkAdapter	Adds a virtual network adapter to a VM.
Disable-VMIntegrationService	Disables specific virtualization features on a virtual machine.
Enable-VMIntegrationService	Enables specific virtualization features on a virtual machine.
Get-VM	Gets a list of virtual machines that are available on a Hyper-V host.
Get-VMIntegrationService	Gets the status of virtualization features for a virtual machine.
Get-VMSwitch	Gets a list of virtual switches that are configured on a Hyper-V host.
New-VFD	Creates a new virtual floppy disk.
New-VM	Creates a new virtual machine on a Hyper-V host.
New-VMSwitch	Creates a new virtual switch on a Hyper-V host.
Rename-VMNetworkAdapter	Changes the name of an existing Hyper-V virtual network adapter.
Set-VMDvdDrive	Adds an ISO image to a Hyper-V VM.

Set-VMFloppyDiskDrive	Attaches a virtual floppy disk to a virtual machine.
Set-VMHost	Configures the Hyper-V host.
Set-VMProcessor	Modifies the number of virtual processors on a Hyper-V virtual machine.
Start-VM	Starts a Hyper-V virtual machine.

Table 16.4.1: Cmdlets that can be used for managing various components of Hyper-V.

Command Line Tools for Managing Windows Server

CLI Command	Purpose
appcmd.exe	AppCmd.exe is a command line tool for managing IIS.
auditpol.exe	Auditpol.exe is a command line tool for managing audit policies on a Windows workstation or server.
certutil.exe	Certutil.exe is a command line tool used for managing certificates and configuration tasks for AD CS.
dcpromo.exe	Dcpromo.exe is a command line tool that is used for installing the AD DS role in earlier versions of Windows Server. This tool has been deprecated.
dism.exe	DISM.exe is a command line tool for managing Windows images, as well as adding and removing features to an existing system.
gpupdate.exe	Gpupdate.exe is a command line tool for managing Group Policy settings on a Windows workstation or server, most often used to refresh GPO.
iisreset.exe	IISReset.exe is a command that is used to manage IIS services from the command line. This command is deprecated and should not be used.
manage-bde.exe	Manage-bde.exe is a command line tool that is used for managing BitLocker on a Windows workstation or server.
net	Net is a command that manages all network tasks on a Windows workstation or server.
sconfig.cmd	SConfig.cmd is a command line tool that is used for managing basic Windows Server functions.

Table 16.5.1: Command line tools that can be used for managing various components of Windows Server.

Graphical Tools Using Windows Server Tools

Command	Purpose
appwiz.cpl	Programs and Features is a Control Panel applet that allows for the installation, modification, and removal of applications.
explorer.exe	Windows File Explorer is used to manage local and remote file systems.
inetmgr.exe	Internet Information Services (IIS) Manager is used to manage IIS services on a Windows device.

ldp.exe	Ldp is a GUI application for connecting to LDAP directories for troubleshooting purposes.
mmc.exe	The Microsoft Management Console is a modular framework for accessing management features within the Windows operating system using Snap-ins.
msinfo32.exe	System Information provides information on the local system, such as hardware, driver, and software versions.
mstsc.exe	Remote Desktop Connection provides a method for connecting to Windows devices using the RDP protocol.
ncpa.cpl	Network Connections is a Control Panel applet that allows for the modification of network adapters that are currently available on a Windows device.
servermanager.exe	Server Manager is a management console that provides access to all roles and features on Windows Server.
regedit.exe	Registry Editor provides a graphical interface for managing the Windows Registry.
vmconnect.exe	The Virtual Machine Connection application provides a graphical interface for managing Hyper-V virtual machines.

Table 16.6.1: Graphical tools that can be used for managing various components of Windows Server.

Graphical Tools Using the Microsoft Management Console

MMC Console	Purpose
adsiedit.msc	ADSI Edit is a tool that is used to connect to, and edit Active Directory objects.
certlm.msc	Certificate Store (local machine) allows management of certificates that are assigned to a workstation or server.
certmgr.msc	Certificate Store (current user) allows management of certificates that are assigned to a user account.
certsrv.msc	Certification Authority provides an interface to issue, revoke and manage certificates for AD CS.
compmgmt.msc	Computer Management provides a single view for tools, storage, and services on a Windows workstation or server.
dnsmgmt.msc	DNS Manager is used to manage DNS Zones that are standalone or integrated with AD DS.
dsa.msc	Active Directory Users and Computers is used to manage AD DS groups, users, workstations, and servers.
dssite.msc	Active Directory Sites and Services is used to manage Active Directory replication as well as AD service nodes.
eventvwr.msc	Event Viewer provides an interface for viewing and searching for events that are stored in Windows.
gpedit.msc	Local Group Policy Editor allows for management of Group Policy settings on a local Windows computer.

gpmc.msc	Group Policy Management allows for the creation and management of Group Policy Objects for Active Directory.
ocsp.msc	Online Responder is used to manage the OCSP settings for Active Directory Certificate Services.
pkiview.msc	Enterprise PKI provides an interface for viewing the overall status of an Enterprise CA in AD CS.
secpol.msc	The Local Security Policy application provides an interface for viewing and modifying security policies.
services.msc	Services provides an interface for viewing services, and provides the ability to start, stop or restart them.
virtmgmt.msc	Hyper-V Manager is used to manage Hyper-V virtual machines on a local or remote server.
wf.msc	Windows Defender Firewall with Advanced Security manager is used to manage settings for the native Windows firewall.

Table 16.7.1: MMC consoles that can be used for managing various components of Windows Server.

Index

www.ingramcontent.com/pod-product-compliance
Lightning Source LLC
Chambersburg PA
CBHW080702220326
41598CB00033B/5279